Open Inventor™ C++ Reference Manual

The Official Reference Document for Open Inventor, Release 2

Open Inventor Architecture Group

Addison-Wesley Publishing Company
Reading, Massachusetts   Menlo Park, California
New York   Don Mills, Ontario   Wokingham, England
Amsterdam   Bonn   Sydney   Singapore   Tokyo   Madrid
San Juan   Paris   Seoul   Milan   Mexico City   Taipei

Library of Congress Cataloging-in-Publication Data

ISBN 0-201-62491-5

Copy Editor: Arthur Evans
Sponsoring Editor: Keith Wollman
Project Editor: Joanne Clapp Fullagar
Cover Image: Rikk Carey
Cover Design: Jean Seal
Text Design: Electric Ink, Ltd., and Kay Maitz

Set in 10-point Stone Serif

Addison-Wesley books are available for bulk purchases by corporations, institutions, and other organizations. For more information, please contact the Corporate, Government and Special Sales Department at
(617) 944-3700 x2915.
First Printing, July 1994
123456789-CRS-9796959493

Contents

About This Book

Open Inventor C++ Reference Manual includes reference pages for the public C++ classes and member functions in the Open Inventor Toolkit, a library of objects and methods used for interactive 3D graphics. These pages are also available online with the Open Inventor product.

For further information about programming with Open Inventor, see *The Inventor Mentor* and *The Inventor Toolmaker*. *The Inventor Mentor* introduces graphics programmers and application developers to Open Inventor. *The Inventor Toolmaker* describes how to create new classes and how to customize existing classes in the Open Inventor Toolkit. Both books include detailed program examples in C++.

Many Inventor classes and member functions are labeled as **SoEXTENDER**, which means they are available to programmers who wish to extend the toolkit. Note that these classes and functions are not documented in the *Open Inventor C++ Reference Manual*. Refer to header files and *The Inventor Toolmaker* for information on them.

Other classes and methods are labeled as **SoINTERNAL**. These are used solely within the Open Inventor library and should not be used in applications. The labels **SoEXTENDER** and **SoINTERNAL** are for documentation purposes only and are not checked by the compiler.

What This Book Contains

This book contains reference pages, in alphabetical order, for all public classes in the Open Inventor Toolkit.

Open Inventor C++ Reference Manual contains the following chapters:

- Chapter 1, "**Class Trees**," shows key portions of the Open Inventor class tree.

- Chapter 2, "**Reference Pages**," which forms the bulk of this manual, contains descriptions of the Open Inventor classes and methods, including file format and default values. Enums, typedefs, and #defines, if any, are listed in the "Include File" section for each class. Each nodekit class lists its catalog parts in a separate section. For the sake of brevity, these parts, which are written out as fields, are not repeated in the "File Format" section for nodekit classes.

Conventions Used in This Book

This book uses **boldface text** font for all Inventor classes, methods, and field names: **SoNode**, **SoMaterial**, **getValue()**, **setValue()**, **ambientColor**, and **center**. Parentheses indicate methods. Include files are in `Courier` font.

Key to Scene Graph Diagrams

Figure I-1 shows the symbols used in the scene graph diagrams that appear throughout this guide.

Figure I-1   Scene Graph Symbols

Class Trees

The figures in this chapter show key portions of the Open Inventor class tree. Node classes are divided into the following categories:

- Shapes
- Properties
- Groups
- Cameras
- Lights

Class trees for the following classes are also included in this chapter:

- Actions
- Highlights
- Events
- Details
- Sensors
- Engines
- Node kits
- Draggers
- Manipulators
- Components
- Errors

The icons used in these figures are explained in the section "About This Book."

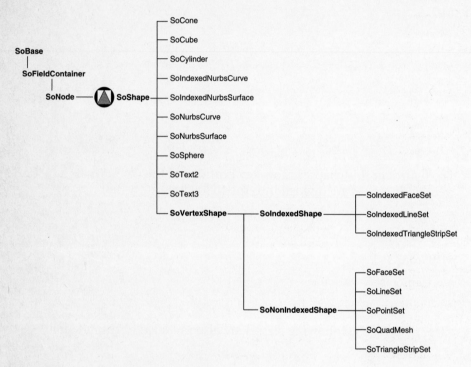

Figure 1-1   Shape-Node Classes

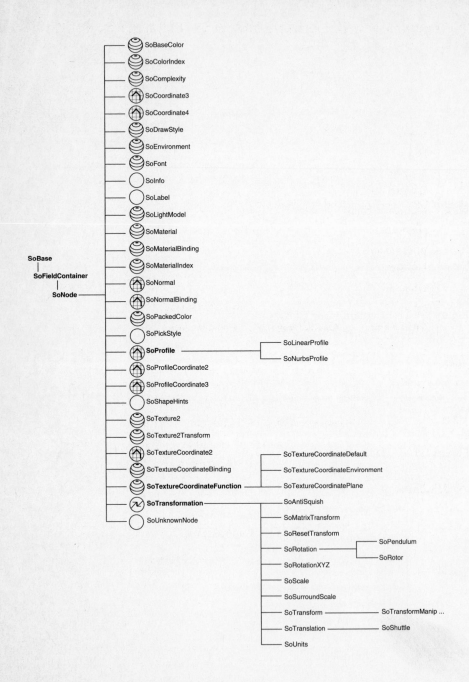

SoBase
|
SoFieldContainer
|
SoNode

SoBaseColor
SoColorIndex
SoComplexity
SoCoordinate3
SoCoordinate4
SoDrawStyle
SoEnvironment
SoFont
SoInfo
SoLabel
SoLightModel
SoMaterial
SoMaterialBinding
SoMaterialIndex
SoNormal
SoNormalBinding
SoPackedColor
SoPickStyle
SoProfile ─── SoLinearProfile
                  SoNurbsProfile
SoProfileCoordinate2
SoProfileCoordinate3
SoShapeHints
SoTexture2
SoTexture2Transform
SoTextureCoordinate2
SoTextureCoordinateBinding
SoTextureCoordinateFunction
SoTransformation
SoUnknownNode

SoTextureCoordinateDefault
SoTextureCoordinateEnvironment
SoTextureCoordinatePlane
SoAntiSquish
SoMatrixTransform
SoResetTransform
SoRotation ─── SoPendulum
               SoRotor
SoRotationXYZ
SoScale
SoSurroundScale
SoTransform ─── SoTransformManip ...
SoTranslation ─── SoShuttle
SoUnits

Figure 1-2   Property-Node Classes

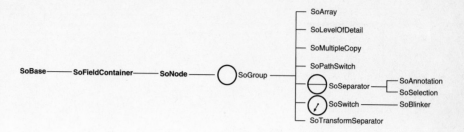

Figure 1-3   Group-Node Classes

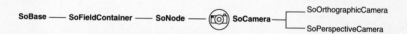

Figure 1-4   Camera-Node Classes

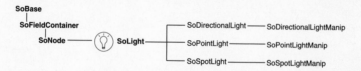

Figure 1-5   Light-Node Classes

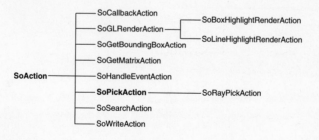

Figure 1-6   Action Classes

SoAction ——— SoGLRenderAction ———┬— SoBoxHighlightRenderAction
└— SoLineHighlightRenderAction

Figure 1-7   Highlight Classes

SoEvent ——┬— SoButtonEvent ———┬— SoKeyboardEvent
│   ├— SoMouseButtonEvent
├— SoLocation2Event   └— SoSpaceballButtonEvent
└— SoMotion3Event

Figure 1-8   Event Classes

SoDetail ——┬— SoConeDetail
├— SoCubeDetail
├— SoCylinderDetail
├— SoFaceDetail
├— SoLineDetail
├— SoNodeKitDetail
├— SoPointDetail
└— SoTextDetail

Figure 1-9   Detail Classes

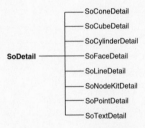
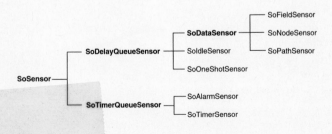

SoSensor ——┬— **SoDelayQueueSensor** ——┬— **SoDataSensor** ——┬— SoFieldSensor
│   │   ├— SoNodeSensor
│   ├— SoIdleSensor └— SoPathSensor
│   └— SoOneShotSensor
│
└— **SoTimerQueueSensor** ——┬— SoAlarmSensor
└— SoTimerSensor

Figure 1-10   Sensor Classes

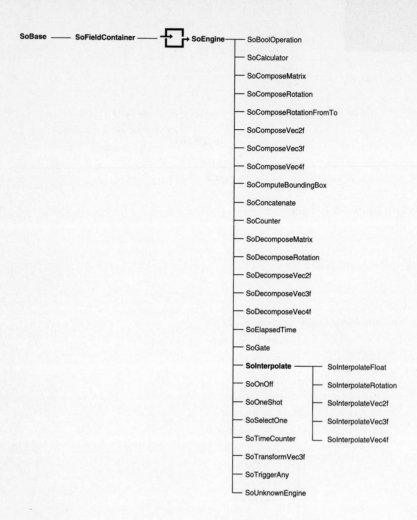

Figure 1-11   Engine Classes

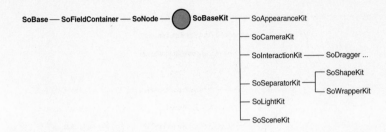

Figure 1-12   Node-kit Classes

Figure 1-13   Dragger Classes

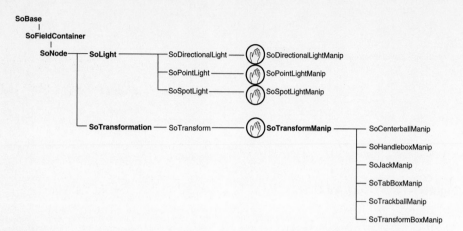

Figure 1-14   Manipulator Classes

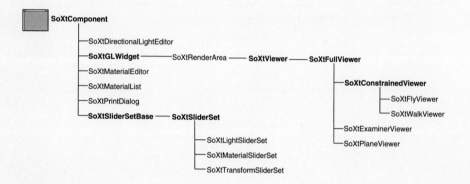

Figure 1-15   Component Classes

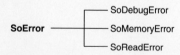

Figure 1-16   Error Classes

Chapter 2

Open Inventor
C++ Reference Pages

This chapter contains the reference pages, in alphabetical order, for all public Open Inventor classes.

SbBool

SbBox2f

SbBox2s

SbBox3f

SbColor

SbCylinder

SbCylinderPlaneProjector

SbCylinderProjector

SbCylinderSectionProjector

SbCylinderSheetProjector

SbLine

SbLineProjector

SbMatrix

SbName

SbPlane

SbPlaneProjector

SbPList

SbProjector

SbRotation

SbSphere

SbSpherePlaneProjector

SbSphereProjector

SbSphereSectionProjector

SbSphereSheetProjector

SbString

SbTime

SbVec2f

SbVec2s

SbVec3f

SbVec4f

SbViewportRegion

SbViewVolume

SbXfBox3f

SoAction

SoAlarmSensor

SoAnnotation

SoAntiSquish

SoAppearanceKit

SoArray

SoBase

SoBaseColor

SoBaseKit

SoBaseList

SoBlinker

SoBoolOperation

SoBoxHighlightRenderAction

SoButtonEvent

SoByteStream

SoCalculator

SoCallback

SoCallbackAction

SoCallbackList

SoCamera

SoCameraKit

SoCenterballDragger

SoCenterballManip

SoClipPlane

SoColorIndex

SoComplexity

SoComposeMatrix

SoComposeRotation

SoComposeRotationFromTo

SoComposeVec2f

SoComposeVec3f

SoComposeVec4f

SoComputeBoundingBox

SoConcatenate

SoCone

SoConeDetail

SoCoordinate3

SoCoordinate4

SoCounter

SoCube
SoCubeDetail
SoCylinder
SoCylinderDetail
SoDataSensor
SoDB
SoDebugError
SoDecomposeMatrix
SoDecomposeRotation
SoDecomposeVec2f
SoDecomposeVec3f
SoDecomposeVec4f
SoDelayQueueSensor
SoDetail
SoDetailList
SoDirectionalLight
SoDirectionalLightDragger
SoDirectionalLightManip
SoDragger
SoDragPointDragger
SoDrawStyle
SoElapsedTime
SoEngine
SoEngineList
SoEngineOutput
SoEngineOutputList
SoEnvironment
SoError
SoEvent
SoEventCallback
SoFaceDetail
SoFaceSet
SoField
SoFieldContainer
SoFieldList
SoFieldSensor

SoFile
SoFont
SoGate
SoGetBoundingBoxAction
SoGetMatrixAction
SoGLRenderAction
SoGroup
SoHandleBoxDragger
SoHandleBoxManip
SoHandleEventAction
SoIdleSensor
SoIndexedFaceSet
SoIndexedLineSet
SoIndexedNurbsCurve
SoIndexedNurbsSurface
SoIndexedShape
SoIndexedTriangleStripSet
SoInfo
SoInput
SoInteraction
SoInteractionKit
SoInterpolate
SoInterpolateFloat
SoInterpolateRotation
SoInterpolateVec2f
SoInterpolateVec3f
SoInterpolateVec4f
SoJackDragger
SoJackManip
SoKeyboardEvent
SoLabel
SoLevelOfDetail
SoLight
SoLightKit
SoLightModel
SoLinearProfile

SoLineDetail
SoLineHighlightRenderAction
SoLineSet
SoLocation2Event
SoMaterial
SoMaterialBinding
SoMaterialIndex
SoMatrixTransform
SoMemoryError
SoMFBitMask
SoMFBool
SoMFColor
SoMFEnum
SoMFFloat
SoMField
SoMFLong
SoMFMatrix
SoMFName
SoMFNode
SoMFPath
SoMFPlane
SoMFRotation
SoMFShort
SoMFString
SoMFTime
SoMFULong
SoMFUShort
SoMFVec2f
SoMFVec3f
SoMFVec4f
SoMotion3Event
SoMouseButtonEvent
SoMultipleCopy
SoNode
SoNodeKit
SoNodekitCatalog

SoNodeKitDetail
SoNodeKitListPart
SoNodeKitPath
SoNodeList
SoNodeSensor
SoNonIndexedShape
SoNormal
SoNormalBinding
SoNurbsCurve
SoNurbsProfile
SoNurbsSurface
SoOffscreenRenderer
SoOneShot
SoOneShotSensor
SoOnOff
SoOrthographicCamera
SoOutput
SoPackedColor
SoPath
SoPathList
SoPathSensor
SoPathSwitch
SoPendulum
SoPerspectiveCamera
SoPickAction
SoPickedPoint
SoPickedPointList
SoPickStyle
SoPointDetail
SoPointLight
SoPointLightDragger
SoPointLightManip
SoPointSet
SoPrimitiveVertex
SoProfile
SoProfileCoordinate2

SoProfileCoordinate3
SoQuadMesh
SoRayPickAction
SoReadError
SoResetTransform
SoRotateCylindricalDragger
SoRotateDiscDragger
SoRotateSphericalDragger
SoRotation
SoRotationXYZ
SoRotor
SoScale
SoScale1Dragger
SoScale2Dragger
SoScale2UniformDragger
SoScaleUniformDragger
SoSceneKit
SoSceneManager
SoSearchAction
SoSelection
SoSelectOne
SoSensor
SoSeparator
SoSeparatorKit
SoSFBitMask
SoSFBool
SoSFColor
SoSFEnum
SoSFFloat
SoSField
SoSFImage
SoSFLong
SoSFMatrix
SoSFName
SoSFNode
SoSFPath

SoSFPlane
SoSFRotation
SoSFShort
SoSFString
SoSFTime
SoSFTrigger
SoSFULong
SoSFUShort
SoSFVec2f
SoSFVec3f
SoSFVec4f
SoShape
SoShapeHints
SoShapeKit
SoShuttle
SoSpaceballButtonEvent
SoSphere
SoSpotLight
SoSpotLightDragger
SoSpotLightManip
SoSurroundScale
SoSwitch
SoTabBoxDragger
SoTabBoxManip
SoTabPlaneDragger
SoText2
SoText3
SoTextDetail
SoTexture2
SoTexture2Transform
SoTextureCoordinate2
SoTextureCoordinateBinding
SoTextureCoordinateDefault
SoTextureCoordinateEnvironment
SoTextureCoordinateFunction
SoTextureCoordinatePlane

SoTimeCounter
SoTimerQueueSensor
SoTimerSensor
SoTrackballDragger
SoTrackballManip
SoTranReceiver
SoTranSender
SoTransform
SoTransformation
SoTransformBoxDragger
SoTransformBoxManip
SoTransformManip
SoTransformSeparator
SoTransformVec3f
SoTranslate1Dragger
SoTranslate2Dragger
SoTranslation
SoTriangleStripSet
SoTriggerAny
SoType
SoTypeList
SoUnits
SoVertexShape
SoWrapperKit
SoWriteAction
SoXt
SoXtClipboard
SoXtComponent
SoXtConstrainedViewer
SoXtDevice
SoXtDirectionalLightEditor
SoXtExaminerViewer
SoXtFlyViewer
SoXtFullViewer
SoXtGLWidget
SoXtInputFocus

SoXtKeyboard
SoXtLightSliderSet
SoXtMaterialEditor
SoXtMaterialList
SoXtMaterialSliderSet
SoXtMouse
SoXtPlaneViewer
SoXtPrintDialog
SoXtRenderArea
SoXtResource
SoXtSliderSet
SoXtSliderSetBase
SoXtSpaceball
SoXtTransformSliderSet
SoXtViewer
SoXtWalkViewer

NAME

SbBool — a Boolean type

INHERITS FROM

SbBool

DESCRIPTION

This typedef is used to represent the Boolean values TRUE and FALSE. **SbBool** is not a class and does not have any methods or variables.

INCLUDE FILE

```
#include <Inventor/SbBasic.h>
```

NAME

SbBox2f — 2D box class

INHERITS FROM

SbBox2f

DESCRIPTION

2D box which has planes parallel to the major axes and is specified by two points (specified as floating point) on a diagonal. This class is part of the standard Inventor datatype classes and is used as input and output to geometry operations.

METHODS

	SbBox2f()
	SbBox2f(float xmin, float ymin, float xmax float ymax)
	SbBox2f(const SbVec2f &min, const SbVec2f &max)
void	**~SbBox2f**()

Constructors and destructor for a 2D float box. *xmin*, *ymin*, *xmax*, and *ymax* are the bounds of the box. *min* and *max* are the corners of the diagonal that define the box.

const SbVec2f &	**getMin**()
const SbVec2f &	**getMax**()

Returns the minimum and maximum points of the box.

SbVec2f	**getCenter**()

Returns the center of the box.

void	**extendBy**(const SbVec2f &point)
void	**extendBy**(const SbBox2f &box)

Extends this box (if necessary) to contain the specified point or other box.

SbBool	**intersect**(const SbVec2f &point)
SbBool	**intersect**(const SbBox2f &box)

Returns TRUE if the specified *point* or *box* intersects this box.

void	**setBounds**(float xmin, float ymin, float xmax, float ymax)
void	**setBounds**(const SbVec2f &min, const SbVec2f &max)

Sets the corners of the box.

void	**getBounds**(float &xmin, float &ymin, float &xmax, float &ymax)
void	**getBounds**(SbVec2f &min, SbVec2f &max)

Gets the corners of the box.

void   **getOrigin**(float &x0, float &y0)
Gets box origin.

void   **getSize**(float &x, float &y)
Gets box size.

float   **getAspectRatio**()
Gets box aspect ratio.

void   **makeEmpty**()
Makes an empty box.

SbBool   **isEmpty**()
Returns TRUE if the box is empty, and FALSE otherwise.

SbBool   **hasArea**()
Returns TRUE if both dimensions of the box have positive size, and FALSE otherwise.

INCLUDE FILE

```
#include <Inventor/SbBox.h>
```

SEE ALSO

SbBox3f, SbXfBox3f, SbBox2s, SbVec3f, SbVec2f, SbVec2s, SbMatrix

NAME

SbBox2s — 2D box class

INHERITS FROM

SbBox2s

DESCRIPTION

2D box which has planes parallel to the major axes and is specified by two points (specified with short integers) on a diagonal. This class is part of the standard Inventor datatype classes and is used as input and output to geometry operations.

METHODS

	SbBox2s()
	SbBox2s(short xmin, short ymin, short xmax, short ymax)
	SbBox2s(const SbVec2s &_min, const SbVec2s &_max)
void	**~SbBox2s**()

Constructors and destructor for a 2D integer box. *xmin, ymin, xmax,* and *ymax* are the bounds of the box. *min* and *max* are the corners of the diagonal that define the box.

const SbVec2s &	**getMin**() const
const SbVec2s &	**getMax**() const

Returns the minimum and maximum points of the box.

void	**extendBy**(const SbVec2s &point)
void	**extendBy**(const SbBox2s &box)

Extends this box (if necessary) to contain the specified *point* or other *box*.

SbBool	**intersect**(const SbVec2s &point) const
SbBool	**intersect**(const SbBox2s &box) const

Returns TRUE if the specified *point* or *box* intersects this box.

void	**setBounds**(short xmin, short ymin, short xmax, short ymax)
void	**setBounds**(const SbVec2s &_min, const SbVec2s &_max)

Sets the corners of the box.

void	**getBounds**(short &xmin, short &ymin, short &xmax, short &ymax) const
void	**getBounds**(SbVec2s &_min, SbVec2s &_max) const

Gets the corners of the box.

void	**getOrigin**(short &originX, short &originY) const

Returns origin (minimum point) of box.

void	**getSize**(short &sizeX, short &sizeY) const	

Returns box size.

float   **getAspectRatio**() const
Returns aspect ratio (ratio of width to height) of box.

void   **makeEmpty**()
Makes an empty box.

int   **operator** ==(const SbBox2s &b1, const SbBox2s &b2)
int   **operator** !=(const SbBox2s &b1, const SbBox2s &b2)
Equality comparisons.

INCLUDE FILE

```
#include <Inventor/SbBox.h>
```

SEE ALSO

SbBox3f, SbXfBox3f, SbBox2f, SbVec3f, SbVec2f, SbVec2s, SbMatrix

NAME

SbBox3f — 3D box class

INHERITS FROM

SbBox3f

DESCRIPTION

3D box which has planes parallel to the major axes and is specified by two points on a diagonal. This class is part of the standard Inventor datatype classes and is used as input and output to geometry operations (see **SoGetBoundingBoxAction**).

METHODS

	SbBox3f()
	SbBox3f(float xmin, float ymin, float zmin float xmax, float ymax, float zmax)
	SbBox3f(const SbVec3f &min, const SbVec3f &max)
void	~**SbBox3f**()

Constructors and destructor for a 3D float box. *xmin, ymin, zmin, xmax, ymax* and *zmax* are the bounds of the box. *min* and *max* are the corners of the diagonal that define the box.

const SbVec3f &	**getMin**()
const SbVec3f &	**getMax**()

Returns the minimum and maximum points of the box. The minimum point is the corner of the box with the lowest X, Y, and Z values. The maximum point is the corner of the box with the highest X, Y, and Z values.

SbVec3f	**getCenter**()

Returns the center of the box.

void	**extendBy**(const SbVec3f &point)
void	**extendBy**(const SbBox3f &box)

Extends this box (if necessary) to contain the specified point or other box.

SbBool	**intersect**(const SbVec3f &point)
SbBool	**intersect**(const SbBox3f &box)

Returns TRUE if the specified *point* or *box* intersects this box.

void	**setBounds**(float xmin, float ymin, float zmin, float xmax, float ymax, float zmax)
void	**setBounds**(const SbVec3f &min, const SbVec3f &max)

Sets the corners of the box.

void	**getBounds**(float &xmin, float &ymin, float &zmin, float &xmax, float &ymax, float &zmax)
void	**getBounds**(SbVec3f &min, SbVec3f &max)

Gets the corners of the box.

void	**getOrigin**(float &x0, float &y0, float &z0)

Gets box origin which is the same as the minimum corner of the box.

void	**getSize**(float &x, float &y, float &z)

Gets box size.

void	**makeEmpty**()

Makes an empty box.

SbBool	**isEmpty**()

Returns TRUE if the box is empty, and FALSE otherwise.

SbBool	**hasVolume**()

Returns TRUE if all three dimensions of the box have positive size, and FALSE otherwise.

void	**getSpan**(SbVec3f &dir, float &dMin, float &dMax)

Finds the span of a box along a specified direction. The span is the total distance the box occupies along a given direction. The total distance is returned in the form of a minimum and maximum distance from the origin of each of the corners of the box along the given direction. The difference between these two values is the span.

void	**transform**(const SbMatrix &mx)

Transforms box by matrix, enlarging box to contain result.

float	**getVolume**()

Returns the volume of the box.

INCLUDE FILE

```
#include <Inventor/SbBox.h>
```

SEE ALSO

SbXfBox3f, SbBox2f, SbBox2s, SbVec3f, SbVec2f, SbVec2s, SbMatrix, SoGetBoundingBoxAction

NAME

SbColor — color vector class

INHERITS FROM

SbVec3f

DESCRIPTION

This class is used to represent an RGB color. Each component of the vector is a floating-point number between 0.0 and 1.0. There are routines to convert back and forth between RGB and HSV.

METHODS

SbColor(const SbVec3f vec3f)
SbColor(const float rgb[3])
SbColor(float r, float g, float b)
Constructors for color vector.

SbColor & **setHSVValue**(float h, float s, float v)
Sets value of color vector from 3 HSV (Hue, Saturation, and Value) components. Value is the same as brightness of the color.

SbColor & **setHSVValue**(const float hsv[3])
Sets value of color vector from array of 3 HSV components

void **getHSVValue**(float &h, float &s, float &v) const
Returns 3 individual HSV components

void **getHSVValue**(float hsv[3]) const
Returns an array of 3 HSV components

SbColor & **setPackedValue**(unsigned long rgba)
RGBA Packed integer color routines. The color format expressed in hexadecimal is 0xaabbggrr, where

aa is the alpha value
bb is the blue value
gg is the green value
rr is the red value

RGBA component values range from 0 to 0xFF (255). Sets value from RGBA packed color. Alpha value is ignored.

unsigned long **getPackedValue**() const
Returns RGBA packed color. Alpha color is always set to 0xFF (255).

Methods from class SbVec3f:

cross, dot, equals, getClosestAxis, getValue, getValue, length, negate, normalize, setValue, setValue, setValue, operator [], operator [], operator *=, operator /=, operator +=, operator -=, operator -, operator *, operator *, operator /, operator +, operator -, operator ==, operator !=

INCLUDE FILE

```
#include <Inventor/SbColor.h>
```

NAME

SbCylinder — class for representing a cylinder

INHERITS FROM

SbCylinder

DESCRIPTION

This class defines a simple cylinder datatype. It is used by the Inventor toolkit for arguments or return values.

METHODS

SbCylinder()
SbCylinder(const SbLine &a, float r)
Constructors. One takes an axis and radius.

void   **setValue**(const SbLine &a, float r)
Change the axis and radius.

void   **setAxis**(const SbLine &a)
void   **setRadius**(float r)
Set just the axis or radius.

const SbLine &   **getAxis**() const
float   **getRadius**() const
Return the axis and radius.

SbBool   **intersect**(const SbLine &l, SbVec3f &intersection) const
SbBool   **intersect**(const SbLine &l, SbVec3f &enter, SbVec3f &exit)
              const
Intersect line and cylinder, returning TRUE if there is an intersection.

INCLUDE FILE

```
#include <Inventor/SbLinear.h>
```

SEE ALSO

SbVec3f, SbLine, SbPlane, SbSphere, SoCylinder

NAME

SbCylinderPlaneProjector — cylinder-plane projector

INHERITS FROM

SbProjector > SbCylinderProjector > SbCylinderSectionProjector >
SbCylinderPlaneProjector

DESCRIPTION

SbCylinderPlaneProjector projects a window space point (usually based on the mouse location) onto a surface defined by a cylinder and plane cutting through the cylinder. Two projected points can produce a rotation along the cylinder's axis. When the mouse position projects onto the plane, the rotations will be as if the plane is being dragged, causing the cylinder to roll beneath it.

Incremental changes (delta rotation) can be computed during interactive sessions. Cylinder projectors are typically used to write interactive 3D manipulators and viewers.

METHODS

SbCylinderPlaneProjector(float edgeTol = .9, SbBool
orientToEye = TRUE)
SbCylinderPlaneProjector(const SbCylinder &cyl, float
edgeTol = .9, SbBool orientToEye = TRUE)

Constructors. The first uses a default cylinder aligned with the Y axis with radius 1.0; the cylinder is supplied in the second. The position of the plane is specified as a fraction of the cylinder radius with the parameter **edgeTol**. A tolerance value of 1.0 positions the plane down the center of the cylinder. A tolerance value of 0.5 defines the longitudinal plane halfway between the center and the outside edge of the cylinder. The default value is .9, so that almost half the cylinder is in front of the plane. The **orientToEye** parameter determines whether the plane is perpendicular to the eye, or perpendicular to the cylinder's Z axis. Setting that parameter to TRUE (the default) specifies that the plane be perpendicular to the eye, which is most often the desired behavior.

The default view volume is undefined, and the working space is identity.

~SbCylinderPlaneProjector()

Destructor.

Methods from class SbCylinderSectionProjector:

setTolerance, getTolerance, isWithinTolerance

Methods from class SbCylinderProjector:

projectAndGetRotation, getRotation, setCylinder, getCylinder,
setOrientToEye, isOrientToEye, setFront, isFront, isPointInFront

Methods from class SbProjector:

project, setViewVolume, getViewVolume, setWorkingSpace,
getWorkingSpace, copy

INCLUDE FILE

```
#include <Inventor/projectors/SbCylinderPlaneProjector.h>
```

SEE ALSO

SbCylinderSheetProjector, SbLineProjector, SbPlaneProjector,
SbSpherePlaneProjector, SbSphereProjector, SbSphereSectionProjector,
SbSphereSheetProjector

NAME

SbCylinderProjector — cylinder projector

INHERITS FROM

SbProjector > SbCylinderProjector

DESCRIPTION

SbCylinderProjector is an abstract base class for projectors that use a cylinder in their projection. The **getRotation**() method for an SbCylinderProjector will always return a rotation that is about the axis of the cylinder. Cylinder projectors are typically used to write interactive 3D manipulators and viewers.

METHODS

~SbCylinderProjector()

Destructor.

SbVec3f   **projectAndGetRotation**(const SbVec2f &point, SbRotation &rot)

Apply the projector using the given point, returning the point in three dimensions that it projects to. This also returns in **rot** a rotation about the axis of the cylinder from the last projected point to this one. The passed **point** should be normalized (i.e. lie in the range [0.0,1.0]), with (0,0) at the lower-left.

virtual SbRotation

getRotation(const SbVec3f &point1, const SbVec3f &point2)

Get a rotation given two points on this cylinder projector. The rotation will be about the axis of the cylinder.

void   **setCylinder**(const SbCylinder &cyl)
const SbCylinder &

getCylinder() const

Set and get the cylinder on which to project points. The default cylinder is aligned with the Y axis and has radius 1.0.

void   **setOrientToEye**(SbBool orientToEye)
SbBool   **isOrientToEye**() const

Set and get whether the projector should always be oriented towards the eye. Set to FALSE if the tolerance should be evaluated in working space.

void	**setFront**(SbBool isFront)
SbBool	**isFront**() const
SbBool	**isPointInFront**(const SbVec3f &point) const

Set and get whether the projector should intersect the half of the cylinder that faces the eye. Set to FALSE if the projector should intersect with the rear half.

Methods from class SbProjector:

project, setViewVolume, getViewVolume, setWorkingSpace, getWorkingSpace, copy

INCLUDE FILE

```
#include <Inventor/projectors/SbCylinderProjector.h>
```

SEE ALSO

SbCylinderPlaneProjector, SbCylinderSectionProjector, SbCylinderSheetProjector, SbLineProjector, SbPlaneProjector, SbSpherePlaneProjector, SbSphereProjector, SbSphereSectionProjector, SbSphereSheetProjector

NAME

SbCylinderSectionProjector — cylinder-section projector

INHERITS FROM

SbProjector > SbCylinderProjector > SbCylinderSectionProjector

DESCRIPTION

SbCylinderSectionProjector projects a window space point (usually based on the mouse location) onto the section of a cylinder that has been sliced by a plane. Two projected points can produce a rotation along the cylinder's axis. The tolerance slice can be specified as a fraction of the radius of the cylinder. The projection point will not extend beyond the sliced portion of the cylinder.

Incremental changes (delta rotation) can be computed during interactive sessions. Cylinder projectors are typically used to write interactive 3D manipulators and viewers.

METHODS

SbCylinderSectionProjector(float edgeTol = .9, SbBool orientToEye = TRUE)

SbCylinderSectionProjector(const SbCylinder &cyl, float edgeTol = .9, SbBool orientToEye = TRUE)

Constructors. The first uses a default cylinder aligned with the Y axis with radius 1.0; the cylinder is supplied in the second. The position of the plane which slices the cylinder into a section is specified as a fraction of the cylinder radius with the parameter **edgeTol**. A tolerance value of 1.0 positions the plane down the center of the cylinder. A tolerance value of 0.5 defines the longitudinal plane halfway between the center and the outside edge of the cylinder. The default value is .9, so that almost half the cylinder is in front of the plane. The **orientToEye** parameter determines whether the plane is perpendicular to the eye, or perpendicular to the cylinder's Z axis. Setting that parameter to TRUE (the default) specifies that the plane be perpendicular to the eye, which is most often the desired behavior.

The default view volume is undefined, and the working space is identity.

~SbCylinderSectionProjector()

Destructor.

void	**setTolerance**(float edgeTol)
float	**getTolerance**() const

Set and get the edge tolerance as a fraction of the radius of the cylinder. If this is 1.0, the projector is a half cylinder. If this is .1, the projector is a slice of the cylinder with radius .1*radius. Default is .9.

SbBool   **isWithinTolerance**(const SbVec3f &point)
  Find whether this point on the cylinder or tolerance plane is within
  tolerance.

Methods from class SbCylinderProjector:

projectAndGetRotation, getRotation, setCylinder, getCylinder,
setOrientToEye, isOrientToEye, setFront, isFront, isPointInFront

Methods from class SbProjector:

project, setViewVolume, getViewVolume, setWorkingSpace,
getWorkingSpace, copy

INCLUDE FILE

```
#include <Inventor/projectors/SbCylinderSectionProjector.h>
```

SEE ALSO

SbCylinderPlaneProjector, SbCylinderSheetProjector, SbLineProjector,
SbPlaneProjector, SbSpherePlaneProjector, SbSphereProjector,
SbSphereSectionProjector, SbSphereSheetProjector

NAME

SbCylinderSheetProjector — cylinder-sheet projector

INHERITS FROM

SbProjector > SbCylinderProjector > SbCylinderSheetProjector

DESCRIPTION

SbCylinderSheetProjector projects a window space point (usually based on the mouse location) onto the surface of a cylinder with a hyperbolic sheet draped over it. This allows smooth transitions onto and off of the cylinder. Two projected points can produce a rotation along the cylinder's axis. When the mouse position projects on to the sheet, the rotations will be as if the sheet is being dragged, causing the cylinder to roll beneath it.

Incremental changes (delta rotation) can be computed during interactive sessions. Cylinder projectors are typically used to write interactive 3D manipulators and viewers.

METHODS

SbCylinderSheetProjector(SbBool orientToEye = TRUE)
SbCylinderSheetProjector(const SbCylinder &cyl, SbBool orientToEye = TRUE)

Constructors. The first uses a default cylinder aligned with the Y axis with radius 1.0; the cylinder is supplied in the second. The **orientToEye** parameter determines whether the sheet is perpendicular to the eye, or perpendicular to the cylinder's Z axis. Setting that parameter to TRUE (the default) specifies that the plane be perpendicular to the eye, which is most often the desired behavior.

The default view volume is undefined, and the working space is identity.

~SbCylinderSheetProjector()

Destructor.

Methods from class SbCylinderProjector:

projectAndGetRotation, getRotation, setCylinder, getCylinder, setOrientToEye, isOrientToEye, setFront, isFront, isPointInFront

Methods from class SbProjector:

project, setViewVolume, getViewVolume, setWorkingSpace, getWorkingSpace, copy

SbCylinderSheetProjector

INCLUDE FILE

```
#include <Inventor/projectors/SbCylinderSheetProjector.h>
```

SEE ALSO

SbCylinderSectionProjector, SbCylinderPlaneProjector, SbLineProjector,
SbPlaneProjector, SbSpherePlaneProjector, SbSphereProjector,
SbSphereSectionProjector, SbSphereSheetProjector

NAME

SbLine — directed line in 3D

INHERITS FROM

SbLine

DESCRIPTION

Represents a directed line in 3D. This is a basic Inventor datatype that is used for representing a 3D line. It is used as input and output by a variety of Inventor classes.

METHODS

SbLine()
SbLine(const SbVec3f &p0, const SbVec3f &p1)
Constructors. To construct a line from a position and direction, use: SbLine(p0, p0 + dir). The line is directed from *p0* to *p1*.

void **setValue**(const SbVec3f &p0, const SbVec3f &p1)
Sets line to pass through points *p0* and *p1*.

SbBool **getClosestPoints**(const SbLine &line2, SbVec3f &ptOnThis, SbVec3f &ptOnLine2) const
Finds the two closest points between this line and *line2*, and loads them into *ptOnThis* and *ptOnLine2*. Returns FALSE if the lines are parallel (results undefined), and returns TRUE otherwise.

SbVec3f **getClosestPoint**(const SbVec3f &point) const
Returns the closest point on the line to the given point.

const SbVec3f & **getPosition**() const
const SbVec3f & **getDirection**() const
Returns position of line origin point and direction vector of line.

INCLUDE FILE

```
#include <Inventor/SbLinear.h>
```

SEE ALSO

SbVec3f, SbPlane

NAME

    SbLineProjector — line projector

INHERITS FROM

    SbProjector > SbLineProjector

DESCRIPTION

    SbLineProjector projects a 2D point, typically the location of the cursor, onto a 3D line.

METHODS

                SbLineProjector()
                ~SbLineProjector()
    Constructor and destructor. The default line passes through the origin and is aligned with the Y axis.

    void   **setLine**(const SbLine &line)
    const SbLine &   **getLine**() const
    Set and get the line on which to project 2D points.

    virtual SbVec3f   **getVector**(const SbVec2f &mousePosition1, const SbVec2f &mousePosition2)
    Get a vector on this line given two normalized mouse points.

    virtual SbVec3f   **getVector**(const SbVec2f &mousePosition)
    Get a vector given the current mouse point. Uses the last point on this projector from the previous call to **getVector()** or **setStartPostion()**. Do not use this if the working space transform is changing since the new point will be in a different space than the old one.

    void   **setStartPosition**(const SbVec2f &mousePosition)
    Set the initial position from a mouse position.

    void   **setStartPosition**(const SbVec3f &point)
    Set the initial position from a point on the projector.

    Methods from class SbProjector:

    project, setViewVolume, getViewVolume, setWorkingSpace, getWorkingSpace, copy

INCLUDE FILE

    `#include <Inventor/projectors/SbLineProjector.h>`

SEE ALSO

SbCylinderProjector, SbCylinderPlaneProjector, SbCylinderSectionProjector,
SbCylinderSheetProjector, SbPlaneProjector, SbSpherePlaneProjector,
SbSphereProjector, SbSphereSectionProjector, SbSphereSheetProjector

NAME

SbMatrix — 4x4 matrix class

INHERITS FROM

SbMatrix

DESCRIPTION

4x4 matrix class/datatype used by many Inventor node and action classes. The matrices are stored in row-major order.

METHODS

SbMatrix()
SbMatrix(float a11, float a12, float a13, float a14, float a21, float a22, float a23, float a24, float a31, float a32, float a33, float a34, float a41, float a42, float a43, float a44)
SbMatrix(const SbMat &m)
Constructors.

void   **setValue**(const SbMat &m)
Sets value from 4x4 array of elements.

void   **getValue**(SbMat &m) const
const SbMat & **getValue**() const
Returns 4x4 array of elements.

void   **makeIdentity**()
Sets matrix to be identity.

static SbMatrix **identity**()
Returns an identity matrix.

void   **setRotate**(const SbRotation &q)
Sets matrix to rotate by given rotation.

void   **setScale**(float s)
Sets matrix to scale by given uniform factor.

void   **setScale**(const SbVec3f &s)
Sets matrix to scale by given vector.

void   **setTranslate**(const SbVec3f &t)
Sets matrix to translate by given vector.

void	**setTransform**(const SbVec3f &t, const SbRotation &r, const SbVec3f &s)
void	**setTransform**(const SbVec3f &t, const SbRotation &r, const SbVec3f &s, const SbRotation &so)
void	**setTransform**(const SbVec3f &translation, const SbRotation &rotation, const SbVec3f &scaleFactor, const SbRotation &scaleOrientation, const SbVec3f &center)

Composes the matrix based on a translation, rotation, scale, orientation for scale, and center. The *center* is the center point for scaling and rotation. The *scaleOrientation* chooses the primary axes for the scale.

void	**getTransform**(SbVec3f &t, SbRotation &r, SbVec3f &s, SbRotation &so) const

Return translation, rotation, scale, and scale orientation components of the matrix.

float	**det3**(int r1, int r2, int r3, int c1, int c2, int c3) const

Returns determinant of 3x3 submatrix composed of given row and column indices (0-3 for each).

float	**det3**() const

Returns determinant of upper-left 3x3 submatrix.

float	**det4**() const

Returns determinant of entire matrix.

SbBool	**factor**(SbMatrix &r, SbVec3f &s, SbMatrix &u, SbVec3f &t, SbMatrix &proj) const

Factors a matrix m into 5 pieces: m = r s r^ u t, where r^ means transpose of r, and r and u are rotations, s is a scale, and t is a translation. Any projection information is returned in *proj*.

SbMatrix	**inverse**() const

Returns inverse of matrix. Results are undefined for singular matrices. Uses LU decomposition.

SbBool	**LUDecomposition**(int index[4], float &d)

Perform in-place LU decomposition of matrix. *index* is index of rows in matrix. *d* is the parity of row swaps. Returns FALSE if singular.

void	**LUBackSubstitution**(int index[4], float b[4]) const

Perform back-substitution on LU-decomposed matrix. Index is permutation of rows from original matrix.

SbMatrix　　　　　　　**transpose**() const
　　　Returns transpose of matrix.

SbMatrix &　　　　　　**multRight**(const SbMatrix &m)
SbMatrix &　　　　　　**multLeft**(const SbMatrix &m)
　　　Multiplies matrix by given matrix on right or left.

void　　　　　　　　　**multMatrixVec**(const SbVec3f &src, SbVec3f &dst) const
　　　Multiplies matrix by given column vector, giving vector result.

void　　　　　　　　　**multVecMatrix**(const SbVec3f &src, SbVec3f &dst) const
　　　Multiplies given row vector by matrix, giving vector result.

void　　　　　　　　　**multDirMatrix**(const SbVec3f &src, SbVec3f &dst) const
　　　Multiplies given row vector by matrix, giving vector result. *src* is assumed to
　　　be a direction vector, so translation part of matrix is ignored.

void　　　　　　　　　**multLineMatrix**(const SbLine &src, SbLine &dst) const
　　　Multiplies the given line's origin by the matrix, and the line's direction by
　　　the rotation portion of the matrix.

void　　　　　　　　　**print**(FILE *fp) const
　　　Prints a formatted version of the matrix to the given file pointer.

float *　　　　　　　　**operator float ***()
　　　Cast: returns pointer to storage of first element.

SbMat　　　　　　　　**operator SbMat &**()
　　　Cast: returns reference to 4x4 array.

float *　　　　　　　　**operator [ ]**(int i)
const float *　　　　　**operator [ ]**(int i) const
　　　Make it look like a usual matrix (so you can do m[3][2]).

SbMatrix &　　　　　　**operator =**(const SbMat &m)
　　　Sets value from 4x4 array of elements.

SbMatrix &　　　　　　**operator =**(const SbMatrix &m)
　　　Set the matrix from another **SbMatrix**.

SbMatrix &　　　　　　**operator =**(const SbRotation &q)
　　　Set the matrix from an **SbRotation**.

SbMatrix   **operator** *=(const SbMatrix &m)
         Performs right multiplication with another matrix.

SbMatrix   **operator** *(const SbMatrix &m1, const SbMatrix &m2)
         Binary multiplication of matrices.

int   **operator** ==(const SbMatrix &m1, const SbMatrix &m2)
int   **operator** !=(const SbMatrix &m1, const SbMatrix &m2)
         Equality comparison operators.

SbBool   **equals**(const SbMatrix &m, float tolerance) const
         Equality comparison within given tolerance, for each component.

INCLUDE FILE
```
#include <Inventor/SbLinear.h>
```

SEE ALSO
SbVec3f, SbRotation

NAME

SbName — character string stored in a hash table

INHERITS FROM

SbName

DESCRIPTION

This class of strings stores the string in a hash table. It is used by the Inventor toolkit for keywords and other unique names. It is not recommended for general use (only in the context of Inventor objects). When a string is stored in this table, a pointer to the storage is returned. Two identical strings will return the same pointer. This means that comparison of two **SbNames** for equality can be accomplished by comparing their identifiers. **SbNames** are used for strings which are expected to show up frequently, such as node names.

METHODS

SbName()
SbName(const char *s)
SbName(const SbString &s)
SbName(const SbName &n)
~**SbName**()
Constructors and destructor.

const char *   **getString**() const
Returns pointer to the character string.

int   **getLength**() const
Returns length of string.

static SbBool   **isIdentStartChar**(char c)
Returns TRUE if given character is a legal starting character for an identifier.

static SbBool   **isIdentChar**(char c)
Returns TRUE if given character is a legal nonstarting character for an identifier.

int   **operator !**() const
Unary "not" operator; returns TRUE if string is empty ("").

int   **operator ==**(const char *s, const SbName &n)
int   **operator ==**(const SbName &n1, const SbName &n2)
int   **operator ==**(const SbName &n, const char *s)
Equality operator for SbName/char* and SbName/SbName comparison.

int	**operator** !=(const char *s, const SbName &n)
int	**operator** !=(const SbName &n1, const SbName &n2)
int	**operator** !=(const SbName &n, const char *s)

Inequality operator for SbName/char* and SbName/SbName comparison.

INCLUDE FILE

```
#include <Inventor/SbString.h>
```

SEE ALSO

SbString

NAME

SbPlane — oriented plane in 3D

INHERITS FROM

SbPlane

DESCRIPTION

Represents an oriented plane in 3D. This is a lightweight class/datatype that is used for arguments to some Inventor objects.

METHODS

SbPlane()
SbPlane(const SbVec3f &p0, const SbVec3f &p1, const SbVec3f &p2)
SbPlane(const SbVec3f &normal, float distance)
SbPlane(const SbVec3f &normal, const SbVec3f &point)
Constructors. *p0*, *p1*, and *p2* represent three points in the plane. *normal* is a normal vector, *distance* is distance from origin to plane along normal vector, and *point* is a point in 3-space for the plane to pass through.

void   **offset**(float d)
Offset a plane by a given distance.

SbBool   **intersect**(const SbLine &l, SbVec3f &intersection) const
Intersect line and plane, returning TRUE if there is an intersection, FALSE if line is parallel to plane.

void   **transform**(const SbMatrix &matrix)
Transforms the plane by the given matrix.

SbBool   **isInHalfSpace**(const SbVec3f &point) const
Returns TRUE if the given point is within the half-space defined by the plane.

const SbVec3f &   **getNormal**() const
Returns normal vector to plane.

float   **getDistanceFromOrigin**() const
Returns distance from origin to plane.

int   **operator** ==(const SbPlane &p1, const SbPlane &p2)
int   **operator** !=(const SbPlane &p1, const SbPlane &p2)
Equality/inequality comparison operators.

INCLUDE FILE

```
#include <Inventor/SbLinear.h>
```

SEE ALSO

SbVec3f, SbLine

SbPlaneProjector

NAME

SbPlaneProjector — plane projector

INHERITS FROM

SbProjector > SbPlaneProjector

DESCRIPTION

SbPlaneProjector projects the mouse onto a plane. This is typically used to write interactive 3D manipulators and viewers.

METHODS

SbPlaneProjector(SbBool orient = FALSE)
Constructor. The default plane passes through the origin and is oriented perpendicular to the Z axis.

SbPlaneProjector(const SbPlane &plane, SbBool orient = FALSE)
Constructor which is passed a plane. If orient to eye is TRUE, the plane will be reoriented to the eye.

~SbPlaneProjector()
Destructor.

void	**setPlane**(const SbPlane &plane)
const SbPlane &	**getPlane**() const

Set and get the plane to use.

void	**setOrientToEye**(SbBool orientToEye)
SbBool	**isOrientToEye**() const

Set and get whether the projector should be oriented towards the eye. If **orientToEye** is set to TRUE, the given plane's direction is ignored, and the plane will be oriented to the eye. It will pass through the same point from the origin defined by the original dir * dist. Set to FALSE if the plane's direction should remain in working space.

virtual SbVec3f   **getVector**(const SbVec2f &mousePosition1, const SbVec2f &mousePosition2)
Get a vector on this plane given two normalized mouse positions.

virtual SbVec3f   **getVector**(const SbVec2f &mousePosition)
Get a vector given the current mouse point. Uses the last point on this projector from the previous call to **getVector**() or **setStartPostion**(). Do not use this if the working space transform is changing since the new point will be in a different space than the old one.

void   **setStartPosition**(const SbVec2f &mousePosition)
Set the initial mouse position.

void   **setStartPosition**(const SbVec3f &point)
Set the initial position from a point on the projector.

Methods from class SbProjector:

project, setViewVolume, getViewVolume, setWorkingSpace, getWorkingSpace, copy

INCLUDE FILE

```
#include <Inventor/projectors/SbPlaneProjector.h>
```

SEE ALSO

SbCylinderProjector, SbCylinderPlaneProjector, SbCylinderSectionProjector, SbCylinderSheetProjector, SbLineProjector, SbSpherePlaneProjector, SbSphereProjector, SbSphereSectionProjector, SbSphereSheetProjector

NAME

SbPList — list of generic (void *) pointers

INHERITS FROM

SbPList

DESCRIPTION

This class manages a dynamic list of generic void * pointers. This class allows random access, insertion, and removal.

METHODS

SbPList()
SbPList(const SbPList &pl)
SbPList(int initSize)
~SbPList()

Constructors and destructor. *initSize* specifies an initial size for the list, which is useful as an optimization if you can estimate the length of the list before you construct it. If another **SbPList** is given, it returns a copy of that list.

void   **append**(void * ptr)
Adds given pointer to end of list.

int   **find**(const void *ptr) const
Returns index of given pointer in list, or -1 if not found.

void   **insert**(void *ptr, int addBefore)
Inserts given pointer in list before pointer with given index.

void   **remove**(int which)
Removes pointer with given index.

int   **getLength**() const
Returns number of pointers in list.

void   **truncate**(int start)
Removes all pointers after one with given index, inclusive.

void   **copy**(const SbPList &pl)
Copy a list.

SbPList &   **operator =**(const SbPList &pl)
Assignment operator; copies list into this list.

void *&   **operator** [ ](int i) const
          Returns pointer with given index.

int   **operator** ==(const SbPList &pl) const
int   **operator** !=(const SbPList &pl) const
          Equality and inequality operators.

INCLUDE FILE

```
#include <Inventor/SbPList.h>
```

NAME

SbProjector — base class for representing projectors

INHERITS FROM

SbProjector

DESCRIPTION

SbProjector is the base class for all projector classes. Projector classes are used to convert from window space (usually based on the mouse location) into a 3D point. This is done by projecting the window coordinate as a 3D vector onto a geometric function in 3-space, and computing the intersection point. Most projectors actually compute incremental changes and produce incremental rotations and translation as needed. Projectors are used to write 3D interactive manipulators and viewers.

METHODS

virtual SbVec3f   **project**(const SbVec2f &point)
> Apply the projector using the given point, returning the point in three dimensions that it projects to. The point should be normalized (lie in the range [0.0,1.0]), with (0,0) at the lower-left.

virtual void   **setViewVolume**(const SbViewVolume &vol)
const SbViewVolume &
> **getViewVolume**() const
> Set and get the view volume to use for the projection. This is typically supplied from **SoCamera::getViewVolume**().

virtual void   **setWorkingSpace**(const SbMatrix &space)
const SbMatrix &
> **getWorkingSpace**() const
> Set and get the transform space to work in. This matrix should transform working space coordinates into world space. The default matrix is identity, meaning that the default working space is world space.

virtual SbProjector *
> **copy**() const
> Creates and returns an exact copy of the projector.

INCLUDE FILE

```
#include <Inventor/projectors/SbProjector.h>
```

SEE ALSO

SbCylinderProjector, SbCylinderPlaneProjector, SbCylinderSectionProjector, SbCylinderSheetProjector, SbLineProjector, SbPlaneProjector, SbSpherePlaneProjector, SbSphereProjector, SbSphereSectionProjector, SbSphereSheetProjector

NAME

SbRotation — class for representing a rotation

INHERITS FROM

SbRotation

DESCRIPTION

Object that stores a rotation. There are several ways to specify a rotation: quaternion (4 floats), 4x4 rotation matrix, or axis and angle. All angles are in radians and all rotations are right-handed.

METHODS

SbRotation()
SbRotation(const float v[4])
SbRotation(float q0, float q1, float q2, float q3)
SbRotation(const SbMatrix &m)
SbRotation(const SbVec3f &axis, float radians)
SbRotation(const SbVec3f &rotateFrom, const SbVec3f &rotateTo)

Constructors for rotation. Matrix constructor requires a valid rotation matrix. Rotation constructor defines rotation that rotates from one vector into another. The *rotateFrom* and *rotateTo* vectors are normalized by the constructor before calculating the rotation.

const float *   **getValue**() const
Returns pointer to array of 4 components defining quaternion.

void   **getValue**(float &q0, float &q1, float &q2, float &q3) const
Returns 4 individual components of rotation quaternion.

SbRotation &   **setValue**(float q0, float q1, float q2, float q3)
Sets value of rotation from 4 individual components of a quaternion.

void   **getValue**(SbVec3f &axis, float &radians) const
Returns corresponding 3D rotation axis vector and angle in radians.

void   **getValue**(SbMatrix &matrix) const
Returns corresponding 4x4 rotation matrix.

SbRotation &   **invert**()
Changes a rotation to be its inverse.

SbRotation   **inverse**() const
Returns the inverse of a rotation.

SbRotation &   **setValue**(const float q[4])
Sets value of rotation from array of 4 components of a quaternion.

SbRotation &   **setValue**(const SbMatrix &m)
Sets value of rotation from a rotation matrix.

SbRotation &   **setValue**(const SbVec3f &axis, float radians)
Sets value of vector from 3D rotation axis vector and angle in radians.

SbRotation &   **setValue**(const SbVec3f &rotateFrom, const SbVec3f &rotateTo)
Sets rotation to rotate one direction vector to another. The *rotateFrom* and *rotateTo* arguments are normalized before the rotation is calculated.

SbRotation &   **operator *=**(const SbRotation &q)
Multiplies by another rotation; results in product of rotations.

int   **operator ==**(const SbRotation &q1, const SbRotation &q2)
int   **operator !=**(const SbRotation &q1, const SbRotation &q2)
Equality comparison operators.

SbBool   **equals**(const SbRotation &r, float tolerance) const
Equality comparison within given tolerance — the square of the length of the maximum distance between the two quaternion vectors.

SbRotation   **operator ***(const SbRotation &q1, const SbRotation &q2)
Multiplication of two rotations; results in product of rotations.

void   **multVec**(const SbVec3f &src, SbVec3f &dst) const
Multiplies the given vector by the matrix of this rotation.

void   **scaleAngle**(float scaleFactor)
Keep the axis the same. Multiply the angle of rotation by the amount *scaleFactor*.

static SbRotation   **slerp**(const SbRotation &rot0, const SbRotation &rot1, float t)
Spherical linear interpolation: as *t* goes from 0 to 1, returned value goes from *rot0* to *rot1*.

static SbRotation   **identity**()
Returns a null rotation.

INCLUDE FILE

```
#include <Inventor/SbLinear.h>
```

NOTES

Rotations are stored internally as quaternions.

SEE ALSO

SbVec3f, SbMatrix

NAME

SbSphere — class for representing a sphere

INHERITS FROM

SbSphere

DESCRIPTION

Represents a sphere in 3D. This is a lightweight datatype that is used for arguments or return values in the Inventor toolkit. See **SoSphere** for a database sphere (used for rendering, picking, etc.).

METHODS

SbSphere()
SbSphere(const SbVec3f &center, float radius)
Constructors.

void   **setValue**(const SbVec3f &center, float radius)
Change the center and radius.

void   **setCenter**(const SbVec3f &center)
void   **setRadius**(float radius)
Set just the center or radius.

const SbVec3f &   **getCenter**() const
float   **getRadius**() const
Return the center and radius.

void   **circumscribe**(const SbBox3f &box)
Return a sphere containing a given box.

SbBool   **intersect**(const SbLine &l, SbVec3f &intersection) const
SbBool   **intersect**(const SbLine &l, SbVec3f &enter, SbVec3f &exit)
          const
Intersect line and sphere, returning TRUE if there is an intersection. The line is treated as a ray.

INCLUDE FILE

```
#include <Inventor/SbLinear.h>
```

SEE ALSO

SbVec3f, SbLine, SoSphere

NAME

SbSpherePlaneProjector — sphere-plane projector

INHERITS FROM

SbProjector > SbSphereProjector > SbSphereSectionProjector >
SbSpherePlaneProjector

DESCRIPTION

SbSpherePlaneProjector projects a window space point (usually based on the mouse location) onto a surface defined by a sphere and plane cutting through the sphere. Two projected points can produce a rotation about the sphere's center. When the mouse position projects onto the plane, the rotations will be as if the plane is being dragged, causing the sphere to roll beneath it.

Incremental changes (delta rotation) can be computed during interactive sessions. Sphere projectors are typically used to write interactive 3D manipulators and viewers.

METHODS

SbSpherePlaneProjector(float edgeTol = .9, SbBool orientToEye = TRUE)
SbSpherePlaneProjector(const SbSphere &sph, float edgeTol = .9, SbBool orientToEye = TRUE)

Constructors. The first uses a default sphere centered at the origin with radius 1.0; the sphere is supplied in the second. The position of the plane is specified as a fraction of the sphere radius with the parameter **edgeTol**. A tolerance value of 1.0 positions the plane down the center of the sphere. A tolerance value of 0.5 defines the longitudinal plane halfway between the center and the outside edge of the sphere. The default value is .9, so that almost half the sphere is in front of the plane. The **orientToEye** parameter determines whether the plane is perpendicular to the eye, or perpendicular to the sphere's Z axis. Setting that parameter to TRUE (the default) specifies that the plane be perpendicular to the eye, which is most often the desired behavior.

The default view volume is undefined, and the working space is identity.

~SbSpherePlaneProjector()

Destructor.

Methods from class SbSphereSectionProjector:

setTolerance, getTolerance, setRadialFactor, getRadialFactor,
isWithinTolerance

Methods from class SbSphereProjector:

projectAndGetRotation, getRotation, setSphere, getSphere, setOrientToEye, isOrientToEye, setFront, isFront, isPointInFront

Methods from class SbProjector:

project, setViewVolume, getViewVolume, setWorkingSpace, getWorkingSpace, copy

INCLUDE FILE

```
#include <Inventor/projectors/SbSpherePlaneProjector.h>
```

SEE ALSO

SbCylinderProjector, SbCylinderPlaneProjector, SbCylinderSectionProjector, SbCylinderSheetProjector, SbLineProjector, SbPlaneProjector, SbSphereSheetProjector

NAME

SbSphereProjector — sphere projector

INHERITS FROM

SbProjector > SbSphereProjector

DESCRIPTION

SbSphereProjector is an abstract base class for projectors that use a sphere in their projection. Sphere projectors are typically used to write interactive 3D manipulators and viewers.

METHODS

SbVec3f   **projectAndGetRotation**(const SbVec2f &point, SbRotation &rot)

Apply the projector using the given point, returning the point in three dimensions that it projects to. This also returns in **rot** a rotation on the surface of the sphere from the last projected point to this one. The passed **point** should be normalized (i.e. lie in the range [0.0,1.0]), with (0,0) at the lower-left.

virtual SbRotation   **getRotation**(const SbVec3f &point1, const SbVec3f &point2)

Get a rotation given two points on this sphere projector. The rotation will be on the surface of the sphere.

void   **setSphere**(const SbSphere &sph)
const SbSphere &   **getSphere**() const

Set and get the sphere on which to project points. The default sphere has radius 1.0.

void   **setOrientToEye**(SbBool orientToEye)
SbBool   **isOrientToEye**() const

Set and get whether the projector should always be oriented towards the eye. Set to FALSE if the tolerance should be evaluated in working space.

void   **setFront**(SbBool isFront)
SbBool   **isFront**() const
SbBool   **isPointInFront**(const SbVec3f &point) const

Set and get whether the projector should intersect the half of the sphere that faces the eye. Set to FALSE if the projector should intersect with the rear half.

Methods from class SbProjector:

project, setViewVolume, getViewVolume, setWorkingSpace,
getWorkingSpace, copy

INCLUDE FILE

```
#include <Inventor/projectors/SbSphereProjector.h>
```

SEE ALSO

SbCylinderProjector, SbCylinderPlaneProjector, SbCylinderSectionProjector,
SbCylinderSheetProjector, SbLineProjector, SbPlaneProjector,
SbSpherePlaneProjector, SbSphereSectionProjector, SbSphereSheetProjector

NAME

SbSphereSectionProjector — sphere-section projector

INHERITS FROM

SbProjector > SbSphereProjector > SbSphereSectionProjector

DESCRIPTION

SbSphereSectionProjector projects a window space point (usually based on the mouse location) onto the section of a sphere that has been sliced by a plane. Two projected points can produce a rotation about the sphere's center. The tolerance slice can be specified as a fraction of the radius of the sphere. The projection point will not extend beyond the sliced portion of the sphere.

Incremental changes (delta rotation) can be computed during interactive sessions. Sphere projectors are typically used to write interactive 3D manipulators and viewers.

METHODS

SbSphereSectionProjector(float edgeTol = .9, SbBool
    orientToEye = TRUE)
SbSphereSectionProjector(const SbSphere &sph, float edgeTol
    = .9, SbBool orientToEye = TRUE)

Constructors. The first uses a default sphere centered at the origin with radius 1.0; the sphere is supplied in the second. The position of the plane which slices the sphere into a section is specified as a fraction of the sphere radius with the parameter **edgeTol**. A tolerance value of 1.0 positions the plane down the center of the sphere. A tolerance value of 0.5 defines the longitudinal plane halfway between the center and the outside edge of the sphere. The default value is .9, so that almost half the sphere is in front of the plane. The **orientToEye** parameter determines whether the plane is perpendicular to the eye, or perpendicular to the sphere's Z axis. Setting that parameter to TRUE (the default) specifies that the plane be perpendicular to the eye, which is most often the desired behavior.

The default view volume is undefined, and the working space is identity.

~SbSphereSectionProjector()

Destructor.

void   **setTolerance**(float edgeTol)
float   **getTolerance**() const

Set and get the edge tolerance as a fraction of the radius of the sphere. If this is 1.0, the projector is a hemisphere. If this is .1, the projector is a slice of the sphere with radius .1*radius. Default is .9.

void	**setRadialFactor**(float radialFactor = 0.0)
float	**getRadialFactor**() const

Set and get the radial rotation factor. When the mouse is dragged off the edge of the sphere, the mouse motion can be classified as either tangential (moving in a circle around the sphere) or radial (moving toward or away from the center). The tangential motion will always map to a rotation around the center, (like the hands of a clock). The radial motion, by default, has no effect. But if you set the **radialFactor** to be > 0.0, this motion will make the sphere rotate as if the mouse is pulling the top of the sphere out toward the mouse. If **radialFactor** = 1.0, then pulling has a 'normal' feel (that is, the mouse motion causes the same amount of rotation as if you had rotated by hitting the actual surface of the sphere). Default is 0.0

SbBool	**isWithinTolerance**(const SbVec3f &point)

Find whether this point on the sphere or tolerance plane is within tolerance.

Methods from class SbSphereProjector:

projectAndGetRotation, getRotation, setSphere, getSphere, setOrientToEye, isOrientToEye, setFront, isFront, isPointInFront

Methods from class SbProjector:

project, setViewVolume, getViewVolume, setWorkingSpace, getWorkingSpace, copy

INCLUDE FILE

```
#include <Inventor/projectors/SbSphereSectionProjector.h>
```

SEE ALSO

SbCylinderProjector, SbCylinderSectionProjector, SbCylinderPlaneProjector, SbCylinderSheetProjector, SbLineProjector, SbPlaneProjector, SbSpherePlaneProjector, SbSphereSheetProjector

NAME

SbSphereSheetProjector — sphere-sheet projector

INHERITS FROM

SbProjector > SbSphereProjector > SbSphereSheetProjector

DESCRIPTION

SbSphereSheetProjector projects a window space point (usually based on the mouse location) onto the surface of a sphere with a hyperbolic sheet draped over it. This allows smooth transitions onto and off of the sphere. Two projected points can produce a rotation about the sphere's center. When the mouse position projects on to the sheet, the rotations will be as if the sheet is being dragged, causing the sphere to roll beneath it.

Incremental changes (delta rotation) can be computed during interactive sessions. Sphere projectors are typically used to write interactive 3D manipulators and viewers.

METHODS

SbSphereSheetProjector(SbBool orientToEye = TRUE)
SbSphereSheetProjector(const SbSphere &sph, SbBool
    orientToEye = TRUE)

Constructors. The first uses a default sphere centered at the origin with radius 1.0; the sphere is supplied in the second. The **orientToEye** parameter determines whether the sheet is perpendicular to the eye, or perpendicular to the sphere's Z axis. Setting that parameter to TRUE (the default) specifies that the sheet be perpendicular to the eye, which is most often the desired behavior.

The default view volume is undefined, and the working space is identity.

~SbSphereSheetProjector()

Destructor.

Methods from class SbSphereProjector:

projectAndGetRotation, getRotation, setSphere, getSphere, setOrientToEye, isOrientToEye, setFront, isFront, isPointInFront

Methods from class SbProjector:

project, setViewVolume, getViewVolume, setWorkingSpace, getWorkingSpace, copy

SbSphereSheetProjector

INCLUDE FILE

    #include <Inventor/projectors/SbSphereSheetProjector.h>

SEE ALSO

SbCylinderProjector, SbCylinderPlaneProjector, SbCylinderSectionProjector, SbCylinderSheetProjector, SbLineProjector, SbPlaneProjector, SbSpherePlaneProjector

NAME

SbString — class for smart character strings

INHERITS FROM

SbString

DESCRIPTION

Strings which have many convenience methods to make string manipulation easier.

METHODS

SbString()
SbString(const char *str)
SbString(const char *str, int start, int end)
SbString(const SbString &str)
SbString(int digitString)
~SbString()

Constructors and destructor. Constructors take a character string, the subset of a character string from start to end (inclusive), or an integer to be turned into a string. For example, SbString(1234) creates the string "1234". SbString("Testing",1,3) creates the string "est".

u_long   **hash**()

Returns a reasonable hash key for string.

int   **getLength**() const

Returns length of string.

void   **makeEmpty**(SbBool freeOld = TRUE)

Sets string to be the empty string (""). If freeOld is TRUE (default), any old storage is freed up.

const char *   **getString**() const

Returns pointer to the character string.

SbString   **getSubString**(int startChar, int endChar = -1) const

Returns new string representing sub-string from *startChar* to *endChar*, inclusive. If *endChar* is -1 (the default), the sub-string from *startChar* until the end is returned.

void   **deleteSubString**(int startChar, int endChar = -1)

Deletes the characters from *startChar* to *endChar*, inclusive, from the string. If *endChar* is -1 (the default), all characters from *startChar* until the end are deleted.

SbString   **operator** =(const char *str)
SbString &   **operator** =(const SbString &str)
      Assignment operators for character string, **SbString**.

SbString &   **operator** +=(const char *str)
SbString &   **operator** +=(const SbString &str)
      Concatenation operators "+=" for string, **SbString**.

int   **operator** !() const
      Unary "not" operator; returns TRUE if string is empty ("").

int   **operator** ==(const char *s, const SbString &str)
int   **operator** ==(const SbString &str, const char *s)
int   **operator** ==(const SbString &str1, const SbString &str2)
      Equality operator for **SbString**/char* and **SbString/SbString** comparison.

int   **operator** !=(const char *s, const SbString &str)
int   **operator** !=(const SbString &str, const char *s)
int   **operator** !=(const SbString &str1, const SbString &str2)
      Inequality operator for **SbString**/char* and **SbString/SbString** comparison.

INCLUDE FILE
      `#include <Inventor/SbString.h>`

SEE ALSO
      SbName

NAME

SbTime — class for representation of a time

INHERITS FROM

SbTime

DESCRIPTION

This class represents and performs operations on time. Operations may be done in seconds, seconds and microseconds, or using a struct timeval (defined in */usr/include/sys/time.h*).

METHODS

SbTime()
SbTime(double sec)
SbTime(long sec, long usec)
SbTime(const struct timeval *tv)

Constructors taking seconds, seconds and microseconds, or a *struct timeval*. NOTE that an integer parameter will not automatically cast to a double to invoke the constructor taking seconds; that is, **SbTime(1)** will result in a compilation error — **SbTime(1.0)** must be used instead. This is to avoid errors in upgrading from an earlier release, in which **SbTime(1)** had different semantics. In future releases, this distinction will be eliminated, and the effect of **SbTime(1.0)** and that of **SbTime(1)** will be identical.

static SbTime   **getTimeOfDay**()
Get the current time (seconds since Jan 1, 1970).

void   **setToTimeOfDay**()
Set to the current time (seconds since Jan 1, 1970).

static SbTime   **zero**()
Get a zero time.

static SbTime   **max**()
Get a time far, far into the future.

void   **setValue**(double sec)
Set time from a double (in seconds).

void   **setValue**(long sec, long usec)
Set time from seconds + microseconds.

void   **setValue**(const struct timeval *tv)
Set time from a *struct timeval*.

void   **setMsecValue**(unsigned long msec)
Set time from milliseconds.

double   **getValue**() const
Get time in seconds as a double.

void   **getValue**(long &sec, long &usec) const
Get time in seconds and microseconds.

void   **getValue**(struct timeval *tv) const
Get time in a *struct timeval*.

unsigned long   **getMsecValue**() const
Get time in milliseconds (for Xt).

SbString   **format**(const char *fmt = "%S.%i") const
Convert to a string. The default format is seconds with 3 digits of fraction precision. *fmt* is a character string that consists of field descriptors and text characters, in a manner analogous to **cftime (3C)** and **printf (3S)**. Each field descriptor consists of a % character followed by another character which specifies the replacement for the field descriptor. All other characters are copied from *fmt* into the result. The following field descriptors are supported:

        %   the '%' character
        D   total number of days
        H   total number of hours
        M   total number of minutes
        S   total number of seconds
        I   total number of milliseconds
        U   total number of microseconds
        h   hours remaining after the days (00-23)
        m   minutes remaining after the hours (00-59)
        s   seconds remaining after the minutes (00-59)
        i   milliseconds remaining after the seconds (000-999)
        u   microseconds remaining after the seconds (000000-999999)

The uppercase descriptors are formatted with a leading '—' for negative times; the lowercase descriptors are formatted fixed width, with leading zeros. For example, a reasonable format string might be "elapsed time: %M minutes, %s seconds". The default value of *fmt*, "%S.%i", formats the time as seconds with 3 digits of fractional precision.

SbString   **formatDate**(const char *fmt = "%A, %D %r") const
    Convert to a date string, interpreting the time as seconds since Jan 1, 1970.
    The default format gives "Tuesday, 01/26/93 11:23:41 AM". See the **cftime()**
    reference page for explanation of the format string.

SbTime   **operator** +(const SbTime &t0, const SbTime &t1)
SbTime   **operator** -(const SbTime &t0, const SbTime &t1)
    Addition and subtraction of two times.

SbTime &   **operator** +=(const SbTime &tm)
SbTime &   **operator** -=(const SbTime &tm)
    Addition and subtraction of two times which modifies the time structure.

SbTime   **operator** -() const
    Unary negation.

SbTime   **operator** *(double s, const SbTime &tm)
SbTime   **operator** *(const SbTime &tm, double s)
SbTime   **operator** /(const SbTime &tm, double s)
    Multiplication and division by scalar.

SbTime &   **operator** *=(double s)
SbTime &   **operator** /=(double s)
    Destructive multiplication and division by scalar.

double   **operator** /(const SbTime &tm) const
    Division by another time.

SbTime   **operator** %(const SbTime &tm) const
    Modulus for two times (remainder when time1 is divided by time2).

int   **operator** ==(const SbTime &tm) const
int   **operator** !=(const SbTime &tm) const
    Equality operators.

SbBool   **operator** <(const SbTime &tm) const
SbBool   **operator** >(const SbTime &tm) const
SbBool   **operator** <=(const SbTime &tm) const
SbBool   **operator** >=(const SbTime &tm) const
    Relational operators.

SbTime

INCLUDE FILE

```
#include <Inventor/SbTime.h>
```

SEE ALSO

cftime

NAME

SbVec2f — 2D vector class

INHERITS FROM

SbVec2f

DESCRIPTION

2D vector class used to store 2D vectors and points. This class is used throughout Inventor for arguments and return values.

METHODS

        SbVec2f()

Default constructor.

        SbVec2f(const float v[2])
        SbVec2f(float x, float y)

Constructor given vector components.

float   **dot**(const SbVec2f &v) const

Returns dot (inner) product of vector and another vector.

SbBool   **equals**(const SbVec2f v, float tolerance) const

Equality comparison within given tolerance — the square of the length of the maximum distance between the two vectors.

const float *   **getValue**() const
void   **getValue**(float &x, float &y) const

Returns vector components.

float   **length**() const

Returns geometric length of vector.

void   **negate**()

Negates each component of vector in place.

float   **normalize**()

Changes vector to be unit length.

SbVec2f &   **setValue**(const float v[2])
SbVec2f &   **setValue**(float x, float y)

Sets the vector components.

float &   **operator** [ ](int i)
const float &   **operator** [ ](int i)
        Accesses indexed component of vector.

SbVec2f &   **operator** *=(float d)
SbVec2f &   **operator** /=(float d)
        Component-wise scalar multiplication and division operators.

SbVec2f &   **operator** +=(const SbVec2f &u)
SbVec2f &   **operator** -=(const SbVec2f &u)
        Component-wise vector addition and subtraction operators.

SbVec2f   **operator** -() const
        Nondestructive unary negation — returns a new vector.

SbVec2f   **operator** *(const SbVec2f &v, float d)
SbVec2f   **operator** *(float d, const SbVec2f &v)
SbVec2f   **operator** /(const SbVec2f &v, float d)
        Component-wise binary scalar multiplication and division operators.

SbVec2f   **operator** +(const SbVec2f &v1, const SbVec2f &v2)
SbVec2f   **operator** -(const SbVec2f &v1, const SbVec2f &v2)
        Component-wise binary vector addition and subtraction operators.

int   **operator** ==(const SbVec2f &v1, const SbVec2f &v2)
int   **operator** !=(const SbVec2f &v1, const SbVec2f &v2)
        Equality comparison operators.

INCLUDE FILE
        #include <Inventor/SbLinear.h>

SEE ALSO
        SbVec3f, SbVec4f, SbVec2s, SbRotation

NAME

SbVec2s — 2D vector class

INHERITS FROM

SbVec2s

DESCRIPTION

2D vector class used to store 2D integer vectors and points. This class is used throughout Inventor for arguments and return values.

METHODS

SbVec2s()
Default constructor.

SbVec2s(const short v[2])
SbVec2s(short x, short y)
Constructor given 2 components.

long   **dot**(const SbVec2f &v) const
Returns dot (inner) product of vector and another vector.

const short *   **getValue**() const
void   **getValue**(short &x, short &y) const
Returns vector components.

void   **negate**()
Negates each component of vector in place.

SbVec2s &   **setValue**(const short v[2])
SbVec2s &   **setValue**(short x, short y)
Sets vector components.

short &   **operator [ ]**(int i)
const short &   **operator [ ]**(int i)
Accesses indexed component of vector.

SbVec2s &   **operator *=**(int d)
SbVec2s &   **operator *=**(double d)
SbVec2s &   **operator /=**(int d)
SbVec2s &   **operator /=**(double d)
Component-wise scalar multiplication and division operators.

SbVec2s   **operator** +=(const SbVec2s &u)
SbVec2s   **operator** -=(const SbVec2s &u)
       Component-wise vector addition and subtraction operators.

SbVec2s   **operator** -() const
       Nondestructive unary negation — returns a new vector.

SbVec2s   **operator** *(const SbVec2s &v, int d)
SbVec2s   **operator** *(const SbVec2s &v, double d)
SbVec2s   **operator** *(int d, const SbVec2s &v)
SbVec2s   **operator** *(double d, const SbVec2s &v)
SbVec2s   **operator** /(const SbVec2s &v, int d)
SbVec2s   **operator** /(const SbVec2s &v, double d)
       Component-wise binary scalar multiplication and division operators.

SbVec2s   **operator** +(const SbVec2s &v1, const SbVec2s &v2)
SbVec2s   **operator** -(const SbVec2s &v1, const SbVec2s &v2)
       Component-wise binary vector addition and subtraction operators.

int   **operator** ==(const SbVec2s &v1, const SbVec2s &v2)
int   **operator** !=(const SbVec2s &v1, const SbVec2s &v2)
       Equality comparison operators.

INCLUDE FILE

```
#include <Inventor/SbLinear.h>
```

SEE ALSO

SbVec3f, SbVec4f, SbVec2f

NAME

    SbVec3f — 3D vector class

INHERITS FROM

    SbVec3f

DESCRIPTION

    3D vector class used to store 3D vectors and points. This class is used throughout Inventor for arguments and return values.

METHODS

                  SbVec3f()
    Default constructor.

                  SbVec3f(const float v[3])
                  SbVec3f(float x, float y, float z)
    Constructor given vector components.

                  SbVec3f(SbPlane &p0, SbPlane &p1, SbPlane &p2)
    Constructor given 3 planes.

SbVec3f   **cross**(const SbVec3f &v) const
    Returns right-handed cross product of vector and another vector.

float   **dot**(const SbVec3f &v) const
    Returns dot (inner) product of vector and another vector.

SbBool   **equals**(const SbVec3f v, float tolerance) const
    Equality comparison within given tolerance — the square of the length of the maximum distance between the two vectors.

SbVec3f   **getClosestAxis**() const
    Returns principal axis that is closest (based on maximum dot product) to this vector.

const float *   **getValue**() const
void   **getValue**(float &x, float &y, float &z) const
    Returns vector components.

float   **length**() const
    Returns geometric length of vector.

void   **negate**()
    Negates each component of vector in place.

float   **normalize**()
Changes vector to be unit length, returning the length before normalization.

SbVec3f &   **setValue**(const float v[3])
SbVec3f &   **setValue**(float x, float y, float z)
Sets the vector components.

SbVec3f &   **setValue**(const SbVec3f &barycentic, const SbVec3f &v0, const
                  SbVec3f &v1, const SbVec3f &v2)
Sets value of vector as the weighted average of 3 other vectors.

float &   **operator** [ ](int i)
const float &   **operator** [ ](int i)
Accesses indexed component of vector.

SbVec3f &   **operator** *=(float d)
SbVec3f &   **operator** /=(float d)
Component-wise scalar multiplication and division operators.

SbVec3f &   **operator** +=(const SbVec3f &u)
SbVec3f &   **operator** -=(const SbVec3f &u)
Component-wise vector addition and subtraction operators.

SbVec3f   **operator** -() const
Nondestructive unary negation — returns a new vector.

SbVec3f   **operator** *(const SbVec3f &v, float d)
SbVec3f   **operator** *(float d, const SbVec3f &v)
SbVec3f   **operator** /(const SbVec3f &v, float d)
Component-wise binary scalar multiplication and division operators.

SbVec3f   **operator** +(const SbVec3f &v1, const SbVec3f &v2)
SbVec3f   **operator** -(const SbVec3f &v1, const SbVec3f &v2)
Component-wise binary vector addition and subtraction operators.

int   **operator** ==(const SbVec3f &v1, const SbVec3f &v2)
int   **operator** !=(const SbVec3f &v1, const SbVec3f &v2)
Equality comparison operators.

INCLUDE FILE

```
#include <Inventor/SbLinear.h>
```

SEE ALSO

SbVec2f, SbVec4f, SbVec2s, SbRotation

NAME

SbVec4f — 4D vector class

INHERITS FROM

SbVec4f

DESCRIPTION

4D vector class used to store homogeneous coordinates. This class is used in Inventor for arguments and return values.

METHODS

> **SbVec4f**()
> Default constructor.

> **SbVec4f**(const float v[4])
> **SbVec4f**(float x, float y, float z, float w)
> Constructor given vector components.

float   **dot**(const SbVec4f &v) const
> Returns dot (inner) product of vector and another vector.

SbBool   **equals**(const SbVec4f v, float tolerance) const
> Equality comparison within given tolerance — the square of the length of the maximum distance between the two vectors.

void   **getReal**(SbVec3f &v) const
> Returns the real portion of the vector by dividing by the fourth value.

const float *   **getValue**() const
void   **getValue**(float &x, float &y, float &z, float &w) const
> Returns vector components.

float   **length**() const
> Returns geometric length of vector.

void   **negate**()
> Negates each component of vector in place.

> **normalize**()
> Changes vector to be unit length.

SbVec4f &   **setValue**(const float v[4])
SbVec4f &   **setValue**(float x, float y, float z, float w)
> Sets the vector components.

float &	**operator** [ ](int i)
const float &	**operator** [ ](int i)

Accesses indexed component of vector.

SbVec4f &	**operator** *=(float d)
SbVec4f &	**operator** /=(float d)

Component-wise scalar multiplication and division operators.

SbVec4f &	**operator** +=(const SbVec4f &u)
SbVec4f &	**operator** -=(const SbVec4f &u)

Component-wise vector addition and subtraction operators.

SbVec4f	**operator** -() const

Nondestructive unary negation — returns a new vector.

SbVec4f	**operator** *(const SbVec4f &v, float d)
SbVec4f	**operator** *(float d, const SbVec4f &v)
SbVec4f	**operator** /(const SbVec4f &v, float d)

Component-wise binary scalar multiplication and division operators.

SbVec4f	**operator** +(const SbVec4f &v1, const SbVec4f &v2)
SbVec4f	**operator** -(const SbVec4f &v1, const SbVec4f &v2)

Component-wise binary vector addition and subtraction operators.

int	**operator** ==(const SbVec4f &v1, const SbVec4f &v2)
int	**operator** !=(const SbVec4f &v1, const SbVec4f &v2)

Equality comparison operators.

INCLUDE FILE

```
#include <Inventor/SbLinear.h>
```

SEE ALSO

SbVec2f, SbVec3f, SbVec2s, SbRotation

NAME

SbViewportRegion — class for representing a viewport

INHERITS FROM

SbViewportRegion

DESCRIPTION

This class represents the active viewport region in a display window. It contains the screen-space size of the window as well as the origin and size of the viewport within the window. By default, the viewport is the same as the full window. Methods allow the viewport to be set either in terms of screen-space pixels or as normalized coordinates, where (0,0) is the lower-left corner of the window and (1,1) is the upper-right corner.

METHODS

SbViewportRegion()
SbViewportRegion(short width, short height)
SbViewportRegion(SbVec2s winSize)
SbViewportRegion(const SbViewportRegion &vpReg)
Constructors of various kinds.

void   **setWindowSize**(short width, short height)
Changes window size to given width and height in pixels.

void   **setWindowSize**(SbVec2s winSize)
Changes window size to given width and height in pixels, given as **SbVec2s.**

void   **setViewport**(float left, float bottom, float width, float height)
Sets viewport to given region, specified as normalized window coordinates: (0,0) is the lower-left corner, (1,1) is the upper-right.

void   **setViewport**(SbVec2f origin, SbVec2f size)
Sets viewport to region with given origin (lower-left corner) and size, given as normalized coordinate vectors.

void   **setViewportPixels**(short left, short bottom, short width, short height)
Sets viewport to given region, specified as pixel coordinates in window: (0,0) is the lower-left corner.

void   **setViewportPixels**(SbVec2s origin, SbVec2s size)
Sets viewport to region with given origin (lower-left corner) and size, given as pixel coordinates.

const SbVec2s &   **getWindowSize**() const
> Returns window size in pixels.

const SbVec2f &   **getViewportOrigin**() const
> Returns viewport origin in normalized coordinates.

const SbVec2s &   **getViewportOriginPixels**() const
> Returns viewport origin in pixels.

const SbVec2f &   **getViewportSize**() const
> Returns viewport size in normalized coordinates.

const SbVec2s &   **getViewportSizePixels**() const
> Returns viewport size in pixels.

float   **getViewportAspectRatio**() const
> Returns aspect ratio (width/height) of viewport.

void   **scaleWidth**(float ratio)
void   **scaleHeight**(float ratio)
> Scales viewport within window to be the given ratio of its current width or height, leaving the resulting viewport centered about the same point as the current one.

void   **setPixelsPerInch**(float ppi)
float   **getPixelsPerInch**() const
> Sets/returns the pixel-per-inch ratio for the display device the viewport is part of. The default value is 72 (1 pixel per printer's point).

float   **getPixelsPerPoint**() const
> Convenience function that returns number of pixels per printer's point.

friend int   **operator ==**(const SbViewportRegion &reg1, const SbViewportRegion &reg2)
> Equality comparison operator.

INCLUDE FILE
> `#include <Inventor/SbViewportRegion.h>`

SEE ALSO
> SbVec2f, SbVec2s

NAME

SbViewVolume — 3D viewing volume class

INHERITS FROM

SbViewVolume

DESCRIPTION

Class used to represent a 3D viewing volume. This class is used to represent viewing frusta and picking volumes. For perspective projection, the view volume is a frustum. For orthographic (parallel) projection, the view volume is a rectangular prism.

METHODS

> **SbViewVolume()**
> **˜SbViewVolume()**

Constructor and destructor.

void	**getMatrices**(SbMatrix &affine, SbMatrix &proj) const

Returns two matrices corresponding to the view volume. The first is a viewing matrix, which is guaranteed to be an affine transformation. The second is suitable for use as a projection matrix in OpenGL.

SbMatrix	**getMatrix**() const

Like the method above, but returns the affine and projection parts together in one matrix (i.e., **affine.multRight(proj))**.

SbMatrix	**getCameraSpaceMatrix**() const

Returns a matrix that transforms the view volume into camera space: it translates the view volume so the viewpoint is at the origin, and rotates it so the view direction is along the negative z axis.

void	**projectPointToLine**(const SbVec2f &pt, SbLine &line) const
void	**projectPointToLine**(const SbVec2f &pt, SbVec3f &line0, SbVec3f &line1) const

Maps a 2D point (in 0 <= x,y <= 1) to a 3D line.

void	**projectToScreen**(const SbVec3f &src, SbVec3f &dst) const

Maps the 3D point in world coordinates to a 2D point in normalized screen coordinates (0 <= x,y,z <= 1, 0 <= z <= 1). The z-screen coordinate represents the homogenized z coordinate which goes (nonlinearly) from 0 at the near clipping plane to 1 at the far clipping plane.

SbPlane	**getPlane**(float distFromEye) const

Returns a plane parallel to the near (or far) plane of the view volume at a given distance from the projection point (eye).

SbVec3f   **getSightPoint**(float distFromEye) const
Returns the point along the line of sight at the given distance from the
projection point (eye).

SbVec3f   **getPlanePoint**(float distFromEye, const SbVec2f &normPoint)
                 const
Returns the projection of a given point in normalized screen coordinates (see
projectToScreen()) onto the plane parallel to the near plane that is at
distFromEye units from the eye.

SbRotation   **getAlignRotation**(SbBool rightAngleOnly = FALSE) const
Returns a rotation that would align a viewed object so that its positive x-axis
(of its object space) is to the right in the view and its positive y-axis is up. If
rightAngleOnly is TRUE, it will come as close as it can to this goal by using
only 90 degree rotations.

float   **getWorldToScreenScale**(const SbVec3f &worldCenter, float
                 normRadius) const
Returns a scale factor that would scale a unit sphere centered at *worldCenter*
so that it would appear to have the given radius in normalized screen
coordinates when projected onto the near plane.

SbVec2f   **projectBox**(const SbBox3f &box) const
Projects the given 3D bounding box onto the near plane and returns the size
(in normalized screen coordinates) of the rectangular region that encloses it.

SbViewVolume   **narrow**(float left, float bottom, float right, float top) const
Given a view volume, narrows the view to the given sub-rectangle of the
near plane. The coordinates of the rectangle are between 0 and 1, where
(0,0) is the lower-left corner of the near plane and (1,1) is the upper-right
corner.

SbViewVolume   **narrow**(const SbBox3f &box) const
Narrows a view volume by the given box. The box must lie inside the unit
cube, and the view will be shrunk according to the size of the box.

void   **ortho**(float left, float right, float bottom, float top, float near,
                 float far)
Sets up an orthographic view volume with the given sides. The parameters
are the same as for the OpenGL **glOrtho()** routine.

void	**perspective**(float fovy, float aspect, float near, float far)

Sets up a perspective view volume with the given field of view and aspect ratio. The parameters are the same as for the OpenGL **gluPerspective()** routine, except that the field of view angle is specified in radians.

void	**rotateCamera**(const SbRotation &q)

Rotate the camera view direction. Note that this accomplishes the reverse of doing an OpenGL **glRotate()** command after defining a camera, which rotates the scene viewed by the camera.

void	**translateCamera**(const SbVec3f &v)

Translate the camera viewpoint. Note that this accomplishes the reverse of doing an OpenGL **glTranslate()** command after defining a camera, which translates the scene viewed by the camera.

SbVec3f	**zVector**() const

Returns the positive z axis in eye space. In this coordinate system, the z value of the near plane should be GREATER than the z value of the far plane.

SbViewVolume	**zNarrow**(float near, float far) const

Returns a narrowed view volume which contains as tightly as possible the given interval on the z axis (in eye space). The returned view volume will never be larger than the current volume, however. *near* and *far* are given in terms of **zVector()**: this means that *near > far* must hold.

void	**scale**(float factor)

Scales width and height of view volume by given factor.

void	**scaleWidth**(float ratio)
void	**scaleHeight**(float ratio)

Scales view volume to be the given ratio of its current width or height, leaving the resulting view volume centered about the same point (in the near plane) as the current one.

ProjectionType	**getProjectionType**() const
const SbVec3f &	**getProjectionPoint**() const
const SbVec3f &	**getProjectionDirection**() const

Returns projection information.

float	**getNearDist**() const

Returns distance from projection point to near plane.

float	**getWidth**() const
float	**getHeight**() const
float	**getDepth**() const

Returns bounds of viewing frustum.

INCLUDE FILE

```
#include <Inventor/SbLinear.h>
```

enum **ProjectionType** {
    SbViewVolume::ORTHOGRAPHIC
                  Orthographic projection
    SbViewVolume::PERSPECTIVE
                  Perspective projection
}

SEE ALSO

SbVec3f, SbVec2f, SbBox3f, SbMatrix, SbRotation

NAME

SbXfBox3f — 3D box with an associated transformation matrix

INHERITS FROM

SbBox3f > SbXfBox3f

DESCRIPTION

A 3D box with an arbitrary transformation applied. This class is useful when a box will be transformed frequently; if an **SbBox3f** is used for this purpose it will expand each time it is transformed in order to keep itself axis-aligned. Transformations can be accumulated on an **SbXfBox3f** without expanding the box, and after all transformations have been done, the box can be expanded to an axis-aligned box if necessary.

METHODS

SbXfBox3f()
SbXfBox3f(const SbVec3f &_min, const SbVec3f &_max)
SbXfBox3f(const SbBox3f &box)
~SbXfBox3f()
Constructors and destructor.

void   **setTransform**(const SbMatrix &m)
Sets the transformation on the box.

const SbMatrix &
   getgetXf() const
const SbMatrix &
   getInverse() const
Gets the transformation on the box, and its inverse.

SbVec3f   **getCenter**() const
Returns the center of the box.

void   **extendBy**(const SbVec3f &pt)
Extends the box (if necessary) to contain the given 3D point.

void   **extendBy**(const SbBox3f &bb)
Extends the box (if necessary) to contain the given **SbBox3f**.

void   **extendBy**(const SbXfBox3f &bb)
Extends the box (if necessary) to contain the given **SbXfBox3f**.

SbBool   **intersect**(const SbVec3f &pt) const
Returns TRUE if intersection of given point and this box is not empty.

SbBool   **intersect**(const SbBox3f &bb) const
Returns TRUE if intersection of given box and this box is not empty.

void   **setBounds**(float xmin, float ymin, float zmin, float xmax, float ymax, float zmax)
void   **setBounds**(const SbVec3f &_min, const SbVec3f &_max)
void   **getBounds**(float &xmin, float &ymin, float &zmin, float &xmax, float &ymax, float &zmax) const
void   **getBounds**(SbVec3f &_min, SbVec3f &_max) const
Set and get the bounds of the box.

void   **getOrigin**(float &originX, float &originY, float &originZ)
Returns origin (minimum point) of the box.

void   **getSize**(float &sizeX, float &sizeY, float &sizeZ)
Returns size of the box.

float   **getVolume**() const
Gives the volume of the box (0 for an empty box).

void   **makeEmpty**()
Sets the box to contain nothing.

SbBool   **isEmpty**() const
Checks if the box is empty (degenerate).

SbBool   **hasVolume**() const
Checks if the box has volume; i.e., all three dimensions have positive size.

void   **getSpan**(const SbVec3f &direction, float &dMin, float &dMax) const
Finds the extent of the box along a particular direction.

void   **transform**(const SbMatrix &m)
Transforms the box by the given matrix.

SbBox3f   **project**() const
Projects an **SbXfBox3f** to an **SbBox3f**

int   **operator ==**(const SbXfBox3f &b1, const SbXfBox3f &b2)
int   **operator !=**(const SbXfBox3f &b1, const SbXfBox3f &b2)
Equality comparisons.

Methods from class SbBox3f:
getMin, getMax

INCLUDE FILE
```
#include <Inventor/SbBox.h>
```

SEE ALSO
SbBox3f, SbBox2f, SbBox2s, SbVec3f, SbVec2f, SbVec2s, SbMatrix, SoGetBoundingBoxAction

NAME

SoAction — abstract base class for all actions

INHERITS FROM

SoAction

DESCRIPTION

SoAction is the abstract base class for all actions. Classes derived from **SoAction** define operations to be applied at each node encountered during traversal of a scene graph. The function that gets called to implement the action for a particular node type is determined by a lookup table in the global database.

METHODS

virtual   **~SoAction**()
Destructor.

virtual void   **apply**(SoNode *node)
virtual void   **apply**(SoPath *path)
virtual void   **apply**(const SoPathList &pathList, SbBool obeysRules = FALSE)
Initiates an action on the graph defined either by a node, path, or list of paths. TRUE can be passed for the *obeysRules* flag if the given path list has the following 4 properties:

1 - All paths have the same head node
2 - Paths are sorted in traversal order
3 - If one path ends at node *A*, no other path
    continues through *A*
4 - No two paths are the same

These rules will be obeyed by path lists returned by picking and by searches for non-group nodes.

static SoType   **getClassTypeId**()
Returns the type identifier for this class.

virtual SoType   **getTypeId**()
Returns the type identifier for a specific instance.

virtual SbBool   **isOfType**(SoType type)
Returns TRUE if this instance is of the type specified in *type* or is derived from that type. Otherwise, it returns FALSE. For example,

actionPtr->isOfType(SoGetMatrixAction::getClassTypeId())

returns TRUE if *actionPtr* is an instance of **SoGetMatrixAction** or one of its subclasses.

virtual void   **invalidateState**()
Invalidates the current traversal state in the action, forcing it to be recreated when the action is next applied. This is typically unnecessary in most applications.

INCLUDE FILE

```
#include <Inventor/actions/SoAction.h>
```

SEE ALSO

SoNode, SoPath, SoPathList, SoCallbackAction, SoGLRenderAction, SoGetBoundingBoxAction, SoGetMatrixAction, SoHandleEventAction, SoPickAction, SoRayPickAction, SoSearchAction, SoWriteAction

NAME

SoAlarmSensor — triggers a callback once sometime in the future

INHERITS FROM

SoSensor > SoTimerQueueSensor > SoAlarmSensor

DESCRIPTION

This type of sensor can be used to schedule a one-time callback for some time in the future. The sensor is not guaranteed to be called at exactly that time, but will be called sometime after the specified time.

METHODS

SoAlarmSensor()
SoAlarmSensor(SoSensorCB *func, void *data)
Creation methods. The second method takes the callback function and data to be called when the sensor is triggered.

~SoAlarmSensor()
Destroys the sensor, freeing up any memory associated with it after unscheduling it.

void   **setTime**(const SbTime &absTime)
Sets the sensor to go off at the specified time. You *must* also call **schedule**() for the sensor to be triggered. If the sensor is already scheduled, it must be unscheduled and then rescheduled for the change in the trigger time to take effect.

void   **setTimeFromNow**(const SbTime &relTime)
Sets the sensor to go off the given amount of time from now. You *must* also call **schedule**() for the sensor to be triggered. If the sensor is already scheduled, it must be unscheduled and then rescheduled for the change in the trigger time to take effect.

const SbTime &   **getTime**() const
Returns the time at which the sensor is set to be triggered. This is similar to the **getTriggerTime** method, but returns the time even if the sensor has not yet been scheduled.

Methods from class SoTimerQueueSensor:

getTriggerTime, schedule, unschedule, isScheduled

Methods from class SoSensor:

setFunction, getFunction, setData, getData

INCLUDE FILE

```
#include <Inventor/sensors/SoAlarmSensor.h>
```

SEE ALSO

SoOneShotSensor, SoTimerSensor, SoTimerQueueSensor, SbTime

NAME

SoAnnotation — Annotation group node

INHERITS FROM

SoBase > SoFieldContainer > SoNode > SoGroup > SoSeparator > SoAnnotation

DESCRIPTION

This group node delays rendering its children until all other nodes have been traversed, turning off depth buffer comparisons first. The result is that the shapes under the annotation node are rendered on top of the rest of the scene. This node is derived from **SoSeparator**, so it saves and restores traversal state for all actions.

Note that if more than one annotation node is present in a graph, the order in which they are traversed determines the stacking order — later nodes are rendered on top of earlier ones. Also note that since depth buffer comparisons are disabled, complex 3D objects may not be rendered correctly when used under annotation nodes.

FIELDS

Fields from class SoSeparator:

renderCaching, boundingBoxCaching, renderCulling, pickCulling

METHODS

SoAnnotation()
Creates an annotation node with default settings.

static SoType   **getClassTypeId**()
Returns type identifier for this class.

Methods from class SoSeparator:

setNumRenderCaches, getNumRenderCaches

Methods from class SoGroup:

addChild, insertChild, getChild, findChild, getNumChildren, removeChild, removeChild, removeAllChildren, replaceChild, replaceChild

Methods from class SoNode:

setOverride, isOverride, copy, affectsState, getByName, getByName

Methods from class SoFieldContainer:

setToDefaults, hasDefaultValues, fieldsAreEqual, copyFieldValues, set, get, getFields, getField, getFieldName, enableNotify, isNotifyEnabled

Methods from class SoBase:

ref, unref, unrefNoDelete, touch, getTypeId, isOfType, setName, getName

ACTION BEHAVIOR
SoGLRenderAction
Delays rendering its children until all other nodes have been traversed, turning off depth buffer comparisons first.

SoCallbackAction, SoGetBoundingBoxAction, SoGetMatrixAction, SoRayPickAction, SoSearchAction
Same as **SoSeparator**

FILE FORMAT/DEFAULTS

```
Annotation {
      renderCaching          AUTO
      boundingBoxCaching     AUTO
      renderCulling          AUTO
      pickCulling            AUTO
}
```

INCLUDE FILE

```
#include <Inventor/nodes/SoAnnotation.h>
```

NAME

SoAntiSquish — transformation node that undoes non-uniform 3D scales

INHERITS FROM

SoBase > SoFieldContainer > SoNode > SoTransformation > SoAntiSquish

DESCRIPTION

This node removes nonuniform 3D scaling from the current transformation matrix when traversed by an action. It is used by draggers such as the **SoTrackballDragger** that need to stay uniformly scaled no matter where they are located in the scene graph.

The magnitude of the new scale is determined by the current transformation matrix and the *sizing* field. This node does not change the translation or rotation in the matrix.

FIELDS

SoSFEnum   **sizing**

Determines which of the algorithms enumerated by the type **Sizing** will be used to select the new scale when the x,y, and z scales are not equal.

METHODS

SoAntiSquish()

Creates an anti-squish node with default settings.

static SoType   **getClassTypeId**()

Returns type identifier for this class.

Methods from class SoNode:

setOverride, isOverride, copy, affectsState, getByName, getByName

Methods from class SoFieldContainer:

setToDefaults, hasDefaultValues, fieldsAreEqual, copyFieldValues, set, get, getFields, getField, getFieldName, enableNotify, isNotifyEnabled

Methods from class SoBase:

ref, unref, unrefNoDelete, touch, getTypeId, isOfType, setName, getName

ACTION BEHAVIOR

SoGLRenderAction, SoCallbackAction, SoGetBoundingBoxAction, SoGetMatrixAction, SoRayPickAction

Replaces the current transformation with an unsquished one.

FILE FORMAT/DEFAULTS

```
AntiSquish {
        sizing  AVERAGE_DIMENSION
}
```

INCLUDE FILE

```
#include <Inventor/nodes/SoAntiSquish.h>
```

enum **Sizing** {

> **SoAntiSquish::AVERAGE_DIMENSION**
>> uses average of 3 scales in the matrix
>
> **SoAntiSquish::BIGGEST_DIMENSION**
>> uses biggest of 3 scales in the matrix
>
> **SoAntiSquish::SMALLEST_DIMENSION**
>> uses smallest of 3 scales in the matrix
>
> **SoAntiSquish::LONGEST_DIAGONAL**
>> accounts for shearing; transforms a cube by the matrix and then
>> uses length of longest diagonal

}

SEE ALSO

SoCenterballDragger, SoJackDragger, SoTrackballDragger, SoTransformation,
SoTransformBoxDragger

NAME

SoAppearanceKit — appearance nodekit class

INHERITS FROM

SoBase > SoFieldContainer > SoNode > SoBaseKit > SoAppearanceKit

DESCRIPTION

The **SoAppearanceKit** is used to create a group of property nodes that will be used to affect subsequent *shape* nodes or nodekits in the scene graph.

This nodekit defines seven new parts: *lightModel, environment, drawStyle, material, complexity, texture2,* and *font*. Note that it does not include *binding* nodes such as **SoMaterialBinding**.

SoAppearanceKit is derived from **SoBaseKit** and thus also includes a *callbackList* part for adding callback nodes.

PARTS

(SoLightModel)　　**lightModel**

An **SoLightModel** node that affects any shapes that follow this nodekit in the scene graph. This part is NULL by default.

(SoEnvironment)

　　　　　　environment

An **SoEnvironment** node that affects any nodes that follow this nodekit in the scene graph. This part is NULL by default.

(SoDrawStyle)　　**drawStyle**

An **SoDrawStyle** node that affects any shapes that follow this nodekit in the scene graph. This part is NULL by default.

(SoMaterial)　　**material**

An **SoMaterial** node that affects any shapes that follow this nodekit in the scene graph. This part is NULL by default.

(SoComplexity)　　**complexity**

An **SoComplexity** node that affects any shapes that follow this nodekit in the scene graph. This part is NULL by default.

(SoTexture2)　　**texture2**

An **SoTexture2** node that affects any shapes that follow this nodekit in the scene graph. This part is NULL by default.

(SoFont)   **font**

An **SoFont** node that affects any text nodes that follow this nodekit in the scene graph. This part is NULL by default.

Parts from class SoBaseKit:

callbackList

METHODS

SoAppearanceKit()

Constructor.

static const SoNodekitCatalog *

getClassNodekitCatalog() const

Returns the **SoNodekitCatalog** for this class

static SoType   **getClassTypeId()**

Returns type identifier for this class.

Methods from class SoBaseKit:

getNodekitCatalog, getPart, getPartString, createPathToPart, setPart, set, set, isSearchingChildren, setSearchingChildren

Methods from class SoNode:

setOverride, isOverride, copy, affectsState, getByName, getByName

Methods from class SoFieldContainer:

setToDefaults, hasDefaultValues, fieldsAreEqual, copyFieldValues, get, getFields, getField, getFieldName, enableNotify, isNotifyEnabled

Methods from class SoBase:

ref, unref, unrefNoDelete, touch, getTypeId, isOfType, setName, getName

MACROS

Macros from class SoBaseKit:

SO_GET_PART, SO_CHECK_PART

CATALOG PARTS

All parts			
Part Name	**Part Type**	**Default Type**	**NULL by Default**
callbackList	NodeKitListPart	--	yes
lightModel	LightModel	--	yes
environment	Environment	--	yes
drawStyle	DrawStyle	--	yes
material	Material	--	yes
complexity	Complexity	--	yes
texture2	Texture2	--	yes
font	Font	--	yes

Extra information for list parts from above table		
Part Name	**Container Type**	**Permissible Types**
callbackList	Separator	Callback, EventCallback

FILE FORMAT/DEFAULTS

```
AppearanceKit {
}
```

INCLUDE FILE

```
#include <Inventor/nodekits/SoAppearanceKit.h>
```

NOTE

Note that **SoSeparatorKit** includes an **SoAppearanceKit** as a part.

SEE ALSO

SoBaseKit, SoCameraKit, SoLightKit, SoNodeKit, SoNodeKitDetail, SoNodeKitListPart, SoNodeKitPath, SoNodekitCatalog, SoSceneKit, SoSeparatorKit, SoShapeKit, SoWrapperKit

NAME

SoArray — group node that creates a regular IxJxK array of copies of its children

INHERITS FROM

SoBase > SoFieldContainer > SoNode > SoGroup > SoArray

DESCRIPTION

This group node traverses its children, in order, several times, creating a regular 3D array of copies of them. The number of copies in each of the three directions is specified by fields, as are the vectors used to separate the copies in each of the three dimensions.

For example, an **SoArray** node can be used to create a 2x3x4 array of copies of its children, where the separation vectors between adjacent copies in the three array dimensions are (1,2,3), (-4,-5,-6), and (7,8,9), respectively. The base point of the array can be set to one of several values, as described in the **origin** field.

Copies are traversed so that the first dimension cycles most quickly, followed by the second, and then the third. This order is important because **SoArray** sets the current switch value to N before traversing the children for the Nth time (for use with inherited switch values - see **SoSwitch**).

FIELDS

SoSFShort	**numElements1**
SoSFShort	**numElements2**
SoSFShort	**numElements3**

Number of elements in each of the three array dimensions.

SoSFVec3f	**separation1**
SoSFVec3f	**separation2**
SoSFVec3f	**separation3**

Separation vector in each of the three array dimensions.

SoSFEnum	**origin**

Defines the base point from which copies are distributed.

METHODS

SoArray()

Creates an array node with default settings.

static SoType　　**getClassTypeId()**

Returns type identifier for this class.

Methods from class SoGroup:

addChild, insertChild, getChild, findChild, getNumChildren, removeChild, removeChild, removeAllChildren, replaceChild, replaceChild

Methods from class SoNode:

setOverride, isOverride, copy, affectsState, getByName, getByName

Methods from class SoFieldContainer:

setToDefaults, hasDefaultValues, fieldsAreEqual, copyFieldValues, set, get, getFields, getField, getFieldName, enableNotify, isNotifyEnabled

Methods from class SoBase:

ref, unref, unrefNoDelete, touch, getTypeId, isOfType, setName, getName

ACTION BEHAVIOR

SoGLRenderAction, SoCallbackAction, SoGetBoundingBoxAction, SoRayPickAction

Traverses all children for each array element, saving and restoring state before and after each traversal.

SoSearchAction

Traverses all children once, setting the inherited switch value to **SO_SWITCH_ALL** first.

FILE FORMAT/DEFAULTS

```
Array {
        numElements1   1
        numElements2   1
        numElements3   1
        separation1    1 0 0
        separation2    0 1 0
        separation3    0 0 1
        origin         FIRST
}
```

INCLUDE FILE

    #include <Inventor/nodes/SoArray.h>

enum **Origin** {

SoArray::FIRST	First copy is rendered at the current local origin; all other copies are distributed relative to it
SoArray::CENTER	Copies are distributed relative to the center of the array
SoArray::LAST	Last copy is rendered at the current local origin; all other copies are distributed relative to it

}

SEE ALSO

SoMultipleCopy, SoSwitch

NAME

SoBase — base class for all nodes, paths, and engines

INHERITS FROM

SoBase

DESCRIPTION

Abstract base class for Inventor node, path, and engine classes. This class handles reference counting, notification, and naming.

METHODS

void	**ref**()
void	**unref**() const
void	**unrefNoDelete**() const

Adds and removes a reference to an instance. Instances should be referenced when they will be used outside of the routine in which they were initialized. (A typical example of this is maintaining a pointer to the root of a graph.) Whenever the reference count for an instance is decremented to 0, the instance is automatically destroyed by the database (unless **unrefNoDelete**() is used to unref it). The reference count of a node is automatically incremented when the node is added as a child of another node or when a path points to the node. Likewise, the reference count is automatically decremented when the node is removed as a child or when a path that points to the node is changed or destroyed.

unrefNoDelete() should be called when it is desired to decrement the reference count, but not delete the instance if this brings the reference count to zero. This is most useful in returning an object to a zero-reference-count state, like it was when it was created by **new**.

| void | **touch**() |

Marks an instance as modified, simulating a change to it. This will notify auditors (parent nodes, connected engines, and so on) of a change to this object and cause attached sensors to be triggered.

| static SoType | **getClassTypeId**() |

Returns type identifier for this class.

| virtual SoType | **getTypeId**() const |

Returns the type identifier for a specific instance.

SbBool isOfType(SoType type) const
Returns TRUE if this object is of the type specified in *type* or is derived from that type. Otherwise, it returns FALSE. For example:

nodePtr->isOfType(SoGroup::getClassTypeId())

returns TRUE if *nodePtr* is an instance of **SoGroup** or one of its subclasses.

virtual void setName(const SbName &name)
Sets the name of an instance. Object names are preserved when objects are written to or read from files.

virtual const SbName &
getName() const
Returns the name of an instance. If the instance has not been named, an empty **SbName** is returned. Objects that are named can be looked up using the **getByName()** methods of **SoNode**, **SoEngine**, or **SoPath**.

INCLUDE FILE
#include <Inventor/misc/SoBase.h>

SEE ALSO
SoFieldContainer, SoNode, SoPath, SoEngine, SoDB

NAME

SoBaseColor — node that defines an object's base color

INHERITS FROM

SoBase > SoFieldContainer > SoNode > SoBaseColor

DESCRIPTION

This node defines the base color (or colors) of subsequent shape nodes in the scene graph. **SoBaseColor** sets only the diffuse color(s) of the current material and has no effect on the material's other attributes.

FIELDS

SoMFColor   **rgb**

RGB color(s).

METHODS

SoBaseColor()

Creates a base color node with default settings.

static SoType   **getClassTypeId()**

Returns type identifier for this class.

Methods from class SoNode:

setOverride, isOverride, copy, affectsState, getByName, getByName

Methods from class SoFieldContainer:

setToDefaults, hasDefaultValues, fieldsAreEqual, copyFieldValues, set, get, getFields, getField, getFieldName, enableNotify, isNotifyEnabled

Methods from class SoBase:

ref, unref, unrefNoDelete, touch, getTypeId, isOfType, setName, getName

ACTION BEHAVIOR

SoGLRenderAction, SoCallbackAction

Sets the current base color in the state.

FILE FORMAT/DEFAULTS

```
BaseColor {
     rgb  0.8 0.8 0.8
}
```

INCLUDE FILE

#include <Inventor/nodes/SoBaseColor.h>

SEE ALSO

SoMaterial, SoPackedColor

NAME

SoBaseKit — base class for all node kits

INHERITS FROM

SoBase > SoFieldContainer > SoNode > SoBaseKit

DESCRIPTION

This is the base class from which all nodekit nodes are derived. Nodekits provide a convenient mechanism for creating groups of scene graph nodes with some larger meaning. When you create a shape node such as an indexed face set, for example, you almost always precede it with a coordinate node. You may also want to add a transform node or specify properties with material, drawing style, material binding, etc. Instead of creating each of these nodes individually and then arranging them into a subgraph, you can use a nodekit of the appropriate type (in this case, **SoShapeKit**).

Each class of nodekit has a *nodekit catalog* (**SoNodekitCatalog**) that describes the nodes in the subgraph, referred to as *parts*. The catalog has an entry for each part, with information such as the *partName*, *partType*, and *nullByDefault* (if FALSE the constructor creates it). The catalog also describes the arrangement of parts in the subgraph. (Other information is described below; a complete description is in the **SoNodekitCatalog** reference page.)

If we regard the scene graph arrangement as a branching tree, then the top node (root) of the arrangement is always the nodekit itself. The leaf nodes are those at the bottom (containing no children). Some leaves of the tree are defined in the catalog to be *public* parts, while other leaves are *private*. All non-leaf parts are considered internal to the nodekit structure and are marked private. Public parts are accessible; they may be requested, changed, or set by the programmer with member functions such as **getPart()**. Private parts are not accessible, so methods such as **getPart()** will have no effect on them. For example, if you call **getPart()** to retrieve a private part, NULL will be returned even when the part exists.

Every nodekit reference page has a Parts section describing the function of each public part it adds to those inherited from its parent class. Also, a Catalog Parts section has tables of often-needed information from the catalog (part type, etc.). These tables include all public parts, both new and inherited. Only the public parts of a nodekit are described in the reference pages. Nodekits take care of the rest for you; they automatically arrange the subgraph, creating and deleting the private parts when necessary. (The **SoNodekitCatalog** reference page has methods for finding out the part names and arrangement of all parts, both public and private.)

The nodekit catalog is a template shared by all instances of a class. They use the shared catalog as a *guide* when creating parts (i.e., constructing actual nodes), but each instance stores its own parts separately. Moreover, nodekits are *not* **SoGroup** nodes, and parts are added as *hidden children*; you can only access parts with the methods of **SoBaseKit** and its derived classes.

Any public part may be retrieved with **getPart()**, installed with **setPart()**, or removed by giving a NULL argument to **setPart()**. Paths from the nodekit down to a part can be created by **createPathToPart()**.

By default, parts are not created until the user requests or sets them. This keeps the subgraph uncluttered and efficient for traversal. Additionally, removing a part (setting it to NULL) has the extra effect of removing any internal parts that are no longer needed.

Since nodekits hide their children, any **SoPath** containing nodekits will end at the topmost nodekit. However, since nodekits may be nested within other nodekits, you may wish to cast an **(SoPath *)** into an **(SoNodeKitPath *)**. The methods of **SoNodeKitPath** allow you to view all nodekits that lie on the path (see the reference page for **SoNodeKitPath**).

Public parts in the nodekit catalog fall into three categories:

[1] *regular nodes*

[2] *nodekits*, or *nested nodekits* (which may nest recursively). Any node which is public in a nested nodekit is accessible to the higher level nodekit(s) that contains it. The description of **getPart()** below shows how to refer to nested parts by name (e.g., *"appearance.material"*). This works for any nodekit method that takes a part name for an argument.

[3] *lists*, or *list parts*. These parts group together children (*list elements*) of a particular type or types. As with nested nodekits, you can refer to individual elements using notation described in **getPart()** (e.g., *"childList[0]"*, or if the list elements are in turn nodekits, *"childList[2].transform"*).

When the catalog denotes that a part is a list, the part itself is always a node of type **SoNodeKitListPart**. The catalog specifies a set of permissible *listItemTypes* and a *listContainerType* for that part. It gives this information to the **SoNodeKitListPart** when it creates it. From then on, the list part will enforce type checking. So even if you retrieve the **SoNodeKitListPart** with **getPart()**, you will not be able to add illegal children. (See the **SoNodeKitListPart** reference page for more information). As an example, the *callbackList* part of **SoBaseKit** has an **SoSeparator** container and allows only **SoCallback** and **SoEventCallback** nodes in the list. Children may be added, retrieved, and removed from an **SoNodeKitListPart** node using methods that parallel those of **SoGroup**. However, type-checking is strictly enforced.

Note that, although all public parts are leaves in the nodekit catalog, you are free to add children to them (assuming that they are groups, nodekits, or list parts). A part's status as a leaf in the catalog just means that the nodekit will not manage the part's children. For example, **SoWrapperKit** has a part called *contents* with a part type of **SoSeparator**. You can put whatever you want underneath the separator, as long as *contents* itself is an **SoSeparator**.

Thus, a nodekit only controls a section of the scene graph. Above and below that section, anything goes.

However, when nodekits are nested, they effectively create a larger 'known' section of the scene graph. For example, the *appearance* part of the **SoSeparatorKit** is a leaf node in the **SoSeparatorKit** catalog. But *appearance* is in turn an **SoAppearanceKit**, containing parts such as *material* and *drawStyle*. The two nodekits combine to make an even larger template, which the **SoSeparatorKit** can examine by looking at the catalogs for both classes. So an **SoSeparatorKit** can successfully return a part named *"material"*; first it finds (or creates) the *appearance* part, then it gets the *material* by calling **getPart**() on the *appearance*.

When the catalog defines the *listItemTypes* of a list part to be nodekits, the name-able space expands further. For example, **SoSeparatorKit** has a part *childList* which permits only **SoSeparatorKits**, so each list element can be further searched. Hence the name "**childList[0].childList[1].childList[2].material**" is perfectly legal.

PARTS

(SoNodeKitListPart)

callbackList

This is the only part that the base class **SoBaseKit** creates. It is a public part that is inherited by *all* nodekits. It provides an easy way to add callbacks for a nodekit to use during action traversal (e.g. **SoHandleEventAction**). It is a list part and may contain numerous **SoCallback** and/or **SoEventCallback** nodes.

METHODS

SoBaseKit()

Constructor.

static const SoNodekitCatalog *
     getClassNodekitCatalog() const
Returns the **SoNodekitCatalog** for the class **SoBaseKit**.

virtual const SoNodekitCatalog *
     getNodekitCatalog() const
Returns the **SoNodekitCatalog** for this instance of **SoBaseKit**. While each instance of a given class creates its own distinct set of parts (which are actual nodes), all instances share the same catalog (which describes the parts but contains no actual node pointers).

virtual SoNode * **getPart**(const SbName &partName, SbBool makeIfNeeded)
Searches the nodekit catalog (and those of all nested nodekits) for the part named *partName*. Returns a pointer to the part if a *match is found*, the part is *public*, and the part has *already been built*. If no match is found, or if the part is *private*, NULL is returned. If *partName* is in the catalog (or that of one of its nested nodekit parts), but the part has not been built yet, the argument *makeIfNeeded* determines the course of action. When *makeIfNeeded* is FALSE, NULL is returned; when *makeIfNeeded* is TRUE, **getPart**() will create the part (as well as any necessary intermediary parts), put it in the correct place, and return a pointer to the newly created part.

Elements of *list parts* and parts within nested nodekits can all be retrieved with **getPart**() The full syntax for legal *partName* arguments is given below.

Part name BNF notation:

partName = singleName | compoundName

compoundName = singleName | compoundName.singleName

singleName = singlePartName | singleListElementName

singlePartName = the name of any single part in the catalog (including those that are lists or nodekits), or in the recursively nested catalogs of any of its parts.

singleListElementName = singleListName[index]

singleListName = the name of any single list-type part in the catalog, or in the recursively nested catalogs of any of its parts.

index = integer

Examples of valid part names are:

"transform", "appearance.material", "childList[2].drawStyle", "foot", "bird.leftLeg.foot", "octopus.leg[4].suctionCup[2].material"

SbString	**getPartString**(const SoBase *part)

Given a node or a path to a node, checks if the part exists in the nodekit, in a nested nodekit, or an element of a list part. If so, returns a string describing the part name; otherwise, returns an empty string ("").

virtual SoNodeKitPath *

createPathToPart(const SbName &partName, SbBool makeIfNeeded, const SoPath *pathToExtend = NULL)

Returns a path that begins at this nodekit and ends at *partName*. Searching for the part is the same as in **getPart**(). NULL is returned if *partName* cannot be found, or if *makeIfNeeded* is FALSE and the part is not yet built. If the the part is retrieved and the argument *pathToExtend* is NULL, the path returned begins at this and ends at *partName*. If *pathToExtend* is not NULL, the path created is a copy of *pathToExtend* with entries appended all the way down to *partName*. It is okay for *pathToExtend* to go beyond the nodekit; extra nodes will be popped off the tail before continuing from this down to *partName*.

virtual SbBool	**setPart**(const SbName &partName, SoNode *newPart)

Inserts the given node (not a copy) as the new part specified by *partName*. See **getPart**() for the syntax of *partName*. This method adds any extra nodes needed to fit the part into the nodekit's catalog. For example, if you call:

mySepKit->setPart("childList[0]", myNewChild);

the kit may need to create the part *childList* before it can install *myNewChild*. Run-time type checking verifies that the node type of *newPart* matches the type called for by *partName*. For example, if *partName* was a *material* for an **SoSeparatorKit**, but *newPart* was an **SoTransform** node, then the node would not be installed, and FALSE would be returned.

If *newPart* is NULL, then the node specified by *partName* is removed. If this renders any private parts useless (as occurs when you remove the last child of an **SoGroup** node), they will also be removed. Hence nodekits do not retain unnecessary nodes.

TRUE is returned on success, and FALSE upon error.

SbBool	**set**(char *partName, char *parameters)
SbBool	**set**(char *nameValuePairs)

These functions allow field values of parts (nodes) to be set. If *partName* and *parameters* are used, then a single part is specified by *partName*; the field values are specified in *parameters*. The format of *paramaters* is the Inventor File Format syntax. For example,

mySepKit->set("material", "diffuseColor 1 0 0 shininess 0.6");

sets the part *material* to the values "diffuseColor 1 0 0 shininess 0.6". The values used in *parameters* must of course be appropriate for the node-type to which *partName* belongs. In this case, the nodekit **SoSeparatorKit** has a part named *material* which is of type **SoMaterial**.

The *nameValuePairs* syntax can be used to set the field values in several different parts simultaneously. In this case, the argument string, *nameValuePairs* contains *name-value* pairs: "partName1 { parameters1 } ... partNameN { parametersN }".

For example,

mySepKit->set("material { diffuseColor 1 1 1 }
        transform { translation 4 3 .6 }");
mySepKit->set("childList[0].material { ambientColor .5 .5 .5 }");

static SbBool	**isSearchingChildren**()
static void	**setSearchingChildren**(SbBool newVal)

Sets and queries if nodekit children are searched during **SoSearchAction** traversal. By default, they are not.

static SoType	**getClassTypeId**()

Returns type identifier for this class.

Methods from class SoNode:

setOverride, isOverride, copy, affectsState, getByName, getByName

Methods from class SoFieldContainer:

setToDefaults, hasDefaultValues, fieldsAreEqual, copyFieldValues, get, getFields, getField, getFieldName, enableNotify, isNotifyEnabled

Methods from class SoBase:

ref, unref, unrefNoDelete, touch, getTypeId, isOfType, setName, getName

MACROS

SO_GET_PART(kit, partName, partClass)

>   Calls **getPart()** with *makeIfNeeded* set to TRUE, then casts the result to the type *partClass*. Note that in the debug library, this macro checks to see if the part is of type *partClass*, while the regular library does no type checking.

SO_CHECK_PART(kit, partName, partClass)

>   Calls **getPart()**, but with *makeIfNeeded* set to FALSE, then casts the result to the type *partClass*. Note that in the debug library, this macro checks to see if the part is of type *partClass*, while the regular library does no type checking.

ACTION BEHAVIOR

SoGLRenderAction, SoCallbackAction, SoGetBoundingBoxAction, SoHandleEventAction

>   Behaves like an **SoGroup**. Traverses each child in order.

SoRayPickAction

>   Traverses each child in order. Then, for any pick containing the kit on its path, makes an **SoNodeKitDetail** as follows: Sets the "detailNodeKit" (retrievable with **SoNodeKitDetail::getNodeKit()**) to be a pointer to itself. Sets the "detailPart" (retrievable with **SoNodeKitDetail::getPart()**) to be a pointer to the kit's leaf-most part that lies on the pickPath. Sets the "detailPartName" (retrievable with **SoNodeKitDetail::getPartName()**) to be the partName of that part, as found in the catalog.

>   Does not descend into nested nodekits. Each nodekit along the path is the "detailPart" in its parent's detail. However, if the pick path goes through a list part, a pointer to the child is used for the "detailPart", and "detailPartName" is of the form *"listName[i]"*.

SoGetMatrixAction

>   Behaves like an **SoGroup**. Does nothing unless the kit is in the middle of the path chain the action is being applied to. If so, the children up to and including the next node in the chain are traversed.

SoSearchAction

>   First, searches itself like an **SoNode**. Then, checks the value of **isSearchingChildren()**. If TRUE, traverses the children in order. If FALSE, returns.

SoWriteAction

>   Begins by writing out regular fields, then writes out the parts. A nodekit does *not* write out its parts the way an **SoGroup** writes out its children. Instead, it

writes each part as an **SoSFNode** field. First the partName is written, then the node being used for that part.

To keep the files terse, nodekits write out as few parts as possible. However, nodekits *always* write a part if another instance or a path is writing it. If this is not the case, parts are left out according to the following rules:

[1] NULL parts only write if the catalog states they are created by default.

[2] Empty **SoGroup** and **SoSeparator** nodes do not write.

[3] Non-leaf parts only write if they have non-default field values.

[4] List parts only write if they have children or if the container node has non-default field values.

[5] Nested nodekit parts only write if they need to write one or more parts, or if they have non-default field values.

CATALOG PARTS

All parts			
Part Name	**Part Type**	**Default Type**	**NULL by Default**
callbackList	NodeKitListPart	--	yes
Extra information for list parts from above table			
Part Name	**Container Type**	**Permissible Types**	
callbackList	Separator	Callback, EventCallback	

FILE FORMAT/DEFAULTS
```
BaseKit {
}
```

INCLUDE FILE
```
#include <Inventor/nodekits/SoBaseKit.h>
```

SEE ALSO

SoAppearanceKit, SoCameraKit, SoLightKit, SoNodeKit, SoNodeKitDetail, SoNodeKitListPart, SoNodeKitPath, SoNodekitCatalog, SoSceneKit, SoSeparatorKit, SoShapeKit, SoWrapperKit

NAME

SoBaseList — maintains a list of pointers to instances of the **SoBase** classes

INHERITS FROM

SbPList > SoBaseList

DESCRIPTION

This subclass of **SbPList** holds lists of pointers to instances of classes derived from **SoBase** (an abstract class). A flag indicates whether adding an instance pointer to the list should add a reference to the instance. If this flag is TRUE, then adding and removing pointers from the list updates reference counts in the corresponding instances.

METHODS

SoBaseList()
Constructor.

SoBaseList(int size)
Constructor that pre-allocates storage for *size* pointers.

SoBaseList(const SoBaseList &l)
Constructor that copies the contents of another list.

~**SoBaseList**()
Destructor.

void   **append**(SoBase *ptr)
Adds a pointer to the end of the list.

void   **insert**(SoBase *ptr, int addBefore)
Inserts given pointer in list before pointer with given index.

void   **remove**(int which)
Removes pointer with given index.

void   **truncate**(int start)
Removes all pointers after one with given index, inclusive.

void   **copy**(const SoBaseList &l)
Copies a list, keeping all reference counts correct.

SoBaseList &   **operator** =(const SoBaseList &l)
Copies a list, keeping all reference counts correct.

SoBase *   **operator** [ ](int i) const
       Accesses an element of a list.

void   **set**(int i, SoBase *ptr)
       Sets an element of a list.

void   **addReferences**(SbBool flag)
       Indicates whether to call **ref**() and **unref**() for bases in the list when
       adding/removing them. The default value is TRUE.

Methods from class SbPList:

       find, getLength, operator ==, operator !=

INCLUDE FILE

       `#include <Inventor/SoLists.h>`

SEE ALSO

       SoBase, SoNodeList, SoPathList

NAME

SoBlinker — animated cycling switch node

INHERITS FROM

SoBase > SoFieldContainer > SoNode > SoGroup > SoSwitch > SoBlinker

DESCRIPTION

The **SoBlinker** class is derived from **SoSwitch**, so it selects one of its children to traverse. Using engines connected to the **realTime** global field, the **whichChild** field is animated over time. If the node has only one child, **whichChild** toggles between SO_SWITCH_NONE and 0, causing the child to be switched on and off repeatedly. If the node has more than one child, they are cycled through continuously.

FIELDS

SoSFFloat   **speed**

Defines the speed of the blinker, in cycles per second.

SoSFBool   **on**

Allows applications to enable or disable the blinking easily.

Fields from class SoSwitch:

whichChild

METHODS

SoBlinker()

Creates a blinker node with default settings.

static SoType   **getClassTypeId**()

Returns type identifier for this class.

Methods from class SoGroup:

addChild, insertChild, getChild, findChild, getNumChildren, removeChild, removeChild, removeAllChildren, replaceChild, replaceChild

Methods from class SoNode:

setOverride, isOverride, copy, affectsState, getByName, getByName

Methods from class SoFieldContainer:

setToDefaults, hasDefaultValues, fieldsAreEqual, copyFieldValues, set, get, getFields, getField, getFieldName, enableNotify, isNotifyEnabled

Methods from class SoBase:

ref, unref, unrefNoDelete, touch, getTypeId, isOfType, setName, getName

ACTION BEHAVIOR

SoGLRenderAction, SoCallbackAction, SoGetBoundingBoxAction, SoGetMatrixAction, SoHandleEventAction, SoRayPickAction, SoSearchAction
Same as for **SoSwitch**.

FILE FORMAT/DEFAULTS

```
Blinker {
        whichChild  0
        speed       1
        on          TRUE
}
```

INCLUDE FILE

```
#include <Inventor/nodes/SoBlinker.h>
```

SoBoolOperation

NAME

> SoBoolOperation — performs Boolean operations

INHERITS FROM

> SoBase > SoFieldContainer > SoEngine > SoBoolOperation

DESCRIPTION

> This engine performs a Boolean operation on two inputs, and returns both the result of the operation and its inverse.
>
> The input fields can have multiple values, allowing the engine to perform several Boolean operations in parallel. One input may have more values than the other. In that case, the last value of the shorter input will be repeated as necessary.

INPUTS

> SoMFBool   **a**
> > First argument to the Boolean operation.
>
> SoMFBool   **b**
> > Second argument to the Boolean operation.
>
> SoMFEnum   **operation**
> > The Boolean operation.

OUTPUTS

> (SoMFBool)   **output**
> > Result of the Boolean operation applied to the inputs.
>
> (SoMFBool)   **inverse**
> > Inverse of **output**.

METHODS

> **SoBoolOperation**()
> Constructor.

> **Methods from class SoEngine:**
>
> > getClassTypeId, getOutputs, getOutput, getOutputName, copy, getByName, getByName

> **Methods from class SoFieldContainer:**
>
> > setToDefaults, hasDefaultValues, fieldsAreEqual, copyFieldValues, set, get, getFields, getField, getFieldName, enableNotify, isNotifyEnabled

Methods from class SoBase:

ref, unref, unrefNoDelete, touch, getTypeId, isOfType, setName, getName

FILE FORMAT/DEFAULTS

```
BoolOperation {
        a         FALSE
        b         FALSE
        operation A
}
```

INCLUDE FILE

```
#include <Inventor/engines/SoBoolOperation.h>
```

enum **Operation** {
    SoBoolOperation::CLEAR
    SoBoolOperation::SET
    SoBoolOperation::A
    SoBoolOperation::NOT_A
    SoBoolOperation::B
    SoBoolOperation::NOT_B
    SoBoolOperation::A_OR_B
    SoBoolOperation::NOT_A_OR_B
    SoBoolOperation::A_OR_NOT_B
    SoBoolOperation::NOT_A_OR_NOT_B
    SoBoolOperation::A_AND_B
    SoBoolOperation::NOT_A_AND_B
    SoBoolOperation::A_AND_NOT_B
    SoBoolOperation::NOT_A_AND_NOT_B
    SoBoolOperation::A_EQUALS_B
    SoBoolOperation::A_NOT_EQUALS_B
}

SEE ALSO

SoEngineOutput, SoCalculator

SoBoxHighlightRenderAction

NAME

SoBoxHighlightRenderAction — a selection highlight style

INHERITS FROM

SoAction > SoGLRenderAction > SoBoxHighlightRenderAction

DESCRIPTION

SoBoxHighlightRenderAction is a render action which renders the specified scene graph, then renders wireframe boxes surrounding each selected object. Selected objects are specified by the first **SoSelection** node in the scene to which this action is applied. If an **SoGetBoundingBoxAction** applied to a selected object produces an empty bounding box, no highlight is rendered for that object. A highlight render action can be passed to the **setGLRenderAction()** method of **SoXtRenderArea** to have an effect on scene graphs.

METHODS

SoBoxHighlightRenderAction()
Constructor.

virtual void   **apply**(SoNode *node)
This renders the passed scene graph, and also renders wireframe boxes around selected objects as specified by the first **SoSelection** node found in the scene graph.

void   **setVisible**(SbBool b)
This provides a convenient mechansim for turning highlights off or on. When *FALSE* is passed, subsequent calls to **apply()** render the scene graph without rendering highlights. The application is responsible for forcing a redraw of the scene after changing this state. The default visibility is on.

SbBool   **isVisible**() const
Returns whether highlights will be rendered or not.

void   **setColor**(const SbColor &c)
SbColor &   **getColor**()
Set and get the color of the highlight. Default is red *(1,0,0)*. Application is responsible for forcing a redraw of the scene to see the effects of this change.

void   **setLinePattern**(unsigned short pattern)
unsigned short   **getLinePattern**()
Set and get the line pattern of the highlight. Default is solid, *0xffff*. The pattern of bits in the passed variable specifies the pattern of the line. See **SoDrawStyle** for a description. Application is responsible for forcing a redraw of the scene to see the effects of this change.

void	**setLineWidth**(float width)
float	**getLineWidth**()

Set and get the line width of the highlight. Default is *3*. Application is responsible for forcing a redraw of the scene to see the effects of this change.

Methods from class SoGLRenderAction:

setViewportRegion, getViewportRegion, setUpdateArea, getUpdateArea, setAbortCallback, setTransparencyType, getTransparencyType, setSmoothing, isSmoothing, setNumPasses, getNumPasses, setPassUpdate, isPassUpdate, setPassCallback, setCacheContext, getCacheContext

Methods from class SoAction:

getClassTypeId, getTypeId, isOfType, invalidateState

INCLUDE FILE

```
#include <Inventor/actions/SoBoxHighlightRenderAction.h>
```

EXAMPLE

Here is an example of how a box highlight can be specified for a particular selection node and render area.

```
SoXtRenderArea *myRenderArea;
SoSelection *mySelection;

// Set the highlight render action
myRenderArea->setGLRenderAction(
    new SoBoxHighlightRenderAction());

// Automatic redraw on selection changes
myRenderArea->redrawOnSelectionChange(mySelection);
```

SEE ALSO

SoLineHighlightRenderAction, SoGLRenderAction, SoSelection, SoXtRenderArea, SoDrawStyle, SoInteraction

NAME

SoButtonEvent — base class for all button events

INHERITS FROM

SoEvent > SoButtonEvent

DESCRIPTION

SoButtonEvent represents generic button press and release events in the Inventor event model. It is the base class for device-specific button events, namely **SoKeyboardEvent**, **SoMouseButtonEvent**, and **SoSpaceballButtonEvent**. This class stores the down/up state of the button when the event occurred.

METHODS

SoButtonEvent()
Constructor.

static SoType   **getClassTypeId**()
Return the type id for the **SoButtonEvent** class.

void   **setState**(SoButtonEvent::State s)
SoButtonEvent::State
    getState() const
Set and get the state of the button.

Methods from class SoEvent:

getTypeId, isOfType, setTime, getTime, setPosition, getPosition, getPosition, getNormalizedPosition, setShiftDown, setCtrlDown, setAltDown, wasShiftDown, wasCtrlDown, wasAltDown

INCLUDE FILE

```
#include <Inventor/events/SoButtonEvent.h>
```

enum **State** {
    SoButtonEvent::UP
       Button up event
    SoButtonEvent::DOWN
       Button down event
    SoButtonEvent::UNKNOWN
       Button in unknown state
}

SEE ALSO

SoEvent, SoKeyboardEvent, SoLocation2Event, SoMotion3Event, SoMouseButtonEvent, SoSpaceballButtonEvent, SoHandleEventAction, SoEventCallback, SoSelection, SoInteraction, SoXtDevice

NAME

SoByteStream — converts scene graph objects to character byte streams

INHERITS FROM

SoByteStream

DESCRIPTION

This class creates a byte stream representation of a scene graph, using an **SoWriteAction** to write path lists to an in-memory buffer. Byte streams are commonly used to transfer data in copy and paste operations. (The **SoXtClipboard** class passes **SoByteStream** data during copy and paste.)

METHODS

SoByteStream()
~**SoByteStream**()

Constructor and destructor.

void	**convert**(SoNode *node, SbBool binaryFormat = TRUE)
void	**convert**(SoPath *path, SbBool binaryFormat = TRUE)
void	**convert**(SoPathList *pathList, SbBool binaryFormat = TRUE)

These convert the passed scene graph object(s) into a byte stream. The caller may specify whether the byte stream is written in binary (TRUE) or ASCII (FALSE) format, and can pass the object(s) by node, path, or pathList.

void *	**getData**()
unsigned long	**getNumBytes**()

These return the data and number of bytes from the last **convert**() operation. This byte stream format is well suited to data transfers, like copy and paste.

static SoPathList *

unconvert(SoByteStream *byteStream)

static SoPathList *

unconvert(void *data, unsigned long numBytes)

These take byte stream data and unconvert it back to scene graph objects. The objects are returned in a path list.

INCLUDE FILE

```
#include <Inventor/misc/SoByteStream.h>
```

SEE ALSO

SoXtClipboard

SoCalculator

NAME

SoCalculator — a general-purpose calculator

INHERITS FROM

SoBase > SoFieldContainer > SoEngine > SoCalculator

DESCRIPTION

This engine is a general-purpose calculator. The calculator operates on floating-point values and 3D floating-point vectors. The engine takes up to eight inputs of each type (**SoMFFloat** and **SoMFVec3f**), and produces up to four outputs of each type.

Each input field (**a-h**, **A-H**) can have multiple values, allowing the engine to evaluate the expression with different values in parallel. Some inputs may have more values than others. In such cases, the last value of the shorter inputs will be repeated as necessary.

The **expression** input string specifies the expression to be evaluated. An expression can consist of multiple subexpressions. Several subexpressions can be specified in one string, separated by semicolons (;). Alternatively, the subexpressions can be stored in separate strings in the multiple-valued input field.

Each subexpression is of the form:

<lhs> = <rhs>

The <lhs> can be any one of the outputs or a temporary variable. The engine provides 8 temporary floating-point variables (ta, tb, tc, td, te, tf, tg, and th), and 8 temporary vector variables (tA, tB, tC, tD, tE, tF, tG, and tH). You can assign a value to one component of a vector output (**A-H**) or a vector variable (**tA-tH**) by using the [] operator. For example, oA[0] = <rhs>, will evaluate the right hand side and assign the value to the first component of the output vector **oA**.

The <rhs> supports arithmetic, logical and conditional operators. They are:

(unary)   !, -
(binary) +, -, *, /, %, <, > <=, >=, ==, !=, &&, ||
(ternary) ? :

The ternary operator is a conditional operator. For example, a ? b : c evaluates to b if a != 0, and to c if a==0.

Valid operands for the <rhs> include the inputs, outputs, temporary variables, and their components (e.g. oA[0]). Operands can also be numeric constants (e.g. 1.0), pre-defined named constants, or pre-defined functions.

The named constants are:

    MAXFLOAT
    MINFLOAT
    M_E
    M_LOG2E
    M_LOG10E
    M_LN2
    M_LN10
    M_PI
    M_SQRT2   = sqrt(2)
    M_SQRT1_2 = sqrt(1/2)

Most of the pre-defined functions come from the math library:

    cos, sin, tan,
    acos, asin, atan, atan2,
    cosh, sinh, tanh,
    sqrt, pow, exp, log, log10,
    ceil, floor, fabs, fmod.

Other functions are defined by **SoCalculator**. They are:

    rand(f) - Random number generator
    cross(v1, v2) - Vector cross product
    dot(v1, v2) - Vector dot product
    length(v) - Vector length
    normalize(v) - Normalize vector
    vec3f(f1, f2, f3) - Generate a vector from 3 floats

The subexpressions are evaluated in order, so a variable set in the <lhs> of an earlier expression may be used in the <rhs> of a later expression.

Note, when the input has multiple values, all the subexpressions specified in the **expression** are applied to all the multiple input values. This is unlike the **SoBoolOperation** engine, where each operation is applied only to the corresponding entries of the input data. Note also, that even though the inputs and outputs can have multiple values the [] operator is only for indexing into the values of a single vector. It does not index into the multiple values of a field. For example, if the floating-point input field **a** has two values: 1.0, and 2.0, then the expression

    "oA[0]=a; oA[1]=a; oA[2]=0.0"

will produce two output vectors in **oA**: (1.0, 1.0, 0.0) and (2.0, 2.0, 0.0).

Examples of expressions:

"ta = oA[0]*floor(a)"
"tb = (a+b)*sin(M_PI)"
"oA = vec3f(ta, tb, ta+tb)"
"oB = normalize(oA)"
"ta = a; tb = sin(ta); oA = vec3f(ta, tb, 0)"

INPUTS

SoMFFloat	**a**
SoMFFloat	**b**
SoMFFloat	**c**
SoMFFloat	**d**
SoMFFloat	**e**
SoMFFloat	**f**
SoMFFloat	**g**
SoMFFloat	**h**

Inputs a-h are the floating-point values.

SoMFVec3f	**A**
SoMFVec3f	**B**
SoMFVec3f	**C**
SoMFVec3f	**D**
SoMFVec3f	**E**
SoMFVec3f	**F**
SoMFVec3f	**G**
SoMFVec3f	**H**

Inputs A-H are the vectors.

SoMFString   **expression**
The expression to be evaluated.

OUTPUTS

(SoMFFloat)	**oa**
(SoMFFloat)	**ob**
(SoMFFloat)	**oc**
(SoMFFloat)	**od**

Outputs oa-od are the floating-point values.

(SoMFVec3f)	**oA**
(SoMFVec3f)	**oB**
(SoMFVec3f)	**oC**
(SoMFVec3f)	**oD**

Outputs oA-oD are the vectors.

METHODS

SoCalculator()

Constructor

Methods from class SoEngine:

getClassTypeId, getOutputs, getOutput, getOutputName, copy, getByName, getByName

Methods from class SoFieldContainer:

setToDefaults, hasDefaultValues, fieldsAreEqual, copyFieldValues, set, get, getFields, getField, getFieldName, enableNotify, isNotifyEnabled

Methods from class SoBase:

ref, unref, unrefNoDelete, touch, getTypeId, isOfType, setName, getName

FILE FORMAT/DEFAULTS

```
Calculator {
        a             0
        b             0
        c             0
        d             0
        e             0
        f             0
        g             0
        h             0
        A             0 0 0
        B             0 0 0
        C             0 0 0
        D             0 0 0
        E             0 0 0
        F             0 0 0
        G             0 0 0
        H             0 0 0
        expression    ""
}
```

SoCalculator

INCLUDE FILE

```
#include <Inventor/engines/SoCalculator.h>
```

SEE ALSO

SoEngineOutput, SoBoolOperation

NAME

SoCallback — provides custom behavior during actions

INHERITS FROM

SoBase > SoFieldContainer > SoNode > SoCallback

DESCRIPTION

This node provides a general mechanism for inserting callback functions into a scene graph. The callback function registered with the node is called each time the node is traversed while performing any scene graph action. The callback function is passed a pointer to the action being performed and a user data pointer registered with the callback function. You can use this node to make nonstandard OpenGL calls while rendering. If you do, be careful not to interfere with Inventor's use of OpenGL.

If you use a callback node for GL rendering, you should be careful to follow render caching rules. If your callback node can make different rendering calls each time it is traversed, it cannot be cached. In such a case, the node should invalidate any open caches, as in the following example:

```
void
myCallbackFunc(void *d, SoAction *action) {
    if (action->isOfType(SoGLRenderAction::getClassTypeId())) {
            // Make my custom GL calls
            ((MyClass *) d)->myRender();

            // Invalidate the state so that a cache is not made
            SoCacheElement::invalidate(action->getState());
    }
}
```

METHODS

SoCallback()
Creates a callback node with default settings.

void   **setCallback(SoCallbackCB *func, void *userData = NULL)**
Sets pointer to callback function and user data. By default, the function pointer in the node is NULL and does nothing.

static SoType   **getClassTypeId()**
Returns type identifier for this class.

Methods from class SoNode:

> setOverride, isOverride, copy, affectsState, getByName, getByName

Methods from class SoFieldContainer:

> setToDefaults, hasDefaultValues, fieldsAreEqual, copyFieldValues, set, get, getFields, getField, getFieldName, enableNotify, isNotifyEnabled

Methods from class SoBase:

> ref, unref, unrefNoDelete, touch, getTypeId, isOfType, setName, getName

ACTION BEHAVIOR

SoGLRenderAction, SoBoundingBoxAction, SoPickAction
Calls the specified callback function for all actions.

FILE FORMAT/DEFAULTS

```
Callback {
}
```

INCLUDE FILE

```
#include <Inventor/nodes/SoCallback.h>
```

typedef void   **SoCallbackCB**(void *userData, SoAction *action)

SEE ALSO

SoAction, SoCallbackAction, SoEventCallback

NAME

SoCallbackAction — performs a generic traversal of the scene graph

INHERITS FROM

SoAction > SoCallbackAction

DESCRIPTION

This action defines a generic traversal of the scene graph. The user can specify callback functions for node types or paths; when those node types or paths are encountered during traversal, the user's callback function is called.

In addition, callback functions can be registered for primitives generated by shapes in the scene graph. Most shape types can generate primitives that represent or approximate their geometries. *Triangle* primitives are used for all surfaces (such as cubes, face sets, or 3D text), *line segment* primitives are used for line shapes, and *point* primitives are used for point shapes. Note that the type of primitives generated for a shape is the same, regardless of drawing style or other properties.

Most of the methods on this class access information from the traversal state. They should be called only by callback functions that are invoked during traversal, so there is a valid state to work with.

METHODS

SoCallbackAction()

The constructor.

void   **addPreCallback**(SoType type, SoCallbackActionCB *cb, void *data)

void   **addPostCallback**(SoType type, SoCallbackActionCB *cb, void *data)

These add a callback function to call when a node of the given type is encountered during traversal. The PreCallback is called just before the node is traversed, and the PostCallback is called just after. The value returned by a callback function indicates whether the action should continue with the traversal.

void   **addPreTailCallback**(SoCallbackActionCB *cb, void *data)

void   **addPostTailCallback**(SoCallbackActionCB *cb, void *data)

These can be used to set up callback functions to call when the action is applied to a path. The functions are called just before or after the node at the tail of the path is traversed.

void	**addTriangleCallback**(SoType type, SoTriangleCB *cb, void *data)
void	**addLineSegmentCallback**(SoType type, SoLineSegmentCB *cb, void *data)
void	**addPointCallback**(SoType type, SoPointCB *cb, void *data)

Routines to add callbacks for generated primitives (triangles, line segments, and points) for all shapes of the given type. The callback function will be called for each primitive generated for all shapes of or derived from that type.

float	**getComplexity**() const
SoComplexity::Type	
	getComplexityType() const

Returns complexity information from the state.

long	**getNumCoordinates**() const
const SbVec3f &	**getCoordinate3**(int index) const
const SbVec4f &	**getCoordinate4**(int index) const

Returns the current coordinates from the state.

SoDrawStyle::Style	
	getDrawStyle() const
unsigned short	**getLinePattern**() const
float	**getLineWidth**() const
float	**getPointSize**() const

Returns the current drawing style information from the state.

const SbName &	**getFontName**() const
float	**getFontSize**() const

Returns the current font information from the state.

SoLightModel::Model	
	getLightModel() const
const SbVec3f &	**getLightAttenuation**() const

Returns the current lighting model information from the state.

void   **getMaterial**(SbColor &ambient, SbColor &diffuse, SbColor &specular, SbColor &emission, float &shininess, float &transparency, int mtlIndex = 0) const

SoMaterialBinding::Binding
                  getMaterialBinding() const

Returns the current material information from the state. Providing a *mtlIndex* will return the material defined for that index.

long   **getNumNormals**() const
const SbVec3f &   **getNormal**(int index) const
SoNormalBinding::Binding
                  getNormalBinding() const

Returns the current normal information from the state.

long   **getNumProfileCoordinates**() const
const SbVec2f &   **getProfileCoordinate2**(int index) const
const SbVec3f &   **getProfileCoordinate3**(int index) const
const SoNodeList &
                  getProfile() const

Returns the current profiles and their coordinates from the state.

SoShapeHints::VertexOrdering
                  getVertexOrdering() const
SoShapeHints::ShapeType
                  getShapeType() const
SoShapeHints::FaceType
                  getFaceType() const
float   **getCreaseAngle**() const

Returns the current shape hints from the state.

long   **getNumTextureCoordinates**() const
const SbVec2f &   **getTextureCoordinate2**(int index) const
const SbVec4f &   **getTextureCoordinate4**(int index) const
SoTextureCoordinateBinding::Binding
                  getTextureCoordinateBinding() const
const SbColor &   **getTextureBlendColor**() const
const unsigned char *
                  getTextureImage(SbVec2s &size, int &numComps) const

Returns texture information from the state. **getNumTextureCoordinates**() returns 0 if texture coordinates are generated by a function. **getTextureImage()** returns NULL if no texture is enabled.

const SbMatrix &	**getTextureMatrix**() const
SoTexture2::Model	**getTextureModel**() const
SoTexture2::Wrap	**getTextureWrapS**() const
SoTexture2::Wrap	**getTextureWrapT**() const

Returns the current texture mapping information from the state.

const SbMatrix &	**getModelMatrix**() const
SoUnits::Units	**getUnits**() const

Returns the current modeling transformation and the current units from the state.

float	**getFocalDistance**() const
const SbMatrix &	**getProjectionMatrix**() const
const SbMatrix &	**getViewingMatrix**() const
const SbViewVolume &	
	getViewVolume() const

Returns the current camera and viewing information from the state.

SoPickStyle::Style	**getPickStyle**() const

Returns the current picking style.

long	**getSwitch**() const

Returns the current switch value.

Methods from class SoAction:

apply, apply, apply, getClassTypeId, getTypeId, isOfType, invalidateState

INCLUDE FILE

```
#include <Inventor/actions/SoCallbackAction.h>
```

typedef void	**SoTriangleCB**(void *userData,
	SoCallbackAction *action,
	const SoPrimitiveVertex *v1,
	const SoPrimitiveVertex *v2,
	const SoPrimitiveVertex *v3)
typedef void	**SoLineSegmentCB**(void *userData,
	SoCallbackAction *action,
	const SoPrimitiveVertex *v1,
	const SoPrimitiveVertex *v2)
typedef void	**SoPointCB**(void *userData,
	SoCallbackAction *action,
	const SoPrimitiveVertex *v)

typedef SoCallbackAction::Response
        SoCallbackActionCB(void *userData,
        SoCallbackAction *action,
        const SoNode *node)

enum **Response** {
    SoCallbackAction::CONTINUE
        Continue traversal as if nothing happened
    SoCallbackAction::ABORT
        Abort traversal
    SoCallbackAction::PRUNE
        Do not traverse node's children, but continue traversal
}

SEE ALSO

SoCallback, SoEventCallback, SoShape

SoCallbackList

NAME

SoCallbackList — manages a list of callback functions and associated data

INHERITS FROM

SoCallbackList

DESCRIPTION

This class manages a list of callback functions and user data. The user can add a callback function to the list, along with user data. When the callback is invoked, it is passed this user data, along with callback data specified by the invoking routine. The type of this callback data is determined by the invoking routine.

METHODS

SoCallbackList()
~SoCallbackList()
Constructor and destructor.

void	**addCallback**(SoCallbackListCB *f, void *userData = NULL)
void	**removeCallback**(SoCallbackListCB *f, void *userData = NULL)

Adds a function to or removes a function from the list of callback functions.

void	**clearCallbacks**()

Clears all callback functions from the list.

int	**getNumCallbacks**() const

Returns the number of callback functions in the list.

void	**invokeCallbacks**(void *callbackData)

Invokes each callback function in the list, passing each function the user data supplied when they were registered here, and *callbackData*, the callback-specific data supplied by the caller.

INCLUDE FILE

```
#include <Inventor/misc/SoCallbackList.h>
```

typedef void	**SoCallbackListCB**(void *userData, void *callbackData)

NAME

SoCamera — abstract base class for camera nodes

INHERITS FROM

SoBase > SoFieldContainer > SoNode > SoCamera

DESCRIPTION

This is the abstract base class for all camera nodes. It defines the common methods and fields that all cameras have. Cameras are used to view a scene. When a camera is encountered during rendering, it sets the projection and viewing matrices and viewport appropriately; it does not draw geometry. Cameras should be placed before any shape nodes or light nodes in a scene graph; otherwise, those shapes or lights cannot be rendered properly. Cameras are affected by the current transformation, so you can position a camera by placing a transformation node before it in the scene graph . The default position and orientation of a camera is at (0,0,1) looking along the negative z-axis.

You can also use a node kit to create a camera; see the reference page for **SoCameraKit**.

FIELDS

SoSFEnum   **viewportMapping**

Defines how to map the rendered image into the current viewport, when the aspect ratio of the camera differs from that of the viewport.

SoSFVec3f   **position**

The location of the camera viewpoint.

SoSFRotation   **orientation**

The orientation of the camera viewpoint, defined as a rotation of the viewing direction from its default (0,0,-1) vector.

SoSFFloat   **aspectRatio**

The ratio of camera viewing width to height. This value must be greater than 0.0. There are several standard camera aspect ratios defined in **SoCamera.h**.

SoSFFloat   **nearDistance**
SoSFFloat   **farDistance**

The distance from the camera viewpoint to the near and far clipping planes.

SoSFFloat   **focalDistance**

The distance from the viewpoint to the point of focus. This is typically ignored during rendering, but may be used by some viewers to define a point of interest.

METHODS

void	**pointAt**(const SbVec3f &targetPoint)

Sets the orientation of the camera so that it points toward the given target point while keeping the "up" direction of the camera parallel to the positive y-axis. If this is not possible, it uses the positive z-axis as "up."

virtual void	**scaleHeight**(float scaleFactor)

Scales the height of the camera. Perspective cameras scale their **heightAngle** fields, and orthographic cameras scale their **height** fields.

virtual SbViewVolume

getViewVolume(float useAspectRatio = 0.0) const

Returns a view volume structure, based on the camera's viewing parameters. If the *useAspectRatio* argument is not 0.0 (the default), the camera uses that ratio instead of the one it has.

void	**viewAll**(SoNode *sceneRoot, const SbViewportRegion &vpRegion, float slack = 1.0)
void	**viewAll**(SoPath *path, const SbViewportRegion &vpRegion, float slack = 1.0)

Sets the camera to view the scene rooted by the given node or defined by the given path. The near and far clipping planes will be positioned *slack* bounding sphere radii away from the bounding box's center. A value of 1.0 will make the clipping planes the tightest around the bounding sphere.

SbViewportRegion

getViewportBounds(const SbViewportRegion &region) const

Returns the viewport region this camera would use to render into the given viewport region, accounting for cropping.

static SoType	**getClassTypeId**()

Returns type identifier for this class.

Methods from class SoNode:

setOverride, isOverride, copy, affectsState, getByName, getByName

Methods from class SoFieldContainer:

setToDefaults, hasDefaultValues, fieldsAreEqual, copyFieldValues, set, get, getFields, getField, getFieldName, enableNotify, isNotifyEnabled

Methods from class SoBase:

ref, unref, unrefNoDelete, touch, getTypeId, isOfType, setName, getName

FILE FORMAT/DEFAULTS

This is an abstract class. See the reference page of a derived class for the format and default values.

INCLUDE FILE

```
#include <Inventor/nodes/SoCamera.h>
```

```
#define SO_ASPECT_SQUARE        1.00
#define SO_ASPECT_VIDEO         1.333333333
#define SO_ASPECT_35mm_ACADEMY  1.371
#define SO_ASPECT_16mm          1.369
#define SO_ASPECT_35mm_FULL     1.33333
#define SO_ASPECT_70mm          2.287
#define SO_ASPECT_CINEMASCOPE   2.35
#define SO_ASPECT_HDTV          1.777777777
#define SO_ASPECT_PANAVISION    2.361
#define SO_ASPECT_35mm          1.5
#define SO_ASPECT_VISTAVISION   2.301
```

```
enum ViewportMapping {
        SoCamera::CROP_VIEWPORT_FILL_FRAME
```
Crops the viewport within the current window, so that the aspect ratio matches that of the camera. As the window size changes, the aspect ratio remains unchanged. The cropped region is drawn as a filled gray area.
```
        SoCamera::CROP_VIEWPORT_LINE_FRAME
```
Crops the viewport, but draws a thin frame around the viewport
```
        SoCamera::CROP_VIEWPORT_NO_FRAME
```
Crops the viewport, but gives no visual feedback as to the viewport dimensions within the window
```
        SoCamera::ADJUST_CAMERA
```
Adjusts the camera aspect ratio and height to make it fit within the given window. (The camera's fields are not affected, just the values sent to the graphics library.)
```
        SoCamera::LEAVE_ALONE
```
Do nothing. Camera image may become stretched out of proportion
```
}
```

SEE ALSO

SoOrthographicCamera, SoPerspectiveCamera, SoCameraKit

NAME

SoCameraKit — camera nodekit class

INHERITS FROM

SoBase > SoFieldContainer > SoNode > SoBaseKit > SoCameraKit

DESCRIPTION

This nodekit class is used to create camera nodes that have a local transformation. **SoCameraKit** adds two public parts to the basic nodekit: *transform* and *camera*.

The *camera* part is created by default as an **SoPerspectiveCamera** node, but may later be changed to any subclass of **SoCamera**.

You can move the camera relative to the rest of the scene by creating and editing the *transform* part.

SoCameraKit also adds a private part, *transformGroup*, which is of type **SoTransformSeparator**. The kit uses this part to contain the effect of *transform* to move only the *camera*, while allowing the *camera* to affect the rest of the scene.

SoCameraKit is derived from **SoBaseKit** and thus also includes a *callbackList* part for adding callback nodes.

PARTS

(SoTransform)   **transform**

A transform that positions and orients the camera relative to the rest of the scene. Private parts keep the effect of the *transform* part localized. This part is NULL by default, but may be set to any subclass of **SoTransform**

(SoCamera)   **camera**

The camera node for this nodekit. The *camera* part is created by default as an **SoPerspectiveCamera** node, but may later be changed to any subclass of **SoCamera**. (e.g., **SoPerspectiveCamera**, **SoOrthographicCamera**).

Parts from class SoBaseKit:

callbackList

METHODS

SoCameraKit()

Constructor.

static const SoNodekitCatalog *
        getClassNodekitCatalog() const
        Returns an **SoNodekitCatalog** for the class **SoCameraKit**.

static SoType   **getClassTypeId**()
        Returns type identifier for this class.

Methods from class SoBaseKit:

        getNodekitCatalog, getPart, getPartString, createPathToPart, setPart, set, set,
        isSearchingChildren, setSearchingChildren

Methods from class SoNode:

        setOverride, isOverride, copy, affectsState, getByName, getByName

Methods from class SoFieldContainer:

        setToDefaults, hasDefaultValues, fieldsAreEqual, copyFieldValues, get,
        getFields, getField, getFieldName, enableNotify, isNotifyEnabled

Methods from class SoBase:

        ref, unref, unrefNoDelete, touch, getTypeId, isOfType, setName, getName

MACROS

        Macros from class SoBaseKit:

        SO_GET_PART, SO_CHECK_PART

CATALOG PARTS

All parts			
Part Name	Part Type	Default Type	NULL by Default
callbackList	NodeKitListPart	--	yes
transform	Transform	--	yes
camera	Camera	PerspectiveCamera	no

Extra information for list parts from above table		
Part Name	**Container Type**	**Permissible Types**
callbackList	Separator	Callback, EventCallback

FILE FORMAT/DEFAULTS

```
CameraKit {
}
```

INCLUDE FILE

```
#include <Inventor/nodekits/SoCameraKit.h>
```

SEE ALSO

SoAppearanceKit, SoBaseKit, SoLightKit, SoNodeKit, SoNodeKitDetail, SoNodeKitListPart, SoNodeKitPath, SoNodekitCatalog, SoSceneKit, SoSeparatorKit, SoShapeKit, SoWrapperKit

NAME

SoCenterballDragger — striped ball you rotate and re-center by dragging with the mouse

INHERITS FROM

SoBase > SoFieldContainer > SoNode > SoBaseKit > SoInteractionKit > SoDragger > SoCenterballDragger

DESCRIPTION

SoCenterballDragger is a composite dragger. Its shape is a sphere defined by three intersecting circles. Where the circles intersect (at the ends of the x, y and z axes) there are sets of small green crosshairs. Dragging a pair of crosshairs translates the entire centerball within the plane of the crosshairs. The interface of the sphere and circles is just like **SoTrackballDragger**. Dragging a circle rotates about a constrained axis and dragging the areas between them rotates the sphere freely about the center. An invisible but pickable sphere initiates the free-rotation dragging.

When you drag the crosshairs, the **center** field is updated; there is no **translation** field. Dragging other parts of the centerball updates the **rotation** field. As with all draggers, if you change the fields the dragger moves in response.

The draggers used for the crosshair parts are **SoTranslate2Draggers**, so pressing the <Shift> key allows you to constrain motion to slide along either the local **x axis** or **y axis** of that crosshair.. The direction is determined by your initial mouse gesture after pressing the key. Releasing the key removes the constraint.

Remember: This is *not* an **SoTransform**! If you want to move other objects with this dragger, you can either:

[a] Use an **SoCenterballManip**, which is subclassed from **SoTransform**. The manipulator creates one of these draggers and uses it as the interface to edit the manipulator's fields. (See the **SoCenterballManip** man page.)

[b] Use field-to-field connections to connect the fields of this dragger to those of any **SoTransformation** node.

You can change the parts in any instance of this dragger using **setPart()**. The default part geometries are defined as resources for this **SoCenterballDragger** class. They are detailed in the Dragger Resources section of the online reference page for this class. You can make your program use different default resources for the parts by copying the file **/usr/share/data/draggerDefaults/centerballDragger.iv** into your own directory, editing the file, and then setting the environment variable **SO_DRAGGER_DIR** to be a path to that directory.

FIELDS

SoSFRotation   **rotation**
> Orientation of the centerball dragger.

SoSFVec3f   **center**
> Center of rotation and scale of the centerball dragger.

Fields from class SoDragger:
> isActive

Fields from class SoInteractionKit:
> renderCaching, boundingBoxCaching, renderCulling, pickCulling

PARTS

Parts from class SoBaseKit:
> callbackList

METHODS

> **SoCenterballDragger**()
Constructor.

static const SoNodekitCatalog *
> **getClassNodekitCatalog**() const
Returns an **SoNodekitCatalog** for this class.

static SoType   **getClassTypeId**()
Returns type identifier for this class.

Methods from class SoDragger:
> addStartCallback, removeStartCallback, addMotionCallback,
> removeMotionCallback, addFinishCallback, removeFinishCallback,
> addValueChangedCallback, removeValueChangedCallback, setMinGesture,
> getMinGesture, setMinScale, getMinScale

Methods from class SoInteractionKit:
> setPartAsPath

Methods from class SoBaseKit:
> getNodekitCatalog, getPart, getPartString, createPathToPart, setPart, set, set,
> isSearchingChildren, setSearchingChildren

Methods from class SoNode:

> setOverride, isOverride, copy, affectsState, getByName, getByName

Methods from class SoFieldContainer:

> setToDefaults, hasDefaultValues, fieldsAreEqual, copyFieldValues, get, getFields, getField, getFieldName, enableNotify, isNotifyEnabled

Methods from class SoBase:

> ref, unref, unrefNoDelete, touch, getTypeId, isOfType, setName, getName

MACROS

Macros from class SoBaseKit:

> SO_GET_PART, SO_CHECK_PART

CATALOG PARTS

All parts			
Part Name	Part Type	Default Type	NULL by Default
callbackList	NodeKitListPart	--	yes
surroundScale	SurroundScale	--	yes
antiSquish	AntiSquish	--	no
translateToCenter	MatrixTransform	--	yes
lightModel	LightModel	--	yes
XAxis	Separator	--	yes
YAxis	Separator	--	yes
ZAxis	Separator	--	yes
rotator	RotateSphericalDragger	--	yes
YRotator	RotateCylindricalDragger	--	yes
ZCenterChanger	Translate2Dragger	--	yes
ZRotator	RotateCylindricalDragger	--	yes
YCenterChanger	Translate2Dragger	--	yes
XCenterChanger	Translate2Dragger	--	yes
XRotator	RotateCylindricalDragger	--	yes

Extra information for list parts from above table		
Part Name	**Container Type**	**Permissible Types**
callbackList	Separator	Callback, EventCallback

FILE FORMAT/DEFAULTS

```
CenterballDragger {
        renderCaching        AUTO
        boundingBoxCaching   AUTO
        renderCulling        AUTO
        pickCulling          AUTO
        isActive             FALSE
        rotation             0 0 1  0
        center               0 0 0
}
```

INCLUDE FILE

```
#include <Inventor/draggers/SoCenterballDragger.h>
```

SEE ALSO

SoInteractionKit, SoDragger, SoDirectionalLightDragger, SoDragPointDragger, SoHandleBoxDragger, SoJackDragger, SoPointLightDragger, SoRotateCylindricalDragger, SoRotateDiscDragger, SoRotateSphericalDragger, SoScale1Dragger, SoScale2Dragger, SoScale2UniformDragger, SoScaleUniformDragger, SoSpotLightDragger, SoTabBoxDragger, SoTabPlaneDragger, SoTrackballDragger, SoTransformBoxDragger, SoTranslate1Dragger, SoTranslate2Dragger

NAME

> SoCenterballManip — transform node with 3D interface for editing rotation and center

INHERITS FROM

> SoBase > SoFieldContainer > SoNode > SoTransformation > SoTransform > SoTransformManip > SoCenterballManip

DESCRIPTION

> **SoCenterballManip** is derived from **SoTransform** (by way of **SoTransformManip**). When its fields change, nodes following it in the scene graph rotate, scale, and/or translate.
>
> As a subclass of **SoTransformManip**, this manipulator also has a 3D interface to edit some of its fields. In this case, the interface edits the **rotation** and **center** fields.
>
> A manipulator differs from a dragger. When you move a dragger, no other nodes are affected. When you move an **SoTransformManip**, other nodes move along with it. (See the reference page for **SoTransformManip**.)
>
> The interface for an **SoCenterballManip** is exactly the same as that of the **SoCenterballDragger**. To find out more about the interface, see the reference page for **SoCenterballDragger**. To find out how the manipulator uses a dragger to provide its interface, see the reference page for **SoTransformManip**.
>
> On screen, this manipulator will surround the objects influenced by its motion. This is because it turns on the *surroundScale* part of the dragger. (See the reference page for **SoSurroundScale**.)

FIELDS

> **Fields from class SoTransform:**
>
>> translation, rotation, scaleFactor, scaleOrientation, center

METHODS

>> **SoCenterballManip**()
>> Constructor.
>
> static SoType   **getClassTypeId**()
>> Returns type identifier for this class.
>
> **Methods from class SoTransformManip:**
>> getDragger, replaceNode, replaceManip

Methods from class SoTransform:

pointAt, getScaleSpaceMatrix, getRotationSpaceMatrix, getTranslationSpaceMatrix, multLeft, multRight, combineLeft, combineRight, setMatrix, recenter

Methods from class SoNode:

setOverride, isOverride, copy, affectsState, getByName, getByName

Methods from class SoFieldContainer:

setToDefaults, hasDefaultValues, fieldsAreEqual, copyFieldValues, set, get, getFields, getField, getFieldName, enableNotify, isNotifyEnabled

Methods from class SoBase:

ref, unref, unrefNoDelete, touch, getTypeId, isOfType, setName, getName

FILE FORMAT/DEFAULTS

```
CenterballManip {
    translation       0 0 0
    rotation          0 0 1 0
    scaleFactor       1 1 1
    scaleOrientation  0 0 1 0
    center            0 0 0
}
```

INCLUDE FILE

```
#include <Inventor/manips/SoCenterballManip.h>
```

SEE ALSO

SoCenterballDragger, SoHandleBoxManip, SoJackManip, SoTabBoxManip, SoTrackballManip, SoTransformBoxManip, SoTransform, SoTransformManip

NAME

SoClipPlane — clipping plane node

INHERITS FROM

SoBase > SoFieldContainer > SoNode > SoClipPlane

DESCRIPTION

This node clips all subsequent shapes in the scene graph to the half-space defined by the **plane** field. The half-space is the side of the plane in the direction of the plane normal. For example, if the plane is positioned at the origin and the normal is pointing down the positive X axis, everything in the negative X space will be clipped away.

Any number of clipping planes may be active simultaneously, although the graphics library may place a limit on this number during rendering.

Note that if any clipping planes are active, backface culling (as set up by the **SoShapeHints** node) will not be performed.

FIELDS

SoSFPlane   **plane**

Plane defining half-space.

SoSFBool   **on**

Whether clipping plane is active.

METHODS

SoClipPlane()

Creates a clip plane node with default settings.

static SoType   **getClassTypeId**()

Returns type identifier for this class.

Methods from class SoNode:

setOverride, isOverride, copy, affectsState, getByName, getByName

Methods from class SoFieldContainer:

setToDefaults, hasDefaultValues, fieldsAreEqual, copyFieldValues, set, get, getFields, getField, getFieldName, enableNotify, isNotifyEnabled

Methods from class SoBase:

ref, unref, unrefNoDelete, touch, getTypeId, isOfType, setName, getName

SoClipPlane

ACTION BEHAVIOR

> **SoGLRenderAction, SoCallbackAction, SoRayPickAction**
>> Adds the plane to the current list of clipping planes in the state.

FILE FORMAT/DEFAULTS

```
ClipPlane {
    plane  1 0 0  0
    on     TRUE
}
```

INCLUDE FILE

```
#include <Inventor/nodes/SoClipPlane.h>
```

SEE ALSO

> SoCamera, SoShapeHints

NAME

SoColorIndex — surface color index node

INHERITS FROM

SoBase > SoFieldContainer > SoNode > SoColorIndex

DESCRIPTION

This node specifies the color to use for subsequent shapes as an index into the current color table. This is used only for BASE_COLOR lighting (see **SoLightModel**) in color index mode. Color index mode may be enabled by the window in which rendering occurs.

Since color indices make sense only in the context of OpenGL rendering, this node implements only a method for the **SoGLRenderAction**.

FIELDS

SoMFLong **index**

Color index.

METHODS

SoColorIndex()

Creates a color index node with default settings.

static SoType **getClassTypeId()**

Returns type identifier for this class.

Methods from class SoNode:

setOverride, isOverride, copy, affectsState, getByName, getByName

Methods from class SoFieldContainer:

setToDefaults, hasDefaultValues, fieldsAreEqual, copyFieldValues, set, get, getFields, getField, getFieldName, enableNotify, isNotifyEnabled

Methods from class SoBase:

ref, unref, unrefNoDelete, touch, getTypeId, isOfType, setName, getName

ACTION BEHAVIOR

SoGLRenderAction

Sets the color index for subsequent shapes rendered with BASE_COLOR lighting.

SoColorIndex

FILE FORMAT/DEFAULTS
```
ColorIndex {
      index  1
}
```
INCLUDE FILE
```
#include <Inventor/nodes/SoColorIndex.h>
```

SEE ALSO

SoBaseColor, SoLightModel, SoMaterialIndex

NAME

SoComplexity — shape complexity node

INHERITS FROM

SoBase > SoFieldContainer > SoNode > SoComplexity

DESCRIPTION

This node sets the current shape complexity value. This is a heuristic value which provides a hint at what geometric complexity to render shape nodes. Values range from 0 to 1, where 0 means minimum complexity and 1 means maximum complexity. Each shape node interprets complexity in its own way.

Shape complexity always affects rendering and primitive generation for the **SoCallbackAction**. For some shapes, it also affects picking.

There are three ways to interpret shape complexity, depending on the **type** field. BOUNDING_BOX complexity ignores the **value** field and renders all shapes as bounding boxes, using the current material, drawing style, etc. The other two types use the **value** field to determine the tessellation of shapes into polygons. OBJECT_SPACE complexity uses **value** directly to determine the tessellation. SCREEN_SPACE complexity depends on **value** and the projected size of the shape on the screen; a **value** of 0 produces the minimum tessellation for a shape, and a **value** of 1 produces a tessellation that is fine enough that each edge of a polygon is about 1 or two pixels in length. Since the projected size depends on the camera position, objects may be tessellated differently every frame if the camera is moving; note that this may have adverse effects on render caching in **SoSeparator** nodes.

The **SoComplexity** node also sets a hint for the quality of textures applied to shapes, based on the value of the **textureQuality** field.

FIELDS

SoSFEnum   **type**

How shape complexity is interpreted.

SoSFFloat   **value**

Complexity value.

SoSFFloat   **textureQuality**

Hint about texture quality. A value of 0 indicates that the fastest texturing should be used, while a value of 1 indicates that the best quality texturing should be used.

METHODS

SoComplexity()
Creates a complexity node with default settings.

static SoType   **getClassTypeId**()
Returns type identifier for this class.

Methods from class SoNode:
setOverride, isOverride, copy, affectsState, getByName, getByName

Methods from class SoFieldContainer:
setToDefaults, hasDefaultValues, fieldsAreEqual, copyFieldValues, set, get, getFields, getField, getFieldName, enableNotify, isNotifyEnabled

Methods from class SoBase:
ref, unref, unrefNoDelete, touch, getTypeId, isOfType, setName, getName

ACTION BEHAVIOR

SoGLRenderAction, SoCallbackAction, SoGetBoundingBoxAction, SoRayPickAction
Sets the current complexity in the state.

FILE FORMAT/DEFAULTS

```
Complexity {
        type            OBJECT_SPACE
        value           0.5
        textureQuality  0.5
}
```

INCLUDE FILE

```
#include <Inventor/nodes/SoComplexity.h>
```

enum **Type** {
     SoComplexity::SCREEN_SPACE
            Set complexity based on screen size
     SoComplexity::OBJECT_SPACE
            Set complexity independent of screen size
     SoComplexity::BOUNDING_BOX
            Draw all shapes as bounding boxes
}

SEE ALSO

SoShape, SoShapeHints, SoTexture2

NAME

SoComposeMatrix — composes a transformation matrix

INHERITS FROM

SoBase > SoFieldContainer > SoEngine > SoComposeMatrix

DESCRIPTION

This engine has inputs that specify values for translation, rotation, scale, and center of transformation. As output, it produces a transformation matrix that transforms objects into the space specified by the scale, rotation, and translation inputs (in that order).

The input fields can have multiple values, allowing the engine to compose several matrices in parallel. Some inputs may have more values than others. In such cases, the last value of the shorter inputs will be repeated as necessary.

INPUTS

SoMFVec3f **translation**
Translation in x, y, and z.

SoMFRotation **rotation**
Rotation.

SoMFVec3f **scaleFactor**
Scale factors in x, y, and z.

SoMFRotation **scaleOrientation**
Rotational space for scaling.

SoMFVec3f **center**
Center point for scaling and rotating.

OUTPUTS

(SoMFMatrix) **matrix**
Transformation matrix that transforms from object space into the space specified by the inputs.

METHODS

SoComposeMatrix()
Constructor

Methods from class SoEngine:

getClassTypeId, getOutputs, getOutput, getOutputName, copy, getByName, getByName

Methods from class SoFieldContainer:

> setToDefaults, hasDefaultValues, fieldsAreEqual, copyFieldValues, set, get, getFields, getField, getFieldName, enableNotify, isNotifyEnabled

Methods from class SoBase:

> ref, unref, unrefNoDelete, touch, getTypeId, isOfType, setName, getName

FILE FORMAT/DEFAULTS

```
ComposeMatrix {
        translation        0 0 0
        rotation           0 0 1  0
        scaleFactor        1 1 1
        scaleOrientation   0 0 1  0
        center             0 0 0
}
```

INCLUDE FILE

```
#include <Inventor/engines/SoCompose.h>
```

SEE ALSO

SoDecomposeMatrix, SoEngineOutput

NAME

SoComposeRotation — composes a rotation from axis and angle values

INHERITS FROM

SoBase > SoFieldContainer > SoEngine > SoComposeRotation

DESCRIPTION

This engine has two inputs, representing an **axis** of rotation and a rotation **angle** in radians. As output, the engine composes the inputs into a rotation field.

The input fields can have multiple values, allowing the engine to compose several rotations in parallel. Some inputs may have more values than others. In such cases, the last value of the shorter inputs will be repeated as necessary.

INPUTS

SoMFVec3f　　　　　**axis**

Axis of rotation.

SoMFFloat　　　　　**angle**

Angle of rotation.

OUTPUTS

(SoMFRotation)　　　**rotation**

Rotation field, defined by the inputs.

METHODS

SoComposeRotation()

Constructor

Methods from class SoEngine:

getClassTypeId, getOutputs, getOutput, getOutputName, copy, getByName, getByName

Methods from class SoFieldContainer:

setToDefaults, hasDefaultValues, fieldsAreEqual, copyFieldValues, set, get, getFields, getField, getFieldName, enableNotify, isNotifyEnabled

Methods from class SoBase:

ref, unref, unrefNoDelete, touch, getTypeId, isOfType, setName, getName

SoComposeRotation

FILE FORMAT/DEFAULTS

```
ComposeRotation {
    axis    0 0 1
    angle   0
}
```

INCLUDE FILE

```
#include <Inventor/engines/SoCompose.h>
```

SEE ALSO

SoComposeRotationFromTo, SoDecomposeRotation, SoEngineOutput

NAME

SoComposeRotationFromTo — composes a rotation that rotates from one vector into another

INHERITS FROM

SoBase > SoFieldContainer > SoEngine > SoComposeRotationFromTo

DESCRIPTION

This engine takes two inputs, representing a vector before and after a rotation has been applied. As output, it produces the rotation value that would cause the first vector to transform into the other.

The input fields can have multiple values, allowing the engine to compose several rotations in parallel. Some inputs may have more values than others. In such cases, the last value of the shorter inputs will be repeated as necessary.

INPUTS

SoMFVec3f   **from**
Vector before the rotation.

SoMFVec3f   **to**
Vector after the rotation.

OUTPUTS

(SoMFRotation)   **rotation**
A rotation that transforms one vector into another.

METHODS

SoComposeRotationFromTo()
Constructor

Methods from class SoEngine:

getClassTypeId, getOutputs, getOutput, getOutputName, copy, getByName, getByName

Methods from class SoFieldContainer:

setToDefaults, hasDefaultValues, fieldsAreEqual, copyFieldValues, set, get, getFields, getField, getFieldName, enableNotify, isNotifyEnabled

Methods from class SoBase:

ref, unref, unrefNoDelete, touch, getTypeId, isOfType, setName, getName

SoComposeRotationFromTo

FILE FORMAT/DEFAULTS

```
ComposeRotationFromTo {
      from  0 0 1
      to    0 0 1
}
```

INCLUDE FILE

```
#include <Inventor/engines/SoCompose.h>
```

SEE ALSO

SoComposeRotation, SoDecomposeRotationFromTo, SoEngineOutput

NAME

SoComposeVec2f — composes 2D vectors from floating-point values

INHERITS FROM

SoBase > SoFieldContainer > SoEngine > SoComposeVec2f

DESCRIPTION

This engine takes two floating-point inputs and composes a 2D floating-point vector.

The input fields can have multiple values, allowing the engine to compose several vectors in parallel. One of the inputs may have more values than others. In such cases, the last value of the shorter input will be repeated as necessary.

INPUTS

SoMFFloat　　　**x**
　　The x component.

SoMFFloat　　　**y**
　　The y component.

OUTPUTS

(SoMFVec2f)　　　**vector**
　　Vector composed of x and y components.

METHODS

　　　　　　SoComposeVec2f()
　　Constructor

Methods from class SoEngine:

　　getClassTypeId, getOutputs, getOutput, getOutputName, copy, getByName, getByName

Methods from class SoFieldContainer:

　　setToDefaults, hasDefaultValues, fieldsAreEqual, copyFieldValues, set, get, getFields, getField, getFieldName, enableNotify, isNotifyEnabled

Methods from class SoBase:

　　ref, unref, unrefNoDelete, touch, getTypeId, isOfType, setName, getName

FILE FORMAT/DEFAULTS

```
ComposeVec2f {
      x   0
      y   0
}
```

INCLUDE FILE

```
#include <Inventor/engines/SoCompose.h>
```

SEE ALSO

SoDecomposeVec2f, SoEngineOutput

NAME

SoComposeVec3f — composes 3D vectors from floating-point values

INHERITS FROM

SoBase > SoFieldContainer > SoEngine > SoComposeVec3f

DESCRIPTION

This engine takes three floating-point inputs and composes a 3D vector.

The input fields can have multiple values, allowing the engine to compose several vectors in parallel. Some inputs may have more values than others. In such cases, the last value of the shorter inputs will be repeated as necessary.

INPUTS

SoMFFloat   x

     The x component

SoMFFloat   y

     The y component

SoMFFloat   z

     The z component.

OUTPUTS

(SoMFVec3f)   **vector**

     Vector composed of x, y, and z.

METHODS

SoComposeVec3f()

Constructor

Methods from class SoEngine:

getClassTypeId, getOutputs, getOutput, getOutputName, copy, getByName, getByName

Methods from class SoFieldContainer:

setToDefaults, hasDefaultValues, fieldsAreEqual, copyFieldValues, set, get, getFields, getField, getFieldName, enableNotify, isNotifyEnabled

Methods from class SoBase:

ref, unref, unrefNoDelete, touch, getTypeId, isOfType, setName, getName

FILE FORMAT/DEFAULTS

```
ComposeVec3f {
        x  0
        y  0
        z  0
}
```

INCLUDE FILE

```
#include <Inventor/engines/SoCompose.h>
```

SEE ALSO

SoDecomposeVec3f, SoEngineOutput

NAME

SoComposeVec4f — composes 4D vectors from floating-point values

INHERITS FROM

SoBase > SoFieldContainer > SoEngine > SoComposeVec4f

DESCRIPTION

This engine takes four floating-point inputs and composes a 4D vector.

The input fields can have multiple values, allowing the engine to compose several vectors in parallel. Some inputs may have more values than others. In such cases, the last value of the shorter inputs will be repeated as necessary.

INPUTS

SoMFFloat   **x**

The x component.

SoMFFloat   **y**

The y component.

SoMFFloat   **z**

The z component.

SoMFFloat   **w**

The w component.

OUTPUTS

(SoMFVec4f)   **vector**

Vector composed of x, y, z, and w.

METHODS

                        SoComposeVec4f()

Constructor

Methods from class SoEngine:

getClassTypeId, getOutputs, getOutput, getOutputName, copy, getByName, getByName

Methods from class SoFieldContainer:

setToDefaults, hasDefaultValues, fieldsAreEqual, copyFieldValues, set, get, getFields, getField, getFieldName, enableNotify, isNotifyEnabled

Methods from class SoBase:

ref, unref, unrefNoDelete, touch, getTypeId, isOfType, setName, getName

SoComposeVec4f

FILE FORMAT/DEFAULTS

```
ComposeVec4f {
        x  0
        y  0
        z  0
        w  0
}
```

INCLUDE FILE

```
#include <Inventor/engines/SoCompose.h>
```

SEE ALSO

SoDecomposeVec4f, SoEngineOutput

NAME

SoComputeBoundingBox — computes the bounding box and center of a scene graph

INHERITS FROM

SoBase > SoFieldContainer > SoEngine > SoComputeBoundingBox

DESCRIPTION

This engine computes the bounding box and center of a scene graph. The scene graph can be defined by a path or by a root node.

If the **path** input is not NULL, the bounding box of the graph defined by the path will be computed. If **path** is NULL, but the **node** input is not NULL, the bounding box is computed on the graph rooted by the node. By default, the two inputs are NULL. If both the inputs are NULL, the outputs are disabled.

The engine uses a default viewport region. If the graph includes screen-based objects (such as **SoText2**) you can call **setViewportRegion()** on the engine instance to set up the correct viewport region to use.

INPUTS

SoSFNode   **node**

Defines the graph for which the bounding box is computed.

SoSFPath   **path**

Alternatively, defines the graph for which the bounding box is computed.

OUTPUTS

(SoSFVec3f)   **min**

Minimum point of the computed bounding box.

(SoSFVec3f)   **max**

Maximum point of the computed bounding box.

(SoSFVec3f)   **boxCenter**

Center of the computed bounding box.

(SoSFVec3f)   **objectCenter**

Center of the objects in the graph.

METHODS

SoComputeBoundingBox()
Constructor

void   **setViewportRegion**(const SbViewportRegion &vpReg);
Sets the viewport region to use for the bounding box computation.

const SbViewportRegion &
getViewportRegion();
Returns the viewport region to use for the bounding box computation.

Methods from class SoEngine:

getClassTypeId, getOutputs, getOutput, getOutputName, copy, getByName, getByName

Methods from class SoFieldContainer:

setToDefaults, hasDefaultValues, fieldsAreEqual, copyFieldValues, set, get, getFields, getField, getFieldName, enableNotify, isNotifyEnabled

Methods from class SoBase:

ref, unref, unrefNoDelete, touch, getTypeId, isOfType, setName, getName

FILE FORMAT/DEFAULTS

```
ComputeBoundingBox {
      node   NULL
      path   NULL
}
```

INCLUDE FILE

```
#include <Inventor/engines/SoComputeBoundingBox.h>
```

SEE ALSO

SoEngineOutput, SoGetBoundingBoxAction, SbBox3f

NAME

SoConcatenate — joins separate fields into a single multiple-value field

INHERITS FROM

SoBase > SoFieldContainer > SoEngine > SoConcatenate

DESCRIPTION

This engine joins up to 10 separate fields of a type into a single multiple-valued field of the same type. The type of the input fields can be any subclass of **SoMField** The type is specified when an instance of the class is created. For example, **SoConcatenate(SoMFFloat::getClassTypeId())** creates an engine that concatenates floating-point values.

The **input** field is a 10-element array, where each element can be connected to single- or multiple-valued fields. All the values in the input are concatenated together to form one multiple-value field. For example, if **input[0]** contains 10 values and **input[1]** contains 3 values, the output will contain 13 values.

Note that, unlike the output of most engines, **output** is a pointer. Note also that by default **input** does not contain any values, and no value is output from the engine.

INPUTS

<inputType>   **input[10]**

OUTPUTS

(<outputType>)   **output**

METHODS

                SoConcatenate(SoType inputType)
Constructor. The argument specifies the type of values to concatenate.

Methods from class SoEngine:

getClassTypeId, getOutputs, getOutput, getOutputName, copy, getByName, getByName

Methods from class SoFieldContainer:

setToDefaults, hasDefaultValues, fieldsAreEqual, copyFieldValues, set, get, getFields, getField, getFieldName, enableNotify, isNotifyEnabled

Methods from class SoBase:

ref, unref, unrefNoDelete, touch, getTypeId, isOfType, setName, getName

SoConcatenate

FILE FORMAT/DEFAULTS

```
Concatenate {
        type            <inputType>
        input0          []
        input1          []
        input2          []
        input3          []
        input4          []
        input5          []
        input6          []
        input7          []
        input8          []
        input9          []
}
```

INCLUDE FILE

```
#include <Inventor/engines/SoConcatenate.h>
```

SEE ALSO

SoEngineOutput, SoGate, SoSelectOne

NAME

SoCone — cone shape node

INHERITS FROM

SoBase > SoFieldContainer > SoNode > SoShape > SoCone

DESCRIPTION

This node represents a simple cone whose central axis is aligned with the y-axis. By default, the cone is centered at (0,0,0) and has a size of -1 to +1 in all three directions. The cone has a radius of 1 at the bottom and a height of 2, with its apex at 1. The cone has two parts: the sides and the bottom.

The cone is transformed by the current cumulative transformation and is drawn with the current lighting model, drawing style, material, and geometric complexity.

If the current material binding is PER_PART or PER_PART_INDEXED, the first current material is used for the sides of the cone, and the second is used for the bottom. Otherwise, the first material is used for the entire cone.

When a texture is applied to a cone, it is applied differently to the sides and bottom. On the sides, the texture wraps counterclockwise (from above) starting at the back of the cone. The texture has a vertical seam at the back, intersecting the yz-plane. For the bottom, a circle is cut out of the texture square and applied to the cone's base circle. The texture appears right side up when the top of the cone is tilted away from the camera.

FIELDS

SoSFBitMask   **parts**

Visible parts of cone.

SoSFFloat   **bottomRadius**
SoSFFloat   **height**

These define the cone's height and the radius of the base circle; values must be greater than 0.0.

METHODS

SoCone()

Creates a cone node with default settings.

void   **addPart**(SoCone::Part part)
void   **removePart**(SoCone::Part part)

These are convenience functions that make it easy to turn on or off a part of the cone.

SbBool   **hasPart**(SoCone::Part part) const

  This convenience function returns whether a given part is on or off.

static SoType **getClassTypeId**()

  Returns type identifier for this class.

Methods from class SoNode:

  setOverride, isOverride, copy, affectsState, getByName, getByName

Methods from class SoFieldContainer:

  setToDefaults, hasDefaultValues, fieldsAreEqual, copyFieldValues, set, get, getFields, getField, getFieldName, enableNotify, isNotifyEnabled

Methods from class SoBase:

  ref, unref, unrefNoDelete, touch, getTypeId, isOfType, setName, getName

ACTION BEHAVIOR

SoGLRenderAction

  Draws cone based on the current coordinates, materials, drawing style, and so on.

SoRayPickAction

  Intersects the ray with the cone. The part of the cone that was picked is available from the **SoConeDetail**.

SoGetBoundingBoxAction

  Computes the bounding box that encloses the cone.

SoCallbackAction

  If any triangle callbacks are registered with the action, they will be invoked for each successive triangle that approximates the cone.

FILE FORMAT/DEFAULTS

```
Cone {
        parts           ALL
        bottomRadius    1
        height          2
}
```

INCLUDE FILE

```
#include <Inventor/nodes/SoCone.h>
```

enum **Part** {

      SoCone::SIDES   The conical part

      SoCone::BOTTOM The bottom circular face

      SoCone::ALL   All parts

}

SEE ALSO

SoConeDetail, SoCube, SoCylinder, SoSphere

SoConeDetail

NAME

SoConeDetail — stores detail information about the SoCone node

INHERITS FROM

SoDetail > SoConeDetail

DESCRIPTION

This class contains detail information about a point on a cone. It contains the part
of the cone that was hit (sides or bottom).

METHODS

SoConeDetail()

virtual **~SoConeDetail**()

Constructor and destructor.

int **getPart**() const

Returns the part in the detail. The returned value is one of the **SoCone** part
flags.

static SoType **getClassTypeId**()

Returns type identifier for this class.

Methods from class SoDetail:

copy, getTypeId, isOfType

INCLUDE FILE

```
#include <Inventor/details/SoConeDetail.h>
```

SEE ALSO

SoCone, SoDetail, SoPickedPoint, SoPrimitiveVertex

NAME

SoCoordinate3 — coordinate point node

INHERITS FROM

SoBase > SoFieldContainer > SoNode > SoCoordinate3

DESCRIPTION

This node defines a set of 3D coordinates to be used by subsequent vertex-based shape nodes (those derived from **SoVertexShape**) or shape nodes that use them as control points (such as NURBS curves and surfaces). This node does not produce a visible result during rendering; it simply replaces the current coordinates in the rendering state for subsequent nodes to use.

FIELDS

SoMFVec3f   **point**

Coordinate point(s).

METHODS

SoCoordinate3()

Creates a coordinate node with default settings.

static SoType   **getClassTypeId**()

Returns type identifier for this class.

Methods from class SoNode:

setOverride, isOverride, copy, affectsState, getByName, getByName

Methods from class SoFieldContainer:

setToDefaults, hasDefaultValues, fieldsAreEqual, copyFieldValues, set, get, getFields, getField, getFieldName, enableNotify, isNotifyEnabled

Methods from class SoBase:

ref, unref, unrefNoDelete, touch, getTypeId, isOfType, setName, getName

ACTION BEHAVIOR

SoGLRenderAction, SoCallbackAction, SoGetBoundingBoxAction, SoRayPickAction

Sets coordinates in current traversal state.

FILE FORMAT/DEFAULTS

```
Coordinate3 {
      point  0 0 0
}
```

SoCoordinate3

INCLUDE FILE

```
#include <Inventor/nodes/SoCoordinate3.h>
```

SEE ALSO

SoCoordinate4, SoVertexShape

NAME

SoCoordinate4 — rational coordinate point node

INHERITS FROM

SoBase > SoFieldContainer > SoNode > SoCoordinate4

DESCRIPTION

This node defines a set of 3D coordinates to be used by subsequent vertex-based shape nodes (those derived from **SoVertexShape**) or shape nodes that use them as control points (such as NURBS curves and surfaces). Coordinates are specifed as rational 4-vectors; the corresponding 3D point is computed by dividing the first three components by the fourth. This node does not produce a visible result during rendering; it simply replaces the current coordinates in the rendering state for subsequent nodes to use.

This node exists primarily for use with NURBS curves and surfaces. However, it can be used to define coordinates for any vertex-based shape.

FIELDS

SoMFVec4f　　　　　**point**

Coordinate point(s).

METHODS

SoCoordinate4()

Creates a coordinate node with default settings.

static SoType　　　　**getClassTypeId**()

Returns type identifier for this class.

Methods from class SoNode:

setOverride, isOverride, copy, affectsState, getByName, getByName

Methods from class SoFieldContainer:

setToDefaults, hasDefaultValues, fieldsAreEqual, copyFieldValues, set, get, getFields, getField, getFieldName, enableNotify, isNotifyEnabled

Methods from class SoBase:

ref, unref, unrefNoDelete, touch, getTypeId, isOfType, setName, getName

ACTION BEHAVIOR

SoGLRenderAction, SoCallbackAction, SoGetBoundingBoxAction, SoRayPickAction

Sets coordinates in current traversal state.

SoCoordinate4

FILE FORMAT/DEFAULTS

```
Coordinate4 {
    point  0 0 0 1
}
```

INCLUDE FILE

```
#include <Inventor/nodes/SoCoordinate4.h>
```

SEE ALSO

SoCoordinate4, SoIndexedNurbsCurve, SoIndexedNurbsSurface, SoNurbsCurve, SoNurbsProfile, SoNurbsSurface, SoVertexShape

NAME

SoCounter — triggered integer counter

INHERITS FROM

SoBase > SoFieldContainer > SoEngine > SoCounter

DESCRIPTION

This engine is a counter that outputs numbers, starting at a minimum value, increasing by a step value, and ending with a number that does not exceed the maximum value. It outputs the next number whenever the **trigger** input is touched. When the maximum number is reached, it starts counting from the beginning again.

At any time the counter can be reset to a specific value by setting the **reset** input field to that value. The next time the counter is triggered it will start counting from there. Note that the counter will always output numbers based on the min, max and step values, and setting the reset value does not affect those input fields. If the reset value is not a legal counter value, the counter will still behave as though it is.

If **reset** is greater than **max**, the counter is set to **max**.
If **reset** is less than **min**, the counter is set to **min**.
If **reset** is between steps, the counter is set to the lower step value.

Each time a counting cycle is started, the **syncOut** output is triggered. This output can be used to synchronize some other event with the counting cycle.

INPUTS

SoSFShort   **min**

Minimum value for the counter.

SoSFShort   **max**

Maximum value for the counter.

SoSFShort   **step**

Counter step value.

SoSFTrigger   **trigger**

Go to the next step.

SoSFShort   **reset**

At the next trigger, reset the counter to the specified value.

OUTPUTS

(SoSFShort) **output**
> Counts min-to-max in step increments.

(SoSFTrigger) **syncOut**
> Triggers at cycle start.

METHODS

SoCounter()
Constructor

Methods from class SoEngine:

> getClassTypeId, getOutputs, getOutput, getOutputName, copy, getByName, getByName

Methods from class SoFieldContainer:

> setToDefaults, hasDefaultValues, fieldsAreEqual, copyFieldValues, set, get, getFields, getField, getFieldName, enableNotify, isNotifyEnabled

Methods from class SoBase:

> ref, unref, unrefNoDelete, touch, getTypeId, isOfType, setName, getName

FILE FORMAT/DEFAULTS

```
Counter {
        min        0
        max        1
        step       1
        trigger
        reset      0
}
```

INCLUDE FILE

```
#include <Inventor/engines/SoCounter.h>
```

SEE ALSO

> SoTimeCounter, SoEngineOutput

NAME

SoCube — cube shape node

INHERITS FROM

SoBase > SoFieldContainer > SoNode > SoShape > SoCube

DESCRIPTION

This node represents a cuboid aligned with the coordinate axes. By default, the cube is centered at (0,0,0) and measures 2 units in each dimension, from -1 to +1. The cube is transformed by the current cumulative transformation and is drawn with the current lighting model, drawing style, material, and geometric complexity.

If the current material binding is PER_PART, PER_PART_INDEXED, PER_FACE, or PER_FACE_INDEXED, materials will be bound to the faces of the cube in this order: front, back, left, right, top, and bottom.

Textures are applied individually to each face of the cube; the entire texture goes on each face. On the front, back, right, and left sides of the cube, the texture is applied right side up. On the top, the texture appears right side up when the top of the cube is tilted toward the camera. On the bottom, the texture appears right side up when the top of the cube is tilted away from the camera.

FIELDS

SoSFFloat	**width**
SoSFFloat	**height**
SoSFFloat	**depth**

Sizes in the x, y, and z dimensions, respectively.

METHODS

SoCube()

Creates a cube node with default settings.

static SoType **getClassTypeId()**

Returns type identifier for this class.

Methods from class SoNode:

setOverride, isOverride, copy, affectsState, getByName, getByName

Methods from class SoFieldContainer:

setToDefaults, hasDefaultValues, fieldsAreEqual, copyFieldValues, set, get, getFields, getField, getFieldName, enableNotify, isNotifyEnabled

Methods from class SoBase:

ref, unref, unrefNoDelete, touch, getTypeId, isOfType, setName, getName

ACTION BEHAVIOR

SoGLRenderAction

Draws cube based on the current coordinates, materials, drawing style, and so on.

SoRayPickAction

Intersects the ray with the cube. The face of the cube that was picked is available from the **SoCubeDetail**.

SoGetBoundingBoxAction

Computes the bounding box that encloses the cube.

SoCallbackAction

If any triangle callbacks are registered with the action, they will be invoked for each successive triangle that approximates the cube.

FILE FORMAT/DEFAULTS

```
Cube {
        width    2
        height   2
        depth    2
}
```

INCLUDE FILE

```
#include <Inventor/nodes/SoCube.h>
```

SEE ALSO

SoCone, SoCubeDetail, SoCylinder, SoSphere

NAME

SoCubeDetail — stores detail information about the SoCube node

INHERITS FROM

SoDetail > SoCubeDetail

DESCRIPTION

This class contains detail information about a point on a cube. It contains the part of the cube that was hit.

Part values are as follows:

0	Front
1	Back
2	Left
3	Right
4	Top
5	Bottom

METHODS

	SoCubeDetail()
virtual	**~SoCubeDetail**()

Constructor and destructor.

int   **getPart**() const

Returns the part in the detail.

static SoType   **getClassTypeId**()

Returns type identifier for this class.

Methods from class SoDetail:

copy, getTypeId, isOfType

INCLUDE FILE

```
#include <Inventor/details/SoCubeDetail.h>
```

SEE ALSO

SoCube, SoDetail, SoPickedPoint, SoPrimitiveVertex

SoCylinder

NAME

SoCylinder — cylinder shape node

INHERITS FROM

SoBase > SoFieldContainer > SoNode > SoShape > SoCylinder

DESCRIPTION

This node represents a simple capped cylinder centered around the y-axis. By default, the cylinder is centered at (0,0,0) and has a default size of -1 to +1 in all three dimensions. You can use the **radius** and **height** fields to create a cylinder with a different size.

The cylinder is transformed by the current cumulative transformation and is drawn with the current lighting model, drawing style, material, and geometric complexity.

If the current material binding is PER_PART or PER_PART_INDEXED, the first current material is used for the sides of the cylinder, the second is used for the top, and the third is used for the bottom. Otherwise, the first material is used for the entire cylinder.

When a texture is applied to a cylinder, it is applied differently to the sides, top, and bottom. On the sides, the texture wraps counterclockwise (from above) starting at the back of the cylinder. The texture has a vertical seam at the back, intersecting the yz-plane. For the top and bottom, a circle is cut out of the texture square and applied to the top or bottom circle. The top texture appears right side up when the top of the cylinder is tilted toward the camera, and the bottom texture appears right side up when the top of the cylinder is tilted away from the camera.

FIELDS

SoSFBitMask   **parts**
Visible parts of cylinder.

SoSFFloat   **radius**
SoSFFloat   **height**
Define the cylinder's height and radius; values must be greater than 0.0.

METHODS

                    SoCylinder()
Creates a cylinder node with default settings.

void   **addPart**(SoCylinder::Part part)
void   **removePart**(SoCylinder::Part part)
These are convenience functions that make it easy to turn on or off a part of the cylinder.

SbBool   **hasPart**(SoCylinder::Part part) const
This convenience function returns whether a given part is on or off.

static SoType   **getClassTypeId**()
Returns type identifier for this class.

Methods from class SoNode:

setOverride, isOverride, copy, affectsState, getByName, getByName

Methods from class SoFieldContainer:

setToDefaults, hasDefaultValues, fieldsAreEqual, copyFieldValues, set, get, getFields, getField, getFieldName, enableNotify, isNotifyEnabled

Methods from class SoBase:

ref, unref, unrefNoDelete, touch, getTypeId, isOfType, setName, getName

ACTION BEHAVIOR

SoGLRenderAction

Draws cylinder based on the current coordinates, materials, drawing style, and so on.

SoRayPickAction

Intersects the ray with the cylinder. The part of the cylinder that was picked is available from the **SoCylinderDetail**.

SoGetBoundingBoxAction

Computes the bounding box that encloses the cylinder.

SoCallbackAction

If any triangle callbacks are registered with the action, they will be invoked for each successive triangle that approximates the cylinder.

FILE FORMAT/DEFAULTS

```
Cylinder {
      parts    ALL
      radius   1
      height   2
}
```

SoCylinder

INCLUDE FILE

```
#include <Inventor/nodes/SoCylinder.h>
```

enum **Part** {
        SoCylinder::SIDES   The cylindrical part
        SoCylinder::TOP   The top circular face
        SoCylinder::BOTTOM The bottom circular face
        SoCylinder::ALL   All parts
}

SEE ALSO

SoCone, SoCube, SoCylinderDetail, SoSphere

NAME

SoCylinderDetail — stores detail information about the SoCylinder node

INHERITS FROM

SoDetail > SoCylinderDetail

DESCRIPTION

This class contains detail information about a point on a cylinder. It contains the part of the cylinder that was hit (sides, top, or bottom).

METHODS

	SoCylinderDetail()
virtual	**~SoCylinderDetail**()

Constructor and destructor.

int **getPart**() const

Returns the part in the detail. The returned value is one of the **SoCylinder** part flags.

static SoType **getClassTypeId**()

Returns type identifier for this class.

Methods from class SoDetail:

copy, getTypeId, isOfType

INCLUDE FILE

```
#include <Inventor/details/SoCylinderDetail.h>
```

SEE ALSO

SoCylinder, SoDetail, SoPickedPoint, SoPrimitiveVertex

NAME

SoDataSensor — abstract base class for sensors attached to parts of a scene

INHERITS FROM

SoSensor > SoDelayQueueSensor > SoDataSensor

DESCRIPTION

Data sensors detect changes to scene graph objects (paths, nodes, or fields) and trigger their callback function when the object changes.

Data sensors provide a delete callback that is called just before the object the data sensor is attached to is deleted; note that the callback should not attempt to modify the object in any way, or core dumps may result.

Priority zero data sensors also provide methods that can be called in the callback function to determine exactly which node, field, or path caused the sensor to be triggered.

METHODS

void   **setDeleteCallback**(SoSensorCB *function, void *data)

Sets a callback that will be called when the object the sensor is sensing is deleted.

SoNode *   **getTriggerNode**() const
SoField *   **getTriggerField**() const

If this is a priority 0 data sensor, returns the node/field that was modified that caused this sensor to trigger. Returns NULL if the sensor was not triggered because a node/field changed (for example, if **schedule**() is called on the sensor) or if this sensor is not a priority 0 sensor. Note that because one change to the scene graph may cause multiple nodes or fields to be modified (because of field-to-field connections), the node or field returned may not be the only one that changed.

SoPath *   **getTriggerPath**() const
void   **setTriggerPathFlag**(SbBool flag)
SbBool   **getTriggerPathFlag**() const

If this is a priority 0 data sensor, returns a path to the node that caused this sensor to trigger. Because recreating the path to the node that changed is relatively expensive, **setTriggerPathFlag(TRUE)** must be called before the sensor is scheduled. If it is not called, or if the sensor wasn't triggered because a node changed, this returns NULL. NULL is also returned if this is not a priority 0 sensor.

Methods from class SoDelayQueueSensor:

setPriority, getPriority, getDefaultPriority, schedule, unschedule, isScheduled

Methods from class SoSensor:

setFunction, getFunction, setData, getData

INCLUDE FILE

```
#include <Inventor/sensors/SoDataSensor.h>
```

SEE ALSO

SoNodeSensor, SoPathSensor, SoFieldSensor, SoDelayQueueSensor

NAME

SoDB — scene graph database class

INHERITS FROM

SoDB

DESCRIPTION

The **SoDB** class holds all scene graphs, each representing a 3D scene used by an application. A scene graph is a collection of SoNode objects which come in several varieties (see **SoNode**). Application programs must initialize the database by calling **SoDB::init()** before calling any other database routines and before constructing any nodes, paths, functions, or actions. Note that **SoDB::init()** is called by **SoInteraction::init()**, **SoNodeKit::init()**, and **SoXt::init()**, so if you are calling any of these methods, you do not need to call **SoDB::init()** directly. All methods on this class are static.

Typical program database initialization and scene reading is as follows:

```
#include <Inventor/SoDB.h>
#include <Inventor/SoInput.h>
#include <Inventor/nodes/SoSeparator.h>

SoSeparator  *rootSep;
SoInput     in;

SoDB::init();
rootSep = SoDB::readAll(&in);
if (rootSep == NULL)
   printf("Error on read...\n");
   ...
```

METHODS

static void   **init**()

Initializes the database. This must be called before calling any other database routines, including the construction of any nodes, paths, engines, or actions.

static const char *

getVersion()

Returns a character string identifying the version of the Inventor library in use.

static SbBool	**read**(SoInput *in, SoNode *&rootNode)
static SbBool	**read**(SoInput *in, SoPath *&path)

Reads a graph from the file specified by the given **SoInput**, returning a pointer to the resulting root node in *rootNode*, or a pointer to the resulting path in *path*. The programmer is responsible for determining which routine to use, based on the contents of the input. These routines return FALSE if any error occurred during reading.

If the passed **SoInput** was used to open a file and the name of the file contains a directory, **SoDB** automatically adds the directory to the end of the current directory search path in the **SoInput**. This means that nested files named in **SoFile** nodes may be found relative to that directory. The directory is removed from the search path when reading is complete.

static SoSeparator *

readAll(SoInput *in)

Reads all graphs from the file specified by the given **SoInput**. If there is only one graph in the file and its root is an **SoSeparator**, a pointer to the root is returned. In all other cases, this creates an **SoSeparator**, adds the root nodes of all graphs read as children of it, and returns a pointer to it. This returns NULL on error. This processes directory paths in the same way as the other reading routines.

static SbBool   **isValidHeader**(const char *testString)

This returns TRUE if the given character string is a valid Inventor file header, either ASCII or binary. Some trivial tests that can be made on the string before calling this are: it must begin with a "#"; it should be no more than 80 characters; it ends at a newline. Characters after the first newline (if any) in the passed string are ignored. The valid ASCII header for Inventor 2.0 is: "#Inventor V2.0 ascii", and the valid binary header is "#Inventor V2.0 binary". Corresponding version 1.0 headers are also considered valid.

static SoField *   **createGlobalField**(const SbName &name, SoType type)

The database maintains a namespace for global fields, making sure that there is at most one instance of a global field with any given name in the database. This routine is used to create new global fields. If there is no global field with the given name, it will create a new global field with the given name and type. If there is already a global field with the given name and type, it will return it. If there is already a global field with the given name but a different type, this returns NULL.

All global fields must be derived from **SoField**; typically the result of this routine is cast into the appropriate type; for example:

SoSFLong *longField =
    (SoSFLong *) SoDB::createGlobalField("Frame",
                      SoSFLong::getClassTypeId());

static SoField *   **getGlobalField**(const SbName &name)

Returns the global field with the given name, or NULL if there is none. The type of the field may be checked using the **SoField::isOfType()**, **SoField::getClassTypeId()**, and **SoField::getTypeId()** methods.

static void   **renameGlobalField**(const SbName &oldName, const SbName &newName)

Renames the global field named *oldName*. Renaming a global field to an empty name ("") deletes it. If there is already a global field with the new name, that field will be deleted (the **getGlobalField** method can be used to guard against this).

static void   **setRealTimeInterval**(const SbTime &deltaT)

The database automatically creates one global field when **SoDB::init()** is called. The **realTime** global field, which is of type **SoSFTime**, can be connected to engines and nodes for real-time animation. The database will automatically update the **realTime** global field 60 times per second, using a timer sensor. Typically, there will be a node sensor on the root of the scene graph which schedules a redraw whenever the scene graph changes; by updating the **realTime** global field periodically, scene graphs that are connected to **realTime** (and are therefore animating) will be redrawn. The rate at which the database updates **realTime** can be controlled with this routine. Passing in a zero time will disable automatic update of **realTime**. Note also that if there are no enabled connections from the **realTime** field to any other field, the sensor is automatically disabled.

static const SbTime &
     getRealTimeInterval()

Returns how often the database is updating **realTime**.

static void   **setDelaySensorTimeout**(const SbTime &t)

This sets the timeout value for sensors that are delay queue sensors (one-shot sensors, data sensors). Delay queue sensors are triggered whenever there is idle time. If a long period of time elapses without any idle time (as when there are continuous events to process), these sensors may not be triggered.

Setting this timeout value ensures that if the specified length of time elapses without any idle time, the delay queue sensors will be processed anyway.

static const SbTime &
getDelaySensorTimeout()
Returns the current delay queue timeout value.

static int **doSelect**(int nfds, fd_set *readfds, fd_set *writefds, fd_set *exceptfds, struct timeval *userTimeOut)
In order to keep timer and idle sensors running as expected, it is necessary that an Inventor application not block waiting for input. If the Inventor application uses the Xt utility library, this can be handled automatically. However, if the application is using its own event loop, this function is provided as a wrapper around **select(2)** that will handle Inventor tasks if necessary instead of blocking.

INCLUDE FILE

```
#include <Inventor/SoDB.h>
```

SEE ALSO

SoBase, SoNode, SoEngine, SoField, SoInput, SoFile, SoPath, SoOneShotSensor, SoDataSensor, SoXt

SoDebugError

NAME

SoDebugError — debug error handling

INHERITS FROM

SoError > SoDebugError

DESCRIPTION

SoDebugError is used for all errors reported from the debugging version of the Inventor library. These errors are typically programmer errors, such as passing a NULL pointer or an out-of-range index. The **post()** method takes the name of the Inventor method that detected the error, to aid the programmer in debugging.

METHODS

static void   **setHandlerCallback**(SoErrorCB *cb, void *data)
static SoErrorCB *

        getHandlerCallback()
static void *   **getHandlerData**()
    Sets/returns handler callback for **SoDebugError** class.

static SoType   **getClassTypeId**()
    Returns type identifier for **SoDebugError** class.

SoDebugError::Severity

        getSeverity() const
    Returns severity of error (for use by handlers).

Methods from class SoError:

    getDebugString, getTypeId, isOfType

INCLUDE FILE

```
#include <Inventor/errors/SoDebugError.h>
```

enum **Severity** {
    SoDebugError::ERROR   Error
    SoDebugError::WARNING Just a warning
    SoDebugError::INFO   No error, just information
}

SEE ALSO

SoMemoryError, SoReadError

NAME

SoDecomposeMatrix — decomposes transformation matrices into values for translation, rotation, and scale

INHERITS FROM

SoBase > SoFieldContainer > SoEngine > SoDecomposeMatrix

DESCRIPTION

This engine takes as input a transformation matrix and a center of transformation. As output the engine produces the translation, rotation and scale values derived from the matrix.

The input fields can have multiple values, allowing the engine to decompose several matrices in parallel. One of the inputs may have more values than the other. In that case, the last value of the shorter input will be repeated as necessary.

INPUTS

SoMFMatrix **matrix**
The 4x4 transformation matrix.

SoMFVec3f **center**
The center of transformations.

OUTPUTS

(SoMFVec3f) **translation**
Derived translation in x, y, and z.

(SoMFRotation) **rotation**
Derived rotation.

(SoMFVec3f) **scaleFactor**
Derived scale values in x, y, and z.

(SoMFRotation) **scaleOrientation**
Derived rotational space for scaling.

METHODS

SoDecomposeMatrix()
Constructor

Methods from class SoEngine:

getClassTypeId, getOutputs, getOutput, getOutputName, copy, getByName, getByName

Methods from class SoFieldContainer:

setToDefaults, hasDefaultValues, fieldsAreEqual, copyFieldValues, set, get, getFields, getField, getFieldName, enableNotify, isNotifyEnabled

Methods from class SoBase:

ref, unref, unrefNoDelete, touch, getTypeId, isOfType, setName, getName

FILE FORMAT/DEFAULTS

```
DecomposeMatrix {
      matrix  1 0 0 0
              0 1 0 0
              0 0 1 0
              0 0 0 1
      center  0 0 0
}
```

INCLUDE FILE

```
#include <Inventor/engines/SoCompose.h>
```

SEE ALSO

SoComposeMatrix, SoEngineOutput

NAME

SoDecomposeRotation — decomposes rotation values

INHERITS FROM

SoBase > SoFieldContainer > SoEngine > SoDecomposeRotation

DESCRIPTION

This engine takes as input a rotation, and decomposes it into an axis value and a rotation angle (in radians).

The input can have multiple values, allowing the engine to decompose several rotations in parallel.

INPUTS

SoMFRotation   **rotation**

Rotation to be decomposed.

OUTPUTS

(SoMFVec3f)   **axis**

Axis of rotation derived from the input.

(SoMFFloat)   **angle**

Angle (in radians) derived from the input.

METHODS

                    SoDecomposeRotation()

Constructor

Methods from class SoEngine:

getClassTypeId, getOutputs, getOutput, getOutputName, copy, getByName, getByName

Methods from class SoFieldContainer:

setToDefaults, hasDefaultValues, fieldsAreEqual, copyFieldValues, set, get, getFields, getField, getFieldName, enableNotify, isNotifyEnabled

Methods from class SoBase:

ref, unref, unrefNoDelete, touch, getTypeId, isOfType, setName, getName

FILE FORMAT/DEFAULTS

```
DecomposeRotation {
    rotation  0 0 1  0
}
```

SoDecomposeRotation

INCLUDE FILE

    #include <Inventor/engines/SoCompose.h>

SEE ALSO

SoDecomposeRotationFromTo, SoComposeRotation, SoEngineOutput

NAME

SoDecomposeVec2f — decomposes 2D vectors into floating-point values

INHERITS FROM

SoBase > SoFieldContainer > SoEngine > SoDecomposeVec2f

DESCRIPTION

This engine takes as input a 2D vector, and decomposes it into two single floating-point values.

The input can have multiple values, allowing the engine to decompose several vectors in parallel.

INPUTS

SoMFVec2f   **vector**

Vector to be decomposed.

OUTPUTS

(SoMFFloat)   **x**

First component of the vector.

(SoMFFloat)   **y**

Second component of the vector.

METHODS

SoDecomposeVec2f()

Constructor

Methods from class SoEngine:

getClassTypeId, getOutputs, getOutput, getOutputName, copy, getByName, getByName

Methods from class SoFieldContainer:

setToDefaults, hasDefaultValues, fieldsAreEqual, copyFieldValues, set, get, getFields, getField, getFieldName, enableNotify, isNotifyEnabled

Methods from class SoBase:

ref, unref, unrefNoDelete, touch, getTypeId, isOfType, setName, getName

FILE FORMAT/DEFAULTS

```
DecomposeVec2f {
      vector  0 0
}
```

SoDecomposeVec2f

INCLUDE FILE

```
#include <Inventor/engines/SoCompose.h>
```

SEE ALSO

SoComposeVec2f, SoEngineOutput

NAME

SoDecomposeVec3f — decomposes 3D vectors into floating-point values

INHERITS FROM

SoBase > SoFieldContainer > SoEngine > SoDecomposeVec3f

DESCRIPTION

This engine takes as input a 3D vector, and decomposes it into three single floating-point values.

The input can have multiple values, allowing the engine to decompose several vectors in parallel.

INPUTS

SoMFVec3f   **vector**

Vector to be decomposed.

OUTPUTS

(SoMFFloat)   **x**

First component of the vector.

(SoMFFloat)   **y**

Second component of the vector.

(SoMFFloat)   **z**

Third component of the vector.

METHODS

                    SoDecomposeVec3f()

Constructor

Methods from class SoEngine:

getClassTypeId, getOutputs, getOutput, getOutputName, copy, getByName, getByName

Methods from class SoFieldContainer:

setToDefaults, hasDefaultValues, fieldsAreEqual, copyFieldValues, set, get, getFields, getField, getFieldName, enableNotify, isNotifyEnabled

Methods from class SoBase:

ref, unref, unrefNoDelete, touch, getTypeId, isOfType, setName, getName

SoDecomposeVec3f

FILE FORMAT/DEFAULTS

```
DecomposeVec3f {
      vector   0 0 0
}
```

INCLUDE FILE

```
#include <Inventor/engines/SoCompose.h>
```

SEE ALSO

SoComposeVec3f, SoEngineOutput

NAME

SoDecomposeVec4f — decomposes 4D vectors into floating-point values

INHERITS FROM

SoBase > SoFieldContainer > SoEngine > SoDecomposeVec4f

DESCRIPTION

This engine takes as input a 4D vector, and decomposes it into four single floating-point values.

The input can have multiple values, allowing the engine to decompose several vectors in parallel.

INPUTS

SoMFVec4f   **vector**

Vector to be decomposed.

OUTPUTS

(SoMFFloat)   **x**

First component of the vector.

(SoMFFloat)   **y**

Second component of the vector.

(SoMFFloat)   **z**

Third component of the vector.

(SoMFFloat)   **w**

Fourth component of the vector.

METHODS

                             SoDecomposeVec4f()

Constructor

Methods from class SoEngine:

getClassTypeId, getOutputs, getOutput, getOutputName, copy, getByName, getByName

Methods from class SoFieldContainer:

setToDefaults, hasDefaultValues, fieldsAreEqual, copyFieldValues, set, get, getFields, getField, getFieldName, enableNotify, isNotifyEnabled

Methods from class SoBase:

ref, unref, unrefNoDelete, touch, getTypeId, isOfType, setName, getName

FILE FORMAT/DEFAULTS

```
DecomposeVec4f {
      vector  0 0 0 0
}
```

INCLUDE FILE

```
#include <Inventor/engines/SoCompose.h>
```

SEE ALSO

SoComposeVec4f, SoEngineOutput

NAME

SoDelayQueueSensor — abstract base class for sensors not dependent on time

INHERITS FROM

SoSensor > SoDelayQueueSensor

DESCRIPTION

Delay queue sensors are separate from timer queue sensors (see **SoTimerQueueSensor**) and provide methods for setting the relative priorities of the sensors in the delay queue (sensors with higher priorities will be triggered first).

Sensors with non-zero priorities are added to the delay queue when scheduled, and are all processed once, in order, when the delay queue is processed, which normally happens as part of your program's main loop (see **SoXt::mainLoop()** or **SoDB::doSelect()**). Typically, the delay queue is processed whenever there are no events waiting to be distributed and there are no timer queue sensors waiting to be triggered. The delay queue also has a timeout to ensure that delay queue sensors are triggered even if there are always events or timer sensors waiting; see **SoDB::setDelaySensorTimeout()**.

Sensors with priority 0 are treated specially. Priority 0 sensors are triggered almost immediately after they are scheduled, before the program returns to the main loop. Priority 0 sensors are not necessarily triggered immediately when they are scheduled, however; if they are scheduled as part of the evaluation of a field connection network they may not be triggered until the evaluation of the network is complete. Also, if a priority 0 sensor is scheduled within the callback method of another priority 0 sensor, it will not be triggered until the callback method is complete (also note that if more than one priority 0 sensor is scheduled, the order in which they fire is undefined).

METHODS

| void | **setPriority**(unsigned long pri) |
| unsigned long | **getPriority**() |

Sets/gets the priority of the sensor. Priorities can be changed at any time; if the priority is changed to zero and it is already scheduled, the sensor is immediately triggered and removed from the queue.

static unsigned long

getDefaultPriority()

Returns the default delay queue sensor priority, which is 100.

virtual void **schedule**()

If this sensor's priority is non-zero, adds this sensor to the list of delay queue sensors ready to be triggered. This is a way of making a sensor fire without changing the thing it is sensing.

Calling **schedule**() within the callback function causes the sensor to be called repeatedly. Because sensors are processed only once every time the delay queue is processed (even if they reschedule themselves), timers and events will still be processed. This should not be done with a priority zero sensor because an infinite loop will result.

virtual void   **unschedule**()
If this sensor is scheduled, removes it from the delay queue so that it will not be triggered.

virtual SbBool   **isScheduled**()
Returns TRUE if this sensor has been scheduled and is waiting in the delay queue to be triggered. Sensors are removed from the queue before their callback function is triggered.

Methods from class SoSensor:

setFunction, getFunction, setData, getData

INCLUDE FILE
```
#include <Inventor/sensors/SoDelayQueueSensor.h>
```

SEE ALSO

SoTimerQueueSensor, SoDataSensor, SoFieldSensor, SoIdleSensor, SoOneShotSensor, SoNodeSensor, SoPathSensor, SoSensorManager

NAME

SoDetail — base class for describing detail information about a shape node

INHERITS FROM

SoDetail

DESCRIPTION

SoDetail is the abstract base class for all detail classes. A detail contains shape-specific information about a particular shape during picking and primitive generation. Subclasses store information based on the particular type of shape.

METHODS

SoDetail *   **copy**() const
Returns an instance that is a copy of this instance. The caller is responsible for deleting the copy when it is no longer needed.

static SoType   **getClassTypeId**()
Returns type identifier for this class.

virtual SoType   **getTypeId**() const
Returns the type identifier for a specific instance.

SbBool   **isOfType**(SoType type) const
Returns TRUE if this object is of the type specified in *type* or is derived from that type. Otherwise, it returns FALSE.

INCLUDE FILE

```
#include <Inventor/details/SoDetail.h>
```

SEE ALSO

SoConeDetail, SoCubeDetail, SoCylinderDetail, SoDetailList, SoFaceDetail, SoLineDetail, SoNodeKitDetail, SoPickedPoint, SoPointDetail, SoPrimitiveVertex, SoTextDetail

NAME

SoDetailList — maintains a list of instances of details

INHERITS FROM

SbPList > SoDetailList

DESCRIPTION

This subclass of **SbPList** holds lists of instances of classes derived from **SoDetail**.

METHODS

SoDetailList()
Constructor.

SoDetailList(int size)
Constructor that pre-allocates storage for *size* pointers.

SoDetailList(const SoDetailList &l)
Constructor that copies the contents of another list.

~**SoDetailList**()
Destructor.

void　　**append**(SoDetail *detail)
Adds a detail to the end of the list.

void　　**insert**(SoDetail *detail, int addBefore)
Inserts given detail in list before detail with given index.

void　　**truncate**(int start)
Removes all details after one with given index, inclusive. Removed detail instances are deleted.

void　　**copy**(const SoDetailList &l)
Copies a list, making a copy of each detail instance in the list.

SoDetailList &　　**operator =**(const SoDetailList &l)
Copies a list, making a copy of each detail instance in the list.

SoDetail *　　**operator [ ]**(int i) const
Accesses an element of a list.

void　　**set**(int i, SoDetail *detail)
Sets an element of a list, deleting the old entry first.

Methods from class SbPList:

find, remove, getLength, operator ==, operator !=

INCLUDE FILE

```
#include <Inventor/SoLists.h>
```

SEE ALSO

SoDetail

NAME

SoDirectionalLight — node representing a directional light source

INHERITS FROM

SoBase > SoFieldContainer > SoNode > SoLight > SoDirectionalLight

DESCRIPTION

This node defines a directional light source that illuminates along rays parallel to a given 3-dimensional vector.

FIELDS

SoSFVec3f **direction**
Illumination direction vector.

Fields from class SoLight:

on, intensity, color

METHODS

SoDirectionalLight()
Creates a directional light source node with default settings.

static SoType **getClassTypeId**()
Returns type identifier for this class.

Methods from class SoNode:

setOverride, isOverride, copy, affectsState, getByName, getByName

Methods from class SoFieldContainer:

setToDefaults, hasDefaultValues, fieldsAreEqual, copyFieldValues, set, get, getFields, getField, getFieldName, enableNotify, isNotifyEnabled

Methods from class SoBase:

ref, unref, unrefNoDelete, touch, getTypeId, isOfType, setName, getName

ACTION BEHAVIOR

SoGLRenderAction

Activates this light (if so specified) during traversal. All shape nodes that come after this light in the scene graph are illuminated by this light. The light's direction is affected by the current transformation.

FILE FORMAT/DEFAULTS

```
DirectionalLight {
        on          TRUE
        intensity   1
        color       1 1 1
        direction   0 0 -1
}
```

INCLUDE FILE

```
#include <Inventor/nodes/SoDirectionalLight.h>
```

SEE ALSO

SoPointLight, SoSpotLight

NAME

SoDirectionalLightDragger — directional icon you rotate and translate by dragging with the mouse

INHERITS FROM

SoBase > SoFieldContainer > SoNode > SoBaseKit > SoInteractionKit > SoDragger > SoDirectionalLightDragger

DESCRIPTION

SoDirectionalLightDragger is a composite dragger. It looks like a sun with a large arrow coming out of it. The arrow can be rotated about the sun by dragging with the mouse; its orientation is given by the **rotation** field. You can also drag the sun (and the arrow with it) through 3-space. The location is stored in the **translation** field.

The dragger uses an **SoRotateSphericalDragger** for changing the rotation. Instead of using the default spherical geometry, this dragger uses an arrow shape.

The sun is an **SoDragPointDragger**. Dragging it edits the **translation** field; conversely, if you change the **translation** field the sun will move to that new location, bringing the arrow with it. The sun looks and behaves just like the sun in an **SoPointLightDragger**, as does the **material** part. See the **SoPointLightDragger** man page for details.

Remember: This is *not* a light source! It just looks like one. If you want to move a light with this dragger, you can either:

[a] Use an **SoDirectionalLightManip**, which is subclassed from **SoLight**. It creates an **SoDirectionalLightDragger** and uses it as the interface to change the **direction** of its light source (see the **SoDirectionalLightManip** man page). The manipulator also edits the **material** part of this dragger to match the color of light the manipulator is producing. However, the directional light manipulator will ignore the **translation** field, because a directional light has no location or translation field. So in this case the translation dragger merely allows you to move the physical arrow to wherever you'd like it to be.

[b] Put an **SoTransform** under an **SoTransformSeparator**. Add the **SoDirectionalLight** as the next child. Use a field-to-field connection between the **rotation** fields of this dragger and the transform node to synchronize the light with this dragger.

[c] Use engines to connect the **rotation** field of this dragger to the **direction** field of an **SoDirectionalLight**. Use the **rotation** as input to an **SoComposeMatrix** engine. Then, use an **SoTransformVec3f** engine to apply that matrix to (0,0,-1), the default light direction.

You can change the parts in any instance of this dragger using **setPart()**. The default part geometries are defined as resources for this **SoDirectionalLightDragger** class. They are detailed in the Dragger Resources section of the online reference page for this class. You can make your program use different default resources for the parts by copying the file **/usr/share/data/draggerDefaults/directionalLightDragger.iv** into your own directory, editing the file, and then setting the environment variable **SO_DRAGGER_DIR** to be a path to that directory.

FIELDS

SoSFRotation   **rotation**
>   Orientation of the rotating part (an arrow by default).

SoSFVec3f   **translation**
>   Position of the origin of the directional light dragger.

Fields from class SoDragger:
>   isActive

Fields from class SoInteractionKit:
>   renderCaching, boundingBoxCaching, renderCulling, pickCulling

PARTS

Parts from class SoBaseKit:
>   callbackList

METHODS

>   **SoDirectionalLightDragger()**
>   Constructor.

static const SoNodekitCatalog *
>   **getClassNodekitCatalog()** const
>   Returns an **SoNodekitCatalog** for this class

static SoType   **getClassTypeId()**
>   Returns type identifier for this class.

Methods from class SoDragger:

addStartCallback, removeStartCallback, addMotionCallback, removeMotionCallback, addFinishCallback, removeFinishCallback, addValueChangedCallback, removeValueChangedCallback, setMinGesture, getMinGesture, setMinScale, getMinScale

Methods from class SoInteractionKit:

setPartAsPath

Methods from class SoBaseKit:

getNodekitCatalog, getPart, getPartString, createPathToPart, setPart, set, set, isSearchingChildren, setSearchingChildren

Methods from class SoNode:

setOverride, isOverride, copy, affectsState, getByName, getByName

Methods from class SoFieldContainer:

setToDefaults, hasDefaultValues, fieldsAreEqual, copyFieldValues, get, getFields, getField, getFieldName, enableNotify, isNotifyEnabled

Methods from class SoBase:

ref, unref, unrefNoDelete, touch, getTypeId, isOfType, setName, getName

MACROS

Macros from class SoBaseKit:

SO_GET_PART, SO_CHECK_PART

CATALOG PARTS

All parts			
Part Name	Part Type	Default Type	NULL by Default
callbackList	NodeKitListPart	--	yes
material	Material	--	yes
translatorRotInv	Rotation	--	yes
translator	DragPointDragger	--	yes
rotator	RotateSphericalDragger	--	yes

Extra information for list parts from above table		
Part Name	Container Type	Permissible Types
callbackList	Separator	Callback, EventCallback

FILE FORMAT/DEFAULTS

```
DirectionalLightDragger {
        renderCaching        AUTO
        boundingBoxCaching   AUTO
        renderCulling        AUTO
        pickCulling          AUTO
        isActive             FALSE
        translation          0 0 0
        rotation             0 0 1  0
}
```

INCLUDE FILE

```
#include <Inventor/draggers/SoDirectionalLightDragger.h>
```

SEE ALSO

SoInteractionKit, SoDragger, SoCenterballDragger, SoDragPointDragger, SoHandleBoxDragger, SoJackDragger, SoPointLightDragger, SoRotateCylindricalDragger, SoRotateDiscDragger, SoRotateSphericalDragger, SoScale1Dragger, SoScale2Dragger, SoScale2UniformDragger, SoScaleUniformDragger, SoSpotLightDragger, SoTabBoxDragger, SoTabPlaneDragger, SoTrackballDragger, SoTransformBoxDragger, SoTranslate1Dragger, SoTranslate2Dragger

SoDirectionalLightManip

NAME

SoDirectionalLightManip — directional light node with 3D interface for editing direction

INHERITS FROM

SoBase > SoFieldContainer > SoNode > SoLight > SoDirectionalLight > SoDirectionalLightManip

DESCRIPTION

SoDirectionalLightManip is the base class for all **SoDirectionalLight** nodes that have a built-in 3D user interface (this is the only such class provided with the Inventor toolkit). Since it is derived from **SoDirectionalLight**, any changes to its fields result in a change of lighting for nodes that follow it in the scene graph. In this case, the interface edits the **direction** field. Also, the color of the manipulator's geometry will reflect the color of the light (but you cannot edit the color using this manipulator).

Typically, you will want to replace a regular **SoDirectionalLight** with an **SoDirectionalLightManip** (as when the user selects a light to be edited), or vice versa (as when the user is done moving the light and the interface should go away). Use the **replaceNode()** method to insert a manipulator into a scene graph, and the **replaceManip()** method to remove it when done.

The **SoDirectionalLightManip** utilizes an **SoDirectionalLightDragger** to provide a 3D interface. However, the manipulator differs from the dragger; it lights other objects in the scene because, as an **SoDirectionalLight**, it alters the state. The field values and movement of the dragger, on the other hand, affect only the dragger itself. To find out more about how the interface works and what each part will do, see the reference page for **SoDirectionalLightDragger**. The interfaces of the dragger and the manipulator are identical.

The **SoDirectionalLightManip** utilizes its dragger by adding it as a hidden child. When an action is applied to the manipulator, such as rendering or handling events, the manipulator first traverses the dragger, and then the manipulator adds its lighting parameters to the state. When you click-drag-release over the manipulator, it passes these events down to the dragger, which moves as a result ("I can't *help* it, I'm a dragger!").

The manipulator maintains consistency between the fields of the dragger and its own fields. Let's say you use the mouse to rotate the *dragger*. Callbacks ensure that the **direction** field of the *manipulator* will change by the same amount, thus changing the lighting of nodes which follow in the scene graph. Similarly, if you set the **direction** field of the **SoDirectionalLightManip**, the manipulator will orient the dragger accordingly.

Because the dragger is a *hidden* child, you can see the dragger on screen and interact with it, but the dragger does not show up when you write the manipulator to file. Also, any **SoPath** will end at the manipulator. (See the Actions section of this reference page for a complete description of when the dragger is traversed).

If you want to get a pointer to the dragger you can get it from the manipulator using the **getDragger()** method. You will need to do this if you want to change the geometry of a manipulator, since the geometry actually belongs to the dragger.

FIELDS

Fields from class SoDirectionalLight:

direction

Fields from class SoLight:

on, intensity, color

METHODS

SoDirectionalLightManip()
Constructor.

SoDragger *   **getDragger()**
Returns a pointer to the dragger being used by this manipulator. Given this pointer, you can customize the dragger just like you would any other dragger. You can change geometry using the **setPart()** method, or add callbacks using the methods found in the **SoDragger** reference page.

SbBool   **replaceNode**(SoPath *p)
Replaces the tail of the path with this manipulator. The tail of the path must be an **SoDirectionalLight** node (or subclass thereof). If the path has a nodekit, this will try to use **setPart()** to insert the manipulator. Otherwise, the manipulator requires that the next to last node in the path chain be a group.

The field values from the directional light node will be copied to this manipulator, and the light node will be replaced.

The manipulator will not call **ref()** on the node it is replacing. The old node will disappear if it has no references other than from the input path *p* and its parent, since this manipulator will be replacing it in both of those places. Nor will the manipulator make any changes to field connections of the old node. The calling process is thus responsible for keeping track of its own nodes and field connections.

SbBool   **replaceManip**(SoPath *p, SoDirectionalLight *newOne) const
Replaces the tail of the path, which must be this manipulator, with the
given **SoDirectionalLight** node. If the path has a nodekit, this will try to use
setPart() to insert the new node. Otherwise, the manipulator requires that
the next to last node in the path chain be a group.

The field values from the manipulator will be copied to the directional light
node, and the manipulator will be replaced.

The manipulator will not call **ref**() or **unref**() on the node which is replacing
it, nor will it make any changes to field connections. The calling process is
thus responsible for keeping track of its own nodes and field connections.

static SoType   **getClassTypeId**()
Returns type identifier for this class.

Methods from class SoNode:

setOverride, isOverride, copy, affectsState, getByName, getByName

Methods from class SoFieldContainer:

setToDefaults, hasDefaultValues, fieldsAreEqual, copyFieldValues, set, get,
getFields, getField, getFieldName, enableNotify, isNotifyEnabled

Methods from class SoBase:

ref, unref, unrefNoDelete, touch, getTypeId, isOfType, setName, getName

ACTION BEHAVIOR

**SoGLRenderAction, SoCallbackAction, SoGetBoundingBoxAction,
SoGetMatrixAction, SoHandleEventAction, SoRayPickAction**

First, traverses the dragger the way an **SoGroup** would. All draggers place
themselves in space, but leave the current transformation unchanged when
finished. Then the **SoDirectionalLightManip** adds a directional light to the
state just like its base class, **SoDirectionalLight**.

SoSearchAction

Searches just like an **SoDirectionalLight**. Does not search the dragger,
which is a hidden child.

SoWriteAction

Writes out just like an **SoDirectionalLight**. Does not write the dragger,
which is a hidden child. If you really need to write valuable information
about the dragger, such as customized geometry, you can retrieve the
dragger with the **getDragger**() method and then write it out separately.

FILE FORMAT/DEFAULTS

```
DirectionalLightManip {
        on          TRUE
        intensity   1
        color       1 1 1
        direction   0 0 -1
}
```

INCLUDE FILE

```
#include <Inventor/manips/SoDirectionalLightManip.h>
```

SEE ALSO

SoDragger, SoDirectionalLight, SoDirectionalLightDragger, SoPointLightManip, SoSpotLightManip

NAME

SoDragger — base class for nodekits that move in response to click-drag-release mouse events

INHERITS FROM

SoBase > SoFieldContainer > SoNode > SoBaseKit > SoInteractionKit > SoDragger

DESCRIPTION

SoDragger is the base class for all nodekits you move by using the mouse to click-drag-and-release. More specifically, they are operated by a start (mouse button 1 pressed over dragger to pick it), followed by dragging (mouse motion events are interpreted by the dragger and result in some form of motion and/or change to a field), followed by finish (mouse up).

Each dragger has a different paradigm for interpreting mouse motion and changing its fields as a result. Draggers map 2D mouse motion into motion of a point on 3D lines, planes, spheres or cylinders. (See the **SbProjector** reference pages.) Then they react to this motion of a point through 3-space by scaling, translating, or rotating. For example, **SoTranslate2Dragger** maps mouse motion onto a 3D plane, then translates to follow the cursor as it moves within that plane.

Every dragger has *fields* that describe its current state. Scaling draggers have a **scaleFactor** field, rotational draggers have a **rotation** field, etc. All draggers have the **isActive** field, defined in this class. It is TRUE while the dragger is being dragged, FALSE otherwise.

Draggers that have only one part to pick and one motion field are called *simple draggers*. Examples are the **SoRotateDiscDragger**, **SoScale1Dragger**, and **SoTranslate2Dragger**.

Draggers that create assemblies out of other draggers and then orchestrate the motion of the whole assembly are call *composite draggers*. **SoTransformBoxDragger** is a composite dragger made entirely of simple draggers. **SoDirectionalLightDragger** contains both a simple dragger (**SoRotateSphericalDragger**) and a composite dragger (**SoDragPointDragger**) When using a composite dragger, the fields of the composite dragger are the ones you should work with. Draggers lower down in the assemblage usually have zeroed out values. For example, when you drag the face of a transformBox, an **SoTranslate2Dragger**, the transformBox "steals" the translation from the child dragger and transfers it up to the top of the composite dragger, where it effects all pieces of the assemblage.

Draggers always keep their fields up to date, including while they are being dragged. So you can use field-to-field connections and engines to connect dragger values to other parts of your scene graph. Hence draggers can be easily utilized as input devices for mouse-driven 3D interface elements. You can also register value-changed callbacks, which are called whenever any of the fields is changed.

Also, if you set the field of a dragger through some method other than dragging, (by calling **setValue()**, for example), the dragger's internal **SoFieldSensor** will sense this and the dragger will move to satisfy that new value. This makes it easy to constrain draggers to keep their fields within certain limits: if the limit is exceeded, just set it back to the exceeded maximum or minimum. You can do this even as the dragger is in use.

When you drag a dragger, the dragger only moves itself. Draggers do not change the state or affect objects that follow in the scene graph. For example a dragger does not ever behave like an **SoTransform** and change the current transformation matrix. Draggers are not transforms, even if they have field names like translation, rotation, scaleFactor. Many draggers, such as **SoTrackballDragger**, have a corresponding **SoTransformManip**, in this case **SoTrackballManip**. The manipulator is a subclass of **SoTransform**, and affects other objects in the scene; it uses a trackball *dragger* to provide its user interface. In this way, draggers are employed extensively by manipulators. Callback functions on the dragger allow its employer to be notified of start, motion, finish, and value changes. In all cases, the callback function is passed a pointer to the dragger which initiated the callback. (See the various man pages for more details on specific draggers and manipulators).

All draggers are nodekits. However, draggers do not list their parts in the Parts section of the reference page. Instead, there is a section called Dragger Resources, more suited to describe the parts made available to the programmer. Because of space limitations, the Dragger Resources section only appears in the online versions of the reference pages. Each dragger has some parts you can pick on, and other parts that replace them when they are *active* or moving. These active parts are often just the same geometry in another color. Draggers also have pieces for displaying feedback. Each of these pieces has a default scene graph, as well as a special function within the dragger. Each part also has a resource name. All this information is contained in the DRAGGER RESOURCES section.

Since draggers are nodekits, you can set the parts in any instance of a dragger using **setPart()**.

But draggers also give each part a *resource name*. When a dragger builds a part, it looks in the global dictionary for the node with that **resourceName**. By putting a new entry in the dictionary, you can override that default. The default part geometries are defined as resources for each class, and each class has a file you can change to alter the defaults. The files are listed in each dragger's man page. You can make your program use different default resources for the parts by copying the listed file from the directory **/usr/share/data/draggerDefaults** into your own directory, editing the file, and then setting the environment variable **SO_DRAGGER_DIR** to be a path to that directory.

FIELDS

SoSFBool **isActive**
TRUE when mouse is down and dragging, else FALSE.

Fields from class SoInteractionKit:
renderCaching, boundingBoxCaching, renderCulling, pickCulling

PARTS

Parts from class SoBaseKit:
callbackList

METHODS

void **addStartCallback**(SoDraggerCB *f, void *userData = NULL)
void **removeStartCallback**(SoDraggerCB *f, void *userData = NULL)
Start callbacks are made after the mouse button 1 goes down and the dragger determines that it has been picked. If it is going to begin dragging, it grabs events and invokes the startCallbacks.

void **addMotionCallback**(SoDraggerCB *f, void *userData = NULL)
void **removeMotionCallback**(SoDraggerCB *f, void *userData = NULL)
Motion callbacks are called after each movement of the mouse during dragging.

void **addFinishCallback**(SoDraggerCB *f, void *userData = NULL)
void **removeFinishCallback**(SoDraggerCB *f, void *userData = NULL)
Finish callbacks are made after dragging ends and the dragger has stopped grabbing events.

void **addValueChangedCallback**(SoDraggerCB *f, void *userData = NULL)
void **removeValueChangedCallback**(SoDraggerCB *f, void *userData = NULL)
Value-changed callbacks are made after a dragger changes any of its fields. This does not include changes to the **isActive** field.

void	**setMinGesture**(int pixels)
int	**getMinGesture**() const

Set and get the number of pixels of movement required to initiate a constraint gesture. Default is 8.

static void	**setMinScale**(float newMinScale)
static float	**getMinScale**()

The smallest scale that any dragger will write. If the user attempts to go below this amount, the dragger will set it to this minimum. Default is .001

static const SoNodekitCatalog *
                    getClassNodekitCatalog() const
Returns an **SoNodekitCatalog** for this class.

static SoType   **getClassTypeId**()
Returns type identifier for this class.

Methods from class SoInteractionKit:

    setPartAsPath

Methods from class SoBaseKit:

    getNodekitCatalog, getPart, getPartString, createPathToPart, setPart, set, set, isSearchingChildren, setSearchingChildren

Methods from class SoNode:

    setOverride, isOverride, copy, affectsState, getByName, getByName

Methods from class SoFieldContainer:

    setToDefaults, hasDefaultValues, fieldsAreEqual, copyFieldValues, get, getFields, getField, getFieldName, enableNotify, isNotifyEnabled

Methods from class SoBase:

    ref, unref, unrefNoDelete, touch, getTypeId, isOfType, setName, getName

MACROS

    Macros from class SoBaseKit:

        SO_GET_PART, SO_CHECK_PART

CATALOG PARTS

All parts			
Part Name	Part Type	Default Type	NULL by Default
callbackList	NodeKitListPart	--	yes

Extra information for list parts from above table		
Part Name	Container Type	Permissible Types
callbackList	Separator	Callback, EventCallback

FILE FORMAT/DEFAULTS

```
Dragger {
        renderCaching       AUTO
        boundingBoxCaching  AUTO
        renderCulling       AUTO
        pickCulling         AUTO
        isActive            FALSE
}
```

INCLUDE FILE

```
#include <Inventor/draggers/SoDragger.h>
```

typedef void   **SoDraggerCB**(void *userData, SoDragger *dragger)

SEE ALSO

SoInteractionKit, SoCenterballDragger, SoDirectionalLightDragger,
SoDragPointDragger, SoHandleBoxDragger, SoJackDragger, SoPointLightDragger,
SoRotateCylindricalDragger, SoRotateDiscDragger, SoRotateSphericalDragger,
SoScale1Dragger, SoScale2Dragger, SoScale2UniformDragger,
SoScaleUniformDragger, SoSpotLightDragger, SoTabBoxDragger, SoTabPlaneDragger,
SoTrackballDragger, SoTransformBoxDragger, SoTranslate1Dragger,
SoTranslate2Dragger

NAME

SoDragPointDragger — object you can translate in 3D by dragging with the mouse

INHERITS FROM

SoBase > SoFieldContainer > SoNode > SoBaseKit > SoInteractionKit > SoDragger > SoDragPointDragger

DESCRIPTION

SoDragPointDragger is a compound dragger that translates in all three dimensions when dragged with the mouse.

It is made up of six smaller draggers, which it displays two at a time. Each pair has one *plane* dragger and one *line* dragger. The line dragger is oriented perpendicular to the plane, so together the *plane/line pair* lets you move through all of 3-space.

DragPoint has a total of three such pairs, oriented along the x, y, and z axes of its local space. You can cycle through the three pairs by hitting the <Alt> key with the cursor over the dragger. (You need not press the mouse button.)

The line draggers are **SoTranslate1Draggers** and the plane draggers are **SoTranslate2Draggers**. So you can use the <Shift> key to constrain the motion of a plane dragger along one of the two axes within the plane, as described in the **SoTranslate2Draggers** man page.

DragPoint adds extra feedback parts to provide a more intuitive idea of where you are placed in three-space. There are three *feedback planes* and three *feedback axes*; each corresponds to one of the plane or line draggers, but spans a much greater distance. When you drag along a line, that line's larger feedback axis is displayed, and remains anchored in space while the dragger slides along it. This helps establish the motion of the dragger relative to the rest of the scene. Similarly, when you drag within a plane, the larger (but transparent) feedback plane establishes a ground plane for you to move upon. The location of the dragger within the plane is pinpointed by two intersecting axes that always cross below the cursor and extend to the edges of the plane. When you move dragPoint to the edge of the feedback plane (or line), the feedback will jump to a new location in that direction, so that the dragger never leaves the feedback behind.

The primary directions of motion are given by the local space of the dragger. Transforms earlier in the scene will affect the dragger, its children, and the orientation of its directions of motion.

This node has a **translation** field which always reflects its position in local space. Setting the field moves the dragger to that point. You can also connect fields of other nodes or engines from this one to make them follow the dragger's motion.

Although the child draggers each have their own resources defining default part geometries, the dragPoint dragger overrides these with a new set of resources. It also defines resources for the feedback parts that it adds. These are detailed in the Dragger Resources section of the online reference page for this class. You can change the parts in any instance of this dragger using **setPart()**.

You can make your program use different default resources for the parts by copying the file **/usr/share/data/draggerDefaults/dragPointDragger.iv** into your own directory, editing the file, and then setting the environment variable **SO_DRAGGER_DIR** to be a path to that directory.

FIELDS

SoSFVec3f   **translation**
>Position of the dragger.

Fields from class SoDragger:
>isActive

Fields from class SoInteractionKit:
>renderCaching, boundingBoxCaching, renderCulling, pickCulling

PARTS

Parts from class SoBaseKit:
>callbackList

METHODS

>**SoDragPointDragger()**

Constructor.

void   **setJumpLimit**(float limit)
float   **getJumpLimit**() const
>Set and get the point at which the feedback axes will jump to a new position. For example, if set to .1 (the default), the feedback axes will jump when the dragger gets within 10% of the end of the axis.

void   **showNextDraggerSet()**
>The dragPoint dragger contains three pairs of draggers, each containing a plane dragger and a line dragger (see the Description above). The dragger starts with the (y-line/xz-plane) pair displayed. Calling this method will cycle next through the (z-line/xy-plane), then the (x-line/yz-plane).

static const SoNodekitCatalog *
         getClassNodekitCatalog() const
Returns an **SoNodekitCatalog** for this class

static SoType   **getClassTypeId**()
Returns type identifier for this class.

Methods from class SoDragger:

addStartCallback, removeStartCallback, addMotionCallback, removeMotionCallback, addFinishCallback, removeFinishCallback, addValueChangedCallback, removeValueChangedCallback, setMinGesture, getMinGesture, setMinScale, getMinScale

Methods from class SoInteractionKit:

setPartAsPath

Methods from class SoBaseKit:

getNodekitCatalog, getPart, getPartString, createPathToPart, setPart, set, set, isSearchingChildren, setSearchingChildren

Methods from class SoNode:

setOverride, isOverride, copy, affectsState, getByName, getByName

Methods from class SoFieldContainer:

setToDefaults, hasDefaultValues, fieldsAreEqual, copyFieldValues, get, getFields, getField, getFieldName, enableNotify, isNotifyEnabled

Methods from class SoBase:

ref, unref, unrefNoDelete, touch, getTypeId, isOfType, setName, getName

MACROS

Macros from class SoBaseKit:

SO_GET_PART, SO_CHECK_PART

CATALOG PARTS

All parts			
Part Name	**Part Type**	**Default Type**	**NULL by Default**
callbackList	NodeKitListPart	--	yes
xTranslator	Translate1Dragger	--	yes
xyTranslator	Translate2Dragger	--	yes
xzTranslator	Translate2Dragger	--	yes
zTranslator	Translate1Dragger	--	yes
yzTranslator	Translate2Dragger	--	yes
yTranslator	Translate1Dragger	--	yes
xFeedback	Separator	--	yes
yFeedback	Separator	--	yes
zFeedback	Separator	--	yes
yzFeedback	Separator	--	yes
xzFeedback	Separator	--	yes
xyFeedback	Separator	--	yes

Extra information for list parts from above table		
Part Name	**Container Type**	**Permissible Types**
callbackList	Separator	Callback, EventCallback

FILE FORMAT/DEFAULTS

```
DragPointDragger {
        renderCaching        AUTO
        boundingBoxCaching   AUTO
        renderCulling        AUTO
        pickCulling          AUTO
        isActive             FALSE
        translation          0 0 0
}
```

INCLUDE FILE

```
#include <Inventor/draggers/SoDragPointDragger.h>
```

SEE ALSO

SoInteractionKit, SoDragger, SoCenterballDragger, SoDragPointDragger,
SoHandleBoxDragger, SoJackDragger, SoPointLightDragger,
SoRotateCylindricalDragger, SoRotateDiscDragger, SoRotateSphericalDragger,
SoScale1Dragger, SoScale2Dragger, SoScale2UniformDragger,
SoScaleUniformDragger, SoSpotLightDragger, SoTabBoxDragger, SoTabPlaneDragger,
SoTrackballDragger, SoTransformBoxDragger, SoTranslate1Dragger,
SoTranslate2Dragger

NAME

SoDrawStyle — node that defines the style to use when rendering

INHERITS FROM

SoBase > SoFieldContainer > SoNode > SoDrawStyle

DESCRIPTION

This node defines the current drawing style for all subsequent shape nodes in a scene graph. **SoDrawStyle** specifies how primitives should be rendered. The drawing style has no effect on picking or callback primitive generation.

Note that if the current drawing style is not filled, backface culling (as set up by the **SoShapeHints** node) will not be performed.

FIELDS

SoSFEnum **style**

Drawing style.

SoSFFloat **pointSize**

Radius of points (for POINTS style).

SoSFFloat **lineWidth**

Width of lines (for LINES style).

SoSFUShort **linePattern**

Stipple pattern for lines (for LINES style). Values can range from 0 (invisible) to 0xffff (solid). This specifies how dashed or dotted lines will be drawn.

METHODS

SoDrawStyle()

Creates a drawing style node with default settings.

static SoType **getClassTypeId()**

Returns type identifier for this class.

Methods from class SoNode:

setOverride, isOverride, copy, affectsState, getByName, getByName

Methods from class SoFieldContainer:

setToDefaults, hasDefaultValues, fieldsAreEqual, copyFieldValues, set, get, getFields, getField, getFieldName, enableNotify, isNotifyEnabled

Methods from class SoBase:

ref, unref, unrefNoDelete, touch, getTypeId, isOfType, setName, getName

ACTION BEHAVIOR

SoGLRenderAction, SoCallbackAction

Sets the current drawing style.

FILE FORMAT/DEFAULTS

```
DrawStyle {
        style          FILLED
        pointSize      0
        lineWidth      0
        linePattern    0xffff
}
```

INCLUDE FILE

```
#include <Inventor/nodes/SoDrawStyle.h>
```

enum **Style** {

SoDrawStyle::FILLED

Draw filled regions

SoDrawStyle::LINES

Draw only outlines (wire frame)

SoDrawStyle::POINTS

Draw points at vertices

SoDrawStyle::INVISIBLE

Do not draw anything at all

}

SEE ALSO

SoLightModel, SoPickStyle, SoShapeHints

NAME

> SoElapsedTime — basic controllable time source

INHERITS FROM

> SoBase > SoFieldContainer > SoEngine > SoElapsedTime

DESCRIPTION

> This engine functions as a stopwatch; it outputs the time that has elapsed since it started running. By default, the **timeIn** input is connected to the **realTime** global field. It can, however, be connected to any other time source.
>
> The ouput from the engine is the time that has elapsed since it started running, or since the **reset** input was last triggered. You can affect the speed of the output time by setting the **speed** scale factor. A value greater than 1.0 will speed up the output, and a value less than 1.0 will slow it down.
>
> If you pause the engine, by setting the **pause** input to TRUE, it stops updating the **timeOut** output. When you turn off the pause, it jumps to its current position without losing time. Alternatively, if you want to stop the engine for a while, and then restart it from where it left off, use the **on** input field.

INPUTS

> SoSFTime   **timeIn**
> > Running time.
>
> SoSFFloat   **speed**
> > Scale factor for time.
>
> SoSFBool   **on**
> > TRUE to start running, FALSE to stop.
>
> SoSFBool   **pause**
> > TRUE to freeze, FALSE to continue running.
>
> SoSFTrigger   **reset**
> > Reset the base time.

OUTPUTS

> (SoSFTime)   **timeOut**
> > Time elapsed, modified by the speed factor.

METHODS

SoElapsedTime()

Constructor.

Methods from class SoEngine:

getClassTypeId, getOutputs, getOutput, getOutputName, copy, getByName, getByName

Methods from class SoFieldContainer:

setToDefaults, hasDefaultValues, fieldsAreEqual, copyFieldValues, set, get, getFields, getField, getFieldName, enableNotify, isNotifyEnabled

Methods from class SoBase:

ref, unref, unrefNoDelete, touch, getTypeId, isOfType, setName, getName

FILE FORMAT/DEFAULTS

```
ElapsedTime {
      timeIn   <current time>
      speed    1
      on       TRUE
      pause    FALSE
      reset
}
```

INCLUDE FILE

```
#include <Inventor/engines/SoElapsedTime.h>
```

SEE ALSO

SoTimeCounter, SoOneShot, SoEngineOutput

NAME
> SoEngine — base class for all engines

INHERITS FROM
> SoBase > SoFieldContainer > SoEngine

DESCRIPTION
> **SoEngine** is the abstract base class for all engines. Engines are objects used for animation and behavior. They are lightweight objects that are connected between nodes, the clock, and other engines to form interesting behaviorial objects (e.g., a spinning windmill).
>
> Engines are used to animate parts of a scene and/or to constrain one part of a scene in relation to some other part of the scene. An engine receives a number of input values, performs some operation on them, and then copies the results into one or more output fields. Both the inputs and the outputs can be connected to other fields or engines in the scene graph. When an engine's output values change, those new values are sent to any fields or engines connected to them.

METHODS
> static SoType   **getClassTypeId**()
> > Returns the type identifier for the SoEngine class.
>
> virtual int   **getOutputs**(SoEngineOutputList &list) const
> > Returns a list of outputs in this engine. Use **getOutputName** to get the names of the outputs, and use **SoEngineOutput::getConnectionType** to determine their types.
>
> SoEngineOutput *
> > **getOutput**(const SbName &outputName) const
> > Returns a pointer to the engine output with the given name. If no such output exists, NULL is returned.
>
> SbBool   **getOutputName**(const SoEngineOutput *output, SbName
> > &outputName) const
> > Returns (in *outputName*) the name of the engine output (*output*). Returns FALSE if the engine output is not contained within the engine instance.
>
> virtual SoEngine *
> > **copy**(SbBool copyConnections = FALSE) const
> > Creates and returns an exact copy of the engine. If the **copyConnections** flag is TRUE, any connections to input fields (but not to outputs) of the engine are also copied.

static SoEngine *   **getByName**(const SbName &name)
static int   **getByName**(const SbName &name, SoEngineList &list)
    Look up engine(s) by name.

Methods from class SoFieldContainer:

setToDefaults, hasDefaultValues, fieldsAreEqual, copyFieldValues, set, get, getFields, getField, getFieldName, enableNotify, isNotifyEnabled

Methods from class SoBase:

ref, unref, unrefNoDelete, touch, getTypeId, isOfType, setName, getName

FILE FORMAT/DEFAULTS

This is an abstract class. See the man page of a derived class for the format and default values.

INCLUDE FILE

```
#include <Inventor/engines/SoEngine.h>
```

SEE ALSO

SoBoolOperation, SoCalculator, SoComposeMatrix, SoComposeRotation, SoComposeRotationFromTo, SoComposeVec2f, SoComposeVec3f, SoComposeVec4f, SoComputeBoundingBox, SoConcatenate, SoCounter, SoDecomposeMatrix, SoDecomposeRotation, SoDecomposeVec2f, SoDecomposeVec3f, SoDecomposeVec4f, SoElapsedTime, SoGate, SoInterpolate, SoOnOff, SoOneShot, SoSelectOne, SoTimeCounter, SoTransformVec3f, SoTriggerAny

NAME

SoEngineList — maintains a list of pointers to engines

INHERITS FROM

SbPList > SoBaseList > SoEngineList

DESCRIPTION

This subclass of **SoBaseList** holds lists of pointers to **SoEngine**s. It updates reference counts to engines in the list whenever adding or removing pointers.

METHODS

SoEngineList()
Constructor.

SoEngineList(int size)
Constructor that pre-allocates storage for *size* pointers.

SoEngineList(const SoEngineList &l)
Constructor that copies the contents of another list.

~**SoEngineList**()
Destructor.

void   **append**(SoEngine *engine)
Adds an engine to the end of the list.

SoEngine *   **operator [ ]**(int i) const
Accesses an element of a list.

SoEngineList &   **operator =**(const SoEngineList &l)
Copies a list, keeping all reference counts correct.

Methods from class SoBaseList:

insert, remove, truncate, copy, set, addReferences

Methods from class SbPList:

find, getLength, operator ==, operator !=

INCLUDE FILE

#include <Inventor/SoLists.h>

SEE ALSO

SoEngine

NAME

SoEngineOutput — class for all engine outputs

INHERITS FROM

SoEngineOutput

DESCRIPTION

SoEngineOuput is the class for all engine output fields. There is no public constructor routine for this class. Only the engine classes create instances of **SoEngineOutput**.

Each engine creates one or more engine outputs. The type of the output is documented in the engine reference pages. There is also an **SoEngineOutput** method for querying the connection type.

The application can at any time enable or disable the engine outputs. By default the engine outputs are enabled.

METHODS

SoType   **getConnectionType**() const
Returns the type of field this output can connect to.

int   **getForwardConnections**(SoFieldList &list) const
Returns the number of fields this output is writing to, and adds pointers to those fields to the given list.

void   **enable**(SbBool flag)
Enables or disables all connections from this ouptut. If the connections are disabled, values will not be output along them. By default, outputs are enabled.

SbBool   **isEnabled**() const
Returns TRUE if this output is currently enabled.

SoEngine*   **getContainer**() const
Returns containing engine.

INCLUDE FILE

```
#include <Inventor/engines/SoEngine.h>
```

SEE ALSO

SoEngine

NAME

SoEngineOutputList — maintains a list of pointers to engine outputs

INHERITS FROM

SbPList > SoEngineOutputList

DESCRIPTION

This subclass of **SbPlist** holds lists of pointers to **SoEngineOutput**s. It updates reference counts to engine outputs in the list whenever adding or removing pointers.

METHODS

SoEngineOutputList()
Constructor.

SoEngineOutputList(int size)
Constructor that pre-allocates storage for *size* pointers.

SoEngineOutputList(const SoEngineOutputList &l)
Constructor that copies the contents of another list.

~**SoEngineOutputList**()
Destructor.

void   **append**(SoEngineOutput *engineOutput)
Adds an engine output to the end of the list.

void   **insert**(SoEngineOutput *engineOutput, int addBefore)
Inserts the given engine output in the list before the element of the given index.

void   **set**(int i, SoEngineOutput *engineOutput)
Sets an element of a list.

SoEngineOutput *

operator [ ](int i) const
Accesses an element of a list.

Methods from class SbPList:

find, remove, getLength, truncate, copy, operator =, operator ==, operator !=

SoEngineOutputList

INCLUDE FILE

```
#include <Inventor/SoLists.h>
```

SEE ALSO

SoEngineOutput

NAME

SoEnvironment — global environment node

INHERITS FROM

SoBase > SoFieldContainer > SoNode > SoEnvironment

DESCRIPTION

This node describes global environmental attributes such as ambient lighting, light attenuation, and fog.

Ambient lighting is the amount of extra light impinging on each surface point when the lighting model is Phong (see **SoLightModel**).

Light attenuation affects all subsequent lights in a scene (see **SoLight**). It is a quadratic function of distance from a light source to a surface point. The three coefficients are specified in the **attenuation** field. Attenuation works only for light sources with a fixed location, such as point and spot lights.

Fog has one of four types, each of which blends each surface point with the specified fog color. Each type interprets the **visibility** field to be the distance at which fog totally obscures objects. A **visibility** value of 0 (the default) causes the **SoEnvironment** node to set up fog so that the visibility is the distance to the far clipping plane of the current camera.

Note that this node has effect only during rendering, and that it does not inherit field values from other **SoEnvironment** nodes.

FIELDS

SoSFFloat   **ambientIntensity**
SoSFColor   **ambientColor**

Intensity and RGB color of ambient lighting (for Phong lighting).

SoSFVec3f   **attenuation**

Squared, linear, and constant light attenuation coefficients (in that order) with respect to distance of light from surface (for Phong lighting).

SoSFEnum   **fogType**
SoSFColor   **fogColor**
SoSFFloat   **fogVisibility**

Type of fog, color of fog, and visibility distance, which is the distance at which fog totally obscures objects.

METHODS

SoEnvironment()
Creates an environment node with default settings.

static SoType **getClassTypeId()**
Returns type identifier for this class.

Methods from class SoNode:
setOverride, isOverride, copy, affectsState, getByName, getByName

Methods from class SoFieldContainer:
setToDefaults, hasDefaultValues, fieldsAreEqual, copyFieldValues, set, get, getFields, getField, getFieldName, enableNotify, isNotifyEnabled

Methods from class SoBase:
ref, unref, unrefNoDelete, touch, getTypeId, isOfType, setName, getName

ACTION BEHAVIOR

SoGLRenderAction
Sets the current environment parameters to those specified with this node. Successive geometries will be rendered using this environment.

FILE FORMAT/DEFAULTS

```
Environment {
        ambientIntensity  0.2
        ambientColor      1 1 1
        attenuation       0 0 1
        fogType           NONE
        fogColor          1 1 1
        fogVisibility     0
}
```

INCLUDE FILE

```
#include <Inventor/nodes/SoEnvironment.h>
```

enum **FogType** {

SoEnvironment::NONE	No fog
SoEnvironment::HAZE	Linear increase in opacity with distance
SoEnvironment::FOG	Exponential increase in opacity
SoEnvironment::SMOKE	Exponential squared increase in opacity

}

SEE ALSO

SoLight, SoLightModel

NAME

SoError — error handling base class

INHERITS FROM

SoError

DESCRIPTION

SoError is the base class for all error classes, which provide error handling for applications. There are two facets to errors: posting and handling. An error is posted when some bad condition occurs. Posting is done primarily by the Inventor library itself, but extenders can post their own errors. Posting an error creates an instance of the appropriate error class (or subclass) and then passes it to the active error handler. The default handler just prints an appropriate message to stderr. Applications can override this behavior by supplying a different handler (by specifying a callback function).

Each subclass of SoError supports the **setHandlerCallback()** method, which is used to set the callback function to handle errors. The callback function for a specfic error class is always used in preference to that of any base classes when handling errors. The error instance passed to a callback is deleted immediately after the callback is called; an application that wishes to save information from the instance has to copy it out first.

Each error class contains a run-time class type id (**SoType**) that can be used to determine the type of an instance. The base class defines a character string that represents a detailed error message that is printed by the default handler. All handlers are called by the **SoError::handleError()** method. When debugging, you can set a breakpoint on this method to stop right before an error is handled.

METHODS

static void   **setHandlerCallback**(SoErrorCB *cb, void *data)
static SoErrorCB *

                      getHandlerCallback()
static void *   **getHandlerData**()
           Sets/returns handler callback for **SoError** class.

const SbString &   **getDebugString**() const
           Returns debug string containing full error information from instance.

static SoType   **getClassTypeId**()
           Returns type identifier for SoError class.

virtual SoType   **getTypeId**() const
           Returns type identifier for error instance.

SbBool   **isOfType**(SoType type) const
         Returns TRUE if instance is of given type or is derived from it.

INCLUDE FILE

    #include <Inventor/errors/SoError.h>

typedef void   **SoErrorCB**(const SoError *error, void *data)

SEE ALSO

SoDebugError, SoMemoryError, SoReadError

NAME

SoEvent — base class for all events

INHERITS FROM

SoEvent

DESCRIPTION

SoEvent is the base class for events in the Inventor event model. An event typically represents a user action, such as a mouse button being pressed or a keyboard key being released. **SoEvent** contains general information found in all Inventor events, including the time the event occurred, the position of the locater when the event occurred, and the state of the modifier keys when the event occurred.

METHODS

	SoEvent()
virtual	**~SoEvent**()

Constructor and destructor.

virtual SoType **getTypeId**() const
Return the type id for this event instance.

static SoType **getClassTypeId**()
Return the type id for the **SoEvent** class.

SbBool **isOfType**(SoType type) const
This returns TRUE if the event is an instance of or derived from an event of the passed type.

void **setTime**(SbTime t)
SbTime **getTime**() const
Set and get the time at which the event occurred.

void **setPosition**(const SbVec2s &p)
const SbVec2s & **getPosition**() const
Set the window pixel location of the cursor when the event occurred. The position is relative to the lower left corner of the window in which the event occurred.

const SbVec2s & **getPosition**(const SbViewportRegion &vpRgn) const
Get the viewport pixel location of the cursor when the event occurred, relative to the specified viewport region.

const SbVec2f & **getNormalizedPosition**(const SbViewportRegion &vpRgn) const
Get the normalized location of the cursor when the event occurred, relative

to the specified viewport region. The returned value will lie between 0.0 and 1.0.

void	**setShiftDown**(SbBool isDown)
void	**setCtrlDown**(SbBool isDown)
void	**setAltDown**(SbBool isDown)

Set whether the modifier keys were down when the event occurred.

SbBool	**wasShiftDown**() const
SbBool	**wasCtrlDown**() const
SbBool	**wasAltDown**() const

Get whether the modifier keys were down when the event occurred.

INCLUDE FILE

```
#include <Inventor/events/SoEvent.h>
```

SEE ALSO

SoButtonEvent, SoKeyboardEvent, SoLocation2Event, SoMotion3Event, SoMouseButtonEvent, SoSpaceballButtonEvent, SoHandleEventAction, SoEventCallback, SoSelection, SoInteraction, SoXtDevice, SoXtRenderArea

NAME

SoEventCallback — node which invokes callbacks for events

INHERITS FROM

SoBase > SoFieldContainer > SoNode > SoEventCallback

DESCRIPTION

SoEventCallback will invoke application supplied callback functions during **SoHandleEventAction** traversal. Methods allow the application to specify which Inventor events should trigger callbacks, and which path must be picked, if any, for the callback invocation to occur. The application callback is able to get information about the event and the pick detail, and may grab events, release events, and set whether the event was handled.

If you register more than one callback function in an **SoEventCallback** node, all the callback functions will be invoked when an event occurs, even if one of the callbacks handles the event. However, if the event is handled by any of the callback functions, no other node in the scene graph will see the event.

METHODS

static SoType   **getClassTypeId**()

Return the type id for the **SoEventCallback** class.

              SoEventCallback()

Constructor creates an event callback node with no event interest and a NULL path.

void   **setPath**(SoPath *path)
const SoPath *   **getPath**()

Set and get the path which must be picked in order for the callbacks to be invoked. If the path is NULL, the callbacks will be invoked for every interesting event, as specified by **addEventCallback**(), regardless of what is picked. The **setPath**() method makes its own copy of the passed path.

void   **addEventCallback**(SoType eventType, SoEventCallbackCB *f,
                  void *userData = NULL)
void   **removeEventCallback**(SoType eventType, SoEventCallbackCB
                  *f, void *userData = NULL)

Specifies the callback functions to be invoked for different event types. When invoked, the callback function will be passed the *userData*, along with a pointer to this **SoEventCallback** node. For example, passing **SoMouseButtonEvent::getClassTypeId**() means callbacks will be invoked only when a mouse button is pressed or released. Passing **SoEvent::getClassTypeId**() for the *eventType* will cause the callback to be invoked for every event which passes through this event callback node.

SoHandleEventAction *
> **getAction**() const
> Returns the **SoHandleEventAction** currently traversing this node, or NULL if traversal is not taking place. This should be called only from callback functions.

const SoEvent *   **getEvent**() const
> Returns the event currently being handled, or NULL if traversal is not taking place. This should be called only from callback functions.

const SoPickedPoint *
> **getPickedPoint**() const
> Returns pick information during **SoHandleEventAction** traversal, or NULL if traversal is not taking place. This should be called only from callback functions.

void   **setHandled**()
> Tells the node the event was handled. The callback function is responsible for setting whether the event was handled or not. If there is more than one callback function registered with an **SoEventCallback** node, all of them will be invoked, regardless of whether one has handled the event or not. This should be called only from callback functions.

SbBool   **isHandled**() const
> Returns whether the event has been handled. This should be called only from callback functions.

void   **grabEvents**()
void   **releaseEvents**()
> Tells the event callback node to grab events or release the grab. While grabbing, the node will consume all events; however, each callback function will only be invoked for events of interest.

Methods from class SoNode:
> setOverride, isOverride, copy, affectsState, getByName, getByName

Methods from class SoFieldContainer:
> setToDefaults, hasDefaultValues, fieldsAreEqual, copyFieldValues, set, get, getFields, getField, getFieldName, enableNotify, isNotifyEnabled

Methods from class SoBase:
> ref, unref, unrefNoDelete, touch, getTypeId, isOfType, setName, getName

FILE FORMAT/DEFAULTS

```
EventCallback {
}
```

INCLUDE FILE

```
#include <Inventor/nodes/SoEventCallback.h>
```

typedef void   **SoEventCallbackCB**(void *userData, SoEventCallback *node)

SEE ALSO

SoInteraction, SoSelection, SoHandleEventAction, SoDragger

NAME

SoFaceDetail — stores detail information about vertex-based shapes made of faces

INHERITS FROM

SoDetail > SoFaceDetail

DESCRIPTION

This class contains detail information about a point on a face in a vertex-based shape made of faces. The information includes the number of points in the face, the points forming the vertices of the face, and the index of the face within the shape.

Note that when an **SoFaceDetail** is returned from picking (in an **SoPickedPoint**), it will contain details for all points defining the face that was intersected. However, when an **SoFaceDetail** is created for a triangle produced during primitive generation (in an **SoPrimitiveVertex**), it will contain details for only the three vertices of the triangle.

METHODS

SoFaceDetail()

virtual   **~SoFaceDetail**()

Constructor and destructor.

long   **getNumPoints**() const

Returns the number of points in the face.

const SoPointDetail *

getPoint(int i) const

Returns information about the point forming the *i*'th vertex of the face, represented as an **SoPointDetail**.

long   **getFaceIndex**() const

Returns the index of the face within the shape.

long   **getPartIndex**() const

Returns the index of the part containing the face within the shape.

static SoType   **getClassTypeId**()

Returns type identifier for this class.

Methods from class SoDetail:

copy, getTypeId, isOfType

INCLUDE FILE

```
#include <Inventor/details/SoFaceDetail.h>
```

SEE ALSO

SoDetail, SoPickedPoint, SoPrimitiveVertex, SoVertexShape

NAME

SoFaceSet — polygonal face shape node

INHERITS FROM

SoBase > SoFieldContainer > SoNode > SoShape > SoVertexShape >
SoNonIndexedShape > SoFaceSet

DESCRIPTION

This node represents a 3D shape formed by constructing faces (polygons) from
vertices located at the current coordinates. **SoFaceSet** uses the current coordinates in
order, starting at the index specified by the **startIndex** field. Each face has a number
of vertices specified by a value in the **numVertices** field. For example, an **SoFaceSet**
with a **startIndex** of 3 and **numVertices** of [3,4,2] would use coordinates 3, 4, and 5
for the first face, coordinates 6, 7, 8, and 9 for the second face, and coordinates 10
and 11 for the third. If the last value in the **numVertices** field is
SO_FACE_SET_USE_REST_OF_VERTICES (-1), all remaining coordinates in the
current coordinates are used as the vertices of the last face.

The number of values in the **numVertices** field indicates the number of faces in the
set.

The coordinates of the face set are transformed by the current cumulative
transformation. The faces are drawn with the current light model and drawing style.

Treatment of the current material and normal binding is as follows: The PER_PART
and PER_FACE bindings specify a material or normal for each face. The _INDEXED
bindings are equivalent to their non-indexed counterparts. The DEFAULT material
binding is equal to OVERALL. The DEFAULT normal binding is equal to
PER_VERTEX. The **startIndex** is also used for materials, normals, or texture
coordinates when the binding indicates that they should be used per vertex.

If the current complexity value is less than 0.5, some faces will be skipped during
rendering.

FIELDS

SoMFLong   **numVertices**
    Number of vertices per face.

Fields from class SoNonIndexedShape:
    startIndex

METHODS

SoFaceSet()
Creates a face set node with default settings.

static SoType   **getClassTypeId**()
Returns type identifier for this class.

Methods from class SoNode:

setOverride, isOverride, copy, affectsState, getByName, getByName

Methods from class SoFieldContainer:

setToDefaults, hasDefaultValues, fieldsAreEqual, copyFieldValues, set, get, getFields, getField, getFieldName, enableNotify, isNotifyEnabled

Methods from class SoBase:

ref, unref, unrefNoDelete, touch, getTypeId, isOfType, setName, getName

ACTION BEHAVIOR

SoGLRenderAction
Draws faces based on the current coordinates, normals, materials, drawing style, and so on.

SoRayPickAction
Picks faces based on the current coordinates and transformation. Details about the intersection are returned in an **SoFaceDetail**.

SoGetBoundingBoxAction
Computes the bounding box that encloses all vertices of the face set with the current transformation applied to them. Sets the center to the average of the coordinates of all vertices.

SoCallbackAction
If any triangle callbacks are registered with the action, they will be invoked for each successive triangle generated from each face in the set.

FILE FORMAT/DEFAULTS

```
FaceSet {
      startIndex    0
      numVertices   -1
}
```

INCLUDE FILE

```
#include <Inventor/nodes/SoFaceSet.h>
```

SEE ALSO

SoCoordinate3, SoDrawStyle, SoIndexedFaceSet, SoFaceDetail

NAME

    SoField — base class for all fields

INHERITS FROM

    SoField

DESCRIPTION

    SoField is the abstract base class for all fields. Fields are the data elements contained within nodes and are the input values for engines. Each node or engine class specifies a set of fields and associates a name with each. These names define the semantics of the field (e.g., the **SoCube** node contains three float fields named width, height, and depth). Field classes provide the access methods that indirectly allow editing and querying of data within nodes.

    There are two abstract subclasses of **SoField**: **SoSField** is the base class for all single-valued field classes and **SoMField** is the base class for all multiple-valued fields, which contain dynamic arrays of values. Subclasses of **SoSField** have an **SoSF** prefix, and subclasses of **SoMField** have an **SoMF** prefix. See the reference pages for **SoSField** and **SoMField** for additional methods.

    Fields are typically constructed only within node or engine instances; if you need a field that is not part of a node or engine, you can create a **GlobalField**; see the methods on **SoDB** for creating global fields.

    Fields can be connected either directly to another field, or can be connected to the output of an engine. The value of a field with a connection will change when the thing it is connected to changes. For example, consider a field "A" that is connected from "B" (by **A->connectFrom(B)**). When B's value is changed, A's value will also change. Note that A and B may have different values, even if they are connected: if A's value is set after B's value, A's value will be different from B's until B's value is set.

    A field can be connected to several other fields, but can be connected from only one source.

    It is possible (and often useful) to create loops of field connections (for example, A connected from B and B connected from A). If there are loops, then the rule is that the last **setValue()** done overrides any connections in to that value. You can think of setting the value of a field as immediately propagating that value forward into all the fields it is connected to, with the propagation stopping at the place where the original **setValue()** occurred if there is a connection loop. (Actually, a more efficient mechanism than this is used, but the semantics are the same.)

If you try to connect two fields of differing types, Inventor will automatically try to insert a field converter engine between them to convert values from one type into the other. Inventor has most reasonable conversions built-in (multiple-valued field to single-valued and vice versa, anything to **SoSFString**, anything to **SoSFTrigger**, float/short/unsigned short/long/unsigned long/etc numeric conversions, etc). You can add field converters using **SoDB**'s extender method **addConverter()**; see the SoDB.h header file for details. You can also find out if a converter is available with the **SoDB::getConverter()** method.

Fields each define their own file format for reading and being written to files, but all fields follow the same conventions:

Fields in a node or engine are written as the name of the field followed by the field's value; fields are not written if they have not been modified since they were created (if they have their default value).

The ignored flag is written as a "~" character after the field's value (if the field's value is its default value, just the "~" is written).

Field connections are written as an "=" followed by the container of the field or engine output that the field is connected to, followed by a "." and the name of the field or engine output. For example:

    DEF node1 Transform { translation 1 1 1 }
    DEF node2 Scale { scaleFactor 1 1 1 = USE node1.translation }

Global fields are written as part of an internal **SoFieldContainer** class called **GlobalField**, which writes out an **SoSFName** field named **type** whose value is the type of the global field, followed by a field of that type whose name is the name of the global field. For example, a global unsigned long field called "FrameCounter" whose value is 494 would be written as:

    GlobalField {
        type SoSFULong
        FrameCounter 494
    }

METHODS

void	**setIgnored**(SbBool ignore)
SbBool	**isIgnored**() const

Sets/gets the ignore flag for this field. When a field's ignore flag is set to TRUE, the field is not used during traversal for rendering and other actions. The default value for this flag is FALSE.

SbBool   **isDefault**() const
> Gets the state of default flag of the field. This flag will be TRUE for any field whose value is not modified after construction and will be FALSE for those that have changed (each node or engine determines what the default values for its fields are). Note: the state of this flag should not be set explicitly from within applications.

static SoType   **getClassTypeId**()
> Return the type identifier for this field class.

virtual SoType   **getTypeId**() const
> Return the type identifier for this field instance (SoField *).

virtual SbBool   **isOfType**(SoType type) const
> Returns TRUE if this field is the given type or derived from that type. This is typically used with the getClassTypeId() method to determine the type of an SoField * at run-time:

>> ```
>> SoField *field = ....;
>> if (field->isOfType(SoSFFloat::getClassTypeId())) {
>>     SoSFFloat *floatField = (SoSFFloat *)field;
>>     floatField->setValue(4.5);
>> }
>> ```

SbBool   **set**(const char *valueString)
> Sets the field to the given value, which is an ASCII string in the Inventor file format. Each field subclass defines its own file format; see their reference pages for information on their file format. The string should contain only the field's value, *not* the field's name (e.g., "1.0", *not* "width 1.0"). This method returns TRUE if the string is valid, FALSE if it is not.

void   **get**(SbString &valueString)
> Returns the value of the field in the Inventor file format, even if the field has its default value.

int   **operator ==**(const SoField &f) const
int   **operator !=**(const SoField &f) const
> Return TRUE (FALSE) if this field is of the same type and has the same value as *f*.

void   **touch**()
> Simulates a change to the field, causing attached sensors to fire, connected fields and engines to be marked as needing evaluation, and so forth. Calling

touch() on an instance of a derived field class is equivalent to calling **setValue(getValue())** using the derived class's methods, except that the field's **isDefault()** status remains unchanged.

SbBool   **connectFrom**(SoField *fromField)
SbBool   **connectFrom**(SoEngineOutput *fromEngine)
Connects this field to another field or from an engine output. If the field was connected to something before, it will be automatically disconnected (a field may have only one connection writing into it at a time). Unless connections to the field are disabled (see **enableConnection()**), the field's value will be set to the value of the thing it is connected to.

void   **disconnect**()
Disconnect the field from whatever it was connected to. This does nothing if the field was not connected.

SbBool   **isConnected**() const
Returns TRUE if the field is connected to anything.

SbBool   **isConnectedFromField**() const
Returns TRUE if the field is connected to another field.

SbBool   **getConnectedField**(SoField *&writingField) const
Returns TRUE if this field is being written into by another field, and returns the field it is connected to in *writingField*. Returns FALSE and does not modify *writingField* if it is not connected to a field.

SbBool   **isConnectedFromEngine**() const
Returns TRUE if the field is connected to an engine's output.

SbBool   **getConnectedEngine**(SoEngineOutput *&engineOutput) const
Returns TRUE if this field is being written into by an engine, and returns the engine output it is connected to in *engineOutput*. Returns FALSE and does not modify *engineOutput* if it is not connected to an engine.

void   **enableConnection**(SbBool flag)
Field connections may be enabled and disabled. Disabling a field's connection is almost exactly like disconnecting it; the only difference is that you can later re-enable the connection by calling enableConnection(TRUE). Note that disconnecting an engine output can cause the engine's reference count to be decremented and the engine to be deleted, but disabling the connection does not decrement its reference count.

Re-enabling a connection will cause the value of the field to be changed to the engine output or field to which it is connected.

A field's connection-enabled status is maintained even if the field is disconnected or reconnected. By default, connections are enabled.

SbBool   **isConnectionEnabled**() const
Returns FALSE if connections to this field are disabled. Note that this may return FALSE even if the field is not connected to anything.

int   **getForwardConnections**(SoFieldList &list) const
Adds pointers to all of the fields that this field is writing into (either fields in nodes, global fields or engine inputs) to the given field list, and returns the number of forward connections.

SoFieldContainer *
            getContainer() const
Returns the object that contains this field. The type of the object will be either **SoNode**, **SoEngine**, or will be a global field container (note that the global field container class is internal to Inventor; see the methods for creating and accessing global fields on **SoDB**). For example:

```
SoFieldContainer *f = field->getContainer();
if (f->isOfType(SoNode::getClassTypeId())) {
    ... do something ...
} else if (f->isOfType(SoEngine::getClassTypeId())) {
    ... do someting else ...
} else {
    ... it must be a global field.  We can figure out its name, but
                        that is about it:
    const SbName &globalFieldName = f->getName();
}
```

INCLUDE FILE
        #include <Inventor/fields/SoField.h>

SEE ALSO
        SoSField, SoMField, SoNode, SoDB

NAME

SoFieldContainer — abstract base class for objects that contain fields

INHERITS FROM

SoBase > SoFieldContainer

DESCRIPTION

SoFieldContainer is the abstract base class for engines and nodes. It contains methods for finding out what fields an object has, controlling notification, and for dealing with all of the fields of an object at once.

The fields of an engine are its inputs. Note that even though an engine's output corresponds to a specific type of field, an engine output is not a field.

METHODS

static SoType   **getClassTypeId**()
Returns the type of this class.

void   **setToDefaults**()
Sets all fields in this object to their default values.

SbBool   **hasDefaultValues**() const
Returns TRUE if all of the object's fields have their default values. This will return TRUE even if a field's **isDefault**() method returns FALSE — for example, if a field's default value is 0.0 and you **setValue(0.0)** that field, the default flag will be set to FALSE (because it would be too slow to compare the field against its default value every time **setValue** is called). However, **hasDefaultValues**() would return TRUE in this case.

SbBool   **fieldsAreEqual**(const SoFieldContainer *fc) const
Returns TRUE if this object's fields are exactly equal to *fc*'s fields. If *fc* is not exactly same type as this object, FALSE is returned.

void   **copyFieldValues**(const SoFieldContainer *fc, SbBool copyConnections = FALSE)
Copies the contents of *fc*'s fields into this object's fields. *fc* must be the same type as this object. If *copyConnections* is TRUE, then if any of *fc*'s fields are connected then this object's fields will also be connected to the same source.

SbBool   **set**(const char *fieldDataString)
Sets one or more fields in this object to the values specified in the given string, which should be a string in the Inventor file format. TRUE is returned if the string was valid Inventor file format. For example, you could set the fields of an **SoCube** by doing:

> SoCube *cube = ...
> cube->set("width 1.0 height 2.0 depth 3.2");

void   **get**(SbString &fieldDataString)
Returns the values of the fields of this object in the Inventor ASCII file format in the given string. Fields whose **isDefault()** bit is set will not be part of the string. You can use the **field->get()** method to get a field's value as a string even if has its default value.

virtual int   **getFields**(SoFieldList &resultList) const
Appends pointers to all of this object's fields to resultList, and returns the number of fields appended. The types of the fields can be determined using **field->isOfType()** and **field->getTypeId()**, and their names can be determined by passing the field pointers to the **getFieldName()** method (see below).

virtual SoField *   **getField**(const SbName &fieldName) const
Returns a pointer to the field of this object whose name is *fieldName*. Returns NULL if there is no field with the given name.

SbBool   **getFieldName**(const SoField *field, SbName &fieldName) const
Returns the name of the given field in the *fieldName* argument. Returns FALSE if field is not a member of this object.

SbBool   **enableNotify**(SbBool flag)
SbBool   **isNotifyEnabled**() const
Notification is the process of telling intersted objects that this object has changed. Notification is needed to make engines and sensors function, is used to keep **SoPaths** up to date when the scene graph's topology changes, and is also used to invalidate rendering or bounding box caches.

Notification is normally enabled, but can be disabled on a node by node (or engine by engine) basis. If you are making extensive changes to a large part of the scene graph then disabling notification can increase performance, at the expense of increased responsibility for making sure that any interested engines, sensors or paths are kept up to date.

For example, if you will be making a lot of changes to a small part of your scene graph and you know that there are no engines or sensors attached to nodes in that part of the scene graph, you might disable notification on the nodes you are changing, modify them, re-enable notification, and then touch() one of the nodes to cause a redraw.

However, you should profile your application and make sure that notification is taking a significant amount of time before going to the trouble of manually controlling notification.

Methods from class SoBase:

ref, unref, unrefNoDelete, touch, getTypeId, isOfType, setName, getName

INCLUDE FILE

```
#include <Inventor/fields/SoFieldContainer.h>
```

SEE ALSO

SoSField, SoMField, SoNode, SoDB

NAME

SoFieldList — maintains a list of pointers to fields

INHERITS FROM

SbPList > SoFieldList

DESCRIPTION

This subclass of **SbPList** holds lists of pointers to instances of classes derived from **SoField**.

METHODS

SoFieldList()
Constructor.

SoFieldList(int size)
Constructor that pre-allocates storage for *size* pointers.

SoFieldList(const SoFieldList &l)
Constructor that copies the contents of another list.

~**SoFieldList**()
Destructor.

void **append**(SoField *ptr)
Adds a pointer to the end of the list.

void **insert**(SoField *ptr, int addBefore)
Inserts given pointer in list before pointer with given index.

SoField * **operator [ ]**(int i) const
Accesses an element of a list.

void **set**(int i, SoField *field)
Sets an element of a list.

Methods from class SbPList:

find, remove, getLength, truncate, copy, operator =, operator ==, operator !=

INCLUDE FILE

```
#include <Inventor/SoLists.h>
```

SEE ALSO

SoField

NAME

SoFieldSensor — sensor class that can be attached to Inventor fields

INHERITS FROM

SoSensor > SoDelayQueueSensor > SoDataSensor > SoFieldSensor

DESCRIPTION

Field sensors detect changes to fields, calling a callback function whenever the field changes. The field may be part of a node, an input of an engine, or a global field.

METHODS

SoFieldSensor()
SoFieldSensor(SoSensorCB *func, void *field)
Creation methods. The second method takes the callback function and field to be called when the sensor is triggered.

~SoFieldSensor()
Destroys the sensor, freeing up any memory associated with it after unscheduling it.

void	**attach**(SoField *field)
void	**detach**()
SoField *	**getAttachedField**() const

The **attach**() method makes this sensor detect changes to the given field. The **detach**() method unschedules this sensor (if it is scheduled) and makes it ignore changes to the scene graph. The **getAttachedField**() method returns the field that this sensor is sensing, or NULL if it is not attached to any field.

Methods from class SoDataSensor:

setDeleteCallback, getTriggerNode, getTriggerField, getTriggerPath, setTriggerPathFlag, getTriggerPathFlag

Methods from class SoDelayQueueSensor:

setPriority, getPriority, getDefaultPriority, schedule, unschedule, isScheduled

Methods from class SoSensor:

setFunction, getFunction, setData, getData

INCLUDE FILE

```
#include <Inventor/sensors/SoFieldSensor.h>
```

SEE ALSO

SoNodeSensor, SoPathSensor, SoDataSensor

NAME

SoFile — node that reads children from a named file

INHERITS FROM

SoBase > SoFieldContainer > SoNode > SoFile

DESCRIPTION

This node represents a subgraph that was read from a named input file. When an **SoFile** node is written out, just the field containing the name of the file is written; no children are written out. When an **SoFile** is encountered during reading, reading continues from the named file, and all nodes read from the file are added as hidden children of the file node.

Whenever the **name** field changes, any existing children are removed and the contents of the new file is read in. The file node remembers what directory the last file was read from and will read the new file from the same directory after checking the standard list of directories (see **SoInput**), assuming the field isn't set to an absolute path name.

The children of an **SoFile** node are hidden; there is no way of accessing or editing them. If you wish to edit the contents of an **SoFile** node, you can modify the contents of the named file and then "touch" the **name** field (see **SoField**). Alternatively, you can use the **copyChildren**() method to get a editable copy of the file node's children. Note that this does not affect the original file on disk, however.

FIELDS

SoSFString   **name**

Name of file from which to read children.

METHODS

              SoFile()

Creates a file node with default settings.

SoGroup *   **copyChildren**() const

Returns a new **SoGroup** containing copies of all of the file node's children.

static SoType   **getClassTypeId**()

Returns type identifier for this class.

Methods from class SoNode:

setOverride, isOverride, copy, affectsState, getByName, getByName

Methods from class SoFieldContainer:

setToDefaults, hasDefaultValues, fieldsAreEqual, copyFieldValues, set, get, getFields, getField, getFieldName, enableNotify, isNotifyEnabled

Methods from class SoBase:

ref, unref, unrefNoDelete, touch, getTypeId, isOfType, setName, getName

ACTION BEHAVIOR

SoGLRenderAction, SoCallbackAction, SoGetBoundingBoxAction, SoGetMatrixAction, SoHandleEventAction
Traverses its children just as **SoGroup** does.

SoRayPickAction
Traverses its hidden children, but, if intersections are found, generates paths that end at the **SoFile** node.

SoWriteAction
Writes just the **name** field and no children.

FILE FORMAT/DEFAULTS

```
File {
      name   "<Undefined file>"
}
```

INCLUDE FILE

```
#include <Inventor/nodes/SoFile.h>
```

SEE ALSO

SoInput, SoPath

NAME

SoFont — node that defines font type and size for text

INHERITS FROM

SoBase > SoFieldContainer > SoNode > SoFont

DESCRIPTION

This node defines the current font type and point size for all subsequent text shapes in the scene graph. Fonts are specified with PostScript names, except for the default font. The default font is called "defaultFont" and is the standard SGI graphics font for 2D text. "Utopia" is the standard Inventor font for 3D text.

FIELDS

SoSFName   **name**

This field defines the font name as a PostScript name. For example, Times Roman would be specified as Times-Roman.

SoSFFloat   **size**

This field defines the font size. The value is in points for 2D text and is in the current units for 3D text.

METHODS

SoFont()

Creates a font node with default settings.

static SoType   **getClassTypeId()**

Returns type identifier for this class.

Methods from class SoNode:

setOverride, isOverride, copy, affectsState, getByName, getByName

Methods from class SoFieldContainer:

setToDefaults, hasDefaultValues, fieldsAreEqual, copyFieldValues, set, get, getFields, getField, getFieldName, enableNotify, isNotifyEnabled

Methods from class SoBase:

ref, unref, unrefNoDelete, touch, getTypeId, isOfType, setName, getName

ACTION BEHAVIOR

SoGLRenderAction, SoCallbackAction, SoGetBoundingBoxAction, SoRayPickAction

Sets the font name and size in the current traversal state.

FILE FORMAT/DEFAULTS

```
Font {
      name    "defaultFont"
      size    10
}
```

INCLUDE FILE

```
#include <Inventor/nodes/SoFont.h>
```

SEE ALSO

SoText2, SoText3

NAME

    SoGate — selectively copies its input to its output

INHERITS FROM

    SoBase > SoFieldContainer > SoEngine > SoGate

DESCRIPTION

    This engine selectively copies its input to its output. The type of the input field can be any subclass of **SoMField**. The type is specified when an instance of the class is created. For example, **SoGate(SoMFFloat::getClassTypeId())** creates an engine that copies floating-point values.

    The **enable** input controls continous flow-through of values. While **enable** is TRUE, the input will be copied to the output. Alternatively, by touching the **trigger** input, you can copy a single value from the input to the output.

    Note that unlike most other engine fields, **input** and **output** are pointers. Note also that by default **input** does not contain any values.

INPUTS

    SoSFBool   **enable**
        Enable continous flow-through.

    SoSFTrigger   **trigger**
        Copy a single value.

    So Field * (handwritten)
    <inputType>   **input**
        The value that is copied to the output when the gate is open.

OUTPUTS *So Field ** (handwritten)

    (<outputType>)   **output**
        Contains a copy of the input value if the gate is open.

METHODS

                SoGate(SoType inputType)
    Constructor. The argument specifies the type of the input field.

    Methods from class SoEngine:
        getClassTypeId, getOutputs, getOutput, getOutputName, copy, getByName, getByName

    Methods from class SoFieldContainer:
        setToDefaults, hasDefaultValues, fieldsAreEqual, copyFieldValues, set, get, getFields, getField, getFieldName, enableNotify, isNotifyEnabled

Methods from class SoBase:

ref, unref, unrefNoDelete, touch, getTypeId, isOfType, setName, getName

FILE FORMAT/DEFAULTS

```
Gate {
        type      <inputType>
        input     []
        enable    FALSE
        trigger
}
```

INCLUDE FILE

```
#include <Inventor/engines/So.h>
```

SEE ALSO

SoEngineOutput, SoConcatenate, SoSelectOne

NAME

SoGetBoundingBoxAction — computes bounding box of a scene

INHERITS FROM

SoAction > SoGetBoundingBoxAction

DESCRIPTION

This class is used to compute a 3D bounding box enclosing objects defined by a scene graph. The box is a rectangular prism. The action also computes the center point, which is defined differently for different objects. (For example, the center of an **SoFaceSet** is the average of its vertices' coordinates.) For a group, the center point is defined as the average of the centers of all shapes in it.

Each bounding box is calculated as a **SbXfBox3f**, where the transformation matrix is defined so that the bounding box can be stored in the object space of the **SoShape**. When two bounding boxes are combined by a group node, the combination is performed so as to produce the smaller untransformed box. The result of the calculation by the action can be returned as an **SbXfBox3f** or as a world-space-aligned **SbBox3f**.

To calculate the bounding box of a subgraph bounded by two paths, specify the left edge of the subgraph with **setResetPath()**, and apply the action to the path that defines the right edge of the subgraph. The accumulated bounding box and transformation will be reset when the tail of the reset path is traversed.

If the subgraph being traversed does not contain any shapes, the returned bounding box will be empty (that is, **box.isEmpty()** will return TRUE).

METHODS

SoGetBoundingBoxAction(const SbViewportRegion &viewportRegion)
Constructor takes viewport region to use for picking. Even though the bounding box computation may not involve a window per se, some nodes need this information to determine their size and placement.

void   **setViewportRegion**(const SbViewportRegion &newRegion)
const SbViewportRegion &
       getViewportRegion() const
Sets/returns current viewport region to use for action.

SbBox3f   **getBoundingBox**() const
Returns computed bounding box in world space.

SbXfBox3f &   **getXfBoundingBox**()
Returns computed bounding box before transformation into world space.

const SbVec3f &   **getCenter**() const
Returns computed center point in world space.

void   **setInCameraSpace**(SbBool flag)
Set this flag to TRUE if you want the returned bounding box to be in the space of whatever camera is in the graph. Camera space is defined to have the viewpoint at the origin, with the direction of view along the negative z axis. This space can be used to determine distances of objects from the camera.

SbBool   **isInCameraSpace**() const
Returns camera space flag.

void   **setResetPath**(const SoPath *path, SbBool resetBefore = TRUE, ResetType what = ALL)
If a non-NULL path is specified, the action will reset the computed bounding box to be empty and/or the current transformation to identity. The *resetBefore* flag indicates whether to perform the reset before or after the tail node of the path is traversed.

const SoPath *   **getResetPath**() const
Returns the current reset path, or NULL.

SbBool   **isResetPath**() const
Returns TRUE if the current reset path is not NULL.

SbBool   **isResetBefore**() const
Returns TRUE if the *resetBefore* flag was specified for the reset path.

SoGetBoundingBoxAction::ResetType
        getWhatReset() const
Returns what flags were specified to be reset for the reset path.

Methods from class SoAction:
apply, apply, apply, getClassTypeId, getTypeId, isOfType, invalidateState

INCLUDE FILE

```
#include <Inventor/actions/SoGetBoundingBoxAction.h>
```

enum **ResetType** {

      SoGetBoundingBoxAction::TRANSFORM

                Transformation

      SoGetBoundingBoxAction::BBOX

                Bounding Box

      SoGetBoundingBoxAction::ALL

                Both Transform and Bounding Box

}

SEE ALSO

SbBox3f, SbXfBox3f, SoGetMatrixAction

NAME

SoGetMatrixAction — computes transformation matrix for subgraph

INHERITS FROM

SoAction > SoGetMatrixAction

DESCRIPTION

This action computes transformation matrices for a given subgraph. It computes the cumulative transformation matrix and its inverse, along with a cumulative texture transformation matrix and its inverse.

This action is unlike most others in that it does not traverse downwards from groups. When applied to a node, it computes the matrix for just that node. (This makes sense for transformation nodes, but not for others, really.) It is much more useful when applied to a path. When applied to a path, it gathers the transformation info for all nodes in the path and those that affect nodes in the path, but it stops when it hits the last node in the path; it does not traverse downwards from it as other actions (such as rendering) do. This behavior makes the most sense for this action.

METHODS

SoGetMatrixAction(const SbViewportRegion &newRegion)
Constructor takes viewport region to use for picking. Even though the matrix computation may not involve a window per se, some nodes need this information to determine their placement.

void   **setViewportRegion**(const SbViewportRegion &newRegion)
const SbViewportRegion &
           getViewportRegion() const
Sets/returns current viewport region to use for action.

SbMatrix &   **getMatrix**()
SbMatrix &   **getInverse**()
Returns cumulative transformation matrix and its inverse.

SbMatrix &   **getTextureMatrix**()
SbMatrix &   **getTextureInverse**()
Returns cumulative texture transformation matrix and its inverse.

Methods from class SoAction:

apply, apply, apply, getClassTypeId, getTypeId, isOfType, invalidateState

INCLUDE FILE

```
#include <Inventor/actions/SoGetMatrixAction.h>
```

SEE ALSO

SoGetBoundingBoxAction

NAME

SoGLRenderAction — renders a scene graph using OpenGL

INHERITS FROM

SoAction > SoGLRenderAction

DESCRIPTION

This class traverses a scene graph and renders it using the OpenGL graphics library. It assumes that a valid window has been created and initialized for proper OpenGL rendering. The **SoXtRenderArea** class or any of its subclasses may be used to create such a window.

METHODS

SoGLRenderAction(const SbViewportRegion &viewportRegion, SbBool useCurrentGLValues = FALSE)
Constructor. The first parameter defines the viewport region into which rendering will take place. The second parameter specifies whether current OpenGL state values (material, line width, etc.) are to be inherited for rendering. If this is FALSE (the default), Inventor will set up its own reasonable default values.

void   **setViewportRegion**(const SbViewportRegion &newRegion)
const SbViewportRegion &
getViewportRegion() const
Changes/returns viewport region to use for rendering.

void   **setUpdateArea**(const SbVec2f &origin, const SbVec2f &size)
void   **getUpdateArea**(SbVec2f &origin, SbVec2f &size) const
Sets/returns the current update area, which is the rectangular area of the viewport region that will actually be rendered into. This can be used for partial updates in applications that can manage them. The update area is specified in normalized viewport coordinates, where (0,0) is the lower left corner of the viewport and (1,1) is the upper right corner. The area is specified or returned as an origin and a size.

void   **setAbortCallback**(SoGLRenderAbortCB *func, void *userData)
Sets callback to call during rendering to test for an abort condition. It will be called for each node that is traversed. This allows applications to terminate rendering prematurely if some condition occurs. The callback function should return TRUE if rendering should abort.

| void | **setTransparencyType**(TransparencyType type) |
| TransparencyType | **getTransparencyType**() const |

Sets/returns transparency quality level to use when rendering. The default is SCREEN_DOOR. (Note that SCREEN_DOOR transparency does not work in the case where transparency values are specified for each vertex of a shape. If this is the case, use one of the other transparency types.)

| void | **setSmoothing**(SbBool smooth) |
| SbBool | **isSmoothing**() const |

Sets/returns smoothing flag. When on, smoothing uses OpenGL's line- and point-smoothing features to provide cheap antialiasing of lines and points. The default is FALSE.

| void | **setNumPasses**(int num) |
| int | **getNumPasses**() const |

Sets/returns number of rendering passes for multipass rendering. Specifying more than one pass will result in antialiasing of the rendered scene, using OpenGL's accumulation buffer. (Camera nodes typically move their viewpoints a little bit for each pass to achieve the antialiasing.) Each additional pass provides better antialiasing, but requires more rendering time The default is 1 pass.

| void | **setPassUpdate**(SbBool flag) |
| SbBool | **isPassUpdate**() const |

Sets/returns a flag indicating whether intermediate results are displayed after each antialiasing pass for progressive improvement (default is FALSE).

| void | **setPassCallback**(SoGLRenderPassCB *func, void *userData) |

Sets a callback function to invoke between passes when antialiasing. Passing NULL (which is the default state) will cause a clear of the color and depth buffers to be performed.

| void | **setCacheContext**(unsigned long context) |
| unsigned long | **getCacheContext**() const |

Sets/returns the OpenGL cache context. A cache context is just an integer identifying when OpenGL display lists (which are used for render caching) can be shared between render actions; for example, see the documentation on GLX contexts for information on when OpenGL display lists can be shared between GLX windows.

Methods from class SoAction:

apply, apply, apply, getClassTypeId, getTypeId, isOfType, invalidateState

INCLUDE FILE

```
#include <Inventor/actions/SoGLRenderAction.h>
```

typedef SbBool   **SoGLRenderAbortCB**(void *userData)
typedef void   **SoGLRenderPassCB**(void *userData)

enum **TransparencyType** {
>   **SoGLRenderAction::SCREEN_DOOR**
>>   Uses stipple patterns for screen-door transparency
>   **SoGLRenderAction::ADD**
>>   Uses additive alpha blending
>   **SoGLRenderAction::DELAYED_ADD**
>>   Uses additive blending, rendering all transparent objects after opaque ones
>   **SoGLRenderAction::SORTED_OBJECT_ADD**
>>   Same as DELAYED_ADD, but sorts transparent objects by distances of bounding boxes from camera
>   **SoGLRenderAction::BLEND**
>>   Uses multiplicative alpha blending
>   **SoGLRenderAction::DELAYED_BLEND**
>>   Uses multiplicative alpha blending, rendering all transparent objects after opaque ones
>   **SoGLRenderAction::SORTED_OBJECT_BLEND**
>>   Same as DELAYED_BLEND, but sorts transparent objects by distances of bounding boxes from camera

}

SEE ALSO

SoSeparator, SoXtRenderArea

NAME

SoGroup — base class for all group nodes

INHERITS FROM

SoBase > SoFieldContainer > SoNode > SoGroup

DESCRIPTION

This node defines the base class for all group nodes. **SoGroup** is a node that contains an ordered list of child nodes. The ordering of the child nodes represents the traversal order for all operations (for example, rendering, picking, and so on). This node is simply a container for the child nodes and does not alter the traversal state in any way. During traversal, state accumulated for a child is passed on to each successive child and then to the parents of the group (**SoGroup** does not push or pop traversal state as **SoSeparator** does).

METHODS

SoGroup()
Creates an empty group node.

SoGroup(int nChildren)
Constructor that takes approximate number of children. Space is allocated for pointers to the children, but the group does not contain any actual child nodes.

void **addChild**(SoNode *child)
Adds a child as last one in group.

void **insertChild**(SoNode *child, int newChildIndex)
Adds a child so that it becomes the one with the given index.

SoNode * **getChild**(int index) const
Returns pointer to child node with the given index.

int **findChild**(const SoNode *child) const
Finds index of given child within group.

int **getNumChildren**() const
Returns number of children.

void **removeChild**(int index)
Removes child with given index from group.

void **removeChild**(SoNode *child)
Removes first instance of given child from group.

void	**removeAllChildren**()

Removes all children from group.

void	**replaceChild**(int index, SoNode *newChild)

Replaces child with given index with new child.

void	**replaceChild**(SoNode *oldChild, SoNode *newChild)

Replaces first instance of given child with new child.

static SoType	**getClassTypeId**()

Returns type identifier for this class.

Methods from class SoNode:

setOverride, isOverride, copy, affectsState, getByName, getByName

Methods from class SoFieldContainer:

setToDefaults, hasDefaultValues, fieldsAreEqual, copyFieldValues, set, get, getFields, getField, getFieldName, enableNotify, isNotifyEnabled

Methods from class SoBase:

ref, unref, unrefNoDelete, touch, getTypeId, isOfType, setName, getName

ACTION BEHAVIOR

SoGLRenderAction, SoCallbackAction, SoGetBoundingBoxAction, SoHandleEventAction, SoRayPickAction

Traverses each child in order.

SoGetMatrixAction

Does nothing unless the group is in the middle of the path chain the action is being applied to. If so, the children up to and including the next node in the chain are traversed.

SoSearchAction

If searching for group nodes, compares with this group. Otherwise, continues to search children.

SoWriteAction

Writes out the group node. This method also deals with any field data associated with the group node. As a result, this method is used for most subclasses of **SoGroup** as well.

FILE FORMAT/DEFAULTS

```
Group {
}
```

INCLUDE FILE

```
#include <Inventor/nodes/SoGroup.h>
```

SEE ALSO

SoArray, SoLevelOfDetail, SoMultipleCopy, SoPathSwitch, SoSeparator, SoSwitch

NAME

SoHandleBoxDragger — box you can scale, stretch and translate by dragging with the mouse

INHERITS FROM

SoBase > SoFieldContainer > SoNode > SoBaseKit > SoInteractionKit > SoDragger > SoHandleBoxDragger

DESCRIPTION

SoHandleBoxDragger is a dragger shaped like a wireframe box with small *corner cubes* mounted on each corner. Click and drag any of these cubes to scale the box uniformly. Six other *center cubes* are centered on the sides of the box; white lines connect them to the center of the dragger. Drag one of the center cubes along its line to stretch the box in that direction. Dragging a face of the box translates the dragger within that plane.

While you drag a face of the box, purple *feedback arrows* display the possible directions of motion. Press the <Shift> key to *constrain* the motion to one of the two major directions in the plane. The constraint direction is chosen based on the next user gesture. Press the <ALT> key and the dragger will translate *perpendicular* to that plane. The **translation** field is modified as the face is dragged.

By default, dragging any of the small cubes scales about the center of the object. Pressing the <ALT> key changes this: A corner cube will scale about its opposite corner. A center cube will scale about the center of its opposite face. Dragging one of the small cubes will usually result in changes to both the **scaleFactor** and **translation** fields. This is because any scale about a point other than the origin has a translation element.

As with all draggers, if you change the fields the dragger will move to match the new settings.

Remember: This is *not* an **SoTransform!**. If you want to move other objects with this dragger, you can either:

[a] Use an **SoHandleBoxManip**, which is subclassed from **SoTransform**. It creates one of these draggers and uses it as the interface to change its fields. (see the **SoHandleBoxManip** reference page).

[b] Use field-to-field connections to connect the fields of this dragger to those of any **SoTransformation** node.

You can change the parts in any instance of this dragger using **setPart()**. The default part geometries are defined as resources for this **SoHandleBoxDragger** class. They are detailed in the Dragger Resources section of the online reference page for this class. You can make your program use different default resources for the parts by copying the file **/usr/share/data/draggerDefaults/handleBoxDragger.iv** into your own directory, editing the file, and then setting the environment variable **SO_DRAGGER_DIR** to be a path to that directory.

FIELDS

SoSFVec3f **scaleFactor**
    Scale of the dragger.

SoSFVec3f **translation**
    Position of the dragger.

Fields from class SoDragger:

    isActive

Fields from class SoInteractionKit:

    renderCaching, boundingBoxCaching, renderCulling, pickCulling

PARTS

Parts from class SoBaseKit:

    callbackList

METHODS

SoHandleBoxDragger()
    Constructor.

static const SoNodekitCatalog *
    getClassNodekitCatalog() const
    Returns an **SoNodekitCatalog** for this class

static SoType **getClassTypeId**()
    Returns type identifier for this class.

Methods from class SoDragger:

    addStartCallback, removeStartCallback, addMotionCallback, removeMotionCallback, addFinishCallback, removeFinishCallback, addValueChangedCallback, removeValueChangedCallback, setMinGesture, getMinGesture, setMinScale, getMinScale

Methods from class SoInteractionKit:

    setPartAsPath

Methods from class SoBaseKit:

getNodekitCatalog, getPart, getPartString, createPathToPart, setPart, set, set, isSearchingChildren, setSearchingChildren

Methods from class SoNode:

setOverride, isOverride, copy, affectsState, getByName, getByName

Methods from class SoFieldContainer:

setToDefaults, hasDefaultValues, fieldsAreEqual, copyFieldValues, get, getFields, getField, getFieldName, enableNotify, isNotifyEnabled

Methods from class SoBase:

ref, unref, unrefNoDelete, touch, getTypeId, isOfType, setName, getName

MACROS

Macros from class SoBaseKit:

SO_GET_PART, SO_CHECK_PART

CATALOG PARTS

All parts			
Part Name	Part Type	Default Type	NULL by Default
callbackList	NodeKitListPart	--	yes
surroundScale	SurroundScale	--	yes
translator1	Separator	--	yes
translator1Active	Separator	--	yes
translator2	Separator	--	yes
translator2Active	Separator	--	yes
translator3	Separator	--	yes
translator3Active	Separator	--	yes
translator4	Separator	--	yes
translator4Active	Separator	--	yes
translator5	Separator	--	yes
translator5Active	Separator	--	yes
translator6	Separator	--	yes
translator6Active	Separator	--	yes

All parts (continued)			
Part Name	Part Type	Default Type	NULL by Default
extruder1	Separator	--	yes
extruder1Active	Separator	--	yes
extruder2	Separator	--	yes
extruder2Active	Separator	--	yes
extruder3	Separator	--	yes
extruder3Active	Separator	--	yes
extruder4	Separator	--	yes
extruder4Active	Separator	--	yes
extruder5	Separator	--	yes
extruder5Active	Separator	--	yes
extruder6	Separator	--	yes
extruder6Active	Separator	--	yes
uniform1	Separator	--	yes
uniform1Active	Separator	--	yes
uniform2	Separator	--	yes
uniform2Active	Separator	--	yes
uniform3	Separator	--	yes
uniform3Active	Separator	--	yes
uniform4	Separator	--	yes
uniform4Active	Separator	--	yes
uniform5	Separator	--	yes
uniform5Active	Separator	--	yes
uniform6	Separator	--	yes
uniform6Active	Separator	--	yes
uniform7	Separator	--	yes
uniform7Active	Separator	--	yes
uniform8	Separator	--	yes
uniform8Active	Separator	--	yes
arrow1	Separator	--	yes
arrow2	Separator	--	yes
arrow3	Separator	--	yes
arrow4	Separator	--	yes
arrow5	Separator	--	yes
arrow6	Separator	--	yes

Extra information for list parts from above table		
Part Name	Container Type	Permissible Types
callbackList	Separator	Callback, EventCallback

FILE FORMAT/DEFAULTS

```
HandleBoxDragger {
        renderCaching        AUTO
        boundingBoxCaching   AUTO
        renderCulling        AUTO
        pickCulling          AUTO
        isActive             FALSE
        translation          0 0 0
        scaleFactor          1 1 1
}
```

INCLUDE FILE

```
#include <Inventor/draggers/SoHandleBoxDragger.h>
```

NOTE

Unlike most multi-function draggers, **SoHandleBoxDragger** is not a compound dragger made up of other draggers that perform its smaller tasks. This is not because it was inappropriate, but because was written before implementation of the methods that synchronize multiple child draggers. The younger **SoTransformBoxDragger** has similarities to the handle box dragger, but the transform box dragger *is* a compound dragger.

SEE ALSO

SoInteractionKit, SoDragger, SoCenterballDragger, SoDirectionalLightDragger, SoDragPointDragger, SoJackDragger, SoPointLightDragger, SoRotateCylindricalDragger, SoRotateDiscDragger, SoRotateSphericalDragger, SoScale1Dragger, SoScale2Dragger, SoScale2UniformDragger, SoScaleUniformDragger, SoSpotLightDragger, SoTabBoxDragger, SoTabPlaneDragger, SoTrackballDragger, SoTransformBoxDragger, SoTranslate1Dragger, SoTranslate2Dragger

NAME

SoHandleBoxManip — transform node with 3D Interface for Editing ScaleFactor and Translation

INHERITS FROM

SoBase > SoFieldContainer > SoNode > SoTransformation > SoTransform > SoTransformManip > SoHandleBoxManip

DESCRIPTION

SoHandleBoxManip is derived from **SoTransform** (by way of **SoTransformManip**). When its fields change, nodes following it in the scene graph rotate, scale, and/or translate.

As a subclass of **SoTransformManip**, this manip also has a 3D interface to edit some of its fields. In this case, the interface edits the **scaleFactor** and **translation** fields.

A manipulator differs from a dragger. When you move a dragger, no other nodes are affected. When you move an **SoTransformManip**, other nodes move along with it. (See the reference page for **SoTransformManip**).

The interface for an **SoHandleBoxManip** is exactly the same as that of the **SoHandleBoxDragger**. To find out more about the interface, see the reference page for **SoHandleBoxDragger**. To find out how the manipulator uses a dragger to provide its interface, see the reference page for **SoTransformManip**.

On screen, this manip will surround the objects influenced by its motion. This is because it turns on the *surroundScale* part of the dragger (See the reference page for **SoSurroundScale**)

FIELDS

Fields from class SoTransform:

translation, rotation, scaleFactor, scaleOrientation, center

METHODS

SoHandleBoxManip()
Constructor.

static SoType   **getClassTypeId**()
Returns type identifier for this class.

Methods from class SoTransformManip:

getDragger, replaceNode, replaceManip

Methods from class SoTransform:

pointAt, getScaleSpaceMatrix, getRotationSpaceMatrix, getTranslationSpaceMatrix, multLeft, multRight, combineLeft, combineRight, setMatrix, recenter

Methods from class SoNode:

setOverride, isOverride, copy, affectsState, getByName, getByName

Methods from class SoFieldContainer:

setToDefaults, hasDefaultValues, fieldsAreEqual, copyFieldValues, set, get, getFields, getField, getFieldName, enableNotify, isNotifyEnabled

Methods from class SoBase:

ref, unref, unrefNoDelete, touch, getTypeId, isOfType, setName, getName

FILE FORMAT/DEFAULTS

```
HandleBoxManip {
        translation       0 0 0
        rotation          0 0 1 0
        scaleFactor       1 1 1
        scaleOrientation  0 0 1 0
        center            0 0 0
}
```

INCLUDE FILE

```
#include <Inventor/manips/SoHandleBoxManip.h>
```

SEE ALSO

SoCenterballManip, SoHandleBoxDragger, SoJackManip, SoTabBoxManip, SoTrackballManip, SoTransformBoxManip, SoTransform, SoTransformManip

NAME

SoHandleEventAction — allows nodes in a graph to receive input events

INHERITS FROM

SoAction > SoHandleEventAction

DESCRIPTION

This class is used to allow nodes in a scene graph to handle input events. It is usually invoked from a component derived from **SoXtRenderArea** when the component receives a window system event.

Manipulator, dragger and selection nodes respond to and process events. Most other group nodes just pass the event to their children, while most other nodes simply ignore the action entirely. Once a node has indicated to the action that it has handled the event, traversal stops.

A node that handles an event can also grab future events. Once it has done so, all events will be sent directly to that node, with no traversal taking place, until the node releases the grab.

METHODS

SoHandleEventAction(const SbViewportRegion &viewportRegion)

Constructor takes viewport region to use; this is needed to perform a pick operation when requested.

void **setViewportRegion**(const SbViewportRegion &newRegion)
const SbViewportRegion &
getViewportRegion() const

Sets/returns current viewport region to use for action.

void **setEvent**(const SoEvent *ev)
const SoEvent * **getEvent**() const

Sets/returns the event being handled.

void **setHandled**()
SbBool **isHandled**() const

Sets/returns whether any node has yet handled the event.

void **setGrabber**(SoNode *node)

Initiates grabbing of future events. All events will be sent to the given node until the grab is released.

void   **releaseGrabber**()
Releases the grab.

SoNode *   **getGrabber**() const
Returns the node that is currently grabbing events, or NULL if there is none.

void   **setPickRoot**(SoNode *node)
SoNode *   **getPickRoot**() const
Sets/returns the root node used for initiating a pick action for those nodes
that want to know what is under the cursor.

void   **setPickRadius**(float radiusInPixels)
Set the radius (in pixels) around the viewport-space point through which the
ray passes when doing ray picking. Ray picking is performed when
getPickedPoint() is called. The pick radius set here is used when testing the
ray against lines and points.

const SoPickedPoint *

                        getPickedPoint()
Returns the frontmost object hit (as an **SoPickedPoint**) by performing a pick
based on the mouse location specified in the event for which the action is
being applied. The first time this is called for a particular event, a
SoRayPickAction is applied to find this object; subsequent calls for the
same event return the same information. The storage for the picked point
remains valid as long as the action is not re-applied or deleted.

const SoPickedPointList &

                        getPickedPointList()
Returns a list of objects intersected by a picking operation, sorted from
nearest to farthest.

Methods from class SoAction:

apply, apply, apply, getClassTypeId, getTypeId, isOfType, invalidateState

INCLUDE FILE

```
#include <Inventor/actions/SoHandleEventAction.h>
```

SEE ALSO

SoEvent, SoPickedPoint, SoRayPickAction

NAME

SoIdleSensor — sensor for one-time only callbacks when the application is idle

INHERITS FROM

SoSensor > SoDelayQueueSensor > SoIdleSensor

DESCRIPTION

An idle sensor is almost exactly like an **SoOneShotSensor**, except that it is only triggered when there are no timer queue sensors waiting to be triggered and there are no events waiting to be processed; that is, idle sensors will not be triggered if the delay queue is processed because the delay queue timeout expires. If the delay queue timeout is disabled (see **SoDB::setDelaySensorTimeout()**.), idle and one-shot sensors are exactly the same.

Note that idle sensors do not reschedule themselves. Inventor 1 idle sensors were always scheduled; call **schedule()** in the callback function to duplicate that behavior.

See the **SoOneShotSensor** manual page for more information.

METHODS

SoIdleSensor()
SoIdleSensor(SoSensorCB *func, void *data)
Creation methods. The second method takes the callback function and data to be called when the sensor is triggered.

~SoIdleSensor()
Destroys the sensor, freeing up any memory associated with it after unscheduling it.

Methods from class SoDelayQueueSensor:

setPriority, getPriority, getDefaultPriority, schedule, unschedule, isScheduled

Methods from class SoSensor:

setFunction, getFunction, setData, getData

INCLUDE FILE

```
#include <Inventor/sensors/SoIdleSensor.h>
```

SEE ALSO

SoOneShotSensor, SoDelayQueueSensor

SoIndexedFaceSet

NAME

SoIndexedFaceSet — indexed polygonal face shape node

INHERITS FROM

SoBase > SoFieldContainer > SoNode > SoShape > SoVertexShape > SoIndexedShape > SoIndexedFaceSet

DESCRIPTION

This node represents a 3D shape formed by constructing faces (polygons) from vertices located at the current coordinates. **SoIndexedFaceSet** uses the indices in the **coordIndex** field (from **SoIndexedShape**) to specify the polygonal faces. An index of SO_END_FACE_INDEX (-1) indicates that the current face has ended and the next one begins.

The vertices of the faces are transformed by the current transformation matrix. The faces are drawn with the current light model and drawing style.

Treatment of the current material and normal binding is as follows: The PER_PART and PER_FACE bindings specify a material or normal for each face. PER_VERTEX specifies a material or normal for each vertex. The corresponding _INDEXED bindings are the same, but use the **materialIndex** or **normalIndex** indices (see **SoIndexedShape**) The DEFAULT material binding is equal to OVERALL. The DEFAULT normal binding is equal to PER_VERTEX_INDEXED; if insufficient normals exist in the state, vertex normals will be generated automatically. Textures are applied as described for the **SoIndexedShape** class.

If the current complexity value is less than 0.5, some faces will be skipped during rendering.

FIELDS

Fields from class SoIndexedShape:

> coordIndex, materialIndex, normalIndex, textureCoordIndex

METHODS

> **SoIndexedFaceSet**()
Creates an indexed face set node with default settings.

static SoType   **getClassTypeId**()
Returns type identifier for this class.

Methods from class SoNode:

> setOverride, isOverride, copy, affectsState, getByName, getByName

Methods from class SoFieldContainer:

setToDefaults, hasDefaultValues, fieldsAreEqual, copyFieldValues, set, get, getFields, getField, getFieldName, enableNotify, isNotifyEnabled

Methods from class SoBase:

ref, unref, unrefNoDelete, touch, getTypeId, isOfType, setName, getName

ACTION BEHAVIOR

SoGLRenderAction

Draws faces based on the current coordinates, normals, materials, drawing style, and so on.

SoRayPickAction

Picks faces based on the current coordinates and transformation. Details about the intersection are returned in an **SoFaceDetail**.

SoGetBoundingBoxAction

Computes the bounding box that encloses all vertices of the face set with the current transformation applied to them. Sets the center to the average of the coordinates of all vertices.

SoCallbackAction

If any triangle callbacks are registered with the action, they will be invoked for each successive triangle generated from each face in the set.

FILE FORMAT/DEFAULTS

```
IndexedFaceSet {
    coordIndex          0
    materialIndex       -1
    normalIndex         -1
    textureCoordIndex   -1
}
```

INCLUDE FILE

```
#include <Inventor/nodes/SoIndexedFaceSet.h>
```

SEE ALSO

SoCoordinate3, SoDrawStyle, SoFaceDetail, SoFaceSet

SoIndexedLineSet

NAME

SoIndexedLineSet — indexed polyline shape node

INHERITS FROM

SoBase > SoFieldContainer > SoNode > SoShape > SoVertexShape > SoIndexedShape
> SoIndexedLineSet

DESCRIPTION

This node represents a 3D shape formed by constructing polylines from vertices
located at the current coordinates. **SoIndexedLineSet** uses the indices in the
coordIndex field (from **SoIndexedShape**) to specify the polylines. An index of
SO_END_LINE_INDEX (-1) indicates that the current polyline has ended and the
next one begins.

The coordinates of the line set are transformed by the current cumulative
transformation. The lines are drawn with the current light model and drawing style
(drawing style FILLED is treated as LINES).

Treatment of the current material and normal binding is as follows: The PER_PART
binding specifies a material or normal for each segment of the line. The PER_FACE
binding specifies a material or normal for each polyline. PER_VERTEX specifies a
material or normal for each vertex. The corresponding _INDEXED bindings are the
same, but use the **materialIndex** or **normalIndex** indices (see **SoIndexedShape**)
The DEFAULT material binding is equal to OVERALL. The DEFAULT normal binding
is equal to PER_VERTEX_INDEXED; if insufficient normals exist in the state, vertex
normals will be generated automatically. Textures are applied as described for the
SoIndexedShape class.

The current complexity value has no effect on the rendering of indexed line sets.

FIELDS

Fields from class SoIndexedShape:

coordIndex, materialIndex, normalIndex, textureCoordIndex

METHODS

SoIndexedLineSet()
Creates an indexed line set node with default settings.

static SoType   **getClassTypeId()**
Returns type identifier for this class.

Methods from class SoNode:

setOverride, isOverride, copy, affectsState, getByName, getByName

Methods from class SoFieldContainer:

> setToDefaults, hasDefaultValues, fieldsAreEqual, copyFieldValues, set, get, getFields, getField, getFieldName, enableNotify, isNotifyEnabled

Methods from class SoBase:

> ref, unref, unrefNoDelete, touch, getTypeId, isOfType, setName, getName

ACTION BEHAVIOR

SoGLRenderAction

Draws lines based on the current coordinates, normals, materials, drawing style, and so on.

SoRayPickAction

Picks lines based on the current coordinates and transformation. Details about the intersection are returned in an **SoLineDetail**.

SoGetBoundingBoxAction

Computes the bounding box that encloses all vertices of the line set with the current transformation applied to them. Sets the center to the average of the coordinates of all vertices.

SoCallbackAction

If any line segment callbacks are registered with the action, they will be invoked for each successive segment in the line set.

FILE FORMAT/DEFAULTS

```
IndexedLineSet {
        coordIndex          0
        materialIndex       -1
        normalIndex         -1
        textureCoordIndex   -1
}
```

INCLUDE FILE

```
#include <Inventor/nodes/SoIndexedLineSet.h>
```

SEE ALSO

SoCoordinate3, SoDrawStyle, SoLineDetail, SoLineSet

NAME

SoIndexedNurbsCurve — indexed NURBS curve shape node

INHERITS FROM

SoBase > SoFieldContainer > SoNode > SoShape > SoIndexedNurbsCurve

DESCRIPTION

This class represents a NURBS curve based on the knot vector and the control points that you specify. The **knotVector** field specifies a floating-point array of values; the values are the coordinates of the knot points in the curve, and you must enter them in non-decreasing order. The **numControlPoints** field specifies the number of control points the curve will have and will use the current coordinates that are indexed from the **coordIndex** field.

You can get a curve of minimum order (2) by specifying two more knots than control points and having at least two control points. This curve would be a set of line segments connecting the control points together.

You can get a curve of maximum order (8) by specifying 8 more knots than control points and having at least 8 control points. In this curve, each control point would have influence on a larger portion of the curve than with curves of lesser order.

The control points of the curve are transformed by the current transformation matrix. The curve is drawn with the current lighting model and drawing style (drawing style FILLED is treated as LINES). The coordinates, normals, and texture coordinates of a NURBS curve are generated, so you cannot bind explicit normals or texture coordinates to a NURBS curve.

The approximation of the curve by line segments is affected by the current complexity value.

FIELDS

SoSFLong   **numControlPoints**
Number of control points for the curve.

SoMFLong   **coordIndex**
Coordinate indices for the control points.

SoMFFloat   **knotVector**
The knot vector for the curve. Values must be in non-decreasing order.

METHODS

SoIndexedNurbsCurve()
Creates an indexed NURBS curve node with default settings.

static SoType   **getClassTypeId()**
Returns type identifier for this class.

Methods from class SoNode:
setOverride, isOverride, copy, affectsState, getByName, getByName

Methods from class SoFieldContainer:
setToDefaults, hasDefaultValues, fieldsAreEqual, copyFieldValues, set, get, getFields, getField, getFieldName, enableNotify, isNotifyEnabled

Methods from class SoBase:
ref, unref, unrefNoDelete, touch, getTypeId, isOfType, setName, getName

ACTION BEHAVIOR

SoGLRenderAction
Draws the curve based on the current coordinates, material, and so on.

SoRayPickAction
Picks the curve based on the current coordinates and transformation.

SoGetBoundingBoxAction
Computes the bounding box that encloses all control points of the curve with the current transformation applied to them. Sets the center to the average of the control points.

SoCallbackAction
If any line segment callbacks are registered with the action, they will be invoked for each successive segment approximating the curve.

FILE FORMAT/DEFAULTS

```
IndexedNurbsCurve {
     numControlPoints   0
     coordIndex         0
     knotVector         0
}
```

SoIndexedNurbsCurve

INCLUDE FILE

        #include <Inventor/nodes/SoIndexedNurbsCurve.h>

SEE ALSO

SoNurbsCurve, SoIndexedNurbsSurface

NAME

SoIndexedNurbsSurface — indexed NURBS surface shape node

INHERITS FROM

SoBase > SoFieldContainer > SoNode > SoShape > SoIndexedNurbsSurface

DESCRIPTION

This shape node represents a NURBS surface based on the knot vectors and the control points that you specify. The **uKnotVector** and **vKnotVector** fields specify floating-point arrays of values; the values are the coordinates of the knot points in the surface, and you must enter them in non-decreasing order. The **numUControlPoints** and **numVControlPoints** fields specify the number of control points the surface will have in the U and V parametric directions, and will use the current coordinates that are indexed from the **coordIndex** field.

You can get a surface of minimum order (2) in the U or V directions by specifying two more knots than control points in that direction and having at least two control points in that direction. This surface would appear creased in one direction.

You can get a surface of maximum order (8) in the U or V directions by specifying eight more knots than control points in that direction and having at least eight control points in that direction.

The control points of the NURBS surface are transformed by the current cumulative transformation. The surface is drawn with the current light model and drawing style. The coordinates, normals, and texture coordinates of a surface are generated, so you cannot bind explicit normals or texture coordinates to a NURBS surface. The first material in the state is applied to the entire surface.

The surface is trimmed according to the currently defined profiles curves.

When default texture coordinates are applied to a NURBS surface, the edges of the texture square are stretched to fit the surface. The axes of the texture are called S and T; S is horizontal and T is vertical. The axes of the NURBS surface are called U and V; U is horizontal and V is vertical. You can also define texture coordinates explicitly with the S,T location point, the knot vectors, and the current texture coordinates.

FIELDS

SoSFLong   **numUControlPoints**
SoSFLong   **numVControlPoints**
Number of control points in the U and V directions.

SoMFLong   **coordIndex**
Coordinate indices.

SoMFFloat   **uKnotVector**
SoMFFloat   **vKnotVector**
The knot vectors in the U and V directions.

SoSFLong   **numSControlPoints**
SoSFLong   **numTControlPoints**
Number of control points in the S and T directions.

SoMFLong   **textureCoordIndex**
Texture coordinate indices.

SoMFFloat   **sKnotVector**
SoMFFloat   **tKnotVector**
The knot vectors in the S and T directions.

METHODS

SoIndexedNurbsSurface()
Creates an indexed NURBS surface node with default settings.

static SoType   **getClassTypeId()**
Returns type identifier for this class.

Methods from class SoNode:

setOverride, isOverride, copy, affectsState, getByName, getByName

Methods from class SoFieldContainer:

setToDefaults, hasDefaultValues, fieldsAreEqual, copyFieldValues, set, get, getFields, getField, getFieldName, enableNotify, isNotifyEnabled

Methods from class SoBase:

ref, unref, unrefNoDelete, touch, getTypeId, isOfType, setName, getName

ACTION BEHAVIOR

SoGLRenderAction
Draws the surface based on the current coordinates, material, and so on.

SoRayPickAction
Picks the surface based on the current coordinates and transformation.

SoGetBoundingBoxAction

Computes the bounding box that encloses all control points of the surface with the current transformation applied to them. Sets the center to the average of the control points.

SoCallbackAction

If any triangle callbacks are registered with the action, they will be invoked for each successive triangle approximating the surface.

FILE FORMAT/DEFAULTS

```
IndexedNurbsSurface {
        numUControlPoints   0
        numVControlPoints   0
        numSControlPoints   0
        numTControlPoints   0
        coordIndex          0
        uKnotVector         0
        vKnotVector         0
        sKnotVector         0
        tKnotVector         0
        textureCoordIndex   -1
}
```

INCLUDE FILE

```
#include <Inventor/nodes/SoIndexedNurbsSurface.h>
```

SEE ALSO

SoIndexedNurbsCurve, SoNurbsSurface, SoProfile

NAME

SoIndexedShape — abstract base class for all indexed vertex-based shapes

INHERITS FROM

SoBase > SoFieldContainer > SoNode > SoShape > SoVertexShape > SoIndexedShape

DESCRIPTION

This node is the abstract base class for all vertex-based shapes that are constructed from indices, including **SoIndexedFaceSet**, **SoIndexedTriangleStripSet**, and **SoIndexedLineSet**. **SoIndexedShape** defines fields that are used in all of its subclasses.

All subclasses of **SoNonIndexedShape** construct objects by using the current coordinates as the object's vertices. The **coordIndex** field defined by this class contains the indices into the current coordinates of the vertices of the shape. These indices are also used for materials, normals, or texture coordinates when the appropriate binding is PER_VERTEX_INDEXED.

Material and normal bindings are interpreted as follows for each subclass:

OVERALL	One material for the entire shape.
PER_PART	Specific to the subclass.
PER_PART_INDEXED	Same as PER_PART, using indices from the **materialIndex** or **normalIndex** field.
PER_FACE	Specific to the subclass.
PER_FACE_INDEXED	Same as PER_FACE, using indices from the **materialIndex** or **normalIndex** field.
PER_VERTEX	One material per vertex.
PER_VERTEX_INDEXED	One material per vertex, using indices from the **materialIndex** or **normalIndex** field.
DEFAULT	Same as OVERALL for materials, or PER_VERTEX_INDEXED for normals.

When any _INDEXED binding is used for materials or normals, the **materialIndex** or **normalIndex** field is used to determine the indices for the materials or normals. If this field contains a single value of -1 (the default), the coordinate indices from the **coordIndex** field are used as well for materials or normals. When the binding is PER_VERTEX_INDEXED, indices in these fields that correspond to negative indices in **coordIndex** are skipped; for other index bindings all the values in the fields are used, in order.

When the normal binding is DEFAULT and there aren't enough normals in the current state to be applied to each vertex, default normals are created. The **creaseAngle** field of the **SoShapeHints** node guides this process.

Explicit texture coordinates (as defined by **SoTextureCoordinate2**) may be bound to vertices of an indexed shape consecutively (if the texture coordinate binding is PER_VERTEX) or by using the indices in the **textureCoordIndex** field (if the binding is PER_VERTEX_INDEXED). As with all vertex-based shapes, if there is a current texture but no texture coordinates are specified, a default texture coordinate mapping is calculated using the bounding box of the shape.

Be sure that the indices contained in the **coordIndex**, **materialIndex**, **normalIndex**, and **textureCoordIndex** fields are valid with respect to the current state, or errors will occur.

FIELDS

SoMFLong   **coordIndex**

The indices of the coordinates that the shape uses as its vertices. The coordinates connect to form faces, lines, or other shapes. Each subclass defines special negative indices to use to indicate separation between faces, lines, and so on.

SoMFLong   **materialIndex**
SoMFLong   **normalIndex**
SoMFLong   **textureCoordIndex**

The indices of the materials, normals, and texture coordinates that are used for the shape. These fields are used only when the appropriate binding is one of the _INDEXED bindings. By default, the values of these fields indicate that the coordinate indices should be used for materials, normals, or texture coordinates as well.

METHODS

static SoType   **getClassTypeId**()
Returns type identifier for this class.

Methods from class SoNode:

setOverride, isOverride, copy, affectsState, getByName, getByName

Methods from class SoFieldContainer:

setToDefaults, hasDefaultValues, fieldsAreEqual, copyFieldValues, set, get, getFields, getField, getFieldName, enableNotify, isNotifyEnabled

Methods from class SoBase:

ref, unref, unrefNoDelete, touch, getTypeId, isOfType, setName, getName

FILE FORMAT/DEFAULTS

This is an abstract class. See the reference page of a derived class for the format and default values.

INCLUDE FILE

```
#include <Inventor/nodes/SoIndexedShape.h>
```

SEE ALSO

SoIndexedFaceSet, SoIndexedLineSet, SoIndexedTriangleStripSet, SoMaterialBinding, SoNonIndexedShape, SoNormalBinding, SoShapeHints, SoTextureCoordinateBinding

NAME

SoIndexedTriangleStripSet — indexed triangle strip set shape node

INHERITS FROM

SoBase > SoFieldContainer > SoNode > SoShape > SoVertexShape > SoIndexedShape > SoIndexedTriangleStripSet

DESCRIPTION

This shape node constructs triangle strips out of vertices located at the current coordinates. **SoIndexedTriangleStripSet** uses the indices in the **coordIndex** field (from **SoIndexedShape**) to specify the vertices of the triangle strips. An index of SO_END_STRIP_INDEX (-1) indicates that the current strip has ended and the next one begins.

The vertices of the faces are transformed by the current transformation matrix. The faces are drawn with the current light model and drawing style.

Treatment of the current material and normal binding is as follows: PER_PART specifies a material or normal per strip. PER_FACE binding specifies a material or normal for each triangle. PER_VERTEX specifies a material or normal for each vertex. The corresponding _INDEXED bindings are the same, but use the **materialIndex** or **normalIndex** indices (see **SoIndexedShape**) The DEFAULT material binding is equal to OVERALL. The DEFAULT normal binding is equal to PER_VERTEX_INDEXED; if insufficient normals exist in the state, vertex normals will be generated automatically. Textures are applied as described for the **SoIndexedShape** class.

If the current complexity value is less than 0.5, some strips will be skipped during rendering.

FIELDS

Fields from class SoIndexedShape:

coordIndex, materialIndex, normalIndex, textureCoordIndex

METHODS

SoIndexedTriangleStripSet()
Creates an indexed triangle strip set node with default settings.

static SoType   **getClassTypeId()**
Returns type identifier for this class.

Methods from class SoNode:

setOverride, isOverride, copy, affectsState, getByName, getByName

Methods from class SoFieldContainer:

setToDefaults, hasDefaultValues, fieldsAreEqual, copyFieldValues, set, get, getFields, getField, getFieldName, enableNotify, isNotifyEnabled

Methods from class SoBase:

ref, unref, unrefNoDelete, touch, getTypeId, isOfType, setName, getName

ACTION BEHAVIOR

SoGLRenderAction

Draws a strip set based on the current coordinates, normals, materials, drawing style, and so on.

SoRayPickAction

Picks on the strip set based on the current coordinates and transformation. Details about the intersection are returned in an **SoFaceDetail**.

SoGetBoundingBoxAction

Computes the bounding box that encloses all vertices of the strip set with the current transformation applied to them. Sets the center to the average of the coordinates of all vertices.

SoCallbackAction

If any triangle callbacks are registered with the action, they will be invoked for each successive triangle forming the strips of the set.

FILE FORMAT/DEFAULTS

```
IndexedTriangleStripSet {
    coordIndex          0
    materialIndex       -1
    normalIndex         -1
    textureCoordIndex   -1
}
```

INCLUDE FILE

```
#include <Inventor/nodes/SoIndexedTriangleStripSet.h>
```

SEE ALSO

SoCoordinate3, SoDrawStyle, SoFaceDetail, SoIndexedFaceSet, SoTriangleStripSet

NAME

SoInfo — node containing information text string

INHERITS FROM

SoBase > SoFieldContainer > SoNode > SoInfo

DESCRIPTION

This class defines a information node in the scene graph. This node has no effect during traversal. It is used to store information in the scene graph, typically for application-specific purposes, copyright messages, or other strings. This node differs from the **SoLabel** node in that it stores its information in an **SbString** instead of an **SbName**; the **SbString** is more efficient for storing long strings that don't have to be accessed very often. Use an **SoLabel** node for short strings that have to be accessed more often.

FIELDS

SoSFString   **string**

Defines the info string value as an **SbString**.

METHODS

                  SoInfo()

Creates an info node with default settings.

static SoType   **getClassTypeId**()

Returns type identifier for this class.

Methods from class SoNode:

setOverride, isOverride, copy, affectsState, getByName, getByName

Methods from class SoFieldContainer:

setToDefaults, hasDefaultValues, fieldsAreEqual, copyFieldValues, set, get, getFields, getField, getFieldName, enableNotify, isNotifyEnabled

Methods from class SoBase:

ref, unref, unrefNoDelete, touch, getTypeId, isOfType, setName, getName

FILE FORMAT/DEFAULTS

```
Info {
      string   "<Undefined info>"
}
```

INCLUDE FILE

```
#include <Inventor/nodes/SoInfo.h>
```

SEE ALSO

SbString, SoLabel

NAME

SoInput — used to read Inventor data files

INHERITS FROM

SoInput

DESCRIPTION

This class is used by the **SoDB** reading routines when reading Inventor data files. It supports both ASCII (default) and binary Inventor formats. It skips over Inventor comments (from '#' to end of line) and can stack input files. When EOF is reached, the stack is popped. This class can also be used to read from a buffer in memory.

METHODS

SoInput()
~SoInput()

Constructor and destructor. The default **SoInput** reads from **stdin**. The destructor closes any files opened by the **SoInput**.

static void	**addDirectoryFirst**(const char *dirName)
static void	**addDirectoryLast**(const char *dirName)
static void	**addEnvDirectoriesFirst**(const char *envVarName)
static void	**addEnvDirectoriesLast**(const char *envVarName)

The **SoInput** class maintains a global list of directories that is searched to find files when opening them. Directories are searched in order. Each of these routines adds directories to the list, either at the beginning ("First") or the end ("Last"). The last two routines add directories named in the value of the given environment variable. Directories may be separated by colons or whitespace in the variable's value.

static void   **removeDirectory**(const char *dirName)
Removes named directory from the list.

static void   **clearDirectories**()
Clears the list of directories (including the current directory).

static const SbStringList &
                   getDirectories()
Returns the list of directories as an **SbStringList**.

void   **setFilePointer**(FILE *newFP)
Sets file pointer to read from. Clears the stack of input files if necessary.

SbBool   **openFile**(const char *fileName, SbBool okIfNotFound = FALSE)
Opens named file, sets file pointer to result. Clears the stack of input files if necessary. This returns FALSE on error; if *okIfNotFound* is FALSE (the default), this prints an error message if the file could not be found.

SbBool   **pushFile**(const char *fileName)
Opens named file, pushing the resulting file pointer onto the stack. Returns FALSE on error.

       closeFile()
Closes all files on stack opened with **openFile**() or **pushFile**().

SbBool   **isValidFile**()
Returns TRUE if the currently open file is a valid Inventor file; that is, it begins with a valid Inventor header.

FILE *   **getCurFile**() const
Returns a pointer to the current file, or NULL if reading from a buffer.

const char *   **getCurFileName**() const
Returns full name (including directory path) of current file, or NULL if reading from a buffer.

void   **setBuffer**(void *bufPointer, size_t bufSize)
Sets an in-memory buffer to read from, along with its size.

INCLUDE FILE

```
#include <Inventor/SoInput.h>
```

SEE ALSO

SoDB, SoOutput, SoTranReceiver

SoInteraction

NAME

SoInteraction — initializes Inventor interaction classes

INHERITS FROM

SoInteraction

DESCRIPTION

SoInteraction consists of one static function which initializes all Inventor interaction classes, as well as nodekits and the database. Note that **SoInteraction::init()** is already called by **SoXt::init()**.

METHODS

static void　　　　**init**()

This calls **SoDB::init()** and **SoNodeKit::init()**, calls **initClasses()** on **SoDragger**, and calls **initClass()** on the following classes: **SoAntiSquish**, **SoBoxHighlightRenderAction, SoCenterballManip, SoDirectionalLightManip, SoHandleBoxManip, SoInteractionKit, SoJackManip, SoLineHighlightRenderAction, SoPointLightManip, SoSelection, SoSpotLightManip, SoSurroundScale, SoTabBoxManip, SoTrackballManip, SoTransformBoxManip**, and **SoTransformManip**.

INCLUDE FILE

```
#include <Inventor/SoInteraction.h>
```

SEE ALSO

SoDB, SoNodeKit, SoXt

NAME

SoInteractionKit — base class for all interaction nodekit classes

INHERITS FROM

SoBase > SoFieldContainer > SoNode > SoBaseKit > SoInteractionKit

DESCRIPTION

This is the base class for all classes of interaction nodekits. Currently, the only subclass is **SoDragger**, which reacts to click-drag-release events from the mouse.

This node has four fields corresponding to those of an **SoSeparator**: They are **renderCaching**, **boundingBoxCaching**, **renderCulling**, and **pickCulling**. They behave the same here as they do for an **SoSeparator**

The **setPartAsPath**() method provides support for creating "stand-in" objects for parts in the interaction kit. The "stand-in", or "surrogate" part, is a path to an object that lies somewhere else in the scene graph.

FIELDS

SoSFEnum   **renderCaching**
Set render caching mode. Default is AUTO.

SoSFEnum   **boundingBoxCaching**
Set bounding box caching mode. Default is ON. Setting this value to AUTO is equivalent to ON - automatic culling is not implemented.

SoSFEnum   **renderCulling**
Set render culling mode. Default is OFF. Setting this value to AUTO is equivalent to ON - automatic culling is not implemented.

SoSFEnum   **pickCulling**
Set pick caching mode. Default is AUTO.

PARTS

Parts from class SoBaseKit:

callbackList

METHODS

                         SoInteractionKit()
Constructor.

virtual SbBool   **setPartAsPath**(const SbName &partName, SoPath
                   *surrogatePath)
Sets any public part in the interaction kit as a "surrogate" path instead. The object at the end of the path serves as a stand-in when a pick occurs, and can thus initiate interaction.

Instead of the usual **setPart()**, which replaces *partName* with a new node, this will remove the node being used for *partName* from the scene and remember the *surrogatePath* you give it. Later, any pick on *surrogatePath* will be regarded as a pick on *partName*.

For example, set the *XRotator* part of an **SoTrackballDragger** to be the path to an object in the scene. The rest of the trackball will look the same, but the *XRotator* stripe will disappear. However, click the mouse on the object at the end of *surrogatePath* and the ball will start to drag in rotation around its X axis.

Note that this is different from setting the part to be the node at the end of the path. When you set the part as a node, a second instance will be drawn in the local space of the interaction kit. When you set it as a path, the object itself is used, not a copy.

The *partName* may be any part name that follows the nodekit syntax for parts, such as *childList[0].shape* or *rotator.rotatorActive*. (See the **getPart()** method in the **SoBaseKit** reference page for a complete description.)

static const SoNodekitCatalog *
           getClassNodekitCatalog() const
Returns an **SoNodekitCatalog** for the class **SoInteractionKit**.

static SoType   **getClassTypeId**()
Returns type identifier for this class.

Methods from class SoBaseKit:

getNodekitCatalog, getPart, getPartString, createPathToPart, setPart, set, set, isSearchingChildren, setSearchingChildren

Methods from class SoNode:

setOverride, isOverride, copy, affectsState, getByName, getByName

Methods from class SoFieldContainer:

setToDefaults, hasDefaultValues, fieldsAreEqual, copyFieldValues, get, getFields, getField, getFieldName, enableNotify, isNotifyEnabled

Methods from class SoBase:

ref, unref, unrefNoDelete, touch, getTypeId, isOfType, setName, getName

MACROS

Macros from class SoBaseKit:

SO_GET_PART, SO_CHECK_PART

CATALOG PARTS

All parts			
Part Name	**Part Type**	**Default Type**	**NULL by Default**
callbackList	NodeKitListPart	--	yes

Extra information for list parts from above table		
Part Name	**Container Type**	**Permissible Types**
callbackList	Separator	Callback, EventCallback

FILE FORMAT/DEFAULTS

```
InteractionKit {
        renderCaching          AUTO
        boundingBoxCaching     AUTO
        renderCulling          AUTO
        pickCulling            AUTO
}
```

INCLUDE FILE

```
#include <Inventor/nodekits/SoInteractionKit.h>
```

enum **CacheEnabled** {

SoInteractionKit::OFF	Never build or use a cache
SoInteractionKit::ON	Always try to build a cache
SoInteractionKit::AUTO	Automatic caching

}

SEE ALSO

SoBaseKit, SoInteraction, SoNodeKitDetail, SoNodeKitPath, SoNodekitCatalog, SoDragger, SoCenterballDragger, SoDirectionalLightDragger, SoDragPointDragger, SoHandleBoxDragger, SoJackDragger, SoPointLightDragger, SoRotateCylindricalDragger, SoRotateDiscDragger, SoRotateSphericalDragger, SoScale1Dragger, SoScale2Dragger, SoScale2UniformDragger, SoScaleUniformDragger, SoSpotLightDragger, SoTabBoxDragger, SoTabPlaneDragger, SoTrackballDragger, SoTransformBoxDragger, SoTranslate1Dragger, SoTranslate2Dragger

NAME

SoInterpolate — base class for all interpolator engines

INHERITS FROM

SoBase > SoFieldContainer > SoEngine > SoInterpolate

DESCRIPTION

SoInterpolate is the abstract base class for all interpolator engines. An interpolator engine linearly interpolates between two values, based on the **alpha** input value. The **alpha** value should be between 0.0 and 1.0. The interpolator engines derived from this class define the input fields that are to be interpolated.

INPUTS

SoSFFloat   **alpha**
> Interpolation control value.

OUTPUTS

(SoMFFloat)   **output**
> Interpolated value. The type of the output value is the same as the type of the input values, which is specified by the derived classes.

METHODS

Methods from class SoEngine:

> getClassTypeId, getOutputs, getOutput, getOutputName, copy, getByName, getByName

Methods from class SoFieldContainer:

> setToDefaults, hasDefaultValues, fieldsAreEqual, copyFieldValues, set, get, getFields, getField, getFieldName, enableNotify, isNotifyEnabled

Methods from class SoBase:

> ref, unref, unrefNoDelete, touch, getTypeId, isOfType, setName, getName

FILE FORMAT/DEFAULTS

This is an abstract class. See the man page of a derived class for the format and default values.

INCLUDE FILE

```
#include <Inventor/engines/SoInterpolate.h>
```

SEE ALSO

SoEngineOutput, SoInterpolateFloat, SoInterpolateRotation, SoInterpolateVec2f, SoInterpolateVec3f, SoInterpolateVec4f

NAME

SoInterpolateFloat — interpolates floating-point values

INHERITS FROM

SoBase > SoFieldContainer > SoEngine > SoInterpolate > SoInterpolateFloat

DESCRIPTION

This engine linearly interpolates between two floating-point values, based on the **alpha** input value. The **alpha** value should be between 0.0 and 1.0.

The input fields can have multiple values, allowing the engine to interpolate several objects in parallel. One of the inputs may have more values than the other. In that case, the last value of the shorter input will be repeated as necessary.

INPUTS

SoMFFloat	**input0**
SoMFFloat	**input1**

The engine linearly interpolates from **input0** to **input1**.

Inputs from class SoInterpolate:

alpha

OUTPUTS

Outputs from class SoInterpolate:

output

METHODS

SoInterpolateFloat()
Constructor.

Methods from class SoEngine:

getClassTypeId, getOutputs, getOutput, getOutputName, copy, getByName, getByName

Methods from class SoFieldContainer:

setToDefaults, hasDefaultValues, fieldsAreEqual, copyFieldValues, set, get, getFields, getField, getFieldName, enableNotify, isNotifyEnabled

Methods from class SoBase:

ref, unref, unrefNoDelete, touch, getTypeId, isOfType, setName, getName

SoInterpolateFloat

FILE FORMAT/DEFAULTS

```
InterpolateFloat {
        alpha   0
        input0  0
        input1  1
}
```

INCLUDE FILE

```
#include <Inventor/engines/SoInterpolate.h>
```

SEE ALSO

SoEngineOutput, SoInterpolateRotation, SoInterpolateVec2f, SoInterpolateVec3f, SoInterpolateVec4f

NAME

SoInterpolateRotation — interpolates rotation values

INHERITS FROM

SoBase > SoFieldContainer > SoEngine > SoInterpolate > SoInterpolateRotation

DESCRIPTION

This engine linearly interpolates between two rotation values, based on the **alpha** input value. The **alpha** value should be between 0.0 and 1.0.

The input fields can have multiple rotations, allowing the engine to interpolate several objects in parallel. One of the inputs may have more values than the other. In that case, the last value of the shorter input will be repeated as necessary.

INPUTS

SoMFRotation   **input0**
SoMFRotation   **input1**
        The engine linearly interpolates from **input0** to **input1**.

Inputs from class SoInterpolate:

        alpha

OUTPUTS

Outputs from class SoInterpolate:

        output

METHODS

                        SoInterpolateRotation()
        Constructor.

Methods from class SoEngine:

        getClassTypeId, getOutputs, getOutput, getOutputName, copy, getByName, getByName

Methods from class SoFieldContainer:

        setToDefaults, hasDefaultValues, fieldsAreEqual, copyFieldValues, set, get, getFields, getField, getFieldName, enableNotify, isNotifyEnabled

Methods from class SoBase:

        ref, unref, unrefNoDelete, touch, getTypeId, isOfType, setName, getName

SoInterpolateRotation

FILE FORMAT/DEFAULTS

```
InterpolateRotation {
    alpha    0
    input0   0 0 1  0
    input1   0 0 1  0
}
```

INCLUDE FILE

```
#include <Inventor/engines/SoInterpolate.h>
```

SEE ALSO

SoEngineOutput, SoInterpolateFloat, SoInterpolateVec2f, SoInterpolateVec3f,
SoInterpolateVec4f

NAME

SoInterpolateVec2f — interpolates 2D floating-point vectors

INHERITS FROM

SoBase > SoFieldContainer > SoEngine > SoInterpolate > SoInterpolateVec2f

DESCRIPTION

This engine linearly interpolates between two 2D vectors, based on the **alpha** input value. The **alpha** value should be between 0.0 and 1.0.

The input fields can have multiple vectors, allowing the engine to interpolate several objects in parallel. One of the inputs may have more values than the other. In that case, the last value of the shorter input will be repeated as necessary.

INPUTS

SoMFVec2f   **input0**
SoMFVec2f   **input1**
The engine linearly interpolates from **input0** to **input1**.

Inputs from class SoInterpolate:

alpha

OUTPUTS

Outputs from class SoInterpolate:

output

METHODS

SoInterpolateVec2f()
Constructor.

Methods from class SoEngine:

getClassTypeId, getOutputs, getOutput, getOutputName, copy, getByName, getByName

Methods from class SoFieldContainer:

setToDefaults, hasDefaultValues, fieldsAreEqual, copyFieldValues, set, get, getFields, getField, getFieldName, enableNotify, isNotifyEnabled

Methods from class SoBase:

ref, unref, unrefNoDelete, touch, getTypeId, isOfType, setName, getName

FILE FORMAT/DEFAULTS

```
InterpolateVec2f {
    alpha    0
    input0   0 0
    input1   0 0
}
```

INCLUDE FILE

```
#include <Inventor/engines/SoInterpolate.h>
```

SEE ALSO

SoEngineOutput, SoInterpolateFloat, SoInterpolateRotation, SoInterpolateVec3f, SoInterpolateVec4f

NAME

SoInterpolateVec3f — interpolates 3D floating-point vectors

INHERITS FROM

SoBase > SoFieldContainer > SoEngine > SoInterpolate > SoInterpolateVec3f

DESCRIPTION

This engine linearly interpolates between two 3D vectors, based on the **alpha** input value. The **alpha** value should be between 0.0 and 1.0.

The input fields can have multiple vectors, allowing the engine to interpolate several objects in parallel. One of the inputs may have more values than the other. In that case, the last value of the shorter input will be repeated as necessary.

INPUTS

SoMFVec3f   **input0**
SoMFVec3f   **input1**

The engine linearly interpolates from **input0** to **input1**.

Inputs from class SoInterpolate:

alpha

OUTPUTS

Outputs from class SoInterpolate:

output

METHODS

SoInterpolateVec3f()
Constructor.

Methods from class SoEngine:

getClassTypeId, getOutputs, getOutput, getOutputName, copy, getByName, getByName

Methods from class SoFieldContainer:

setToDefaults, hasDefaultValues, fieldsAreEqual, copyFieldValues, set, get, getFields, getField, getFieldName, enableNotify, isNotifyEnabled

Methods from class SoBase:

ref, unref, unrefNoDelete, touch, getTypeId, isOfType, setName, getName

SoInterpolateVec3f

FILE FORMAT/DEFAULTS

```
InterpolateVec3f {
      alpha    0
      input0   0 0 0
      input1   0 0 0
}
```

INCLUDE FILE

```
#include <Inventor/engines/SoInterpolate.h>
```

SEE ALSO

SoEngineOutput, SoInterpolateFloat, SoInterpolateRotation, SoInterpolateVec2f, SoInterpolateVec4f

NAME

SoInterpolateVec4f — interpolates 4D floating-point vectors

INHERITS FROM

SoBase > SoFieldContainer > SoEngine > SoInterpolate > SoInterpolateVec4f

DESCRIPTION

This engine linearly interpolates between two 4D vectors, based on the **alpha** input value. The **alpha** value should be between 0.0 and 1.0.

The input fields can have multiple vectors, allowing the engine to interpolate several objects in parallel. One of the inputs may have more values than the other. In that case, the last value of the shorter input will be repeated as necessary.

INPUTS

SoMFVec4f   **input0**
SoMFVec4f   **input1**

The engine linearly interpolates from **input0** to **input1**.

Inputs from class SoInterpolate:

alpha

OUTPUTS

Outputs from class SoInterpolate:

output

METHODS

SoInterpolateVec4f()

Constructor.

Methods from class SoEngine:

getClassTypeId, getOutputs, getOutput, getOutputName, copy, getByName, getByName

Methods from class SoFieldContainer:

setToDefaults, hasDefaultValues, fieldsAreEqual, copyFieldValues, set, get, getFields, getField, getFieldName, enableNotify, isNotifyEnabled

Methods from class SoBase:

ref, unref, unrefNoDelete, touch, getTypeId, isOfType, setName, getName

SoInterpolateVec4f

FILE FORMAT/DEFAULTS

```
InterpolateVec4f {
      alpha   0
      input0  0 0 0 0
      input1  0 0 0 0
}
```

INCLUDE FILE

```
#include <Inventor/engines/SoInterpolate.h>
```

SEE ALSO

SoEngineOutput, SoInterpolateFloat, SoInterpolateRotation, SoInterpolateVec2f, SoInterpolateVec3f

NAME

SoJackDragger — jack-shaped object you rotate, translate, or scale by dragging with the mouse

INHERITS FROM

SoBase > SoFieldContainer > SoNode > SoBaseKit > SoInteractionKit > SoDragger > SoJackDragger

DESCRIPTION

SoJackDragger is a composite dragger in the shape of a jack from the children's game jacks. Three lines along the x, y, and z axes form the central star shape, which you can drag with the mouse to rotate the jack. Dragging any of the small cubes mounted at the end of the axes will scale the jack uniformly in all 3 dimensions. At the core of the jack is an **SoDragPointDragger** for translating the jack.

Each of these shapes is a different dragger with the default geometry changed. All of them are parts of the jack dragger, which keeps them moving together. The star is an **SoRotateSphericalDragger**, and dragging it updates the **rotation** field of the jack dragger. The small cubes are an **SoScaleUniformDragger**, tied to the **scaleFactor** field. The position of the **SoDragPointDragger** is given by the **translation** field. As with all draggers, if you change the fields the dragger will move to match the new settings.

Remember: This is *not* an **SoTransform**!. If you want to move other objects with this dragger, you can either:

[a] Use an **SoJackManip**, which is subclassed from **SoTransform**. It creates one of these draggers and uses it as the interface to change its fields. (see the **SoJackManip** man page).

[b] Use field-to-field connections to connect the fields of this dragger to those of any **SoTransformation** node.

You can change the parts in any instance of this dragger using **setPart()**. The default part geometries are defined as resources for this **SoJackDragger** class. They are detailed in the Dragger Resources section of the online reference page for this class. You can make your program use different default resources for the parts by copying the file **/usr/share/data/draggerDefaults/jackDragger.iv** into your own directory, editing the file, and then setting the environment variable **SO_DRAGGER_DIR** to be a path to that directory.

FIELDS

SoSFRotation   **rotation**

    Orientation of the dragger.

SoSFVec3f   **scaleFactor**
Scale of the dragger.

SoSFVec3f   **translation**
Position of the dragger.

Fields from class SoDragger:
isActive

Fields from class SoInteractionKit:
renderCaching, boundingBoxCaching, renderCulling, pickCulling

PARTS

Parts from class SoBaseKit:
callbackList

METHODS

SoJackDragger()
Constructor.

static const SoNodekitCatalog *
getClassNodekitCatalog() const
Returns an **SoNodekitCatalog** for this class

static SoType   **getClassTypeId**()
Returns type identifier for this class.

Methods from class SoDragger:
addStartCallback, removeStartCallback, addMotionCallback, removeMotionCallback, addFinishCallback, removeFinishCallback, addValueChangedCallback, removeValueChangedCallback, setMinGesture, getMinGesture, setMinScale, getMinScale

Methods from class SoInteractionKit:
setPartAsPath

Methods from class SoBaseKit:
getNodekitCatalog, getPart, getPartString, createPathToPart, setPart, set, set, isSearchingChildren, setSearchingChildren

Methods from class SoNode:
setOverride, isOverride, copy, affectsState, getByName, getByName

Methods from class SoFieldContainer:

> setToDefaults, hasDefaultValues, fieldsAreEqual, copyFieldValues, get, getFields, getField, getFieldName, enableNotify, isNotifyEnabled

Methods from class SoBase:

> ref, unref, unrefNoDelete, touch, getTypeId, isOfType, setName, getName

MACROS

Macros from class SoBaseKit:

> SO_GET_PART, SO_CHECK_PART

CATALOG PARTS

All parts			
Part Name	**Part Type**	**Default Type**	**NULL by Default**
callbackList	NodeKitListPart	--	yes
surroundScale	SurroundScale	--	yes
antiSquish	AntiSquish	--	no
scaler	ScaleUniformDragger	--	yes
rotator	RotateSphericalDragger	--	yes
translator	DragPointDragger	--	yes

Extra information for list parts from above table		
Part Name	**Container Type**	**Permissible Types**
callbackList	Separator	Callback, EventCallback

FILE FORMAT/DEFAULTS

```
JackDragger {
      renderCaching        AUTO
      boundingBoxCaching   AUTO
      renderCulling        AUTO
      pickCulling          AUTO
      isActive             FALSE
      rotation             0 0 1  0
      translation          0 0 0
      scaleFactor          1 1 1
}
```

INCLUDE FILE

```
#include <Inventor/draggers/SoJackDragger.h>
```

SEE ALSO

SoInteractionKit, SoDragger, SoCenterballDragger, SoDirectionalLightDragger, SoDragPointDragger, SoHandleBoxDragger, SoPointLightDragger, SoRotateCylindricalDragger, SoRotateDiscDragger, SoRotateSphericalDragger, SoScale1Dragger, SoScale2Dragger, SoScale2UniformDragger, SoScaleUniformDragger, SoSpotLightDragger, SoTabBoxDragger, SoTabPlaneDragger, SoTrackballDragger, SoTransformBoxDragger, SoTranslate1Dragger, SoTranslate2Dragger

NAME

SoJackManip — transform node with 3D interface for rotating, scaling, and translating

INHERITS FROM

SoBase > SoFieldContainer > SoNode > SoTransformation > SoTransform > SoTransformManip > SoJackManip

DESCRIPTION

SoJackManip is derived from **SoTransform** (by way of **SoTransformManip**). When its fields change, nodes following it in the scene graph rotate, scale, and/or translate.

As a subclass of **SoTransformManip**, this manip also has a 3D interface to edit some of its fields. In this case, the interface edits the **scaleFactor**, **rotation** and **translation** fields.

A manipulator differs from a dragger. When you move a dragger, no other nodes are affected. When you move an **SoTransformManip**, other nodes move along with it. (See the reference page for **SoTransformManip**).

The interface for an **SoJackManip** is exactly the same as that of the **SoJackDragger**. To find out more about the interface, see the reference page for **SoJackDragger**. To find out how the manipulator uses a dragger to provide its interface, see the reference page for **SoTransformManip**.

On screen, this manip will surround the objects influenced by its motion. This is because it turns on the *surroundScale* part of the dragger (See the reference page for **SoSurroundScale**)

FIELDS

Fields from class SoTransform:

translation, rotation, scaleFactor, scaleOrientation, center

METHODS

SoJackManip()
Constructor.

static SoType   **getClassTypeId()**
Returns type identifier for this class.

Methods from class SoTransformManip:

getDragger, replaceNode, replaceManip

Methods from class SoTransform:

> pointAt, getScaleSpaceMatrix, getRotationSpaceMatrix, getTranslationSpaceMatrix, multLeft, multRight, combineLeft, combineRight, setMatrix, recenter

Methods from class SoNode:

> setOverride, isOverride, copy, affectsState, getByName, getByName

Methods from class SoFieldContainer:

> setToDefaults, hasDefaultValues, fieldsAreEqual, copyFieldValues, set, get, getFields, getField, getFieldName, enableNotify, isNotifyEnabled

Methods from class SoBase:

> ref, unref, unrefNoDelete, touch, getTypeId, isOfType, setName, getName

FILE FORMAT/DEFAULTS

```
JackManip {
        translation       0 0 0
        rotation          0 0 1  0
        scaleFactor       1 1 1
        scaleOrientation  0 0 1  0
        center            0 0 0
}
```

INCLUDE FILE

```
#include <Inventor/manips/SoJackManip.h>
```

SEE ALSO

> SoCenterballManip, SoHandleBoxManip, SoJackDragger, SoTabBoxManip, SoTrackballManip, SoTransformBoxManip, SoTransform, SoTransformManip

NAME

SoKeyboardEvent — keyboard key press and release events

INHERITS FROM

SoEvent > SoButtonEvent > SoKeyboardEvent

DESCRIPTION

SoKeyboardEvent represents keyboard key press and release events in the Inventor event model.

METHODS

SoKeyboardEvent()
Constructor.

static SoType   **getClassTypeId**()
Return the type id for the **SoKeyboardEvent** class.

void   **setKey**(SoKeyboardEvent::Key whichKey)
SoKeyboardEvent::Key
     getKey() const
Set and get which key generated the event.

static SbBool   **isKeyPressEvent**(const SoEvent *e, SoKeyboardEvent::Key
         whichKey)
static SbBool   **isKeyReleaseEvent**(const SoEvent *e, SoKeyboardEvent::Key
         whichKey)
Returns whether the passed event is a keyboard press or release event of the passed key. When **SoKeyboardEvent::ANY** is passed, this returns TRUE if the event represents a keyboard press or release of any key.

char   **getPrintableCharacter**() const
Convenience routine that returns the character representing the key, if it's printable. If not, this returns NULL ('\0').

Methods from class SoButtonEvent:

setState, getState

Methods from class SoEvent:

getTypeId, isOfType, setTime, getTime, setPosition, getPosition, getPosition, getNormalizedPosition, setShiftDown, setCtrlDown, setAltDown, wasShiftDown, wasCtrlDown, wasAltDown

SoKeyboardEvent

INCLUDE FILE

```
#include <Inventor/events/SoKeyboardEvent.h>

#define SO_KEY_PRESS_EVENT(EVENT,KEY)
    (SoKeyboardEvent::isKeyPressEvent(EVENT,SoKeyboardEvent::KEY))
#define SO_KEY_RELEASE_EVENT(EVENT,KEY)
    (SoKeyboardEvent::isKeyReleaseEvent(EVENT,SoKeyboardEvent::KEY))
```

enum **Key** {

SoKeyboardEvent::ANY	Special constant for any key
SoKeyboardEvent::LEFT_SHIFT	Modifiers
SoKeyboardEvent::RIGHT_SHIFT	
SoKeyboardEvent::LEFT_CONTROL	
SoKeyboardEvent::RIGHT_CONTROL	
SoKeyboardEvent::LEFT_ALT	
SoKeyboardEvent::RIGHT_ALT	
SoKeyboardEvent::NUMBER_0	Numbers
SoKeyboardEvent::NUMBER_1	
SoKeyboardEvent::NUMBER_2	
SoKeyboardEvent::NUMBER_3	
SoKeyboardEvent::NUMBER_4	
SoKeyboardEvent::NUMBER_5	
SoKeyboardEvent::NUMBER_6	
SoKeyboardEvent::NUMBER_7	
SoKeyboardEvent::NUMBER_8	
SoKeyboardEvent::NUMBER_9	
SoKeyboardEvent::A	Letters
SoKeyboardEvent::B	
SoKeyboardEvent::C	
SoKeyboardEvent::D	
SoKeyboardEvent::E	
SoKeyboardEvent::F	
SoKeyboardEvent::G	
SoKeyboardEvent::H	
SoKeyboardEvent::I	
SoKeyboardEvent::J	
SoKeyboardEvent::K	
SoKeyboardEvent::L	
SoKeyboardEvent::M	
SoKeyboardEvent::N	
SoKeyboardEvent::O	

SoKeyboardEvent::P
SoKeyboardEvent::Q
SoKeyboardEvent::R
SoKeyboardEvent::S
SoKeyboardEvent::T
SoKeyboardEvent::U
SoKeyboardEvent::V
SoKeyboardEvent::W
SoKeyboardEvent::X
SoKeyboardEvent::Y
SoKeyboardEvent::Z
SoKeyboardEvent::HOME   Cursor control and motion
SoKeyboardEvent::LEFT_ARROW
SoKeyboardEvent::UP_ARROW
SoKeyboardEvent::RIGHT_ARROW
SoKeyboardEvent::DOWN_ARROW
SoKeyboardEvent::PAGE_UP
SoKeyboardEvent::PAGE_DOWN
SoKeyboardEvent::PRIOR
SoKeyboardEvent::NEXT
SoKeyboardEvent::END
SoKeyboardEvent::PAD_ENTER   Keypad functions
SoKeyboardEvent::PAD_F1
SoKeyboardEvent::PAD_F2
SoKeyboardEvent::PAD_F3
SoKeyboardEvent::PAD_F4
SoKeyboardEvent::PAD_0
SoKeyboardEvent::PAD_1
SoKeyboardEvent::PAD_2
SoKeyboardEvent::PAD_3
SoKeyboardEvent::PAD_4
SoKeyboardEvent::PAD_5
SoKeyboardEvent::PAD_6
SoKeyboardEvent::PAD_7
SoKeyboardEvent::PAD_8
SoKeyboardEvent::PAD_9
SoKeyboardEvent::PAD_ADD
SoKeyboardEvent::PAD_SUBTRACT
SoKeyboardEvent::PAD_MULTIPLY
SoKeyboardEvent::PAD_DIVIDE
SoKeyboardEvent::PAD_SPACE

```
            SoKeyboardEvent::PAD_TAB
            SoKeyboardEvent::PAD_INSERT
            SoKeyboardEvent::PAD_DELETE
            SoKeyboardEvent::PAD_PERIOD
            SoKeyboardEvent::F1                  Function keys
            SoKeyboardEvent::F2
            SoKeyboardEvent::F3
            SoKeyboardEvent::F4
            SoKeyboardEvent::F5
            SoKeyboardEvent::F6
            SoKeyboardEvent::F7
            SoKeyboardEvent::F8
            SoKeyboardEvent::F9
            SoKeyboardEvent::F10
            SoKeyboardEvent::F11
            SoKeyboardEvent::F12
            SoKeyboardEvent::BACKSPACE           Miscellaneous
            SoKeyboardEvent::TAB
            SoKeyboardEvent::RETURN
            SoKeyboardEvent::ENTER
            SoKeyboardEvent::PAUSE
            SoKeyboardEvent::SCROLL_LOCK
            SoKeyboardEvent::ESCAPE
            SoKeyboardEvent::DELETE
            SoKeyboardEvent::PRINT
            SoKeyboardEvent::INSERT
            SoKeyboardEvent::NUM_LOCK
            SoKeyboardEvent::CAPS_LOCK
            SoKeyboardEvent::SHIFT_LOCK
            SoKeyboardEvent::SPACE
            SoKeyboardEvent::APOSTROPHE
            SoKeyboardEvent::COMMA
            SoKeyboardEvent::MINUS
            SoKeyboardEvent::PERIOD
            SoKeyboardEvent::SLASH
            SoKeyboardEvent::SEMICOLON
            SoKeyboardEvent::EQUAL
            SoKeyboardEvent::BRACKETLEFT
            SoKeyboardEvent::BACKSLASH
            SoKeyboardEvent::BRACKETRIGHT
            SoKeyboardEvent::GRAVE
    }
```

SEE ALSO

SoEvent, SoButtonEvent, SoLocation2Event, SoMotion3Event, SoMouseButtonEvent, SoSpaceballButtonEvent, SoHandleEventAction, SoEventCallback, SoSelection, SoInteraction, SoXtDevice

NAME

SoLabel — node containing label text string

INHERITS FROM

SoBase > SoFieldContainer > SoNode > SoLabel

DESCRIPTION

This class defines a label node in the scene graph. This node has no effect during traversal. It is used to store text labels in the scene graph, typically for application-specific identification of subgraphs when node naming is not appropriate.

FIELDS

SoSFName   **label**

Defines the label string value as an **SbName**.

METHODS

   SoLabel()

Creates a label node with default settings.

static SoType   **getClassTypeId**()

Returns type identifier for this class.

Methods from class SoNode:

setOverride, isOverride, copy, affectsState, getByName, getByName

Methods from class SoFieldContainer:

setToDefaults, hasDefaultValues, fieldsAreEqual, copyFieldValues, set, get, getFields, getField, getFieldName, enableNotify, isNotifyEnabled

Methods from class SoBase:

ref, unref, unrefNoDelete, touch, getTypeId, isOfType, setName, getName

FILE FORMAT/DEFAULTS

```
Label {
    label   "<Undefined label>"
}
```

INCLUDE FILE

```
#include <Inventor/nodes/SoLabel.h>
```

SEE ALSO

SbName, SoInfo

NAME

SoLevelOfDetail — level-of-detail switching group node

INHERITS FROM

SoBase > SoFieldContainer > SoNode > SoGroup > SoLevelOfDetail

DESCRIPTION

This group node is used to allow applications to switch between various representations of objects automatically. The children of this node typically represent the same object or objects at varying levels of detail, from highest detail to lowest. The size of the objects when projected into the viewport is used to determine which version to use (i.e., which child to traverse).

The size is computed as the area of the screen rectangle enclosing the projection of the 3D bounding box that encloses all of the children. When rendering, this size is compared to the values in the **screenArea** field. If the size is greater than the first value, child 0 is traversed. If it is smaller than the first, but greater than the second, child 1 is traversed, and so on. If there are fewer children than are required by this rule, the last child is traversed. The **screenArea** field contains just 0 by default, so the first child is always traversed.

The size calculation takes the current complexity into account. If the complexity is 0 or is of type BOUNDING_BOX, the last child is always traversed. If the complexity is less than .5, the computed size is scaled down appropriately to use (possibly) a less detailed representation. If the complexity is greater than .5, the size is scaled up. At complexity 1, the first child is always used.

FIELDS

SoMFFloat   **screenArea**

Areas to use for comparison

METHODS

SoLevelOfDetail()

Creates a level-of-detail node with default settings.

static SoType   **getClassTypeId**()

Returns type identifier for this class.

Methods from class SoGroup:

addChild, insertChild, getChild, findChild, getNumChildren, removeChild, removeChild, removeAllChildren, replaceChild, replaceChild

Methods from class SoNode:

setOverride, isOverride, copy, affectsState, getByName, getByName

Methods from class SoFieldContainer:

> setToDefaults, hasDefaultValues, fieldsAreEqual, copyFieldValues, set, get, getFields, getField, getFieldName, enableNotify, isNotifyEnabled

Methods from class SoBase:

> ref, unref, unrefNoDelete, touch, getTypeId, isOfType, setName, getName

ACTION BEHAVIOR

SoGLRenderAction, SoRayPickAction, SoCallbackAction
> Only the child with the appropriate level of detail is traversed.

SoGetBoundingBoxAction
> The box that encloses all children is computed. (This is the box that is needed to compute the projected size.)

others
> All implemented as for **SoGroup**, except that **SoLevelOfDetail** saves/restores state (like **SoSeparator**) when applying any action.

FILE FORMAT/DEFAULTS

```
LevelOfDetail {
    screenArea  0
}
```

INCLUDE FILE

```
#include <Inventor/nodes/SoLevelOfDetail.h>
```

SEE ALSO

> SoComplexity, SoSwitch, SoSeparator

NAME

SoLight — abstract base class for all light source nodes

INHERITS FROM

SoBase > SoFieldContainer > SoNode > SoLight

DESCRIPTION

SoLight is the abstract base class for all light nodes. A light node defines an illumination source that may affect subsequent shapes in the scene graph, depending on the current lighting style. Light sources are affected by the current transformation. A light node under a separator does not affect any objects outside that separator.

You can also use a node kit to create a light; see the reference page for **SoLightKit**.

FIELDS

SoSFBool **on**

Determines whether the source is active or inactive. When inactive, the source does not illuminate at all.

SoSFFloat **intensity**

Illumination intensity of light source. Valid values range from 0.0 (no illumination) to 1.0 (maximum illumination).

SoSFColor **color**

Light source illumination color.

METHODS

static SoType **getClassTypeId()**

Returns type identifier for this class.

Methods from class SoNode:

setOverride, isOverride, copy, affectsState, getByName, getByName

Methods from class SoFieldContainer:

setToDefaults, hasDefaultValues, fieldsAreEqual, copyFieldValues, set, get, getFields, getField, getFieldName, enableNotify, isNotifyEnabled

Methods from class SoBase:

ref, unref, unrefNoDelete, touch, getTypeId, isOfType, setName, getName

ACTION BEHAVIOR

SoGLRenderAction

Activates this light (if so specified) during traversal. All shape nodes that come after this light in the scene graph are illuminated by this light.

FILE FORMAT/DEFAULTS

This is an abstract class. See the reference page of a derived class for the format and default values.

INCLUDE FILE

```
#include <Inventor/nodes/SoLight.h>
```

SEE ALSO

SoDirectionalLight, SoEnvironment, SoLightKit, SoLightModel, SoMaterial, SoPointLight, SoSpotLight

NAME

SoLightKit — light nodekit class

INHERITS FROM

SoBase > SoFieldContainer > SoNode > SoBaseKit > SoLightKit

DESCRIPTION

This nodekit class is used to create light nodes that have a local transformation and a geometry icon to represent the light source. **SoLightKit** adds three public parts to the basic nodekit: *transform*, *light*, and *icon*.

SoLightKit creates an **SoDirectionalLight** as the *light* part by default - all other parts are NULL at creation.

You can move the light relative to the rest of the scene by creating and editing the *transform* part.

You can add a geometrical representation for the light by setting the *icon* part to be any scene graph you like.

SoLightKit also adds two private parts. An **SoTransformSeparator** contains the effect of *transform* to move only the *light* and *icon*, while allowing the *light* to illuminate the rest of the scene. The second private part is an **SoSeparator**, which keeps property nodes within the *icon* geometry from affecting the rest of the scene. It also serves to cache the *icon* even when the *light* or *transform* is changing.

SoLightKit is derived from **SoBaseKit** and thus also includes a *callbackList* part for adding callback nodes.

PARTS

(SoTransform) **transform**

This part positions and orients the light and icon relative to the rest of the scene. Its effect is kept local to this nodekit by a private part of type **SoTransformSeparator**. The *transform* part is NULL by default. If you ask for *transform* using **getPart()**, an **SoTransform** will be returned. But you may set the part to be any subclass of **SoTransform**. For example, set the *transform* to be an **SoDragPointManip** and the *light* to be an **SoPointLight**. Then you can move the light by dragging the manipulator with the mouse.

(SoLight) **light**

The light node for this nodekit. This can be set to any node derived from **SoLight**. An **SoDirectionalLight** is created by default, and it is also the type of light returned when the you request that the nodekit build a light for you.

(SoNode)   **icon**
> This part is a user-supplied scene graph that represents the light source. It is NULL by default — an **SoCube** is created by the lightkit when a method requires it to build the part itself.

Parts from class SoBaseKit:
> callbackList

METHODS

SoLightKit()
> Constructor.

static const SoNodekitCatalog *
> **getClassNodekitCatalog**() const
> Returns an **SoNodekitCatalog** for the class **SoLightKit**.

static SoType   **getClassTypeId**()
> Returns type identifier for this class.

Methods from class SoBaseKit:
> getNodekitCatalog, getPart, getPartString, createPathToPart, setPart, set, set, isSearchingChildren, setSearchingChildren

Methods from class SoNode:
> setOverride, isOverride, copy, affectsState, getByName, getByName

Methods from class SoFieldContainer:
> setToDefaults, hasDefaultValues, fieldsAreEqual, copyFieldValues, get, getFields, getField, getFieldName, enableNotify, isNotifyEnabled

Methods from class SoBase:
> ref, unref, unrefNoDelete, touch, getTypeId, isOfType, setName, getName

MACROS
Macros from class SoBaseKit:
> SO_GET_PART, SO_CHECK_PART

CATALOG PARTS

All parts			NULL by
Part Name	Part Type	Default Type	Default
callbackList	NodeKitListPart	--	yes
transform	Transform	--	yes
light	Light	DirectionalLight	no
icon	Node	Cube	yes

Extra information for list parts from above table		
Part Name	Container Type	Permissible Types
callbackList	Separator	Callback, EventCallback

FILE FORMAT/DEFAULTS

```
LightKit {
}
```

INCLUDE FILE

```
#include <Inventor/nodekits/SoLightKit.h>
```

SEE ALSO

SoAppearanceKit, SoBaseKit, SoCameraKit, SoNodeKit, SoNodeKitDetail,
SoNodeKitListPart, SoNodeKitPath, SoNodekitCatalog, SoSceneKit, SoSeparatorKit,
SoShapeKit, SoWrapperKit

NAME

SoLightModel — node that defines the lighting model to use when rendering

INHERITS FROM

SoBase > SoFieldContainer > SoNode > SoLightModel

DESCRIPTION

This node defines the lighting model to be used when rendering subsequent shapes. The lighting model is specified in the **model** field. When the default model (Phong lighting) is used, light sources are required in a scene for objects to be easily visible.

FIELDS

SoSFEnum   **model**

    Lighting model to use

METHODS

    SoLightModel()

Creates a light model node with default settings.

static SoType   **getClassTypeId**()

    Returns type identifier for this class.

Methods from class SoNode:

setOverride, isOverride, copy, affectsState, getByName, getByName

Methods from class SoFieldContainer:

setToDefaults, hasDefaultValues, fieldsAreEqual, copyFieldValues, set, get, getFields, getField, getFieldName, enableNotify, isNotifyEnabled

Methods from class SoBase:

ref, unref, unrefNoDelete, touch, getTypeId, isOfType, setName, getName

ACTION BEHAVIOR

SoGLRenderAction, SoCallbackAction

    Sets the current lighting model in the state.

FILE FORMAT/DEFAULTS

```
LightModel {
    model   PHONG
}
```

INCLUDE FILE

```
#include <Inventor/nodes/SoLightModel.h>
```

enum **Model** {

      SoLightModel::BASE_COLOR

                    Use only the base (diffuse) object color

      SoLightModel::PHONG

                    Use Phong lighting model

}

SEE ALSO

SoBaseColor, SoEnvironment, SoLight, SoMaterial

NAME

SoLinearProfile — Piecewise-linear profile curve

INHERITS FROM

SoBase > SoFieldContainer > SoNode > SoProfile > SoLinearProfile

DESCRIPTION

this node specifies a piecewise-linear curve that is used as a profile.

FIELDS

Fields from class SoProfile:

index, linkage

METHODS

SoLinearProfile()

Creates a linear profile node with default settings.

static SoType **getClassTypeId()**

Returns type identifier for this class.

Methods from class SoNode:

setOverride, isOverride, copy, affectsState, getByName, getByName

Methods from class SoFieldContainer:

setToDefaults, hasDefaultValues, fieldsAreEqual, copyFieldValues, set, get, getFields, getField, getFieldName, enableNotify, isNotifyEnabled

Methods from class SoBase:

ref, unref, unrefNoDelete, touch, getTypeId, isOfType, setName, getName

ACTION BEHAVIOR

SoGLRenderAction, SoRayPickAction, SoCallbackAction

Adds a profile to the current state.

FILE FORMAT/DEFAULTS

```
LinearProfile {
    index     0
    linkage   START_FIRST
}
```

INCLUDE FILE

#include <Inventor/nodes/SoLinearProfile.h>

SEE ALSO

SoNurbsProfile, SoProfileCoordinate2, SoProfileCoordinate3

NAME

    SoLineDetail — stores detail information about vertex-based shapes made of line segments

INHERITS FROM

    SoDetail > SoLineDetail

DESCRIPTION

    This class contains detail information about a point on a line segment in a vertex-based shape made of line segments. The information includes the points at the ends of the segment, and the index of the segment within the shape.

METHODS

                         SoLineDetail()
    virtual   **˜SoLineDetail**()
    Constructor and destructor.

    const SoPointDetail *
                         getPoint0() const
    const SoPointDetail *
                         getPoint1() const
    These return information about the two points forming the end vertices of the line segment, represented as an **SoPointDetail**.

    long   **getLineIndex**() const
    Returns the index of the line the segment is part of within a shape, such as the third line within an **SoLineSet**.

    long   **getPartIndex**() const
    Returns the index of the part containing the line segment within the shape. Usually, the part index is the same as the line segment index, such as the fifth segment overall within an **SoLineSet**.

    static SoType   **getClassTypeId**()
    Returns type identifier for this class.

    Methods from class SoDetail:

    copy, getTypeId, isOfType

INCLUDE FILE

    `#include <Inventor/details/SoLineDetail.h>`

SEE ALSO

    SoDetail, SoPickedPoint, SoPrimitiveVertex, SoVertexShape

SoLineHighlightRenderAction

NAME

SoLineHighlightRenderAction — selection highlight style

INHERITS FROM

SoAction > SoGLRenderAction > SoLineHighlightRenderAction

DESCRIPTION

SoLineHighlightRenderAction is a render action which renders the specified scene graph, then renders each selected object again in wireframe. Selected objects are specified by the first **SoSelection** node in the scene to which this action is applied. If there is no renderable geometry in a selected object, no highlight is rendered for that object. A highlight render action can be passed to the **setGLRenderAction()** method of **SoXtRenderArea** to have an affect on scene graphs.

METHODS

SoLineHighlightRenderAction()

Constructor.

virtual void   **apply**(SoNode *node)

This renders the passed scene graph, and also renders each selected object in wireframe, as specified by the first **SoSelection** node found in the scene graph.

void   **setVisible**(SbBool b)

This provides a convenient mechansim for turning highlights off or back on. When FALSE is passed, subsequent calls to apply() render the scene graph without rendering highlights. The application is responsible for forcing a redraw of the scene after changing this state. The default visibility is on.

SbBool   **isVisible**() const

Returns whether highlights will be rendered or not.

void   **setColor**(const SbColor &c)

SbColor &   **getColor**()

Set and get the color of the highlight. Default is red *(1,0,0)*. The application is responsible for forcing a redraw of the scene to see the affects of this change.

void   **setLinePattern**(unsigned short pattern)

unsigned short   **getLinePattern**()

Set and get the line pattern of the highlight. Default is solid, *0xffff*. The pattern of bits in the passed variable specifies the pattern of the line. See **SoDrawStyle** for more information. The application is responsible for forcing a redraw of the scene to see the affects of this change.

void	**setLineWidth**(float width)
float	**getLineWidth**()

Set and get the line width of the highlight. Default is *3*. The application is responsible for forcing a redraw of the scene to see the affects of this change.

Methods from class SoGLRenderAction:

setViewportRegion, getViewportRegion, setUpdateArea, getUpdateArea, setAbortCallback, setTransparencyType, getTransparencyType, setSmoothing, isSmoothing, setNumPasses, getNumPasses, setPassUpdate, isPassUpdate, setPassCallback, setCacheContext, getCacheContext

Methods from class SoAction:

getClassTypeId, getTypeId, isOfType, invalidateState

INCLUDE FILE

```
#include <Inventor/actions/SoLineHighlightRenderAction.h>
```

EXAMPLE

Here is an example of how a line highlight can be specified for a particular selection node and render area.

```
SoXtRenderArea *myRenderArea;
SoSelection *mySelection;

// Set the highlight render action
myRenderArea->setGLRenderAction(
   new SoLineHighlightRenderAction());

// Automatic redraw on selection changes
myRenderArea->redrawOnSelectionChange(mySelection);
```

SEE ALSO

SoBoxHighlightRenderAction, SoGLRenderAction, SoSelection, SoXtRenderArea, SoDrawStyle, SoInteraction

NAME

SoLineSet — polyline shape node

INHERITS FROM

SoBase > SoFieldContainer > SoNode > SoShape > SoVertexShape >
SoNonIndexedShape > SoLineSet

DESCRIPTION

This node represents a 3D shape formed by constructing polylines from vertices
located at the current coordinates. **SoLineSet** uses the current coordinates in order,
starting at the index specified by the **startIndex** field. Each line has a number of
vertices specified by a value in the **numVertices** field. For example, an **SoLineSet**
with a **startIndex** of 3 and **numVertices** of [3,4,2] would use coordinates 3, 4, and 5
for the first line, coordinates 6, 7, 8, and 9 for the second line, and coordinates 10
and 11 for the third. If the last value in the **numVertices** field is
SO_LINE_SET_USE_REST_OF_VERTICES (-1), all remaining coordinates in the
current coordinates are used as the vertices of the last line.

The number of values in the **numVertices** field indicates the number of polylines in
the set.

The coordinates of the line set are transformed by the current cumulative
transformation. The lines are drawn with the current light model and drawing style
(drawing style FILLED is treated as LINES).

Treatment of the current material and normal binding is as follows: The PER_PART
binding specifies a material or normal for each segment of the line. The PER_FACE
binding specifies a material or normal for each polyline. The _INDEXED bindings
are equivalent to their non-indexed counterparts. The DEFAULT material binding is
equal to OVERALL. The DEFAULT normal binding is equal to PER_VERTEX. The
startIndex is also used for materials, normals, or texture coordinates when the
binding indicates that they should be used per vertex.

The current complexity value has no effect on the rendering of line sets.

FIELDS

SoMFLong   **numVertices**

Number of vertices per polyline.

Fields from class SoNonIndexedShape:

startIndex

METHODS

SoLineSet()
Creates a line set node with default settings.

static SoType **getClassTypeId**()
Returns type identifier for this class.

Methods from class SoNode:

setOverride, isOverride, copy, affectsState, getByName, getByName

Methods from class SoFieldContainer:

setToDefaults, hasDefaultValues, fieldsAreEqual, copyFieldValues, set, get, getFields, getField, getFieldName, enableNotify, isNotifyEnabled

Methods from class SoBase:

ref, unref, unrefNoDelete, touch, getTypeId, isOfType, setName, getName

ACTION BEHAVIOR

SoGLRenderAction
Draws lines based on the current coordinates, normals, materials, drawing style, and so on.

SoRayPickAction
Picks lines based on the current coordinates and transformation. Details about the intersection are returned in an **SoLineDetail**.

SoGetBoundingBoxAction
Computes the bounding box that encloses all vertices of the line set with the current transformation applied to them. Sets the center to the average of the coordinates of all vertices.

SoCallbackAction
If any line segment callbacks are registered with the action, they will be invoked for each successive segment in the line set.

FILE FORMAT/DEFAULTS

```
LineSet {
    startIndex    0
    numVertices   -1
}
```

SoLineSet

INCLUDE FILE

```
#include <Inventor/nodes/SoLineSet.h>
```

SEE ALSO

SoCoordinate3, SoDrawStyle, SoIndexedLineSet, SoLineDetail

NAME

SoLocation2Event — 2D location events

INHERITS FROM

SoEvent > SoLocation2Event

DESCRIPTION

SoLocation2Event represents 2D location events in the Inventor event model.

METHODS

SoLocation2Event()
Constructor.

static SoType   **getClassTypeId**()
Return the type id for the **SoLocation2Event** class.

Methods from class SoEvent:

getTypeId, isOfType, setTime, getTime, setPosition, getPosition, getPosition, getNormalizedPosition, setShiftDown, setCtrlDown, setAltDown, wasShiftDown, wasCtrlDown, wasAltDown

INCLUDE FILE

```
#include <Inventor/events/SoLocation2Event.h>
```

SEE ALSO

SoEvent, SoButtonEvent, SoKeyboardEvent, SoMotion3Event, SoMouseButtonEvent, SoSpaceballButtonEvent, SoHandleEventAction, SoEventCallback, SoSelection, SoInteraction, SoXtDevice

NAME

SoMaterial — surface material definition node

INHERITS FROM

SoBase > SoFieldContainer > SoNode > SoMaterial

DESCRIPTION

This node defines the current surface material properties for all subsequent shapes. **SoMaterial** sets several components of the current material during traversal. Different shapes interpret materials with multiple values differently. To bind materials to shapes, use an **SoMaterialBinding** node.

FIELDS

SoMFColor   **ambientColor**
    Ambient color(s) of the surface.

SoMFColor   **diffuseColor**
    Diffuse color(s) of the surface.

SoMFColor   **specularColor**
    Specular color(s) of the surface.

SoMFColor   **emissiveColor**
    Emissive color(s) of the surface.

SoMFFloat   **shininess**
    Shininess coefficient(s) of the surface. Values can range from 0.0 for no shininess (a diffuse surface) to 1.0 for maximum shininess (a highly polished surface).

SoMFFloat   **transparency**
    Transparency value(s) of the surface. Values can range from 0.0 for opaque surfaces to 1.0 for completely transparent surfaces.

METHODS

     SoMaterial()
    Creates a material node with default settings.

static SoType   **getClassTypeId**()
    Returns type identifier for this class.

Methods from class SoNode:

    setOverride, isOverride, copy, affectsState, getByName, getByName

Methods from class SoFieldContainer:

> setToDefaults, hasDefaultValues, fieldsAreEqual, copyFieldValues, set, get, getFields, getField, getFieldName, enableNotify, isNotifyEnabled

Methods from class SoBase:

> ref, unref, unrefNoDelete, touch, getTypeId, isOfType, setName, getName

ACTION BEHAVIOR
SoGLRenderAction, SoCallbackAction

> Sets the ambient color, the diffuse color, the specular color, the emissive color, the shininess, and the transparency of the current material.

FILE FORMAT/DEFAULTS

```
Material {
        ambientColor    0.2 0.2 0.2
        diffuseColor    0.8 0.8 0.8
        specularColor   0 0 0
        emissiveColor   0 0 0
        shininess       0.2
        transparency    0
}
```

INCLUDE FILE

```
#include <Inventor/nodes/SoMaterial.h>
```

SEE ALSO

SoBaseColor, SoLightModel, SoMaterialBinding, SoPackedColor

SoMaterialBinding

NAME

NAME

SoMaterialBinding — node that specifies how multiple materials are bound to shapes

INHERITS FROM

SoBase > SoFieldContainer > SoNode > SoMaterialBinding

DESCRIPTION

This node specifies how the current materials are bound to shapes that follow in the scene graph. Each shape node may interpret bindings differently. The current material always has a base value, which is defined by the first value of all material fields. Since material fields may have multiple values, the binding determines how these values are distributed over a shape.

The bindings for faces and vertices are meaningful only for shapes that are made from faces and vertices. Similarly, the indexed bindings are only used by the shapes that allow indexing.

When multiple material values are bound, the values are cycled through, based on the period of the material component with the most values. For example, the following table shows the values used when cycling through (or indexing into) a material with 2 ambient colors, 3 diffuse colors, and 1 of all other components in the current material. (The period of this material cycle is 3):

Material	Ambient color	Diffuse color	Other
0	0	0	0
1	1	1	0
2	1	2	0
3 (same as 0)	0	0	0

FIELDS

SoSFEnum   **value**

Specifies how to bind materials to shapes.

METHODS

SoMaterialBinding()

Creates a material binding node with default settings.

static SoType   **getClassTypeId()**

Returns type identifier for this class.

Methods from class SoNode:

setOverride, isOverride, copy, affectsState, getByName, getByName

Methods from class SoFieldContainer:

setToDefaults, hasDefaultValues, fieldsAreEqual, copyFieldValues, set, get, getFields, getField, getFieldName, enableNotify, isNotifyEnabled

Methods from class SoBase:

ref, unref, unrefNoDelete, touch, getTypeId, isOfType, setName, getName

ACTION BEHAVIOR

SoGLRenderAction, SoCallbackAction

Sets the current material binding type.

FILE FORMAT/DEFAULTS

```
MaterialBinding {
     value   DEFAULT
}
```

INCLUDE FILE

```
#include <Inventor/nodes/SoMaterialBinding.h>
```

enum **Binding** {

SoMaterialBinding::DEFAULT

Use default binding

SoMaterialBinding::OVERALL

Whole object has same material

SoMaterialBinding::PER_PART

One material for each part of object

SoMaterialBinding::PER_PART_INDEXED

One material for each part, indexed

SoMaterialBinding::PER_FACE

One material for each face of object

SoMaterialBinding::PER_FACE_INDEXED

One material for each face, indexed

SoMaterialBinding::PER_VERTEX

One material for each vertex of object

SoMaterialBinding::PER_VERTEX_INDEXED

One material for each vertex, indexed

}

SEE ALSO

SoMaterial, SoNormalBinding, SoShape, SoTextureCoordinateBinding

SoMaterialIndex

NAME

    SoMaterialIndex — surface material node for color index mode

INHERITS FROM

    SoBase > SoFieldContainer > SoNode > SoMaterialIndex

DESCRIPTION

    This node is used to define surface materials for scenes to be rendered in OpenGL's color index mode (as opposed to RGB mode). The fields of this node set up indices into the current color map for OpenGL lighting. Refer to the OpenGL manuals for lighting information. The application is responsible for setting up a color map that will work for lighting.

    The index fields have multiple values, and are bound to shapes in the same manner as are the fields of the **SoMaterial** node. Note that the three index fields should contain the same number of values.

    When using both **SoMaterialIndex** and **SoMaterial**, fields common to the two nodes (that is, **shininess** and **transparency** are overridden, but other fields are not. Therefore, it is possible to use both nodes in the same graph.

FIELDS

    SoMFLong   **ambientIndex**
        Ambient index(ices) of the surface.

    SoMFLong   **diffuseIndex**
        Diffuse index(ices) of the surface.

    SoMFLong   **specularIndex**
        Specular index(ices) of the surface.

    SoMFFloat   **shininess**
        Shininess coefficient(s) of the surface. Values can range from 0.0 for no shininess (a diffuse surface) to 1.0 for maximum shininess (a highly polished surface).

    SoMFFloat   **transparency**
        Transparency value(s) of the surface. Values can range from 0.0 for opaque surfaces to 1.0 for completely transparent surfaces.

METHODS

                SoMaterialIndex()
        Creates a material index node with default settings.

static SoType   **getClassTypeId**()
> Returns type identifier for this class.

Methods from class SoNode:
> setOverride, isOverride, copy, affectsState, getByName, getByName

Methods from class SoFieldContainer:
> setToDefaults, hasDefaultValues, fieldsAreEqual, copyFieldValues, set, get, getFields, getField, getFieldName, enableNotify, isNotifyEnabled

Methods from class SoBase:
> ref, unref, unrefNoDelete, touch, getTypeId, isOfType, setName, getName

ACTION BEHAVIOR

SoGLRenderAction, SoCallbackAction
> Sets the ambient index, the diffuse index, the specular index, the the shininess, and the transparency of the current material.

FILE FORMAT/DEFAULTS

```
MaterialIndex {
        ambientIndex    1
        diffuseIndex    2
        specularIndex   3
        shininess       0.2
        transparency    0
}
```

INCLUDE FILE

```
#include <Inventor/nodes/SoMaterialIndex.h>
```

SEE ALSO
> SoColorIndex, SoMaterial, SoMaterialBinding, SoXtRenderArea

NAME

SoMatrixTransform — node that specifies a 3D geometric transformation as a matrix

INHERITS FROM

SoBase > SoFieldContainer > SoNode > SoTransformation > SoMatrixTransform

DESCRIPTION

This node defines a geometric 3D transformation with a single **SbMatrix**. Note that some matrices (such as singular ones) may result in errors in bounding boxes, picking, and lighting.

FIELDS

SoSFMatrix **matrix**
Transformation matrix.

METHODS

SoMatrixTransform()
Creates a matrix transformation node with default settings.

static SoType **getClassTypeId()**
Returns type identifier for this class.

Methods from class SoNode:

setOverride, isOverride, copy, affectsState, getByName, getByName

Methods from class SoFieldContainer:

setToDefaults, hasDefaultValues, fieldsAreEqual, copyFieldValues, set, get, getFields, getField, getFieldName, enableNotify, isNotifyEnabled

Methods from class SoBase:

ref, unref, unrefNoDelete, touch, getTypeId, isOfType, setName, getName

ACTION BEHAVIOR

SoGLRenderAction, SoCallbackAction, SoGetBoundingBoxAction, SoRayPickAction
Concatenates matrix given in the **matrix** field with the current transformation matrix.

SoGetMatrixAction
Returns transformation matrix specified in the **matrix** field.

FILE FORMAT/DEFAULTS

```
MatrixTransform {
      matrix  1 0 0 0
              0 1 0 0
              0 0 1 0
              0 0 0 1
}
```

INCLUDE FILE

```
#include <Inventor/nodes/SoMatrixTransform.h>
```

SEE ALSO

SoTransform, SoMultipleCopy

NAME

SoMemoryError — memory error handling

INHERITS FROM

SoError > SoMemoryError

DESCRIPTION

SoMemoryError is used for errors reported due to lack of memory.

METHODS

static void   **setHandlerCallback**(SoErrorCB *cb, void *data)
static SoErrorCB *

                                  getHandlerCallback()
static void *   **getHandlerData**()

Sets/returns handler callback for **SoMemoryError** class.

static SoType   **getClassTypeId**()

Returns type identifier for SoMemoryError class.

Methods from class SoError:

getDebugString, getTypeId, isOfType

INCLUDE FILE

```
#include <Inventor/errors/SoMemoryError.h>
```

SEE ALSO

SoDebugError, SoReadError

NAME

SoMFBitMask — multiple-value field containing any number of masks of bit flags

INHERITS FROM

SoField > SoMField > SoMFEnum > SoMFBitMask

DESCRIPTION

A multiple-value field that contains any number of masks of bit flags, stored as ints. Nodes or engines that use this field class define mnemonic names for the bit flags. These names should be used when setting or testing the values of the field, even though the values are treated as integers in the methods.

The bit-wise "&" and "|" operators should be used when testing and setting flags in a mask.

SoMFBitMasks are written to file as one or more mnemonic enumerated type names, in this format:

(flag1 | flag2 | ...)

If only one flag is used in a mask, the parentheses are optional. These names differ among uses of this field in various node or engine classes. See the reference pages for specific nodes or engines for the names.

The field values may also be represented as integers, but this is not guaranteed to be portable.

When more than one value is present, all of the values are enclosed in square brackets and separated by commas.

METHODS

static SoType   **getClassTypeId**()
virtual void   **getTypeId**() const
　　　　Returns the type for this class or a particular object of this class.

int   **operator [ ]**(int i) const
　　　　Returns the *i*'th value of the field. Indexing past the end of the field (passing in *i* greater than **getNum**()) will return garbage.

const int *   **getValues**(int start) const
　　　　Returns a pointer into the array of values in the field, starting at index *start*. The values are read-only; see the **startEditing**()/**finishEditing**() methods for a way of modifying values in place.

int   **find**(int targetValue, SbBool addIfNotFound = FALSE)
Finds the given value in the array and returns the index of that value in the array. If the value is not found, -1 is returned. If *addIfNotFound* is set, then *targetValue* is added to the end of the array (but -1 is still returned).

void   **setValues**(int start, int num, const int *newValues)
Sets *num* values starting at index *start* to the values in *newValues*. The array will be automatically be made larger to accomodate the new values, if necessary.

void   **set1Value**(int index, int newValue)
Sets the *index*'th value in the array to *newValue*. The array will be automatically expanded, if necessary.

int   **operator =**(int newValue)
void   **setValue**(int newValue)
Sets the first value in the array to *newValue*, and deletes the second and subsequent values.

int   **operator ==**(const SoMFBitMask &f) const
int   **operator !=**(const SoMFBitMask &f) const
Returns TRUE if all of the values of this field equal (do not equal) those of the given field. If the fields are different types FALSE will always be returned (even if one field is an **SoMFFloat** with one value of 1.0 and the other is an **SoMFInt** with a value of 1, for example).

int *   **startEditing**()
void   **finishEditing**()
startEditing() returns a pointer to the internally-maintained array that can be modified. The values in the array may be changed, but values cannot be added or removed. It is illegal to call any other editing methods between **startEditing**() and **finishEditing**() (e.g. **set1Value**(), **setValue**(), etc).

Fields, engines or sensors connected to this field and sensors are not notified that this field has changed until **finishEditing**() is called. Calling **finishEditing**() always sets the **isDefault**() flag to FALSE and informs engines and sensors that the field changed, even if none of the values actually were changed.

Methods from class SoMField:

getNum, setNum, deleteValues, insertSpace, set1, get1

Methods from class SoField:

setIgnored, isIgnored, isDefault, isOfType, set, get, touch, connectFrom, connectFrom, disconnect, isConnected, isConnectedFromField, getConnectedField, isConnectedFromEngine, getConnectedEngine, enableConnection, isConnectionEnabled, getForwardConnections, getContainer

INCLUDE FILE

```
#include <Inventor/fields/SoMFBitMask.h>
```

NAME

SoMFBool — multiple-value field containing any number of boolean values

INHERITS FROM

SoField > SoMField > SoMFBool

DESCRIPTION

A multiple-value field that contains any number of boolean values.

SoMFBools are written to file as one or more boolean values, which are written as "0" (representing a false value), "1", "TRUE", or "FALSE".

When more than one value is present, all of the values are enclosed in square brackets and separated by commas; for example:

[0, FALSE, 1, TRUE]

METHODS

static SoType   **getClassTypeId**()
virtual void   **getTypeId**() const
Returns the type for this class or a particular object of this class.

SbBool   **operator [ ]**(int i) const
Returns the i'th value of the field. Indexing past the end of the field (passing in i greater than **getNum**()) will return garbage.

const SbBool *   **getValues**(int start) const
Returns a pointer into the array of values in the field, starting at index *start*. The values are read-only; see the **startEditing**()/**finishEditing**() methods for a way of modifying values in place.

int   **find**(SbBool targetValue, SbBool addIfNotFound = FALSE)
Finds the given value in the array and returns the index of that value in the array. If the value is not found, -1 is returned. If *addIfNotFound* is set, then *targetValue* is added to the end of the array (but -1 is still returned).

void   **setValues**(int start, int num, const SbBool *newValues)
Sets *num* values starting at index *start* to the values in *newValues*. The array will be automatically be made larger to accomodate the new values, if necessary.

void	**set1Value**(int index, SbBool newValue)

Sets the *index*'th value in the array to *newValue*. The array will be automatically expanded, if necessary.

SbBool	**operator =**(SbBool newValue)
void	**setValue**(SbBool newValue)

Sets the first value in the array to *newValue*, and deletes the second and subsequent values.

int	**operator ==**(const SoMFBool &f) const
int	**operator !=**(const SoMFBool &f) const

Returns TRUE if all of the values of this field equal (do not equal) those of the given field. If the fields are different types FALSE will always be returned (even if one field is an **SoMFFloat** with one value of 1.0 and the other is an **SoMFInt** with a value of 1, for example).

SbBool *	**startEditing**()
void	**finishEditing**()

startEditing() returns a pointer to the internally-maintained array that can be modified. The values in the array may be changed, but values cannot be added or removed. It is illegal to call any other editing methods between **startEditing**() and **finishEditing**() (e.g. **set1Value**(), **setValue**(), etc).

Fields, engines or sensors connected to this field and sensors are not notified that this field has changed until **finishEditing**() is called. Calling **finishEditing**() always sets the **isDefault**() flag to FALSE and informs engines and sensors that the field changed, even if none of the values actually were changed.

Methods from class SoMField:

getNum, setNum, deleteValues, insertSpace, set1, get1

Methods from class SoField:

setIgnored, isIgnored, isDefault, isOfType, set, get, touch, connectFrom, connectFrom, disconnect, isConnected, isConnectedFromField, getConnectedField, isConnectedFromEngine, getConnectedEngine, enableConnection, isConnectionEnabled, getForwardConnections, getContainer

INCLUDE FILE

```
#include <Inventor/fields/SoMFBool.h>
```

NAME

SoMFColor — multiple-value field containing any number of RGB colors stored as three floats

INHERITS FROM

SoField > SoMField > SoMFColor

DESCRIPTION

A multiple-value field that contains any number of RGB colors, stored as instances of **SbColor**. Values may be set in either RGB (red, green, blue) or HSV (hue, saturation, value) color spaces.

SoMFColors are written to file as one or more RGB triples of floating point numbers in standard scientific notation. When more than one value is present, all of the values are enclosed in square brackets and separated by commas. For example:

[1.0 0.0 0.0, 0 1 0, 0 0 1]

represents the three colors red, green, and blue.

METHODS

| void | **setValues**(int start, int num, const float rgb[ ][3]) |
| void | **setHSVValues**(int start, int num, const float hsv[ ][3]) |

Sets *num* values starting at index *start* to the RGB (or HSV) values specified by the given array of floats. Each float should be in the range 0.0 to 1.0, and there must be 3*num floats in the array.

void	**setValue**(const SbVec3f &vec)
void	**setValue**(float red, float green, float blue)
void	**setHSVValue**(float hue, float saturation, float value)
void	**setValue**(const float rgb[3])
void	**setHSVValue**(const float hsv[3])

Sets the field to contain one and only one value, the given color (expressed as either RGB or HSV floating point values in the range 0.0 to 1.0), and deletes the second and subsequent values.

void	**set1Value**(index, const SbVec3f &vec)
void	**set1Value**(index, float r, float g, float b)
void	**set1HSVValue**(index, float h, float s, float v)
void	**set1Value**(index, const float rgb[3])
void	**set1HSVValue**(index, const float hsv[3])

Sets one value in the array to the given color. The array will be expanded and filled with zeroes as necessary.

static SoType   **getClassTypeId**()
virtual void   **getTypeId**() const
> Returns the type for this class or a particular object of this class.

const SbColor &   **operator** [ ](int i) const
> Returns the *i*'th value of the field. Indexing past the end of the field (passing in *i* greater than **getNum**()) will return garbage.

const SbColor *   **getValues**(int start) const
> Returns a pointer into the array of values in the field, starting at index *start*. The values are read-only; see the **startEditing**()/**finishEditing**() methods for a way of modifying values in place.

int   **find**(const SbColor & targetValue, SbBool addIfNotFound = FALSE)
> Finds the given value in the array and returns the index of that value in the array. If the value is not found, -1 is returned. If *addIfNotFound* is set, then *targetValue* is added to the end of the array (but -1 is still returned).

void   **setValues**(int start, int num, const SbColor *newValues)
> Sets *num* values starting at index *start* to the values in *newValues*. The array will be automatically be made larger to accomodate the new values, if necessary.

void   **set1Value**(int index, const SbColor & newValue)
> Sets the *index*'th value in the array to *newValue*. The array will be automatically expanded, if necessary.

const SbColor &   **operator** =(const SbColor & newValue)
void   **setValue**(const SbColor & newValue)
> Sets the first value in the array to *newValue*, and deletes the second and subsequent values.

int   **operator** ==(const SoMFColor &f) const
int   **operator** !=(const SoMFColor &f) const
> Returns TRUE if all of the values of this field equal (do not equal) those of the given field. If the fields are different types FALSE will always be returned (even if one field is an **SoMFFloat** with one value of 1.0 and the other is an **SoMFInt** with a value of 1, for example).

SbColor *	**startEditing**()
void	**finishEditing**()

startEditing() returns a pointer to the internally-maintained array that can be modified. The values in the array may be changed, but values cannot be added or removed. It is illegal to call any other editing methods between **startEditing**() and **finishEditing**() (e.g. **set1Value**(), **setValue**(), etc).

Fields, engines or sensors connected to this field and sensors are not notified that this field has changed until **finishEditing**() is called. Calling **finishEditing**() always sets the **isDefault**() flag to FALSE and informs engines and sensors that the field changed, even if none of the values actually were changed.

Methods from class SoMField:

getNum, setNum, deleteValues, insertSpace, set1, get1

Methods from class SoField:

setIgnored, isIgnored, isDefault, isOfType, set, get, touch, connectFrom, connectFrom, disconnect, isConnected, isConnectedFromField, getConnectedField, isConnectedFromEngine, getConnectedEngine, enableConnection, isConnectionEnabled, getForwardConnections, getContainer

SEE ALSO

SbColor

NAME

SoMFEnum — multiple-value field containing any number of enumerated type values

INHERITS FROM

SoField > SoMField > SoMFEnum

DESCRIPTION

A multiple-value field that contains any number of enumerated type values, stored as ints. Nodes that use this field class define mnemonic names for values. These names should be used when setting or testing the values of the field, even though the values are treated as integers in the methods.

SoMFEnums are written to file as a set of mnemonic enumerated type names. These names differ among uses of this field in various node classes. See the reference pages for specific nodes for the names.

When more than one value is present, all of the values are enclosed in square brackets and separated by commas.

METHODS

void   **setValue**(const SbName &name)

Sets this field to contain one and only one value, which is the mnemonic name as a string.

void   **set1Value**(int index, const SbName &name)

Sets the *index*'th value to be the integer corresponding to the mnemonic name in the given string.

static SoType   **getClassTypeId**()
virtual void   **getTypeId**() const

Returns the type for this class or a particular object of this class.

int   **operator [ ]**(int i) const

Returns the *i*'th value of the field. Indexing past the end of the field (passing in *i* greater than **getNum**()) will return garbage.

const int *   **getValues**(int start) const

Returns a pointer into the array of values in the field, starting at index *start*. The values are read-only; see the **startEditing**()/**finishEditing**() methods for a way of modifying values in place.

int	**find**(int targetValue, SbBool addIfNotFound = FALSE)

Finds the given value in the array and returns the index of that value in the array. If the value is not found, -1 is returned. If *addIfNotFound* is set, then *targetValue* is added to the end of the array (but -1 is still returned).

void	**setValues**(int start, int num, const int *newValues)

Sets *num* values starting at index *start* to the values in *newValues*. The array will be automatically be made larger to accomodate the new values, if necessary.

void	**set1Value**(int index, int newValue)

Sets the *index*'th value in the array to *newValue*. The array will be automatically expanded, if necessary.

int	**operator** =(int newValue)
void	**setValue**(int newValue)

Sets the first value in the array to *newValue*, and deletes the second and subsequent values.

int	**operator** ==(const SoMFEnum &f) const
int	**operator** !=(const SoMFEnum &f) const

Returns TRUE if all of the values of this field equal (do not equal) those of the given field. If the fields are different types FALSE will always be returned (even if one field is an **SoMFFloat** with one value of 1.0 and the other is an **SoMFInt** with a value of 1, for example).

int *	**startEditing**()
void	**finishEditing**()

startEditing() returns a pointer to the internally-maintained array that can be modified. The values in the array may be changed, but values cannot be added or removed. It is illegal to call any other editing methods between **startEditing**() and **finishEditing**() (e.g. set1Value(), setValue(), etc).

Fields, engines or sensors connected to this field and sensors are not notified that this field has changed until **finishEditing**() is called. Calling **finishEditing**() always sets the **isDefault**() flag to FALSE and informs engines and sensors that the field changed, even if none of the values actually were changed.

Methods from class SoMField:

getNum, setNum, deleteValues, insertSpace, set1, get1

Methods from class SoField:

setIgnored, isIgnored, isDefault, isOfType, set, get, touch, connectFrom, connectFrom, disconnect, isConnected, isConnectedFromField, getConnectedField, isConnectedFromEngine, getConnectedEngine, enableConnection, isConnectionEnabled, getForwardConnections, getContainer

NAME

SoMFFloat — multiple-value field containing any number of floating point values

INHERITS FROM

SoField > SoMField > SoMFFloat

DESCRIPTION

A multiple-value field that contains any number of floating point values.

SoMFFloats are written to file as one or more values in standard scientific notation. When more than one value is present, all of the values are enclosed in square brackets and separated by commas; for example:

[1.0, 2.3, 5, 6.2e4, -100,]

The last comma is optional.

METHODS

static SoType **getClassTypeId**()
virtual void **getTypeId**() const
Returns the type for this class or a particular object of this class.

float **operator** [ ](int i) const
Returns the *i*'th value of the field. Indexing past the end of the field (passing in *i* greater than **getNum**()) will return garbage.

const float * **getValues**(int start) const
Returns a pointer into the array of values in the field, starting at index *start*. The values are read-only; see the **startEditing**()/**finishEditing**() methods for a way of modifying values in place.

int **find**(float targetValue, SbBool addIfNotFound = FALSE)
Finds the given value in the array and returns the index of that value in the array. If the value is not found, -1 is returned. If *addIfNotFound* is set, then *targetValue* is added to the end of the array (but -1 is still returned).

void **setValues**(int start, int num, const float *newValues)
Sets *num* values starting at index *start* to the values in *newValues*. The array will be automatically be made larger to accomodate the new values, if necessary.

void **set1Value**(int index, float newValue)
Sets the *index*'th value in the array to *newValue*. The array will be automatically expanded, if necessary.

| float | **operator** =(float newValue) |
| void | **setValue**(float newValue) |

Sets the first value in the array to *newValue*, and deletes the second and subsequent values.

| int | **operator** ==(const SoMFFloat &f) const |
| int | **operator** !=(const SoMFFloat &f) const |

Returns TRUE if all of the values of this field equal (do not equal) those of the given field. If the fields are different types FALSE will always be returned (even if one field is an **SoMFFloat** with one value of 1.0 and the other is an **SoMFInt** with a value of 1, for example).

| float * | **startEditing**() |
| void | **finishEditing**() |

startEditing() returns a pointer to the internally-maintained array that can be modified. The values in the array may be changed, but values cannot be added or removed. It is illegal to call any other editing methods between **startEditing**() and **finishEditing**() (e.g. **set1Value**(), **setValue**(), etc).

Fields, engines or sensors connected to this field and sensors are not notified that this field has changed until **finishEditing**() is called. Calling **finishEditing**() always sets the **isDefault**() flag to FALSE and informs engines and sensors that the field changed, even if none of the values actually were changed.

Methods from class SoMField:

getNum, setNum, deleteValues, insertSpace, set1, get1

Methods from class SoField:

setIgnored, isIgnored, isDefault, isOfType, set, get, touch, connectFrom, connectFrom, disconnect, isConnected, isConnectedFromField, getConnectedField, isConnectedFromEngine, getConnectedEngine, enableConnection, isConnectionEnabled, getForwardConnections, getContainer

INCLUDE FILE

```
#include <Inventor/fields/SoMFFloat.h>
```

NAME

SoMField — base class for all multiple-valued fields

INHERITS FROM

SoField > SoMField

DESCRIPTION

Each class derived from **SoMField** begins with an **SoMF** prefix and contains a dynamic array of values of a particular type. Each has a **setValues()** method that is passed a pointer to a const array of values of the correct type; these values are copied into the array in the field, making extra room in the array if necessary. The start and num parameters to this method indicate the starting array index to copy into and the number of values to copy.

The **getValues()** method for a multiple-value field returns a const pointer to the array of values in the field. (Because this pointer is const, it cannot be used to change values in this array.)

In addition, the indexing operator "[]" is overloaded to return the *i*'th value in the array; because it returns a const reference, it can be used only to get values, not to set them.

Methods are provided for getting the number of values in the field, inserting space for new values in the middle, and deleting values.

There are other methods that allow you to set only one value of several in the field and to set the field to contain one and only one value.

Two other methods can be used to make several changes to a multiple-value field without the overhead of copying values into and out of the fields. The **startEditing()** method returns a non-const pointer to the array of values in the field; this pointer can then be used to change (but not add or remove) any values in the array. The **finishEditing()** method indicates that the editing is done and notifies any sensors or engines that may be connected to the field.

SoMFields are written to file as a series of values separated by commas, all enclosed in square brackets. If the field has no values (**getNum()** returns zero), then only the square brackets ("[]") are written. The last value may optionally be followed by a comma. Each field subtype defines how the values are written; for example, a field whose values are integers might be written as:

    [1, 2, 3, 4]
      or:
    [1, 2, 3, 4,]

METHODS

int **getNum**() const
Returns the number of values currently in the field.

void **setNum**(int num)
Forces this field to have exactly num values, inserting or deleting values as necessary.

virtual void **deleteValues**(int start, int num = -1)
Deletes *num* values beginning at index *start* (index *start* through *start+num*-1 will be deleted, and any leftover values will be moved down to fill in the gap created). A *num* of -1 means delete all values from *start* to the last value in the field; **getNum**() will return *start* as the number of values in the field after this operation (**deleteValues(0, -1) empties the field**).

virtual void **insertSpace**(int start, int num)
Inserts space for *num* values at index *start*. Index *start* through *start+num*-1 will be moved up to make room. For example, to make room for 7 new values at the beginning of the field call **insertSpace(0, 10)**.

SbBool **set1**(int index, const char *valueString)
void **get1**(int index, SbString &valueString)
These are equivalent to the **set**() and **get**() methods of **SoField**, but they operate on only one value. See the **SoField** methods for details.

static SoType **getClassTypeId**()
Return the type identifier for this field class.

Methods from class SoField:

setIgnored, isIgnored, isDefault, getTypeId, isOfType, set, get, operator ==, operator !=, touch, connectFrom, connectFrom, disconnect, isConnected, isConnectedFromField, getConnectedField, isConnectedFromEngine, getConnectedEngine, enableConnection, isConnectionEnabled, getForwardConnections, getContainer

INCLUDE FILE

```
#include <Inventor/fields/SoField.h>
```

SEE ALSO

SoNode, SoEngine

NAME

SoMFLong — multiple-value field containing any number of long integers

INHERITS FROM

SoField > SoMField > SoMFLong

DESCRIPTION

A multiple-value field that contains any number of long (32-bit) integers.

SoMFLongs are written to file as one or more integer values, in decimal, hexadecimal or octal format. When more than one value is present, all of the values are enclosed in square brackets and separated by commas; for example:

[17, -0xE20, -518820]

METHODS

static SoType **getClassTypeId**()
virtual void **getTypeId**() const
  Returns the type for this class or a particular object of this class.

long **operator [ ]**(int i) const
  Returns the *i*'th value of the field. Indexing past the end of the field (passing in *i* greater than **getNum**()) will return garbage.

const long * **getValues**(int start) const
  Returns a pointer into the array of values in the field, starting at index *start*. The values are read-only; see the **startEditing**()/**finishEditing**() methods for a way of modifying values in place.

int **find**(long targetValue, SbBool addIfNotFound = FALSE)
  Finds the given value in the array and returns the index of that value in the array. If the value is not found, -1 is returned. If *addIfNotFound* is set, then *targetValue* is added to the end of the array (but -1 is still returned).

void **setValues**(int start, int num, const long *newValues)
  Sets *num* values starting at index *start* to the values in *newValues*. The array will be automatically be made larger to accomodate the new values, if necessary.

void **set1Value**(int index, long newValue)
  Sets the *index*'th value in the array to *newValue*. The array will be automatically expanded, if necessary.

long	**operator** =(long newValue)
void	**setValue**(long newValue)

Sets the first value in the array to *newValue,* and deletes the second and subsequent values.

int	**operator** ==(const SoMFLong &f) const
int	**operator** !=(const SoMFLong &f) const

Returns TRUE if all of the values of this field equal (do not equal) those of the given field. If the fields are different types FALSE will always be returned (even if one field is an **SoMFFloat** with one value of 1.0 and the other is an **SoMFInt** with a value of 1, for example).

long *	**startEditing**()
void	**finishEditing**()

startEditing() returns a pointer to the internally-maintained array that can be modified. The values in the array may be changed, but values cannot be added or removed. It is illegal to call any other editing methods between **startEditing**() and **finishEditing**() (e.g. **set1Value**(), **setValue**(), etc).

Fields, engines or sensors connected to this field and sensors are not notified that this field has changed until **finishEditing**() is called. Calling **finishEditing**() always sets the **isDefault**() flag to FALSE and informs engines and sensors that the field changed, even if none of the values actually were changed.

Methods from class SoMFField:

getNum, setNum, deleteValues, insertSpace, set1, get1

Methods from class SoField:

setIgnored, isIgnored, isDefault, isOfType, set, get, touch, connectFrom, connectFrom, disconnect, isConnected, isConnectedFromField, getConnectedField, isConnectedFromEngine, getConnectedEngine, enableConnection, isConnectionEnabled, getForwardConnections, getContainer

INCLUDE FILE

```
#include <Inventor/fields/SoMFLong.h>
```

NAME

SoMFMatrix — multiple-value field containing any number of 4x4 matrices

INHERITS FROM

SoField > SoMField > SoMFMatrix

DESCRIPTION

A multiple-value field that contains any number of 4x4 matrices.

SoMFMatrices are written to file as sets of 16 floating point numbers separated by whitespace. When more than one value is present, all of the values are enclosed in square brackets and separated by commas; for example, two identity matrices might be written as:

    [1 0 0 0 0 1 0 0 0 0 1 0 0 0 0 1,
      1 0 0 0 0 1 0 0 0 0 1 0 0 0 0 1]

METHODS

void   **setValue**(float a11, float a12, float a13, float a14, float a21, float a22, float a23, float a24, float a31, float a32, float a33, float a34, float a41, float a42, float a43, float a44)
Makes this field contain one and only one value, which is the matrix given by the 16 values.

static SoType   **getClassTypeId**()
virtual void   **getTypeId**() const
Returns the type for this class or a particular object of this class.

const SbMatrix &

                 operator [ ](int i) const
Returns the i'th value of the field. Indexing past the end of the field (passing in i greater than **getNum**()) will return garbage.

const SbMatrix *   **getValues**(int start) const
Returns a pointer into the array of values in the field, starting at index start. The values are read-only; see the **startEditing**()/**finishEditing**() methods for a way of modifying values in place.

int   **find**(const SbMatrix & targetValue, SbBool addIfNotFound = FALSE)
Finds the given value in the array and returns the index of that value in the array. If the value is not found, -1 is returned. If *addIfNotFound* is set, then *targetValue* is added to the end of the array (but -1 is still returned).

void   **setValues**(int start, int num, const SbMatrix *newValues)
Sets *num* values starting at index *start* to the values in *newValues*. The array
will be automatically be made larger to accomodate the new values, if
necessary.

void   **set1Value**(int index, const SbMatrix & newValue)
Sets the *index*'th value in the array to *newValue*. The array will be
automatically expanded, if necessary.

const SbMatrix &
                operator =(const SbMatrix & newValue)
void   **setValue**(const SbMatrix & newValue)
Sets the first value in the array to *newValue*, and deletes the second and
subsequent values.

int   **operator** ==(const SoMFMatrix &f) const
int   **operator** !=(const SoMFMatrix &f) const
Returns TRUE if all of the values of this field equal (do not equal) those of
the given field. If the fields are different types FALSE will always be returned
(even if one field is an **SoMFFloat** with one value of 1.0 and the other is an
SoMFInt with a value of 1, for example).

SbMatrix *   **startEditing**()
void   **finishEditing**()
startEditing() returns a pointer to the internally-maintained array that can
be modified. The values in the array may be changed, but values cannot be
added or removed. It is illegal to call any other editing methods between
startEditing() and **finishEditing**() (e.g. **set1Value**(), **setValue**(), etc).

Fields, engines or sensors connected to this field and sensors are not notified
that this field has changed until **finishEditing**() is called. Calling
finishEditing() always sets the **isDefault**() flag to FALSE and informs
engines and sensors that the field changed, even if none of the values
actually were changed.

Methods from class SoMField:

getNum, setNum, deleteValues, insertSpace, set1, get1

Methods from class SoField:

setIgnored, isIgnored, isDefault, isOfType, set, get, touch, connectFrom, connectFrom, disconnect, isConnected, isConnectedFromField, getConnectedField, isConnectedFromEngine, getConnectedEngine, enableConnection, isConnectionEnabled, getForwardConnections, getContainer

INCLUDE FILE

```
#include <Inventor/fields/SoMFMatrix.h>
```

NAME

SoMFName — multiple-value field containing any number of names

INHERITS FROM

SoField > SoMFField > SoMFName

DESCRIPTION

A multiple-valued field containing any number of names. Names are short series of characters generally used for labels or names, and are stored in a special table designed to allow fast lookup and comparison. For most purposes, an **SoMFString** field is probably more appropriate.

SoMFNames are written to file as one or more strings of characters. Names must begin with an underscore or alphabetic character, and must consist entirely of underscores, alphabetic characters, or numbers. When more than one value is present, all of the values are enclosed in square brackets and separated by commas; for example:

[Fred, Wilma, _Part_01, translationField]

METHODS

void **setValues**(int start, int num, const char *strings[])
Sets *num* values beginning at index *start* to the names contained in the given set of character strings.

void **setValue**(const char *string)
Sets this field to contain one and only one value, given by *string*.

static SoType **getClassTypeId**()
virtual void **getTypeId**() const
Returns the type for this class or a particular object of this class.

const SbName & **operator [ ]**(int i) const
Returns the *i*'th value of the field. Indexing past the end of the field (passing in *i* greater than **getNum**()) will return garbage.

const SbName * **getValues**(int start) const
Returns a pointer into the array of values in the field, starting at index *start*. The values are read-only; see the **startEditing**()/**finishEditing**() methods for a way of modifying values in place.

int	**find**(const SbName & targetValue, SbBool addIfNotFound = FALSE)

Finds the given value in the array and returns the index of that value in the array. If the value is not found, -1 is returned. If *addIfNotFound* is set, then *targetValue* is added to the end of the array (but -1 is still returned).

void	**setValues**(int start, int num, const SbName *newValues)

Sets *num* values starting at index *start* to the values in *newValues*. The array will be automatically be made larger to accomodate the new values, if necessary.

void	**set1Value**(int index, const SbName & newValue)

Sets the *index*'th value in the array to *newValue*. The array will be automatically expanded, if necessary.

const SbName &	**operator=**(const SbName & newValue)
void	**setValue**(const SbName & newValue)

Sets the first value in the array to *newValue*, and deletes the second and subsequent values.

int	**operator ==**(const SoMFName &f) const
int	**operator !=**(const SoMFName &f) const

Returns TRUE if all of the values of this field equal (do not equal) those of the given field. If the fields are different types FALSE will always be returned (even if one field is an **SoMFFloat** with one value of 1.0 and the other is an **SoMFInt** with a value of 1, for example).

SbName *	**startEditing**()
void	**finishEditing**()

startEditing() returns a pointer to the internally-maintained array that can be modified. The values in the array may be changed, but values cannot be added or removed. It is illegal to call any other editing methods between **startEditing**() and **finishEditing**() (e.g. **set1Value**(), **setValue**(), etc).

Fields, engines or sensors connected to this field and sensors are not notified that this field has changed until **finishEditing**() is called. Calling **finishEditing**() always sets the **isDefault**() flag to FALSE and informs engines and sensors that the field changed, even if none of the values actually were changed.

Methods from class SoMField:

getNum, setNum, deleteValues, insertSpace, set1, get1

Methods from class SoField:

setIgnored, isIgnored, isDefault, isOfType, set, get, touch, connectFrom, connectFrom, disconnect, isConnected, isConnectedFromField, getConnectedField, isConnectedFromEngine, getConnectedEngine, enableConnection, isConnectionEnabled, getForwardConnections, getContainer

INCLUDE FILE

```
#include <Inventor/fields/SoMFName.h>
```

NAME

SoMFNode — multiple-value field containing any number of pointers to nodes

INHERITS FROM

SoField > SoMField > SoMFNode

DESCRIPTION

This field maintains a set of pointers to **SoNode** instances, correctly maintaining their reference counts.

SoMFNodes are written to file as one or more nodes. When more than one value is present, all of the values are enclosed in square brackets and separated by commas; for example:

[Cube { }, Sphere { radius 2.0 }, USE myTranslation]

METHODS

static SoType   **getClassTypeId**()
virtual void   **getTypeId**() const
    Returns the type for this class or a particular object of this class.

SoNode *   **operator [ ]**(int i) const
    Returns the *i*'th value of the field. Indexing past the end of the field (passing in *i* greater than **getNum**()) will return garbage.

const SoNode * *   **getValues**(int start) const
    Returns a pointer into the array of values in the field, starting at index *start*. The values are read-only; see the **startEditing**()/**finishEditing**() methods for a way of modifying values in place.

int   **find**(SoNode * targetValue, SbBool addIfNotFound = FALSE)
    Finds the given value in the array and returns the index of that value in the array. If the value is not found, -1 is returned. If *addIfNotFound* is set, then *targetValue* is added to the end of the array (but -1 is still returned).

void   **setValues**(int start, int num, const SoNode * *newValues)
    Sets num values starting at index *start* to the values in *newValues*. The array will be automatically be made larger to accomodate the new values, if necessary.

void   **set1Value**(int index, SoNode * newValue)
    Sets the *index*'th value in the array to *newValue*. The array will be automatically expanded, if necessary.

SoNode *	**operator** =(SoNode * newValue)
void	**setValue**(SoNode * newValue)

Sets the first value in the array to *newValue*, and deletes the second and subsequent values.

int	**operator** ==(const SoMFNode &f) const
int	**operator** !=(const SoMFNode &f) const

Returns TRUE if all of the values of this field equal (do not equal) those of the given field. If the fields are different types FALSE will always be returned (even if one field is an **SoMFFloat** with one value of 1.0 and the other is an **SoMFInt** with a value of 1, for example).

SoNode * *	**startEditing**()
void	**finishEditing**()

startEditing() returns a pointer to the internally-maintained array that can be modified. The values in the array may be changed, but values cannot be added or removed. It is illegal to call any other editing methods between **startEditing**() and **finishEditing**() (e.g. **set1Value**(), **setValue**(), etc).

Fields, engines or sensors connected to this field and sensors are not notified that this field has changed until **finishEditing**() is called. Calling **finishEditing**() always sets the **isDefault**() flag to FALSE and informs engines and sensors that the field changed, even if none of the values actually were changed.

Methods from class SoMFField:

getNum, setNum, deleteValues, insertSpace, set1, get1

Methods from class SoField:

setIgnored, isIgnored, isDefault, isOfType, set, get, touch, connectFrom, connectFrom, disconnect, isConnected, isConnectedFromField, getConnectedField, isConnectedFromEngine, getConnectedEngine, enableConnection, isConnectionEnabled, getForwardConnections, getContainer

INCLUDE FILE

```
#include <Inventor/fields/SoMFNode.h>
```

NAME

SoMFPath — multiple-value field containing any number of pointers to paths

INHERITS FROM

SoField > SoMField > SoMFPath

DESCRIPTION

This field maintains a set of pointers to **SoPath** instances, correctly maintaining their reference counts.

SoMFPaths are written to file as one or more paths (see the **SoPath** manual page for a description of the file format for a path). When more than one value is present, all of the values are enclosed in square brackets and separated by commas.

METHODS

static SoType   **getClassTypeId**()
virtual void   **getTypeId**() const
Returns the type for this class or a particular object of this class.

SoPath *   **operator [ ]**(int i) const
Returns the *i*'th value of the field. Indexing past the end of the field (passing in *i* greater than **getNum**()) will return garbage.

const SoPath * *   **getValues**(int start) const
Returns a pointer into the array of values in the field, starting at index *start*. The values are read-only; see the **startEditing**()/**finishEditing**() methods for a way of modifying values in place.

int   **find**(SoPath * targetValue, SbBool addIfNotFound = FALSE)
Finds the given value in the array and returns the index of that value in the array. If the value is not found, -1 is returned. If *addIfNotFound* is set, then *targetValue* is added to the end of the array (but -1 is still returned).

void   **setValues**(int start, int num, const SoPath * *newValues)
Sets *num* values starting at index *start* to the values in *newValues*. The array will be automatically be made larger to accomodate the new values, if necessary.

void   **set1Value**(int index, SoPath * newValue)
Sets the *index*'th value in the array to *newValue*. The array will be automatically expanded, if necessary.

SoPath *	**operator =**(SoPath * newValue)
void	**setValue**(SoPath * newValue)

Sets the first value in the array to *newValue*, and deletes the second and subsequent values.

int	**operator ==**(const SoMFPath &f) const
int	**operator !=**(const SoMFPath &f) const

Returns TRUE if all of the values of this field equal (do not equal) those of the given field. If the fields are different types FALSE will always be returned (even if one field is an **SoMFFloat** with one value of 1.0 and the other is an **SoMFInt** with a value of 1, for example).

SoPath * *	**startEditing**()
void	**finishEditing**()

startEditing() returns a pointer to the internally-maintained array that can be modified. The values in the array may be changed, but values cannot be added or removed. It is illegal to call any other editing methods between **startEditing**() and **finishEditing**() (e.g. **set1Value**(), **setValue**(), etc).

Fields, engines or sensors connected to this field and sensors are not notified that this field has changed until **finishEditing**() is called. Calling **finishEditing**() always sets the **isDefault**() flag to FALSE and informs engines and sensors that the field changed, even if none of the values actually were changed.

Methods from class SoMFIeld:

getNum, setNum, deleteValues, insertSpace, set1, get1

Methods from class SoField:

setIgnored, isIgnored, isDefault, isOfType, set, get, touch, connectFrom, connectFrom, disconnect, isConnected, isConnectedFromField, getConnectedField, isConnectedFromEngine, getConnectedEngine, enableConnection, isConnectionEnabled, getForwardConnections, getContainer

INCLUDE FILE

```
#include <Inventor/fields/SoMFPath.h>
```

NAME

SoMFPlane — field containing several plane equations

INHERITS FROM

SoField > SoMField > SoMFPlane

DESCRIPTION

A field containing one or more plane equations.

SoMFPlanes are written to file as groups of four floating point values separated by whitespace. In each set of four values, the first three are the normal direction of the plane, the fourth is the distance of the plane from the origin (in the direction of the normal).

When more than one value is present, all of the values are enclosed in square brackets and separated by commas; for example:

[1 0 0 0, .707 .707 0 100,]

METHODS

static SoType   **getClassTypeId**()

virtual void   **getTypeId**() const

Returns the type for this class or a particular object of this class.

SbPlane   **operator [ ]**(int i) const

Returns the *i*'th value of the field. Indexing past the end of the field (passing in *i* greater than *getNum()*) will return garbage.

const SbPlane *   **getValues**(int start) const

Returns a pointer into the array of values in the field, starting at index *start*. The values are read-only; see the **startEditing**()/**finishEditing**() methods for a way of modifying values in place.

int   **find**(SbPlane targetValue, SbBool addIfNotFound = FALSE)

Finds the given value in the array and returns the index of that value in the array. If the value is not found, -1 is returned. If *addIfNotFound* is set, then *targetValue* is added to the end of the array (but -1 is still returned).

void   **setValues**(int start, int num, const SbPlane *newValues)

Sets num values starting at index *start* to the values in *newValues*. The array will be automatically be made larger to accomodate the new values, if necessary.

void	**set1Value**(int index, SbPlane newValue)

Sets the *index*'th value in the array to *newValue*. The array will be automatically expanded, if necessary.

SbPlane	**operator =**(SbPlane newValue)
void	**setValue**(SbPlane newValue)

Sets the first value in the array to *newValue*, and deletes the second and subsequent values.

int	**operator ==**(const SoMFPlane &f) const
int	**operator !=**(const SoMFPlane &f) const

Returns TRUE if all of the values of this field equal (do not equal) those of the given field. If the fields are different types FALSE will always be returned (even if one field is an **SoMFFloat** with one value of 1.0 and the other is an **SoMFInt** with a value of 1, for example).

SbPlane *	**startEditing**()
void	**finishEditing**()

startEditing() returns a pointer to the internally-maintained array that can be modified. The values in the array may be changed, but values cannot be added or removed. It is illegal to call any other editing methods between **startEditing**() and **finishEditing**() (e.g. **set1Value**(), **setValue**(), etc).

Fields, engines or sensors connected to this field and sensors are not notified that this field has changed until **finishEditing**() is called. Calling **finishEditing**() always sets the **isDefault**() flag to FALSE and informs engines and sensors that the field changed, even if none of the values actually were changed.

Methods from class SoMFField:

getNum, setNum, deleteValues, insertSpace, set1, get1

Methods from class SoField:

setIgnored, isIgnored, isDefault, isOfType, set, get, touch, connectFrom, connectFrom, disconnect, isConnected, isConnectedFromField, getConnectedField, isConnectedFromEngine, getConnectedEngine, enableConnection, isConnectionEnabled, getForwardConnections, getContainer

INCLUDE FILE

```
#include <Inventor/fields/SoMFPlane.h>
```

NAME

SoMFRotation — Multiple-value field containing any number of SbRotations.

INHERITS FROM

SoField > SoMField > SoMFRotation

DESCRIPTION

multiple-value field that contains any number of SbRotations.

SoMFRotations are written to file as one or more sets of four floating point values. Each set of 4 values is an axis of rotation followed by the amount of right-handed rotation about that axis, in radians.

When more than one value is present, all of the values are enclosed in square brackets and separated by commas; for example:

[1 0 0 0, -.707 -.707 0 1.57]

METHODS

void	**set1Value**(int index, const SbVec3f &axis, float angle)

Sets the *index*'th value to the given axis/angle.

void	**setValue**(const SbVec3f &axis, float angle)

Makes this field have exactly one value, given by *axis* and *angle*.

void	**set1Value**(int index, float q0, float q1, float q2, float q3)
void	**set1Value**(int index, const float q[4])

Sets the *index*'th value to the given quaternion.

void	**setValue**(float q0, float q1, float q2, float q3)
void	**setValue**(float q[4])

Makes this field have exactly one value, given by the quaternion.

static SoType	**getClassTypeId**()
virtual void	**getTypeId**() const

Returns the type for this class or a particular object of this class.

const SbRotation &
                 operator [ ](int i) const

Returns the *i*'th value of the field. Indexing past the end of the field (passing in *i* greater than **getNum**()) will return garbage.

const SbRotation *
    getValues(int start) const
Returns a pointer into the array of values in the field, starting at index *start*.
The values are read-only; see the **startEditing()/finishEditing()** methods for
a way of modifying values in place.

int
    find(const SbRotation & targetValue, SbBool addIfNotFound =
    FALSE)
Finds the given value in the array and returns the index of that value in the
array. If the value is not found, -1 is returned. If *addIfNotFound* is set, then
targetValue is added to the end of the array (but -1 is still returned).

void
    setValues(int start, int num, const SbRotation *newValues)
Sets *num* values starting at index *start* to the values in *newValues*. The array
will be automatically be made larger to accomodate the new values, if
necessary.

void
    set1Value(int index, const SbRotation & newValue)
Sets the *index*'th value in the array to *newValue*. The array will be
automatically expanded, if necessary.

const SbRotation &
    operator =(const SbRotation & newValue)
void
    setValue(const SbRotation & newValue)
Sets the first value in the array to *newValue*, and deletes the second and
subsequent values.

int
    operator ==(const SoMFRotation &f) const
int
    operator !=(const SoMFRotation &f) const
Returns TRUE if all of the values of this field equal (do not equal) those of
the given field. If the fields are different types FALSE will always be returned
(even if one field is an **SoMFFloat** with one value of 1.0 and the other is an
SoMFInt with a value of 1, for example).

SbRotation *
    startEditing()
void
    finishEditing()
startEditing() returns a pointer to the internally-maintained array that can
be modified. The values in the array may be changed, but values cannot be
added or removed. It is illegal to call any other editing methods between
startEditing() and **finishEditing**() (e.g. **set1Value**(), **setValue**(), etc).

Fields, engines or sensors connected to this field and sensors are not notified
that this field has changed until **finishEditing**() is called. Calling

finishEditing() always sets the **isDefault()** flag to FALSE and informs engines and sensors that the field changed, even if none of the values actually were changed.

Methods from class SoMField:

getNum, setNum, deleteValues, insertSpace, set1, get1

Methods from class SoField:

setIgnored, isIgnored, isDefault, isOfType, set, get, touch, connectFrom, connectFrom, disconnect, isConnected, isConnectedFromField, getConnectedField, isConnectedFromEngine, getConnectedEngine, enableConnection, isConnectionEnabled, getForwardConnections, getContainer

INCLUDE FILE

```
#include <Inventor/fields/SoMFRotation.h>
```

SEE ALSO

SbRotation

NAME

SoMFShort — multiple-value field containing any number of short integers

INHERITS FROM

SoField > SoMField > SoMFShort

DESCRIPTION

A multiple-value field that contains any number of short (16-bit) integers.

SoMFShorts are written to file as one or more short integer values, represented as decimal, hexadecimal (beginning with '0x') or octal (beginning with '0') values. When more than one value is present, all of the values are enclosed in square brackets and separated by commas; for example:

[-7, 0xFF, -033]

METHODS

static SoType   **getClassTypeId**()
virtual void   **getTypeId**() const
Returns the type for this class or a particular object of this class.

short   **operator [ ]**(int i) const
Returns the *i*'th value of the field. Indexing past the end of the field (passing in *i* greater than *getNum()*) will return garbage.

const short *   **getValues**(int start) const
Returns a pointer into the array of values in the field, starting at index *start*. The values are read-only; see the **startEditing**()/**finishEditing**() methods for a way of modifying values in place.

int   **find**(short targetValue, SbBool addIfNotFound = FALSE)
Finds the given value in the array and returns the index of that value in the array. If the value is not found, -1 is returned. If *addIfNotFound* is set, then *targetValue* is added to the end of the array (but -1 is still returned).

void   **setValues**(int start, int num, const short *newValues)
Sets *num* values starting at index *start* to the values in *newValues*. The array will be automatically be made larger to accomodate the new values, if necessary.

void   **set1Value**(int index, short newValue)
Sets the *index*'th value in the array to *newValue*. The array will be automatically expanded, if necessary.

short	**operator** =(short newValue)
void	**setValue**(short newValue)

Sets the first value in the array to *newValue*, and deletes the second and subsequent values.

int	**operator** ==(const SoMFShort &f) const
int	**operator** !=(const SoMFShort &f) const

Returns TRUE if all of the values of this field equal (do not equal) those of the given field. If the fields are different types FALSE will always be returned (even if one field is an **SoMFFloat** with one value of 1.0 and the other is an **SoMFInt** with a value of 1, for example).

short *	**startEditing**()
void	**finishEditing**()

startEditing() returns a pointer to the internally-maintained array that can be modified. The values in the array may be changed, but values cannot be added or removed. It is illegal to call any other editing methods between **startEditing**() and **finishEditing**() (e.g. **set1Value**(), **setValue**(), etc).

Fields, engines or sensors connected to this field and sensors are not notified that this field has changed until **finishEditing**() is called. Calling **finishEditing**() always sets the **isDefault**() flag to FALSE and informs engines and sensors that the field changed, even if none of the values actually were changed.

Methods from class SoMFField:

getNum, setNum, deleteValues, insertSpace, set1, get1

Methods from class SoField:

setIgnored, isIgnored, isDefault, isOfType, set, get, touch, connectFrom, connectFrom, disconnect, isConnected, isConnectedFromField, getConnectedField, isConnectedFromEngine, getConnectedEngine, enableConnection, isConnectionEnabled, getForwardConnections, getContainer

INCLUDE FILE

```
#include <Inventor/fields/SoMFShort.h>
```

NAME

SoMFString — multiple-value field containing any number of strings

INHERITS FROM

SoField > SoMField > SoMFString

DESCRIPTION

A multiple-value field that contains any number of strings.

SoMFStrings are written to file as one or more strings within double quotes. Any characters (including newlines) may appear within the quotes. To include a double quote character within the string, precede it with a backslash. For example:

[cowEnizer , "Scene Boy" , "He said, \"I did not!\""]

METHODS

setValues(int start, int num, const char *strings[])
Sets *num* values, starting at index *start*, to the strings in the given character arrays.

setValue(const char *string)
Deletes all values currently in this field and sets this field to contain only the given string.

static SoType   **getClassTypeId**()
virtual void   **getTypeId**() const
Returns the type for this class or a particular object of this class.

const SbString &   **operator** [ ](int i) const
Returns the *i*'th value of the field. Indexing past the end of the field (passing in *i* greater than **getNum**()) will return garbage.

const SbString *   **getValues**(int start) const
Returns a pointer into the array of values in the field, starting at index *start*. The values are read-only; see the **startEditing**()/**finishEditing**() methods for a way of modifying values in-place.

int   **find**(const SbString & targetValue, SbBool addIfNotFound = FALSE)
Finds the given value in the array and returns the index of that value in the array. If the value is not found, -1 is returned. If *addIfNotFound* is set, then targetValue will be added to the end of the array (but -1 is still returned).

void   **setValues**(int start, int num, const SbString *newValues)
Sets *num* values starting at index *start* to the values in *newValues*. The array will be automatically be made larger to accomodate the new values, if necessary.

void   **set1Value**(int index, const SbString & newValue)
Sets the *index*'th value in the array to *newValue*. The array will be automatically expanded, if necessary.

const SbString &   **operator =**(const SbString & newValue)
void   **setValue**(const SbString & newValue)
Sets the first value in the array to *newValue*, and deletes the second and subsequent values.

int   **operator ==**(const SoMFString &f) const
int   **operator !=**(const SoMFString &f) const
Returns TRUE if all of the values of this field equal (do not equal) those of the given field. If the fields are different types FALSE will always be returned (even if one field is an **SoMFFloat** with one value of 1.0 and the other is an **SoMFInt** with a value of 1, for example).

SbString *   **startEditing**()
void   **finishEditing**()
startEditing() returns a pointer to the internally-maintained array that can be modified. The values in the array may be changed, but values cannot be added or removed. It is illegal to call any other editing methods between **startEditing**() and **finishEditing**() (e.g. **set1Value**(), **setValue**(), etc).

Fields, engines or sensors connected to this field and sensors are not notified that this field has changed until **finishEditing**() is called. Calling **finishEditing**() always sets the **isDefault**(). flag to FALSE and informs engines and sensors that the field changed, even if none of the values actually were changed.

Methods from class SoMField:
getNum, setNum, deleteValues, insertSpace, set1, get1

Methods from class SoField:

setIgnored, isIgnored, isDefault, isOfType, set, get, touch, connectFrom, connectFrom, disconnect, isConnected, isConnectedFromField, getConnectedField, isConnectedFromEngine, getConnectedEngine, enableConnection, isConnectionEnabled, getForwardConnections, getContainer

INCLUDE FILE

```
#include <Inventor/fields/SoMFString.h>
```

NAME

SoMFTime — multiple-value field containing any number of SbTime values

INHERITS FROM

SoField > SoMField > SoMFTime

DESCRIPTION

A multiple-value field that contains any number of SbTime values.

SoMFTimes are written to file as one or more double-precision floating point values representing the length of time in seconds. Absolute times are measured relative to 00:00:00 GMT, January 1, 1970.

When more than one value is present, all of the values are enclosed in square brackets and separated by commas; for example:

[1.0, 1345600.1200055, 99.8]

METHODS

static SoType   **getClassTypeId**()
virtual void   **getTypeId**() const
Returns the type for this class or a particular object of this class.

const SbTime &   **operator [ ]**(int i) const
Returns the *i*'th value of the field. Indexing past the end of the field (passing in *i* greater than **getNum**()) will return garbage.

const SbTime *   **getValues**(int start) const
Returns a pointer into the array of values in the field, starting at index *start*. The values are read-only; see the **startEditing**()/**finishEditing**() methods for a way of modifying values in place.

int   **find**(const SbTime & targetValue, SbBool addIfNotFound = FALSE)
Finds the given value in the array and returns the index of that value in the array. If the value is not found, -1 is returned. If *addIfNotFound* is set, then *targetValue* is added to the end of the array (but -1 is still returned).

void   **setValues**(int start, int num, const SbTime *newValues)
Sets *num* values starting at index *start* to the values in *newValues*. The array will be automatically be made larger to accomodate the new values, if necessary.

void	**set1Value**(int index, const SbTime & newValue)

Sets the *index*'th value in the array to *newValue*. The array will be automatically expanded, if necessary.

const SbTime &	**operator =**(const SbTime & newValue)
void	**setValue**(const SbTime & newValue)

Sets the first value in the array to *newValue*, and deletes the second and subsequent values.

int	**operator ==**(const SoMFTime &f) const
int	**operator !=**(const SoMFTime &f) const

Returns TRUE if all of the values of this field equal (do not equal) those of the given field. If the fields are different types FALSE will always be returned (even if one field is an **SoMFFloat** with one value of 1.0 and the other is an **SoMFInt** with a value of 1, for example).

SbTime *	**startEditing**()
void	**finishEditing**()

startEditing() returns a pointer to the internally-maintained array that can be modified. The values in the array may be changed, but values cannot be added or removed. It is illegal to call any other editing methods between **startEditing**() and **finishEditing**() (e.g. **set1Value**(), **setValue**(), etc).

Fields, engines or sensors connected to this field and sensors are not notified that this field has changed until **finishEditing**() is called. Calling **finishEditing**() always sets the **isDefault**() flag to FALSE and informs engines and sensors that the field changed, even if none of the values actually were changed.

Methods from class SoMField:

getNum, setNum, deleteValues, insertSpace, set1, get1

Methods from class SoField:

setIgnored, isIgnored, isDefault, isOfType, set, get, touch, connectFrom, connectFrom, disconnect, isConnected, isConnectedFromField, getConnectedField, isConnectedFromEngine, getConnectedEngine, enableConnection, isConnectionEnabled, getForwardConnections, getContainer

SoMFTime

INCLUDE FILE

```
#include <Inventor/fields/SoMFTime.h>
```

SEE ALSO

SbTime

NAME

SoMFULong — multiple-value field containing any number of unsigned long integers

INHERITS FROM

SoField > SoMField > SoMFULong

DESCRIPTION

A multiple-value field that contains any number of unsigned long (32-bit) integers.

SoMFULongs are written to file as one or more unsigned long integers, in decimal, hexadecimal or octal format.

When more than one value is present, all of the values are enclosed in square brackets and separated by commas; for example:

[17, 0xFFFFE0, 0755]

METHODS

static SoType   **getClassTypeId**()
virtual void   **getTypeId**() const
   Returns the type for this class or a particular object of this class.

unsigned long   **operator[]**(int i) const
   Returns the *i*'th value of the field. Indexing past the end of the field (passing in *i* greater than **getNum**()) will return garbage.

const unsigned long *
     getValues(int start) const
   Returns a pointer into the array of values in the field, starting at index *start*. The values are read-only; see the **startEditing**()/**finishEditing**() methods for a way of modifying values in place.

int   **find**(unsigned long targetValue, SbBool addIfNotFound = FALSE)
   Finds the given value in the array and returns the index of that value in the array. If the value is not found, -1 is returned. If *addIfNotFound* is set, then *targetValue* is added to the end of the array (but -1 is still returned).

void   **setValues**(int start, int num, const unsigned long *newValues)
   Sets *num* values starting at index *start* to the values in *newValues*. The array will be automatically be made larger to accomodate the new values, if necessary.

void	**set1Value**(int index, unsigned long newValue)

Sets the *index*'th value in the array to *newValue*. The array will be automatically expanded, if necessary.

unsigned long	**operator =**(unsigned long newValue)
void	**setValue**(unsigned long newValue)

Sets the first value in the array to *newValue*, and deletes the second and subsequent values.

int	**operator ==**(const SoMFULong &f) const
int	**operator !=**(const SoMFULong &f) const

Returns TRUE if all of the values of this field equal (do not equal) those of the given field. If the fields are different types FALSE will always be returned (even if one field is an **SoMFFloat** with one value of 1.0 and the other is an **SoMFInt** with a value of 1, for example).

unsigned long *	**startEditing**()
void	**finishEditing**()

startEditing() returns a pointer to the internally-maintained array that can be modified. The values in the array may be changed, but values cannot be added or removed. It is illegal to call any other editing methods between **startEditing**() and **finishEditing**() (e.g. **set1Value**(), **setValue**(), etc).

Fields, engines or sensors connected to this field and sensors are not notified that this field has changed until **finishEditing**() is called. Calling **finishEditing**() always sets the **isDefault**() flag to FALSE and informs engines and sensors that the field changed, even if none of the values actually were changed.

Methods from class SoMField:

getNum, setNum, deleteValues, insertSpace, set1, get1

Methods from class SoField:

setIgnored, isIgnored, isDefault, isOfType, set, get, touch, connectFrom, connectFrom, disconnect, isConnected, isConnectedFromField, getConnectedField, isConnectedFromEngine, getConnectedEngine, enableConnection, isConnectionEnabled, getForwardConnections, getContainer

INCLUDE FILE

```
#include <Inventor/fields/SoMFULong.h>
```

NAME

SoMFUShort — multiple-value field containing any number of unsigned short integers

INHERITS FROM

SoField > SoMField > SoMFUShort

DESCRIPTION

A multiple-value field that contains any number of unsigned short integers.

SoMFUShorts are written to file as one or more unsigned short integer values, represented as decimal, hexadecimal (beginning with '0x') or octal (beginning with '0') values. When more than one value is present, all of the values are enclosed in square brackets and separated by commas; for example:

[7, 0xFF, 033]

METHODS

static SoType   **getClassTypeId**()
virtual void   **getTypeId**() const
Returns the type for this class or a particular object of this class.

unsigned short   **operator [ ]**(int i) const
Returns the *i*'th value of the field. Indexing past the end of the field (passing in *i* greater than **getNum**()) will return garbage.

const unsigned short *
     getValues(int start) const
Returns a pointer into the array of values in the field, starting at index *start*. The values are read-only; see the **startEditing**()/**finishEditing**() methods for a way of modifying values in place.

int   **find**(unsigned short targetValue, SbBool addIfNotFound = FALSE)
Finds the given value in the array and returns the index of that value in the array. If the value is not found, -1 is returned. If *addIfNotFound* is set, then *targetValue* is added to the end of the array (but -1 is still returned).

void   **setValues**(int start, int num, const unsigned short *newValues)
Sets *num* values starting at index *start* to the values in *newValues*. The array will be automatically be made larger to accomodate the new values, if necessary.

void	**set1Value**(int index, unsigned short newValue)

Sets the *index*'th value in the array to *newValue*. The array will be automatically expanded, if necessary.

unsigned short	**operator =**(unsigned short newValue)
void	**setValue**(unsigned short newValue)

Sets the first value in the array to *newValue*, and deletes the second and subsequent values.

int	**operator ==**(const SoMFUShort &f) const
int	**operator !=**(const SoMFUShort &f) const

Returns TRUE if all of the values of this field equal (do not equal) those of the given field. If the fields are different types FALSE will always be returned (even if one field is an **SoMFFloat** with one value of 1.0 and the other is an **SoMFInt** with a value of 1, for example).

unsigned short *	**startEditing**()
void	**finishEditing**()

startEditing() returns a pointer to the internally-maintained array that can be modified. The values in the array may be changed, but values cannot be added or removed. It is illegal to call any other editing methods between **startEditing**() and **finishEditing**() (e.g. **set1Value**(), **setValue**(), etc).

Fields, engines or sensors connected to this field and sensors are not notified that this field has changed until **finishEditing**() is called. Calling **finishEditing**() always sets the **isDefault**() flag to FALSE and informs engines and sensors that the field changed, even if none of the values actually were changed.

Methods from class SoMField:

getNum, setNum, deleteValues, insertSpace, set1, get1

Methods from class SoField:

setIgnored, isIgnored, isDefault, isOfType, set, get, touch, connectFrom, connectFrom, disconnect, isConnected, isConnectedFromField, getConnectedField, isConnectedFromEngine, getConnectedEngine, enableConnection, isConnectionEnabled, getForwardConnections, getContainer

INCLUDE FILE

```
#include <Inventor/fields/SoMFUShort.h>
```

NAME

SoMFVec2f — multiple-value field containing any number of two-dimensional vectors

INHERITS FROM

SoField > SoMField > SoMFVec2f

DESCRIPTION

A multiple-value field that contains any number of two-dimensional vectors.

SoMFVec2fs are written to file as one or more pairs of floating point values separated by whitespace. When more than one value is present, all of the values are enclosed in square brackets and separated by commas; for example:

[0 0, 1.2 3.4, 98.6 -4e1]

METHODS

void   **setValues**(int start, int num, const float xy[ ][2])
Sets *num* values starting at index *start* to the given floating point values. There must be *num**2 values in the passed array.

void   **set1Value**(int index, float x, float y)
void   **set1Value**(int index, const float xy[2])
Set the *index*'th value to the given floating point values.

void   **setValue**(float x, float y)
void   **setValue**(const float xy[2])
Sets the field to contain the given value and only the given value (if the array had multiple values before, they are deleted).

static SoType **getClassTypeId**()
virtual void **getTypeId**() const
Returns the type for this class or a particular object of this class.

const SbVec2f & **operator** [ ](int i) const
Returns the *i*'th value of the field. Indexing past the end of the field (passing in *i* greater than **getNum**()) will return garbage.

const SbVec2f * **getValues**(int start) const
Returns a pointer into the array of values in the field, starting at index *start*. The values are read-only; see the **startEditing**()/**finishEditing**() methods for a way of modifying values in place.

int	**find**(const SbVec2f & targetValue, SbBool addIfNotFound = FALSE)

Finds the given value in the array and returns the index of that value in the array. If the value is not found, -1 is returned. If *addIfNotFound* is set, then *targetValue* is added to the end of the array (but -1 is still returned).

void	**setValues**(int start, int num, const SbVec2f *newValues)

Sets *num* values starting at index *start* to the values in *newValues*. The array will be automatically be made larger to accomodate the new values, if necessary.

void	**set1Value**(int index, const SbVec2f & newValue)

Sets the *index*'th value in the array to *newValue*. The array will be automatically expanded, if necessary.

const SbVec2f &	**operator =**(const SbVec2f & newValue)
void	**setValue**(const SbVec2f & newValue)

Sets the first value in the array to *newValue*, and deletes the second and subsequent values.

int	**operator ==**(const SoMFVec2f &f) const
int	**operator !=**(const SoMFVec2f &f) const

Returns TRUE if all of the values of this field equal (do not equal) those of the given field. If the fields are different types FALSE will always be returned (even if one field is an **SoMFFloat** with one value of 1.0 and the other is an **SoMFInt** with a value of 1, for example).

SbVec2f *	**startEditing**()
void	**finishEditing**()

startEditing() returns a pointer to the internally-maintained array that can be modified. The values in the array may be changed, but values cannot be added or removed. It is illegal to call any other editing methods between **startEditing**() and **finishEditing**() (e.g. **set1Value**(), **setValue**(), etc).

Fields, engines or sensors connected to this field and sensors are not notified that this field has changed until **finishEditing**() is called. Calling **finishEditing**() always sets the **isDefault**() flag to FALSE and informs engines and sensors that the field changed, even if none of the values actually were changed.

Methods from class SoMField:

getNum, setNum, deleteValues, insertSpace, set1, get1

Methods from class SoField:

setIgnored, isIgnored, isDefault, isOfType, set, get, touch, connectFrom, connectFrom, disconnect, isConnected, isConnectedFromField, getConnectedField, isConnectedFromEngine, getConnectedEngine, enableConnection, isConnectionEnabled, getForwardConnections, getContainer

INCLUDE FILE

```
#include <Inventor/fields/SoMFVec2f.h>
```

NAME

SoMFVec3f — multiple-value field containing any number of three-dimensional vectors

INHERITS FROM

SoField > SoMField > SoMFVec3f

DESCRIPTION

A multiple-value field that contains any number of three-dimensional vectors.

SoMFVec3fs are written to file as one or more triples of floating point values separated by whitespace.

When more than one value is present, all of the values are enclosed in square brackets and separated by commas; for example:

[0 0 0, 1.2 3.4 5.6, 98.6 -4e1 212]

METHODS

void   **setValues**(int start, int num, const float xyz[ ][3])
Sets *num* values starting at index *start* to the given floating point values. There must be *num**3 values in the passed array.

void   **set1Value**(int index, float x, float y, float z)
void   **set1Value**(int index, const float xyz[3])
Set the *index*'th value to the given floating point values.

void   **setValue**(float x, float y, float z)
void   **setValue**(const float xyz[3])
Sets the field to contain the given value and only the given value (if the array had multiple values before, they are deleted).

static SoType   **getClassTypeId**()
virtual void   **getTypeId**() const
Returns the type for this class or a particular object of this class.

const SbVec3f &   **operator** [ ](int i) const
Returns the *i*'th value of the field. Indexing past the end of the field (passing in *i* greater than **getNum**()) will return garbage.

const SbVec3f *   **getValues**(int start) const
> Returns a pointer into the array of values in the field, starting at index *start*. The values are read-only; see the **startEditing()/finishEditing()** methods for a way of modifying values in place.

int   **find**(const SbVec3f & targetValue, SbBool addIfNotFound = FALSE)
> Finds the given value in the array and returns the index of that value in the array. If the value is not found, -1 is returned. If *addIfNotFound* is set, then *targetValue* is added to the end of the array (but -1 is still returned).

void   **setValues**(int start, int num, const SbVec3f *newValues)
> Sets *num* values starting at index *start* to the values in *newValues*. The array will be automatically be made larger to accomodate the new values, if necessary.

void   **set1Value**(int index, const SbVec3f & newValue)
> Sets the *index*'th value in the array to *newValue*. The array will be automatically expanded, if necessary.

const SbVec3f &   **operator** =(const SbVec3f & newValue)
void   **setValue**(const SbVec3f & newValue)
> Sets the first value in the array to *newValue*, and deletes the second and subsequent values.

int   **operator** ==(const SoMFVec3f &f) const
int   **operator** !=(const SoMFVec3f &f) const
> Returns TRUE if all of the values of this field equal (do not equal) the given field. If the fields are different types FALSE will always be returned (even if one field is an **SoMFFloat** with one value of 1.0 and the other is an **SoMFInt** with a value of 1, for example).

SbVec3f *   **startEditing**()
void   **finishEditing**()
> **startEditing**() returns a pointer to the internally-maintained array that can be modified. The values in the array may be changed, but values cannot be added or removed. It is illegal to call any other editing methods between **startEditing**() and **finishEditing**() (e.g. **set1Value**(), **setValue**(), etc).

> Fields, engines or sensors connected to this field and sensors are not notified that this field has changed until **finishEditing**() is called. Calling

finishEditing() always sets the **isDefault()** flag to FALSE and informs engines and sensors that the field changed, even if none of the values actually were changed.

Methods from class SoMField:

getNum, setNum, deleteValues, insertSpace, set1, get1

Methods from class SoField:

setIgnored, isIgnored, isDefault, isOfType, set, get, touch, connectFrom, connectFrom, disconnect, isConnected, isConnectedFromField, getConnectedField, isConnectedFromEngine, getConnectedEngine, enableConnection, isConnectionEnabled, getForwardConnections, getContainer

INCLUDE FILE

```
#include <Inventor/fields/SoMFVec3f.h>
```

NAME

SoMFVec4f — multiple-value field containing any number of four-dimensional vectors

INHERITS FROM

SoField > SoMField > SoMFVec4f

DESCRIPTION

A multiple-value field that contains any number of four-dimensional vectors.

SoMFVec4fs are written to file as one or more triples of floating point values separated by whitespace.

When more than one value is present, all of the values are enclosed in square brackets and separated by commas; for example:

[0 0 0, 1.2 3.4 5.6, 98.6 -4e1 212]

METHODS

void	**setValues**(int start, int num, const float xyzw[ ][4])

Sets *num* values starting at index *start* to the given floating point values. There must be *num**4 values in the passed array.

void	**set1Value**(int index, float x, float y, float z, float w)
void	**set1Value**(int index, const float xyzw[4])

Set the *index*'th value to the given floating point values.

void	**setValue**(float x, float y, float z, float w)
void	**setValue**(const float xyzw[4])

Sets the field to contain the given value and only the given value (if the array had multiple values before, they are deleted).

static SoType	**getClassTypeId**()
virtual void	**getTypeId**() const

Returns the type for this class or a particular object of this class.

const SbVec4f &	**operator** [ ](int i) const

Returns the *i*'th value of the field. Indexing past the end of the field (passing in *i* greater than **getNum**()) will return garbage.

const SbVec4f *   **getValues**(int start) const
> Returns a pointer into the array of values in the field, starting at index *start*. The values are read-only; see the **startEditing()**/**finishEditing()** methods for a way of modifying values in place.

int   **find**(const SbVec4f & targetValue, SbBool addIfNotFound = FALSE)
> Finds the given value in the array and returns the index of that value in the array. If the value is not found, -1 is returned. If *addIfNotFound* is set, then *targetValue* is added to the end of the array (but -1 is still returned).

void   **setValues**(int start, int num, const SbVec4f *newValues)
> Sets *num* values starting at index *start* to the values in *newValues*. The array will be automatically be made larger to accomodate the new values, if necessary.

void   **set1Value**(int index, const SbVec4f & newValue)
> Sets the *index*'th value in the array to *newValue*. The array will be automatically expanded, if necessary.

const SbVec4f &   **operator =**(const SbVec4f & newValue)
void   **setValue**(const SbVec4f & newValue)
> Sets the first value in the array to *newValue*, and deletes the second and subsequent values.

int   **operator ==**(const SoMFVec4f &f) const
int   **operator !=**(const SoMFVec4f &f) const
> Returns TRUE if all of the values of this field equal (do not equal) those of the given field. If the fields are different types FALSE will always be returned (even if one field is an **SoMFFloat** with one value of 1.0 and the other is an **SoMFInt** with a value of 1, for example).

SbVec4f *   **startEditing**()
void   **finishEditing**()
> **startEditing**() returns a pointer to the internally-maintained array that can be modified. The values in the array may be changed, but values cannot be added or removed. It is illegal to call any other editing methods between **startEditing**() and **finishEditing**() (e.g. **set1Value**(), **setValue**(), etc).
>
> Fields, engines or sensors connected to this field and sensors are not notified that this field has changed until **finishEditing**() is called. Calling **finishEditing**() always sets the **isDefault**() flag to FALSE and informs engines and sensors that the field changed, even if none of the values actually were changed.

Methods from class SoMFField:

getNum, setNum, deleteValues, insertSpace, set1, get1

Methods from class SoField:

setIgnored, isIgnored, isDefault, isOfType, set, get, touch, connectFrom, connectFrom, disconnect, isConnected, isConnectedFromField, getConnectedField, isConnectedFromEngine, getConnectedEngine, enableConnection, isConnectionEnabled, getForwardConnections, getContainer

INCLUDE FILE

```
#include <Inventor/fields/SoMFVec4f.h>
```

NAME

SoMotion3Event — 3D motion events

INHERITS FROM

SoEvent > SoMotion3Event

DESCRIPTION

SoMotion3Event represents 3D relative motion events in the Inventor event model.

METHODS

SoMotion3Event()
Constructor.

static SoType   **getClassTypeId**()
Return the type id for the **SoMotion3Event** class.

void   **setTranslation**(const SbVec3f &t)
const SbVec3f &   **getTranslation**() const
Set and get the relative change in translation since the last translation event.

void   **setRotation**(const SbRotation &r)
const SbRotation &

getRotation() const
Set and get the relative change in rotation since the last rotation event.

Methods from class SoEvent:

getTypeId, isOfType, setTime, getTime, setPosition, getPosition, getPosition, getNormalizedPosition, setShiftDown, setCtrlDown, setAltDown, wasShiftDown, wasCtrlDown, wasAltDown

INCLUDE FILE

```
#include <Inventor/events/SoMotion3Event.h>
```

SEE ALSO

SoEvent, SoButtonEvent, SoKeyboardEvent, SoLocation2Event, SoMouseButtonEvent, SoSpaceballButtonEvent, SoHandleEventAction, SoEventCallback, SoSelection, SoInteraction, SoXtDevice

NAME

SoMouseButtonEvent — mouse button press and release events

INHERITS FROM

SoEvent > SoButtonEvent > SoMouseButtonEvent

DESCRIPTION

SoMouseButtonEvent represents mouse button press and release events in the Inventor event model.

METHODS

SoMouseButtonEvent()

Constructor.

static SoType   **getClassTypeId**()

Return the type id for the **SoMouseButtonEvent** class.

void   **setButton**(SoMouseButtonEvent::Button b)
SoMouseButtonEvent::Button
     getButton() const

Set and get which mouse button generated the event.

static SbBool   **isButtonPressEvent**(const SoEvent *e,
         SoMouseButtonEvent::Button whichButton)
static SbBool   **isButtonReleaseEvent**(const SoEvent *e,
         SoMouseButtonEvent::Button whichButton)

Returns whether the passed event is a mouse button press or release event of the passed button. When **SoMouseButtonEvent::ANY** is passed, this returns TRUE if the event represents a button press or release of any mouse button.

Methods from class SoButtonEvent:

setState, getState

Methods from class SoEvent:

getTypeId, isOfType, setTime, getTime, setPosition, getPosition, getPosition, getNormalizedPosition, setShiftDown, setCtrlDown, setAltDown, wasShiftDown, wasCtrlDown, wasAltDown

INCLUDE FILE

```
#include <Inventor/events/SoMouseButtonEvent.h>
```

```
#define SO_MOUSE_PRESS_EVENT(EVENT,BUTTON) \
    (SoMouseButtonEvent::isButtonPressEvent(EVENT,SoMouseButtonEvent::BUTTON))
#define SO_MOUSE_RELEASE_EVENT(EVENT,BUTTON) \
    (SoMouseButtonEvent::isButtonReleaseEvent(EVENT,SoMouseButtonEvent::BUTTON))
```

enum **Button** {
> **SoMouseButtonEvent::ANY**
>> Any button
> **SoMouseButtonEvent::BUTTON1**
>> First mouse button
> **SoMouseButtonEvent::BUTTON2**
>> Second mouse button
> **SoMouseButtonEvent::BUTTON3**
>> Third mouse button

}

SEE ALSO

> SoEvent, SoButtonEvent, SoKeyboardEvent, SoLocation2Event, SoMotion3Event, SoSpaceballButtonEvent, SoHandleEventAction, SoEventCallback, SoSelection, SoInteraction, SoXtDevice

NAME

SoMultipleCopy — group node that traverses multiple times, applying matrices

INHERITS FROM

SoBase > SoFieldContainer > SoNode > SoGroup > SoMultipleCopy

DESCRIPTION

This group node traverses its children, in order, several times, applying a different matrix each time. The matrices are stored in the multiple-value **matrix** field. Each matrix is concatenated to the current transformation matrix, and all of the children are traversed. This allows the user to put multiple copies of the same data in different locations easily and efficiently.

Traversing the Nth child sets the current switch value to N, for use with inherited switch values (see **SoSwitch**).

FIELDS

SoMFMatrix   **matrix**

Set of matrices to apply to children.

METHODS

SoMultipleCopy()

Creates a multiple copy node with default settings.

static SoType   **getClassTypeId()**

Returns type identifier for this class.

Methods from class SoGroup:

addChild, insertChild, getChild, findChild, getNumChildren, removeChild, removeChild, removeAllChildren, replaceChild, replaceChild

Methods from class SoNode:

setOverride, isOverride, copy, affectsState, getByName, getByName

Methods from class SoFieldContainer:

setToDefaults, hasDefaultValues, fieldsAreEqual, copyFieldValues, set, get, getFields, getField, getFieldName, enableNotify, isNotifyEnabled

Methods from class SoBase:

ref, unref, unrefNoDelete, touch, getTypeId, isOfType, setName, getName

SoMultipleCopy

ACTION BEHAVIOR

SoGLRenderAction, SoCallbackAction, SoGetBoundingBoxAction, SoRayPickAction

Traverses all children for each matrix, saving and restoring state before and after each traversal.

SoSearchAction

Traverses all children once, setting the inherited switch value to SO_SWITCH_ALL first.

FILE FORMAT/DEFAULTS

```
MultipleCopy {
      matrix  1 0 0 0
              0 1 0 0
              0 0 1 0
              0 0 0 1
}
```

INCLUDE FILE

```
#include <Inventor/nodes/SoMultipleCopy.h>
```

SEE ALSO

SoArray, SoSwitch

NAME

SoNode — abstract base class for all database nodes

INHERITS FROM

SoBase > SoFieldContainer > SoNode

DESCRIPTION

This is the abstract base class from which all scene graph node classes are derived.

METHODS

void   **setOverride**(SbBool state)

Turns override flag on or off.

SbBool   **isOverride**() const

Returns the state of the override flag.

virtual SoNode * **copy**(SbBool copyConnections = FALSE) const

Creates and returns an exact copy of the node. If the node is a group, it copies the children as well. If *copyConnections* is TRUE (it is FALSE by default), any connections to (but not from) fields of the node are copied, as well.

virtual SbBool **affectsState**() const

Returns TRUE if a node has an effect on the state during traversal. The default method returns TRUE. Node classes (such as **SoSeparator**) that isolate their effects from the rest of the graph override this method to return FALSE.

static SoNode * **getByName**(const SbName &name)

static int   **getByName**(const SbName &name, SoNodeList &list)

A node's name can be set using **SoBase::setName**(). These methods allow nodes to be looked up by name. The first one returns the last node given the specified name. The second one returns the number of nodes with the given name, and adds to *list* pointers to those nodes.

static SoType **getClassTypeId**()

Returns type identifier for the **SoNode** class.

Methods from class SoFieldContainer:

setToDefaults, hasDefaultValues, fieldsAreEqual, copyFieldValues, set, get, getFields, getField, getFieldName, enableNotify, isNotifyEnabled

Methods from class SoBase:

ref, unref, unrefNoDelete, touch, getTypeId, isOfType, setName, getName

ACTION BEHAVIOR

> **SoSearchAction**
>> If the node pointer, type, or name matches the search criteria, returns a path to the node.
>
> **SoWriteAction**
>> Writes the contents of the node to the current **SoOutput**.

FILE FORMAT/DEFAULTS

> This is an abstract class. See the reference page of a derived class for the format and default values.

INCLUDE FILE

> `#include <Inventor/nodes/SoNode.h>`

SEE ALSO

> SoPath, SoAction, SoNodeKit

NAME

    SoNodeKit — initializes nodekit classes

INHERITS FROM

    SoNodeKit

DESCRIPTION

    This class is used to initialize all nodekit classes.

METHODS

    static void   **init**()

        Initialize all nodekit classes by registering them with the database. This
        function needs to be called before *any* other nodekit class may be
        constructed or accessed. Note that this is called automatically by
        SoInteraction::init() and **SoXt::init()**, so if you have made either of these
        calls, there is no need to call **SoNodeKit::init()** directly.

INCLUDE FILE

    `#include <Inventor/nodekits/SoNodeKit.h>`

SEE ALSO

    SoAppearanceKit, SoBaseKit, SoCameraKit, SoInteraction, SoLightKit,
    SoNodeKitDetail, SoNodeKitListPart, SoNodeKitPath, SoNodekitCatalog, SoSceneKit,
    SoSeparatorKit, SoShapeKit, SoWrapperKit, SoXt

NAME

SoNodekitCatalog — nodekit catalog class

INHERITS FROM

SoNodekitCatalog

DESCRIPTION

This class describes the parts and structure of a nodekit. Each class of nodekit has one **SoNodekitCatalog** (a static variable for the class). Internally, the catalog contains one entry for each "part" in the nodekit's structure. Users can query the catalog for information about each entry in the catalog. This information can be obtained either by part name (an **SbName** unique for the part within the catalog) or by part number (an index into an array of parts).

Note that, although the catalog for a nodekit class may contain many entries, each instance of that class is not initially created with all of these parts intact. Rather, each instance of the class has its own parts list which keeps track of which parts the user has created. The nodekit uses the catalog as a guide in creating new nodes as its descendants; the standard **addChild()**, **removeChild()** and other **SoGroup** methods are protected, so that users must create descendants indirectly by asking the nodekit to get and/or set the different "parts" in the catalog.

The first entry in any **SoNodekitCatalog** corresponds to the nodekit itself. Its *partName* is "this" and its *partNumber* is 0. All other parts in the catalog are described relative to "this."

METHODS

static void   **initClass**()
        Initializes this object.

int   **getNumEntries**() const
        Returns number of entries in the catalog.

int   **getPartNumber**(const SbName &theName) const
        Given the name of a part, returns its part number in the catalog.

const SbName &   **getName**(int thePartNumber) const
        Given the part number of a part, returns its name in the catalog.

SoType	**getType**(int thePartNumber) const
SoType	**getType**(const SbName &theName) const
SoType	**getDefaultType**(int thePartNumber) const
SoType	**getDefaultType**(const SbName &theName) const
SbBool	**isNullByDefault**(int thePartNumber) const
SbBool	**isNullByDefault**(const SbName &theName) const
SbBool	**isLeaf**(int thePartNumber) const
SbBool	**isLeaf**(const SbName &theName) const
const SbName &	**getParentName**(int thePartNumber) const
const SbName &	**getParentName**(const SbName &theName) const
int	**getParentPartNumber**(int thePartNumber) const
int	**getParentPartNumber**(const SbName &theName) const
const SbName &	**getRightSiblingName**(int thePartNumber) const
const SbName &	**getRightSiblingName**(const SbName &theName) const
int	**getRightSiblingPartNumber**(int thePartNumber) const
int	**getRightSiblingPartNumber**(const SbName &theName) const
SbBool	**isList**(int thePartNumber) const
SbBool	**isList**(const SbName &theName) const
SoType	**getListContainerType**(int thePartNumber) const
SoType	**getListContainerType**(const SbName &theName) const
const SoTypeList &	
	getListItemTypes(int thePartNumber) const
const SoTypeList &	
	getListItemTypes(const SbName &theName) const
SbBool	**isPublic**(int thePartNumber) const
SbBool	**isPublic**(const SbName &theName) const

A full set of methods for finding out all parameters in the catalog, given either the part name or the part number.

INCLUDE FILE

```
#include <Inventor/nodekits/SoNodekitCatalog.h>
```

```
#define SO_CATALOG_NAME_NOT_FOUND -1
#define SO_CATALOG_THIS_PART_NUM   0
```

SEE ALSO

SoAppearanceKit, SoBaseKit, SoCameraKit, SoLightKit, SoNodeKit, SoNodeKitDetail, SoNodeKitListPart, SoNodeKitPath, SoSceneKit, SoSeparatorKit, SoShapeKit, SoWrapperKit

SoNodeKitDetail

NAME

SoNodeKitDetail — stores detail information about a nodekit

INHERITS FROM

SoDetail > SoNodeKitDetail

DESCRIPTION

This class contains detail information about a nodekit. This consists of a pointer to the nodekit, a pointer to the child part within the nodekit, and the name of the child part.

During a pick action, each nodekit along the picked path creates its own **SoNodeKitDetail**. Together, the full set of details gives you complete picture of the pickpath.

Since nodekits have hidden children (See the reference page for **SoBaseKit**), a regular **SoPath** ends at the topmost nodekit in the path. If you cast the pickpath from an **SoPath** pointer to an **SoNodeKitPath** pointer, you can then retrieve all nodekits along the path and examine their corresponding details.

METHODS

	SoNodeKitDetail()
virtual	**~SoNodeKitDetail**()

Constructor and destructor.

SoBaseKit * **getNodeKit**() const
Returns a pointer to the nodekit that created this detail.

SoNode * **getPart**() const
Returns a pointer to the part selected within the nodekit that created this detail.

const SbName & **getPartName**() const
Returns the name of the part selected within the nodekit that created this detail. (See **SoRayPickAction** in the ACTIONS section of the **SoBaseKit** reference page for more information).

Methods from class SoDetail:

copy, getClassTypeId, getTypeId, isOfType

INCLUDE FILE

```
#include <Inventor/details/SoNodeKitDetail.h>
```

SEE ALSO

SoBaseKit, SoNodeKitPath, SoDetail, SoPickedPoint

NAME

NAME

SoNodeKitListPart — group node with restricted children

INHERITS FROM

SoBase > SoFieldContainer > SoNode > SoNodeKitListPart

DESCRIPTION

This node class is very similar to **SoGroup** with the exception that it specifies restrictions on the type of children that it allows. It is used by nodekits to restrict child types within *list parts* (see the reference page for **SoBaseKit**).

By default, any kind of child may be added. Methods of this class allow you to restrict the type of allowable children, and to lock down the types so that this type list may no longer be altered.

Inside the **SoNodeKitListPart** is a *container* node, which in turn contains the *children*. The *container* node is a hidden child, and the type of node used may be set with **setContainerType()**. In this way, you can make the nodekitlist behave like a group, a separator, or any other subclass of group. The *container* is not accessible so that the nodekitlist may retain control over what kinds of children are added.

METHODS

      SoNodeKitListPart()

Constructor.

SoType   **getContainerType()** const

void   **setContainerType**(SoType newContainerType)

Gets and sets the type of node used as the *container*.

const SoTypeList &

      getChildTypes() const

Returns the permitted child node types. By default, any type of node is permitted, so the list contains one entry of type **SoNode**.

void   **addChildType**(SoType typeToAdd)

Permits the node type *typeToAdd* as a child. The first time the **addChildType()** method is called, the default of **SoNode** is overridden and only the new *typeToAdd* is permitted. In subsequent calls to **addChildType()**, the *typeToAdd* is added to the existing types.

SbBool   **isTypePermitted**(SoType typeToCheck) const

Returns whether a node of type *typeToCheck* may be added as a child.

SbBool   **isChildPermitted**(const SoNode *child) const
Returns whether the node *child* may be added to this list. This will return
TRUE if the type of *child* is one of the permissible child types.

void   **containerSet**(const char *fieldDataString)
Sends a string to the **set**() method on the container node. This is how you
can set the value of a switch node if the container node is an **SoSwitch**, for
example.

void   **lockTypes**()
This function permanently locks the permitted child types and the container
type permanently. Calls to **setContainerType**() and **addChildType**() will
have no effect after this function is called.

SbBool   **isTypeLocked**() const
Returns whether the permitted child types and the container type are locked
(i.e. cannot be changed). See **lockTypes**()

void   **addChild**(SoNode *child)
void   **insertChild**(SoNode *child, int childIndex)
SoNode *   **getChild**(int index) const
int   **findChild**(SoNode *child) const
int   **getNumChildren**() const
void   **removeChild**(int index)
void   **removeChild**(SoNode *child)
void   **replaceChild**(int index, SoNode *newChild)
void   **replaceChild**(SoNode *oldChild, SoNode *newChild)
These are the functions used to edit the children. They parallel those of
SoGroup, except that they always check the child types against those which
are permissible. See **SoGroup** for details.

static SoType   **getClassTypeId**()
Returns type identifier for this class.

Methods from class SoNode:

setOverride, isOverride, copy, affectsState, getByName, getByName

Methods from class SoFieldContainer:

setToDefaults, hasDefaultValues, fieldsAreEqual, copyFieldValues, set, get,
getFields, getField, getFieldName, enableNotify, isNotifyEnabled

Methods from class SoBase:

ref, unref, unrefNoDelete, touch, getTypeId, isOfType, setName, getName

FILE FORMAT/DEFAULTS

```
NodeKitListPart {
      containerTypeName   "Group"
      childTypeNames      ""
      containerNode       NULL
}
```

INCLUDE FILE

```
#include <Inventor/nodekits/SoNodeKitListPart.h>
```

SEE ALSO

SoBaseKit, SoNodeKit, SoNodeKitDetail, SoNodeKitPath, SoNodekitCatalog, SoSceneKit, SoSeparatorKit, SoShapeKit, SoWrapperKit

NAME

SoNodeKitPath — path that points to a list of hierarchical nodekits

INHERITS FROM

SoBase > SoPath > SoNodeKitPath

DESCRIPTION

SoNodeKitPath is a subclass of **SoPath** that lets you look at nodekits below the top nodekit in the path. Since nodekits have hidden children, when you call **getTail()** on a regular path, it returns the top-most nodekit on the path. This occurs even though the path might contain extra internal information leading to a node far deeper in the scene graph. For example, when picking an object inside an **SoSceneKit**, the *regular* path would end at the scenekit. But a *nodekit* path would continue further down listing the other nodekits below it in the path.

Intermediary (private) nodes between nodekits are not included in the nodekit path.

Note that there is no constructor for an **SoNodeKitPath**, so you can not create one. Rather, you cast an **(SoPath *)** into an **(SoNodeKitPath *)**, which returns nodekit-style values from all the same questions as **SoPath**.

Also, some methods of **SoPath** may not be called on an **SoNodeKitPath**. Any methods which take a regular **SoNode** as an argument (except for **setHead()**) are not accessible, and replaced by methods that take an **SoBaseKit** as an argument instead. Methods which allow the programmer to refer to the child index of a node beneath its parent are also inaccessible; since a **SoNodeKitPath** only shows nodekits and hides any private parts, successive nodekits in the path may not actually be parent and child.

METHODS

void	**append**(SoBaseKit *childKit)

Adds *childKit* to end of chain; uses first occurrence of *childKit* as a part within current last nodekit. If the path is empty, this is equivalent to **setHead(childKit)**.

void	**append**(const SoNodeKitPath *fromPath)

Adds all nodekits in *fromPath*'s chain to end of chain; the head node of *fromPath* must be the same as or a child of the current tail node.

void	**pop()**

Pops the last nodekit off the end of the path.

SoNode *   **getTail**() const
>   Return the last nodekit in a path chain. Note that **getHead()** is not redefined
>   from **SoPath**, since an **SoNodeKitPath** need not begin with a nodekit; the
>   restriction is placed only on successive nodes on the path.

SoNode *   **getNode**(int i) const
>   Returns a pointer to the *i*'th node in the nodekit path.

SoNode *   **getNodeFromTail**(int i) const
>   Returns a pointer to the *i*'th nodekit in the chain, counting backward from
>   the tail nodekit. Passing 0 for *i* returns the tail nodekit.

int   **getLength**() const
>   Returns length of path chain (number of nodekits).

void   **truncate**(int start)
>   Truncates the path chain, removing all nodes from index *start* on. Calling
>   **truncate(0)** empties the path entirely.

SbBool   **containsNode**(const SoNodeKit *nodeKit) const
>   Returns TRUE if the passed nodekit is found anywhere in the path chain.

int   **findFork**(const SoNodeKitPath *path) const
>   If the two paths have different head nodes, this returns -1. Otherwise, it
>   returns the path chain index of the last nodekit (starting at the head) that is
>   the same for both paths.

friend int   **operator** ==(const SoNodeKitPath &p1, const SoNodeKitPath
>   &p2)
>   Returns TRUE if all node pointers in the two nodekit path chains are equal.

Methods from class SoPath:

setHead, getHead, containsPath, copy, getByName, getByName

Methods from class SoBase:

ref, unref, unrefNoDelete, touch, getClassTypeId, getTypeId, isOfType,
setName, getName

INCLUDE FILE

    #include <Inventor/SoNodeKitPath.h>

SEE ALSO

SoBaseKit, SoPath, SoRayPickAction, SoSearchAction

SoNodeList

NAME

SoNodeList — maintains a list of pointers to nodes

INHERITS FROM

SbPList > SoBaseList > SoNodeList

DESCRIPTION

This subclass of **SoBaseList** holds lists of pointers to **SoNode**s. It updates reference counts to nodes in the list whenever adding or removing pointers.

METHODS

SoNodeList()
Constructor.

SoNodeList(int size)
Constructor that pre-allocates storage for *size* pointers.

SoNodeList(const SoNodeList &l)
Constructor that copies the contents of another list.

~**SoNodeList**()
Destructor.

void   **append**(SoNode *node)
Adds a pointer to the end of the list.

SoNode *   **operator [ ]**(int i) const
Accesses an element of a list.

SoNodeList &   **operator =**(const SoNodeList &l)
Copies a list, keeping all reference counts correct.

Methods from class SoBaseList:

insert, remove, truncate, copy, set, addReferences

Methods from class SbPList:

find, getLength, operator ==, operator !=

INCLUDE FILE

```
#include <Inventor/SoLists.h>
```

SEE ALSO

SoNode

NAME

SoNodeSensor — sensor class that can be attached to Inventor nodes

INHERITS FROM

SoSensor > SoDelayQueueSensor > SoDataSensor > SoNodeSensor

DESCRIPTION

Node sensors detect changes to nodes, calling a callback function whenever any field of the node or, if the node is a group node, any children of the node change.

METHODS

SoNodeSensor()
SoNodeSensor(SoSensorCB *func, void *data)

Creation methods. The second method takes the callback function and data to be called when the sensor is triggered.

~SoNodeSensor()

Destroys the sensor, freeing up any memory associated with it after unscheduling it.

void	**attach**(SoNode *node)
void	**detach**()
SoNode *	**getAttachedNode**() const

The **attach**() method makes this sensor detect changes to the given node. The **detach**() method unschedules this sensor (if it is scheduled) and makes it ignore changes to the scene graph. The **getAttachedNode**() method returns the node that this sensor is sensing, or NULL if it is not attached to any node.

Methods from class SoDataSensor:

setDeleteCallback, getTriggerNode, getTriggerField, getTriggerPath, setTriggerPathFlag, getTriggerPathFlag

Methods from class SoDelayQueueSensor:

setPriority, getPriority, getDefaultPriority, schedule, unschedule, isScheduled

Methods from class SoSensor:

setFunction, getFunction, setData, getData

INCLUDE FILE

#include <Inventor/sensors/SoNodeSensor.h>

SEE ALSO

SoFieldSensor, SoPathSensor, SoDataSensor

NAME

SoNonIndexedShape — abstract base class for all non-indexed vertex-based shapes

INHERITS FROM

SoBase > SoFieldContainer > SoNode > SoShape > SoVertexShape > SoNonIndexedShape

DESCRIPTION

This node is the abstract base class for all vertex-based shapes that are not constructed from indices, such as **SoFaceSet**, **SoLineSet**, and **SoQuadMesh**.

All subclasses of **SoNonIndexedShape** construct objects by using the current coordinates as the object's vertices. The **startIndex** field defined by this class contains the index of the coordinate to use for the first vertex. This index is also used for materials, normals, or texture coordinates when the binding indicates that they should be used per vertex.

The subclass decides what to do with this and any subsequent coordinates. The shape is drawn with the current lighting model and drawing style and is transformed by the current transformation matrix.

Material, normal, and texture coordinate bindings for shapes derived from this class ignore any index specifications. That is, a binding value of PER_FACE_INDEXED is treated the same way as PER_FACE, and so on.

If there aren't sufficient values in the current coordinates, material, or texture coordinates, errors will occur.

FIELDS

SoSFLong   **startIndex**
Index of first coordinate of shape.

METHODS

static SoType   **getClassTypeId**()
Returns type identifier for this class.

Methods from class SoNode:

setOverride, isOverride, copy, affectsState, getByName, getByName

Methods from class SoFieldContainer:

setToDefaults, hasDefaultValues, fieldsAreEqual, copyFieldValues, set, get, getFields, getField, getFieldName, enableNotify, isNotifyEnabled

Methods from class SoBase:

ref, unref, unrefNoDelete, touch, getTypeId, isOfType, setName, getName

FILE FORMAT/DEFAULTS

This is an abstract class. See the reference page of a derived class for the format and default values.

INCLUDE FILE

```
#include <Inventor/nodes/SoNonIndexedShape.h>
```

SEE ALSO

SoFaceSet, SoIndexedShape, SoLineSet, SoPointSet, SoQuadMesh, SoTriangleStripSet

SoNormal

NAME

SoNormal — node that defines surface normals for shapes

INHERITS FROM

SoBase > SoFieldContainer > SoNode > SoNormal

DESCRIPTION

This node defines a set of 3D surface normal vectors to be used by vertex-based shape nodes that follow it in the scene graph. This node does not produce a visible result during rendering; it simply replaces the current normals in the rendering state for subsequent nodes to use. This node contains one multiple-valued field that contains the normal vectors.

Surface normals are needed to compute lighting when the Phong lighting model is used. Most vertex-based shapes that use normals can compute default normals if none are specified, depending on the current normal binding.

FIELDS

SoMFVec3f   **vector**

Surface normal vectors.

METHODS

SoNormal()

Creates a surface normal node with default settings.

static SoType   **getClassTypeId**()

Returns type identifier for this class.

Methods from class SoNode:

setOverride, isOverride, copy, affectsState, getByName, getByName

Methods from class SoFieldContainer:

setToDefaults, hasDefaultValues, fieldsAreEqual, copyFieldValues, set, get, getFields, getField, getFieldName, enableNotify, isNotifyEnabled

Methods from class SoBase:

ref, unref, unrefNoDelete, touch, getTypeId, isOfType, setName, getName

ACTION BEHAVIOR

SoGLRenderAction, SoCallbackAction, SoRayPickAction

Sets the current normals in the traversal state.

FILE FORMAT/DEFAULTS

```
Normal {
    vector  0 0 1
}
```

INCLUDE FILE

```
#include <Inventor/nodes/SoNormal.h>
```

SEE ALSO

SoCoordinate3, SoLightModel, SoNormalBinding, SoVertexShape

NAME

SoNormalBinding — node that specifies how multiple surface normals are bound to shapes

INHERITS FROM

SoBase > SoFieldContainer > SoNode > SoNormalBinding

DESCRIPTION

This node specifies how the current normals are bound to shapes that follow in the scene graph. Each shape node may interpret bindings differently.

The bindings for faces and vertices are meaningful only for shapes that are made from faces and vertices. Similarly, the indexed bindings are only used by the shapes that allow indexing. For bindings that require multiple normals, be sure to have at least as many normals defined as are necessary; otherwise, errors will occur.

FIELDS

SoSFEnum   **value**

Specifies how to bind normals to shapes.

METHODS

               SoNormalBinding()

Creates a normal binding node with default settings.

static SoType   **getClassTypeId**()

Returns type identifier for this class.

Methods from class SoNode:

setOverride, isOverride, copy, affectsState, getByName, getByName

Methods from class SoFieldContainer:

setToDefaults, hasDefaultValues, fieldsAreEqual, copyFieldValues, set, get, getFields, getField, getFieldName, enableNotify, isNotifyEnabled

Methods from class SoBase:

ref, unref, unrefNoDelete, touch, getTypeId, isOfType, setName, getName

ACTION BEHAVIOR

SoGLRenderAction, SoCallbackAction, SoRayPickAction

Sets the current normal binding type.

FILE FORMAT/DEFAULTS

```
NormalBinding {
      value   DEFAULT
}
```

INCLUDE FILE

```
#include <Inventor/nodes/SoNormalBinding.h>
```

enum **Binding** {

    SoNormalBinding::DEFAULT

        Use default binding

    SoNormalBinding::OVERALL

        Whole object has same normal

    SoNormalBinding::PER_PART

        One normal for each part of object

    SoNormalBinding::PER_PART_INDEXED

        One normal for each part, indexed

    SoNormalBinding::PER_FACE

        One normal for each face of object

    SoNormalBinding::PER_FACE_INDEXED

        One normal for each face, indexed

    SoNormalBinding::PER_VERTEX

        One normal for each vertex of object

    SoNormalBinding::PER_VERTEX_INDEXED

        One normal for each vertex, indexed

}

SEE ALSO

SoMaterialBinding, SoNormal, SoTextureCoordinateBinding, SoVertexShape

NAME

SoNurbsCurve — NURBS curve shape node

INHERITS FROM

SoBase > SoFieldContainer > SoNode > SoShape > SoNurbsCurve

DESCRIPTION

This class represents a NURBS curve, based on the knot vector and the control points that you specify. The **knotVector** field specifies a floating-point array of values; the values are the coordinates of the knot points in the curve, and you must enter them in non-decreasing order. The curve will use the first **numControlPoints** values in the current coordinates as control points.

If you specify *n* knots, you can specify up to *n-8* control points. The number of knots minus the number of control points is known as the order of the curve. A NURBS curve can have an order of up to 8.

The control points of the curve are transformed by the current transformation matrix. The curve is drawn with the current lighting model and drawing style (drawing style FILLED is treated as LINES). The coordinates, normals, and texture coordinates of a NURBS curve are generated, so you cannot bind explicit normals or texture coordinates to a NURBS curve.

The approximation of the curve by line segments is affected by the current complexity value.

FIELDS

SoSFLong   **numControlPoints**
Number of control points.

SoMFFloat   **knotVector**
The knot vector.

METHODS

SoNurbsCurve()
Creates a NURBS curve node with default settings.

static SoType   **getClassTypeId**()
Returns type identifier for this class.

Methods from class SoNode:

setOverride, isOverride, copy, affectsState, getByName, getByName

Methods from class SoFieldContainer:

> setToDefaults, hasDefaultValues, fieldsAreEqual, copyFieldValues, set, get, getFields, getField, getFieldName, enableNotify, isNotifyEnabled

Methods from class SoBase:

> ref, unref, unrefNoDelete, touch, getTypeId, isOfType, setName, getName

ACTION BEHAVIOR

SoGLRenderAction

Draws the curve based on the current coordinates, material, and so on.

SoRayPickAction

Picks the curve based on the current coordinates and transformation.

SoGetBoundingBoxAction

Computes the bounding box that encloses all control points of the curve with the current transformation applied to them. Sets the center to the average of the control points.

SoCallbackAction

If any line segment callbacks are registered with the action, they will be invoked for each successive segment approximating the curve.

FILE FORMAT/DEFAULTS

```
NurbsCurve {
        numControlPoints   0
        knotVector         0
}
```

INCLUDE FILE

```
#include <Inventor/nodes/SoNurbsCurve.h>
```

SEE ALSO

SoIndexedNurbsCurve, SoNurbsSurface

NAME

SoNurbsProfile — NURBS profile curve

INHERITS FROM

SoBase > SoFieldContainer > SoNode > SoProfile > SoNurbsProfile

DESCRIPTION

This node specifies a NURBS curve that is used as a profile. The curve is defined in the same way as a standard **SoNurbsCurve**, except that the control points are constructed from the current set of profile coordinates, using the **index** field.

FIELDS

SoMFFloat **knotVector**

The knot vector for the NURBS curve. It must be a list of non-decreasing floating point values.

Fields from class SoProfile:

index, linkage

METHODS

SoNurbsProfile()

Creates a NURBS profile curve node with default settings.

static SoType **getClassTypeId()**

Returns type identifier for this class.

Methods from class SoNode:

setOverride, isOverride, copy, affectsState, getByName, getByName

Methods from class SoFieldContainer:

setToDefaults, hasDefaultValues, fieldsAreEqual, copyFieldValues, set, get, getFields, getField, getFieldName, enableNotify, isNotifyEnabled

Methods from class SoBase:

ref, unref, unrefNoDelete, touch, getTypeId, isOfType, setName, getName

ACTION BEHAVIOR

SoGLRenderAction, SoCallbackAction, SoRayPickAction

Adds a profile to the current traversal state.

FILE FORMAT/DEFAULTS

```
NurbsProfile {
      index        0
      linkage      START_FIRST
      knotVector   0
}
```

INCLUDE FILE

```
#include <Inventor/nodes/SoNurbsProfile.h>
```

SEE ALSO

SoLinearProfile, SoNurbsCurve, SoProfileCoordinate2, SoProfileCoordinate3

NAME

SoNurbsSurface — NURBS surface shape node

INHERITS FROM

SoBase > SoFieldContainer > SoNode > SoShape > SoNurbsSurface

DESCRIPTION

This shape node represents a NURBS surface based on the node's knot vectors and on control points constructed from the current coordinates. The current coordinates are used in row-major order (the V direction corresponds to the rows). The number of coordinates used is determined by the **numUControlPoints** and **numVControlPoints** fields. The **uKnotVector** and **vKnotVector** fields contain floating point arrays of non-decreasing values.

The order of the surface in the U and V directions is defined as the number of knots minus the number of control points in the particular direction. The largest order allowed for a NURBS surface is 8.

The control points of the NURBS surface are transformed by the current cumulative transformation. The surface is drawn with the current light model and drawing style. The coordinates, normals, and texture coordinates of a surface are generated, so you cannot bind explicit normals or texture coordinates to a NURBS surface. The first material in the state is applied to the entire surface.

The surface is trimmed according to the currently defined profile's curves.

When default texture coordinates are applied to a NURBS surface, the edges of the texture square are stretched to fit the surface. The axes of the texture are called S and T; S is horizontal and T is vertical. The axes of the NURBS surface are called U and V; U is horizontal and V is vertical. You can also define texture coordinates explicitly with the S,T location point, the knot vectors, and the current texture coordinates.

The approximation of the surface by polygons is affected by the current complexity value.

FIELDS

SoSFLong	**numUControlPoints**
SoSFLong	**numVControlPoints**

Number of control points in the U and V directions.

SoSFLong	**numSControlPoints**
SoSFLong	**numTControlPoints**

Number of control points in the S and T directions.

SoMFFloat   **uKnotVector**
SoMFFloat   **vKnotVector**
> The knot vectors in the U and V directions.

SoMFFloat   **sKnotVector**
SoMFFloat   **tKnotVector**
> The knot vectors in the S and T directions.

METHODS

SoNurbsSurface()
> Creates a NURBS surface node with default settings.

static SoType   **getClassTypeId()**
> Returns type identifier for this class.

Methods from class SoNode:

> setOverride, isOverride, copy, affectsState, getByName, getByName

Methods from class SoFieldContainer:

> setToDefaults, hasDefaultValues, fieldsAreEqual, copyFieldValues, set, get, getFields, getField, getFieldName, enableNotify, isNotifyEnabled

Methods from class SoBase:

> ref, unref, unrefNoDelete, touch, getTypeId, isOfType, setName, getName

ACTION BEHAVIOR

SoGLRenderAction
> Draws the surface based on the current coordinates, material, and so on.

SoRayPickAction
> Picks the surface based on the current coordinates and transformation.

SoGetBoundingBoxAction
> Computes the bounding box that encloses all control points of the surface with the current transformation applied to them. Sets the center to the average of the control points.

SoCallbackAction
> If any triangle callbacks are registered with the action, they will be invoked for each successive triangle approximating the surface.

FILE FORMAT/DEFAULTS

```
NurbsSurface {
        numUControlPoints   0
        numVControlPoints   0
        numSControlPoints   0
        numTControlPoints   0
        uKnotVector         0
        vKnotVector         0
        sKnotVector         0
        tKnotVector         0
}
```

INCLUDE FILE

```
#include <Inventor/nodes/SoNurbsSurface.h>
```

SEE ALSO

SoIndexedNurbsSurface, SoNurbsCurve, SoProfile

NAME

SoOffScreenRenderer — renders to an off-screen buffer for printing or generating textures

INHERITS FROM

SoOffScreenRenderer

DESCRIPTION

This class is used to render into an off-screen buffer to create a printable image or to generate a texture image. It uses X Pixmaps for rendering. Methods are provided to write the buffer to a file, either as an RGB image or an encapsulated PostScript description.

METHODS

static float   **getScreenPixelsPerInch**()

Returns the number of pixels per inch (in the horizontal direction) of the current X device screen.

void   **setComponents**(Components components)
Components   **getComponents**() const

Sets or returns the components to be rendered.

void   **setViewportRegion**(const SbViewportRegion &region)
const SbViewportRegion &
                         getViewportRegion() const

Sets or returns the viewport region used for rendering.

void   **setBackgroundColor**(const SbColor &c)
const SbColor &   **getBackgroundColor**() const

Sets or returns the background color for rendering.

SbBool   **render**(SoNode *scene)
SbBool   **render**(SoPath *scene)

Renders the given scene, specified as a node or a path, into an off-screen buffer.

unsigned char *   **getBuffer**() const

Returns the buffer containing the rendered image.

SbBool   **writeToRGB**(FILE *fp) const

Writes the buffer as a .rgb file to the given file pointer.

SbBool	**writeToPostScript**(FILE *fp) const
SbBool	**writeToPostScript**(FILE *fp, const SbVec2f &printSize) const

Writes the buffer as encapsulated PostScript. If a print size is not given, the size of the image in the buffer is adjusted so it is the same as the apparent size of the viewport region on the current device.

INCLUDE FILE

```
#include <Inventor/misc/SoOffScreenRenderer.h>
```

enum **Components** {
    SoOffScreenRenderer::LUMINANCE
    SoOffScreenRenderer::LUMINANCE_TRANSPARENCY
    SoOffScreenRenderer::RGB
    SoOffScreenRenderer::RGB_TRANSPARENCY
}

NAME

SoOneShot — timer that runs for a pre-set amount of time

INHERITS FROM

SoBase > SoFieldContainer > SoEngine > SoOneShot

DESCRIPTION

This engine is a timer that runs for a pre-set amount of time and then stops. By default, the **timeIn** input is connected to the **realTime** global field. It can, however, by connected to any other time source.

The timer is started when the **trigger** input is touched. It then runs for the specified **duration**, and updates the **timeOut** output with the time that has elapsed. During that time, the **ramp** output is also updated. The **ramp** output starts at 0.0 at the beginning of the cycle, and linearly increases until it reaches 1.0 at the end of the cycle.

You can disable the timer by setting the **disable** input to TRUE. The output value remains 0.0 while the timer is disabled. If the timer is disabled in the middle of a cycle the output values will be set to 0.0.

The **flags** input contains control flags. Using the flags you can set the timer to be retriggerable in the middle of a cycle, and set the output values to stay high after the cycle has been completed. By default, these flags are not set.

INPUTS

SoSFTime **timeIn**

Running time.

SoSFTime **duration**

Duration of the active cycle.

SoSFTrigger **trigger**

Start the cycle. The trigger will be ignored if it is touched in the middle of a cycle and the RETRIGGERABLE flag is not set.

SoSFBitMask **flags**

Control flags.

SoSFBool **disable**

If TRUE, the timer is disabled.

OUTPUTS

> (SoSFTime)   **timeOut**
> Elapsed time from the start.

> (SoSFBool)   **isActive**
> Is TRUE during the active cycle.

> (SoSFFloat)   **ramp**
> Ramps linearly from 0.0 to 1.0.

METHODS

>   **SoOneShot()**
> Constructor

> **Methods from class SoEngine:**
>
> getClassTypeId, getOutputs, getOutput, getOutputName, copy, getByName, getByName

> **Methods from class SoFieldContainer:**
>
> setToDefaults, hasDefaultValues, fieldsAreEqual, copyFieldValues, set, get, getFields, getField, getFieldName, enableNotify, isNotifyEnabled

> **Methods from class SoBase:**
>
> ref, unref, unrefNoDelete, touch, getTypeId, isOfType, setName, getName

FILE FORMAT/DEFAULTS

```
OneShot {
        duration  1
        trigger
        flags     ()
        disable   FALSE
        timeIn    <current time>
}
```

INCLUDE FILE

```
#include <Inventor/engines/So.h>
```

> enum **Flags** {
>
>   **SoOneShot::RETRIGGERABLE**   Can start over during the cycle
>   **SoOneShot::HOLD_FINAL**   Output values stay high after cycle
> }

SEE ALSO

> SoElapsedTime, SoEngineOutput

NAME

SoOneShotSensor — sensor for one-time only callbacks

INHERITS FROM

SoSensor > SoDelayQueueSensor > SoOneShotSensor

DESCRIPTION

A one-shot sensor is triggered once after it is scheduled, when the delay queue is processed. Like all delay queue sensors, one-shot sensors with a non-zero priority are just added to the delay queue when scheduled; if they are scheduled again before the delay queue is processed nothing happens, and they are guaranteed to be called only once when the delay queue is processed. For example, a one-shot sensor whose callback function redraws the scene might be scheduled whenever the scene graph changes and whenever a window-system event reporting that the window changed size occurs. By using a one-shot, the scene will only be redrawn once even if a window-changed-size event occurs just after the scene graph is modified (or if several window-changed-size events occur in a row).

Calling **schedule()** in the callback function is a useful way of getting something to happen repeatedly as often as possible, while still handling events and timeouts.

A priority 0 one-shot sensor isn't very useful, since scheduling it is exactly the same as directly calling its callback function.

METHODS

SoOneShotSensor()
SoOneShotSensor(SoSensorCB *func, void *data)
Creation methods. The second method takes the callback function and data to be called when the sensor is triggered.

~SoOneShotSensor()
Destroys the sensor, freeing up any memory associated with it after unscheduling it.

Methods from class SoDelayQueueSensor:

setPriority, getPriority, getDefaultPriority, schedule, unschedule, isScheduled

Methods from class SoSensor:

setFunction, getFunction, setData, getData

INCLUDE FILE

```
#include <Inventor/sensors/SoOneShotSensor.h>
```

SEE ALSO

SoIdleSensor, SoDelayQueueSensor

NAME

SoOnOff — engine that functions as an on/off switch

INHERITS FROM

SoBase > SoFieldContainer > SoEngine > SoOnOff

DESCRIPTION

This engine has three triggers as input and two Boolean values as output. The **isOn** output is a switch that can be turned **on** or **off** by triggering the corresponding input. You can toggle the value by triggering the **toggle** input. By default **isOn** is FALSE. The **isOff** output value is the inverse of **isOn**

INPUTS

SoSFTrigger **on**
  Turn the **isOn** switch on.

SoSFTrigger **off**
  Turn the **isOn** switch off.

SoSFTrigger **toggle**
  Toggle the switch value.

OUTPUTS

(SoSFBool) **isOn**
  Switch value.

(SoSFBool) **isOff**
  The inverse of **isOn**.

METHODS

SoOnOff()
  Constructor.

Methods from class SoEngine:

  getClassTypeId, getOutputs, getOutput, getOutputName, copy, getByName, getByName

Methods from class SoFieldContainer:

  setToDefaults, hasDefaultValues, fieldsAreEqual, copyFieldValues, set, get, getFields, getField, getFieldName, enableNotify, isNotifyEnabled

Methods from class SoBase:

  ref, unref, unrefNoDelete, touch, getTypeId, isOfType, setName, getName

FILE FORMAT/DEFAULTS

```
OnOff {
      on
      off
      toggle
}
```

INCLUDE FILE

```
#include <Inventor/engines/SoOnOff.h>
```

SEE ALSO

SoEngineOutput

NAME

SoOrthographicCamera — orthographic camera node

INHERITS FROM

SoBase > SoFieldContainer > SoNode > SoCamera > SoOrthographicCamera

DESCRIPTION

An orthographic camera defines a parallel projection from a viewpoint. This camera does not diminish objects with distance, as an **SoPerspectiveCamera** does. The viewing volume for an orthographic camera is a rectangular parallelepiped (a box).

By default, the camera is located at (0,0,1) and looks along the negative z-axis; the **position** and **orientation** fields can be used to change these values. The **height** field defines the total height of the viewing volume; this and the **aspectRatio** field determine its width.

FIELDS

SoSFFloat   **height**

Height of the viewing volume.

Fields from class SoCamera:

viewportMapping, position, orientation, aspectRatio, nearDistance, farDistance, focalDistance

METHODS

SoOrthographicCamera()

Creates an orthographic camera node with default settings.

static SoType   **getClassTypeId**()

Returns type identifier for this class.

Methods from class SoCamera:

pointAt, scaleHeight, getViewVolume, viewAll, viewAll, getViewportBounds

Methods from class SoNode:

setOverride, isOverride, copy, affectsState, getByName, getByName

Methods from class SoFieldContainer:

setToDefaults, hasDefaultValues, fieldsAreEqual, copyFieldValues, set, get, getFields, getField, getFieldName, enableNotify, isNotifyEnabled

Methods from class SoBase:

ref, unref, unrefNoDelete, touch, getTypeId, isOfType, setName, getName

ACTION BEHAVIOR

SoGLRenderAction, SoCallbackAction, SoGetBoundingBoxAction, SoHandleEventAction, SoRayPickAction
Sets the viewport and camera information in the state.

FILE FORMAT/DEFAULTS

```
OrthographicCamera {
        viewportMapping   ADJUST_CAMERA
        position          0 0 1
        orientation       0 0 1  0
        aspectRatio       1
        nearDistance      1
        farDistance       10
        focalDistance     5
        height            2
}
```

INCLUDE FILE

```
#include <Inventor/nodes/SoOrthographicCamera.h>
```

SEE ALSO

SbViewVolume, SoPerspectiveCamera

NAME

SoOutput — used to write Inventor data files

INHERITS FROM

SoOutput

DESCRIPTION

This class is used for writing Inventor data files. It supports both ASCII (default) and binary formats and provides some convenience functions for handling files. It can also write to a buffer in memory as well as to a file pointer. An instance of **SoOutput** is contained in an **SoWriteAction**; this is typically the only instance needed.

METHODS

SoOutput()
~SoOutput()
Constructor and destructor. The default **SoOutput** writes to **stdout**. The destructor closes any files opened by the **SoOutput**.

void   **setFilePointer**(FILE *newFP)
Sets file pointer to write to.

FILE *   **getFilePointer**() const
Returns the file pointer in use, or NULL if using a buffer.

SbBool   **openFile**(const char *fileName)
Opens named file, sets file pointer to result. This returns FALSE on error.

closeFile()
Closes current file if opened with **openFile**().

void   **setBuffer**(void *bufPointer, size_t initSize, SoOutputReallocCB *reallocFunc, long offset = 0)
Sets up memory buffer to write to, initial size, reallocation function (which is called if there is not enough room in the buffer), and offset in the buffer at which to begin writing. If the reallocation function returns NULL, writing will be disabled.

SbBool   **getBuffer**(void *&bufPointer, size_t &nBytes) const
Returns pointer to memory buffer being written to and the new size of the buffer. Returns FALSE if not writing into a buffer.

size_t   **getBufferSize**() const
The total number of bytes allocated to a memory buffer may be larger than the number of bytes written. This returns that total number.

void   **resetBuffer**()
> Resets buffer for output again. Output starts over at beginning of buffer.

void   **setBinary**(SbBool flag)
> Sets whether output should be ASCII (default) or binary.

SbBool   **isBinary**() const
> Returns current state of binary flag.

static float   **isASCIIHeader**(const char *string)
static float   **isBinaryHeader**(const char *string)
> Returns non-zero if given string matches the ASCII or binary file header. The value returned is the file format version number.

INCLUDE FILE
> #include <Inventor/SoOutput.h>

> typedef void *   **SoOutputReallocCB**(void *ptr, size_t newSize)

SEE ALSO
> SoInput, SoWriteAction, SoTranSender

NAME

SoPackedColor — node that defines base colors using packed representation

INHERITS FROM

SoBase > SoFieldContainer > SoNode > SoPackedColor

DESCRIPTION

SoPackedColor is similar to **SoBaseColor** in that it sets the diffuse color component of the current material. However, it also changes the transparency component. The color and transparency information is packed into unsigned long integers: 0xaabbggrr, where aa represents the alpha (0x00 = fully transparent, 0xff = opaque), and bb, gg, and rr represent the blue, green, and red components of the color, respectively.

SoPackedColor uses less memory than **SoBaseColor** or **SoMaterial** to store multiple color and transparency values. It can be used in cases where space is critical.

FIELDS

SoMFULong **rgba**
Defines the packed colors.

METHODS

SoPackedColor()
Creates a packed color node with default settings.

static SoType **getClassTypeId**()
Returns type identifier for this class.

Methods from class SoNode:

setOverride, isOverride, copy, affectsState, getByName, getByName

Methods from class SoFieldContainer:

setToDefaults, hasDefaultValues, fieldsAreEqual, copyFieldValues, set, get, getFields, getField, getFieldName, enableNotify, isNotifyEnabled

Methods from class SoBase:

ref, unref, unrefNoDelete, touch, getTypeId, isOfType, setName, getName

ACTION BEHAVIOR

SoGLRenderAction, SoCallbackAction
Sets the current base (diffuse) color(s) in the state.

FILE FORMAT/DEFAULTS

```
PackedColor {
    rgba   0xffcccccc
}
```

INCLUDE FILE

```
#include <Inventor/nodes/SoPackedColor.h>
```

SEE ALSO

SoBaseColor, SoMaterial

NAME

SoPath — path that points to a list of hierarchical nodes

INHERITS FROM

SoBase > SoPath

DESCRIPTION

A path represents a scene graph or subgraph. It contains a list of pointers to nodes forming a chain from some root to some descendent. Each node in the chain is a child of the previous node. Paths are used to refer to some object in a scene graph precisely and unambiguously, even if there are many instances of the object. Therefore, paths are returned by both the **SoRayPickAction** and **SoSearchAction**.

When an action is applied to a path, only the nodes in the subgraph defined by the path are traversed. These include: the nodes in the path chain, all nodes (if any) below the last node in the path, and all nodes whose effects are inherited by any of these nodes.

SoPath attempts to maintain consistency of paths even when the structure of the scene graph changes. For example, removing a child from its parent when both are in a path chain cuts the path chain at that point, leaving the top part intact. Removing the node to the left of a node in a path adjusts the index for that node. Replacing a child of a node when both the parent and the child are in the chain replaces the child in the chain with the new child, truncating the path below the new child.

Note that only public children of nodes are accessible from an **SoPath**. Nodes like node kits that limit access to their children may provide other ways to get more information, such as by using the **SoNodeKitPath** class.

METHODS

SoPath()
Constructs an empty path.

SoPath(int approxLength)
Constructs a path with a hint to length (number of nodes in chain).

SoPath(SoNode *node)
Constructs a path and sets the head node to the given node.

void   **setHead**(SoNode *node)
Sets head node (first node in chain). The head node must be set before the **append**() or **push**() methods may be called.

void	**append**(int childIndex)

Adds node to end of chain; the node is the *childIndex*'th child of the current tail node.

void	**append**(SoNode *childNode)

Adds node to end of chain; uses the first occurrence of *childNode* as child of current tail node. If the path is empty, this is equivalent to **setHead(childNode)**.

void	**append**(const SoPath *fromPath)

Adds all nodes in *fromPath*'s chain to end of chain; the head node of *fromPath* must be the same as or a child of the current tail node.

void	**push**(int childIndex)
void	**pop**()

These allow a path to be treated as a stack; they push a node at the end of the chain and pop the last node off.

SoNode *	**getHead**() const
SoNode *	**getTail**() const

These return the first and last nodes in a path chain.

SoNode *	**getNode**(int i) const
int	**getIndex**(int i) const

These return a pointer to the *i*'th node or the index of the *i*'th node (within its parent) in the chain. Calling **getNode(0)** is equivalent to calling **getHead()**.

SoNode *	**getNodeFromTail**(int i) const
int	**getIndexFromTail**(int i) const

These return a pointer to the *i*'th node or the index of the *i*'th node (within its parent) in the chain, counting backward from the tail node. Passing 0 for *i* returns the tail node or its index.

int	**getLength**() const

Returns length of path chain (number of nodes).

void	**truncate**(int start)

Truncates the path chain, removing all nodes from index *start* on. Calling **truncate(0)** empties the path entirely.

SbBool   **containsNode**(const SoNode *node) const
Returns TRUE if the node is found anywhere in the path chain.

SbBool   **containsPath**(const SoPath *path) const
Returns TRUE if the nodes in the chain in the passed path are contained (in consecutive order) in this path chain.

int   **findFork**(const SoPath *path) const
If the two paths have different head nodes, this returns -1. Otherwise, it returns the path chain index of the last node (starting at the head) that is the same for both paths.

SoPath *   **copy**(int startFromNodeIndex = 0, int numNodes = 0) const
Creates and returns a new path that is a copy of some or all of this path. Copying starts at the given index (default is 0, which is the head node). A *numNodes* of 0 (the default) means copy all nodes from the starting index to the end. Returns NULL on error.

friend int   **operator ==**(const SoPath &p1, const SoPath &p2)
Returns TRUE if all node pointers in the two path chains are identical.

static SoPath *   **getByName**(const SbName &name)
static int   **getByName**(const SbName &name, SoPathList &list)
These methods lookup and return paths with a given name. Paths are named by calling their **setName()** method (defined by the **SoBase** class). The first form returns the last path that was given that name, either by **setName()** or by reading in a named path from a file. If there is no path with the given name, NULL will be returned. The second form appends all paths with the given name to the given path list and returns the number of paths that were added. If there are no paths with the given name, zero will be returned and nothing will be added to the list.

Methods from class SoBase:

ref, unref, unrefNoDelete, touch, getClassTypeId, getTypeId, isOfType, setName, getName

FILE FORMAT/DEFAULTS

```
SoPath {
    [head node]
    [number of remaining indices]
    [index]
    ...
    [index]
}
```

Note that the indices in a written path are adjusted based on the nodes that are actually written to a file. Since nodes in the graph that have no effect on the path (such as some separator nodes) are not written, the siblings of such nodes must undergo index adjustment when written. The actual nodes in the graph remain unchanged.

INCLUDE FILE

```
#include <Inventor/SoPath.h>
```

SEE ALSO

SoNode, SoRayPickAction, SoSearchAction, SoNodeKitPath

NAME

SoPathList — maintains a list of pointers to paths

INHERITS FROM

SbPList > SoBaseList > SoPathList

DESCRIPTION

This subclass of **SoBaseList** holds lists of pointers to **SoPath**s. It updates reference counts to paths in the list whenever adding or removing pointers.

METHODS

SoPathList()
Constructor.

SoPathList(int size)
Constructor that pre-allocates storage for *size* pointers.

SoPathList(const SoPathList &l)
Constructor that copies the contents of another list.

~**SoPathList**()
Destructor.

void   **append**(SoPath *path)
Adds a path to the end of the list.

SoPath *   **operator [ ]**(int i) const
Accesses an element of a list.

SoPathList &   **operator =**(const SoPathList &l)
Copies a list, keeping all reference counts correct.

int   **findPath**(const SoPath &path)
Returns the index of the matching path in the list, or -1 if not found.

void   **sort**()
Sorts list in place based on (1) increasing address of head node, then (2) increasing indices of children.

void   **uniquify**()
Given a sorted list, removes any path that (1) is a duplicate, or (2) goes through a node that is the tail of another path.

Methods from class SoBaseList:

insert, remove, truncate, copy, set, addReferences

Methods from class SbPList:

find, getLength, operator ==, operator !=

INCLUDE FILE

```
#include <Inventor/SoLists.h>
```

SEE ALSO

SoPath

NAME

SoPathSensor — sensor class that can be attached to Inventor paths

INHERITS FROM

SoSensor > SoDelayQueueSensor > SoDataSensor > SoPathSensor

DESCRIPTION

Path sensors detect changes to paths, calling a callback function whenever the path or any node in the path changes. The definition of "in the path" is the same as the definition used when applying an action to the path — any node that can possibly affect the node at the end of the path chain is considered in the path. See the **SoPath** manual page for more information on paths.

METHODS

SoPathSensor()
SoPathSensor(SoSensorCB *func, void *data)
Creation methods. The second method takes the callback function and data to be called when the sensor is triggered.

~SoPathSensor()
Destroys the sensor, freeing up any memory associated with it after unscheduling it.

void	**attach**(SoPath *path)
void	**detach**()
SoPath *	**getAttachedPath**() const

The **attach**() method makes this sensor detect changes to the given path. The **detach**() method unschedules this sensor (if it is scheduled) and makes it ignore changes to the scene graph. The **getAttachedPath**() method returns the path that this sensor is sensing, or NULL if it is not attached to any path.

Methods from class SoDataSensor:

setDeleteCallback, getTriggerNode, getTriggerField, getTriggerPath, setTriggerPathFlag, getTriggerPathFlag

Methods from class SoDelayQueueSensor:

setPriority, getPriority, getDefaultPriority, schedule, unschedule, isScheduled

Methods from class SoSensor:

setFunction, getFunction, setData, getData

INCLUDE FILE

```
#include <Inventor/sensors/SoPathSensor.h>
```

SEE ALSO

SoNodeSensor, SoPathSensor, SoDataSensor

NAME

SoPathSwitch — group node that traverses only when traversed along a given path

INHERITS FROM

SoBase > SoFieldContainer > SoNode > SoGroup > SoPathSwitch

DESCRIPTION

SoPathSwitch is a group node that traverses its children only if the current traversal path matches the **SoPath** in the **path** field. This can be used, for example, to affect only one instance of a subgraph. The **path** field contains the path up to (but not including) the **SoPathSwitch**. The path need not go all the way back to the root; if it does not, then only the number of ancestors that are in the path are compared to see if the children should be traversed. A NULL path means that the children are never traversed.

FIELDS

SoSFPath **path**

The path that must match the current traversal path.

METHODS

SoPathSwitch()

Creates a path switch node with default settings.

SoPathSwitch(int nChildren)

Constructor that takes approximate number of children.

static SoType **getClassTypeId**()

Returns type identifier for this class.

Methods from class SoGroup:

addChild, insertChild, getChild, findChild, getNumChildren, removeChild, removeChild, removeAllChildren, replaceChild, replaceChild

Methods from class SoNode:

setOverride, isOverride, copy, affectsState, getByName, getByName

Methods from class SoFieldContainer:

setToDefaults, hasDefaultValues, fieldsAreEqual, copyFieldValues, set, get, getFields, getField, getFieldName, enableNotify, isNotifyEnabled

Methods from class SoBase:

ref, unref, unrefNoDelete, touch, getTypeId, isOfType, setName, getName

ACTION BEHAVIOR

SoGLRenderAction, SoCallbackAction, SoGetBoundingBoxAction, SoRayPickAction, SoHandleEventAction
Traverses the children if the paths match.

FILE FORMAT/DEFAULTS

```
PathSwitch {
    path  NULL
}
```

INCLUDE FILE

```
#include <Inventor/nodes/SoPathSwitch.h>
```

SEE ALSO

SoPath, SoSwitch

NAME

SoPendulum — animated oscillating rotation node

INHERITS FROM

SoBase > SoFieldContainer > SoNode > SoTransformation > SoRotation > SoPendulum

DESCRIPTION

The **SoPendulum** class is derived from **SoRotation**, so it applies a rotation to the current transformation. Using engines connected to the **realTime** global field, the rotation value is animated over time between two fixed rotations, achieving the effect of a swinging pendulum. The period of the swing can be adjusted by changing the **speed** field. The current rotation at any time is available in the **rotation** field, inherited from **SoRotation**

FIELDS

SoSFRotation   **rotation0**
SoSFRotation   **rotation1**
      These define the two fixed rotations that are interpolated to create the pendular motion.

SoSFFloat   **speed**
      Defines the speed of the pendulum, in cycles per second.

SoSFBool   **on**
      Allows applications to enable or disable the motion easily.

Fields from class SoRotation:

      rotation

METHODS

      SoPendulum()
      Creates a pendulum node with default settings.

static SoType   **getClassTypeId**()
      Returns type identifier for this class.

Methods from class SoNode:

      setOverride, isOverride, copy, affectsState, getByName, getByName

Methods from class SoFieldContainer:

      setToDefaults, hasDefaultValues, fieldsAreEqual, copyFieldValues, set, get, getFields, getField, getFieldName, enableNotify, isNotifyEnabled

Methods from class SoBase:

> ref, unref, unrefNoDelete, touch, getTypeId, isOfType, setName, getName

ACTION BEHAVIOR

**SoGLRenderAction, SoCallbackAction, SoGetBoundingBoxAction,
SoRayPickAction**

Concatenates interpolated rotation value with the current transformation
matrix.

SoGetMatrixAction

Returns transformation matrix specified by the interpolated rotation.

FILE FORMAT/DEFAULTS

```
Pendulum {
        rotation   0 0 1   3.14159
        rotation0  0 0 1   3.14159
        rotation1  0 0 1   3.14159
        speed      1
        on         TRUE
}
```

INCLUDE FILE

```
#include <Inventor/nodes/SoPendulum.h>
```

SEE ALSO

SoRotor, SoShuttle

NAME

SoPerspectiveCamera — perspective camera node

INHERITS FROM

SoBase > SoFieldContainer > SoNode > SoCamera > SoPerspectiveCamera

DESCRIPTION

A perspective camera defines a perspective projection from a viewpoint. The viewing volume for a perspective camera is a truncated right pyramid.

By default, the camera is located at (0,0,1) and looks along the negative z-axis; the **position** and **orientation** fields can be used to change these values. The **heightAngle** field defines the total vertical angle of the viewing volume; this and the **aspectRatio** field determine the horizontal angle.

FIELDS

SoSFFloat   **heightAngle**
> Vertical angle of the viewing volume.

Fields from class SoCamera:

> viewportMapping, position, orientation, aspectRatio, nearDistance, farDistance, focalDistance

METHODS

SoPerspectiveCamera()
> Creates a perspective camera node with default settings.

static SoType   **getClassTypeId()**
> Returns type identifier for this class.

Methods from class SoCamera:

> pointAt, scaleHeight, getViewVolume, viewAll, viewAll, getViewportBounds

Methods from class SoNode:

> setOverride, isOverride, copy, affectsState, getByName, getByName

Methods from class SoFieldContainer:

> setToDefaults, hasDefaultValues, fieldsAreEqual, copyFieldValues, set, get, getFields, getField, getFieldName, enableNotify, isNotifyEnabled

Methods from class SoBase:

> ref, unref, unrefNoDelete, touch, getTypeId, isOfType, setName, getName

ACTION BEHAVIOR

> SoGLRenderAction, SoCallbackAction, SoGetBoundingBoxAction,
> SoHandleEventAction, SoRayPickAction
>
> > Sets the viewport and camera information in the state.

FILE FORMAT/DEFAULTS

```
PerspectiveCamera {
        viewportMapping   ADJUST_CAMERA
        position          0 0 1
        orientation       0 0 1  0
        aspectRatio       1
        nearDistance      1
        farDistance       10
        focalDistance     5
        heightAngle       0.785398
}
```

INCLUDE FILE

> #include <Inventor/nodes/SoPerspectiveCamera.h>

SEE ALSO

> SbViewVolume, SoOrthographicCamera

NAME

SoPickAction — abstract base class for picking objects in a scene

INHERITS FROM

SoAction > SoPickAction

DESCRIPTION

This is an abstract base class for all picking actions. Currently, the only supported subclass is the **SoRayPickAction**.

METHODS

void   **setViewportRegion**(const SbViewportRegion &newRegion)
const SbViewportRegion &
                    getViewportRegion() const
Sets/returns current viewport region to use for action. Even though the picking operation may not involve a window per se, some nodes need this information to determine their size and placement.

Methods from class SoAction:

apply, apply, apply, getClassTypeId, getTypeId, isOfType, invalidateState

INCLUDE FILE

```
#include <Inventor/actions/SoPickAction.h>
```

SEE ALSO

SoRayPickAction

NAME

SoPickedPoint — represents point on surface of picked object

INHERITS FROM

SoPickedPoint

DESCRIPTION

An **SoPickedPoint** represents a point on the surface of an object that was picked by applying an **SoRayPickAction** to a scene. It contains a path to the picked shape, the point of intersection, the surface normal and texture coordinates at that point, and other information.

Each node in the picked path may have a corresponding instance of a detail subclass. These detail instances are stored in the **SoPickedPoint**.

METHODS

SoPickedPoint(const SoPickedPoint &pp)

Copy constructor.

~SoPickedPoint()

Destructor.

const SbVec3f & **getPoint**() const
const SbVec3f & **getNormal**() const
const SbVec4f & **getTextureCoords**() const

These return the intersection point and surface normal in world space, and the texture coordinates in image space.

int **getMaterialIndex**() const

Returns the index into the current set of materials of the material active at the intersection point. Note that if the materials are interpolated between vertices, the index will correspond to the material at one of the vertices.

SoPath * **getPath**() const

Returns the path to the object that was intersected.

SbBool **isOnGeometry**() const

Returns whether the intersection is actually on the geometry of the character that was hit, as opposed to being on the bounding box. The pick style (see **SoPickStyle**) affects this decision.

const SoDetail * **getDetail**(const SoNode *node = NULL) const

Returns the detail that corresponds to the given node in the path returned by **getPath**(). If the node pointer is NULL (the default), the detail corresponding to the tail of the path is returned.

const SbMatrix   **getObjectToWorld**(const SoNode *node = NULL) const
const SbMatrix   **getWorldToObject**(const SoNode *node = NULL) const
These return the transformation matrices between world space and the object space corresponding to the given node in the path. If the node pointer is NULL (the default), the matrix corresponding to the tail of the path is returned.

const SbMatrix   **getObjectToImage**(const SoNode *node = NULL) const
const SbMatrix   **getImageToObject**(const SoNode *node = NULL) const
These return the texture transformation matrices between image space and the object space corresponding to the given node in the path. If the node pointer is NULL (the default), the matrix corresponding to the tail of the path is returned.

const SbVec3f   **getObjectPoint**(const SoNode *node = NULL) const
const SbVec3f   **getObjectNormal**(const SoNode *node = NULL) const
const SbVec4f   **getObjectTextureCoords**(const SoNode *node=NULL) const
These return the intersection point, surface normal, and texture coordinates in the object space corresponding to the given node in the path. If the node pointer is NULL (the default), the information corresponding to the tail of the path is returned.

INCLUDE FILE

```
#include <Inventor/SoPickedPoint.h>
```

SEE ALSO

SoRayPickAction, SoPickStyle, SoDetail, SoPath

NAME

SoPickedPointList — maintains a list of pointers to **SoPickedPoint** instances

INHERITS FROM

SbPList > SoPickedPointList

DESCRIPTION

This subclass of **SbPList** holds lists of pointers to instances of classes derived from **SoPickedPoint**. It is used primarily to return information from picking with the **SoRayPickAction** class.

METHODS

SoPickedPointList()
Constructor.

SoPickedPointList(int size)
Constructor that pre-allocates storage for *size* pointers.

SoPickedPointList(const SoPickedPointList &l)
Constructor that copies the contents of another list.

~SoPickedPointList()
Destructor.

void   **append**(SoPickedPoint *ptr)
Adds a pointer to the end of the list.

void   **insert**(SoPickedPoint *ptr, int addBefore)
Inserts given pointer in list before pointer with given index.

void   **truncate**(int start)
Removes all pointers after one with given index, inclusive, deleting all instances removed from the list.

SoPickedPoint *   **operator [ ]**(int i) const
Accesses an element of a list.

void   **set**(int i, SoPickedPoint *pickedPoint)
Sets an element of a list.

Methods from class SbPList:

find, remove, getLength, copy, operator =, operator ==, operator !=

SoPickedPointList

INCLUDE FILE

```
#include <Inventor/SoLists.h>
```

SEE ALSO

SoPickedPoint, SoRayPickAction

NAME

SoPickStyle — picking style node

INHERITS FROM

SoBase > SoFieldContainer > SoNode > SoPickStyle

DESCRIPTION

This node determines how subsequent geometry nodes in the scene graph are to be picked, as indicated by the **style** field.

Note that this is the only way to change the pick behavior of shapes; drawing style, complexity, and other rendering-related properties have no effect on picking.

FIELDS

SoSFEnum   **style**

Picking style.

METHODS

SoPickStyle()

Creates a pick style node with default settings.

static SoType   **getClassTypeId**()

Returns type identifier for this class.

Methods from class SoNode:

setOverride, isOverride, copy, affectsState, getByName, getByName

Methods from class SoFieldContainer:

setToDefaults, hasDefaultValues, fieldsAreEqual, copyFieldValues, set, get, getFields, getField, getFieldName, enableNotify, isNotifyEnabled

Methods from class SoBase:

ref, unref, unrefNoDelete, touch, getTypeId, isOfType, setName, getName

ACTION BEHAVIOR

SoRayPickAction, SoCallbackAction

Sets the current pick style in the state.

FILE FORMAT/DEFAULTS

```
PickStyle {
      style  SHAPE
}
```

SoPickStyle

INCLUDE FILE

```
#include <Inventor/nodes/SoPickStyle.h>
```

enum **Style** {

    SoPickStyle::SHAPE

        Points on the surfaces of shapes may be picked

    SoPickStyle::BOUNDING_BOX

        Points on the surfaces of 3D bounding boxes of shapes may be picked

    SoPickStyle::UNPICKABLE

        Subsequent objects are transparent to picks

}

SEE ALSO

SoComplexity, SoDrawStyle, SoRayPickAction

NAME

SoPointDetail — stores detail information about vertex-based shapes made of points

INHERITS FROM

SoDetail > SoPointDetail

DESCRIPTION

This class contains detail information about a point in a vertex-based shape made of points. It is used for returning information about an intersection with or primitives generated by a set of points. It is also used by **SoFaceDetail** and **SoLineDetail** to return information about the vertices of faces and line segments.

METHODS

| | **SoPointDetail**() |
| virtual | **~SoPointDetail**() |

Constructor and destructor.

long **getCoordinateIndex**() const

Returns the index of the point within the relevant coordinate node.

long **getMaterialIndex**() const

Returns the index of the material for the point within the relevant material node.

long **getNormalIndex**() const

Returns the index of the surface normal at the point within the relevant normal node. Note that if normals have been generated for a shape, the index may not be into an existing normal node.

long **getTextureCoordIndex**() const

Returns the index of the texture coordinates for the point within the relevant normal node. Note that if texture coordinates have been generated for a shape, the index may not be into an existing texture coordinate node.

Methods from class SoDetail:

copy, getClassTypeId, getTypeId, isOfType

INCLUDE FILE

```
#include <Inventor/details/SoPointDetail.h>
```

SEE ALSO

SoDetail, SoPickedPoint, SoPrimitiveVertex, SoVertexShape, SoFaceDetail, SoLineDetail

NAME

SoPointLight — node representing a point light source

INHERITS FROM

SoBase > SoFieldContainer > SoNode > SoLight > SoPointLight

DESCRIPTION

This node defines a point light source at a fixed 3D location. A point source illuminates equally in all directions; that is, it is omni-directional.

FIELDS

SoSFVec3f **location**

Location of the source.

Fields from class SoLight:

on, intensity, color

METHODS

SoPointLight()

Creates a point light source node with default settings.

static SoType **getClassTypeId**()

Returns type identifier for this class.

Methods from class SoNode:

setOverride, isOverride, copy, affectsState, getByName, getByName

Methods from class SoFieldContainer:

setToDefaults, hasDefaultValues, fieldsAreEqual, copyFieldValues, set, get, getFields, getField, getFieldName, enableNotify, isNotifyEnabled

Methods from class SoBase:

ref, unref, unrefNoDelete, touch, getTypeId, isOfType, setName, getName

ACTION BEHAVIOR

SoGLRenderAction

Activates this light (if so specified) during traversal. All shape nodes that come after this light in the scene graph are illuminated by this light. The light's location is affected by the current transformation.

FILE FORMAT/DEFAULTS

```
PointLight {
        on          TRUE
        intensity   1
        color       1 1 1
        location    0 0 1
}
```

INCLUDE FILE

```
#include <Inventor/nodes/SoPointLight.h>
```

SEE ALSO

SoDirectionalLight, SoSpotLight

NAME

SoPointLightDragger — sun-shaped icon you can translate in 3D by dragging with the mouse

INHERITS FROM

SoBase > SoFieldContainer > SoNode > SoBaseKit > SoInteractionKit > SoDragger > SoPointLightDragger

DESCRIPTION

SoPointLightDragger is a dragger that looks like a point light source, can be translated in three directions, and has a **translation** field that always reflects its position in local space. The point light dragger also has a special *material* part which can be used to make it take on the color of a light source.

Remember: This is *not* a light source! It just looks like one. If you want to move a light with this dragger, you can either:

[a] Use an **SoPointLightManip**, which is subclassed from **SoLight**. It creates one of these draggers and uses it as the interface to change the **location** of its light source (see the **SoPointLightManip** reference page). The manipulator also edits the **material** part of this dragger to match the color of light the manipulator is producing.

[b] Use a field-to-field connection to connect the **location** of a light source from this dragger's **translation** field.

This dragger contains an **SoDragPointDragger**, which you drag through 3-space using an integrated set of linear and planar draggers. (For detailed information on how to use **SoDragPointDragger**, see its reference page.) The point light dragger sets the planar translation parts of this dragPoint dragger with a new default that looks like a shining sun emanating rays of light (okay, so use your imagination).

By changing the **material** part you can change the color of the sun shape, because the default part contains no **SoMaterial** nodes. This fact enables the **SoPointLightManip** (not the dragger, the manipulator) to color its dragger to match the color of the light it is emanating. Recall that a point light *manip* is derived from **SoLight** and creates a point light *dragger* to provide an interface and geometrical presence on screen. The manipulator also has a **color** field; when the light color changes, it changes the **material** part of its dragger so that they match.

You can change the parts in any instance of this dragger using **setPart()**.

The default part geometries are defined as resources for this **SoPointLightDragger** class. They are detailed in the Dragger Resources section of the online reference page for this class. You can make your program use different default resources for the parts by copying the file **/usr/share/data/draggerDefaults/pointLightDragger.iv** into your own directory, editing the file, and then setting the environment variable **SO_DRAGGER_DIR** to be a path to that directory.

FIELDS

SoSFVec3f   **translation**
        Position of the dragger.

Fields from class SoDragger:
        isActive

Fields from class SoInteractionKit:
        renderCaching, boundingBoxCaching, renderCulling, pickCulling

PARTS

Parts from class SoBaseKit:
        callbackList

METHODS

                SoPointLightDragger()
        Constructor.

static const SoNodekitCatalog *
                getClassNodekitCatalog() const
        Returns an **SoNodekitCatalog** for this class

static SoType   **getClassTypeId**()
        Returns type identifier for this class.

Methods from class SoDragger:
        addStartCallback, removeStartCallback, addMotionCallback,
        removeMotionCallback, addFinishCallback, removeFinishCallback,
        addValueChangedCallback, removeValueChangedCallback, setMinGesture,
        getMinGesture, setMinScale, getMinScale

Methods from class SoInteractionKit:
        setPartAsPath

Methods from class SoBaseKit:
        getNodekitCatalog, getPart, getPartString, createPathToPart, setPart, set, set,
        isSearchingChildren, setSearchingChildren

Methods from class SoNode:

setOverride, isOverride, copy, affectsState, getByName, getByName

Methods from class SoFieldContainer:

setToDefaults, hasDefaultValues, fieldsAreEqual, copyFieldValues, get, getFields, getField, getFieldName, enableNotify, isNotifyEnabled

Methods from class SoBase:

ref, unref, unrefNoDelete, touch, getTypeId, isOfType, setName, getName

MACROS

Macros from class SoBaseKit:

SO_GET_PART, SO_CHECK_PART

CATALOG PARTS

All parts			
Part Name	**Part Type**	**Default Type**	**NULL by Default**
callbackList	NodeKitListPart	--	yes
material	Material	--	yes
translator	DragPointDragger	--	yes

Extra information for list parts from above table		
Part Name	**Container Type**	**Permissible Types**
callbackList	Separator	Callback, EventCallback

FILE FORMAT/DEFAULTS

```
PointLightDragger {
      renderCaching        AUTO
      boundingBoxCaching   AUTO
      renderCulling        AUTO
      pickCulling          AUTO
      isActive             FALSE
      translation          0 0 0
}
```

INCLUDE FILE

```
#include <Inventor/draggers/SoPointLightDragger.h>
```

SEE ALSO

SoInteractionKit, SoDragger, SoCenterballDragger, SoDirectionalLightDragger, SoDragPointDragger, SoHandleBoxDragger, SoJackDragger, SoRotateCylindricalDragger, SoRotateDiscDragger, SoRotateSphericalDragger, SoScale1Dragger, SoScale2Dragger, SoScale2UniformDragger, SoScaleUniformDragger, SoSpotLightDragger, SoTabBoxDragger, SoTabPlaneDragger, SoTrackballDragger, SoTransformBoxDragger, SoTranslate1Dragger, SoTranslate2Dragger

NAME

SoPointLightManip — point light node with 3D interface for editing location

INHERITS FROM

SoBase > SoFieldContainer > SoNode > SoLight > SoPointLight > SoPointLightManip

DESCRIPTION

SoPointLightManip is the base class for all **SoPointLight** nodes that have a built-in 3D user interface (this is the only such class provided with the Inventor toolkit). Since it is derived from **SoPointLight**, any changes to its fields result in a change of lighting for nodes that follow it in the scene graph. In this case, the interface edits the **location** field. Also, the color of the manipulator's geometry will reflect the color of the light (but you can not edit the color using this manipulator).

Typically, you will want to replace a regular **SoPointLight** with an **SoPointLightManip** (as when the user selects a light to be edited), or vice versa (as when the user is done moving the light and the interface should go away). Use the **replaceNode()** method to insert a manipulator into a scene graph, and the **replaceManip()** method to remove it when done.

The **SoPointLightManip** utilizes an **SoPointLightDragger** to provide a 3D interface. However, the manipulator differs from the dragger; it lights other objects in the scene because, as an **SoPointLight**, it alters the state. The fields values and movement of the dragger, on the other hand, affect only the dragger itself. To find out more about how the interface works and what each part will do, see the reference page for **SoPointLightDragger**. The interfaces of the dragger and the manipulator are identical.

The **SoPointLightManip** utilizes its dragger by adding it as a hidden child. When an action is applied to the manipulator, such as rendering or handling events, the manipulator first traverses the dragger, and then the manipulator adds its lighting parameters to the state. When you click-drag-release over the manipulator, it passes these events down to the dragger, which moves as a result ("I can't *help* it, I'm a dragger!").

The manipulator maintains consistency between the fields of the dragger and its own fields. Let's say you use the mouse to translate the *dragger*. Callbacks insure that the **location** field of the *manipulator* will change by the same amount, thus changing the lighting of nodes which follow in the scene graph. Similarly, if you set the **location** field of the **SoPointLightManip**, the manipulator will place the dragger accordingly.

Because the dragger is a *hidden* child, you can see the dragger on screen and interact with it, but the dragger does not show up when you write the manipulator to file.

Also, any **SoPath** will end at the manipulator. (See the Actions section of this reference page for a complete description of when the dragger is traversed).

If you want to get a pointer to the dragger you can get it from the manipulator using the **getDragger()** method. You will need to do this if you want to change the geometry of a manipulator, since the geometry actually belongs to the dragger.

FIELDS

Fields from class SoPointLight:

location

Fields from class SoLight:

on, intensity, color

METHODS

SoPointLightManip()
Constructor.

SoDragger *   **getDragger()**
Returns a pointer to the dragger being used by this manipulator. Given this pointer, you can customize the dragger just like you would any other dragger. You can change geometry using the **setPart()** method, or add callbacks using the methods found in the **SoDragger** reference page.

SbBool   **replaceNode(SoPath *p)**
Replaces the tail of the path with this manipulator. The tail of the path must be an **SoPointLight** node (or subclass thereof). If the path has a nodekit, this will try to use **setPart()** to insert the manipulator. Otherwise, the manipulator requires that the next to last node in the path chain be a group.

The field values from the point light node will be copied to this manipulator, and the light node will be replaced.

The manipulator will not call **ref()** on the node it is replacing. The old node will disappear if it has no references other than from the input path *p* and its parent, since this manipulator will be replacing it in both of those places. Nor will the manipulator make any changes to field connections of the old node. The calling process is thus responsible for keeping track of its own nodes and field connections.

SbBool   **replaceManip(SoPath *p, SoPointLight *newOne)** const
Replaces the tail of the path, which must be this manipulator, with the given **SoPointLight** node. If the path has a nodekit, this will try to use

    setPart() to insert the new node. Otherwise, the manipulator requires that the next to last node in the path chain be a group.

    The field values from the manipulator will be copied to the point light node, and the manipulator will be replaced.

    The manipulator will not call **ref**() or **unref**() on the node which is replacing it, nor will it make any changes to field connections. The calling process is thus responsible for keeping track of its own nodes and field connections.

static SoType   **getClassTypeId**()
Returns type identifier for this class.

Methods from class SoNode:

    setOverride, isOverride, copy, affectsState, getByName, getByName

Methods from class SoFieldContainer:

    setToDefaults, hasDefaultValues, fieldsAreEqual, copyFieldValues, set, get, getFields, getField, getFieldName, enableNotify, isNotifyEnabled

Methods from class SoBase:

    ref, unref, unrefNoDelete, touch, getTypeId, isOfType, setName, getName

ACTION BEHAVIOR

SoGLRenderAction, SoCallbackAction, SoGetBoundingBoxAction, SoGetMatrixAction, SoHandleEventAction, SoRayPickAction

    First, traverses the dragger the way an **SoGroup** would. All draggers place themselves in space, but leave the current transformation unchanged when finished. Then the **SoPointLightManip** adds a point light into the state, just like its base class, **SoPointLight**.

SoSearchAction

    Searches just like an **SoPointLight**. Does not search the dragger, which is a hidden child.

SoWriteAction

    Writes out just like an **SoPointLight**. Does not write the dragger, which is a hidden child. If you really need to write valuable information about the dragger, such as customized geometry, you can retrieve the dragger with the **getDragger**() method and then write it out separately.

FILE FORMAT/DEFAULTS

```
PointLightManip {
        on          TRUE
        intensity   1
        color       1 1 1
        location    0 0 1
}
```

INCLUDE FILE

```
#include <Inventor/manips/SoPointLightManip.h>
```

SEE ALSO

SoDragger, SoPointLight, SoPointLightDragger, SoDirectionalLightManip,
SoSpotLightManip

NAME

SoPointSet — point set shape node

INHERITS FROM

SoBase > SoFieldContainer > SoNode > SoShape > SoVertexShape >
SoNonIndexedShape > SoPointSet

DESCRIPTION

This node represents a set of points located at the current coordinates. **SoPointSet**
uses the current coordinates in order, starting at the index specified by the
startIndex field. The number of points in the set is specified by the **numPoints**
field. A value of SO_POINT_SET_USE_REST_OF_POINTS (-1) for this field indicates
that all remaining values in the current coordinates are to be used as points.

The coordinates of the point set are transformed by the current cumulative
transformation. The points are drawn with the current light model and drawing
style (drawing styles FILLED and LINES are treated as POINTS).

Treatment of the current material and normal binding is as follows: PER_PART,
PER_FACE, and PER_VERTEX bindings bind one material or normal to each point.
The DEFAULT material binding is equal to OVERALL. The DEFAULT normal binding
is equal to PER_VERTEX. The **startIndex** is also used for materials, normals, or
texture coordinates when the binding indicates that they should be used per vertex.

If the current complexity value is less than 0.5, some points will be skipped during
rendering.

FIELDS

SoSFLong   **numPoints**
          Number of points.

Fields from class SoNonIndexedShape:
          startIndex

METHODS

                    SoPointSet()
          Creates a point set node with default settings.

static SoType   **getClassTypeId**()
          Returns type identifier for this class.

Methods from class SoNode:
          setOverride, isOverride, copy, affectsState, getByName, getByName

Methods from class SoFieldContainer:

> setToDefaults, hasDefaultValues, fieldsAreEqual, copyFieldValues, set, get, getFields, getField, getFieldName, enableNotify, isNotifyEnabled

Methods from class SoBase:

> ref, unref, unrefNoDelete, touch, getTypeId, isOfType, setName, getName

ACTION BEHAVIOR

SoGLRenderAction

Draws points based on the current coordinates, normals, materials, drawing style, and so on.

SoRayPickAction

Picks points based on the current coordinates and transformation. Details about the intersection are returned in an **SoPointDetail**.

SoGetBoundingBoxAction

Computes the bounding box that encloses all points in the set with the current transformation applied to them. Sets the center to the average of the coordinates of all points.

SoCallbackAction

If any point callbacks are registered with the action, they will be invoked for each point in the set.

FILE FORMAT/DEFAULTS

```
PointSet {
      startIndex   0
      numPoints    -1
}
```

INCLUDE FILE

```
#include <Inventor/nodes/SoPointSet.h>
```

SEE ALSO

SoCoordinate3, SoDrawStyle, SoIndexedPointSet, SoPointDetail

NAME

SoPrimitiveVertex — represents a vertex of a generated primitive

INHERITS FROM

SoPrimitiveVertex

DESCRIPTION

An **SoPrimitiveVertex** represents a vertex of a primitive (triangle, line segment, or point) that is being generated by an **SoCallbackAction**. It contains an object-space point, normal, texture coordinates, material index, and a pointer to an instance of an **SoDetail** subclass. This detail may contain more information about the vertex, or may be a NULL pointer if there is no such info.

Instances of **SoPrimitiveVertex** are typically created on the stack by shape classes while they are generating primitives. Anyone who wants to save them as return values from **SoCallbackAction** should probably make copies of them.

METHODS

SoPrimitiveVertex()
SoPrimitiveVertex(const SoPrimitiveVertex &pv)
~**SoPrimitiveVertex**()

Constructors and destructor. Note that copying a primitive vertex copies the detail pointer, and not the detail itself.

const SbVec3f & **getPoint**() const
const SbVec3f & **getNormal**() const
const SbVec4f & **getTextureCoords**() const

These return the surface point, normal, and texture coordinates in object space.

int **getMaterialIndex**() const

Returns the index into the current set of materials of the material active at the vertex.

const SoDetail * **getDetail**() const

Returns the detail giving more information about the vertex. Note that this pointer may be NULL if there is no more info.

SoPrimitiveVertex &
operator =(const SoPrimitiveVertex &pv)
Copies the given vertex. Note that just the pointer to the detail is copied, and not the detail itself.

INCLUDE FILE

```
#include <Inventor/SoPrimitiveVertex.h>
```

NAME

SoProfile — abstract base class for all profile nodes

INHERITS FROM

SoBase > SoFieldContainer > SoNode > SoProfile

DESCRIPTION

This node is the abstract base class for all profile nodes, which define 2D curves. A profile is not itself geometry, but is used to change or delimit the geometry of something else. For an **SoText3** node, the profile determines the cross-section of the side of each text character. For an **SoNurbsSurface** node, the profile is used to specify trim curves for the surface.

The current profile state can consist of one or more profiles, each of which can be made up of one or more instances of **SoProfile** subclass nodes. Each profile node specifies (in the **index** field) a set of indices that refer to the current set of profile coordinates, specified using either an **SoProfileCoordinate2** or an **SoProfileCoordinate3** node. No profile curve should intersect itself or another profile curve.

Profiles are part of the state, just like all other properties. The state contains a current list of profiles. Depending on the **linkage** field, a profile can clear the list and begin a new profile, begin a new profile at the end of those already in the list, or append to the last profile in the current list. Note that when appending profile B to the end of profile A, B must begin at the same 2D point at which A ends.

FIELDS

SoMFLong   **index**
Indices into profile coordinates.

SoSFEnum   **linkage**
Specifies connectivity of profile curve with respect to profiles in current list in state.

METHODS

static SoType   **getClassTypeId**()
Returns type identifier for this class.

Methods from class SoNode:

setOverride, isOverride, copy, affectsState, getByName, getByName

Methods from class SoFieldContainer:

setToDefaults, hasDefaultValues, fieldsAreEqual, copyFieldValues, set, get, getFields, getField, getFieldName, enableNotify, isNotifyEnabled

Methods from class SoBase:

ref, unref, unrefNoDelete, touch, getTypeId, isOfType, setName, getName

ACTION BEHAVIOR

SoGLRenderAction, SoCallbackAction, SoGetBoundingBoxAction, SoRayPickAction

Adds profile to current traversal state.

FILE FORMAT/DEFAULTS

This is an abstract class. See the reference page of a derived class for the format and default values.

INCLUDE FILE

```
#include <Inventor/nodes/SoProfile.h>
```

enum **Profile** {
    SoProfile::START_FIRST
                Start a new profile and remove any existing profiles from the current list
    SoProfile::START_NEW
                Start a new profile and add it to the current list
    SoProfile::ADD_TO_CURRENT
                Add to end of the last profile in the current list
}

SEE ALSO

SoLinearProfile, SoNurbsProfile, SoNurbsSurface, SoProfileCoordinate2, SoProfileCoordinate3, SoText3

NAME

SoProfileCoordinate2 — profile coordinate node

INHERITS FROM

SoBase > SoFieldContainer > SoNode > SoProfileCoordinate2

DESCRIPTION

This node defines a set of 2D coordinates to be used by subsequent **SoProfile** nodes. This node does not produce a visible result during rendering; it simply replaces the current profile coordinates in the traversal state for subsequent nodes to use.

FIELDS

SoMFVec2f   **point**

2D profile coordinate points.

METHODS

SoProfileCoordinate2()

Creates a profile coordinate node with default settings.

static SoType   **getClassTypeId**()

Returns type identifier for this class.

Methods from class SoNode:

setOverride, isOverride, copy, affectsState, getByName, getByName

Methods from class SoFieldContainer:

setToDefaults, hasDefaultValues, fieldsAreEqual, copyFieldValues, set, get, getFields, getField, getFieldName, enableNotify, isNotifyEnabled

Methods from class SoBase:

ref, unref, unrefNoDelete, touch, getTypeId, isOfType, setName, getName

ACTION BEHAVIOR

SoGLRenderAction, SoCallbackAction, SoGetBoundingBoxAction, SoRayPickAction

Sets profile coordinates in current traversal state.

FILE FORMAT/DEFAULTS

```
ProfileCoordinate2 {
     point  0 0
}
```

INCLUDE FILE

```
#include <Inventor/nodes/SoProfileCoordinate2.h>
```

SEE ALSO

SoProfile, SoProfileCoordinate3

SoProfileCoordinate3

NAME

SoProfileCoordinate3 — rational profile coordinate node

INHERITS FROM

SoBase > SoFieldContainer > SoNode > SoProfileCoordinate3

DESCRIPTION

This node defines a set of rational 3D coordinates to be used by subsequent **SoProfile** nodes. (These coordinates may be used for any type of profile; they may be useful in some cases for specifying control points for **SoNurbsProfile** nodes.) This node does not produce a visible result during rendering; it simply replaces the current profile coordinates in the traversal state for subsequent nodes to use.

FIELDS

SoMFVec3f   **point**

Rational 3D profile coordinate points.

METHODS

SoProfileCoordinate3()

Creates a profile coordinate node with default settings.

static SoType   **getClassTypeId**()

Returns type identifier for this class.

Methods from class SoNode:

setOverride, isOverride, copy, affectsState, getByName, getByName

Methods from class SoFieldContainer:

setToDefaults, hasDefaultValues, fieldsAreEqual, copyFieldValues, set, get, getFields, getField, getFieldName, enableNotify, isNotifyEnabled

Methods from class SoBase:

ref, unref, unrefNoDelete, touch, getTypeId, isOfType, setName, getName

ACTION BEHAVIOR

SoGLRenderAction, SoCallbackAction, SoGetBoundingBoxAction, SoRayPickAction

Sets profile coordinates in current traversal state.

FILE FORMAT/DEFAULTS

```
ProfileCoordinate3 {
      point  0 0 1
}
```

INCLUDE FILE

```
#include <Inventor/nodes/SoProfileCoordinate3.h>
```

SEE ALSO

SoProfile, SoProfileCoordinate2

NAME

      SoQuadMesh — quadrilateral mesh shape node

INHERITS FROM

      SoBase > SoFieldContainer > SoNode > SoShape > SoVertexShape >
      SoNonIndexedShape > SoQuadMesh

DESCRIPTION

      This shape node constructs quadrilaterals out of vertices located at the current
      coordinates. **SoQuadMesh** uses the current coordinates, in order, starting at the
      index specified by the **startIndex** field. The number of vertices in the columns and
      rows of the mesh are specified by the **verticesPerColumn** and **verticesPerRow**
      fields. (Note that these numbers are 1 greater than the number of quadrilaterals per
      row and per column.)

      For example, an **SoQuadMesh** with a **startIndex** of 3, **verticesPerColumn** of 3, and
      verticesPerRow of 4 would use coordinates 3, 4, 5, and 6 for the first row of vertices,
      coordinates 7, 8, 9, and 10 for the second row, and coordinates 11, 12, 13, and 14
      for the third (last) row. The result is a mesh of 3 quadrilaterals across by 2 down.
      Note: non-planar quadrilaterals formed by a quad mesh may cause interesting but
      unpredictable results.

      The coordinates of the mesh are transformed by the current cumulative
      transformation. The mesh is drawn with the current light model and drawing style.

      Treatment of the current material and normal binding is as follows: The PER_PART
      binding specifies a material or normal for each row of the mesh. The PER_FACE
      binding specifies a material or normal for each quadrilateral. The _INDEXED
      bindings are equivalent to their non-indexed counterparts. The DEFAULT material
      binding is equal to OVERALL. The DEFAULT normal binding is equal to
      PER_VERTEX. The **startIndex** is also used for materials, normals, or texture
      coordinates when the binding indicates that they should be used per vertex.

      If the current complexity value is less than 0.5, some rows will be skipped during
      rendering.

FIELDS

      SoSFLong   **verticesPerColumn**
      SoSFLong   **verticesPerRow**
           Number of vertices per column and row.

      Fields from class SoNonIndexedShape:
           startIndex

METHODS

SoQuadMesh()

Creates a quadrilateral mesh node with default settings.

static SoType   **getClassTypeId()**

Returns type identifier for this class.

Methods from class SoNode:

setOverride, isOverride, copy, affectsState, getByName, getByName

Methods from class SoFieldContainer:

setToDefaults, hasDefaultValues, fieldsAreEqual, copyFieldValues, set, get, getFields, getField, getFieldName, enableNotify, isNotifyEnabled

Methods from class SoBase:

ref, unref, unrefNoDelete, touch, getTypeId, isOfType, setName, getName

ACTION BEHAVIOR

SoGLRenderAction

Draws a mesh based on the current coordinates, normals, materials, drawing style, and so on.

SoRayPickAction

Picks on the mesh based on the current coordinates and transformation. Details about the intersection are returned in an **SoFaceDetail**.

SoGetBoundingBoxAction

Computes the bounding box that encloses all vertices of the mesh with the current transformation applied to them. Sets the center to the average of the coordinates of all vertices.

SoCallbackAction

If any triangle callbacks are registered with the action, they will be invoked for each successive triangle forming the quadrilaterals of the mesh.

FILE FORMAT/DEFAULTS

```
QuadMesh {
      startIndex          0
      verticesPerColumn   1
      verticesPerRow      1
}
```

SoQuadMesh

INCLUDE FILE

    #include <Inventor/nodes/SoQuadMesh.h>

SEE ALSO

SoCoordinate3, SoDrawStyle, SoFaceDetail, SoFaceSet, SoTriangleStripSet

NAME

SoRayPickAction — intersects objects with a ray cast into scene

INHERITS FROM

SoAction > SoPickAction > SoRayPickAction

DESCRIPTION

This class performs picking by casting a ray into a scene and performing intersection tests with each object. The ray is extended to be a cone or cylinder, depending on the camera type, for intersection with points and lines. Each intersection is returned as an **SoPickedPoint** instance.

The picking ray can be specified as either a ray from the camera location through a particular viewport pixel, or as a world-space ray. In the former case, a valid camera must be encountered during traversal of the graph to determine the location of the ray in world space.

Callers can cause the action to compute all intersections along the ray (sorted closest to farthest) by setting the **pickAll** flag to TRUE. By default, the action computes only the closest intersection. In either case, the intersections are returned in an **SoPickedPointList**. Each intersection can be examined by accessing the appropriate **SoPickedPoint** in the list. The **SoPickedPoint** class provides methods to get the intersection point, normal, and other info.

METHODS

SoRayPickAction(const SbViewportRegion &viewportRegion)
Constructor takes viewport region to use for picking. Even though the picking operation may not involve a window per se, some nodes need this information to determine their size and placement.

void   **setPoint**(const SbVec2s &viewportPoint)
Sets the viewport-space point through which the ray passes, starting at the camera's viewpoint. Viewport coordinates range from (0,0) at the lower left to (width-1,height-1) at the upper right.

void   **setNormalizedPoint**(const SbVec2f &normPoint)
Sets the viewport point in normalized coordinates, which range from (0,0) at the lower left to (1,1) at the upper right.

void   **setRadius**(float radiusInPixels)
Set the radius (in pixels) around the point. This is used when testing the ray against lines and points. By default, the radius is 5 pixels. For perspective cameras, the ray is extended to be a cone when testing against lines and points. For orthographic cameras, the ray is extended to be a cylinder. The radius has no effect for shapes of other types.

| void | **setRay**(const SbVec3f &start, const SbVec3f &direction, float nearDistance = -1.0, float farDistance = -1.0) |

Sets a world-space ray along which to pick. The ray is defined as a world space starting point and direction vector. The direction vector will be normalized automatically. The last two arguments are the parametric distances between which intersections along the ray must occur. The distances are measured as if the direction vector is unit length; e.g., if *nearDistance* is 2.0, the intersection must occur past (*start* + 2*(length of the direction vector)) units along the ray. These distances can be used to achieve near and far plane clipping. A negative distance (such as the default values) means disable clipping to that plane.

| void | **setPickAll**(SbBool flag) |
| SbBool | **isPickAll**() const |

Sets/returns whether the action will return all objects intersected or just the closest one.

| const SoPickedPointList & | **getPickedPointList**() const |

Returns list of picked points.

| SoPickedPoint * | **getPickedPoint**(int index = 0) const |

Returns the indexed picked point from the list.

Methods from class SoPickAction:

setViewportRegion, getViewportRegion

Methods from class SoAction:

apply, apply, apply, getClassTypeId, getTypeId, isOfType, invalidateState

INCLUDE FILE

```
#include <Inventor/actions/SoRayPickAction.h>
```

SEE ALSO

SoPickedPoint, SoPickedPointList

NAME

SoReadError — read error handling

INHERITS FROM

SoError > SoReadError

DESCRIPTION

SoReadError is used for errors reported while reading Inventor data files.

METHODS

static void   **setHandlerCallback**(SoErrorCB *cb, void *data)
static SoErrorCB *

                getHandlerCallback()
static void *   **getHandlerData**()
Sets/returns handler callback for **SoReadError** class.

static SoType   **getClassTypeId**()
Returns type identifier for SoReadError class.

Methods from class SoError:

getDebugString, getTypeId, isOfType

INCLUDE FILE

#include <Inventor/errors/SoReadError.h>

SEE ALSO

SoDebugError, SoMemoryError

NAME

SoResetTransform — node that resets the current transformation to identity

INHERITS FROM

SoBase > SoFieldContainer > SoNode > SoTransformation > SoResetTransform

DESCRIPTION

This node resets the current transformation to identity. It can be used to apply an absolute world space transformation afterwards, such as translating to a specific point from within a hierarchy. An **SoResetTransform** node should probably be used under an **SoSeparator** or **SoTransformSeparator** so it won't change transformations for the rest of the scene graph. An **SoResetTransform** node can also be used to reset the current bounding box to empty during traversal of an **SoGetBoundingBoxAction**, if the **whatToReset** field has the **BBOX** bit set.

FIELDS

SoSFBitMask   **whatToReset**

Specifies which items to reset when the node is traversed.

METHODS

SoResetTransform()

Creates a reset transformation node with default settings.

static SoType   **getClassTypeId**()

Returns type identifier for this class.

Methods from class SoNode:

setOverride, isOverride, copy, affectsState, getByName, getByName

Methods from class SoFieldContainer:

setToDefaults, hasDefaultValues, fieldsAreEqual, copyFieldValues, set, get, getFields, getField, getFieldName, enableNotify, isNotifyEnabled

Methods from class SoBase:

ref, unref, unrefNoDelete, touch, getTypeId, isOfType, setName, getName

ACTION BEHAVIOR

SoGLRenderAction, SoCallbackAction, SoRayPickAction

If specified, resets current transformation matrix to identity.

SoGetBoundingBoxAction

If specified, resets current transformation matrix to identity and current computed bounding box to be empty.

> **SoGetMatrixAction**
> Returns identity matrix.

FILE FORMAT/DEFAULTS

```
ResetTransform {
        whatToReset   TRANSFORM
}
```

INCLUDE FILE

```
#include <Inventor/nodes/SoResetTransform.h>
```

enum **ResetType** {
> **SoResetTransform::TRANSFORM**
> > Reset the current transformation to identity
> **SoResetTransform::BBOX**
> > Reset the bounding box to empty

}

SEE ALSO

SoTransform

NAME

SoRotateCylindricalDragger — object you rotate along a cylindrical surface by dragging with the mouse

INHERITS FROM

SoBase > SoFieldContainer > SoNode > SoBaseKit > SoInteractionKit > SoDragger > SoRotateCylindricalDragger

DESCRIPTION

SoRotateCylindricalDragger is a simple dragger that rotates about the y axis of its local space. The feel of the rotation is as if you were spinning a cylinder about its axis of rotation. The local space is determined by its location in the scene graph. Transformation nodes placed before it will affect both the dragger and the direction of motion.

This node has a **rotation** field which always reflects its orientation in local space. If you set the field, the dragger will rotate accordingly. You can also connect fields of other nodes or engines from this one to make them follow the dragger's orientation.

This dragger contains four parts, *rotator*, *rotatorActive*, *feedback*, and *feedbackActive*.

Each of these is set by default from a resource described in the Dragger Resources section of the online reference page for this class. You can change the parts in any instance of this dragger using **setPart()**.

You can make your program use different default resources for the parts by copying the file **/usr/share/data/draggerDefaults/rotateCylindricalDragger.iv** into your own directory, editing the file, and then setting the environment variable **SO_DRAGGER_DIR** to be a path to that directory.

FIELDS

SoSFRotation   **rotation**
        Orientation of the dragger.

Fields from class SoDragger:
        isActive

Fields from class SoInteractionKit:
        renderCaching, boundingBoxCaching, renderCulling, pickCulling

PARTS

Parts from class SoBaseKit:
        callbackList

METHODS

SoRotateCylindricalDragger()
Constructor.

void **setProjector**(SbCylinderProjector *p)
const SbCylinderProjector *
getProjector() const
Set and get a different cylinder projector. See the **SbCylinderProjector** man pages to find out how each kind affects the feel of your dragger's motion. The default uses an **SbCylinderPlaneProjector**.

Passing in NULL will cause this default type of projector to be used. Any projector you pass in will be deleted by this dragger when this dragger is deleted. Note that the axis and radius of the cylinder are determined by the dragger, based on the **y-axis** in local space and how far the initial mouse click occured from the center of rotation.

static const SoNodekitCatalog *
getClassNodekitCatalog() const
Returns an **SoNodekitCatalog** for this class

static SoType **getClassTypeId**()
Returns type identifier for this class.

Methods from class SoDragger:

addStartCallback, removeStartCallback, addMotionCallback, removeMotionCallback, addFinishCallback, removeFinishCallback, addValueChangedCallback, removeValueChangedCallback, setMinGesture, getMinGesture, setMinScale, getMinScale

Methods from class SoInteractionKit:

setPartAsPath

Methods from class SoBaseKit:

getNodekitCatalog, getPart, getPartString, createPathToPart, setPart, set, set, isSearchingChildren, setSearchingChildren

Methods from class SoNode:

setOverride, isOverride, copy, affectsState, getByName, getByName

Methods from class SoFieldContainer:

setToDefaults, hasDefaultValues, fieldsAreEqual, copyFieldValues, get, getFields, getField, getFieldName, enableNotify, isNotifyEnabled

Methods from class SoBase:

ref, unref, unrefNoDelete, touch, getTypeId, isOfType, setName, getName

MACROS

Macros from class SoBaseKit:

SO_GET_PART, SO_CHECK_PART

CATALOG PARTS

All parts			
Part Name	Part Type	Default Type	NULL by Default
callbackList	NodeKitListPart	--	yes
rotator	Separator	--	yes
rotatorActive	Separator	--	yes
feedback	Separator	--	yes
feedbackActive	Separator	--	yes
Extra information for list parts from above table			
Part Name	Container Type	Permissible Types	
callbackList	Separator	Callback, EventCallback	

FILE FORMAT/DEFAULTS

```
RotateCylindricalDragger {
        renderCaching       AUTO
        boundingBoxCaching  AUTO
        renderCulling       AUTO
        pickCulling         AUTO
        isActive            FALSE
        rotation            0 0 1  0
}
```

INCLUDE FILE

```
#include <Inventor/draggers/SoRotateCylindricalDragger.h>
```

SEE ALSO

SoInteractionKit, SoDragger, SoCenterballDragger, SoDirectionalLightDragger, SoDragPointDragger, SoHandleBoxDragger, SoJackDragger, SoPointLightDragger, SoRotateDiscDragger, SoRotateSphericalDragger, SoScale1Dragger, SoScale2Dragger, SoScale2UniformDragger, SoScaleUniformDragger, SoSpotLightDragger, SoTabBoxDragger, SoTabPlaneDragger, SoTrackballDragger, SoTransformBoxDragger, SoTranslate1Dragger, SoTranslate2Dragger

NAME

SoRotateDiscDragger — object you can rotate like a knob by dragging With the mouse

INHERITS FROM

SoBase > SoFieldContainer > SoNode > SoBaseKit > SoInteractionKit > SoDragger > SoRotateDiscDragger

DESCRIPTION

SoRotateDiscDragger is a simple dragger that rotates about the z axis of its local space. The feel of the rotation is as if you were spinning a record on a turntable or rotating the volume knob of a radio. The local space is determined by its location in the scene graph. Transformation nodes placed before it will affect both the dragger and the direction of motion.

This node has a **rotation** field which always reflects its orientation in local space. If you set the field, the dragger will rotate accordingly. You can also connect fields of other nodes or engines from this one to make them follow the dragger's rotation.

This dragger contains four parts, *rotator*, *rotatorActive*, *feedback*, and *feedbackActive*.

Each of these is set by default from a resource described in the Dragger Resources section of the online reference page for this class. You can change the parts in any instance of this dragger using **setPart()**.

You can make your program use different default resources for the parts by copying the file **/usr/share/data/draggerDefaults/rotateDiscDragger.iv** into your own directory, editing the file, and then setting the environment variable **SO_DRAGGER_DIR** to be a path to that directory.

FIELDS

SoSFRotation   **rotation**

Orientation of the dragger.

Fields from class SoDragger:

isActive

Fields from class SoInteractionKit:

renderCaching, boundingBoxCaching, renderCulling, pickCulling

PARTS

Parts from class SoBaseKit:

callbackList

METHODS

> **SoRotateDiscDragger**()
> Constructor.

static const SoNodekitCatalog *
> **getClassNodekitCatalog**() const
> Returns an **SoNodekitCatalog** for this class

static SoType   **getClassTypeId**()
> Returns type identifier for this class.

Methods from class SoDragger:

> addStartCallback, removeStartCallback, addMotionCallback, removeMotionCallback, addFinishCallback, removeFinishCallback, addValueChangedCallback, removeValueChangedCallback, setMinGesture, getMinGesture, setMinScale, getMinScale

Methods from class SoInteractionKit:

> setPartAsPath

Methods from class SoBaseKit:

> getNodekitCatalog, getPart, getPartString, createPathToPart, setPart, set, set, isSearchingChildren, setSearchingChildren

Methods from class SoNode:

> setOverride, isOverride, copy, affectsState, getByName, getByName

Methods from class SoFieldContainer:

> setToDefaults, hasDefaultValues, fieldsAreEqual, copyFieldValues, get, getFields, getField, getFieldName, enableNotify, isNotifyEnabled

Methods from class SoBase:

> ref, unref, unrefNoDelete, touch, getTypeId, isOfType, setName, getName

MACROS

Macros from class SoBaseKit:

> SO_GET_PART, SO_CHECK_PART

CATALOG PARTS

All parts			
Part Name	**Part Type**	**Default Type**	**NULL by Default**
callbackList	NodeKitListPart	--	yes
rotator	Separator	--	yes
rotatorActive	Separator	--	yes
feedback	Separator	--	yes
feedbackActive	Separator	--	yes

Extra information for list parts from above table		
Part Name	**Container Type**	**Permissible Types**
callbackList	Separator	Callback, EventCallback

FILE FORMAT/DEFAULTS

```
RotateDiscDragger {
        renderCaching          AUTO
        boundingBoxCaching     AUTO
        renderCulling          AUTO
        pickCulling            AUTO
        isActive               FALSE
        rotation               0 0 1  0
}
```

INCLUDE FILE

```
#include <Inventor/draggers/SoRotateDiscDragger.h>
```

SEE ALSO

SoInteractionKit, SoDragger, SoCenterballDragger, SoDirectionalLightDragger, SoDragPointDragger, SoHandleBoxDragger, SoJackDragger, SoPointLightDragger, SoRotateCylindricalDragger, SoRotateSphericalDragger, SoScale1Dragger, SoScale2Dragger, SoScale2UniformDragger, SoScaleUniformDragger, SoSpotLightDragger, SoTabBoxDragger, SoTabPlaneDragger, SoTrackballDragger, SoTransformBoxDragger, SoTranslate1Dragger, SoTranslate2Dragger

NAME

SoRotateSphericalDragger — object you can rotate about a spherical surface by dragging with the mouse

INHERITS FROM

SoBase > SoFieldContainer > SoNode > SoBaseKit > SoInteractionKit > SoDragger > SoRotateSphericalDragger

DESCRIPTION

SoRotateSphericalDragger is a simple dragger that rotates freely in all directions. The feel of the rotation is as if you were rolling a ball. The center of rotation is the origin of the local space, determined by the dragger's location in the scene graph. Transformation nodes placed before it will affect both the dragger and the direction of motion.

This node has a **rotation** field which always reflects its orientation in local space. If you set the field, the dragger will rotate accordingly. You can also connect fields of other nodes or engines from this one to make them follow the dragger's orientation.

This dragger contains four parts, *rotator*, *rotatorActive*, *feedback*, and *feedbackActive*.

Each of these is set by default from a resource described in the Dragger Resources section of the online reference page for this class. You can change the parts in any instance of this dragger using **setPart()**.

You can make your program use different default resources for the parts by copying the file **/usr/share/data/draggerDefaults/rotateSphericalDragger.iv** into your own directory, editing the file, and then setting the environment variable **SO_DRAGGER_DIR** to be a path to that directory.

FIELDS

SoSFRotation   **rotation**

Orientation of the dragger.

Fields from class SoDragger:

isActive

Fields from class SoInteractionKit:

renderCaching, boundingBoxCaching, renderCulling, pickCulling

PARTS

Parts from class SoBaseKit:

callbackList

METHODS

SoRotateSphericalDragger()
Constructor.

void **setProjector**(SbSphereProjector *p)
const SbSphereProjector *
getProjector() const
Set and get a different sphere projector. See the **SbSphereProjector** man pages to find out how each kind affects the feel of your dragger's motion. The default uses an **SbSpherePlaneProjector**.

Passing in NULL will cause the default type of projector to be used. Any projector you pass in will be deleted by this dragger when this dragger is deleted. Note that the center and radius of the sphere are determined by the dragger, based on the origin of the local space and the distance between the initial mouse click and that origin.

static const SoNodekitCatalog *
getClassNodekitCatalog() const
Returns an **SoNodekitCatalog** for this class

static SoType **getClassTypeId**()
Returns type identifier for this class.

Methods from class SoDragger:

addStartCallback, removeStartCallback, addMotionCallback, removeMotionCallback, addFinishCallback, removeFinishCallback, addValueChangedCallback, removeValueChangedCallback, setMinGesture, getMinGesture, setMinScale, getMinScale

Methods from class SoInteractionKit:

setPartAsPath

Methods from class SoBaseKit:

getNodekitCatalog, getPart, getPartString, createPathToPart, setPart, set, set, isSearchingChildren, setSearchingChildren

Methods from class SoNode:

setOverride, isOverride, copy, affectsState, getByName, getByName

Methods from class SoFieldContainer:

setToDefaults, hasDefaultValues, fieldsAreEqual, copyFieldValues, get, getFields, getField, getFieldName, enableNotify, isNotifyEnabled

Methods from class SoBase:

ref, unref, unrefNoDelete, touch, getTypeId, isOfType, setName, getName

MACROS

Macros from class SoBaseKit:

SO_GET_PART, SO_CHECK_PART

CATALOG PARTS

All parts			
Part Name	Part Type	Default Type	NULL by Default
callbackList	NodeKitListPart	--	yes
rotator	Separator	--	yes
rotatorActive	Separator	--	yes
feedback	Separator	--	yes
feedbackActive	Separator	--	yes
Extra information for list parts from above table			
Part Name	Container Type	Permissible Types	
callbackList	Separator	Callback, EventCallback	

FILE FORMAT/DEFAULTS

```
RotateSphericalDragger {
      renderCaching        AUTO
      boundingBoxCaching   AUTO
      renderCulling        AUTO
      pickCulling          AUTO
      isActive             FALSE
      rotation             0 0 1 0
}
```

INCLUDE FILE

```
#include <Inventor/draggers/SoRotateSphericalDragger.h>
```

SEE ALSO

SoInteractionKit, SoDragger, SoCenterballDragger, SoDirectionalLightDragger,
SoDragPointDragger, SoHandleBoxDragger, SoJackDragger, SoPointLightDragger,
SoRotateCylindricalDragger, SoRotateDiscDragger, SoScale1Dragger,
SoScale2Dragger, SoScale2UniformDragger, SoScaleUniformDragger,
SoSpotLightDragger, SoTabBoxDragger, SoTabPlaneDragger, SoTrackballDragger,
SoTransformBoxDragger, SoTranslate1Dragger, SoTranslate2Dragger

NAME

SoRotation — node representing a 3D rotation about an arbitrary axis

INHERITS FROM

SoBase > SoFieldContainer > SoNode > SoTransformation > SoRotation

DESCRIPTION

This node defines a 3D rotation about an arbitrary axis through the origin. The rotation is accumulated into the current transformation, which is applied to subsequent shapes. The **rotation** field provides a variety of methods for specifying the rotation.

FIELDS

SoSFRotation **rotation**
Rotation specification.

METHODS

SoRotation()
Creates a rotation node with default settings.

static SoType **getClassTypeId()**
Returns type identifier for this class.

Methods from class SoNode:

setOverride, isOverride, copy, affectsState, getByName, getByName

Methods from class SoFieldContainer:

setToDefaults, hasDefaultValues, fieldsAreEqual, copyFieldValues, set, get, getFields, getField, getFieldName, enableNotify, isNotifyEnabled

Methods from class SoBase:

ref, unref, unrefNoDelete, touch, getTypeId, isOfType, setName, getName

ACTION BEHAVIOR

SoGLRenderAction, SoCallbackAction, SoGetBoundingBoxAction, SoRayPickAction
Accumulates rotation transformation into the current transformation.

SoGetMatrixAction
Returns the matrix corresponding to the rotation.

SoRotation

FILE FORMAT/DEFAULTS

```
Rotation {
      rotation  0 0 1  0
}
```

INCLUDE FILE

```
#include <Inventor/nodes/SoRotation.h>
```

SEE ALSO

SoRotationXYZ, SoTransform

NAME

SoRotationXYZ — node representing a 3D rotation about the x-, y-, or z-axis

INHERITS FROM

SoBase > SoFieldContainer > SoNode > SoTransformation > SoRotationXYZ

DESCRIPTION

This node defines a 3D rotation about one of the three principal axes. The rotation is accumulated into the current transformation, which is applied to subsequent shapes.

FIELDS

SoSFEnum   **axis**
Rotation axis.

SoSFFloat   **angle**
Rotation angle (in radians), using the right-hand rule.

METHODS

        SoRotationXYZ()
Creates a rotation node with default settings.

SbRotation   **getRotation**() const
Returns an **SbRotation** equivalent to the specified rotation.

static SoType   **getClassTypeId**()
Returns type identifier for this class.

Methods from class SoNode:

setOverride, isOverride, copy, affectsState, getByName, getByName

Methods from class SoFieldContainer:

setToDefaults, hasDefaultValues, fieldsAreEqual, copyFieldValues, set, get, getFields, getField, getFieldName, enableNotify, isNotifyEnabled

Methods from class SoBase:

ref, unref, unrefNoDelete, touch, getTypeId, isOfType, setName, getName

ACTION BEHAVIOR

SoGLRenderAction, SoCallbackAction, SoGetBoundingBoxAction, SoRayPickAction
Accumulates rotation transformation into the current transformation.

SoGetMatrixAction
Returns the matrix corresponding to the rotation.

FILE FORMAT/DEFAULTS

```
RotationXYZ {
      axis    X
      angle   0
}
```

INCLUDE FILE

```
#include <Inventor/nodes/SoRotationXYZ.h>
```

enum **Axis** {
      SoRotationXYZ::X The x-axis
      SoRotationXYZ::Y The y-axis
      SoRotationXYZ::Z The z-axis
}

SEE ALSO
SoRotation, SoTransform

NAME

SoRotor — animated rotation node

INHERITS FROM

SoBase > SoFieldContainer > SoNode > SoTransformation > SoRotation > SoRotor

DESCRIPTION

The **SoRotor** class is derived from **SoRotation**, so it applies a rotation to the current transformation. Using engines connected to the **realTime** global field, the rotation value is animated over time, achieving a spinning effect. The period of the rotation can be adjusted by changing the **speed** field.

The current rotation at any time is available in the **rotation** field, inherited from **SoRotation**. This field can also be set to specify the axis of rotation. Note that unless a non-zero rotation is specified for the rotation, the node will not know which axis to use. For example, to set a rotor to spin about the y-axis, use the following:

    rotor->rotation.setValue(axis, 0.1);

where *axis* is a vector containing (0,1,0). Any non-zero angle can be used in this code.

FIELDS

SoSFFloat   **speed**

Defines the speed of the rotor, in revolutions per second.

SoSFBool   **on**

Allows applications to enable or disable the motion easily.

Fields from class SoRotation:

rotation

METHODS

SoRotor()

Creates a rotor node with default settings.

static SoType   **getClassTypeId()**

Returns type identifier for this class.

Methods from class SoNode:

setOverride, isOverride, copy, affectsState, getByName, getByName

Methods from class SoFieldContainer:

setToDefaults, hasDefaultValues, fieldsAreEqual, copyFieldValues, set, get, getFields, getField, getFieldName, enableNotify, isNotifyEnabled

Methods from class SoBase:

ref, unref, unrefNoDelete, touch, getTypeId, isOfType, setName, getName

ACTION BEHAVIOR

SoGLRenderAction, SoCallbackAction, SoGetBoundingBoxAction, SoRayPickAction

Concatenates current rotation value with the current transformation matrix.

SoGetMatrixAction

Returns transformation matrix specified by the rotation.

FILE FORMAT/DEFAULTS

```
Rotor {
      rotation   0 0 1  0
      speed      1
      on         TRUE
}
```

INCLUDE FILE

```
#include <Inventor/nodes/SoRotor.h>
```

SEE ALSO

SoPendulum, SoShuttle

NAME

SoScale — node representing a 3D geometric scaling

INHERITS FROM

SoBase > SoFieldContainer > SoNode > SoTransformation > SoScale

DESCRIPTION

This node defines a 3D scaling about the origin. If the components of the scaling vector are not all the same, this produces a non-uniform scale.

FIELDS

SoSFVec3f   **scaleFactor**

The scaling factors in the x, y, and z dimensions. Non-positive values may cause undesirable results.

METHODS

                 SoScale()

Creates a scale node with default settings.

static SoType   **getClassTypeId()**

Returns type identifier for this class.

Methods from class SoNode:

setOverride, isOverride, copy, affectsState, getByName, getByName

Methods from class SoFieldContainer:

setToDefaults, hasDefaultValues, fieldsAreEqual, copyFieldValues, set, get, getFields, getField, getFieldName, enableNotify, isNotifyEnabled

Methods from class SoBase:

ref, unref, unrefNoDelete, touch, getTypeId, isOfType, setName, getName

ACTION BEHAVIOR

SoGLRenderAction, SoCallbackAction, SoGetBoundingBoxAction, SoRayPickAction

Accumulates scaling transformation into the current transformation.

SoGetMatrixAction

Returns the matrix corresponding to the scaling.

FILE FORMAT/DEFAULTS

```
Scale {
    scaleFactor  1 1 1
}
```

SoScale

INCLUDE FILE

```
#include <Inventor/nodes/SoScale.h>
```

SEE ALSO

SoTransform, SoUnits

NAME

SoScale1Dragger — object you can scale in one dimension by dragging with the mouse

INHERITS FROM

SoBase > SoFieldContainer > SoNode > SoBaseKit > SoInteractionKit > SoDragger > SoScale1Dragger

DESCRIPTION

SoScale1Dragger is a simple dragger that scales in one dimension when dragged with the mouse. It moves along the x axis of its local space, as determined by its location in the scene graph. Transformation nodes placed before it will affect both the dragger and the direction of motion.

This node has a **scaleFactor** field which always reflects its size in local space. If you set the field, the dragger will change accordingly. You can also connect fields of other nodes or engines from this one to make them follow the dragger's motion.

This dragger contains four parts, *scaler*, *scalerActive*, *feedback*, and *feedbackActive*.

Each of these is set by default from a resource described in the Dragger Resources section of the online reference page for this class. You can change the parts in any instance of this dragger using **setPart()**.

You can make your program use different default resources for the parts by copying the file **/usr/share/data/draggerDefaults/scale1Dragger.iv** into your own directory, editing the file, and then setting the environment variable **SO_DRAGGER_DIR** to be a path to that directory.

FIELDS

SoSFVec3f   **scaleFactor**

Scale factor affecting the dragger.

Fields from class SoDragger:

isActive

Fields from class SoInteractionKit:

renderCaching, boundingBoxCaching, renderCulling, pickCulling

PARTS

Parts from class SoBaseKit:

callbackList

METHODS

SoScale1Dragger()
Constructor.

static const SoNodekitCatalog *
getClassNodekitCatalog() const
Returns an **SoNodekitCatalog** for this class

static SoType   **getClassTypeId**()
Returns type identifier for this class.

Methods from class SoDragger:

addStartCallback, removeStartCallback, addMotionCallback, removeMotionCallback, addFinishCallback, removeFinishCallback, addValueChangedCallback, removeValueChangedCallback, setMinGesture, getMinGesture, setMinScale, getMinScale

Methods from class SoInteractionKit:

setPartAsPath

Methods from class SoBaseKit:

getNodekitCatalog, getPart, getPartString, createPathToPart, setPart, set, set, isSearchingChildren, setSearchingChildren

Methods from class SoNode:

setOverride, isOverride, copy, affectsState, getByName, getByName

Methods from class SoFieldContainer:

setToDefaults, hasDefaultValues, fieldsAreEqual, copyFieldValues, get, getFields, getField, getFieldName, enableNotify, isNotifyEnabled

Methods from class SoBase:

ref, unref, unrefNoDelete, touch, getTypeId, isOfType, setName, getName

MACROS

Macros from class SoBaseKit:

SO_GET_PART, SO_CHECK_PART

CATALOG PARTS

All parts			
Part Name	**Part Type**	**Default Type**	**NULL by Default**
callbackList	NodeKitListPart	--	yes
scaler	Separator	--	yes
scalerActive	Separator	--	yes
feedback	Separator	--	yes
feedbackActive	Separator	--	yes

Extra information for list parts from above table		
Part Name	**Container Type**	**Permissible Types**
callbackList	Separator	Callback, EventCallback

FILE FORMAT/DEFAULTS

```
Scale1Dragger {
        renderCaching          AUTO
        boundingBoxCaching     AUTO
        renderCulling          AUTO
        pickCulling            AUTO
        isActive               FALSE
        scaleFactor            1 1 1
}
```

INCLUDE FILE

```
#include <Inventor/draggers/SoScale1Dragger.h>
```

SEE ALSO

SoInteractionKit, SoDragger, SoCenterballDragger, SoDirectionalLightDragger, SoDragPointDragger, SoHandleBoxDragger, SoJackDragger, SoPointLightDragger, SoRotateCylindricalDragger, SoRotateDiscDragger, SoRotateSphericalDragger, SoScale2Dragger, SoScale2UniformDragger, SoScaleUniformDragger, SoSpotLightDragger, SoTabBoxDragger, SoTabPlaneDragger, SoTrackballDragger, SoTransformBoxDragger, SoTranslate1Dragger, SoTranslate2Dragger

NAME

SoScale2Dragger — object you can scale in two dimensions by dragging with the mouse

INHERITS FROM

SoBase > SoFieldContainer > SoNode > SoBaseKit > SoInteractionKit > SoDragger > SoScale2Dragger

DESCRIPTION

SoScale2Dragger is a simple dragger that scales freely and independently in two dimensions when dragged with the mouse. It moves within the x-y plane of its local space, as determined by its location in the scene graph. Transformation nodes placed before it will affect both the dragger and the plane of motion.

This node has a **scaleFactor** field which always reflects its size in local space. If you set the field, the dragger will change accordingly. You can also connect fields of other nodes or engines from this one to make them follow the dragger's motion.

This dragger contains four parts, *scaler*, *scalerActive*, *feedback*, and *feedbackActive*.

Each of these is set by default from a resource described in the Dragger Resources section of the online reference page for this class. You can change the parts in any instance of this dragger using **setPart()**.

You can make your program use different default resources for the parts by copying the file **/usr/share/data/draggerDefaults/scale2Dragger.iv** into your own directory, editing the file, and then setting the environment variable **SO_DRAGGER_DIR** to be a path to that directory.

FIELDS

SoSFVec3f   **scaleFactor**
  Scale factor affecting the dragger.

Fields from class SoDragger:
  isActive

Fields from class SoInteractionKit:
  renderCaching, boundingBoxCaching, renderCulling, pickCulling

PARTS

Parts from class SoBaseKit:
  callbackList

METHODS

SoScale2Dragger()
Constructor.

static const SoNodekitCatalog *
getClassNodekitCatalog() const
Returns an **SoNodekitCatalog** for this class

static SoType **getClassTypeId**()
Returns type identifier for this class.

Methods from class SoDragger:

addStartCallback, removeStartCallback, addMotionCallback, removeMotionCallback, addFinishCallback, removeFinishCallback, addValueChangedCallback, removeValueChangedCallback, setMinGesture, getMinGesture, setMinScale, getMinScale

Methods from class SoInteractionKit:

setPartAsPath

Methods from class SoBaseKit:

getNodekitCatalog, getPart, getPartString, createPathToPart, setPart, set, set, isSearchingChildren, setSearchingChildren

Methods from class SoNode:

setOverride, isOverride, copy, affectsState, getByName, getByName

Methods from class SoFieldContainer:

setToDefaults, hasDefaultValues, fieldsAreEqual, copyFieldValues, get, getFields, getField, getFieldName, enableNotify, isNotifyEnabled

Methods from class SoBase:

ref, unref, unrefNoDelete, touch, getTypeId, isOfType, setName, getName

MACROS

Macros from class SoBaseKit:

SO_GET_PART, SO_CHECK_PART

CATALOG PARTS

All parts			
Part Name	Part Type	Default Type	NULL by Default
callbackList	NodeKitListPart	--	yes
scaler	Separator	--	yes
scalerActive	Separator	--	yes
feedback	Separator	--	yes
feedbackActive	Separator	--	yes

Extra information for list parts from above table		
Part Name	Container Type	Permissible Types
callbackList	Separator	Callback, EventCallback

FILE FORMAT/DEFAULTS

```
Scale2Dragger {
        renderCaching          AUTO
        boundingBoxCaching     AUTO
        renderCulling          AUTO
        pickCulling            AUTO
        isActive               FALSE
        scaleFactor            1 1 1
}
```

INCLUDE FILE

```
#include <Inventor/draggers/SoScale2Dragger.h>
```

SEE ALSO

SoInteractionKit, SoDragger, SoCenterballDragger, SoDirectionalLightDragger, SoDragPointDragger, SoHandleBoxDragger, SoJackDragger, SoPointLightDragger, SoRotateCylindricalDragger, SoRotateDiscDragger, SoRotateSphericalDragger, SoScale1Dragger, SoScale2UniformDragger, SoScaleUniformDragger, SoSpotLightDragger, SoTabBoxDragger, SoTabPlaneDragger, SoTrackballDragger, SoTransformBoxDragger, SoTranslate1Dragger, SoTranslate2Dragger

NAME

SoScale2UniformDragger — object you can scale uniformly in two dimensions by dragging with the mouse

INHERITS FROM

SoBase > SoFieldContainer > SoNode > SoBaseKit > SoInteractionKit > SoDragger > SoScale2UniformDragger

DESCRIPTION

SoScale2UniformDragger is a simple dragger that scales uniformly in the x and y dimensions when dragged within the x-y plane with the mouse. The local space is determined by its location in the scene graph. Transformation nodes placed before it will affect both the dragger and the plane of motion.

This node has a **scaleFactor** field which always reflects its size in local space. If you set the field, the dragger will change accordingly. You can also connect fields of other nodes or engines from this one to make them follow the dragger's motion.

This dragger contains four parts, *scaler*, *scalerActive*, *feedback*, and *feedbackActive*.

Each of these is set by default from a resource described in the Dragger Resource section of the online reference page for this class. You can change the parts in any instance of this dragger using **setPart()**.

You can make your program use different default resources for the parts by copying the file **/usr/share/data/draggerDefaults/scale2UniformDragger.iv** into your own directory, editing the file, and then setting the environment variable **SO_DRAGGER_DIR** to be a path to that directory.

FIELDS

SoSFVec3f   **scaleFactor**

Scale factor affecting the dragger.

Fields from class SoDragger:

isActive

Fields from class SoInteractionKit:

renderCaching, boundingBoxCaching, renderCulling, pickCulling

PARTS

Parts from class SoBaseKit:

callbackList

METHODS

SoScale2UniformDragger()
Constructor.

static const SoNodekitCatalog *
getClassNodekitCatalog() const
Returns an **SoNodekitCatalog** for this class

static SoType **getClassTypeId**()
Returns type identifier for this class.

Methods from class SoDragger:

addStartCallback, removeStartCallback, addMotionCallback, removeMotionCallback, addFinishCallback, removeFinishCallback, addValueChangedCallback, removeValueChangedCallback, setMinGesture, getMinGesture, setMinScale, getMinScale

Methods from class SoInteractionKit:

setPartAsPath

Methods from class SoBaseKit:

getNodekitCatalog, getPart, getPartString, createPathToPart, setPart, set, set, isSearchingChildren, setSearchingChildren

Methods from class SoNode:

setOverride, isOverride, copy, affectsState, getByName, getByName

Methods from class SoFieldContainer:

setToDefaults, hasDefaultValues, fieldsAreEqual, copyFieldValues, get, getFields, getField, getFieldName, enableNotify, isNotifyEnabled

Methods from class SoBase:

ref, unref, unrefNoDelete, touch, getTypeId, isOfType, setName, getName

MACROS

Macros from class SoBaseKit:

SO_GET_PART, SO_CHECK_PART

CATALOG PARTS

All parts			
Part Name	Part Type	Default Type	NULL by Default
callbackList	NodeKitListPart	--	yes
scaler	Separator	--	yes
scalerActive	Separator	--	yes
feedback	Separator	--	yes
feedbackActive	Separator	--	yes

Extra information for list parts from above table		
Part Name	Container Type	Permissible Types
callbackList	Separator	Callback, EventCallback

FILE FORMAT/DEFAULTS

```
Scale2UniformDragger {
        renderCaching          AUTO
        boundingBoxCaching     AUTO
        renderCulling          AUTO
        pickCulling            AUTO
        isActive               FALSE
        scaleFactor            1 1 1
}
```

INCLUDE FILE

```
#include <Inventor/draggers/SoScale2UniformDragger.h>
```

SEE ALSO

SoInteractionKit, SoDragger, SoCenterballDragger, SoDirectionalLightDragger, SoDragPointDragger, SoHandleBoxDragger, SoJackDragger, SoPointLightDragger, SoRotateCylindricalDragger, SoRotateDiscDragger, SoRotateSphericalDragger, SoScale1Dragger, SoScale2Dragger, SoScaleUniformDragger, SoSpotLightDragger, SoTabBoxDragger, SoTabPlaneDragger, SoTrackballDragger, SoTransformBoxDragger, SoTranslate1Dragger, SoTranslate2Dragger

NAME

SoScaleUniformDragger — object you can scale uniformly in 3D by dragging with the mouse

INHERITS FROM

SoBase > SoFieldContainer > SoNode > SoBaseKit > SoInteractionKit > SoDragger > SoScaleUniformDragger

DESCRIPTION

SoScaleUniformDragger is a simple dragger that scales uniformly in all 3 dimensions when dragged with the mouse. The local space is determined by its location in the scene graph. Transformation nodes placed before it will affect both the dragger and the plane of motion.

This node has a **scaleFactor** field which always reflects its size in local space. If you set the field, the dragger will change accordingly. You can also connect fields of other nodes or engines from this one to make them follow the dragger's motion.

This dragger contains four parts, *scaler*, *scalerActive*, *feedback*, and *feedbackActive*.

Each of these is set by default from a resource described in the Dragger Resources section of the online reference page for this class. You can change the parts in any instance of this dragger using **setPart()**.

You can make your program use different default resources for the parts by copying the file **/usr/share/data/draggerDefaults/scaleUniformDragger.iv** into your own directory, editing the file, and then setting the environment variable **SO_DRAGGER_DIR** to be a path to that directory.

FIELDS

Fields from class SoDragger:

isActive

Fields from class SoInteractionKit:

renderCaching, boundingBoxCaching, renderCulling, pickCulling

PARTS

Parts from class SoBaseKit:

callbackList

METHODS

Methods from class SoDragger:

addStartCallback, removeStartCallback, addMotionCallback,
removeMotionCallback, addFinishCallback, removeFinishCallback,

addValueChangedCallback, removeValueChangedCallback, setMinGesture, getMinGesture, setMinScale, getMinScale, getClassNodekitCatalog, getClassTypeId

Methods from class SoInteractionKit:

setPartAsPath

Methods from class SoBaseKit:

getNodekitCatalog, getPart, getPartString, createPathToPart, setPart, set, set, isSearchingChildren, setSearchingChildren

Methods from class SoNode:

setOverride, isOverride, copy, affectsState, getByName, getByName

Methods from class SoFieldContainer:

setToDefaults, hasDefaultValues, fieldsAreEqual, copyFieldValues, get, getFields, getField, getFieldName, enableNotify, isNotifyEnabled

Methods from class SoBase:

ref, unref, unrefNoDelete, touch, getTypeId, isOfType, setName, getName

MACROS

Macros from class SoBaseKit:

SO_GET_PART, SO_CHECK_PART

CATALOG PARTS

All parts			
Part Name	**Part Type**	**Default Type**	**NULL by Default**
callbackList	NodeKitListPart	--	yes
scaler	Separator	--	yes
scalerActive	Separator	--	yes
feedback	Separator	--	yes
feedbackActive	Separator	--	yes

<table>
<tr><td colspan="3" align="center">Extra information for list parts from above table</td></tr>
<tr><td>Part Name</td><td>Container Type</td><td>Permissible Types</td></tr>
<tr><td>callbackList</td><td>Separator</td><td>Callback, EventCallback</td></tr>
</table>

FILE FORMAT/DEFAULTS

```
ScaleUniformDragger {
        renderCaching          AUTO
        boundingBoxCaching     AUTO
        renderCulling          AUTO
        pickCulling            AUTO
        isActive               FALSE
        scaleFactor            1 1 1
}
```

INCLUDE FILE

```
#include <Inventor/draggers/SoScaleUniformDragger.h>
```

SEE ALSO

SoInteractionKit, SoDragger, SoCenterballDragger, SoDirectionalLightDragger, SoDragPointDragger, SoHandleBoxDragger, SoJackDragger, SoPointLightDragger, SoRotateCylindricalDragger, SoRotateDiscDragger, SoRotateSphericalDragger, SoScale1Dragger, SoScale2Dragger, SoScale2UniformDragger, SoSpotLightDragger, SoTabBoxDragger, SoTabPlaneDragger, SoTrackballDragger, SoTransformBoxDragger, SoTranslate1Dragger, SoTranslate2Dragger

NAME

SoSceneKit — scene nodekit class

INHERITS FROM

SoBase > SoFieldContainer > SoNode > SoBaseKit > SoSceneKit

DESCRIPTION

This nodekit is used to organize camera, (**SoCameraKit**), light, (**SoLightKit**), and object, (**SoShapeKit**, **SoSeparatorKit**, and **SoWrapperKit**) nodekits into a scene. A scene is composed of a list of cameras, a list of lights, and a list of children. There are three parts created by this nodekit: *cameraList*, *lightList*, and *childList*.

The *cameraList* part is a *list part* of **SoCameraKit** nodes. The list itself is an **SoNodeKitListPart**, and since only one camera can be active at a time, the *container* of the *list part* is an **SoSwitch** node. Use **setCameraNumber()**, and the scene kit will set the switch to make that camera active.

The *lightList* part is a list of **SoLightKit** nodes. The *lightList* is used to illuminate the objects contained in the *childList* part.

The *childList* part contains a set of **SoSeparatorKit** nodes. You can add any kind of **SoSeparatorKit** to this list, including **SoShapeKit** and **SoWrapperKit**. Since each **SoSeparatorKit** in turn contains a *childList*, this part is used to describe a hierarchical scene. (See the reference page for **SoSeparatorKit**). All members of *childList* are lit by the lights in *lightList* and rendered by the active camera in *cameraList*.

PARTS

(SoNodeKitListPart)

cameraList

This part is an **SoNodeKitListPart** It has a *container* that is an **SoSwitch** node. The list may contain only **SoCameraKit** nodekits. The active child of the **SoSwitch** is the *active* camera. This part is NULL by default, but is automatically created whenever you add a camera, as with **setPart("cameraList[0]", myNewCamera)** .

(SoNodeKitListPart)

lightList

This part is an **SoNodeKitListPart** that uses an defines an **SoGroup** as its *container* The list may contain only **SoLightKit** nodekits. Add **SoLightKits** to this list and they will light the members of the *childList* of this **SoSceneKit**. This part is NULL by default, but is automatically created when you add a light.

(SoNodeKitListPart)

childList

This part is an **SoNodeKitListPart** that uses an **SoGroup** for its *container*. The list may contain only **SoSeparatorKit** nodekits or nodekits derived from **SoSeparatorKit** (e.g., **SoShapeKit** and **SoWrapperKit**). These children represent the objects in the scene. This part is NULL by default, but is automatically created whenever you add a child to the *childList*. Also, when asked to build a member of the *childList*, the scenekit will build an **SoShapeKit** by default. So if the *childList* part is NULL, and you call: **getPart("childList[0]", TRUE)** . the scene kit will create the *childList* and add an **SoShapeKit** as the new element in the list.

Parts from class SoBaseKit:

callbackList

METHODS

SoSceneKit()

Constructor.

static const SoNodekitCatalog *

getClassNodekitCatalog() const

Returns an **SoNodekitCatalog** for the class **SoSceneKit**.

| int | **getCameraNumber()** |
| void | **setCameraNumber**(int camNum) |

Gets and sets current camera index. This index refers to which child is active in the *cameraList* part (**SoSwitch** node).

static SoType   **getClassTypeId()**

Returns type identifier for this class.

Methods from class SoBaseKit:

getNodekitCatalog, getPart, getPartString, createPathToPart, setPart, set, set, isSearchingChildren, setSearchingChildren

Methods from class SoNode:

setOverride, isOverride, copy, affectsState, getByName, getByName

Methods from class SoFieldContainer:

setToDefaults, hasDefaultValues, fieldsAreEqual, copyFieldValues, get, getFields, getField, getFieldName, enableNotify, isNotifyEnabled

Methods from class SoBase:

>ref, unref, unrefNoDelete, touch, getTypeId, isOfType, setName, getName

MACROS

Macros from class SoBaseKit:

>SO_GET_PART, SO_CHECK_PART

CATALOG PARTS

All parts			
Part Name	**Part Type**	**Default Type**	**NULL by Default**
callbackList	NodeKitListPart	--	yes
cameraList	NodeKitListPart	--	yes
lightList	NodeKitListPart	--	yes
childList	NodeKitListPart	--	yes

Extra information for list parts from above table		
Part Name	**Container Type**	**Permissible Types**
callbackList	Separator	Callback, EventCallback
cameraList	Switch	CameraKit
lightList	Group	LightKit
childList	Group	ShapeKit, SeparatorKit

FILE FORMAT/DEFAULTS

```
SceneKit {
}
```

INCLUDE FILE

```
#include <Inventor/nodekits/SoSceneKit.h>
```

SEE ALSO

SoAppearanceKit, SoBaseKit, SoCameraKit, SoLightKit, SoNodeKit, SoNodeKitDetail, SoNodeKitListPart, SoNodeKitPath, SoNodekitCatalog, SoSeparatorKit, SoShapeKit, SoWrapperKit

NAME

SoSceneManager — manages scene graph rendering and event handling

INHERITS FROM

SoSceneManager

DESCRIPTION

SoSceneManager provides Inventor rendering and event handling inside a window provided by the caller. The scene manager is able to render in only a portion of a window if desired. The **SoXtRenderArea** class employs a **SoSceneManager**, and handles most all the details for setting up a window, converting X events to Inventor events, automatically redrawing the scene when necessary, and so on. It is simplest to use a render area when rendering in an entire window. The **SoSceneManager** class is available for programmers not working with the *Inventor Xt Component and Utility Library.*

METHODS

SoSceneManager(SbBool useCurrentGLValues = FALSE)
~SoSceneManager()

Constructor and destructor. The parameter specifies whether current GL values (material, line width, etc.) are to be used for rendering. If this is FALSE (the default), Inventor will set up its own reasonable values.

virtual void **render**(SbBool clearWindow = TRUE, SbBool clearZbuffer = TRUE)

Apply an **SoGLRenderAction** to the scene graph managed here. The caller is responsible for setting up a window to render into. If *clearWindow* is *TRUE*, this clears the graphics window before rendering. If *clearZbuffer* is *TRUE*, the z buffer will be cleared before rendering.

virtual SbBool **processEvent**(const SoEvent *event)

Process the passed event by applying an **SoHandleEventAction** to the scene graph managed here. Returns TRUE if the event was handled by a node.

void **reinitialize**()

Reinitialize graphics. This should be called, for instance, when there is a new window.

void **scheduleRedraw**()

Schedule a redraw for some time in the near future. If there is no render callback set, or this is not active, no redraw will be scheduled.

virtual void	**setSceneGraph**(SoNode *newScene)
virtual SoNode *	**getSceneGraph**() const

Set and get the scene graph which is managed here. This is the Inventor scene which will be traversed for rendering and event processing.

void	**setWindowSize**(const SbVec2s &newSize)
const SbVec2s &	**getWindowSize**() const

Set and get the size of the window in which the scene manager should render. This size must be set before **render()** and **processEvent()** are called.

void	**setSize**(const SbVec2s &newSize)
const SbVec2s &	**getSize**() const
void	**setOrigin**(const SbVec2s &newOrigin)
const SbVec2s &	**getOrigin**() const

Set and get the size and origin of the viewport within the window. Default is to render the entire window region. The origin (0,0) is the lower left corner of the window.

void	**setBackgroundColor**(const SbColor &c)
const SbColor &	**getBackgroundColor**() const

Set and get the window background color when in RGB mode. This is the color the scene manager viewport is cleared to when **render()** is called with *clearWindow* set to *TRUE*. Default is black (0,0,0).

void	**setBackgroundIndex**(int index)
int	**getBackgroundIndex**() const

Set and get the window background color when in color index mode. This is the color the scene manager viewport is cleared to when **render()** is called with *clearWindow* set to *TRUE*. Default is black (index 0).

void	**setRGBMode**(SbBool onOrOff)
SbBool	**isRGBMode**() const

Set and get the color mode (TRUE — RGB mode, FALSE — color map mode). Default is RGB mode. Only a subset of Inventor nodes will render correctly in color map mode. Basically, when in color index mode, lighting should be turned off (the **model** field of **SoLightModel** should be set to *BASE_COLOR*), and the **SoColorIndex** node should be used to specify colors.

virtual void	**activate**()
virtual void	**deactivate**()

Activate and deactivate the scene manager. The scene manager will only employ sensors for automatic redraw while it is active. Typically, the scene manager should be activated whenever its window is visible on the screen, and deactivated when its window is closed or iconified.

void   **setRenderCallback**(SoSceneManagerRenderCB *f, void *userData = NULL)

The render callback provides a mechanism for automatically redrawing the scene in response to changes in the scene graph. The scene manager employs a sensor to monitor scene graph changes. When the sensor is triggered, the render callback registered here is invoked. The callback should set up its graphics window, then call the scene manager **render()** method. If the callback is set to NULL (the default), auto-redraw is turned off.

SbBool   **isAutoRedraw**() const

Returns *TRUE* if there is currently a render callback registered.

void   **setRedrawPriority**(unsigned long priority)
unsigned long   **getRedrawPriority**() const
static unsigned long

                             getDefaultRedrawPriority()

Set and get the priority of the redraw sensor. Sensors are processed based on priority, with priority values of 0 processed immediately. The default priority for the scene manager redraw sensor is 10000.

void   **setAntialiasing**(SbBool smoothing, int numPasses)
void   **getAntialiasing**(SbBool &smoothing, int &numPasses) const

Set/get the antialiasing for rendering. There are two kinds of antialiasing available: smoothing and multipass antialiasing. If *smoothing* is set to TRUE, smoothing is enabled. Smoothing uses OpenGL's line- and point-smoothing features to provide cheap antialiasing of lines and points. The value of *numPasses* controls multipass antialiasing. Each time a render action is applied, Inventor renders the scene *numPasses* times from slightly different camera positions, averaging the results. *numPasses* can be from one to 255, inclusive. Setting *numPasses* to one disables multipass antialiasing. You can use either, both, or neither of these antialiasing techniques. By default, both smoothing and multipass antialiasing are disabled.

INCLUDE FILE

```
#include <Inventor/SoSceneManager.h>
```

typedef void   **SoSceneManagerRenderCB**(void *userData, SoSceneManager *mgr)

SEE ALSO

SoXtRenderArea, SoGLRenderAction, SoHandleEventAction

NAME

SoSearchAction — searches for nodes in a scene graph

INHERITS FROM

SoAction > SoSearchAction

DESCRIPTION

This class is used to search scene graphs for specific nodes, nodes of a specific type, nodes with a specific name, or any combination of these. It can search for just the first or last node satisfying the criteria or for all such nodes. The actions return paths to each node found.

METHODS

SoSearchAction()
Constructor.

void	**setNode**(SoNode *n)
SoNode *	**getNode**() const

Sets/returns the node to search for.

void	**setType**(SoType t, int derivedIsOk = TRUE)
SoType	**getType**(int &derivedIsOk) const

Sets/returns the node type to search for. If *derivedIsOk* is TRUE, a node that is of a type that is derived from *t* will pass this search criterion.

void	**setName**(const SbName &n)
const SbName &	**getName**() const

Sets/returns the name of the node to search for.

void	**setFind**(int what)
int	**getFind**()

Sets/returns what to look for; *what* is a bitmask of LookFor enum values. Default is no flags at all. Note that setting a node, type, and/or name to search for activates the relevant flag, so you may never need to call this method directly.

void	**setInterest**(Interest interest)
Interest	**getInterest**() const

Sets/returns which paths to return. Default is FIRST.

void	**setSearchingAll**(SbBool flag)
SbBool	**isSearchingAll**() const

Sets/returns whether searching uses regular traversal or whether it traverses every single node. For example, if this flag is FALSE, an **SoSwitch** node will traverse only the child or children it would normally traverse for an action.

If the flag is TRUE, the switch would always traverse all of its children. The default is FALSE.

SoPath *   **getPath**() const
Returns resulting path, or NULL if no path was found. This should be used if the interest is FIRST or LAST.

SoPathList &   **getPaths**()
Returns resulting path list. This should be used if the interest is ALL.

void   **reset**()
Resets options back to default values; clears list of returned paths. This can be used to apply the action again with a different set of search criteria.

Methods from class SoAction:

apply, apply, apply, getClassTypeId, getTypeId, isOfType, invalidateState

INCLUDE FILE

```
#include <Inventor/actions/SoSearchAction.h>
```

enum **LookFor** {
    SoSearchAction::NODE
                    Search for a particular node (by pointer)
    SoSearchAction::TYPE
                    Search for a particular type of node
    SoSearchAction::NAME
                    Search for a node with a particular name
}

enum **Interest** {
    SoSearchAction::FIRST
                    Return only the first path found
    SoSearchAction::LAST
                    Return only the last path found
    SoSearchAction::ALL
                    Return all paths found
}

SEE ALSO

SoPath

NAME

    SoSelection — manages a list of selected objects

INHERITS FROM

    SoBase > SoFieldContainer > SoNode > SoGroup > SoSeparator > SoSelection

DESCRIPTION

    SoSelection defines a node which can be inserted into a scene graph and will generate and manage a selection list from picks on any node in the subgraph below it. Nodes are selected based on a current selection policy. Callback functions report back to the application when a path has been selected or deselected. The selection list can also be managed programatically.

    When handling events, **SoSelection** makes sure that the mouse release event was over the same object as the mouse press event before changing the list of selected objects. This allows users to mouse down on an object, change their mind and move the cursor off the object, then release the mouse button without altering the selection.

    The selection can be highlighted automatically through the **SoXtRenderArea**, or the application can provide custom highlights. Please see the chapter "Creating a Selection Highlight Style" in the *Inventor Toolmaker*.

FIELDS

    SoSFEnum   **policy**

    Selection policy that is followed in response to user interaction. This can be set to SoSelection::SINGLE, SoSelection::TOGGLE, or SoSelection::SHIFT.

    Fields from class SoSeparator:

    renderCaching, boundingBoxCaching, renderCulling, pickCulling

METHODS

                SoSelection()
                SoSelection(int nChildren)
    Constructor. The second constructor allows the programmer to pass in the approximate number of children to the node.

    static SoType   **getClassTypeId**()
    Return the type id for the **SoSelection** class.

    void   **select**(const SoPath *path)
    Select the passed path by adding it to the selection list. The selection node must lie in the path. The path is copied and truncated such that the selection node is the head of the path. If the selection node does not lie in

the path, the selection list remains unchanged. This method ignores the current selection policy.

void **select**(SoNode *node)
Select the passed node by creating a path to it, and adding the path to the selection list by calling **select(path)**. If there is more than one instance of *node* beneath the selection node, the created path will be the first instance found.

void **deselect**(const SoPath *path)
Deselect the passed path by removing it from the selection list.

void **deselect**(int which)
Deselect a path by removing it from the selection list. The argument *which* specifies which path in the list to be removed.

void **deselect**(SoNode *node)
Deselect the passed node by creating a path to it, and removing the node from the selection list by calling **deselect(path)**. If there is more than one instance of *node* beneath the selection node, the created path will be the first instance found.

void **toggle**(const SoPath *path)
Toggle the selection status of the passed path — if the path is in the selection list, it is removed; if not in the list, it is added.

void **toggle**(SoNode *node)
Toggle the selection status of the passed node by creating a path to it, then calling **toggle(path)**. If there is more than one instance of *node* beneath the selection node, the created path will be the first instance found.

SbBool **isSelected**(const SoPath *path) const
Returns *TRUE* if the passed path is selected, that is, if it is in the selection list.

SbBool **isSelected**(SoNode *node) const
Returns *TRUE* if the passed node is selected by creating a path to it, then calling **isSelected()**. If there is more than one instance of *node* beneath the selection node, the created path will be the first instance found.

void **deselectAll**()
Deselect all paths in the selection list, that is, clear the list.

int	**getNumSelected**() const

Return the number of paths in the selection list.

const SoPathList *	
	getList() const

Return the list of selected paths.

SoPath *	**getPath**(int index) const
SoPath *	**operator** [ ](int i) const

Return the *i*th path in the selection list.

void	**addSelectionCallback**(SoSelectionPathCB *f, void *userData = NULL)
void	**removeSelectionCallback**(SoSelectionPathCB *f, void *userData = NULL)

The selection callbacks are invoked every time an object is selected, whether it be from user interaction or from method call. The callbacks are invoked after the object has been added to the selection list.

void	**addDeselectionCallback**(SoSelectionPathCB *f, void *userData = NULL)
void	**removeDeselectionCallback**(SoSelectionPathCB *f, void *userData = NULL)

The deselection callbacks are invoked every time an object is deselected, whether it be from user interaction or from method call. This is invoked after the object has been removed from the selection list.

void	**addStartCallback**(SoSelectionClassCB *f, void *userData = NULL)
void	**removeStartCallback**(SoSelectionClassCB *f, void *userData = NULL)

The start callbacks are invoked when the user has initiated an interactive change to the selection list (by picking objects). This will be followed by invocations of the select and/or deselect callbacks, finally followed by each finish callback. A start callback can be used, for instance, to save the current selection for later restoration (e.g. undo/redo). The start callbacks are not called when the selection list is changed programatically.

void	**addFinishCallback**(SoSelectionClassCB *f, void *userData = NULL)
void	**removeFinishCallback**(SoSelectionClassCB *f, void *userData = NULL)

The finish callbacks are invoked when the user has finished interactively changing the selection list (by picking objects). This was preceeded by an invocation of each start callback, and invocations of the select and/or deselect callbacks. The finish callbacks are not called when the selection list is changed programatically.

void	**setPickFilterCallback**(SoSelectionPickCB *f, void *userData = NULL, SbBool callOnlyIfSelectable = TRUE)

The pick filter callback is invoked when a pick has occurred and the selection node is about to change the selection list. The callback function returns the path that the selection node should use when selecting and deselecting. If no pick callback is registered (the default), the selection node will use the path returned by **SoPickedPoint::getPath**() on the picked point associated with the event being processed. The returned path should not be ref'd - selection will **ref**() and **unref**() it. (See **SoPath::unrefNoDelete**().)

Note that a picked object may or may not be a child of the selection node. A selection node will only select paths that pass through it. Possible return values from the callback:

[a] NULL — selection behaves as if nothing was picked (i.e. for SINGLE and SHIFT policies, this clears the selection list). Handle event action traversal halts.

[b] Path — this path will be selected/deselected according to the selection policy (it must lie under the selection node). Handle event action traversal halts.

[c] Path containing *only* the selection node — apply the selection policy as if nothing was picked. Handle event action traversal continues.

[d] Path not passing through the selection node — selection ignores this pick event and no change is made to the selection list. Handle event action traversal continues.

A simple way to tell selection to ignore the pick is to return an **SoPath** with no nodes in it. (i.e. **return new SoPath;**) Selection will always ref the path returned by the callback, make a copy of the path, then unref the path.

The *callOnlyIfSelectable* argument, when set to TRUE, means the pick callback function will only be invoked on picks which pass through the selection node. When FALSE, all picks will be passed to the callback whether they pass through the selection or not.

void	**setPickMatching**(SbBool pickTwice)
SbBool	**getPickMatching**() const

SoSelection will pick once on mouse down and once on mouse up, and make sure the picks match before changing the selection list. This allows the user to pick down on an object, change their mind and drag off the object, release the mouse button and not affect the selection. Pass TRUE to enable this behavior. Pass FALSE to disable this, meaning whatever is picked on a mouse release is added to/removed from the selection list. Default is pick-matching on.

Methods from class SoSeparator:

setNumRenderCaches, getNumRenderCaches

Methods from class SoGroup:

addChild, insertChild, getChild, findChild, getNumChildren, removeChild, removeChild, removeAllChildren, replaceChild, replaceChild

Methods from class SoNode:

setOverride, isOverride, copy, affectsState, getByName, getByName

Methods from class SoFieldContainer:

setToDefaults, hasDefaultValues, fieldsAreEqual, copyFieldValues, set, get, getFields, getField, getFieldName, enableNotify, isNotifyEnabled

Methods from class SoBase:

ref, unref, unrefNoDelete, touch, getTypeId, isOfType, setName, getName

FILE FORMAT/DEFAULTS

```
Selection {
        renderCaching          AUTO
        boundingBoxCaching     AUTO
        renderCulling          AUTO
        pickCulling            AUTO
        policy                 SHIFT
}
```

SoSelection

INCLUDE FILE

```
#include <Inventor/nodes/SoSelection.h>
```

typedef void	**SoSelectionPathCB**(void *userData, SoPath *path)
typedef void	**SoSelectionClassCB**(void *userData, SoSelection *sel)
typedef SoPath *	**SoSelectionPickCB**(void *userData, const SoPickedPoint *pick)

enum **Policy** {

SoSelection::SINGLE	Left mouse pick on object clears selection, then selects object. Left mouse pick on nothing clears selection. Only one object may be selected at a time.
SoSelection::TOGGLE	Left mouse pick on object toggles its selection status. Left mouse pick on nothing does nothing. Multiple objects may be selected.
SoSelection::SHIFT	When shift key is down, selection policy is TOGGLE. When shift key is up, selection policy is SINGLE. Multiple objects may be selected.

}

SEE ALSO

SoEventCallback, SoXtRenderArea, SoBoxHighlightRenderAction, SoLineHighlightRenderAction

NAME

SoSelectOne — selects one value from a multiple-value field.

INHERITS FROM

SoBase > SoFieldContainer > SoEngine > SoSelectOne

DESCRIPTION

This engine selects a single value from a multiple-value field, based on the input field **index**. The type of the input field can be any subclass of **SoMField**. The type is specified when an instance of the class is created. For example, **SoSelectOne(SoMFFloat::getClassTypeId())** creates an engine that selects one floating-point value.

Note that unlike most other engine fields, the **input** field and **output** are pointers. Note also that by default **input** does not contain any values, and no value is output from the engine.

INPUTS

SoSFLong   **index**

Index of the value to select from the multiple-value field.

<inputType>   **input**

The multiple-value field from which the value will be selected.

OUTPUTS

(<outputType>)   **output**

The single value selected.

METHODS

                         SoSelectOne(SoType inputType)

Constructor. The argument specifies the type of the multiple-value input field.

Methods from class SoEngine:

getClassTypeId, getOutputs, getOutput, getOutputName, copy, getByName, getByName

Methods from class SoFieldContainer:

setToDefaults, hasDefaultValues, fieldsAreEqual, copyFieldValues, set, get, getFields, getField, getFieldName, enableNotify, isNotifyEnabled

Methods from class SoBase:

ref, unref, unrefNoDelete, touch, getTypeId, isOfType, setName, getName

SoSelectOne

FILE FORMAT/DEFAULTS

```
SelectOne {
        type    <inputType>
        input   []
        index   0
}
```

INCLUDE FILE

```
#include <Inventor/engines/SoSelectOne.h>
```

SEE ALSO

SoEngineOutput, SoConcatenate, SoGate

NAME

SoSensor — abstract base class for Inventor sensors

INHERITS FROM

SoSensor

DESCRIPTION

Sensors detect changes either to time or to Inventor objects in a scene graph, and call a user-defined callback function. Sensors are *scheduled* when the thing they are attached to changes, and sometime after they are scheduled they are *triggered*, calling the user's callback function.

METHODS

void   **setFunction**(SoSensorCB *callbackFunction)

Sets the callback function that is called when the sensor is triggered. The function must take two arguments — user-supplied callback data (of type void *) and a pointer to the sensor that is triggering the function (of type SoSensor *).

SoSensorCB *   **getFunction**() const

Returns the callback function that will be called when the sensor is triggered.

void   **setData**(void *callbackData)

Sets the callback data passed to the callback function.

void *   **getData**() const

Returns the user-supplied pointer that will be passed to the callback function.

INCLUDE FILE

```
#include <Inventor/sensors/SoSensor.h>
```

typedef void   **SoSensorCB**(void *data, SoSensor *sensor)

SEE ALSO

SoAlarmSensor, SoDataSensor, SoFieldSensor, SoIdleSensor, SoNodeSensor, SoPathSensor, SoSensorManager

NAME

SoSeparator — group node that saves and restores traversal state

INHERITS FROM

SoBase > SoFieldContainer > SoNode > SoGroup > SoSeparator

DESCRIPTION

This group node performs a push (save) of the traversal state before traversing its children and a pop (restore) after traversing them. This isolates the separator's children from the rest of the scene graph. A separator can include lights, cameras, coordinates, normals, bindings, and all other properties. Separators are relatively inexpensive, so they can be used freely within scenes.

The **SoSeparator** node provides caching of state during rendering and bounding box computation. This feature can be enabled by setting the **renderCaching** and **boundingBoxCaching** fields. By default, these are set to AUTO, which means that Inventor decides whether to build a cache based on internal heuristics.

Separators can also perform culling during rendering and picking. Culling skips over traversal of the separator's children if they are not going to be rendered or picked, based on the comparison of the separator's bounding box with the current view volume. Culling is controlled by the **renderCulling** and **pickCulling** fields. These are also set to AUTO by default; however, render culling can be expensive (and can interfere with render caching), so the AUTO heuristics leave it disabled unless specified otherwise.

FIELDS

SoSFEnum **renderCaching**
Whether to cache during rendering traversal.

SoSFEnum **boundingBoxCaching**
Whether to cache during bounding box traversal.

SoSFEnum **renderCulling**
Whether to cull during rendering traversal.

SoSFEnum **pickCulling**
Whether to cull during picking traversal.

METHODS

SoSeparator()
Creates a separator node with default settings.

SoSeparator(int nChildren)
Constructor that takes approximate number of children.

static void   **setNumRenderCaches**(int howMany)
By default, each separator node maintains 2 render caches. (This is to allow two different representations, such as filled and wire-frame, to both be cached.) The **setNumRenderCaches**() method sets the number of render caches each separator will have. Each render cache uses memory, so increasing this number may increase the memory requirements of the application. This method affects only separators that are created after it is called, not separators that were created before. Setting the number of caches to 0 turns off render caching globally from then on.

static int   **getNumRenderCaches**()
Returns the current number of render caches.

static SoType   **getClassTypeId**()
Returns type identifier for this class.

Methods from class SoGroup:

addChild, insertChild, getChild, findChild, getNumChildren, removeChild, removeChild, removeAllChildren, replaceChild, replaceChild

Methods from class SoNode:

setOverride, isOverride, copy, affectsState, getByName, getByName

Methods from class SoFieldContainer:

setToDefaults, hasDefaultValues, fieldsAreEqual, copyFieldValues, set, get, getFields, getField, getFieldName, enableNotify, isNotifyEnabled

Methods from class SoBase:

ref, unref, unrefNoDelete, touch, getTypeId, isOfType, setName, getName

ACTION BEHAVIOR

SoGLRenderAction, SoCallbackAction, SoGetBoundingBoxAction, SoGetMatrixAction, SoHandleEventAction, SoRayPickAction, SoSearchAction
Saves the current traversal state, traverses all children, and restores the previous traversal state.

FILE FORMAT/DEFAULTS

```
Separator {
        renderCaching          AUTO
        boundingBoxCaching     AUTO
        renderCulling          AUTO
        pickCulling            AUTO
}
```

INCLUDE FILE

```
#include <Inventor/nodes/SoSeparator.h>
```

enum **CacheEnabled** {

SoSeparator::OFF	Never build a cache
SoSeparator::ON	Always try to build a cache
SoSeparator::AUTO	Decide whether to cache based on some heuristic

}

SEE ALSO

SoSelection, SoTransformSeparator

NAME

SoSeparatorKit — separator nodekit class

INHERITS FROM

SoBase > SoFieldContainer > SoNode > SoBaseKit > SoSeparatorKit

DESCRIPTION

A nodekit that is used for creating nodekit hierarchies. **SoSeparatorKit** contains a *transform* part, a *childList* part, and a few others in its catalog. The *transform* part (an **SoTransform** node) affects all of the children in the childList. Each of these children must be an **SoSeparatorKit** or from a class that is derived from **SoSeparatorKit** (e.g., **SoShapeKit** and **SoWrapperKit**). Since all members of the *childList* are in turn **SoSeparatorKit**s, and each contains a *transform*, these nested lists allow you to create a hierarchy of motion, in which each *transform* affects an entire subgraph of nodekits.

The other parts added to the catalog for the **SoSeparatorKit** are *pickStyle*, *appearance*, *units* and *texture2Transform*. Furthermore, since **SoSeparator** is derived from **SoBaseKit**, it inherits an the *callbackList* part. This is a list of **SoCallback** and/or **SoEventCallback** nodes which enable the **SoSeparatorKit** to perform special callbacks whenever an is applied to it.

By creating the *pickStyle* part, a user can alter the pick style for the entire nodekit hierarchy. The *appearance* part is an **SoAppearanceKit** nodekit. Note that all parts contained in the **SoAppearanceKit** catalog can be accessed as if they were part of the **SoSeparatorKit**. For example:

    myMtl = mySepKit->getPart("material",TRUE)

and

    mySepKit->setPart("material",myMtl)

See **SoBaseKit** for further explanation.

FIELDS

SoSFEnum   **renderCaching**

Set render caching mode. Default is AUTO.

SoSFEnum   **boundingBoxCaching**

Set bounding box caching mode. Default is ON. Setting this value to AUTO is equivalent to ON — automatic culling is not implemented.

SoSFEnum   **renderCulling**

Set render culling mode. Default is OFF. Setting this value to AUTO is equivalent to ON — automatic culling is not implemented.

SoSFEnum   **pickCulling**

Set pick culling mode. Default is AUTO.

PARTS

(SoPickStyle)   **pickStyle**

An **SoPickStyle** property node that can be used to set the picking style of its children. This part is NULL by default, but is created automatically if necessary.

(SoAppearanceKit)

appearance

An **SoAppearanceKit** nodekit which can be used to set the appearance properties of its children. This part is NULL by default, but is created automatically if necessary.

(SoUnits)   **units**

An **SoUnits** node which can be used to set the types of units, (e.g., feet), of its children. This part is NULL by default, but is created automatically if necessary.

(SoTransform)   **transform**

An **SoTransform** node which can be used to set the overall position, orientation, and scale of its children. This part is NULL by default, but is created automatically if necessary.

(SoTexture2Transform)

texture2Transform

An **SoTexture2Transform** node which can be used to apply a transformation to any textures used by its children. This part is NULL by default, but is created automatically if necessary.

(SoNodeKitListPart)

childList

This part contains the children nodekits of this **SoSeparatorKit**. This part is a *list part* and can have multiple children. This part is NULL by default, but is created automatically when the first child is added to the *childList*. Also, when asked to build a member of the *childList*, the separatorKit will build an **SoShapeKit** by default. So if the *childList* part is NULL, and you call: **getPart("childList[0]", TRUE)**, the separator kit will create the *childList* and add an **SoShapeKit** as the new element in the list.

Parts from class SoBaseKit:

> callbackList

METHODS

> **SoSeparatorKit**()
> Constructor.

> static const SoNodekitCatalog *
> **getClassNodekitCatalog**() const
> Returns an **SoNodekitCatalog** for the class **SoSeparatorKit**.

> static SoType **getClassTypeId**()
> Returns type identifier for this class.

Methods from class SoBaseKit:

> getNodekitCatalog, getPart, getPartString, createPathToPart, setPart, set, set, isSearchingChildren, setSearchingChildren

Methods from class SoNode:

> setOverride, isOverride, copy, affectsState, getByName, getByName

Methods from class SoFieldContainer:

> setToDefaults, hasDefaultValues, fieldsAreEqual, copyFieldValues, get, getFields, getField, getFieldName, enableNotify, isNotifyEnabled

Methods from class SoBase:

> ref, unref, unrefNoDelete, touch, getTypeId, isOfType, setName, getName

MACROS

Macros from class SoBaseKit:

> SO_GET_PART, SO_CHECK_PART

CATALOG PARTS

All parts			
Part Name	**Part Type**	**Default Type**	**NULL by Default**
callbackList	NodeKitListPart	--	yes
pickStyle	PickStyle	--	yes
appearance	AppearanceKit	--	yes
units	Units	--	yes
transform	Transform	--	yes
texture2Transform	Texture2Transform	--	yes
childList	NodeKitListPart	--	yes

Extra information for list parts from above table		
Part Name	**Container Type**	**Permissible Types**
callbackList	Separator	Callback, EventCallback
childList	Separator	ShapeKit, SeparatorKit

FILE FORMAT/DEFAULTS

```
SeparatorKit {
        renderCaching          AUTO
        boundingBoxCaching     AUTO
        renderCulling          AUTO
        pickCulling            AUTO
}
```

INCLUDE FILE

```
#include <Inventor/nodekits/SoSeparatorKit.h>
```

enum **CacheEnabled** {

    SoSeparatorKit::OFF   Never build or use a cache

    SoSeparatorKit::ON   Always try to build a cache

    SoSeparatorKit::AUTO   Automatic caching

}

SEE ALSO

SoAppearanceKit, SoBaseKit, SoCameraKit, SoLightKit, SoNodeKit, SoNodeKitDetail, SoNodeKitListPart, SoNodeKitPath, SoNodekitCatalog, SoSceneKit, SoShapeKit, SoWrapperKit

NAME

SoSFBitMask — single-value field containing a set of bit flags

INHERITS FROM

SoField > SoSField > SoSFEnum > SoSFBitMask

DESCRIPTION

A single-value field that contains a mask of bit flags, stored as an integer. Nodes that use this field class define mnemonic names for the bit flags. These names should be used when setting or testing the values of the field, even though the values are treated as integers in the methods.

The bit-wise "&" and "|" operators should be used when testing and setting flags in a mask. For example, to turn on the sides of a 3D text node and turn off the back you would write:

```
text3->parts = text3->parts.getValue() | SoText3::SIDES;
text3->parts = text3->parts.getValue() & ~SoText3::BACK;
```

SoSFBitMasks are written to file as one or more mnemonic enumerated type names, in this format:

(flag1 | flag2 | ...)

If only one flag is used in a mask, the parentheses are optional. These names differ among uses of this field in various node or engine classes. See their man pages for the names.

The field values may also be represented as integers, but this is not guaranteed to be portable.

METHODS

static SoType	**getClassTypeId**()
virtual void	**getTypeId**() const

Returns the type for this class or a particular object of this class.

int	**getValue**() const

Returns this field's value.

void	**setValue**(int newValue)
int	**operator =**(int newValue)

Sets this field to *newValue*.

int	**operator** ==(const SoSFBitMask &f) const
int	**operator** !=(const SoSFBitMask &f) const

Returns TRUE if *f* is of the same type and has the same value as this field.

Methods from class SoField:

setIgnored, isIgnored, isDefault, isOfType, set, get, touch, connectFrom, connectFrom, disconnect, isConnected, isConnectedFromField, getConnectedField, isConnectedFromEngine, getConnectedEngine, enableConnection, isConnectionEnabled, getForwardConnections, getContainer

INCLUDE FILE

```
#include <Inventor/fields/SoSFBitMask.h>
```

SEE ALSO

SoField, SoSField, SoMFBitMask

NAME

SoSFBool — field containing a single boolean value

INHERITS FROM

SoField > SoSField > SoSFBool

DESCRIPTION

A field containing a single boolean (true or false) value.

SoSFBools may be written to file as "0" (representing FALSE), "1", "TRUE", or "FALSE".

METHODS

static SoType	**getClassTypeId**()
virtual void	**getTypeId**() const

Returns the type for this class or a particular object of this class.

SbBool	**getValue**() const

Returns this field's value.

SbBool	**operator** =(SbBool newValue)
void	**setValue**(SbBool newValue)

Sets this field to *newValue*.

int	**operator** ==(const SoSFBool &f) const
int	**operator** !=(const SoSFBool &f) const

Returns TRUE if *f* is of the same type and has the same value as this field.

Methods from class SoField:

setIgnored, isIgnored, isDefault, isOfType, set, get, touch, connectFrom, connectFrom, disconnect, isConnected, isConnectedFromField, getConnectedField, isConnectedFromEngine, getConnectedEngine, enableConnection, isConnectionEnabled, getForwardConnections, getContainer

INCLUDE FILE

```
#include <Inventor/fields/SoSFBool.h>
```

SEE ALSO

SoField, SoSField, SoMFBool

NAME

SoSFColor — field containing an RGB color

INHERITS FROM

SoField > SoSField > SoSFColor

DESCRIPTION

A single-value field containing an **SbColor**. Values may be set in either RGB (red, green, blue) or HSV (hue, saturation, value) color spaces.

SoSFColors are written to file as an RGB triple of floating point numbers in standard scientific notation, in the range 0.0 to 1.0.

METHODS

void	**setValue**(const SbVec3f &vec)
void	**setValue**(float red, float green, float blue)
void	**setValue**(const float rgb[3])
void	**setHSVValue**(float hue, float saturation, float value)
void	**setHSVValue**(const float hsv[3])

Convenience methods for setting the value.

static SoType	**getClassTypeId**()
virtual void	**getTypeId**() const

Returns the type for this class or a particular object of this class.

const SbColor &	**getValue**() const

Returns this field's value.

const SbColor &	**operator =**(const SbColor & newValue)
void	**setValue**(const SbColor & newValue)

Sets this field to *newValue*.

int	**operator ==**(const SoSFColor &f) const
int	**operator !=**(const SoSFColor &f) const

Returns TRUE if *f* is of the same type and has the same value as this field.

Methods from class SoField:

setIgnored, isIgnored, isDefault, isOfType, set, get, touch, connectFrom, connectFrom, disconnect, isConnected, isConnectedFromField, getConnectedField, isConnectedFromEngine, getConnectedEngine, enableConnection, isConnectionEnabled, getForwardConnections, getContainer

SEE ALSO

SoField, SoSField, SoMFColor, SbColor

NAME

SoSFEnum — field containing an enumerated value

INHERITS FROM

SoField > SoSField > SoSFEnum

DESCRIPTION

A single-value field that contains an enumerated type value, stored as an integer. Nodes that use this field class define mnemonic names for the values. These names should be used when setting or testing the values of the field, even though the values are treated as integers in the methods.

SoSFEnums are written to file as a mnemonic enumerated type name. The name differs among uses of this field in various node or engine classes. See the man pages for specific nodes or engines for the names (e.g. **SoDrawStyle**).

METHODS

void   **setValue**(const SbName &name)
Sets this field to contain the given mnemonic name, passed in as a name or string.

static SoType · **getClassTypeId**()
virtual void   **getTypeId**() const
Returns the type for this class or a particular object of this class.

int   **getValue**() const
Returns this field's value.

int   **operator =**(int newValue)
void   **setValue**(int newValue)
Sets this field to *newValue*.

int   **operator ==**(const SoSFEnum &f) const
int   **operator !=**(const SoSFEnum &f) const
Returns TRUE if *f* is of the same type and has the same value as this field.

Methods from class SoField:

setIgnored, isIgnored, isDefault, isOfType, set, get, touch, connectFrom, connectFrom, disconnect, isConnected, isConnectedFromField, getConnectedField, isConnectedFromEngine, getConnectedEngine, enableConnection, isConnectionEnabled, getForwardConnections, getContainer

SEE ALSO

SoField, SoSField, SoMFEnum

NAME

SoSFFloat — field containing a floating-point value

INHERITS FROM

SoField > SoSField > SoSFFloat

DESCRIPTION

A field that contains one single-precision floating point number.

SoSFFloats are written to file in standard scientific notation.

METHODS

static SoType	**getClassTypeId**()
virtual void	**getTypeId**() const

Returns the type for this class or a particular object of this class.

float	**getValue**() const

Returns this field's value.

float	**operator =**(float newValue)
void	**setValue**(float newValue)

Sets this field to *newValue.*

int	**operator ==**(const SoSFFloat &f) const
int	**operator !=**(const SoSFFloat &f) const

Returns TRUE if *f* is of the same type and has the same value as this field.

Methods from class SoField:

setIgnored, isIgnored, isDefault, isOfType, set, get, touch, connectFrom, connectFrom, disconnect, isConnected, isConnectedFromField, getConnectedField, isConnectedFromEngine, getConnectedEngine, enableConnection, isConnectionEnabled, getForwardConnections, getContainer

INCLUDE FILE

```
#include <Inventor/fields/SoSFFloat.h>
```

SEE ALSO

SoField, SoSField, SoMFFloat

NAME

SoSField — abstract base class for all single-value fields

INHERITS FROM

SoField > SoSField

DESCRIPTION

Each class derived from **SoSField** begins with an **SoSF** prefix and contains one value of a particular type. Each has **setValue()** and **getValue()** methods that are used to change or access this value. In addition, some field classes have extra convenience routines that allow values to be set or retrieved in other related formats (see below).

In addition to **setValue()**, all single-value fields overload the "=" assignment operator to set the field value from the correct datatype or from another field instance of the same type.

The value of a single-value field is written to file in a format dependent on the field type; see the subclass man pages for details.

A field that is ignored has a tilde (˜) either in place of the value (if the actual value is the default) or after it (otherwise).

METHODS

static SoType   **getClassTypeId()**
> Return the type identifier for this field class.

Methods from class SoField:

> setIgnored, isIgnored, isDefault, getTypeId, isOfType, set, get, operator ==, operator !=, touch, connectFrom, connectFrom, disconnect, isConnected, isConnectedFromField, getConnectedField, isConnectedFromEngine, getConnectedEngine, enableConnection, isConnectionEnabled, getForwardConnections, getContainer

INCLUDE FILE

```
#include <Inventor/fields/SoField.h>
```

SEE ALSO

SoField, SoMField

SoSFImage

NAME

SoSFImage — Field containing a 2D image

INHERITS FROM

SoField > SoSField > SoSFImage

DESCRIPTION

A field containing a two-dimensional image. Images can be greyscale (intensity), greyscale with transparency information, RGB, or RGB with transparency. Each component of the image (intensity, red, green, blue or transparency (alpha)) can have an unsigned one-byte value from 0 to 255.

Values are returned as arrays of unsigned chars. The image is stored in this array starting at the bottom left corner of the image with the intensity or red component of that pixel, followed by either the alpha, the green and blue, or the green, blue and alpha components (depending on the number of components in the image). The next value is the first component of the next pixel to the right.

SoSFImages are written to file as three integers representing the width, height and number of components in the image, followed by width*height hexadecimal values representing the pixels in the image, separated by whitespace. A one-component image will have one-byte hexadecimal values representing the intensity of the image. For example, 0xFF is full intensity, 0x00 is no intensity. A two-component image puts the intensity in the first (high) byte and the transparency in the second (low) byte. Pixels in a three-component image have the red component in the first (high) byte, followed by the green and blue components (so 0xFF0000 is red). Four-component images put the transparency byte after red/green/blue (so 0x0000FF80 is semi-transparent blue). Note: each pixel is actually read as a single unsigned number, so a 3-component pixel with value "0x0000FF" can also be written as "0xFF" or "255" (decimal).

For example,

          1 2 1 0xFF 0x00

is a 1 pixel wide by 2 pixel high greyscale image, with the bottom pixel white and the top pixel black. And:

          2 4 3 0xFF0000 0xFF00 0 0 0 0 0xFFFFFF 0xFFFF00

is a 2 pixel wide by 4 pixel high RGB image, with the bottom left pixel red, the bottom right pixel green, the two middle rows of pixels black, the top left pixel white, and the top right pixel yellow.

METHODS

const unsigned char *

getValue(SbVec2s &size, int &nc) const
Returns the pixels in the image as an array of unsigned chars. The *size* and *nc* arguments are filled in with the dimensions of the image and the number of components in the image; the number of bytes in the array returned will be *size*[0]**size*[1]**nc*.

void **setValue**(const SbVec2s &size, int nc, const unsigned char
*bytes)
Sets the value of this field to be an image of the given size, with the given number of components, and with the given pixel values. *size*[0]**size*[1]**nc* bytes from the given array will be copied into internal storage maintained by the **SoSFImage** field.

unsigned char * **startEditing**(SbVec2s &size, int &nc)
void **finishEditing**()
These methods can be used to efficiently edit the values in an image field. **startEditing**() returns the size of the image in the *size* and *nc* arguments; writing past the end of the array returned is a good way to cause hard-to-find core dumps.

Methods from class SoSField:

getClassTypeId

Methods from class SoField:

setIgnored, isIgnored, isDefault, getTypeId, isOfType, set, get, operator ==, operator !=, touch, connectFrom, connectFrom, disconnect, isConnected, isConnectedFromField, getConnectedField, isConnectedFromEngine, getConnectedEngine, enableConnection, isConnectionEnabled, getForwardConnections, getContainer

INCLUDE FILE

```
#include <Inventor/fields/SoSFImage.h>
```

SEE ALSO

SoField, SoSField

NAME

SoSFLong — field containing a long integer

INHERITS FROM

SoField > SoSField > SoSFLong

DESCRIPTION

A field containing a single long (32-bit) integer.

SoSFLongs are written to file as an integer in decimal, hexadecimal (beginning with '0x') or octal (beginning with '0') format.

METHODS

static SoType   **getClassTypeId**()
virtual void   **getTypeId**() const
          Returns the type for this class or a particular object of this class.

long   **getValue**() const
          Returns this field's value.

long   **operator** =(long newValue)
void   **setValue**(long newValue)
          Sets this field to *newValue*.

int   **operator** ==(const SoSFLong &f) const
int   **operator** !=(const SoSFLong &f) const
          Returns TRUE if *f* is of the same type and has the same value as this field.

Methods from class SoField:

setIgnored, isIgnored, isDefault, isOfType, set, get, touch, connectFrom, connectFrom, disconnect, isConnected, isConnectedFromField, getConnectedField, isConnectedFromEngine, getConnectedEngine, enableConnection, isConnectionEnabled, getForwardConnections, getContainer

INCLUDE FILE

```
#include <Inventor/fields/SoSFLong.h>
```

SEE ALSO

SoField, SoSField, SoMFLong, SoSFULong

NAME

SoSFMatrix — field containing a 4x4 matrix

INHERITS FROM

SoField > SoSField > SoSFMatrix

DESCRIPTION

A field containing a transformation matrix (an **SbMatrix**).

SoSFMatrices are written to file as 16 floating point numbers separated by whitespace. For example, an identity matrix is written as:

1 0 0 0 0 1 0 0 0 0 1 0 0 0 0 1

METHODS

void **setValue**(float a11, float a12, float a13, float a14, float a21, float a22, float a23, float a24, float a31, float a32, float a33, float a34, float a41, float a42, float a43, float a44)

Sets this field to contain the matrix given by the 16 values. For a translation matrix, the x, y and z translations should be in the a41, a42, and a43 arguments.

static SoType **getClassTypeId**()
virtual void **getTypeId**() const

Returns the type for this class or a particular object of this class.

const SbMatrix &
getValue() const

Returns this field's value.

const SbMatrix &
operator =(const SbMatrix & newValue)
void **setValue**(const SbMatrix & newValue)

Sets this field to *newValue*.

int **operator** ==(const SoSFMatrix &f) const
int **operator** !=(const SoSFMatrix &f) const

Returns TRUE if *f* is of the same type and has the same value as this field.

Methods from class SoField:

setIgnored, isIgnored, isDefault, isOfType, set, get, touch, connectFrom, connectFrom, disconnect, isConnected, isConnectedFromField, getConnectedField, isConnectedFromEngine, getConnectedEngine,

enableConnection, isConnectionEnabled, getForwardConnections,
getContainer

INCLUDE FILE

```
#include <Inventor/fields/SoSFMatrix.h>
```

SEE ALSO

SoField, SoSField, SoMFMatrix, SbMatrix

NAME

SoSFName — field containing a name

INHERITS FROM

SoField > SoSField > SoSFName

DESCRIPTION

A field containing a name. Names are short series of characters generally used for labels or names, and are stored in a special table designed to allow fast lookup and comparison. For most purposes, an **SoSFString** field is probably more appropriate.

SoSFNames are written to file as a string of characters. Names must begin with an underscore or alphabetic character, and must consist entirely of underscores, alphabetic characters, or numbers.

METHODS

void	**setValue**(const char *string)

Set this field to the name equivalent to the given string.

static SoType	**getClassTypeId**()
virtual void	**getTypeId**() const

Returns the type for this class or a particular object of this class.

const SbName &	**getValue**() const

Returns this field's value.

const SbName &	**operator =**(const SbName & newValue)
void	**setValue**(const SbName & newValue)

Sets this field to *newValue*.

int	**operator ==**(const SoSFName &f) const
int	**operator !=**(const SoSFName &f) const

Returns TRUE if *f* is of the same type and has the same value as this field.

Methods from class SoField:

setIgnored, isIgnored, isDefault, isOfType, set, get, touch, connectFrom, connectFrom, disconnect, isConnected, isConnectedFromField, getConnectedField, isConnectedFromEngine, getConnectedEngine, enableConnection, isConnectionEnabled, getForwardConnections, getContainer

SoSFName

INCLUDE FILE

```
#include <Inventor/fields/SoSFName.h>
```

SEE ALSO

SoField, SoSField, SoMFName

NAME

SoSFNode — field containing a pointer to a node

INHERITS FROM

SoField > SoSField > SoSFNode

DESCRIPTION

This field maintains a pointer to an **SoNode** instance, correctly maintaining its reference count.

SoSFNodes are written to file as the node they are pointing to. For example:

mySoSFNodeField Cube {}

is an SoSFNode field named 'mySoSFNodeField', pointing to an SoCube node. If the node is used elsewhere, the regular DEF/USE instancing mechanism applies:

anotherSoSFNodeField USE topSeparator

is an SoSFNode field that points to a node named 'topSeparator' that was DEF'ed earlier in the scene.

METHODS

static SoType	**getClassTypeId**()
virtual void	**getTypeId**() const

Returns the type for this class or a particular object of this class.

SoNode *	**getValue**() const

Returns this field's value.

SoNode *	**operator =**(SoNode * newValue)
void	**setValue**(SoNode * newValue)

Sets this field to *newValue*.

int	**operator ==**(const SoSFNode &f) const
int	**operator !=**(const SoSFNode &f) const

Returns TRUE if *f* is of the same type and has the same value as this field.

Methods from class SoField:

setIgnored, isIgnored, isDefault, isOfType, set, get, touch, connectFrom, connectFrom, disconnect, isConnected, isConnectedFromField, getConnectedField, isConnectedFromEngine, getConnectedEngine, enableConnection, isConnectionEnabled, getForwardConnections, getContainer

SoSFNode

INCLUDE FILE

```
#include <Inventor/fields/SoSFNode.h>
```

SEE ALSO

SoField, SoSField, SoMFNode, SoNode

NAME

SoSFPath — field containing a pointer to an SoPath

INHERITS FROM

SoField > SoSField > SoSFPath

DESCRIPTION

This field maintains a pointer to an **SoPath** instance, correctly maintaining its reference count.

SoSFPaths are written to file as the path they point to. See the **SoPath** manual page for a description of the file format for a path.

METHODS

static SoType	**getClassTypeId**()
virtual void	**getTypeId**() const

Returns the type for this class or a particular object of this class.

SoPath *	**getValue**() const

Returns this field's value.

SoPath *	**operator** =(SoPath * newValue)
void	**setValue**(SoPath * newValue)

Sets this field to *newValue*.

int	**operator** ==(const SoSFPath &f) const
int	**operator** !=(const SoSFPath &f) const

Returns TRUE if *f* is of the same type and has the same value as this field.

Methods from class SoField:

setIgnored, isIgnored, isDefault, isOfType, set, get, touch, connectFrom, connectFrom, disconnect, isConnected, isConnectedFromField, getConnectedField, isConnectedFromEngine, getConnectedEngine, enableConnection, isConnectionEnabled, getForwardConnections, getContainer

INCLUDE FILE

```
#include <Inventor/fields/SoSFPath.h>
```

SEE ALSO

SoField, SoSField, SoMFPath, SoPath

SoSFPlane

NAME

SoSFPlane — field containing a plane equation

INHERITS FROM

SoField > SoSField > SoSFPlane

DESCRIPTION

A field containing a plane equation (an SbPlane).

SoSFPlanes are written to file as four floating point values separated by whitespace. The first three are the normal direction of the plane, the fourth is the distance of the plane from the origin (in the direction of the normal).

METHODS

static SoType	**getClassTypeId**()
virtual void	**getTypeId**() const

Returns the type for this class or a particular object of this class.

const SbPlane &	**getValue**() const

Returns this field's value.

const SbPlane &	**operator** =(const SbPlane & newValue)
void	**setValue**(const SbPlane & newValue)

Sets this field to *newValue*.

int	**operator** ==(const SoSFPlane &f) const
int	**operator** !=(const SoSFPlane &f) const

Returns TRUE if *f* is of the same type and has the same value as this field.

Methods from class SoField:

setIgnored, isIgnored, isDefault, isOfType, set, get, touch, connectFrom, connectFrom, disconnect, isConnected, isConnectedFromField, getConnectedField, isConnectedFromEngine, getConnectedEngine, enableConnection, isConnectionEnabled, getForwardConnections, getContainer

INCLUDE FILE

```
#include <Inventor/fields/SoSFPlane.h>
```

SEE ALSO

SbPlane, SoField, SoSField, SoMFPlane

NAME
SoSFRotation — field containing a rotation

INHERITS FROM
SoField > SoSField > SoSFRotation

DESCRIPTION
A field containing a single **SbRotation** (an arbitrary rotation).

SoSFRotations are written to file as four floating point values separated by whitespace. The 4 values represent an axis of rotation followed by the amount of right-handed rotation about that axis, in radians. For example, a 180 degree rotation about the Y axis is:

    0 1 0 3.14159265

METHODS

void   **getValue**(const SbVec3f &axis, float angle) const
Gets the value of the field as an axis/angle.

void   **setValue**(float q0, float q1, float q2, float q3)
      setValue(float q[4])
Set the field to the given quaternion.

void   **setValue**(const SbVec3f &axis, float angle)
Set the field to the rotation given by axis/angle.

static SoType   **getClassTypeId**()
virtual void   **getTypeId**() const
      Returns the type for this class or a particular object of this class.

const SbRotation &
      getValue() const
Returns this field's value.

const SbRotation &
      operator =(const SbRotation & newValue)
void   **setValue**(const SbRotation & newValue)
      Sets this field to *newValue*.

int   **operator** ==(const SoSFRotation &f) const
int   **operator** !=(const SoSFRotation &f) const
    Returns TRUE if *f* is of the same type and has the same value as this field.

Methods from class SoField:

setIgnored, isIgnored, isDefault, isOfType, set, get, touch, connectFrom, connectFrom, disconnect, isConnected, isConnectedFromField, getConnectedField, isConnectedFromEngine, getConnectedEngine, enableConnection, isConnectionEnabled, getForwardConnections, getContainer

INCLUDE FILE

```
#include <Inventor/fields/SoSFRotation.h>
```

SEE ALSO

SbRotation, SoField, SoSField, SoMFRotation

NAME

SoSFShort — field containing a short integer

INHERITS FROM

SoField > SoSField > SoSFShort

DESCRIPTION

A field containing a short (16-bit) integer.

SoSFShorts are written to file as a single short integer value, represented as decimal, hexadecimal (beginning with '0x') or octal (beginning with '0') value.

METHODS

static SoType	**getClassTypeId**()
virtual void	**getTypeId**() const

Returns the type for this class or a particular object of this class.

short	**getValue**() const

Returns this field's value.

short	**operator** =(short newValue)
void	**setValue**(short newValue)

Sets this field to *newValue*.

int	**operator** ==(const SoSFShort &f) const
int	**operator** !=(const SoSFShort &f) const

Returns TRUE if *f* is of the same type and has the same value as this field.

Methods from class SoField:

setIgnored, isIgnored, isDefault, isOfType, set, get, touch, connectFrom, connectFrom, disconnect, isConnected, isConnectedFromField, getConnectedField, isConnectedFromEngine, getConnectedEngine, enableConnection, isConnectionEnabled, getForwardConnections, getContainer

INCLUDE FILE

```
#include <Inventor/fields/SoSFShort.h>
```

SEE ALSO

SoField, SoSField, SoMFShort, SoSFUShort, SoSFLong

NAME

    SoSFString — field containing a string

INHERITS FROM

    SoField > SoSField > SoSFString

DESCRIPTION

    A field containing an ASCII string (sequence of characters). Inventor does not support non-ASCII strings.

    SoSFStrings are written to file as a sequence of ASCII characters in double quotes (optional if the string doesn't contain any whitespace). Any characters (including newlines) may appear within the quotes. To include a double quote character within the string, precede it with a backslash. For example:

```
Testing
"One, Two, Three"
"He said, \"Immel did it!\""
```

    are all valid strings.

METHODS

                    setValue(const char *string)
    Convenience method to set the field's value given a character array.

    static SoType   **getClassTypeId**()
    virtual void   **getTypeId**() const
    Returns the type for this class or a particular object of this class.

    const SbString &   **getValue**() const
    Returns this field's value.

    const SbString &   **operator** =(const SbString & newValue)
    void   **setValue**(const SbString & newValue)
    Sets this field to *newValue*.

    int   **operator** ==(const SoSFString &f) const
    int   **operator** !=(const SoSFString &f) const
    Returns TRUE if *f* is of the same type and has the same value as this field.

    Methods from class SoField:

    setIgnored, isIgnored, isDefault, isOfType, set, get, touch, connectFrom, connectFrom, disconnect, isConnected, isConnectedFromField,

getConnectedField, isConnectedFromEngine, getConnectedEngine,
enableConnection, isConnectionEnabled, getForwardConnections,
getContainer

INCLUDE FILE

```
#include <Inventor/fields/SoSFString.h>
```

SEE ALSO

SbString, SoField, SoSField, SoMFString

SoSFTime

NAME

SoSFTime — field containing an SbTime

INHERITS FROM

SoField > SoSField > SoSFTime

DESCRIPTION

A multiple-value field that contains any number of time values.

SoSFTimes are written to file as a double-precision floating point value representing the length of time in seconds. Absolute times are measured relative to 00:00:00 GMT, January 1, 1970.

METHODS

static SoType	**getClassTypeId**()
virtual void	**getTypeId**() const

Returns the type for this class or a particular object of this class.

const SbTime &	**getValue**() const

Returns this field's value.

const SbTime &	**operator** =(const SbTime & newValue)
void	**setValue**(const SbTime & newValue)

Sets this field to *newValue*.

int	**operator** ==(const SoSFTime &f) const
int	**operator** !=(const SoSFTime &f) const

Returns TRUE if *f* is of the same type and has the same value as this field.

Methods from class SoField:

setIgnored, isIgnored, isDefault, isOfType, set, get, touch, connectFrom, connectFrom, disconnect, isConnected, isConnectedFromField, getConnectedField, isConnectedFromEngine, getConnectedEngine, enableConnection, isConnectionEnabled, getForwardConnections, getContainer

INCLUDE FILE

```
#include <Inventor/fields/SoSFTime.h>
```

SEE ALSO

SbTime, SoField, SoSField, SoMFTime

NAME

SoSFTrigger — field used to trigger engines or connection networks

INHERITS FROM

SoField > SoSField > SoSFTrigger

DESCRIPTION

This class can be used to start or to synchronize a network of field connections. It is the "null" field — a field with no values. It is typically used as the "start button" for engines that change over time.

Triggers can be connected from any other type of field, and will notify any engines or nodes they are part of (or any other triggers they are connected to) whenever the value of the field changes or the field is **touch()**'ed.

Since they have no value, **SoSFTriggers** are not written to file. A node or engine containing an **SoSFTrigger** field will write only the field's name.

METHODS

void   **setValue()**
Starts the notification process; this is equivalent to calling **touch()**.

void   **getValue()**
Forces any connected engines or fields to evaluate themselves.

int   **operator ==**(const SoSFTrigger &t) const
int   **operator !=**(const SoSFTrigger &t) const
All trigger fields are equal; these methods always return TRUE and FALSE, respectively.

Methods from class SoSField:

getClassTypeId

Methods from class SoField:

setIgnored, isIgnored, isDefault, getTypeId, isOfType, set, get, touch, connectFrom, connectFrom, disconnect, isConnected, isConnectedFromField, getConnectedField, isConnectedFromEngine, getConnectedEngine, enableConnection, isConnectionEnabled, getForwardConnections, getContainer

INCLUDE FILE

```
#include <Inventor/fields/SoSFTrigger.h>
```

SEE ALSO

SoSFBool, SoMFBool

NAME

SoSFULong — field containing an unsinged long integer

INHERITS FROM

SoField > SoSField > SoSFULong

DESCRIPTION

A single-value field containg an unsigned 32-bit integer, representing a number from 0 to 4,294,967,295.

SoSFULongs are written to file as a single unsigned long (32-bit) integer in decimal, hexadecimal or octal format.

METHODS

static SoType   **getClassTypeId**()
virtual void   **getTypeId**() const
     Returns the type for this class or a particular object of this class.

long unsigned long
     getValue() const
     Returns this field's value.

long unsigned long
     operator =(long unsigned long newValue)
void   **setValue**(long unsigned long newValue)
     Sets this field to *newValue*.

int   **operator ==**(const SoSFULong &f) const
int   **operator !=**(const SoSFULong &f) const
     Returns TRUE if *f* is of the same type and has the same value as this field.

Methods from class SoField:

setIgnored, isIgnored, isDefault, isOfType, set, get, touch, connectFrom, connectFrom, disconnect, isConnected, isConnectedFromField, getConnectedField, isConnectedFromEngine, getConnectedEngine, enableConnection, isConnectionEnabled, getForwardConnections, getContainer

INCLUDE FILE

#include <Inventor/fields/SoSFULong.h>

SEE ALSO

SoField, SoSField, SoMFULong

NAME

SoSFUShort — field containing an unsigned short integer

INHERITS FROM

SoField > SoSField > SoSFUShort

DESCRIPTION

A single-value field containing a short (16-bit) integer.

SoSFUShorts are written to file in decimal, hexadecimal (beginning with '0x') or octal (beginning with '0') values.

METHODS

static SoType	**getClassTypeId**()
virtual void	**getTypeId**() const

Returns the type for this class or a particular object of this class.

short unsigned short
                getValue() const

Returns this field's value.

short unsigned short
                operator =(short unsigned short newValue)

void
                setValue(short unsigned short newValue)

Sets this field to *newValue*.

int
                operator ==(const SoSFUShort &f) const

int
                operator !=(const SoSFUShort &f) const

Returns TRUE if *f* is of the same type and has the same value as this field.

Methods from class SoField:

setIgnored, isIgnored, isDefault, isOfType, set, get, touch, connectFrom, connectFrom, disconnect, isConnected, isConnectedFromField, getConnectedField, isConnectedFromEngine, getConnectedEngine, enableConnection, isConnectionEnabled, getForwardConnections, getContainer

INCLUDE FILE

```
#include <Inventor/fields/SoSFUShort.h>
```

SEE ALSO

SoField, SoSField, SoMFUShort

NAME

SoSFVec2f — Field containing a two-dimensional vector

INHERITS FROM

SoField > SoSField > SoSFVec2f

DESCRIPTION

Field containing a two-dimensional vector.

SoSFVec2fs are written to file as a pair of floating point values separated by whitespace.

METHODS

void	**setValue**(float x, float y)
void	**setValue**(const float xy[2])

Sets the field to the given value.

static SoType	**getClassTypeId**()
virtual void	**getTypeId**() const

Returns the type for this class or a particular object of this class.

const SbVec2f &	**getValue**() const

Returns this field's value.

const SbVec2f &	**operator =**(const SbVec2f & newValue)
void	**setValue**(const SbVec2f & newValue)

Sets this field to *newValue.*

int	**operator ==**(const SoSFVec2f &f) const
int	**operator !=**(const SoSFVec2f &f) const

Returns TRUE if *f* is of the same type and has the same value as this field.

Methods from class SoField:

setIgnored, isIgnored, isDefault, isOfType, set, get, touch, connectFrom, connectFrom, disconnect, isConnected, isConnectedFromField, getConnectedField, isConnectedFromEngine, getConnectedEngine, enableConnection, isConnectionEnabled, getForwardConnections, getContainer

INCLUDE FILE

```
#include <Inventor/fields/SoSFVec2f.h>
```

SEE ALSO

SoField, SoSField, SoMFVec2f

NAME

SoSFVec3f — field containing a three-dimensional vector

INHERITS FROM

SoField > SoSField > SoSFVec3f

DESCRIPTION

Field containing a three-dimensional vector.

SoSFVec3fs are written to file as three floating point values separated by whitespace.

METHODS

void	**setValue**(float x, float y, float z)
void	**setValue**(const float xyz[3])

Sets the field to the given value.

static SoType	**getClassTypeId**()
virtual void	**getTypeId**() const

Returns the type for this class or a particular object of this class.

const SbVec3f &	**getValue**() const

Returns this field's value.

const SbVec3f &	**operator** =(const SbVec3f & newValue)
void	**setValue**(const SbVec3f & newValue)

Sets this field to *newValue*.

int	**operator** ==(const SoSFVec3f &f) const
int	**operator** !=(const SoSFVec3f &f) const

Returns TRUE if *f* is of the same type and has the same value as this field.

Methods from class SoField:

setIgnored, isIgnored, isDefault, isOfType, set, get, touch, connectFrom, connectFrom, disconnect, isConnected, isConnectedFromField, getConnectedField, isConnectedFromEngine, getConnectedEngine, enableConnection, isConnectionEnabled, getForwardConnections, getContainer

INCLUDE FILE

#include <Inventor/fields/SoSFVec3f.h>

SEE ALSO

SoField, SoSField, SoMFVec3f

NAME

SoSFVec4f — field containing a homogeneous three-dimensional vector

INHERITS FROM

SoField > SoSField > SoSFVec4f

DESCRIPTION

Field containing a homogeneous three-dimensional vector.

SoSFVec4fs are written to file as four floating point values separated by whitespace.

METHODS

| void | **setValue**(float x, float y, float z, float w) |
| void | **setValue**(const float xyzw[4]) |

Sets the field to the given value.

| static SoType | **getClassTypeId**() |
| virtual void | **getTypeId**() const |

Returns the type for this class or a particular object of this class.

| const SbVec4f & | **getValue**() const |

Returns this field's value.

| const SbVec4f & | **operator =**(const SbVec4f & newValue) |
| void | **setValue**(const SbVec4f & newValue) |

Sets this field to *newValue*.

| int | **operator ==**(const SoSFVec4f &f) const |
| int | **operator !=**(const SoSFVec4f &f) const |

Returns TRUE if *f* is of the same type and has the same value as this field.

Methods from class SoField:

setIgnored, isIgnored, isDefault, isOfType, set, get, touch, connectFrom, connectFrom, disconnect, isConnected, isConnectedFromField, getConnectedField, isConnectedFromEngine, getConnectedEngine, enableConnection, isConnectionEnabled, getForwardConnections, getContainer

INCLUDE FILE

```
#include <Inventor/fields/SoSFVec4f.h>
```

SEE ALSO

SoField, SoSField, SoMFVec4f

NAME

SoShape — abstract base class for all shape nodes

INHERITS FROM

SoBase > SoFieldContainer > SoNode > SoShape

DESCRIPTION

This node is the abstract base class for all shape (geometry) nodes. All classes derived from **SoShape** draw geometry during render traversal.

METHODS

static SoType   **getClassTypeId**()
> Returns type identifier for this class.

Methods from class SoNode:

> setOverride, isOverride, copy, affectsState, getByName, getByName

Methods from class SoFieldContainer:

> setToDefaults, hasDefaultValues, fieldsAreEqual, copyFieldValues, set, get, getFields, getField, getFieldName, enableNotify, isNotifyEnabled

Methods from class SoBase:

> ref, unref, unrefNoDelete, touch, getTypeId, isOfType, setName, getName

FILE FORMAT/DEFAULTS

This is an abstract class. See the reference page of a derived class for the format and default values.

INCLUDE FILE

`#include <Inventor/nodes/SoShape.h>`

SEE ALSO

SoCone, SoCube, SoCylinder, SoIndexedNurbsCurve, SoIndexedNurbsSurface, SoNurbsCurve, SoNurbsSurface, SoShapeHints, SoShapeKit, SoSphere, SoText2, SoText3, SoVertexShape

NAME

SoShapeHints — node that provides hints about shapes

INHERITS FROM

SoBase > SoFieldContainer > SoNode > SoShapeHints

DESCRIPTION

By default, Inventor assumes very little about the shapes it renders. You can use the **SoShapeHints** node to indicate that vertex-based shapes (those derived from **SoVertexShape**) are solid, contain ordered vertices, or contain convex faces.

These hints allow Inventor to optimize certain rendering features. Optimizations that may be performed include enabling back-face culling and disabling two-sided lighting. For example, if an object is solid and has ordered vertices, Inventor turns on backface culling and turns off two-sided lighting. If the object is not solid but has ordered vertices, it turns off backface culling and turns on two-sided lighting. In all other cases, both backface culling and two-sided lighting are off. Note that if the current drawing style is not filled or any clipping planes are in effect, backface culling will not be performed.

The **SoShapeHints** node also affects how default normals are generated. When a node derived from **SoVertexShape** has to generate default normals, it uses the **creaseAngle** field to determine which edges should be smooth-shaded and which ones should have a sharp crease. The crease angle is the angle between surface normals on adjacent polygons. For example, a crease angle of .5 radians (the default value) means that an edge between two adjacent polygonal faces will be smooth shaded if the normals to the two faces form an angle that is less than .5 radians (about 30 degrees). Otherwise, it will be faceted.

FIELDS

SoSFEnum   **vertexOrdering**

Indicates how the vertices of faces are ordered. CLOCKWISE ordering means that the vertices of each face form a clockwise loop around the face, when viewed from the outside (the side toward which the normal points).

SoSFEnum   **shapeType**

Indicates whether the shape is known to enclose a volume (SOLID) or not. If the inside (the side away from the surface normal) of any part of the shape is visible, the shape is not solid.

SoSFEnum   **faceType**

Indicates whether each face is convex. Because the penalty for non-convex faces is very steep (faces must be triangulated expensively), the default assumes all faces are convex. Therefore, shapes with concave faces may not be displayed correctly unless this hint is set to UNKNOWN_FACE_TYPE.

SoSFFloat   **creaseAngle**
> Indicates the minimum angle (in radians) between two adjacent face
> normals required to form a sharp crease at the edge when default normals
> are computed and used.

METHODS

SoShapeHints()
> Creates a shape hints node with default settings.

static SoType   **getClassTypeId()**
> Returns type identifier for this class.

Methods from class SoNode:
> setOverride, isOverride, copy, affectsState, getByName, getByName

Methods from class SoFieldContainer:
> setToDefaults, hasDefaultValues, fieldsAreEqual, copyFieldValues, set, get,
> getFields, getField, getFieldName, enableNotify, isNotifyEnabled

Methods from class SoBase:
> ref, unref, unrefNoDelete, touch, getTypeId, isOfType, setName, getName

ACTION BEHAVIOR
SoGLRenderAction, SoCallbackAction, SoRayPickAction,
SoGetBoundingBoxAction
> Sets the state to contain the hints; sets up optimizations based on the hints.

FILE FORMAT/DEFAULTS

```
ShapeHints {
        vertexOrdering   UNKNOWN_ORDERING
        shapeType        UNKNOWN_SHAPE_TYPE
        faceType         CONVEX
        creaseAngle      0.5
}
```

SoShapeHints

INCLUDE FILE

        #include <Inventor/nodes/SoShapeHints.h>

        enum **VertexOrdering** {
                SoShapeHints::UNKNOWN_ORDERING
                                Ordering of vertices is unknown
                SoShapeHints::CLOCKWISE
                                Face vertices are ordered clockwise (from the outside)
                SoShapeHints::COUNTERCLOCKWISE
                                Face vertices are ordered counterclockwise (from the outside)
        }

        enum **ShapeType** {
                SoShapeHints::UNKNOWN_SHAPE_TYPE
                                Nothing is known about the shape
                SoShapeHints::SOLID
                                The shape encloses a volume
        }

        enum **FaceType** {
                SoShapeHints::UNKNOWN_FACE_TYPE
                                Nothing is known about faces
                SoShapeHints::CONVEX
                                All faces are convex
        }

SEE ALSO

        SoClipPlane, SoDrawStyle, SoVertexShape

NAME

SoShapeKit — shape nodekit class

INHERITS FROM

SoBase > SoFieldContainer > SoNode > SoBaseKit > SoSeparatorKit > SoShapeKit

DESCRIPTION

A nodekit that is used for creating a shape (i.e. geometry). **SoShapeKit** is derived from **SoSeparatorKit** and **SoBaseKit**, and thus inherits all the parts defined by these classes.

Furthermore, **SoShapeKit** adds numerous parts that can be used to define a variety of *shape* objects, a *localTransform* part, and of course a *shape* part.

All of the property nodes requires to define any of the Inventor shapes are included as parts in this class. Not all of these parts (nodes) are needed for any one type of shape. For example, if you set the *shape* part to be an **SoSphere** node, then it is not necessary to create a *profileCoordinate3* part since it will be ignored in drawing the sphere. (And the unneeded parts will not be created, so there is no performance penalty for using this class of node.

This class contains two private parts. They are both **SoSeparator** nodes. One of them sits just below the nodekit itself, and serves to contain all properties within this nodekit from affecting nodes that come after this nodekit. The second separator sits above the *shape* and *localTransform* parts, and serves to cache them even when the *transform* and *appearance* parts are changing.

FIELDS

Fields from class SoSeparatorKit:

renderCaching, boundingBoxCaching, renderCulling, pickCulling

PARTS

(SoSeparator)   **shapeSeparator**

This is a private part. The parent node of the actual shape part. It is a **SoSeparator** and is NULL by default, but is created automatically if necessary.

(SoMaterialBinding)

materialBinding

An **SoMaterialBinding** node that can be used to set the material binding for the shape. This part is NULL by default, but is created automatically if necessary.

(SoNormalBinding)
normalBinding
An **SoNormalBinding** node that can be used to set the normal binding for the shape. This part is NULL by default, but is created automatically if necessary.

(SoTextureCoordinateBinding)
textureCoordinateBinding
An **SoTextureCoordinateBinding** node that can be used to set the texture coordinate binding for the shape. This part is NULL by default, but is created automatically if necessary.

(SoShapeHints) **shapeHints**
An **SoShapeHints** node that can be used to set the shape hints for the shape. This part is NULL by default, but is created automatically if necessary.

(SoCoordinate3) **coordinate3**
An **SoCoordinate3** node that can be used to set the 3D coordinates for a vertex-based shape. This part is NULL by default, but is created automatically if necessary.

(SoCoordinate4) **coordinate4**
An **SoCoordinate4** node that can be used to set the 4D coordinates for a NURBS shapes. This part is NULL by default, but is created automatically if necessary.

(SoNormal) **normal**
An **SoNormal** node that can be used to set the normal vectors for a vertex-based shape. This part is NULL by default, but is created automatically if necessary.

(SoTextureCoordinate2)
textureCoordinate2
An **SoTextureCoordinate2** node that can be used to set the texture coordinates for a vertex-based shape. This part is NULL by default, but is created automatically if necessary.

(SoTextureCoordinateFunction)
textureCoordinateFunction
An **SoTextureCoordinateFunction** node that can be used to set the a procedural texture coordinates function for a vertex-based shape. This part is NULL by default, but is created automatically if necessary.

(SoProfileCoordinate2)
profileCoordinate2
An **SoProfileCoordinate2** node that can be used to set the 2D profile coordinates for a shape that uses them, (e.g., **SoText3**). This part is NULL by default, but is created automatically if necessary.

(SoProfileCoordinate3)
profileCoordinate3
An **SoProfileCoordinate3** node that can be used to set the 3D profile coordinates for a shape that uses them, (e.g., **SoSoNURBSCurve**). This part is NULL by default, but is created automatically if necessary.

(SoNodeKitListPart)
profileList
An **SoProfileList** node that can be used to set the profile curve for a shape that uses them, (e.g., **SoNurbsCurve**). This part is NULL by default, but is created automatically if necessary.

(SoTransform)   **localTransform**
An **SoTransform** node that can be used to set a local tranformation on the shape. This part is NULL by default, but is created automatically if necessary.

(SoShape)   **shape**
This is the part which specifies the actual shape node. This can be any node derived from **SoShape** By default, an **SoCube** is created. It is important to set all of the appropriate parts within this nodekit to suit the type of **SoShape** that is used. For example, if the *shape* part is set to an **SoFaceSet**, then the *coordinate3* shape and probably the *normal* shape would be set as well. See the reference page of the shape used for details on which other nodes are necessary.

Parts from class SoSeparatorKit:
pickStyle, appearance, units, transform, texture2Transform, childList

Parts from class SoBaseKit:
callbackList

METHODS

SoShapeKit()
Constructor.

static const SoNodekitCatalog *
getClassNodekitCatalog() const
Returns an **SoNodekitCatalog** for the class **SoShapeKit**.

static SoType   **getClassTypeId**()
Returns type identifier for this class.

Methods from class SoBaseKit:

getNodekitCatalog, getPart, getPartString, createPathToPart, setPart, set, set, isSearchingChildren, setSearchingChildren

Methods from class SoNode:

setOverride, isOverride, copy, affectsState, getByName, getByName

Methods from class SoFieldContainer:

setToDefaults, hasDefaultValues, fieldsAreEqual, copyFieldValues, get, getFields, getField, getFieldName, enableNotify, isNotifyEnabled

Methods from class SoBase:

ref, unref, unrefNoDelete, touch, getTypeId, isOfType, setName, getName

MACROS

Macros from class SoBaseKit:

SO_GET_PART, SO_CHECK_PART

CATALOG PARTS

All parts			
Part Name	**Part Type**	**Default Type**	**NULL by Default**
callbackList	NodeKitListPart	--	yes
pickStyle	PickStyle	--	yes
appearance	AppearanceKit	--	yes
units	Units	--	yes
transform	Transform	--	yes
texture2Transform	Texture2Transform	--	yes
childList	NodeKitListPart	--	yes
materialBinding	MaterialBinding	--	yes
normalBinding	NormalBinding	--	yes
textureCoordinate- Binding	TextureCoordinate- Binding	--	yes
shapeHints	ShapeHints	--	yes
coordinate3	Coordinate3	--	yes
coordinate4	Coordinate4	--	yes
normal	Normal	--	yes
textureCoordinate2	TextureCoordinate2	--	yes
textureCoordinate- Function	TextureCoordinate- Function	TextureCoordinate- Default	yes
profileCoordinate2	ProfileCoordinate2	--	yes
profileCoordinate3	ProfileCoordinate3	--	yes
profileList	NodeKitListPart	--	yes
localTransform	Transform	--	yes
shape	Shape	Cube	no

Extra information for list parts from above table		
Part Name	**Container Type**	**Permissible Types**
callbackList	Separator	Callback, EventCallback
childList	Separator	ShapeKit, SeparatorKit
profileList	Group	Profile

FILE FORMAT/DEFAULTS

```
ShapeKit {
        renderCaching          AUTO
        boundingBoxCaching     AUTO
        renderCulling          AUTO
        pickCulling            AUTO
}
```

INCLUDE FILE

```
#include <Inventor/nodekits/SoShapeKit.h>
```

SEE ALSO

SoAppearanceKit, SoBaseKit, SoCameraKit, SoLightKit, SoNodeKit, SoNodeKitDetail, SoNodeKitListPart, SoNodeKitPath, SoNodekitCatalog, SoSceneKit, SoSeparatorKit, SoWrapperKit, SoCone, SoCube, SoCylinder, SoIndexedNurbsCurve, SoIndexedNurbsSurface, SoNurbsCurve, SoNurbsSurface, SoShapeHints, SoSphere, SoText2, SoText3, SoVertexShape

NAME

SoShuttle — animated oscillating translation node

INHERITS FROM

SoBase > SoFieldContainer > SoNode > SoTransformation > SoTranslation > SoShuttle

DESCRIPTION

The **SoShuttle** class is derived from **SoTranslation**, so it applies a translation to the current transformation. Using engines connected to the **realTime** global field, the translation value is animated over time between two fixed translations, achieving a shuttling effect. The period of the motion can be adjusted by changing the **speed** field. The current translation at any time is available in the **translation** field, inherited from **SoTranslation**

FIELDS

SoSFVec3f   **translation0**
SoSFVec3f   **translation1**
   These define the two fixed translations that are interpolated to create the shuttling motion.

SoSFFloat   **speed**
   Defines the speed of the shuttle, in cycles per second.

SoSFBool   **on**
   Allows applications to enable or disable the motion easily.

Fields from class SoTranslation:

   translation

METHODS

                  SoShuttle()
   Creates a shuttle node with default settings.

static SoType   **getClassTypeId()**
   Returns type identifier for this class.

Methods from class SoNode:

   setOverride, isOverride, copy, affectsState, getByName, getByName

Methods from class SoFieldContainer:

   setToDefaults, hasDefaultValues, fieldsAreEqual, copyFieldValues, set, get, getFields, getField, getFieldName, enableNotify, isNotifyEnabled

Methods from class SoBase:

ref, unref, unrefNoDelete, touch, getTypeId, isOfType, setName, getName

ACTION BEHAVIOR

SoGLRenderAction, SoCallbackAction, SoGetBoundingBoxAction, SoRayPickAction

Concatenates interpolated translation value with the current transformation matrix.

SoGetMatrixAction

Returns transformation matrix specified by the interpolated translation.

FILE FORMAT/DEFAULTS

```
Shuttle {
        translation   0 0 0
        translation0  0 0 0
        translation1  0 0 0
        speed         1
        on            TRUE
}
```

INCLUDE FILE

```
#include <Inventor/nodes/SoShuttle.h>
```

SEE ALSO

SoPendulum, SoRotor

NAME

SoSpaceballButtonEvent — spaceball button press and release events

INHERITS FROM

SoEvent > SoButtonEvent > SoSpaceballButtonEvent

DESCRIPTION

SoSpaceballButtonEvent represents spaceball button press and release events in the Inventor event model.

METHODS

SoSpaceballButtonEvent()

Constructor.

static SoType   **getClassTypeId**()

Return the type id for the **SoSpaceballButtonEvent** class.

void   **setButton**(SoSpaceballButtonEvent::Button b)
SoSpaceballButtonEvent::Button

getButton() const

Set and get which spaceball button generated the event.

static SbBool   **isButtonPressEvent**(const SoEvent *e,
        SoSpaceballButtonEvent::Button whichButton)
static SbBool   **isButtonReleaseEvent**(const SoEvent *e,
        SoSpaceballButtonEvent::Button whichButton)

Returns whether the passed event is a spaceball button press or release event of the passed button. When *SoSpaceballButtonEvent::ANY* is passed, this returns *TRUE* if the event represents a button press or release of any spaceball button.

Methods from class SoButtonEvent:

setState, getState

Methods from class SoEvent:

getTypeId, isOfType, setTime, getTime, setPosition, getPosition, getPosition, getNormalizedPosition, setShiftDown, setCtrlDown, setAltDown, wasShiftDown, wasCtrlDown, wasAltDown

SoSpaceballButtonEvent

INCLUDE FILE

```
#include <Inventor/events/SoSpaceballButtonEvent.h>

#define SO_SPACEBALL_PRESS_EVENT(EVENT,BUTTON)
    (SoSpaceballButtonEvent::isButtonPressEvent(EVENT,
                    SoSpaceballButtonEvent::BUTTON))
#define SO_SPACEBALL_RELEASE_EVENT(EVENT,BUTTON)
    (SoSpaceballButtonEvent::isButtonReleaseEvent(EVENT,
                    SoSpaceballButtonEvent::BUTTON))

enum Button {
```

SoSpaceballButtonEvent::ANY	Any spaceball button
SoSpaceballButtonEvent::BUTTON1	Spaceball button 1
SoSpaceballButtonEvent::BUTTON2	Spaceball button 2
SoSpaceballButtonEvent::BUTTON3	Spaceball button 3
SoSpaceballButtonEvent::BUTTON4	Spaceball button 4
SoSpaceballButtonEvent::BUTTON5	Spaceball button 5
SoSpaceballButtonEvent::BUTTON6	Spaceball button 6
SoSpaceballButtonEvent::BUTTON7	Spaceball button 7
SoSpaceballButtonEvent::BUTTON8	Spaceball button 8
SoSpaceballButtonEvent::PICK	Spaceball pick button

```
}
```

SEE ALSO

SoEvent, SoButtonEvent, SoKeyboardEvent, SoLocation2Event, SoMotion3Event, SoMouseButtonEvent, SoHandleEventAction, SoEventCallback, SoSelection, SoInteraction, SoXtDevice

NAME

SoSphere — sphere shape node

INHERITS FROM

SoBase > SoFieldContainer > SoNode > SoShape > SoSphere

DESCRIPTION

This node represents a sphere. By default, the sphere is centered at the origin and has a radius of 1. The sphere is transformed by the current cumulative transformation and is drawn with the current lighting model, drawing style, material, and geometric complexity.

A sphere does not have faces or parts. Therefore, the sphere ignores material and normal bindings, using the first material for the entire sphere and using its own normals. When a texture is applied to a sphere, the texture covers the entire surface, wrapping counterclockwise from the back of the sphere. The texture has a seam at the back on the yz-plane.

FIELDS

SoSFFloat   **radius**

Radius of sphere. This must be greater than 0.

METHODS

SoSphere()

Creates a sphere node with default settings.

static SoType   **getClassTypeId()**

Returns type identifier for this class.

Methods from class SoNode:

setOverride, isOverride, copy, affectsState, getByName, getByName

Methods from class SoFieldContainer:

setToDefaults, hasDefaultValues, fieldsAreEqual, copyFieldValues, set, get, getFields, getField, getFieldName, enableNotify, isNotifyEnabled

Methods from class SoBase:

ref, unref, unrefNoDelete, touch, getTypeId, isOfType, setName, getName

ACTION BEHAVIOR

SoGLRenderAction

Draws sphere based on the current coordinates, materials, drawing style, and so on.

SoRayPickAction
> Intersects the ray with the sphere. No details are created for intersections.

SoGetBoundingBoxAction
> Computes the bounding box that encloses the sphere.

SoCallbackAction
> If any triangle callbacks are registered with the action, they will be invoked for each successive triangle that approximates the sphere.

FILE FORMAT/DEFAULTS

```
Sphere {
      radius  1
}
```

INCLUDE FILE

```
#include <Inventor/nodes/SoSphere.h>
```

SEE ALSO

SoCone, SoCube, SoCylinder

NAME

SoSpotLight — node representing a spotlight source

INHERITS FROM

SoBase > SoFieldContainer > SoNode > SoLight > SoSpotLight

DESCRIPTION

This node defines a spotlight style light source. A spotlight is placed at a fixed location in 3-space and illuminates in a cone along a particular direction. The intensity of the illumination drops off exponentially as a ray of light diverges from this direction toward the edges of the cone. The rate of drop-off and the angle of the cone are controlled by the **dropOffRate** and **cutOffAngle** fields.

FIELDS

SoSFVec3f   **location**
Location of the source.

SoSFVec3f   **direction**
Principal direction of illumination (center axis of cone).

SoSFFloat   **dropOffRate**
Rate of intensity drop-off per change in angle from primary direction: 0 = constant intensity, 1 = very sharp drop-off

SoSFFloat   **cutOffAngle**
Angle (in radians) outside of which intensity is zero, measured from the center axis of the cone to an edge.

Fields from class SoLight:

on, intensity, color

METHODS

         SoSpotLight()
Creates a spotlight source node with default settings.

static SoType   **getClassTypeId()**
Returns type identifier for this class.

Methods from class SoNode:

setOverride, isOverride, copy, affectsState, getByName, getByName

Methods from class SoFieldContainer:

setToDefaults, hasDefaultValues, fieldsAreEqual, copyFieldValues, set, get, getFields, getField, getFieldName, enableNotify, isNotifyEnabled

Methods from class SoBase:

ref, unref, unrefNoDelete, touch, getTypeId, isOfType, setName, getName

ACTION BEHAVIOR
SoGLRenderAction

Activates this light (if so specified) during traversal. All shape nodes that come after this light in the scene graph are illuminated by this light. The light's location is affected by the current transformation.

FILE FORMAT/DEFAULTS

```
SpotLight {
        on              TRUE
        intensity       1
        color           1 1 1
        location        0 0 1
        direction       0 0 -1
        dropOffRate     0
        cutOffAngle     0.785398
}
```

INCLUDE FILE

```
#include <Inventor/nodes/SoSpotLight.h>
```

SEE ALSO

SoDirectionalLight, SoPointLight

NAME

SoSpotLightDragger — spotlight shaped dragger that allows you to change position, direction, and width of the beam

INHERITS FROM

SoBase > SoFieldContainer > SoNode > SoBaseKit > SoInteractionKit > SoDragger > SoSpotLightDragger

DESCRIPTION

SoSpotLightDragger is a composite dragger. It is shaped like a beam of light emanating from a sun-like ball. An arrow runs along the axis of the beam and extends past the end of the beam.

When you click and drag the beam, it opens and closes with an umbrella-like motion. The angle between the center and edge of the beam is stored in the **angle** field of this dragger; setting the **angle** field causes the beam to widen or narrow in response. The spotlight dragger does not use a standard dragger class to execute this motion. More details are given later in this section.

Dragging the arrow rotates it arount the sun, and the beam moves with it. The arrow is an **SoRotateSphericalDragger** that controls the **rotation** field. See the reference page for **SoDirectionalLightDragger**, which works the same way, for details.

The sun-shape can be dragged to translate all three pieces together through 3-space. Its movement controls the **translation** field and works exactly as described in the reference pages for **SoDirectionalLightDragger** and **SoPointLightDragger** (which goes into more detail).

Remember: This is *not* a light source! It just looks like one. If you want to move a light with this dragger, you can do the following:

[a] Use an **SoSpotLightManip**, which is subclassed from **SoLight**. It creates an **SoSpotLightDragger** and uses it as the interface to change the **location**, **direction**, and **cutOffAngle** of its light source (see the **SoSpotLightManip** man page). The manip also edits the **material** part of this dragger to match the color of light the manip is producing.

[b] Connect the **angle** field of this dragger to the **cutOffAngle** field of an **SoSpotLight** with a field-to-field connection.

See the **SoPointLightDragger** and **SoDirectionalLightDragger** man pages for other ways to control light parameters with the **rotation** and **translation** fields.

This class creates its own projector and handles mouse events to do it's own dragging of the beam angle. When the mouse picks a point on the beam, that point is dragged in a circle just like in an **SoRotateDiscDragger**, but the plane of the disc is re-defined every time a drag is initiated. Imagine placing the metal tip of a compass at the apex of the cone and the pencil tip at the picked point. If you swing an arc through the central axis of the cone, you will be drawing the arc used to drag the beam open and closed.

The beam is opened and closed not by rotating, but by scaling. The dragger scales the beam-cone so that the height and radius change to move the picked point along the circle. Then the **angle** field is calculated from the height and radius.

You can change the geometry of parts in any instance of this dragger using **setPart()**. The default part geometries are defined as resources for this **SoSpotLightDragger** class. They are detailed below in the DRAGGER RESOURCE section. You can make your program use different default resources for the parts by copying the file **/usr/share/data/draggerDefaults/spotLightDragger.iv** into your own directory, editing the file, and then setting the environment variable **SO_DRAGGER_DIR** to be a path to that directory.

FIELDS

SoSFRotation   **rotation**
        Orientation of the rotating part (an arrow by default).

SoSFVec3f   **translation**
        Position of the dragger.

SoSFFloat   **angle**
        Angle between center and edge of beam.

Fields from class SoDragger:
        isActive

Fields from class SoInteractionKit:
        renderCaching, boundingBoxCaching, renderCulling, pickCulling

PARTS

Parts from class SoBaseKit:
        callbackList

METHODS

SoSpotLightDragger()
Constructor.

static const SoNodekitCatalog *
getClassNodekitCatalog() const
Returns an **SoNodekitCatalog** for this class

static SoType   getClassTypeId()
Returns type identifier for this class.

Methods from class SoDragger:

addStartCallback, removeStartCallback, addMotionCallback, removeMotionCallback, addFinishCallback, removeFinishCallback, addValueChangedCallback, removeValueChangedCallback, setMinGesture, getMinGesture, setMinScale, getMinScale

Methods from class SoInteractionKit:

setPartAsPath

Methods from class SoBaseKit:

getNodekitCatalog, getPart, getPartString, createPathToPart, setPart, set, set, isSearchingChildren, setSearchingChildren

Methods from class SoNode:

setOverride, isOverride, copy, affectsState, getByName, getByName

Methods from class SoFieldContainer:

setToDefaults, hasDefaultValues, fieldsAreEqual, copyFieldValues, get, getFields, getField, getFieldName, enableNotify, isNotifyEnabled

Methods from class SoBase:

ref, unref, unrefNoDelete, touch, getTypeId, isOfType, setName, getName

MACROS

Macros from class SoBaseKit:

SO_GET_PART, SO_CHECK_PART

CATALOG PARTS

<table>
<tr><th colspan="4">All parts</th></tr>
<tr><th>Part Name</th><th>Part Type</th><th>Default Type</th><th>NULL by Default</th></tr>
<tr><td>callbackList</td><td>NodeKitListPart</td><td>--</td><td>yes</td></tr>
<tr><td>material</td><td>Material</td><td>--</td><td>yes</td></tr>
<tr><td>translator</td><td>DragPointDragger</td><td>--</td><td>yes</td></tr>
<tr><td>rotator</td><td>RotateSphericalDragger</td><td>--</td><td>yes</td></tr>
<tr><td>beamPlacement</td><td>Translation</td><td>--</td><td>yes</td></tr>
<tr><td>beamScale</td><td>Scale</td><td>--</td><td>yes</td></tr>
<tr><td>beam</td><td>Separator</td><td>--</td><td>yes</td></tr>
<tr><td>beamActive</td><td>Separator</td><td>--</td><td>yes</td></tr>
</table>

<table>
<tr><th colspan="3">Extra information for list parts from above table</th></tr>
<tr><th>Part Name</th><th>Container Type</th><th>Permissible Types</th></tr>
<tr><td>callbackList</td><td>Separator</td><td>Callback, EventCallback</td></tr>
</table>

FILE FORMAT/DEFAULTS

```
SpotLightDragger {
        renderCaching        AUTO
        boundingBoxCaching   AUTO
        renderCulling        AUTO
        pickCulling          AUTO
        isActive             FALSE
        rotation             0 0 1  0
        translation          0 0 0
        angle                1
}
```

INCLUDE FILE

```
#include <Inventor/draggers/SoSpotLightDragger.h>
```

SEE ALSO

SoInteractionKit, SoDragger, SoCenterballDragger, SoDirectionalLightDragger, SoDragPointDragger, SoHandleBoxDragger, SoJackDragger, SoPointLightDragger, SoRotateCylindricalDragger, SoRotateDiscDragger, SoRotateSphericalDragger, SoScale1Dragger, SoScale2Dragger, SoScale2UniformDragger, SoScaleUniformDragger, SoTabBoxDragger, SoTabPlaneDragger, SoTrackballDragger, SoTransformBoxDragger, SoTranslate1Dragger, SoTranslate2Dragger

NAME

SoSpotLightManip — spotlight node with 3D interface for editing location, direction, and beam width

INHERITS FROM

SoBase > SoFieldContainer > SoNode > SoLight > SoSpotLight > SoSpotLightManip

DESCRIPTION

SoSpotLightManip is the base class for all **SoSpotLight** nodes that have a built-in 3D user interface (this is the only such class provided with the Inventor toolkit). Since it is derived from **SoSpotLight**, any changes to its fields result in a change of lighting for nodes that follow it in the scene graph. In this case, the interface edits the **location**, **direction**, and **cutOffAngle** fields. Also, the color of the manipulator's geometry will reflect the color of the light (but you can not edit the color using this manipulator).

Typically, you will want to replace a regular **SoSpotLight** with an **SoSpotLightManip** (as when the user selects a light to be edited), or vice versa (as when the user is done moving the light and the interface should go away). Use the **replaceNode()** method to insert a manipulator into a scene graph, and the **replaceManip()** method to remove it when done.

The **SoSpotLightManip** utilizes an **SoSpotLightDragger** to provide a 3D interface. However, the manipulator differs from the dragger; it lights other objects in the scene because, as an **SoSpotLight**, it alters the state. The fields values and movement of the dragger, on the other hand, affect only the dragger itself. To find out more about how the interface works and what each part will do, see the reference page for **SoSpotLightDragger**. The interfaces of the dragger and the manipulator are identical.

The **SoSpotLightManip** utilizes its dragger by adding it as a hidden child. When an action is applied to the manipulator, such as rendering or handling events, the manipulator first traverses the dragger, and then the manipulator adds its lighting parameters to the state. When you click-drag-release over the manipulator, it passes these events down to the dragger, which moves as a result ("I can't *help* it, I'm a dragger!").

The manipulator maintains consistency between the fields of the dragger and its own fields. Let's say you use the mouse to widen the cone of the *dragger*. Callbacks insure that the **cutOffAngle** field of the *manipulator* will change by the same amount, thus changing the lighting of nodes which follow in the scene graph. Similarly, if you set the **cutOffAngle** field of the **SoSpotLightManip**, the manipulator will widen the beam of the dragger accordingly.

Because the dragger is a *hidden* child, you can see the dragger on screen and interact with it, but the dragger does not show up when you write the manipulator to file. Also, any **SoPath** will end at the manipulator. (See the Actions section of this reference page for a complete description of when the dragger is traversed).

If you want to get a pointer to the dragger you can get it from the manipulator using the **getDragger()** method. You will need to do this if you want to change the geometry of a manipulator, since the geometry actually belongs to the dragger.

FIELDS

Fields from class SoSpotLight:

location, direction, dropOffRate, cutOffAngle

Fields from class SoLight:

on, intensity, color

METHODS

SoSpotLightManip()
Constructor.

SoDragger *   **getDragger()**
Returns a pointer to the dragger being used by this manipulator. Given this pointer, you can customize the dragger just like you would any other dragger. You can change geometry using the **setPart()** method, or add callbacks using the methods found in the **SoDragger** reference page.

SbBool   **replaceNode**(SoPath *p)
Replaces the tail of the path with this manipulator. The tail of the path must be an **SoSpotLight** node (or subclass thereof). If the path has a nodekit, this will try to use **setPart()** to insert the manipulator. Otherwise, the manipulator requires that the next to last node in the path chain be a group.

The field values from the spotlight node will be copied to this manipulator, and the light node will be replaced.

The manipulator will not call **ref()** on the node it is replacing. The old node will disappear if it has no references other than from the input path *p* and its parent, since this manipulator will be replacing it in both of those places. Nor will the manipulator make any changes to field connections of the old node. The calling process is thus responsible for keeping track of its own nodes and field connections.

SbBool   **replaceManip**(SoPath *p, SoSpotLight *newOne) const

Replaces the tail of the path, which must be this manipulator, with the given **SoSpotLight** node. If the path has a nodekit, this will try to use **setPart**() to insert the new node. Otherwise, the manipulator requires that the next to last node in the path chain be a group.

The field values from the manipulator will be copied to the spotlight node, and the manipulator will be replaced.

The manipulator will not call **ref**() or **unref**() on the node which is replacing it, nor will it make any changes to field connections. The calling process is thus responsible for keeping track of its own nodes and field connections.

static SoType   **getClassTypeId**()

Returns type identifier for this class.

Methods from class SoNode:

setOverride, isOverride, copy, affectsState, getByName, getByName

Methods from class SoFieldContainer:

setToDefaults, hasDefaultValues, fieldsAreEqual, copyFieldValues, set, get, getFields, getField, getFieldName, enableNotify, isNotifyEnabled

Methods from class SoBase:

ref, unref, unrefNoDelete, touch, getTypeId, isOfType, setName, getName

ACTION BEHAVIOR

SoGLRenderAction, SoCallbackAction, SoGetBoundingBoxAction, SoGetMatrixAction, SoHandleEventAction, SoRayPickAction

First, traverses the dragger the way an **SoGroup** would. All draggers place themselves in space, but leave the current transformation unchanged when finished. Then the **SoSpotLightManip** adds a spotlight to the state, just like its base class, **SoSpotLight**.

SoSearchAction

Searches just like an **SoSpotLight**. Does not search the dragger, which is a hidden child.

SoWriteAction

Writes out just like an **SoSpotLight**. Does not write the dragger, which is a hidden child. If you really need to write valuable information about the dragger, such as customized geometry, you can retrieve the dragger with the **getDragger**() method and then write it out separately.

FILE FORMAT/DEFAULTS

```
SpotLightManip {
        on              TRUE
        intensity       1
        color           1 1 1
        location        0 0 1
        direction       0 0 -1
        dropOffRate     0
        cutOffAngle     0.785398
}
```

INCLUDE FILE

```
#include <Inventor/manips/SoSpotLightManip.h>
```

SEE ALSO

SoDragger, SoSpotLight, SoSpotLightDragger, SoDirectionalLightManip, SoPointLightManip

NAME

SoSurroundScale — transformation node that adjusts the current matrix so a default cube will surround other objects

INHERITS FROM

SoBase > SoFieldContainer > SoNode > SoTransformation > SoSurroundScale

DESCRIPTION

When traversed by an action, this node appends a transformation to the current transformation matrix so that a default size cube will surround the objects specified by its fields. Transform manipulators, such as **SoHandleBoxManip**, use these nodes to make themselves surround other objects.

This node only recalculates after the **invalidate()** method has been called. Otherwise it uses a saved scale and translation.

When calculating what to surround, the **SoSurroundScale** looks at the current path in the action and at its own field values. Then **SoSurroundScale** applies an **SoGetBoundingBoxAction** to the node that is **numNodesUpToContainer** nodes above it on the path. **SoSurroundScale** also tells the action to reset the bounding box upon traversal of the node located **numNodesUpToReset** nodes above it in the path. The **SoSurroundScale** then appends a translation and scale to the current transformation so that a default size **SoCube** will translate and scale to fit this bounding box.

For example, when an **SoHandleBoxManip** wants to surround the objects it is going to move, the scene graph will look something like this:

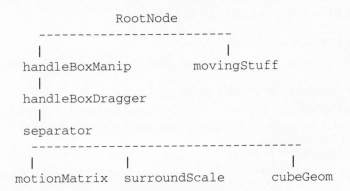

The **SoHandleBoxDragger** wants to transform the *cubeGeom* so that it surrounds the *movingStuff*. So it sets the *surroundScale* fields to:

>   **numNodesUpToContainer** = 4;
>   **numNodesUpToReset** = 3;

The **SoBoundingBoxAction** will then be applied to *RootNode*, with a reset after traversing the **SoHandleBoxManip**. So the **SoSurroundScale** will surround the objects below *separator*, and to the right of *handleBoxManip*, producing the desired effect.

FIELDS

SoSFLong   **numNodesUpToContainer**

When traversed by an action, if surroundScale needs to calculate a new box, surroundScale looks at the current path in the action. It travels up this path a distance of **numNodesUpToContainer** and applies an **SoGetBoundingBoxAction** to the node that it finds there.

SoSFLong   **numNodesUpToReset**

Before applying the **SoGetBoundingBoxAction** (see the **numNodesUpToContainer** field aove) the surroundScale node travels up the path a distance of **numNodesUpToReset** and tells the action to reset the bounding box upon traversal of that node.

METHODS

                            SoSurroundScale()

Creates a surround scale node with default settings.

void   **invalidate**()

If you call this, then next time an action is applied the node will re-calculate it's cached translation and scale values.

static SoType   **getClassTypeId**()

Returns type identifier for this class.

Methods from class SoNode:

setOverride, isOverride, copy, affectsState, getByName, getByName

Methods from class SoFieldContainer:

setToDefaults, hasDefaultValues, fieldsAreEqual, copyFieldValues, set, get, getFields, getField, getFieldName, enableNotify, isNotifyEnabled

Methods from class SoBase:

ref, unref, unrefNoDelete, touch, getTypeId, isOfType, setName, getName

ACTION BEHAVIOR

SoGLRenderAction, SoCallbackAction, SoGetBoundingBoxAction, SoRayPickAction

Accumulates scaling and translation transformations into the current transformation.

SoGetMatrixAction
Returns the matrix corresponding to the scaling and translation.

FILE FORMAT/DEFAULTS

```
SurroundScale {
      numNodesUpToContainer   0
      numNodesUpToReset       0
}
```

INCLUDE FILE

```
#include <Inventor/nodes/SoSurroundScale.h>
```

SEE ALSO

SoTransformation, SoTransformManip, SoCenterballDragger, SoCenterballManip, SoHandleBoxDragger, SoHandleBoxManip, SoJackDragger, SoJackManip, SoTabBoxDragger, SoTabBoxManip, SoTrackballDragger, SoTrackballManip, SoTransformBoxDragger, SoTransformBoxManip

NAME

    SoSwitch — group node that traverse one chosen child

INHERITS FROM

    SoBase > SoFieldContainer > SoNode > SoGroup > SoSwitch

DESCRIPTION

    This group node usually traverses only one or none of its children. It implements an operation similar to the switch statement in C. One can use this node to switch on and off the effects of some properties or to switch between different properties.

    The **whichChild** field specifies the index of the child to traverse, where the first child has index 0.

    A value of SO_SWITCH_NONE (-1, the default) means do not traverse any children. A value of SO_SWITCH_INHERIT (-2) allows the index to be inherited from a previously-encountered **SoSwitch** node or from certain other nodes (such as **SoArray** or **SoMultipleCopy**) that set the switch value. A value of SO_SWITCH_ALL (-3) traverses all children, making the switch behave exactly like a regular **SoGroup**.

FIELDS

SoSFLong   **whichChild**

    Index of the child to traverse, or one of SO_SWITCH_NONE, SO_SWITCH_INHERIT, or SO_SWITCH_ALL.

METHODS

        SoSwitch()
    Creates a switch node with default settings.

        SoSwitch(int nChildren)
    Constructor that takes approximate number of children.

static SoType   **getClassTypeId**()
    Returns type identifier for this class.

Methods from class SoGroup:

    addChild, insertChild, getChild, findChild, getNumChildren, removeChild, removeChild, removeAllChildren, replaceChild, replaceChild

Methods from class SoNode:

    setOverride, isOverride, copy, affectsState, getByName, getByName

Methods from class SoFieldContainer:

setToDefaults, hasDefaultValues, fieldsAreEqual, copyFieldValues, set, get, getFields, getField, getFieldName, enableNotify, isNotifyEnabled

Methods from class SoBase:

ref, unref, unrefNoDelete, touch, getTypeId, isOfType, setName, getName

ACTION BEHAVIOR

SoGLRenderAction, SoCallbackAction, SoGetBoundingBoxAction, SoGetMatrixAction, SoHandleEventAction, SoRayPickAction
Traverses the chosen child or children.

SoSearchAction
If the action's Searching-All flag is set, always traverses all children. Otherwise, traverses just the chosen child or children.

FILE FORMAT/DEFAULTS

```
Switch {
    whichChild  -1
}
```

INCLUDE FILE

```
#include <Inventor/nodes/SoSwitch.h>
```

SEE ALSO

SoArray, SoLevelOfDetail, SoMultipleCopy, SoPathSwitch

NAME

SoTabBoxDragger — cubic object you can translate and scale by dragging with the mouse

INHERITS FROM

SoBase > SoFieldContainer > SoNode > SoBaseKit > SoInteractionKit > SoDragger > SoTabBoxDragger

DESCRIPTION

SoTabBoxDragger is a composite dragger shaped like a box. Inside it are six **SoTabPlaneDraggers** which the dragger positions and orients to form a cube. The operations available in an **SoTabPlaneDragger** (translation, 1D scaling and 2D scaling) are available on each face of the cube. Since they each move in their local space, the dragger may be easily translated or scaled in any direction.

As a composite dragger, this class makes sure that when one plane is dragged, the entire box moves together.

As each sub-dragger is moved, the **SoTabBoxDragger** updates its **scaleFactor** and **translation** fields. As with all draggers, if you change a field the dragger will move to match the new settings.

Remember: This is *not* an **SoTransform**!. If you want to move other objects with this dragger, you can either:

[a] Use an **SoTabBoxManip**, which is subclassed from **SoTransform**. It creates one of these draggers and uses it as the interface to change its fields. (see the **SoTabBoxManip** man page).

[b] Use field-to-field connections to connect the fields of this dragger to those of any **SoTransformation** node.

You can change the parts in any instance of this dragger using **setPart()**. The default part geometries are defined as resources for this **SoTabBoxDragger** class. They are detailed below in the Dragger Resources section of the online reference page for this class. You can make your program use different default resources for the parts by copying the file **/usr/share/data/draggerDefaults/tabBoxDragger.iv** into your own directory, editing the file, and then setting the environment variable **SO_DRAGGER_DIR** to be a path to that directory.

FIELDS

SoSFVec3f   **scaleFactor**
           Scale of the dragger.

SoSFVec3f   **translation**
> Position of the dragger.

Fields from class SoDragger:
> isActive

Fields from class SoInteractionKit:
> renderCaching, boundingBoxCaching, renderCulling, pickCulling

PARTS

Parts from class SoBaseKit:
> callbackList

METHODS

> **SoTabBoxDragger**()
>
> Constructor.

void   **adjustScaleTabSize**()
> Cause the scale tab sizes to be re-adjusted on all 6 **SoTabPlaneDragger**s so that they remain a near constant screen space size. This happens automatically upon dragger finish. Call this to adjust the scale tab sizes at other times, for instance after the camera has changed in a viewer finish callback.

static const SoNodekitCatalog *
> **getClassNodekitCatalog**() const
>
> Returns an **SoNodekitCatalog** for this class

static SoType   **getClassTypeId**()
> Returns type identifier for this class.

Methods from class SoDragger:
> addStartCallback, removeStartCallback, addMotionCallback, removeMotionCallback, addFinishCallback, removeFinishCallback, addValueChangedCallback, removeValueChangedCallback, setMinGesture, getMinGesture, setMinScale, getMinScale

Methods from class SoInteractionKit:
> setPartAsPath

Methods from class SoBaseKit:

getNodekitCatalog, getPart, getPartString, createPathToPart, setPart, set, set, isSearchingChildren, setSearchingChildren

Methods from class SoNode:

setOverride, isOverride, copy, affectsState, getByName, getByName

Methods from class SoFieldContainer:

setToDefaults, hasDefaultValues, fieldsAreEqual, copyFieldValues, get, getFields, getField, getFieldName, enableNotify, isNotifyEnabled

Methods from class SoBase:

ref, unref, unrefNoDelete, touch, getTypeId, isOfType, setName, getName

MACROS

Macros from class SoBaseKit:

SO_GET_PART, SO_CHECK_PART

CATALOG PARTS

All parts			
Part Name	**Part Type**	**Default Type**	**NULL by Default**
callbackList	NodeKitListPart	--	yes
surroundScale	SurroundScale	--	yes
tabPlane1	TabPlaneDragger	--	yes
tabPlane2	TabPlaneDragger	--	yes
tabPlane3	TabPlaneDragger	--	yes
tabPlane4	TabPlaneDragger	--	yes
tabPlane5	TabPlaneDragger	--	yes
tabPlane6	TabPlaneDragger	--	yes
boxGeom	Separator	--	yes

Extra information for list parts from above table		
Part Name	Container Type	Permissible Types
callbackList	Separator	Callback, EventCallback

FILE FORMAT/DEFAULTS

```
TabBoxDragger {
        renderCaching          AUTO
        boundingBoxCaching     AUTO
        renderCulling          AUTO
        pickCulling            AUTO
        isActive               FALSE
        translation            0 0 0
        scaleFactor            1 1 1
}
```

INCLUDE FILE

```
#include <Inventor/draggers/SoTabBoxDragger.h>
```

SEE ALSO

SoInteractionKit, SoDragger, SoCenterballDragger, SoDirectionalLightDragger, SoDragPointDragger, SoHandleBoxDragger, SoJackDragger, SoPointLightDragger, SoRotateCylindricalDragger, SoRotateDiscDragger, SoRotateSphericalDragger, SoScale1Dragger, SoScale2Dragger, SoScale2UniformDragger, SoScaleUniformDragger, SoSpotLightDragger, SoTabPlaneDragger, SoTrackballDragger, SoTransformBoxDragger, SoTranslate1Dragger, SoTranslate2Dragger

NAME

SoTabBoxManip — transform node with 3D Interface for editing scale and translation

INHERITS FROM

SoBase > SoFieldContainer > SoNode > SoTransformation > SoTransform > SoTransformManip > SoTabBoxManip

DESCRIPTION

SoTabBoxManip is derived from **SoTransform** (by way of **SoTransformManip**). When its fields change, nodes following it in the scene graph scale, and/or translate.

As a subclass of **SoTransformManip**, this manip also has a 3D interface to edit some of its fields. In this case, the interface edits the **scaleFactor** and **translation** fields.

A manipulator differs from a dragger. When you move a dragger, no other nodes are affected. When you move an **SoTransformManip**, other nodes move along with it. (See the reference page for **SoTransformManip**.)

The interface for an **SoTabBoxManip** is exactly the same as that of the **SoTabBoxDragger**. To find out more about the interface, see the reference page for **SoTabBoxDragger**. To find out how the manipulator uses a dragger to provide its interface, see the reference page for **SoTransformManip**.

On screen, this manip will surround the objects influenced by its motion. This is because it turns on the *surroundScale* part of the dragger (See the reference page for **SoSurroundScale**)

FIELDS

Fields from class SoTransform:

translation, rotation, scaleFactor, scaleOrientation, center

METHODS

SoTabBoxManip()
Constructor.

static SoType **getClassTypeId()**
Returns type identifier for this class.

Methods from class SoTransformManip:

getDragger, replaceNode, replaceManip

Methods from class SoTransform:

> pointAt, getScaleSpaceMatrix, getRotationSpaceMatrix, getTranslationSpaceMatrix, multLeft, multRight, combineLeft, combineRight, setMatrix, recenter

Methods from class SoNode:

> setOverride, isOverride, copy, affectsState, getByName, getByName

Methods from class SoFieldContainer:

> setToDefaults, hasDefaultValues, fieldsAreEqual, copyFieldValues, set, get, getFields, getField, getFieldName, enableNotify, isNotifyEnabled

Methods from class SoBase:

> ref, unref, unrefNoDelete, touch, getTypeId, isOfType, setName, getName

FILE FORMAT/DEFAULTS

```
TabBoxManip {
        translation        0 0 0
        rotation           0 0 1  0
        scaleFactor        1 1 1
        scaleOrientation   0 0 1  0
        center             0 0 0
}
```

INCLUDE FILE

```
#include <Inventor/manips/SoTabBoxManip.h>
```

SEE ALSO

> SoCenterballManip, SoHandleBoxManip, SoJackManip, SoTabBoxDragger, SoTrackballManip, SoTransformBoxManip, SoTransform, SoTransformManip

NAME

SoTabPlaneDragger — object you can translate or scale within a plane by dragging with the mouse

INHERITS FROM

SoBase > SoFieldContainer > SoNode > SoBaseKit > SoInteractionKit > SoDragger > SoTabPlaneDragger

DESCRIPTION

SoTabPlaneDragger is a dragger which allows the user to interactively translate and scale in a plane. It looks like a square white outline with smaller green squares (or *tabs*) set in the corners and along the center of each edge. Dragging a **corner tab** scales the dragger in 2D by scaling about the opposite corner. Dragging an **edge tab** performs 1D scaling about the opposite edge. The rest of the dragger is invisible but pickable; selecting it initiates translation within the plane.

The dragger tries to keep the small tabs a constant size in screen space. Every time a drag begins or ends, the size is recalculated based on the viewing and modeling matrix.

When dragging the translator part, press the <Shift> key and you can constrain motion to either the local **x axis** or the **y axis**. The direction is determined by your initial mouse gesture after pressing the key. Releasing the key removes the constraint.

When the translator part drags, the dragger updates its **translation** field. The various scaling parts cause changes to both the **scaleFactor** and **translation** field, since scaling about a point other than the center adds translation to the center of the dragger. If you set the field, the dragger will move accordingly. You can also connect fields of other nodes or engines from this one to make them follow the dragger's motion.

You can not change the shape used to draw the tabs. This part is kept privately and may not be changed; the coordinates for the tabs are edited during **adjustScaleTabSize()**.

The **SoTabPlaneDragger** class does contain three other parts you can change: *tabPlaneTranslator*, *tabPlaneScaleTabMaterial* and *tabPlaneScaleTabHints*.

Each of these is set by default from a resource described in the Dragger Resources section of the online reference page for this class. You can change the parts in any instance of this dragger using **setPart()**.

You can make your program use different default resources for the parts by copying the file **/usr/share/data/draggerDefaults/tabPlaneDragger.iv** into your own directory, editing the file, and then setting the environment variable **SO_DRAGGER_DIR** to be a path to that directory.

FIELDS

SoSFVec3f   **scaleFactor**
        Scale factor affecting the dragger.

SoSFVec3f   **translation**
        Position of the dragger.

Fields from class SoDragger:
        isActive

Fields from class SoInteractionKit:
        renderCaching, boundingBoxCaching, renderCulling, pickCulling

PARTS

Parts from class SoBaseKit:
        callbackList

METHODS

                SoTabPlaneDragger()
        Constructor.

void   **adjustScaleTabSize()**
        Cause the scale tab sizes to be re-adjusted so that they remain a near constant screen space size. This happens automatically upon dragger finish. Call this to adjust the scale tab sizes at other times, for instance after the camera has changed in a viewer finish callback.

static const SoNodekitCatalog *
                getClassNodekitCatalog() const
        Returns an **SoNodekitCatalog** for this class

static SoType   **getClassTypeId()**
        Returns type identifier for this class.

Methods from class SoDragger:

addStartCallback, removeStartCallback, addMotionCallback, removeMotionCallback, addFinishCallback, removeFinishCallback, addValueChangedCallback, removeValueChangedCallback, setMinGesture, getMinGesture, setMinScale, getMinScale

Methods from class SoInteractionKit:

setPartAsPath

Methods from class SoBaseKit:

getNodekitCatalog, getPart, getPartString, createPathToPart, setPart, set, set, isSearchingChildren, setSearchingChildren

Methods from class SoNode:

setOverride, isOverride, copy, affectsState, getByName, getByName

Methods from class SoFieldContainer:

setToDefaults, hasDefaultValues, fieldsAreEqual, copyFieldValues, get, getFields, getField, getFieldName, enableNotify, isNotifyEnabled

Methods from class SoBase:

ref, unref, unrefNoDelete, touch, getTypeId, isOfType, setName, getName

MACROS

Macros from class SoBaseKit:

SO_GET_PART, SO_CHECK_PART

CATALOG PARTS

All parts			
Part Name	Part Type	Default Type	NULL by Default
callbackList	NodeKitListPart	--	yes
translator	Separator	--	yes
scaleTabMaterial	Material	--	yes
scaleTabHints	ShapeHints	--	yes

Extra information for list parts from above table		
Part Name	Container Type	Permissible Types
callbackList	Separator	Callback, EventCallback

FILE FORMAT/DEFAULTS

```
TabPlaneDragger {
        renderCaching       AUTO
        boundingBoxCaching  AUTO
        renderCulling       AUTO
        pickCulling         AUTO
        isActive            FALSE
        translation         0 0 0
        scaleFactor         1 1 1
}
```

INCLUDE FILE

```
#include <Inventor/draggers/SoTabPlaneDragger.h>
```

SEE ALSO

SoInteractionKit, SoDragger, SoCenterballDragger, SoDirectionalLightDragger,
SoDragPointDragger, SoHandleBoxDragger, SoJackDragger, SoPointLightDragger,
SoRotateCylindricalDragger, SoRotateDiscDragger, SoRotateSphericalDragger,
SoScale1Dragger, SoScale2Dragger, SoScale2UniformDragger,
SoScaleUniformDragger, SoSpotLightDragger, SoTabBoxDragger, SoTrackballDragger,
SoTransformBoxDragger, SoTranslate1Dragger, SoTranslate2Dragger

NAME

SoText2 — screen-aligned 2D text shape node

INHERITS FROM

SoBase > SoFieldContainer > SoNode > SoShape > SoText2

DESCRIPTION

This node defines one or more strings of 2D text. The text is always aligned horizontally with the screen and does not change size with distance in a perspective projection. The text origin is at (0,0,0) after applying the current transformation. Rotations and scales have no effect on the orientation or size of 2D text, just the location.

SoText2 uses the current font to determine the typeface and size. The text is always drawn with the diffuse color of the current material; it is not lit, regardless of the lighting model. Furthermore, 2D text can not be textured, and it ignores the current drawing style and complexity.

Because 2D text is screen-aligned, it has some unusual characteristics. For example, the 3D bounding box surrounding a 2D text string depends on the current camera and the current viewport size, since changing the field of view or the mapping onto the window changes the relative size of the text with respect to the rest of the scene. This has implications for caching as well, since a render cache in an **SoSeparator** that contains an **SoText2** node depends on the current camera.

FIELDS

SoMFString   **string**

The text string(s) to display. Each string will appear on its own line.

SoSFFloat   **spacing**

Defines the distance (in the negative y direction) between the base points of successive strings, measured with respect to the current font height. A value of 1 indicates single spacing, a value of 2 indicates double spacing, and so on.

SoSFEnum   **justification**

Indicates placement and alignment of strings. With LEFT justification, the left edge of the first line is at the (transformed) origin, and all left edges are aligned. RIGHT justification is similar. CENTER justification places the center of the first string at the (transformed) origin, with the centers of all remaining strings aligned under it.

METHODS

SoText2()
Creates a 2D text node with default settings.

static SoType **getClassTypeId()**
Returns type identifier for this class.

Methods from class SoNode:
setOverride, isOverride, copy, affectsState, getByName, getByName

Methods from class SoFieldContainer:
setToDefaults, hasDefaultValues, fieldsAreEqual, copyFieldValues, set, get, getFields, getField, getFieldName, enableNotify, isNotifyEnabled

Methods from class SoBase:
ref, unref, unrefNoDelete, touch, getTypeId, isOfType, setName, getName

ACTION BEHAVIOR

SoGLRenderAction
Draws text based on the current font, at a location based on the current transformation.

SoRayPickAction
Performs a pick on the text. Text will be picked if the picking ray intersects the bounding box of the strings. The string index and character position are available from the **SoTextDetail**.

SoGetBoundingBoxAction
Computes the bounding box that encloses the text.

FILE FORMAT/DEFAULTS

```
Text2 {
      string          " "
      spacing         1
      justification   LEFT
}
```

INCLUDE FILE

```
#include <Inventor/nodes/SoText2.h>
```

enum **Justification** {
        SoText2::LEFT   Left edges of all strings are aligned
        SoText2::RIGHT   Right edges of all strings are aligned
        SoText2::CENTER Centers of all strings are aligned
}

SEE ALSO

SoFont, SoText3, SoTextDetail

NAME
SoText3 — 3D text shape node

INHERITS FROM
SoBase > SoFieldContainer > SoNode > SoShape > SoText3

DESCRIPTION
This node defines one or more strings of 3D text. In contrast with **SoText2**, 3D text can be rotated, scaled, lighted, and textured, just like all other 3D shapes. Each character in a 3D text string is created by extruding an outlined version of the character (in the current typeface) along the current profile, as defined by nodes derived from **SoProfile**. The default text profile, if none is specified, is a straight line segment one unit long.

The text origin is at (0,0,0) after applying the current transformation. The scale of the text is affected by the **size** field of the current **SoFont** as well as the current transformation.

SoText3 uses the current set of materials when rendering. If the material binding is OVERALL, then the whole text is drawn with the first material. If it is PER_PART or PER_PART_INDEXED, the front part of the text is drawn with the first material, the sides with the second, and the back with the third.

Textures are applied to 3D text as follows. On the front and back faces of the text, the texture origin is at the base point of the first string; the base point is at the lower left for justification LEFT, at the lower right for RIGHT, and at the lower center for CENTER. The texture is scaled equally in both S and T dimensions, with the font height representing 1 unit. S increases to the right on the front faces and to the left on the back faces. On the sides, the texture is scaled the same as on the front and back. S is equal to 0 at the rear edge of the side faces. The T origin can occur anywhere along each character, depending on how that character's outline is defined.

FIELDS

SoMFString   **string**
The text string(s) to display. Each string will appear on its own line.

SoSFFloat   **spacing**
Defines the distance (in the negative y direction) between the base points of successive strings, measured with respect to the current font height. A value of 1 indicates single spacing, a value of 2 indicates double spacing, and so on.

SoSFBitMask **parts**
> Which parts of text are visible. Note that, for speed, the default for this field is FRONT only.

SoSFEnum **justification**
> Indicates placement and alignment of strings. With LEFT justification, the left edge of the first line is at the (transformed) origin, and all left edges are aligned. RIGHT justification is similar. CENTER justification places the center of the first string at the (transformed) origin, with the centers of all remaining strings aligned under it.

METHODS

SoText3()
> Creates a 3D text node with default settings.

static SoType **getClassTypeId()**
> Returns type identifier for this class.

Methods from class SoNode:

> setOverride, isOverride, copy, affectsState, getByName, getByName

Methods from class SoFieldContainer:

> setToDefaults, hasDefaultValues, fieldsAreEqual, copyFieldValues, set, get, getFields, getField, getFieldName, enableNotify, isNotifyEnabled

Methods from class SoBase:

> ref, unref, unrefNoDelete, touch, getTypeId, isOfType, setName, getName

ACTION BEHAVIOR

SoGLRenderAction
> Draws text based on the current font, profiles, transformation, drawing style, material, texture, complexity, and so on.

SoRayPickAction
> Performs a pick on the text. The string index and character position are available from the **SoTextDetail**.

SoGetBoundingBoxAction
> Computes the bounding box that encloses the text.

SoCallbackAction
> If any triangle callbacks are registered with the action, they will be invoked for each successive triangle used to approximate the text geometry.

FILE FORMAT/DEFAULTS

```
Text3 {
        string              " "
        spacing             1
        justification       LEFT
        parts               FRONT
}
```

INCLUDE FILE

```
#include <Inventor/nodes/SoText3.h>
```

enum **Justification** {

SoText3::LEFT	Left edges of all strings are aligned
SoText3::RIGHT	Right edges of all strings are aligned
SoText3::CENTER	Centers of all strings are aligned

}

enum **Part** {

SoText3::FRONT	Front faces of characters
SoText3::SIDES	Extruded sides of characters
SoText3::BACK	Back faces of characters
SoText3::ALL	All parts

}

SEE ALSO

SoFont, SoProfile, SoText2, SoTextDetail

SoTextDetail

NAME

SoTextDetail — stores detail information about a text node

INHERITS FROM

SoDetail > SoTextDetail

DESCRIPTION

This class contains detail information about a point on a text shape (**SoText2** or **SoText3**). It contains the part of the text, string, and character that were hit or generated.

METHODS

| | **SoTextDetail**() |
| virtual | **~SoTextDetail**() |

Constructor and destructor.

| long | **getStringIndex**() const |

Returns the index of the relevant string within a multiple-value **string** field of a text node.

| long | **getCharacterIndex**() const |

Returns the index of the relevant character within the string. For example, if the character of detail was the "u" within "Splurmph", the character index would be 3.

| SoText3::Part | **getPart**() const |

For **SoText3**, this returns which part was picked or generated.

| SbBox3f | **getBoundingBox**() const |
| SbXfBox3f | **getXfBoundingBox**() const |

When the detail is returned from picking, these return the object-space bounding box of the character that was intersected. Otherwise, they return an empty box. The second method returns an **SbXfBox3f** instead of a **SbBox3f**. These methods are implemented only for 3D text.

| static SoType | **getClassTypeId**() |

Returns type identifier for this class.

Methods from class SoDetail:

copy, getTypeId, isOfType

INCLUDE FILE

```
#include <Inventor/details/SoTextDetail.h>
```

SEE ALSO

SoText2, SoText3, SoDetail, SoPickedPoint, SoPrimitiveVertex

NAME

SoTexture2 — texture mapping node

INHERITS FROM

SoBase > SoFieldContainer > SoNode > SoTexture2

DESCRIPTION

This property node defines a texture map and parameters for that map. This map is used to apply texture to subsequent shapes as they are rendered.

The texture can be read from the file specified by the **filename** field. Once the texture has been read, the **image** field contains the texture data. However, this field is marked so the image is not written out when the texture node is written to a file. To turn off texturing, set the **filename** field to an empty string ("").

Textures can also be specified in memory by setting the **image** field to contain the texture data. Doing so resets the **filename** to the empty string.

The quality of the texturing is affected by the **textureQuality** field of the **SoComplexity** node. The **textureQuality** field affects what kind of filtering is done to the texture when it must be minified or magnified.

If the texture image's width or height is not a power of 2, then the image will be automatically scaled to the next higher power of 2 before being given to OpenGL, since OpenGL only handles images with dimensions that are powers of 2. This automatic scaling can cause suprising results, especially for small images, since the pixels are linearly interpolated to produce the larger image.

FIELDS

SoSFString   **filename**

Names file from which to read texture image. Currently only SGI .rgb files are supported. If the filename is not an absolute path name, the list of directories maintained by **SoInput** is searched. If the texture is not found in any of those directories, then the file is searched for relative to the directory from which the **SoTexture2** node was read. For example, if an **SoTexture2** node with a filename of "../tofu.rgb" is read from /usr/people/bob/models/food.iv, then /usr/people/bob/tofu.rgb will be read (assuming tofu.rgb isn't found in the directories maintained by **SoInput**).

SoSFImage   **image**

Contains an in-memory representation of the texture map. It is either the contents of the file read from **filename**, an image read directly from an Inventor file, or an image set programmatically using the methods provided by **SoSFImage**.

SoSFEnum **wrapS**
SoSFEnum **wrapT**
> Indicates what to do when texture coordinates in the S (horizontal) or T (vertical) direction lie outside the range 0-1.

SoSFEnum **model**
> Specifies how to map texture onto surface.

SoSFColor **blendColor**
> Color used for BLEND model.

METHODS
> **SoTexture2()**
> Creates a texture node with default settings.

static SoType **getClassTypeId()**
> Returns type identifier for this class.

Methods from class SoNode:
> setOverride, isOverride, copy, affectsState, getByName, getByName

Methods from class SoFieldContainer:
> setToDefaults, hasDefaultValues, fieldsAreEqual, copyFieldValues, set, get, getFields, getField, getFieldName, enableNotify, isNotifyEnabled

Methods from class SoBase:
> ref, unref, unrefNoDelete, touch, getTypeId, isOfType, setName, getName

ACTION BEHAVIOR
SoGLRenderAction, SoCallbackAction
> Sets current texture in state.

FILE FORMAT/DEFAULTS
```
Texture2 {
        filename    ""
        image       0 0 0
        wrapS       REPEAT
        wrapT       REPEAT
        model       MODULATE
        blendColor  0 0 0
}
```

SoTexture2

INCLUDE FILE

```
#include <Inventor/nodes/SoTexture2.h>
```

enum **Model** {

    SoTexture2::MODULATE

          The texture color is multiplied by the surface color

    SoTexture2::DECAL

          The texture color replaces the surface color

    SoTexture2::BLEND

          Blends between the surface color and a specified blend color

}

enum **Wrap** {

    SoTexture2::REPEAT

          Repeats texture outside 0-1 texture coordinate range

    SoTexture2::CLAMP

          Clamps texture coordinates to lie within 0-1 range

}

SEE ALSO

SoComplexity, SoMaterial, SoTexture2Transform, SoTextureCoordinate2, SoTextureCoordinateBinding, SoTextureCoordinateFunction

NAME

SoTexture2Transform — 2D texture transformation node

INHERITS FROM

SoBase > SoFieldContainer > SoNode > SoTexture2Transform

DESCRIPTION

This node defines a 2D transformation applied to texture coordinates. This affects the way textures are applied to the surfaces of subsequent shapes. The transformation consists of (in order) a non-uniform scale about an arbitrary center point, a rotation about that same point, and a translation. (Note: while the transformations can be thought of as being applied in that order, the GL matrices are actually premultiplied in the opposite order. Therefore, the operations are listed in the reverse order throughout this reference page.) This allows a user to change the size and position of the textures on objects.

FIELDS

SoSFVec2f   **translation**
Translation in S and T.

SoSFFloat   **rotation**
Counter-clockwise rotation of the coordinate space, in radians. This results in a clockwise rotation of the texture on the object.

SoSFVec2f   **scaleFactor**
Scaling factors in S and T.

SoSFVec2f   **center**
Center point used for scaling and rotation.

METHODS

               SoTexture2Transform()
Creates a texture transformation node with default settings.

static SoType   **getClassTypeId()**
Returns type identifier for this class.

Methods from class SoNode:

setOverride, isOverride, copy, affectsState, getByName, getByName

Methods from class SoFieldContainer:

setToDefaults, hasDefaultValues, fieldsAreEqual, copyFieldValues, set, get, getFields, getField, getFieldName, enableNotify, isNotifyEnabled

SoTexture2Transform

Methods from class SoBase:
ref, unref, unrefNoDelete, touch, getTypeId, isOfType, setName, getName

ACTION BEHAVIOR
SoGLRenderAction, SoCallbackAction
Concatenates transformation with the current texture transformation.

FILE FORMAT/DEFAULTS
```
Texture2Transform {
        translation  0 0
        rotation     0
        scaleFactor  1 1
        center       0 0
}
```

INCLUDE FILE
```
#include <Inventor/nodes/SoTexture2Transform.h>
```

SEE ALSO
SoTexture2, SoTextureCoordinate2, SoTextureCoordinateFunction

NAME

SoTextureCoordinate2 — 2D texture coordinate node

INHERITS FROM

SoBase > SoFieldContainer > SoNode > SoTextureCoordinate2

DESCRIPTION

This node defines a set of 2D coordinates to be used to map textures to subsequent vertex-based shapes (those derived from **SoVertexShape**). It replaces the current texture coordinates in the rendering state for the shapes to use.

The current texture coordinate binding (see **SoTextureCoordinateBinding**) determines how texture coordinates are mapped to vertices of shapes. An alternative to using explicit texture coordinates is to generate them using a function; see **SoTextureCoordinateFunction**.

Texture coordinates range from 0 to 1 across the texture. The horizontal coordinate, called S, is specified first, followed by the vertical coordinate, T.

FIELDS

SoMFVec2f   **point**

Texture coordinate points.

METHODS

SoTextureCoordinate2()

Creates a texture coordinate node with default settings.

static SoType   **getClassTypeId()**

Returns type identifier for this class.

Methods from class SoNode:

setOverride, isOverride, copy, affectsState, getByName, getByName

Methods from class SoFieldContainer:

setToDefaults, hasDefaultValues, fieldsAreEqual, copyFieldValues, set, get, getFields, getField, getFieldName, enableNotify, isNotifyEnabled

Methods from class SoBase:

ref, unref, unrefNoDelete, touch, getTypeId, isOfType, setName, getName

ACTION BEHAVIOR

SoGLRenderAction, SoCallbackAction

Sets the current texture coordinates in the state.

SoTextureCoordinate2

FILE FORMAT/DEFAULTS

```
TextureCoordinate2 {
    point   0 0
}
```

INCLUDE FILE

```
#include <Inventor/nodes/SoTextureCoordinate2.h>
```

SEE ALSO

SoTexture2, SoTextureCoordinateBinding, SoTextureCoordinateFunction,
SoVertexShape

NAME

SoTextureCoordinateBinding — node that specifies how texture coordinates are bound to shapes

INHERITS FROM

SoBase > SoFieldContainer > SoNode > SoTextureCoordinateBinding

DESCRIPTION

This node specifies how the current texture coordinates are bound to vertex-based shapes that follow in the scene graph. The DEFAULT binding causes each shape to define its own default coordinates. These default coordinates typically cause a texture to be mapped across the whole surface of a shape.

FIELDS

SoSFEnum **value**

Specifies how to bind texture coordinates to shapes.

METHODS

SoTextureCoordinateBinding()

Creates a texture coordinate binding node with default settings.

static SoType **getClassTypeId**()

Returns type identifier for this class.

Methods from class SoNode:

setOverride, isOverride, copy, affectsState, getByName, getByName

Methods from class SoFieldContainer:

setToDefaults, hasDefaultValues, fieldsAreEqual, copyFieldValues, set, get, getFields, getField, getFieldName, enableNotify, isNotifyEnabled

Methods from class SoBase:

ref, unref, unrefNoDelete, touch, getTypeId, isOfType, setName, getName

ACTION BEHAVIOR

SoGLRenderAction, SoCallbackAction

Sets the current texture coordinate binding type.

FILE FORMAT/DEFAULTS

```
TextureCoordinateBinding {
      value   DEFAULT
}
```

SoTextureCoordinateBinding

INCLUDE FILE

```
#include <Inventor/nodes/SoTextureCoordinateBinding.h>
```

enum **Binding** {

    SoTextureCoordinateBinding::DEFAULT

          Shape defines texture coordinates

    SoTextureCoordinateBinding::PER_VERTEX

          Current texture coordinates are applied sequentially to vertices of shape

    SoTextureCoordinateBinding::PER_VERTEX_INDEXED

          Current texture coordinates are indexed per vertex

}

SEE ALSO

SoMaterialBinding, SoNormalBinding, SoTexture2, SoTexture2Transform, SoTextureCoordinate2, SoTextureCoordinateFunction, SoVertexShape

NAME

SoTextureCoordinateDefault — node that removes texture coordinates from state

INHERITS FROM

SoBase > SoFieldContainer > SoNode > SoTextureCoordinateFunction > SoTextureCoordinateDefault

DESCRIPTION

This node changes the current traversal state to indicate that there are no currently defined texture coordinates or texture coordinate function. This forces subsequent shapes to use their own default texture coordinates. The net result is that this node turns off any previous texture coordinate specification.

METHODS

SoTextureCoordinateDefault()
Creates a node with default settings.

static SoType **getClassTypeId()**
Returns type identifier for this class.

Methods from class SoNode:

setOverride, isOverride, copy, affectsState, getByName, getByName

Methods from class SoFieldContainer:

setToDefaults, hasDefaultValues, fieldsAreEqual, copyFieldValues, set, get, getFields, getField, getFieldName, enableNotify, isNotifyEnabled

Methods from class SoBase:

ref, unref, unrefNoDelete, touch, getTypeId, isOfType, setName, getName

ACTION BEHAVIOR

SoGLRenderAction, SoCallbackAction, SoRayPickAction
Removes any texture coordinates or function.

FILE FORMAT/DEFAULTS

```
TextureCoordinateDefault {
}
```

INCLUDE FILE

```
#include <Inventor/nodes/SoTextureCoordinateDefault.h>
```

SEE ALSO

SoTexture2, SoTexture2Transform, SoTextureCoordinateCube,
SoTextureCoordinateCylinder, SoTextureCoordinateEnvironment,
SoTextureCoordinatePlane, SoTextureCoordinateSphere

NAME

SoTextureCoordinateEnvironment — node that specifies texture coordinates by projection from a environment

INHERITS FROM

SoBase > SoFieldContainer > SoNode > SoTextureCoordinateFunction > SoTextureCoordinateEnvironment

DESCRIPTION

This node creates texture coordinates by projecting points on an object's surface to the interior of a surrounding sphere, along the reflection across the surface normal of the vector from the camera point to the surface. If the current texture image represents a spherical reflection map of the current surrounding environment, subsequent shapes will appear to reflect that environment.

METHODS

SoTextureCoordinateEnvironment()
Creates a texture function node with default settings.

static SoType **getClassTypeId**()
Returns type identifier for this class.

Methods from class SoNode:

setOverride, isOverride, copy, affectsState, getByName, getByName

Methods from class SoFieldContainer:

setToDefaults, hasDefaultValues, fieldsAreEqual, copyFieldValues, set, get, getFields, getField, getFieldName, enableNotify, isNotifyEnabled

Methods from class SoBase:

ref, unref, unrefNoDelete, touch, getTypeId, isOfType, setName, getName

ACTION BEHAVIOR

SoGLRenderAction, SoCallbackAction, SoRayPickAction
Sets the current texture function in the state.

FILE FORMAT/DEFAULTS

```
TextureCoordinateEnvironment {
}
```

INCLUDE FILE

```
#include <Inventor/nodes/SoTextureCoordinateEnvironment.h>
```

SoTextureCoordinateEnvironment

SEE ALSO

SoTexture2, SoTexture2Transform, SoTextureCoordinateCube,
SoTextureCoordinateCylinder, SoTextureCoordinateDefault,
SoTextureCoordinatePlane, SoTextureCoordinateSphere

NAME

SoTextureCoordinateFunction — abstract base class for texture coordinate function nodes

INHERITS FROM

SoBase > SoFieldContainer > SoNode > SoTextureCoordinateFunction

DESCRIPTION

This is an abstract base class for texture coordinate functions. The subclasses of this node enable texture coordinates to be created by mapping object-space points on the surfaces of shapes into texture space, according to some function.

METHODS

static SoType   **getClassTypeId**()
>Returns type identifier for this class.

Methods from class SoNode:

>setOverride, isOverride, copy, affectsState, getByName, getByName

Methods from class SoFieldContainer:

>setToDefaults, hasDefaultValues, fieldsAreEqual, copyFieldValues, set, get, getFields, getField, getFieldName, enableNotify, isNotifyEnabled

Methods from class SoBase:

>ref, unref, unrefNoDelete, touch, getTypeId, isOfType, setName, getName

FILE FORMAT/DEFAULTS

```
TextureCoordinateFunction {
}
```

INCLUDE FILE

```
#include <Inventor/nodes/SoTextureCoordinateFunction.h>
```

SEE ALSO

SoTexture2, SoTexture2Transform SoTextureCoordinate2, SoTextureCoordinateBinding, SoTextureCoordinateCube, SoTextureCoordinateCylinder, SoTextureCoordinateDefault, SoTextureCoordinateEnvironment, SoTextureCoordinatePlane, SoTextureCoordinateSphere,

NAME

SoTextureCoordinatePlane — node that specifies texture coordinates by projection from a plane

INHERITS FROM

SoBase > SoFieldContainer > SoNode > SoTextureCoordinateFunction > SoTextureCoordinatePlane

DESCRIPTION

This node creates texture coordinates for points on an object's surface by projecting them onto a plane. The **directionS** and **directionT** fields define the plane. The S coordinate is computed as the distance from the object-space origin along the vector specified in the **directionS** field. The T coordinate is computed similarly, using the **directionT** field.

The length of the direction vector is also taken into account. For example, assume **directionS** is (0.5, 0, 0) and **directionT** is (0, 1, 0). The square defined by the (x, y, z) vertices:

(-1, -1, 0) (1, -1, 0) (1, 1, 0) (-1, 1, 0)

will be assigned the (s, t) texture coordinates:

(-2, -1) (2, -1) (2, 1) (-2, 1)

FIELDS

SoSFVec3f **directionS**
SoSFVec3f **directionT**
Directions of projection for S and T coordinates.

METHODS

SoTextureCoordinatePlane()
Creates a texture function node with default settings.

static SoType **getClassTypeId()**
Returns type identifier for this class.

Methods from class SoNode:
setOverride, isOverride, copy, affectsState, getByName, getByName

Methods from class SoFieldContainer:

setToDefaults, hasDefaultValues, fieldsAreEqual, copyFieldValues, set, get, getFields, getField, getFieldName, enableNotify, isNotifyEnabled

Methods from class SoBase:

ref, unref, unrefNoDelete, touch, getTypeId, isOfType, setName, getName

ACTION BEHAVIOR

SoGLRenderAction, SoCallbackAction, SoRayPickAction
Sets the current texture function in the state.

FILE FORMAT/DEFAULTS

```
TextureCoordinatePlane {
      directionS  1 0 0
      directionT  0 1 0
}
```

INCLUDE FILE

```
#include <Inventor/nodes/SoTextureCoordinatePlane.h>
```

SEE ALSO

SoTexture2, SoTexture2Transform, SoTextureCoordinateCube, SoTextureCoordinateCylinder, SoTextureCoordinateDefault, SoTextureCoordinateEnvironment, SoTextureCoordinateSphere

SoTimeCounter

NAME

SoTimeCounter — timed integer counter

INHERITS FROM

SoBase > SoFieldContainer > SoEngine > SoTimeCounter

DESCRIPTION

This engine is a counter that outputs numbers, starting at a minimum value, increasing by a step value, and ending with a number that does not exceed the maximum value. When the maximum number is reached, it starts counting from the beginning again.

The difference between this engine and the **SoCounter** engine, is that this engine also has a **timeIn** input, which allows the counting cycles to be timed. This engine counts automatically over time; it does not need to be triggered to go to the next step. By default, the **timeIn** input is connected to the **realTime** global field. It can, however, be connected to any time source.

The **frequency** input field controls how many min-to-max cycles are performed per second. For example, a **frequency** value of 0.5 means that it will take 2 seconds to complete a single min-to-max cycle.

The steps in the count cycle do not necessarily all have the same duration. Using the **duty** input field, you can arbitrarily split the time period of the count cycle between the steps. For example, if there are 5 steps in the cycle, a duty input of (1., 2., 2., 2., 1.) will make the second, third, and fourth steps take twice as long as the first and last steps.

At any time the counter can be reset to a specific value. If you set the **reset** input field to a value, the engine will continue counting from there. Note that the counter will always output numbers based on the **min**, **max** and **step** values, and setting the **reset** value does not affect the those input fields. If the reset value is not a legal counter value, the counter will still behave as though it is:

> If **reset** is greater than **max**, the counter is set to **max**.
> If **reset** is less than **min**, the counter is set to **min**.
> If **reset** is between step values, the counter is set to the lower step.

Each time a counting cycle is started, the **syncOut** output is triggered. This output can be used to synchronize some other event with the counting cycle. Other events can also synchronize the counter by triggering the **syncIn** input.

You can pause the engine, by setting the **on** input to FALSE, and it will stop updating the output field. When you turn off the pause, by setting **on** to TRUE, it will start counting again from where it left off.

INPUTS

SoSFTime **timeIn**
Running time.

SoSFShort **min**
Minimum value for the counter.

SoSFShort **max**
Maximum value for the counter.

SoSFShort **step**
Counter step value.

SoSFBool **on**
Counter pauses if this is set to FALSE.

SoSFFloat **frequency**
Number of **min**-to-**max** cycles per second.

SoMFFloat **duty**
Duty cycle values.

SoSFShort **reset**
Reset the counter to the specified value.

SoSFTrigger **syncIn**
Restart at the beginning of the cycle.

OUTPUTS

(SoSFShort) **output**
Counts **min**-to-**max**, in **step** increments.

(SoSFTrigger) **syncOut**
Triggers at cycle start.

METHODS

SoTimeCounter()
Constructor

Methods from class SoEngine:

getClassTypeId, getOutputs, getOutput, getOutputName, copy, getByName, getByName

Methods from class SoFieldContainer:

setToDefaults, hasDefaultValues, fieldsAreEqual, copyFieldValues, set, get, getFields, getField, getFieldName, enableNotify, isNotifyEnabled

Methods from class SoBase:

ref, unref, unrefNoDelete, touch, getTypeId, isOfType, setName, getName

FILE FORMAT/DEFAULTS

```
TimeCounter {
        min          0
        max          1
        step         1
        on           TRUE
        frequency    1
        duty         1
        timeIn       <current time>
        syncIn
        reset        0
}
```

INCLUDE FILE

```
#include <Inventor/engines/SoTimeCounter.h>
```

SEE ALSO

SoCounter, SoElapsedTime, SoEngineOutput

NAME

SoTimerQueueSensor — abstract base class for sensors dependent on time

INHERITS FROM

SoSensor > SoTimerQueueSensor

DESCRIPTION

Timer queue sensors are sensors that trigger themselves at specific times. The timer queue is normally processed as part of a programs main loop when the program is not busy doing something else. Note that processing the timer queue is not asynchronous — the program must re-enter its main loop for timers to be triggered. When the timer queue is processed, all timers scheduled to go off at or before the current time are triggered once, in order from earliest to latest.

METHODS

const SbTime &   **getTriggerTime()**

Returns the time at which this sensor is scheduled to be triggered. If the sensor is not scheduled the results are undefined.

virtual void   **schedule()**

Adds this sensor to the timer queue. Subclasses provide methods for setting when the sensor will be triggered.

virtual void   **unschedule()**

If this sensor is scheduled, removes it from the timer queue so that it will not be triggered.

virtual SbBool   **isScheduled()**

Returns TRUE if this sensor has been scheduled and is waiting in the timer queue to be triggered.

Methods from class SoSensor:

setFunction, getFunction, setData, getData

INCLUDE FILE

```
#include <Inventor/sensors/SoTimerQueueSensor.h>
```

SEE ALSO

SoTimerSensor, SoAlarmSensor, SoIdleSensor, SoOneShotSensor, SoDataSensor

NAME

SoTimerSensor — sensor that triggers callback repeatedly at regular intervals

INHERITS FROM

SoSensor > SoTimerQueueSensor > SoTimerSensor

DESCRIPTION

Timer sensors trigger their callback function at regular intervals. For example, a timer might be setup to call its callback function every second on the second by setting the base time to **SbTime(0.0)** and the interval to **SbTime(1.0)**. Timers are guaranteed to be triggered only once when the timer queue is processed, so if the application only processes the timer queue once every 5 seconds (because it is busy doing something else) the once-a-second sensor's callback will be called only once every 5 seconds.

Note also that **SoTimers** always schedule themselves to be triggered the next even multiple of the interval time after the base time; so, for example, if the once-a-second sensor is triggered at time 2.9 (because the application way busy doing something at time 2.0 and didn't get around to processing the sensor queue for a while) it will reschedule itself to go off at time 3.0, not at time 3.9. If the base time was never set, the sensor would be scheduled for time 3.9.

METHODS

SoTimerSensor()
SoTimerSensor(SoSensorCB *func, void *data)
Creation methods. The second method takes the callback function and data to be called when the sensor is triggered.

~SoTimerSensor()
Destroys the sensor, freeing up any memory associated with it after unscheduling it.

void	**setBaseTime**(const SbTime &base)
const SbTime &	**getBaseTime**() const
void	**setInterval**(const SbTime &interval)
const SbTime &	**getInterval**() const

Sets/gets the base time and the interval. The default base time is the time when the sensor is scheduled or rescheduled, and the default interval is 1/30th of a second.

Methods from class SoTimerQueueSensor:

getTriggerTime, schedule, unschedule, isScheduled

Methods from class SoSensor:

setFunction, getFunction, setData, getData

INCLUDE FILE

```
#include <Inventor/sensors/SoTimerSensor.h>
```

SEE ALSO

SoOneShotSensor, SoAlarmSensor, SoTimerQueueSensor, SbTime

NAME

SoTrackballDragger — striped ball you can rotate or scale uniformly by dragging with the mouse

INHERITS FROM

SoBase > SoFieldContainer > SoNode > SoBaseKit > SoInteractionKit > SoDragger > SoTrackballDragger

DESCRIPTION

SoTrackballDragger is a ball wrapped in three circular stripes. The stripes are oriented like wheels that spin around the x, y, and z axes. Drag the stripes to rotate the trackball around those axes. You do not have to hit the lines; pick anywhere within the stripe's outline. To rotate the trackball freely in 3 dimensions, click the area between the stripes and then drag. An invisible but pickable sphere initiates this dragging. If the mouse is still moving when you release it, the trackball will continue to spin.

Press the <Alt> key to scale the trackball uniformly instead of rotating.

Press the <Shift> key and the *user axis* appears; this is a draggable axis with an extra stripe around it. Moving the mouse along the surface of the sphere drags the 'pole' of the axis. Release the <Shift> key and the user axis remains; drag the new stripe for constrained rotation around the user axis. To make the user axis disappear, press <Shift> and drag the pole to where two of other stripes intersect. This aligns the user axis with a primary axis, at which point the user axis disappears.

As you drag the trackball, it updates its **rotation** field, or its **scaleFactor** field if the <Alt> key is down. As with all draggers, if you change the fields the dragger moves in response.

Remember: This is *not* an **SoTransform**!. If you want to move other objects with this dragger, you can either:

[a] Use an **SoTrackballManip**, which is subclassed from **SoTransform**. The manipulator creates one of these draggers and uses it as the interface to edit the manipulator's fields. (see the **SoTrackballManip** reference page).

[b] Use field-to-field connections to connect the fields of this dragger to those of any **SoTransformation** node.

You can change the parts in any instance of this dragger using **setPart()**. The default part geometries are defined as resources for this **SoTrackballDragger** class. They are detailed in the Dragger Resources section of the online reference page for this class. You can make your program use different default resources for the parts by copying the file **/usr/share/data/draggerDefaults/trackballDragger.iv** into your own directory, editing the file, and then setting the environment variable **SO_DRAGGER_DIR** to be a path to that directory.

FIELDS

SoSFVec3f   **scaleFactor**
> Scale of the dragger.

SoSFRotation   **rotation**
> Orientation of the dragger.

Fields from class SoDragger:
> isActive

Fields from class SoInteractionKit:
> renderCaching, boundingBoxCaching, renderCulling, pickCulling

PARTS

Parts from class SoBaseKit:
> callbackList

METHODS

> **SoTrackballDragger()**
Constructor.

SbBool   **isAnimationEnabled()**
void   **setAnimationEnabled**(SbBool newVal)
> If the mouse is moving while you release it, the trackball will continue to spin afterwards. These two methods will query and set whether this feature is turned on or off. By default, the animation feature is turned on.

static const SoNodekitCatalog *
> **getClassNodekitCatalog()** const
Returns an **SoNodekitCatalog** for this class

static SoType   **getClassTypeId()**
> Returns type identifier for this class.

Methods from class SoDragger:
> addStartCallback, removeStartCallback, addMotionCallback, removeMotionCallback, addFinishCallback, removeFinishCallback, addValueChangedCallback, removeValueChangedCallback, setMinGesture, getMinGesture, setMinScale, getMinScale

Methods from class SoInteractionKit:

setPartAsPath

Methods from class SoBaseKit:

getNodekitCatalog, getPart, getPartString, createPathToPart, setPart, set, set, isSearchingChildren, setSearchingChildren

Methods from class SoNode:

setOverride, isOverride, copy, affectsState, getByName, getByName

Methods from class SoFieldContainer:

setToDefaults, hasDefaultValues, fieldsAreEqual, copyFieldValues, get, getFields, getField, getFieldName, enableNotify, isNotifyEnabled

Methods from class SoBase:

ref, unref, unrefNoDelete, touch, getTypeId, isOfType, setName, getName

MACROS

Macros from class SoBaseKit:

SO_GET_PART, SO_CHECK_PART

CATALOG PARTS

All parts			NULL by
Part Name	Part Type	Default Type	Default
callbackList	NodeKitListPart	--	yes
surroundScale	SurroundScale	--	yes
antiSquish	AntiSquish	--	no
rotator	Separator	--	yes
rotatorActive	Separator	--	yes
XRotator	Separator	--	yes
XRotatorActive	Separator	--	yes
YRotator	Separator	--	yes
YRotatorActive	Separator	--	yes
ZRotator	Separator	--	yes
ZRotatorActive	Separator	--	yes
userAxis	Separator	--	yes
userAxisActive	Separator	--	yes
userRotator	Separator	--	yes
userRotatorActive	Separator	--	yes

Extra information for list parts from above table		
Part Name	Container Type	Permissible Types
callbackList	Separator	Callback, EventCallback

FILE FORMAT/DEFAULTS

```
TrackballDragger {
        renderCaching      AUTO
        boundingBoxCaching AUTO
        renderCulling      AUTO
        pickCulling        AUTO
        isActive           FALSE
        rotation           0 0 1  0
        scaleFactor        1 1 1
}
```

INCLUDE FILE

```
#include <Inventor/draggers/SoTrackballDragger.h>
```

NOTE

Unlike most multi-function draggers, **SoTrackballDragger** is not a compound dragger made up of other draggers that perform its smaller tasks. This is not because it was inappropriate, but because the trackball was written before implementation of the methods that take care of synchronizing multiple child draggers. The younger **SoCenterballDragger** is similar in form to the trackball, but the centerball *is* a compound dragger.

SEE ALSO

SoInteractionKit, SoDragger, SoCenterballDragger, SoDirectionalLightDragger, SoDragPointDragger, SoHandleBoxDragger, SoJackDragger, SoPointLightDragger, SoRotateCylindricalDragger, SoRotateDiscDragger, SoRotateSphericalDragger, SoScale1Dragger, SoScale2Dragger, SoScale2UniformDragger, SoScaleUniformDragger, SoSpotLightDragger, SoTabBoxDragger, SoTabPlaneDragger, SoTransformBoxDragger, SoTranslate1Dragger, SoTranslate2Dragger

NAME

SoTrackballManip — transform node with 3D interface for changing rotation and scaling

INHERITS FROM

SoBase > SoFieldContainer > SoNode > SoTransformation > SoTransform > SoTransformManip > SoTrackballManip

DESCRIPTION

SoTrackballManip is derived from **SoTransform** (by way of **SoTransformManip**). When its fields change, nodes following it in the scene graph rotate, scale, and/or translate.

As a subclass of **SoTransformManip**, this manipulator also has a 3D interface to edit some of its fields. In this case, the interface edits the **rotation** and **scaleFactor** fields.

A manipulator differs from a dragger. When you move a dragger, no other nodes are affected. When you move an **SoTransformManip**, other nodes move along with it. (See the reference page for **SoTransformManip**).

The interface for an **SoTrackballManip** is exactly the same as that of the **SoTrackballDragger**. To find out more about the interface, see the reference page for **SoTrackballDragger**. To find out how the manipulator uses a dragger to provide its interface, see the reference page for **SoTransformManip**.

On screen, this manipulator will surround the objects influenced by its motion. This is because it turns on the *surroundScale* part of the dragger (See the reference page for **SoSurroundScale**)

FIELDS

Fields from class SoTransform:

translation, rotation, scaleFactor, scaleOrientation, center

METHODS

SoTrackballManip()
Constructor.

static SoType **getClassTypeId()**
Returns type identifier for this class.

Methods from class SoTransformManip:

getDragger, replaceNode, replaceManip

Methods from class SoTransform:

pointAt, getScaleSpaceMatrix, getRotationSpaceMatrix, getTranslationSpaceMatrix, multLeft, multRight, combineLeft, combineRight, setMatrix, recenter

Methods from class SoNode:

setOverride, isOverride, copy, affectsState, getByName, getByName

Methods from class SoFieldContainer:

setToDefaults, hasDefaultValues, fieldsAreEqual, copyFieldValues, set, get, getFields, getField, getFieldName, enableNotify, isNotifyEnabled

Methods from class SoBase:

ref, unref, unrefNoDelete, touch, getTypeId, isOfType, setName, getName

FILE FORMAT/DEFAULTS

```
TrackballManip {
        translation       0 0 0
        rotation          0 0 1  0
        scaleFactor       1 1 1
        scaleOrientation  0 0 1  0
        center            0 0 0
}
```

INCLUDE FILE

```
#include <Inventor/manips/SoTrackballManip.h>
```

SEE ALSO

SoCenterballManip, SoHandleBoxManip, SoJackManip, SoTabBoxManip, SoTrackballDragger, SoTransformBoxManip, SoTransform, SoTransformManip

NAME

SoTranReceiver — interprets database changes for transcription

INHERITS FROM

SoTranReceiver

DESCRIPTION

This class is used for transcribing Inventor data. Transcription is the process of packaging changes to a database and sending them over a "wire" to another database.

The **SoTranReceiver** class is used on the receiving side of transcription. It interprets changes to a Inventor database packaged up by an **SoTranSender**.

METHODS

SoTranReceiver(SoGroup *rootNode)
The constructor takes a pointer to an SoGroup instance that is the root node of the scene graph on the receiving end. All changes to the database are made relative to this root.

~SoTranReceiver()
Destructor.

SbBool   **interpret**(SoInput *in)
Interprets the transcription commands found in the given input stream. Returns FALSE on any error. Note: some errors (such as invalid node references) are recoverable, while others (such as syntax errors) are not.

INCLUDE FILE

```
#include <Inventor/misc/SoTranscribe.h>
```

SEE ALSO

SoInput, SoTranSender

NAME

SoTranSender — sends database changes for transcription

INHERITS FROM

SoTranSender

DESCRIPTION

This class is used for transcribing Inventor data. Transcription is the process of packaging changes to a database and sending them over a "wire" to another database.

The **SoTranSender** class is used on the sending side of transcription. It packages up changes to a Inventor database into a file or memory area defined by an **SoOutput** instance. It supports a limited set of changes to a database; each change is stored as a command in the transcription area. The **SoTranReceiver** class can be used at the other end to interpret the transcribed commands.

METHODS

SoTranSender(SoOutput *output)
The constructor takes a pointer to an **SoOutput** instance that determines what the transcription area is (file or memory).

~**SoTranSender**()
Destructor.

SoOutput *   **getOutput**() const
Returns pointer to current **SoOutput** instance.

void   **insert**(SoNode *node)
Adds an INSERT command to the transcription area. The given node will be added as the last child of the root node on the receiving end.

void   **insert**(SoNode *node, SoNode *parent, int n)
Adds an INSERT command to the transcription area. The given node will be added as the *n*th child of the given parent node on the receiving end. A NULL parent node causes the node to be added to the receiving end's root node.

void   **remove**(SoNode *parent, int n)
Adds a REMOVE command to the transcription area. The *n*th child of the given (non-NULL) parent node on the receiving end will be removed.

void   **replace**(SoNode *parent, int n, SoNode *newNode)
Adds a REPLACE command to the transcription area. The *n*th child of the
given (non-NULL) parent node on the receiving end will be replaced with
newNode.

void   **modify**(SoNode *node)
Adds a MODIFY command to the transcription area. Updates the field data
for the given node to the new contents. Note that this changes only field
data; children of groups are not affected, nor is any non-field instance data.

void   **prepareToSend**()
Prepares a **SoTranSender** instance for transcription, making sure the
transcription area is complete and all packaged to go. This must be called
before the transcription can be performed.

INCLUDE FILE
```
#include <Inventor/misc/SoTranscribe.h>
```

SEE ALSO
SoOutput, SoTranReceiver

NAME

SoTransform — general 3D geometric transformation node

INHERITS FROM

SoBase > SoFieldContainer > SoNode > SoTransformation > SoTransform

DESCRIPTION

This node defines a geometric 3D transformation consisting of (in order) a (possibly) non-uniform scale about an arbitrary point, a rotation about an arbitrary point and axis, and a translation. (While the transformations can be thought of as being applied in that order, matrices are actually premultiplied in the opposite order. Therefore, the operations are listed in the reverse order throughout this reference page.)

FIELDS

SoSFVec3f **translation**
Translation vector.

SoSFRotation **rotation**
Rotation specification.

SoSFVec3f **scaleFactor**
Scale factors.

SoSFRotation **scaleOrientation**
Rotational orientation for scale.

SoSFVec3f **center**
Origin for scale and rotation.

METHODS

SoTransform()
Creates a transformation node with default settings.

void **pointAt**(const SbVec3f &fromPoint, const SbVec3f &toPoint)
Sets the node to translate the origin to the **fromPoint** and rotate the negative z-axis (0,0,-1) to lie on the vector from **fromPoint** to **toPoint**. This always tries to keep the "up" direction the positive y-axis, unless that is impossible. All current field values in the node are replaced.

void	**getScaleSpaceMatrix**(SbMatrix &mat, SbMatrix &inv) const
void	**getRotationSpaceMatrix**(SbMatrix &mat, SbMatrix &inv) const
void	**getTranslationSpaceMatrix**(SbMatrix &mat, SbMatrix &inv) const

These return composite matrices that transform from object space to each of the spaces after the scale, rotation, or translation.

void	**multLeft**(const SbMatrix &mat)
void	**multRight**(const SbMatrix &mat)

These are convenience functions that combine the effects of a matrix transformation into the current transformation stored in this node. The first method premultiplies the transformation and the second postmultiplies it.

void	**combineLeft**(SoTransformation *nodeOnLeft)
void	**combineRight**(SoTransformation *nodeOnRight)

These are convenience functions that combine the effects of another transformation node into the current transformation stored in this node. The first method premultiplies the transformation and the second postmultiplies it.

void	**setMatrix**(const SbMatrix &mat)

Sets the fields in the node to implement the transformation represented by the given matrix. Note that invalid matrices (such as singular ones) have undefined results.

void	**recenter**(const SbVec3f &newCenter)

Changes the center of the transformation to the given point without affecting the overall effect of the transformation.

static SoType	**getClassTypeId**()

Returns type identifier for this class.

Methods from class SoNode:

setOverride, isOverride, copy, affectsState, getByName, getByName

Methods from class SoFieldContainer:

setToDefaults, hasDefaultValues, fieldsAreEqual, copyFieldValues, set, get, getFields, getField, getFieldName, enableNotify, isNotifyEnabled

Methods from class SoBase:

ref, unref, unrefNoDelete, touch, getTypeId, isOfType, setName, getName

SoTransform

ACTION BEHAVIOR

**SoGLRenderAction, SoCallbackAction, SoGetBoundingBoxAction,
SoRayPickAction**

Accumulates transformation into the current transformation.

SoGetMatrixAction

Returns the matrix corresponding to the total transformation.

FILE FORMAT/DEFAULTS

```
Transform {
        translation       0 0 0
        rotation          0 0 1  0
        scaleFactor       1 1 1
        scaleOrientation  0 0 1  0
        center            0 0 0
}
```

INCLUDE FILE

```
#include <Inventor/nodes/SoTransform.h>
```

SEE ALSO

SoMatrixTransform, SoResetTransform, SoRotation, SoRotationXYZ, SoScale,
SoTransformManip, SoTransformSeparator, SoTranslation

NAME

SoTransformation — Abstract base class for all geometric transformation nodes

INHERITS FROM

SoBase > SoFieldContainer > SoNode > SoTransformation

DESCRIPTION

This is the abstract base class for all nodes that perform geometric transformations. It exists only to make it easy for applications to test whether a particular node is a transformation node (that is, is derived from this class).

METHODS

static SoType   **getClassTypeId**()
    Returns type identifier for this class.

Methods from class SoNode:

setOverride, isOverride, copy, affectsState, getByName, getByName

Methods from class SoFieldContainer:

setToDefaults, hasDefaultValues, fieldsAreEqual, copyFieldValues, set, get, getFields, getField, getFieldName, enableNotify, isNotifyEnabled

Methods from class SoBase:

ref, unref, unrefNoDelete, touch, getTypeId, isOfType, setName, getName

FILE FORMAT/DEFAULTS

This is an abstract class. See the reference page of a derived class for the format and default values.

INCLUDE FILE

```
#include <Inventor/nodes/SoTransformation.h>
```

SEE ALSO

SoAntiSquish, SoMatrixTransform, SoResetTransform, SoRotation, SoRotationXYZ, SoScale, SoSurroundScale, SoTransform, SoTransformManip, SoTransformSeparator, SoTranslation SoUnits

NAME

SoTransformBoxDragger — box-like object you scale, rotate, and translate by dragging with the mouse

INHERITS FROM

SoBase > SoFieldContainer > SoNode > SoBaseKit > SoInteractionKit > SoDragger > SoTransformBoxDragger

DESCRIPTION

SoTransformBoxDragger is a composite dragger shaped like a box with small cubes at the corners. Click and drag any of these cubes to scale the box uniformly. Drag any edge of the box to rotate the whole dragger about its center, along an axis parallel to that edge. Pick any face of the box for 2D translation in the plane of that face.

Although the box looks just about like a wireframe cube, it is composed of many different simple draggers arranged in a composite assembly. When one part is dragged, the transformBox makes sure they all move together. Each of the parts of the box is a different dragger with the default geometry changed. The faces of the box are **SoTranslate2Draggers**, the edges are **SoRotateCylindricalDraggers**, and the cubes are an **SoScaleUniformDragger**. Drag them and the dragger will update its **translation**, **rotation** and **scaleFactor** fields to reflect the changes. As with all draggers, if you change the fields the dragger will move to match the new settings.

Remember: This is *not* an **SoTransform**!. If you want to move other objects with this dragger, you can either:

[a] Use an **SoTransformBoxManip**, which is subclassed from **SoTransform**. It creates one of these draggers and uses it as the interface to change its fields. (see the **SoTransformBoxManip** man page).

[b] Use field-to-field connections to connect the fields of this dragger to those of any **SoTransformation** node.

You can change the parts in any instance of this dragger using **setPart()**. The default part geometries are defined as resources for this **SoTransformBoxDragger** class. They are detailed in the Dragger Resources section of the online reference page for this class. You can make your program use different default resources for the parts by copying the file **/usr/share/data/draggerDefaults/transformBoxDragger.iv** into your own directory, editing the file, and then setting the environment variable **SO_DRAGGER_DIR** to be a path to that directory.

FIELDS

SoSFRotation **rotation**
Orientation of the dragger.

SoSFVec3f **translation**
Position of the dragger.

SoSFVec3f **scaleFactor**
Scale of the dragger.

Fields from class SoDragger:
isActive

Fields from class SoInteractionKit:
renderCaching, boundingBoxCaching, renderCulling, pickCulling

PARTS

Parts from class SoBaseKit:
callbackList

METHODS

SoTransformBoxDragger()
Constructor.

static const SoNodekitCatalog *
getClassNodekitCatalog() const
Returns an **SoNodekitCatalog** for this class

static SoType **getClassTypeId()**
Returns type identifier for this class.

Methods from class SoDragger:
addStartCallback, removeStartCallback, addMotionCallback,
removeMotionCallback, addFinishCallback, removeFinishCallback,
addValueChangedCallback, removeValueChangedCallback, setMinGesture,
getMinGesture, setMinScale, getMinScale

Methods from class SoInteractionKit:
setPartAsPath

Methods from class SoBaseKit:

getNodekitCatalog, getPart, getPartString, createPathToPart, setPart, set, set, isSearchingChildren, setSearchingChildren

Methods from class SoNode:

setOverride, isOverride, copy, affectsState, getByName, getByName

Methods from class SoFieldContainer:

setToDefaults, hasDefaultValues, fieldsAreEqual, copyFieldValues, get, getFields, getField, getFieldName, enableNotify, isNotifyEnabled

Methods from class SoBase:

ref, unref, unrefNoDelete, touch, getTypeId, isOfType, setName, getName

MACROS

Macros from class SoBaseKit:

SO_GET_PART, SO_CHECK_PART

CATALOG PARTS

All parts			
Part Name	**Part Type**	**Default Type**	**NULL by Default**
callbackList	NodeKitListPart	--	yes
surroundScale	SurroundScale	--	yes
antiSquish	AntiSquish	--	no
scaler	ScaleUniformDragger	--	yes
rotator1	RotateCylindricalDragger	--	yes
rotator2	RotateCylindricalDragger	--	yes
rotator3	RotateCylindricalDragger	--	yes
translator1	Translate2Dragger	--	yes
translator2	Translate2Dragger	--	yes
translator3	Translate2Dragger	--	yes
translator4	Translate2Dragger	--	yes
translator5	Translate2Dragger	--	yes
translator6	Translate2Dragger	--	yes

Extra information for list parts from above table		
Part Name	**Container Type**	**Permissible Types**
callbackList	Separator	Callback, EventCallback

FILE FORMAT/DEFAULTS

```
TransformBoxDragger {
        renderCaching        AUTO
        boundingBoxCaching   AUTO
        renderCulling        AUTO
        pickCulling          AUTO
        isActive             FALSE
        rotation             0 0 1  0
        translation          0 0 0
        scaleFactor          1 1 1
}
```

INCLUDE FILE

```
#include <Inventor/draggers/SoTransformBoxDragger.h>
```

SEE ALSO

SoInteractionKit, SoDragger, SoCenterballDragger, SoDirectionalLightDragger,
SoDragPointDragger, SoHandleBoxDragger, SoJackDragger, SoPointLightDragger,
SoRotateCylindricalDragger, SoRotateDiscDragger, SoRotateSphericalDragger,
SoScale1Dragger, SoScale2Dragger, SoScale2UniformDragger,
SoScaleUniformDragger, SoSpotLightDragger, SoTabBoxDragger, SoTabPlaneDragger,
SoTrackballDragger, SoTranslate1Dragger, SoTranslate2Dragger

SoTransformBoxManip

NAME

SoTransformBoxManip — transform node with 3D interface for changing scaling, rotation, and translation

INHERITS FROM

SoBase > SoFieldContainer > SoNode > SoTransformation > SoTransform > SoTransformManip > SoTransformBoxManip

DESCRIPTION

SoTransformBoxManip is derived from **SoTransform** (by way of **SoTransformManip**). When its fields change, nodes following it in the scene graph rotate, scale, and/or translate.

As a subclass of **SoTransformManip**, this manipulator also has a 3D interface to edit some of its fields. In this case, the interface edits the **scaleFactor**, **rotation** and **translation** fields.

A manipulator differs from a dragger. When you move a dragger, no other nodes are affected. When you move an **SoTransformManip**, other nodes move along with it. (See the reference page for **SoTransformManip**).

The interface for an **SoTransformBoxManip** is exactly the same as that of the **SoTransformBoxDragger**. To find out more about the interface, see the reference page for **SoTransformBoxDragger**. To find out how the manipulator uses a dragger to provide its interface, see the reference page for **SoTransformManip**.

On screen, this manipulator will surround the objects influenced by its motion. This is because it turns on the *surroundScale* part of the dragger (See the reference page for **SoSurroundScale**)

FIELDS

Fields from class SoTransform:

translation, rotation, scaleFactor, scaleOrientation, center

METHODS

SoTransformBoxManip()
Constructor.

static SoType   **getClassTypeId**()
Returns type identifier for this class.

Methods from class SoTransformManip:

getDragger, replaceNode, replaceManip

Methods from class SoTransform:

pointAt, getScaleSpaceMatrix, getRotationSpaceMatrix, getTranslationSpaceMatrix, multLeft, multRight, combineLeft, combineRight, setMatrix, recenter

Methods from class SoNode:

setOverride, isOverride, copy, affectsState, getByName, getByName

Methods from class SoFieldContainer:

setToDefaults, hasDefaultValues, fieldsAreEqual, copyFieldValues, set, get, getFields, getField, getFieldName, enableNotify, isNotifyEnabled

Methods from class SoBase:

ref, unref, unrefNoDelete, touch, getTypeId, isOfType, setName, getName

FILE FORMAT/DEFAULTS

```
TransformBoxManip {
        translation       0 0 0
        rotation          0 0 1 0
        scaleFactor       1 1 1
        scaleOrientation  0 0 1 0
        center            0 0 0
}
```

INCLUDE FILE

```
#include <Inventor/manips/SoTransformBoxManip.h>
```

SEE ALSO

SoCenterballManip, SoHandleBoxManip, SoJackManip, SoTabBoxManip, SoTrackballManip, SoTransform, SoTransformBoxDragger, SoTransformManip

NAME

SoTransformManip — base class for all transform Nodes with built-in 3D user interfaces

INHERITS FROM

SoBase > SoFieldContainer > SoNode > SoTransformation > SoTransform > SoTransformManip

DESCRIPTION

SoTransformManip is the base class for all **SoTransform** nodes that have a built-in 3D user interface. Since it is derived from **SoTransform**, any changes to its fields result in the rotation, scaling, and/or translation of nodes that follow it in the scene graph.

Typically, you will want to replace a regular **SoTransform** with an **SoTransformManip** (as when the user selects an object to be moved), or vice versa (as when the object is deselected, and the motion interface should go away). Use the **replaceNode()** method to insert a manipulator into a scene graph, and the **replaceManip()** method to remove it when done.

Every subclass of **SoTransformManip** utilizes a dragger of some sort to provide a 3D interface. (This class does not have dragger; but all the subclasses do.) However a manipulator differs from a dragger; it influences other objects in the scene because, as an **SoTransform**, it alters the state. The fields values and movement of a dragger, on the other hand, affect only the dragger itself.

Each **SoTransformManip** subclass utilizes its dragger by adding it as a hidden child. When an action is applied to the manipulator, such as rendering or handling events, the manipulator first traverses the dragger, and then the manipulator adds its transformation matrix to the state. When you click-drag-release over the manipulator, it passes these events down to the dragger, which moves as a result ("I can't *help* it, I'm a dragger!").

The manipulator maintains consistency between the fields of the dragger and its own fields. Let's say you use the mouse to rotate the *dragger*. Callbacks insure that the **rotation** field of the *manipulator* will change by the same amount, resulting in the rotation of nodes which follow in the scene graph. Similarly, if you set any of the **SoTransformManip** fields the manipulator will move the dragger accordingly. You can use this feature to impose constraints on a manipulator: If the user moves the manipulator so that a field value becomes too large, you can set the field back to your desired maximum, and the whole thing will move back to where you specified.

Since each **SoTransformManip** uses a dragger to provide its interface, you will generally be told to look at the dragger's reference page for details of how it moves and what the different parts are for. The interface for the dragger and the manipulator will always be exactly the same. Usually, a **SoTransformManip** will surround the objects that it influences (i.e., those that move along with it). This is because the manipulator turns on the *surroundScale* part of its dragger; so the dragger geometry expands to envelope the other objects (see the reference page for **SoSurroundScale**).

Because the dragger is a *hidden* child, you can see the dragger on screen and interact with it, but the dragger does not show up when you write the manipulator to file. Also, any **SoPath** will end at the manipulator. (See the Actions section of this reference page for a complete description of when the dragger is traversed).

If you want to get a pointer to the dragger you can get it from the manipulator using the **getDragger()** method. You will need to do this if you want to change the geometry of a manipulator, since the geometry actually belongs to the dragger.

FIELDS

Fields from class SoTransform:

translation, rotation, scaleFactor, scaleOrientation, center

METHODS

SoTransformManip()

Constructor.

SoDragger *   getDragger()

Returns a pointer to the dragger being used by this manipulator. Given this pointer, you can customize the dragger just like you would any other dragger. You can change geometry using the **setPart()** method, or add callbacks using the methods found in the **SoDragger** reference page.

SbBool   replaceNode(SoPath *p)

Replaces the tail of the path with this manipulator. The tail of the path must be an **SoTransform** node (or subclass thereof). If the path has a nodekit, this will try to use **setPart()** to insert the manipulator. Otherwise, the manipulator requires that the next to last node in the path chain be a group.

The field values from the transform node will be copied to this manipulator, and the transform will be replaced.

The manipulator will not call **ref()** on the node it is replacing. The old node will disappear if it has no references other than from the input path *p* and its parent, since this manipulator will be replacing it in both of those places. Nor will the manipulator make any changes to field connections of the old node. The calling process is thus responsible for keeping track of its own nodes and field connections.

SbBool **replaceManip**(SoPath *p, SoTransform *newOne) const
Replaces the tail of the path, which must be this manipulator, with the given **SoTransform** node. If the path has a nodekit, this will try to use **setPart**() to insert the new node. Otherwise, the manipulator requires that the next to last node in the path chain be a group.

The field values from the manipulator will be copied to the transform node, and the manipulator will be replaced.

The manipulator will not call **ref**() or **unref**() on the node which is replacing it, nor will it make any changes to field connections. The calling process is thus responsible for keeping track of its own nodes and field connections.

static SoType **getClassTypeId**()
Returns type identifier for this class.

Methods from class SoTransform:

pointAt, getScaleSpaceMatrix, getRotationSpaceMatrix, getTranslationSpaceMatrix, multLeft, multRight, combineLeft, combineRight, setMatrix, recenter

Methods from class SoNode:

setOverride, isOverride, copy, affectsState, getByName, getByName

Methods from class SoFieldContainer:

setToDefaults, hasDefaultValues, fieldsAreEqual, copyFieldValues, set, get, getFields, getField, getFieldName, enableNotify, isNotifyEnabled

Methods from class SoBase:

ref, unref, unrefNoDelete, touch, getTypeId, isOfType, setName, getName

ACTION BEHAVIOR

SoGLRenderAction, SoCallbackAction, SoGetBoundingBoxAction, SoGetMatrixAction, SoHandleEventAction, SoRayPickAction
First, traverses the dragger the way an **SoGroup** would. All draggers place themselves in space, but leave the current transformation unchanged when finished. Then the **SoTransformManip** accumulates a transformation into the current transformation just like its base class, **SoTransform**.

SoSearchAction

Searches just like an **SoTransform**. Does not search the dragger, which is a hidden child.

SoWriteAction

Writes out just like an **SoTransform**. Does not write the dragger, which is a hidden child. If you really need to write valuable information about the dragger, such as customized geometry, you can retrieve the dragger with the **getDragger()** method and then write it out separately.

FILE FORMAT/DEFAULTS

```
TransformManip {
        translation        0 0 0
        rotation           0 0 1  0
        scaleFactor        1 1 1
        scaleOrientation   0 0 1  0
        center             0 0 0
}
```

INCLUDE FILE

```
#include <Inventor/manips/SoTransformManip.h>
```

SEE ALSO

SoDragger, SoTransform, SoCenterballManip, SoHandleBoxManip, SoJackManip, SoSurroundScale, SoTabBoxManip, SoTrackballManip, SoTransformBoxManip

NAME

SoTransformSeparator — group node that saves and restores transformation state

INHERITS FROM

SoBase > SoFieldContainer > SoNode > SoGroup > SoTransformSeparator

DESCRIPTION

This group node is similar to the **SoSeparator** node in that it saves state before traversing its children and restores it afterwards. However, it saves only the current transformation; all other state is left as is. This node can be useful for positioning a camera, since the transformations to the camera will not affect the rest of the scene, even through the camera will view the scene. Similarly, this node can be used to isolate transformations to light sources or other objects.

METHODS

SoTransformSeparator()
Creates a transform separator node with default settings.

SoTransformSeparator(int nChildren)
Constructor that takes approximate number of children.

static SoType   **getClassTypeId**()
Returns type identifier for this class.

Methods from class SoGroup:

addChild, insertChild, getChild, findChild, getNumChildren, removeChild, removeChild, removeAllChildren, replaceChild, replaceChild

Methods from class SoNode:

setOverride, isOverride, copy, affectsState, getByName, getByName

Methods from class SoFieldContainer:

setToDefaults, hasDefaultValues, fieldsAreEqual, copyFieldValues, set, get, getFields, getField, getFieldName, enableNotify, isNotifyEnabled

Methods from class SoBase:

ref, unref, unrefNoDelete, touch, getTypeId, isOfType, setName, getName

ACTION BEHAVIOR

SoGLRenderAction, SoCallbackAction, SoGetBoundingBoxAction, SoGetMatrixAction, SoRayPickAction

Saves the current transformation state, traverses all children, and restores the previous transformation state.

FILE FORMAT/DEFAULTS

```
TransformSeparator {
}
```

INCLUDE FILE

```
#include <Inventor/nodes/SoTransformSeparator.h>
```

SEE ALSO

SoResetTransform, SoTransformation

NAME

SoTransformVec3f — transforms a 3D vector by a 4x4 matrix

INHERITS FROM

SoBase > SoFieldContainer > SoEngine > SoTransformVec3f

DESCRIPTION

This engine takes as input a three dimensional floating-point vector and a transformation matrix. The vector is assumed to be a row vector.

The engine multiplies the vector by the matrix and returns the result in the output **point**. The output **direction** contains the result when the matrix multiplication assumes the vector is a direction, and therefore ignores the translation part of the matrix. The output **normalDirection** contains the normalized **direction**

INPUTS

SoMFVec3f **vector**
Input row vector.

SoMFMatrix **matrix**
Input transformation matrix.

OUTPUTS

(SoMFVec3f) **point**
Vector transformed by matrix.

(SoMFVec3f) **direction**
Vector transformed by matrix, ignoring translation.

(SoMFVec3f) **normalDirection**
Normalized direction.

METHODS

SoTransformVec3f()
Constructor

Methods from class SoEngine:

getClassTypeId, getOutputs, getOutput, getOutputName, copy, getByName, getByName

Methods from class SoFieldContainer:

setToDefaults, hasDefaultValues, fieldsAreEqual, copyFieldValues, set, get, getFields, getField, getFieldName, enableNotify, isNotifyEnabled

Methods from class SoBase:

    ref, unref, unrefNoDelete, touch, getTypeId, isOfType, setName, getName

FILE FORMAT/DEFAULTS

```
TransformVec3f {
      vector  0 0 0
      matrix  1 0 0 0
              0 1 0 0
              0 0 1 0
              0 0 0 1
}
```

INCLUDE FILE

```
#include <Inventor/engines/SoTransformVec3f.h>
```

SEE ALSO

    SoEngineOutput

NAME

SoTranslate1Dragger — object you can translate along a line by dragging With the mouse

INHERITS FROM

SoBase > SoFieldContainer > SoNode > SoBaseKit > SoInteractionKit > SoDragger > SoTranslate1Dragger

DESCRIPTION

SoTranslate1Dragger is a simple dragger that translates in one dimension when dragged with the mouse. It moves along the x axis of its local space, determined by its location in the scene graph. Transformation nodes placed before it will affect both the dragger and the direction of motion.

This node has a **translation** field which always reflects its position in local space. If you set the field, the dragger will move accordingly. You can also connect fields of other nodes or engines from this one to make them follow the dragger's motion.

This dragger contains four parts, *translator*, *translatorActive*, *feedback*, and *feedbackActive*.

Each of these is set by default from a resource described in the Dragger Resources section of the online reference page for this class. You can change the parts in any instance of this dragger using **setPart()**.

You can make your program use different default resources for the parts by copying the file **/usr/share/data/draggerDefaults/translate1Dragger.iv** into your own directory, editing the file, and then setting the environment variable **SO_DRAGGER_DIR** to be a path to that directory.

FIELDS

SoSFVec3f   **translation**
    Position of the dragger.

Fields from class SoDragger:
    isActive

Fields from class SoInteractionKit:
    renderCaching, boundingBoxCaching, renderCulling, pickCulling

PARTS

Parts from class SoBaseKit:
    callbackList

METHODS

SoTranslate1Dragger()
Constructor.

static const SoNodekitCatalog *
getClassNodekitCatalog() const
Returns an **SoNodekitCatalog** for this class

static SoType   **getClassTypeId()**
Returns type identifier for this class.

Methods from class SoDragger:

addStartCallback, removeStartCallback, addMotionCallback, removeMotionCallback, addFinishCallback, removeFinishCallback, addValueChangedCallback, removeValueChangedCallback, setMinGesture, getMinGesture, setMinScale, getMinScale

Methods from class SoInteractionKit:

setPartAsPath

Methods from class SoBaseKit:

getNodekitCatalog, getPart, getPartString, createPathToPart, setPart, set, set, isSearchingChildren, setSearchingChildren

Methods from class SoNode:

setOverride, isOverride, copy, affectsState, getByName, getByName

Methods from class SoFieldContainer:

setToDefaults, hasDefaultValues, fieldsAreEqual, copyFieldValues, get, getFields, getField, getFieldName, enableNotify, isNotifyEnabled

Methods from class SoBase:

ref, unref, unrefNoDelete, touch, getTypeId, isOfType, setName, getName

MACROS
Macros from class SoBaseKit:

SO_GET_PART, SO_CHECK_PART

CATALOG PARTS

All parts			
Part Name	Part Type	Default Type	NULL by Default
callbackList	NodeKitListPart	--	yes
translator	Separator	--	yes
translatorActive	Separator	--	yes
feedback	Separator	--	yes
feedbackActive	Separator	--	yes

Extra information for list parts from above table		
Part Name	Container Type	Permissible Types
callbackList	Separator	Callback, EventCallback

FILE FORMAT/DEFAULTS

```
Translate1Dragger {
        renderCaching        AUTO
        boundingBoxCaching   AUTO
        renderCulling        AUTO
        pickCulling          AUTO
        isActive             FALSE
        translation          0 0 0
}
```

INCLUDE FILE

```
#include <Inventor/draggers/SoTranslate1Dragger.h>
```

SEE ALSO

SoInteractionKit, SoDragger, SoCenterballDragger, SoDirectionalLightDragger, SoDragPointDragger, SoHandleBoxDragger, SoJackDragger, SoPointLightDragger, SoRotateCylindricalDragger, SoRotateDiscDragger, SoRotateSphericalDragger, SoScale1Dragger, SoScale2Dragger, SoScale2UniformDragger, SoScaleUniformDragger, SoSpotLightDragger, SoTabBoxDragger, SoTabPlaneDragger, SoTrackballDragger, SoTransformBoxDragger, SoTranslate2Dragger

NAME

SoTranslate2Dragger — object you can translate within a plane by dragging with the mouse

INHERITS FROM

SoBase > SoFieldContainer > SoNode > SoBaseKit > SoInteractionKit > SoDragger > SoTranslate2Dragger

DESCRIPTION

SoTranslate2Dragger is a simple dragger that translates in two dimensions when dragged with the mouse. It moves within the x-y plane of its local space, determined by its location in the scene graph. Transformation nodes placed before it will affect both the dragger and the direction of motion.

Pressing the <Shift> key allows you to constrain motion to either the x axis or the y axis. The direction is determined by your initial mouse gesture after pressing the key. Releasing the key removes the constraint.

This node has a **translation** field which always reflects its position in local space. If you set the field, the dragger will move accordingly. You can also connect fields of other nodes or engines from this one to make them follow the dragger's motion.

This dragger contains six parts, *translator*, *translatorActive*, *feedback*, *feedbackActive*, *xAxisFeedback*, and *yAxisFeedback*. The last two parts are only displayed during motion, and only when their direction of motion is enabled. (Pressing the <Shift> key and then dragging disables one of the two directions.)

Each of these is set by default from a resource described in the Dragger Resources section of the online reference page for this class. You can change the parts in any instance of this dragger using **setPart()**.

You can make your program use different default resources for the parts by copying the file **/usr/share/data/draggerDefaults/translate2Dragger.iv** into your own directory, editing the file, and then setting the environment variable **SO_DRAGGER_DIR** to be a path to that directory.

FIELDS

SoSFVec3f   **translation**
> Position of the dragger.

Fields from class SoDragger:
> isActive

Fields from class SoInteractionKit:
> renderCaching, boundingBoxCaching, renderCulling, pickCulling

PARTS

Parts from class SoBaseKit:

callbackList

METHODS

SoTranslate2Dragger()
Constructor.

static const SoNodekitCatalog *
getClassNodekitCatalog() const
Returns an **SoNodekitCatalog** for this class

static SoType   **getClassTypeId**()
Returns type identifier for this class.

Methods from class SoDragger:

addStartCallback, removeStartCallback, addMotionCallback,
removeMotionCallback, addFinishCallback, removeFinishCallback,
addValueChangedCallback, removeValueChangedCallback, setMinGesture,
getMinGesture, setMinScale, getMinScale

Methods from class SoInteractionKit:

setPartAsPath

Methods from class SoBaseKit:

getNodekitCatalog, getPart, getPartString, createPathToPart, setPart, set, set,
isSearchingChildren, setSearchingChildren

Methods from class SoNode:

setOverride, isOverride, copy, affectsState, getByName, getByName

Methods from class SoFieldContainer:

setToDefaults, hasDefaultValues, fieldsAreEqual, copyFieldValues, get,
getFields, getField, getFieldName, enableNotify, isNotifyEnabled

Methods from class SoBase:

ref, unref, unrefNoDelete, touch, getTypeId, isOfType, setName, getName

MACROS

Macros from class SoBaseKit:

SO_GET_PART, SO_CHECK_PART

CATALOG PARTS

All parts			
Part Name	Part Type	Default Type	NULL by Default
callbackList	NodeKitListPart	--	yes
translator	Separator	--	yes
translatorActive	Separator	--	yes
feedback	Separator	--	yes
feedbackActive	Separator	--	yes
xAxisFeedback	Separator	--	yes
yAxisFeedback	Separator	--	yes

Extra information for list parts from above table		
Part Name	Container Type	Permissible Types
callbackList	Separator	Callback, EventCallback

FILE FORMAT/DEFAULTS

```
Translate2Dragger {
        renderCaching      AUTO
        boundingBoxCaching AUTO
        renderCulling      AUTO
        pickCulling        AUTO
        isActive           FALSE
        translation        0 0 0
}
```

INCLUDE FILE

```
#include <Inventor/draggers/SoTranslate2Dragger.h>
```

SEE ALSO

SoInteractionKit, SoDragger, SoCenterballDragger, SoDirectionalLightDragger, SoDragPointDragger, SoHandleBoxDragger, SoJackDragger, SoPointLightDragger, SoRotateCylindricalDragger, SoRotateDiscDragger, SoRotateSphericalDragger, SoScale1Dragger, SoScale2Dragger, SoScale2UniformDragger, SoScaleUniformDragger, SoSpotLightDragger, SoTabBoxDragger, SoTabPlaneDragger, SoTrackballDragger, SoTransformBoxDragger, SoTranslate1Dragger

NAME

SoTranslation — node representing a 3D translation

INHERITS FROM

SoBase > SoFieldContainer > SoNode > SoTransformation > SoTranslation

DESCRIPTION

This node defines a translation by a 3D vector.

FIELDS

SoSFVec3f **translation**
Translation vector.

METHODS

SoTranslation()
Creates a translation node with default settings.

static SoType **getClassTypeId()**
Returns type identifier for this class.

Methods from class SoNode:

setOverride, isOverride, copy, affectsState, getByName, getByName

Methods from class SoFieldContainer:

setToDefaults, hasDefaultValues, fieldsAreEqual, copyFieldValues, set, get, getFields, getField, getFieldName, enableNotify, isNotifyEnabled

Methods from class SoBase:

ref, unref, unrefNoDelete, touch, getTypeId, isOfType, setName, getName

ACTION BEHAVIOR

SoGLRenderAction, SoCallbackAction, SoGetBoundingBoxAction, SoRayPickAction
Accumulates translation into the current transformation.

SoGetMatrixAction
Returns the matrix corresponding to the translation.

FILE FORMAT/DEFAULTS

```
Translation {
     translation  0 0 0
}
```

INCLUDE FILE

```
#include <Inventor/nodes/SoTranslation.h>
```

SEE ALSO

SoTransform

NAME

SoTriangleStripSet — triangle strip set shape node

INHERITS FROM

SoBase > SoFieldContainer > SoNode > SoShape > SoVertexShape > SoNonIndexedShape > SoTriangleStripSet

DESCRIPTION

This shape node constructs triangle strips out of vertices located at the current coordinates. It is one of the fastest ways of drawing polygonal objects in Inventor. **SoTriangleStripSet** uses the current coordinates, in order, starting at the index specified by the **startIndex** field. The values in the **numVertices** field indicate the number of vertices to use for each triangle strip in the set. The number of values in this field determines the number of strips.

For example, if the **startIndex** field contains the value 3 and **numVertices** has the values [3,5], coordinates 3, 4, and 5 would be used for the first triangle strip and coordinates 6, 7, 8, 9, and 10 would be used for the second strip. This would result in 1 triangle in the first strip and 3 in the second.

If the last value in the **numVertices** field is SO_TRI_STRIP_SET_USE_REST_OF_VERTICES (-1), all remaining values in the current coordinates are used as the vertices of the last triangle strip.

The coordinates of the strips are transformed by the current cumulative transformation. The strips are drawn with the current light model and drawing style.

Treatment of the current material and normal binding is as follows: The PER_PART binding specifies a material or normal for each strip of the set. The PER_FACE binding specifies a material or normal for each triangle. The _INDEXED bindings are equivalent to their non-indexed counterparts. The DEFAULT material binding is equal to OVERALL. The DEFAULT normal binding is equal to PER_VERTEX. The **startIndex** is also used for materials, normals, or texture coordinates when the binding indicates that they should be used per vertex.

If the current complexity value is less than 0.5, some strips will be skipped during rendering.

FIELDS

SoMFLong   **numVertices**

Number of vertices in each triangle strip. The number of strips is equal to the number of values in this field.

Fields from class SoNonIndexedShape:

startIndex

METHODS

SoTriangleStripSet()
Creates a triangle strip set node with default settings.

static SoType   **getClassTypeId()**
Returns type identifier for this class.

Methods from class SoNode:

setOverride, isOverride, copy, affectsState, getByName, getByName

Methods from class SoFieldContainer:

setToDefaults, hasDefaultValues, fieldsAreEqual, copyFieldValues, set, get, getFields, getField, getFieldName, enableNotify, isNotifyEnabled

Methods from class SoBase:

ref, unref, unrefNoDelete, touch, getTypeId, isOfType, setName, getName

ACTION BEHAVIOR

SoGLRenderAction
Draws a strip set based on the current coordinates, normals, materials, drawing style, and so on.

SoRayPickAction
Picks on the strip set based on the current coordinates and transformation. Details about the intersection are returned in an **SoFaceDetail**.

SoGetBoundingBoxAction
Computes the bounding box that encloses all vertices of the strip set with the current transformation applied to them. Sets the center to the average of the coordinates of all vertices.

SoCallbackAction
If any triangle callbacks are registered with the action, they will be invoked for each successive triangle forming the strips of the set.

FILE FORMAT/DEFAULTS

```
TriangleStripSet {
        startIndex   0
        numVertices  -1
}
```

INCLUDE FILE

```
#include <Inventor/nodes/SoTriangleStripSet.h>
```

SEE ALSO

SoCoordinate3, SoDrawStyle, SoFaceDetail, SoFaceSet, SoIndexedTriangleStripSet, SoQuadMesh

NAME

SoTriggerAny — provides fan-in for triggers

INHERITS FROM

SoBase > SoFieldContainer > SoEngine > SoTriggerAny

DESCRIPTION

This engine takes up to 10 input triggers, and produces one trigger output. The output is triggered whenever one of the inputs is touched.

INPUTS

SoSFTrigger	**input0**
SoSFTrigger	**input1**
SoSFTrigger	**input2**
SoSFTrigger	**input3**
SoSFTrigger	**input4**
SoSFTrigger	**input5**
SoSFTrigger	**input6**
SoSFTrigger	**input7**
SoSFTrigger	**input8**
SoSFTrigger	**input9**

OUTPUTS

(SoSFTrigger)   **output**

Triggered when any of the inputs is touched.

METHODS

SoTriggerAny()

Constructor

Methods from class SoEngine:

getClassTypeId, getOutputs, getOutput, getOutputName, copy, getByName, getByName

Methods from class SoFieldContainer:

setToDefaults, hasDefaultValues, fieldsAreEqual, copyFieldValues, set, get, getFields, getField, getFieldName, enableNotify, isNotifyEnabled

Methods from class SoBase:

ref, unref, unrefNoDelete, touch, getTypeId, isOfType, setName, getName

FILE FORMAT/DEFAULTS

```
TriggerAny {
        input0
        input1
        input2
        input3
        input4
        input5
        input6
        input7
        input8
        input9
}
```

INCLUDE FILE

```
#include <Inventor/engines/SoSoTriggerAny.h>
```

SEE ALSO

SoEngineOutput, SoSFTrigger

NAME

SoType — stores runtime type information

INHERITS FROM

SoType

DESCRIPTION

The **SoType** class keeps track of runtime type information in Inventor. Each type is associated with a given name, so lookup is possible in either direction.

Many Inventor classes request a unique **SoType** when they are initialized. This type can then be used to find out the actual class of an instance when only its base class is known, or to obtain an instance of a particular class given its type or name.

Note that the names associated with types of Inventor classes do not contain the "So" prefix.

METHODS

static SoType   **fromName**(SbName name)
     Returns the type associated with the given name.

SbName   **getName**() const
     Returns the name associated with a type.

SoType   **getParent**() const
     Returns the type of the parent class.

static SoType   **badType**()
     Returns an always-illegal type. Useful for returning errors.

SbBool   **isBad**() const
     Returns TRUE if the type is a bad type.

SbBool   **isDerivedFrom**(SoType t) const
     Returns TRUE if the type is derived from type *t*.

static int   **getAllDerivedFrom**(SoType type, SoTypeList &list)
     Adds all types derived from the given type to the given type list. Returns the number of types added.

SbBool   **canCreateInstance**() const
     Some types are able to create instances; for example, most nodes and engines (those which are not abstract classes) can be created this way. This method returns TRUE if the type supports such creation.

void * **createInstance**() const
Creates and returns a pointer to an instance of the type. Returns NULL if an instance could not be created for some reason. The pointer is returned as a generic pointer, but can be cast to the appropriate type. For example:

SoCube *c = (SoCube *) SoCube::getClassTypeId().createInstance();

is a convoluted way of creating a new instance of an **SoCube**.

int **operator ==**(const SoType t) const
int **operator !=**(const SoType t) const
Returns TRUE if this type is the same as or not the same as the given type.

int **operator <**(const SoType t) const
Less-than comparison operator that can be used to sort types. This is pretty useless otherwise.

INCLUDE FILE

```
#include <Inventor/SoType.h>
```

SEE ALSO

SoAction, SoBase, SoDetail, SoError, SoEvent, SoField

NAME
>   SoTypeList — maintains a list of **SoTypes**

INHERITS FROM
>   SbPList > SoTypeList

DESCRIPTION
>   This subclass of **SbPList** holds lists of **SoType** type identifiers.

METHODS

>>   **SoTypeList**()
>   Constructor.

>>   **SoTypeList**(int size)
>   Constructor that pre-allocates storage for *size* types.

>>   **SoTypeList**(const SoTypeList &l)
>   Constructor that copies the contents of another list.

>>   **~SoTypeList**()
>   Destructor.

>   void   **append**(SoType type)
>   Adds a type to the end of the list.

>   void   **insert**(SoType *type, int addBefore)
>   Inserts given type in list before type with given index.

>   void   **set**(int i, SoType *type)
>   Sets an element of a list.

>   int   **find**(SoType typeId) const
>   Returns index of given type in list, or -1 if not found.

>   SoType   **operator [ ]**(int i) const
>   Accesses an element of a list.

>   **Methods from class SbPList:**

>>   remove, getLength, truncate, copy, operator =, operator ==, operator !=

INCLUDE FILE
>   #include <Inventor/SoLists.h>

SEE ALSO
>   SoType

NAME

SoUnits — node that scales to convert units of length

INHERITS FROM

SoBase > SoFieldContainer > SoNode > SoTransformation > SoUnits

DESCRIPTION

This node defines a uniform 3D scale about the origin relative to the previously defined units. The default units for all data are meters. Adding a units node with the value INCHES will have the same effect as adding an **SoScale** node with the **scaleFactor** of (.0254, .0254, .0254). Any subsequent **SoUnits** node will take the previous units into account. When building a composite object out of a bunch of pieces, it would be a good practice to add an **SoUnits** node at the beginning of each of the pieces, under an **SoSeparator** node, to make sure all the pieces fit together with the same scale.

FIELDS

SoSFEnum   **units**

Defines the current unit.

METHODS

SoUnits()

Creates a unit conversion node with default settings.

static SoType   **getClassTypeId()**

Returns type identifier for this class.

Methods from class SoNode:

setOverride, isOverride, copy, affectsState, getByName, getByName

Methods from class SoFieldContainer:

setToDefaults, hasDefaultValues, fieldsAreEqual, copyFieldValues, set, get, getFields, getField, getFieldName, enableNotify, isNotifyEnabled

Methods from class SoBase:

ref, unref, unrefNoDelete, touch, getTypeId, isOfType, setName, getName

ACTION BEHAVIOR

SoGLRenderAction, SoCallbackAction, SoGetBoundingBoxAction, SoRayPickAction

Accumulates the scale that is the ratio of the size from the previous unit to the current unit into the current transformation.

SoGetMatrixAction

Returns the matrix corresponding to the units scaling.

FILE FORMAT/DEFAULTS

```
Units {
        units  METERS
}
```

INCLUDE FILE

```
#include <Inventor/nodes/SoUnits.h>
```

enum **Units** {
      SoUnits::METERS
      SoUnits::CENTIMETERS
      SoUnits::MILLIMETERS
      SoUnits::MICROMETERS
      SoUnits::MICRONS
      SoUnits::NANOMETERS
      SoUnits::ANGSTROMS
      SoUnits::KILOMETERS
      SoUnits::FEET
      SoUnits::INCHES
      SoUnits::POINTS
      SoUnits::YARDS
      SoUnits::MILES
      SoUnits::NAUTICAL_MILES
}

SEE ALSO

SoScale, SoTransform

NAME

SoVertexShape — abstract base class for all vertex-based shape nodes

INHERITS FROM

SoBase > SoFieldContainer > SoNode > SoShape > SoVertexShape

DESCRIPTION

This node is the abstract base class for all vertex-based shape (geometry) nodes. There are no public fields; it is used only as a repository for convenience functions for subclasses and to provide a type identifier to make it easy to determine whether a shape is vertex-based.

All subclasses of this node draw objects constructed from vertices located at the current coordinates. The coordinates of the shape are transformed by the current transformation matrix and are drawn with the current light model and drawing style.

Subclasses that construct polygons from vertices may not render or pick correctly if any of their polygons are self-intersecting or non-planar.

All vertex shape subclasses use the bounding box of the shape to determine default texture coordinates. The longest dimension of the bounding box defines the S coordinates, and the next longest defines the T coordinates. The value of the S coordinate ranges from 0 to 1, from one end of the bounding box to the other. The T coordinate ranges between 0 and the ratio of the second greatest dimension of the bounding box to the greatest dimension.

When a vertex-based shape is picked with an **SoRayPickAction**, a detail is always returned. If the shape is composed of faces (such as **SoFaceSet** or **SoTriangleStripSet**), an **SoFaceDetail** is returned. If the shape is composed of line segments (such as **SoLineSet**), an **SoLineDetail** is returned. If the shape is composed of points (such as **SoPointSet**), an **SoPointDetail** is returned. Note that the type of detail returned is not affected by the current drawing style.

Similarly, each class of vertex-based shape invokes appropriate callbacks if those callbacks are registered with the **SoCallbackAction**. Shapes made of faces invoke triangle callbacks for each generated triangle. (Faces may be triangulated to create these triangles.) Shapes made of line segments invoke line segment callbacks for each segment, and shapes made of points invoke point callbacks.

Two subclasses, **SoIndexedShape** and **SoNonIndexedShape**, are base classes for vertex-based shapes that do or no not index into the current set of coordinates.

METHODS

static SoType   **getClassTypeId**()
> Returns type identifier for this class.

Methods from class SoNode:

> setOverride, isOverride, copy, affectsState, getByName, getByName

Methods from class SoFieldContainer:

> setToDefaults, hasDefaultValues, fieldsAreEqual, copyFieldValues, set, get, getFields, getField, getFieldName, enableNotify, isNotifyEnabled

Methods from class SoBase:

> ref, unref, unrefNoDelete, touch, getTypeId, isOfType, setName, getName

FILE FORMAT/DEFAULTS

This is an abstract class. See the reference page of a derived class for the format and default values.

INCLUDE FILE

```
#include <Inventor/nodes/SoVertexShape.h>
```

SEE ALSO

SoIndexedShape, SoNonIndexedShape

NAME

SoWrapperKit — wrapper nodekit class

INHERITS FROM

SoBase > SoFieldContainer > SoNode > SoBaseKit > SoSeparatorKit > SoWrapperKit

DESCRIPTION

SoWrapperKit is derived from **SoSeparatorKit**. It adds the capability to wrap an arbitrary scene graph, (non-nodekit), within an **SoSeparatorKit**, so that it may be used along with other shape kits in a hierarchy. There are two additional parts included in **SoWrapperKit**: *localTransform* and *contents*.

The part *contents* is an **SoSeparator** node beneath which any arbitrary scene graph can be added. This is especially useful for importing scene graphs of unknown structure (non-nodekits) into nodekit format.

Since an **SoWrapperKit** is a class descended from **SoSeparatorKit**, it may be put into another **SoSeparatorKit**'s *childList*.

FIELDS

Fields from class SoSeparatorKit:

renderCaching, boundingBoxCaching, renderCulling, pickCulling

PARTS

(SoTransform)   **localTransform**

This part is an **SoTransform** node that is used to affect the scene graph defined in *contents* part. This part is NULL by default and is automatically created if requested.

(SoSeparator)   **contents**

This part is an **SoSeparator** node that contains a user-supplied scene graph. This scene graph can contain any nodes. This part is NULL by default and an **SoSeparatoir** is automatically created if the user asks the nodekit to build the part.

Parts from class SoSeparatorKit:

pickStyle, appearance, units, transform, texture2Transform, childList

Parts from class SoBaseKit:

callbackList

METHODS

> **SoWrapperKit**()
> Constructor.

> static const SoNodekitCatalog *
> > **getClassNodekitCatalog**() const
> > Returns an **SoNodekitCatalog** for the class **SoWrapperKit**.

> static SoType **getClassTypeId**()
> Returns type identifier for this class.

Methods from class SoBaseKit:

> getNodekitCatalog, getPart, getPartString, createPathToPart, setPart, set, set, isSearchingChildren, setSearchingChildren

Methods from class SoNode:

> setOverride, isOverride, copy, affectsState, getByName, getByName

Methods from class SoFieldContainer:

> setToDefaults, hasDefaultValues, fieldsAreEqual, copyFieldValues, get, getFields, getField, getFieldName, enableNotify, isNotifyEnabled

Methods from class SoBase:

> ref, unref, unrefNoDelete, touch, getTypeId, isOfType, setName, getName

MACROS

Macros from class SoBaseKit:

> SO_GET_PART, SO_CHECK_PART

CATALOG PARTS

All parts			
Part Name	**Part Type**	**Default Type**	**NULL by Default**
callbackList	NodeKitListPart	--	yes
pickStyle	PickStyle	--	yes
appearance	AppearanceKit	--	yes
units	Units	--	yes
transform	Transform	--	yes
texture2Transform	Texture2Transform	--	yes
childList	NodeKitListPart	--	yes
localTransform	Transform	--	yes
contents	Separator	--	yes

Extra information for list parts from above table		
Part Name	**Container Type**	**Permissible Types**
callbackList	Separator	Callback, EventCallback
childList	Separator	ShapeKit, SeparatorKit

FILE FORMAT/DEFAULTS

```
WrapperKit {
      renderCaching         AUTO
      boundingBoxCaching    AUTO
      renderCulling         AUTO
      pickCulling           AUTO
}
```

INCLUDE FILE

```
#include <Inventor/nodekits/SoWrapperKit.h>
```

SEE ALSO

SoAppearanceKit, SoBaseKit, SoCameraKit, SoLightKit, SoNodeKit, SoNodeKitDetail, SoNodeKitListPart, SoNodeKitPath, SoNodekitCatalog, SoSceneKit, SoSeparatorKit, SoShapeKit

NAME

SoWriteAction — Writes a scene graph to a file

INHERITS FROM

SoAction > SoWriteAction

DESCRIPTION

This class is used for writing scene graphs to files. It contains an **SoOutput** instance that by default writes to the standard output. Methods on the **SoOutput** can be called to specify what file or memory buffer to write to.

METHODS

SoWriteAction()
Constructor.

SoWriteAction(SoOutput *out)
Constructor that takes an **SoOutput** to use for output.

SoOutput *   **getOutput**() const
Returns pointer to **SoOutput** instance in action.

Methods from class SoAction:

apply, apply, apply, getClassTypeId, getTypeId, isOfType, invalidateState

INCLUDE FILE

```
#include <Inventor/actions/SoWriteAction.h>
```

SEE ALSO

SoOutput

NAME

SoXt — routines for Inventor/Xt compatibility.

INHERITS FROM

SoXt

DESCRIPTION

The SoXt class initializes Inventor for use with the Xt toolkit and Motif. **SoXt::init()** must be called in order for Inventor to work properly with Xt. **SoXt::mainLoop()** must be called in order for extension device events to be passed to Inventor render areas. The other methods are convenience functions.

Refer to the **SoXtComponent** man pages for examples on how this class should be used when using Inventor Xt components.

METHODS

static Widget   **init**(const char *appName, const char *className = "Inventor")
This is called to initialize Inventor and Xt, and bind Inventor with Xt event handling so that Inventor sensors will work correctly. This returns the top level shell widget. This method will call **SoDB::init()**, **SoNodeKit::init()**, **SoInteraction::init()** and **XtAppInitialize()**.

static void   **init**(Widget topLevelWidget)
This alternate form of init allows the application to initialize Xt. The passed widget should be the top level shell widget returned from the Xt initializiation. This method will call **SoDB::init()**, **SoNodeKit::init()**, **SoInteraction::init()** and **XtAppInitialize()**.

static void   **mainLoop**()
This retrieves and dispatches events (loops forever). Unlike Xt which ignores extension devices (i.e. any device besides mouse and keyboard), this main loop will dispatch events from input extension devices like the spaceball. It calls **SoXt::nextEvent()** and **SoXt::dispatchEvent()** to do this. If only the mouse and keyboard devices are used, this is equivalent to calling **XtAppMainLoop()**.

static void   **nextEvent**(XtAppContext appContext, XEvent *event)
Get the nextEvent by calling **XtAppNextEvent()**. The **appContext** can be had by calling **SoXt::getAppContext()**.

static Boolean   **dispatchEvent**(XEvent *event)
Dispatch the passed event to a handler. Mouse and keyboard events are dispatched by calling **XtDispatchEvent()**. Events from input extension devices are dispatched by code implemented in this routine. This returns True if a handler was found, else it returns False.

static XtAppContext
>>>>>>>>>>>>>>> **getAppContext**()
static Display * >>>> **getDisplay**()
static Widget >>>>>> **getTopLevelWidget**()
>>>> These return information based on the top level widget returned by or
>>>> passed to init.

static void >>>>>>>> **show**(Widget widget)
static void >>>>>>>> **hide**(Widget widget)
>>>> Convenience routines to show and hide the passed widget.

>>>> For a shell widget, this is equivalent to calling **RealizeWidget**() +
>>>> **XMapWindow**() or **XMapRaised**() if window already exists (raise and de-
>>>> iconify). **hide**() will then call **XUnrealizeWidget**().

>>>> For a subwidget, those simply calls **XtManageChild**() and
>>>> **XtUnmanageChild**().

static XmString >>>> **encodeString**(char *s)
static char * >>>>>> **decodeString**(XmString xs)
>>>> These are convenience routines for encoding a character string as an
>>>> **XmString**, and decoding an **XmString** back to a character string. (**XmString**
>>>> is a Motif string). The application is responsible for freeing up the memory
>>>> pointed to by these return values. Use **XmStringFree**() to free an **XmString**,
>>>> and **free**() to free a character pointer.

static void >>>>>>>> **setWidgetSize**(Widget w, const SbVec2s &size)
static SbVec2s >>>>>> **getWidgetSize**(Widget w)
>>>> Convenience routines to set/get the size of the given widget. Those are
>>>> equivalent to calling **XtSetValues**() and **XtGetValues**() on **XtNheight** and
>>>> **XtNwidth** widget resources.

static Widget >>>>>> **getShellWidget**(Widget w)
>>>> Convenience routine which will return the ShellWidget containing the
>>>> given widget. The widget tree is traversed up until a shell widget is found
>>>> using **XtIsShell**().

static void >>>>>>>> **createSimpleErrorDialog**(Widget widget, char *dialogTitle,
>>>>>>>>>>>>>>>>>> char *errorStr1, char *errorStr2 = NULL)
>>>> Convenience routine which brings a simple motif error dialog box
>>>> displaying the given error string(s) and window title. The OK button, which
>>>> destroys the dialog, is the only button displayed. The widget argument is
>>>> used to create and center the dialog (using **XmCreateErrorDialog**()).

static void   **getPopupArgs**(Display *d, int scr, ArgList args, int *n)
Convenience routine which gets visual args for the popup planes. These args can then be passed in to **XmCreatePulldownMenu()** or **XmCreatePopupMenu()** to create menus in the popup planes. **addColormapToShell()** has to be called on the main popup window so set the proper color map.

static void   **addColormapToShell**(Widget widget, Widget shell)
Convenience routine to append the given widget colormap onto the supplied shell widget. This will not replace the existing installed colormaps (or list of windows), but instead append the new colormap to the existing list using **XGetWMColormapWindows()** and **XSetWMColormapWindows()**.

INCLUDE FILE

```
#include <Inventor/Xt/SoXt.h>
```

SEE ALSO

SoXtComponent

NAME

SoXtClipboard — Supports copy/paste for Inventor using Xt

INHERITS FROM

SoXtClipboard

DESCRIPTION

This class manages data transfers for copy and paste. Transfers may occur within the same widget, from one widget to another widget, and from process to process. This uses the ICCCM protocol for the transfer of data.

METHODS

SoXtClipboard(Widget w, Atom selectionAtom = _XA_CLIPBOARD_)
~SoXtClipboard()

Constructor and destructor. **w** is the Xt widget which this clipboard acts as an agent for. *selectionAtom* is the X selection through which data should be transferred. For quick data transfers, this should be XA_PRIMARY. The default is to use the X clipboard selection.

void	**copy**(SoNode *node, Time eventTime)
void	**copy**(SoPath *path, Time eventTime)
void	**copy**(SoPathList *pathList, Time eventTime)

This copies the passed scene graph object, and tells the X server that the clipboard now owns the selection which was specified by *selectionAtom* in the constructor. When a paste happens (in this window, another window, or another process), the X server will ask this clipboard for the data it copied here. The *eventTime* should be the time found in the X event structure which triggered the copy operation, and is used to insure synchronization of copy and paste requests. Data targets supported for export are INVENTOR, XA_STRING, and TARGETS.

void	**paste**(Time eventTime, SoXtClipboardPasteCB *pasteDoneFunc, void *userData = NULL)

This makes a request to the X server for data to paste from the selection atom specified in the constructor (*selectionAtom*), then returns. When the data is retrieved from the selection owner, the *pasteDoneFunc* callback is invoked. The newly pasted data is passed as the callback function's *pathList* argument (an **SoPathList**). Data targets supported for import are INVENTOR, XA_STRING, and TARGETS.

SoXtClipboard

INCLUDE FILE

```
#include <Inventor/Xt/SoXtClipboard.h>
```

typedef void   **SoXtClipboardPasteCB**(void *userData, SoPathList *pathList)

#define _XA_CLIPBOARD_ ((Atom) 0)

SEE ALSO

SoSelection, SoXt, X Selections

NAME

SoXtComponent — abstract base class for all Inventor Xt components

INHERITS FROM

SoXtComponent

DESCRIPTION

Abstract base class from which all Inventor Xt components are derived. This class provides a basic C++ protocol for building and displaying Motif components. Components are used to encapsulate some function or task into a reusable package in the form of a Motif widget that can be used in any Inventor Xt program. See the Example section on how to build and use **SoXtComponents**.

METHODS

virtual void	**show**()
virtual void	**hide**()

This shows and hides the component. If this is a topLevelShell component, then **show**() will Realize and Map the window, otherwise it will simply Manage the widget. **hide**() calls the appropriate unmap or unmanage routines.

In addition, **show**() will also pop the component window to the top and de-iconify if necessary, to make sure the component is visible by the user.

SbBool   **isVisible**()

Returns TRUE if this component is mapped onto the screen. For a component to be visible, it's widget and the shell containing this widget must be mapped (which is FALSE when the component is iconified).

Subclasses should call this routine before redrawing anything and in any sensor trigger methods. Calling this will check the current visibility (which is really cheap) and invoke the visibility changed callbacks if the state changes (see **addVisibilityChangeCallback**()).

Widget   **getWidget**() const

This returns the base widget for this component. If the component created its own shell, this returns the topmost widget beneath the shell. Call **getShellWidget**() to obtain the shell.

SbBool	**isTopLevelShell**() const
Widget	**getShellWidget**() const

Returns TRUE if this component is a top level shell component (has its own window). Subclasses may use this to decide if they are allowed to resize themselves. Also method to return the shell widget (NULL if the shell hasn't been created by this component).

Widget   **getParentWidget**() const
     Return the parent widget, be it a shell or not

void   **setSize**(const SbVec2s &size)
SbVec2s   **getSize**()
     Convenience routines on the widget — setSize calls XtSetValue

Display *   **getDisplay**()
     Returns the X display associated with this components widget.

void   **setTitle**(const char *newTitle)
const char *   **getTitle**() const
void   **setIconTitle**(const char *newIconTitle)
const char *   **getIconTitle**() const
     The window and icon title can be set for topLevelShell components or
     components which are directly under a shell widget (i.e. components which
     have their own window).

void   **setWindowCloseCallback**(SoXtComponentCB *func, void
        *data = NULL)
     Sets which callback to call when the user closes this component (double
     click in the upper left corner) — by default **hide**() is called on this
     component, unless a callback is set to something other than NULL. A
     pointer to this class will be passed as the callback data.

     Note: this callback is supplied because the user may wish to delete this
     component when it is closed.

static SoXtComponent *
      getComponent(Widget w)
     This returns the **SoXtComponent** for this widget. If the widget is not an
     Inventor component, then NULL is returned.

const char *   **getWidgetName**() const
const char *   **getClassName**() const
     Routines which return the widget name and the class name. The widget
     name is passed to the build method. The class name is predefined by each
     component. These names are used when retrieving X resource values for the
     component.

INCLUDE FILE

```
#include <Inventor/Xt/SoXtComponent.h>
```

typedef void   **SoXtComponentCB**(void *userData, SoXtComponent *comp)

EXAMPLE

This example shows how an Inventor component can be built inside a program using the Xt widget set. The example uses the **SoXtExaminerViewer** widget to view some simple geometry.

```
#include <Inventor/Xt/SoXt.h>
#include <Inventor/nodes/SoCone.h>
#include <Inventor/Xt/viewers/SoXtExaminerViewer.h>

void main(int, char **argv)
{
    // Initialize Inventor and Xt, which must be done
    // before any Inventor calls are made.
    Widget myWindow = SoXt::init(argv[0]);

    // create the viewer in the toplevel window
    // and set some scene to display
    SoXtExaminerViewer *myViewer = new SoXtExaminerViewer(myWindow);
    myViewer->setSceneGraph( new SoCone() );

    // manage and map window on screen
    myViewer->show();
    SoXt::show(myWindow); // calls XtRealizeWidget()

    // Loop forever
    SoXt::mainLoop();
}
```

SEE ALSO

SoXt, SoXtRenderArea, SoXtViewer, SoXtMaterialEditor

NAME

SoXtConstrainedViewer — base viewer class which adds camera constraints given a world up direction

INHERITS FROM

SoXtComponent > SoXtGLWidget > SoXtRenderArea > SoXtViewer > SoXtFullViewer > SoXtConstrainedViewer

DESCRIPTION

This is a base class for the **SoXtWalkViewer** and **SoXtFlyViewer** component viewers. This class adds methods and convenience routines available to subclasses to constrain the camera given a world up direction. This prevents the camera from looking upside down. By default the +Y direction is used.

METHODS

void   **setUpDirection**(const SbVec3f &newUpDirection)
SbVec3f   **getUpDirection**()

Specifies the upward direction of the viewer. This up direction is used by the viewers to constrain the camera when tilting up/down, and also used when rotating the camera right/left. The default is the +Y (0,1,0) direction.

Methods from class SoXtFullViewer:

setDecoration, isDecoration, setPopupMenuEnabled, isPopupMenuEnabled, getAppPushButtonParent, addAppPushButton, insertAppPushButton, removeAppPushButton, findAppPushButton, lengthAppPushButton, getRenderAreaWidget

Methods from class SoXtViewer:

setCamera, getCamera, setCameraType, getCameraType, viewAll, saveHomePosition, resetToHomePosition, setHeadlight, isHeadlight, getHeadlight, setDrawStyle, getDrawStyle, setBufferingType, getBufferingType, setViewing, isViewing, setAutoClipping, isAutoClipping, setStereoViewing, isStereoViewing, setStereoOffset, getStereoOffset, setDetailSeek, isDetailSeek, setSeekTime, getSeekTime, addStartCallback, addFinishCallback, re moveStartCallback, removeFinishCallback, copyView, pasteView

Methods from class SoXtRenderArea:

setSceneGraph, getSceneGraph, setOverlaySceneGraph, getOverlaySceneGraph, registerDevice, unregisterDevice, setBackgroundColor, getBackgroundColor, setBackgroundIndex, getBackgroundIndex, setOverlayBackgroundIndex, getOverlayBackgroundIndex, setColorMap, setOverlayColorMap, setViewportRegion, getViewportRegion, setTransparencyType, getTransparencyType, setAntialiasing, getAntialiasing, setClearBeforeRender,

isClearBeforeRender, setClearBe foreOverlayRender,
isClearBeforeOverlayRender, setAutoRedraw, isAutoRedraw,
setRedrawPriority, getRedrawPriority, getDefaultRedrawPriority, render,
renderOverlay, scheduleRedraw, scheduleOverlayRedraw,
redrawOnSelectionChange, redrawOverlayOnSelectionChange,
setEventCallback, setGLRenderAction, getGLRenderAction,
setOverlayGLRenderAction, getOverlayGLRenderAction, setSceneManager,
getSceneManager, setOverlaySceneManager, getOverlaySceneManager

Methods from class SoXtGLWidget:

setBorder, isBorder, setDoubleBuffer, isDoubleBuffer, getNormalWindow,
getOverlayWindow, getNormalContext, getOverlayContext,
getNormalWidget, getOverlayWidget, setNormalVisual, getNormalVisual,
setOverlayVisual, getOverlayVisual

Methods from class SoXtComponent:

show, hide, isVisible, getWidget, isTopLevelShell, getShellWidget,
getParentWidget, setSize, getSize, getDisplay, setTitle, getTitle, setIconTitle,
getIconTitle, setWindowCloseCallback, getComponent, getWidgetName,
getClassName

INCLUDE FILE
```
#include <Inventor/Xt/viewers/SoXtConstrainedViewer.h>
```

SEE ALSO
SoXtFullViewer, SoXtViewer, SoXtComponent, SoXtRenderArea, SoXtWalkViewer,
SoXtFlyViewer

SoXtDevice

NAME

SoXtDevice — abstract base class device for use with the **SoXtRenderArea**

INHERITS FROM

SoXtDevice

DESCRIPTION

This is the abstract base class for devices in the Inventor Xt component and utility library. When a device is registered with an **SoXtRenderArea**, the device is able to generate events in the render area window.

METHODS

virtual void   **enable**(Widget w, XtEventHandler f, XtPointer data, Window win = NULL)

virtual void   **disable**(Widget w, XtEventHandler f, XtPointer data)

Enable and disable the device for the passed widget. When enabled, the callback function *f* will be invoked when events occur in the widget. *data* is the *clientData* which will be passed.

virtual const SoEvent *

          translateEvent(XAnyEvent *xevent)

This attempts to convert the passed X event into an **SoEvent**. If the event was not generated by this device, then NULL is returned.

void   **setWindowSize**(const SbVec2s &size)

const SbVec2s &   **getWindowSize**() const

Set and get the window size of the widget this device is registered for. This allows the device to correctly convert position information from X window coordinates (origin at top left) to Inventor window coordinates (origin at bottom left). (**SoXtRenderArea** will automatically call this method for each device registered on it whenever the window size changes.)

INCLUDE FILE

```
#include <Inventor/Xt/devices/SoXtDevice.h>
```

SEE ALSO

SoXtMouse, SoXtKeyboard, SoXtSpaceball, SoXtInputFocus, SoXtRenderArea

NAME

SoXtDirectionalLightEditor — component for editing directional lights

INHERITS FROM

SoXtComponent > SoXtDirectionalLightEditor

DESCRIPTION

This class is used to edit an **SoDirectionalLight** node (color, intensity, and direction are changed). In addition to directly editing directional light nodes, the editor can also be used with callbacks which will be called whenever the light is changed. The component consists of a render area and a value slider in the main window, with controls to display a color picker. In the render area there appears a sphere representing the world, and a directional light manipulator representing the direction of the light. Picking on the manipulator and moving the mouse provides direct manipulation of the light direction. The color picker is used to edit the color, and the value slider edits the intensity.

The editor can currently be attached to only one light at a time. Attaching to two different lights will automatically detach the first one before attaching the second.

METHODS

SoXtDirectionalLightEditor(Widget parent = NULL, const char *name = NULL, SbBool buildInsideParent = TRUE)
~**SoXtDirectionalLightEditor**()

Constructor and destructor.

void	**attach**(SoPath *pathToLight)
void	**detach**()

Attach/detach the editor to/from a directional light. When attached, changes made in the editor directly affect the attached light.

SbBool	**isAttached**()

Returns TRUE if the editor is attached.

void	**addLightChangedCallback**(SoXtDirectionalLightEditorCB *f, void *userData = NULL)
void	**removeLightChangedCallback**(SoXtDirectionalLightEditorCB *f, void *userData = NULL)

Additional way of using the directional light editor, by registering a callback and setting the light.

void   **setLight**(const SoDirectionalLight &newLight)
const SoDirectionalLight &
                getLight() const
Set new light values, and get the current light values.

Methods from class SoXtComponent:

show, hide, isVisible, getWidget, isTopLevelShell, getShellWidget, getParentWidget, setSize, getSize, getDisplay, setTitle, getTitle, setIconTitle, getIconTitle, setWindowCloseCallback, getComponent, getWidgetName, getClassName

INCLUDE FILE

```
#include <Inventor/Xt/SoXtDirectionalLightEditor.h>
```

typedef void   **SoXtDirectionalLightEditorCB**(void *userData, const SoDirectionalLight *light)

SEE ALSO

SoXtComponent, SoDirectionalLight

NAME

SoXtExaminerViewer — viewer component which uses a virtual trackball to view the data

INHERITS FROM

SoXtComponent > SoXtGLWidget > SoXtRenderArea > SoXtViewer > SoXtFullViewer > SoXtExaminerViewer

DESCRIPTION

The Examiner viewer component allows you to rotate the view around a point of interest using a virtual trackball. The viewer uses the camera **focalDistance** field to figure out the point of rotation, which is usually set to be at the center of the scene. In addition to allowing you to rotate the camera around the point of interest, this viewer also allows you to translate the camera in the viewer plane, as well as dolly (move forward and backward) to get closer to or further away from the point of interest. The viewer also supports seek to quickly move the camera to a desired object or point.

METHODS

SoXtExaminerViewer(Widget parent = NULL, const char *name = NULL, SbBool buildInsideParent = TRUE, SoXtFullViewer::BuildFlag flag = BUILD_ALL, SoXtViewer::Type type = BROWSER)

~SoXtExaminerViewer()

Constructor and destructor which specifies the viewer type. Please refer to the **SoXtViewer** reference page for a description of the viewer types.

void	**setFeedbackVisibility**(SbBool onOrOff)
SbBool	**isFeedbackVisible**() const

Show/Hide the point of rotation feedback, which only appears while in viewing mode (default in off).

void	**setFeedbackSize**(int newSize)
int	**getFeedbackSize**() const

Set/get the point of rotation feedback size in pixels (default 20 pix).

void	**setAnimationEnabled**(SbBool onOrOff)
SbBool	**isAnimationEnabled**()

Enable/disable the spinning animation feature of the viewer (enabled by default).

void	**stopAnimating**()
SbBool	**isAnimating**()

Stop animation, if it is occurring, and query if the viewer is currently animating.

Methods from class SoXtFullViewer:

setDecoration, isDecoration, setPopupMenuEnabled, isPopupMenuEnabled, getAppPushButtonParent, addAppPushButton, insertAppPushButton, removeAppPushButton, findAppPushButton, lengthAppPushButton, getRenderAreaWidget

Methods from class SoXtViewer:

setCamera, getCamera, setCameraType, getCameraType, viewAll, saveHomePosition, resetToHomePosition, setHeadlight, isHeadlight, getHeadlight, setDrawStyle, getDrawStyle, setBufferingType, getBufferingType, setViewing, isViewing, setAutoClipping, isAutoClipping, setStereoViewing, isStereoViewing, setStereoOffset, getStereoOffset, setDetailSeek, isDetailSeek, setSeekTime, getSeekTime, addStartCallback, addFinishCallback, re moveStartCallback, removeFinishCallback, copyView, pasteView

Methods from class SoXtRenderArea:

setSceneGraph, getSceneGraph, setOverlaySceneGraph, getOverlaySceneGraph, registerDevice, unregisterDevice, setBackgroundColor, getBackgroundColor, setBackgroundIndex, getBackgroundIndex, setOverlayBackgroundIndex, getOverlayBackgroundIndex, setColorMap, setOverlayColorMap, setViewportRegion, getViewportRegion, setTransparencyType, getTransparencyType, setAntialiasing, getAntialiasing, setClearBeforeRender, isClearBeforeRender, setClearBe foreOverlayRender, isClearBeforeOverlayRender, setAutoRedraw, isAutoRedraw, setRedrawPriority, getRedrawPriority, getDefaultRedrawPriority, render, renderOverlay, scheduleRedraw, scheduleOverlayRedraw, redrawOnSelectionChange, redrawOverlayOnSelectionChange, setEventCallback, setGLRenderAction, getGLRenderAction, setOverlayGLRenderAction, getOverlayGLRenderAction, setSceneManager, getSceneManager, setOverlaySceneManager, getOverlaySceneManager

Methods from class SoXtGLWidget:

setBorder, isBorder, setDoubleBuffer, isDoubleBuffer, getNormalWindow, getOverlayWindow, getNormalContext, getOverlayContext, getNormalWidget, getOverlayWidget, setNormalVisual, getNormalVisual, setOverlayVisual, getOverlayVisual

Methods from class SoXtComponent:

show, hide, isVisible, getWidget, isTopLevelShell, getShellWidget, getParentWidget, setSize, getSize, getDisplay, setTitle, getTitle, setIconTitle, getIconTitle, setWindowCloseCallback, getComponent, getWidgetName, getClassName

INCLUDE FILE

```
#include <Inventor/Xt/viewers/SoXtExaminerViewer.h>
```

RESOURCES

*SoXtExaminerViewer.spinAnimation: on (on | off)
*SoXtExaminerViewer.pointOfRotationAxes: off (on | off)
*SoXtExaminerViewer.axesSize: 20 (short, pixels if axes is on)
*SoXtExaminerViewer.decoration: on (on | off)
*SoXtExaminerViewer.seekAnimationTime: 2.0 (float)
*SoXtExaminerViewer.seekTo: point (point | object)
*SoXtExaminerViewer.seekDistanceUsage: percentage (percentage | absolute)
*SoXtExaminerViewer.zoomMin: 1.0 (float)
*SoXtExaminerViewer.zoomMax: 179.0 (float)
*SoXtExaminerViewer.autoClipping: on (on | off)
*SoXtExaminerViewer.nearDistance: 2.4 (float, when autoClipping is off)
*SoXtExaminerViewer.farDistance: 2.8 (float, when autoClipping is off)
*SoXtExaminerViewer*BackgroundColor: black (color name or hex value)

USAGE

Left Mouse: Rotate the virtual trackball.

Ctrl + Left Mouse: Used for roll action (rotates around the viewer forward direction).

<s> + Left Mouse: Alternative to the Seek button. Press (but do not hold down) the <s> key, then click on a target object.

Middle Mouse: Translate up, down, left and right.

Left + Middle Mouse: Dolly in and out (gets closer to and further away from the object).

Right Mouse: Open the popup menu.

SEE ALSO

SoXtFullViewer, SoXtViewer, SoXtComponent, SoXtRenderArea, SoXtWalkViewer, SoXtFlyViewer, SoXtPlaneViewer

NAME

SoXtFlyViewer — viewer component for flying through space, with a constant world up

INHERITS FROM

SoXtComponent > SoXtGLWidget > SoXtRenderArea > SoXtViewer > SoXtFullViewer > SoXtConstrainedViewer > SoXtFlyViewer

DESCRIPTION

Fly Viewer — this viewer is intended to simulate flight through space, with a constant world up direction. The viewer only constrains the camera to keep the user from flying upside down. No mouse buttons need to be pressed in order to fly. The mouse position is used only for steering, while mouse clicks are used to increase or decrease the viewer speed.

The viewer allows you to tilt your head up/down/right/left and move in the direction you are looking (forward or backward). The viewer also supports seek to quickly move the camera to a desired object or point.

METHODS

> **SoXtFlyViewer**(Widget parent = NULL, const char *name = NULL, SbBool buildInsideParent = TRUE, SoXtFullViewer::BuildFlag flag = BUILD_ALL, SoXtViewer::Type type = BROWSER)
> **~SoXtFlyViewer**()

Constructor and destructor which specifies the viewer type. Please refer to the **SoXtViewer** reference page for a description of the viewer types.

Methods from class SoXtConstrainedViewer:

setUpDirection, getUpDirection

Methods from class SoXtFullViewer:

setDecoration, isDecoration, setPopupMenuEnabled, isPopupMenuEnabled, getAppPushButtonParent, addAppPushButton, insertAppPushButton, removeAppPushButton, findAppPushButton, lengthAppPushButton, getRenderAreaWidget

Methods from class SoXtViewer:

setCamera, getCamera, setCameraType, getCameraType, viewAll, saveHomePosition, resetToHomePosition, setHeadlight, isHeadlight, getHeadlight, setDrawStyle, getDrawStyle, setBufferingType, getBufferingType, setViewing, isViewing, setAutoClipping, isAutoClipping, setStereoViewing, isStereoViewing, setStereoOffset, getStereoOffset, setDetailSeek, isDetailSeek, setSeekTime, getSeekTime, addStartCallback, addFinishCallback, re moveStartCallback, removeFinishCallback, copyView, pasteView

Methods from class SoXtRenderArea:

setSceneGraph, getSceneGraph, setOverlaySceneGraph, getOverlaySceneGraph, registerDevice, unregisterDevice, setBackgroundColor, getBackgroundColor, setBackgroundIndex, getBackgroundIndex, setOverlayBackgroundIndex, getOverlayBackgroundIndex, setColorMap, setOverlayColorMap, setViewportRegion, getViewportRegion, setTransparencyType, getTransparencyType, setAntialiasing, getAntialiasing, setClearBeforeRender, isClearBeforeRender, setClearBe foreOverlayRender, isClearBeforeOverlayRender, setAutoRedraw, isAutoRedraw, setRedrawPriority, getRedrawPriority, getDefaultRedrawPriority, render, renderOverlay, scheduleRedraw, scheduleOverlayRedraw, redrawOnSelectionChange, redrawOverlayOnSelectionChange, setEventCallback, setGLRenderAction, getGLRenderAction, setOverlayGLRenderAction, getOverlayGLRenderAction, setSceneManager, getSceneManager, setOverlaySceneManager, getOverlaySceneManager

Methods from class SoXtGLWidget:

setBorder, isBorder, setDoubleBuffer, isDoubleBuffer, getNormalWindow, getOverlayWindow, getNormalContext, getOverlayContext, getNormalWidget, getOverlayWidget, setNormalVisual, getNormalVisual, setOverlayVisual, getOverlayVisual

Methods from class SoXtComponent:

show, hide, isVisible, getWidget, isTopLevelShell, getShellWidget, getParentWidget, setSize, getSize, getDisplay, setTitle, getTitle, setIconTitle, getIconTitle, setWindowCloseCallback, getComponent, getWidgetName, getClassName

INCLUDE FILE

```
#include <Inventor/Xt/viewers/SoXtFlyViewer.h>
```

RESOURCES

*SoXtFlyViewer.decoration: on (on | off)
*SoXtFlyViewer.seekAnimationTime: 2.0 (float)
*SoXtFlyViewer.seekTo: point (point | object)
*SoXtFlyViewer.seekDistanceUsage: percentage (percentage | absolute)
*SoXtFlyViewer.zoomMin: 1.0 (float)
*SoXtFlyViewer.zoomMax: 179.0 (float)
*SoXtFlyViewer.autoClipping: on (on | off)
*SoXtFlyViewer.nearDistance: 2.4 (float, when autoClipping is off)
*SoXtFlyViewer.farDistance: 2.8 (float, when autoClipping is off)
*SoXtFlyViewer*BackgroundColor: black (color name or hex value)

USAGE

Left Mouse: Click to increase speed.

<s> + Left Mouse: Alternative to the Seek button. Press (but do not hold down) the <s> key, then click on a target object.

<u> + Left Mouse: Press (but do not hold down) the <u> key, then click on a target object to set the "up" direction to the surface normal. By default +y is the "up" direction.

Middle Mouse: Click to decrease speed.

Left and Middle Mouse: Click boths simultaneously to stop.

Ctrl: Hold the key down to temporary stop and rotate the viewpoint.

Right Mouse: Open the popup menu.

SEE ALSO

SoXtFullViewer, SoXtViewer, SoXtComponent, SoXtRenderArea, SoXtWalkViewer, SoXtExaminerViewer, SoXtPlaneViewer

NAME

SoXtFullViewer — base viewer class which adds a decoration around the rendering area

INHERITS FROM

SoXtComponent > SoXtGLWidget > SoXtRenderArea > SoXtViewer > SoXtFullViewer

DESCRIPTION

This is a base class used by all viewer components. The class adds a decoration around the rendering area which includes thumb wheels, a zoom slider and push buttons. This base class also includes a viewer popup menu and a preference sheet with generic viewing functions. The constructors for the various subclasses of **SoXtFullViewer** provide a flag for specifying whether the decoration and popup menus should be built.

METHODS

void	**setDecoration**(SbBool onOrOff)
SbBool	**isDecoration**()

Show/hide the viewer component trim (default on). See the viewer constructor to prevent the decoration from being built.

void	**setPopupMenuEnabled**(SbBool trueOrFalse)
SbBool	**isPopupMenuEnabled**()

Enable/disable the viewer popup menu (default enabled). See the viewer constructor to prevent the popup menu from being built.

Widget	**getAppPushButtonParent**() const

Returns the parent widget, which is needed when creating new buttons. Note: that if the decoration is *not* created in the constructor, this will be NULL until the decoration is shown.

void	**addAppPushButton**(Widget newButton)
void	**insertAppPushButton**(Widget newButton, int index)
void	**removeAppPushButton**(Widget oldButton)
int	**findAppPushButton**(Widget oldButton)
int	**lengthAppPushButton**()

Add/remove push buttons for the application, which will be placed in the left hand side decoration trim. Adding buttons appends them to the end of the list, while inserting them places them at the desired index.

Note: the button pixmaps should be 24-by-24 pixels size to nicely fit into the decoration trim like the other viewer buttons.

Widget   **getRenderAreaWidget**()
Returns the render area widget.

Methods from class SoXtViewer:

setCamera, getCamera, setCameraType, getCameraType, viewAll,
saveHomePosition, resetToHomePosition, setHeadlight, isHeadlight,
getHeadlight, setDrawStyle, getDrawStyle, setBufferingType,
getBufferingType, setViewing, isViewing, setAutoClipping, isAutoClipping,
setStereoViewing, isStereoViewing, setStereoOffset, getStereoOffset,
setDetailSeek, isDetailSeek, setSeekTime, getSeekTime, addStartCallback,
addFinishCallback, re moveStartCallback, removeFinishCallback, copyView,
pasteView

Methods from class SoXtRenderArea:

setSceneGraph, getSceneGraph, setOverlaySceneGraph,
getOverlaySceneGraph, registerDevice, unregisterDevice,
setBackgroundColor, getBackgroundColor, setBackgroundIndex,
getBackgroundIndex, setOverlayBackgroundIndex,
getOverlayBackgroundIndex, setColorMap, setOverlayColorMap,
setViewportRegion, getViewportRegion, setTransparencyType,
getTransparencyType, setAntialiasing, getAntialiasing, setClearBeforeRender,
isClearBeforeRender, setClearBe foreOverlayRender,
isClearBeforeOverlayRender, setAutoRedraw, isAutoRedraw,
setRedrawPriority, getRedrawPriority, getDefaultRedrawPriority, render,
renderOverlay, scheduleRedraw, scheduleOverlayRedraw,
redrawOnSelectionChange, redrawOverlayOnSelectionChange,
setEventCallback, setGLRenderAction, getGLRenderAction,
setOverlayGLRenderAction, getOverlayGLRenderAction, setSceneManager,
getSceneManager, setOverlaySceneManager, getOverlaySceneManager

Methods from class SoXtGLWidget:

setBorder, isBorder, setDoubleBuffer, isDoubleBuffer, getNormalWindow,
getOverlayWindow, getNormalContext, getOverlayContext,
getNormalWidget, getOverlayWidget, setNormalVisual, getNormalVisual,
setOverlayVisual, getOverlayVisual

Methods from class SoXtComponent:

show, hide, isVisible, getWidget, isTopLevelShell, getShellWidget,
getParentWidget, setSize, getSize, getDisplay, setTitle, getTitle, setIconTitle,
getIconTitle, setWindowCloseCallback, getComponent, getWidgetName,
getClassName

INCLUDE FILE

```
#include <Inventor/Xt/viewers/SoXtFullViewer.h>
```

enum **BuildFlag** {

    SoXtFullViewer::BUILD_NONE
        doesn't build anything extra

    SoXtFullViewer::BUILD_DECORATION
        build the decoration only

    SoXtFullViewer::BUILD_POPUP
        build the popup menu only

    SoXtFullViewer::BUILD_ALL
        build everything by default

}

SEE ALSO

SoXtViewer, SoXtComponent, SoXtRenderArea, SoXtExaminerViewer, SoXtWalkViewer, SoXtFlyViewer, SoXtPlaneViewer

NAME

SoXtGLWidget — wrapper around GLwMDraw for OpenGL rendering in a motif widget

INHERITS FROM

SoXtComponent > SoXtGLWidget

DESCRIPTION

This abstract base class provides a C++ wrapper around the **GLwMDraw** widget. It allows OpenGL rendering to be performed within a motif widget and is used by the **SoXtRenderArea**. **SoXtGlWidget** uses a form widget around two separate **GLwMDraw** widgets (one for single and one for double buffering), with routines to return the appropriate windows.

Subclasses only need to redefine the **redraw()** routine for rendering and **processEvent()** routine if they are interested in receiving X events.

METHODS

void	**setBorder**(SbBool onOrOff)
SbBool	**isBorder**() const

Show and hide the border around the glx widgets (thickness 3). Default is no border (FALSE). (The **SoXtRenderArea** subclass defaults turns the border on by default.)

void	**setDoubleBuffer**(SbBool onOrOff)
SbBool	**isDoubleBuffer**()

Routine which dynamically changes between single and double buffering. Default is double buffer off. (The **SoXtRenderArea** subclass makes it double buffer by default.)

Window	**getNormalWindow**()
Window	**getOverlayWindow**()
GLXContext	**getNormalContext**()
GLXContext	**getOverlayContext**()
Widget	**getNormalWidget**()
Widget	**getOverlayWidget**()

Get the current normal and overlay GLX windows, contexes and widgets, which are needed as arguments to glXMakeCurrent() when doing drawing in the normal or overlay planes.

Note: These should *not* be cached by users because they will change as single/double buffering changes.

virtual void	**setNormalVisual**(XVisualInfo *vis)
XVisualInfo *	**getNormalVisual**()
virtual void	**setOverlayVisual**(XVisualInfo *vis)
XVisualInfo *	**getOverlayVisual**()

Specify exactly what the visual should be for the normal and overlay window. This allows the user to create all possible visuals supported by OpenGL. The **XVisualInfo** structure should be a valid OpenGL visual returned by **glXChooseVisual**(). This structure will be copied by the **SoXtGLWidget**; the application is responsible for freeing the visual info with **XFree**() when done. (The methods for setting the visual are virtual so that derived classes can know when the visual is changing.)

Methods from class SoXtComponent:

show, hide, isVisible, getWidget, isTopLevelShell, getShellWidget, getParentWidget, setSize, getSize, getDisplay, setTitle, getTitle, setIconTitle, getIconTitle, setWindowCloseCallback, getComponent, getWidgetName, getClassName

INCLUDE FILE

```
#include <Inventor/Xt/SoXtGLWidget.h>
```

SEE ALSO

SoXtComponent, SoXtRenderArea

SoXtInputFocus

NAME

SoXtInputFocus — reports input focus change events

INHERITS FROM

SoXtDevice > SoXtInputFocus

DESCRIPTION

This class reports input focus change events (i.e. when the cursor crosses into or out of the window). There are no input focus events in Inventor, so this always returns NULL when asked to translate events. When this class is registered on a render area, the render area will receive X input focus change events. (This class is extensively employed by the viewer classes.)

METHODS

SoXtInputFocus(EventMask mask =
SO_XT_ALL_FOCUS_EVENTS)
~SoXtInputFocus()

Constructor and destructor. To the constructor, pass which input focus events you are interested in as a bitwise OR of the following values:

EnterWindowMask — Input focus entered the window

LeaveWindowMask — Input focus left the window

Or simply pass the defined value SO_XT_ALL_FOCUS_EVENTS for all input focus events.

Methods from class SoXtDevice:

enable, disable, translateEvent, setWindowSize, getWindowSize

INCLUDE FILE

```
#include <Inventor/Xt/devices/SoXtInputFocus.h>
```

#define SO_XT_ALL_FOCUS_EVENTS (EnterWindowMask | LeaveWindowMask)

SEE ALSO

SoXtDevice

NAME

SoXtKeyboard — translates and reports events for the keyboard

INHERITS FROM

SoXtDevice > SoXtKeyboard

DESCRIPTION

This class manages events generated by the keyboard, including key press and release events (**SoKeyboardEvent**).

METHODS

SoXtKeyboard(EventMask mask =
SO_XT_ALL_KEYBOARD_EVENTS)
~**SoXtKeyboard**()

Constructor and destructor. To the constructor, pass which keyboard events you are interested in as a bitwise OR of the following values:

KeyPressMask — Key press events

KeyReleaseMask — Key release events

Or simply pass the defined value SO_XT_ALL_KEYBOARD_EVENTS for all keyboard events. The device will only report events of this type for the widget it is enabled on.

Methods from class SoXtDevice:

enable, disable, translateEvent, setWindowSize, getWindowSize

INCLUDE FILE

```
#include <Inventor/Xt/devices/SoXtKeyboard.h>
```

#define SO_XT_ALL_KEYBOARD_EVENTS (KeyPressMask | KeyReleaseMask)

SEE ALSO

SoXtDevice, SoKeyboardEvent

SoXtLightSliderSet

NAME

SoXtLightSliderSet — component with Motif sliders for editing SoLight nodes

INHERITS FROM

SoXtComponent > SoXtSliderSetBase > SoXtSliderSet > SoXtLightSliderSet

DESCRIPTION

This class is used to manipulate the intensity and color of an **SoLight** node using an arrangement of Motif sliders and buttons.

METHODS

SoXtLightSliderSet(Widget parent = NULL, const char *name = NULL, SbBool buildInsideParent = TRUE, SoNode *newEditNode = NULL)

~SoXtLightSliderSet()

Constructor and destructor. At construction time the light node to edit can be supplied.

Methods from class SoXtSliderSetBase:

setNode, getNode

Methods from class SoXtComponent:

show, hide, isVisible, getWidget, isTopLevelShell, getShellWidget, getParentWidget, setSize, getSize, getDisplay, setTitle, getTitle, setIconTitle, getIconTitle, setWindowCloseCallback, getComponent, getWidgetName, getClassName

INCLUDE FILE

```
#include <Inventor/Xt/SoXtLightSliderSet.h>
```

SEE ALSO

SoXtSliderSet, SoXtSliderSetBase, SoXtComponent, SoLight, SoNode

NAME

 SoXtMaterialEditor — Component which lets you edit a material interactively

INHERITS FROM

SoXtComponent > SoXtMaterialEditor

DESCRIPTION

This class is used to edit the material properties of an **SoMaterial** node. The editor can also directly be used using callbacks instead of attaching it to a node. The component consists of a render area displaying a test sphere, some sliders, a set of radio buttons, and a menu. The sphere displays the current material being edited. There is one slider for each material coefficient. Those fields are ambient, diffuse, specular, emissive (all of which are colors); and transparency and shininess (which are scalar values). A color editor can be opened to edit the color slider base color. A material list displays palettes of predefined materials from which to choose.

The editor can currently be attached to only one material at a time. Attaching two different materials will automatically detach the first one before attaching the second.

METHODS

 SoXtMaterialEditor(Widget parent = NULL, const char *name = NULL, SbBool buildInsideParent = TRUE)
 ~SoXtMaterialEditor()
Constructor and destructor.

void **attach**(SoMaterial *material, int index = 0)
void **detach**()
Attach/detach the editor to a material node and edit the material of the given index.

SbBool **isAttached**()
Returns TRUE if the editor is attached.

void **addMaterialChangedCallback**(SoXtMaterialEditorCB *f, void *userData = NULL)
void **removeMaterialChangedCallback**(SoXtMaterialEditorCB *f, void *userData = NULL)
Additional way of using the material editor, by registering a callback which will be called whenever the material changes (check the **UpdateFrequency** to find when the callbacks will be called).

void   **setUpdateFrequency**(SoXtMaterialEditor::UpdateFrequency
                            freq)
SoXtMaterialEditor::UpdateFrequency
                  getUpdateFrequency()
Sets/gets the update frequency. See the **UpdateFrequency** enum declaration.

void   **setMaterial**(const SoMaterial &mtl)
const SoMaterial &
                  getMaterial() const
Set a new material value, and get the current material value.

Methods from class SoXtComponent:

show, hide, isVisible, getWidget, isTopLevelShell, getShellWidget,
getParentWidget, setSize, getSize, getDisplay, setTitle, getTitle, setIconTitle,
getIconTitle, setWindowCloseCallback, getComponent, getWidgetName,
getClassName

INCLUDE FILE

```
#include <Inventor/Xt/SoXtMaterialEditor.h>
```

typedef void   **SoXtMaterialEditorCB**(void *userData, const SoMaterial *mtl)

enum **UpdateFrequency** {
        SoXtMaterialEditor::CONTINUOUS
                  send updates with every mouse motion
        SoXtMaterialEditor::AFTER_ACCEPT
                  only send updates after user hits accept button
}

RESOURCES

*SoXtMaterialEditor.tile1Color: #4c4c4c (color name or hex value)
*SoXtMaterialEditor.tile2Color: #999999 (color name or hex value)
*SoXtMaterialEditor.light1Color: white (color name or hex value)
*SoXtMaterialEditor.light2Color: white (color name or hex value)
*SoXtMaterialEditor.updateFrequency: continuous (continuous | manual)

SEE ALSO

SoXtComponent, SoXtMaterialList, SoXtDirLightEditor, SoMaterial

NAME

SoXtMaterialList — component which lets you edit a material interactively

INHERITS FROM

SoXtComponent > SoXtMaterialList

DESCRIPTION

This class is used to choose an **SoMaterial** from palettes of predefined materials (for example, gold, silver, or bronze from the metal palette; emerald, pearl, or ruby from the stones palette). The chosen material is passed to callback functions registered with this component.

METHODS

SoXtMaterialList(Widget parent = NULL, const char *name = NULL, SbBool buildInsideParent = TRUE, const char *dir = NULL)

~SoXtMaterialList()

The constructor is passed a directory name which serves as the home directory for the material palettes. You can have any number of palettes in this directory. A palette is a subdirectory that contains Inventor data files, where each file describes one material. Predefined Inventor materials are found in /usr/share/data/materials.

addCallback(SoXtMaterialListCB *f, void *userData = NULL)

removeCallback(SoXtMaterialListCB *f, void *userData = NULL)

Register functions that will be called whenever the user chooses a new material from the list. Each callback when invoked will be passed the **userData** pointer, along with a pointer to the newly selected material.

Methods from class SoXtComponent:

show, hide, isVisible, getWidget, isTopLevelShell, getShellWidget, getParentWidget, setSize, getSize, getDisplay, setTitle, getTitle, setIconTitle, getIconTitle, setWindowCloseCallback, getComponent, getWidgetName, getClassName

INCLUDE FILE

```
#include <Inventor/Xt/SoXtMaterialList.h>
```

typedef void   **SoXtMaterialListCB**(void *userData, const SoMaterial *mtl)

SEE ALSO

SoXtComponent, SoCallbackList, SoMaterial, SoXtMaterialEditor

SoXtMaterialSliderSet

NAME

SoXtMaterialSliderSet — component with Motif sliders for editing SoMaterial nodes

INHERITS FROM

SoXtComponent > SoXtSliderSetBase > SoXtSliderSet > SoXtMaterialSliderSet

DESCRIPTION

This class defines an editor that uses Motif Sliders to edit the fields in an **SoMaterial** node. There are sliders for editing the RGB values of **ambientColor**, **diffuseColor**, **specularColor** and **emissiveColor**, as well as for editing the **transparency** and **shininess** values.

METHODS

SoXtMaterialSliderSet(Widget parent = NULL, const char *name = NULL, SbBool buildInsideParent = TRUE, SoNode *newEditNode = NULL)
~**SoXtMaterialSliderSet**()
Constructor and destructor. At construction time the material node to edit can be supplied.

Methods from class SoXtSliderSetBase:

setNode, getNode

Methods from class SoXtComponent:

show, hide, isVisible, getWidget, isTopLevelShell, getShellWidget, getParentWidget, setSize, getSize, getDisplay, setTitle, getTitle, setIconTitle, getIconTitle, setWindowCloseCallback, getComponent, getWidgetName, getClassName

INCLUDE FILE

```
#include <Inventor/Xt/SoXtMaterialSliderSet.h>
```

SEE ALSO

SoXtMaterialEditor, SoXtSliderSet, SoXtSliderSetBase, SoXtComponent, SoMaterial, SoNode

NAME

SoXtMouse — translates and reports events for the mouse

INHERITS FROM

SoXtDevice > SoXtMouse

DESCRIPTION

This class manages events generated by the mouse, including mouse motion
(**SoLocation2Event**), and mouse button press and release events
(**SoMouseButtonEvent**).

METHODS

SoXtMouse(EventMask mask = SO_XT_ALL_MOUSE_EVENTS)
~SoXtMouse()

Constructor and destructor. To the constructor, pass which mouse events
you are interested in as a bitwise OR of the following values:

ButtonPressMask — Mouse press events

ButtonReleaseMask — Mouse release events

PointerMotionMask — Mouse motion with no buttons

ButtonMotionMask — Mouse motion with buttons pressed

Or simply pass the defined value SO_XT_ALL_MOUSE_EVENTS for all mouse
events. The device will only report events of this type for the widget it is
enabled on.

Methods from class SoXtDevice:

enable, disable, translateEvent, setWindowSize, getWindowSize

INCLUDE FILE

```
#include <Inventor/Xt/devices/SoXtMouse.h>
```

#define SO_XT_ALL_MOUSE_EVENTS \
    (ButtonPressMask | ButtonReleaseMask | PointerMotionMask | ButtonMotionMask)

SEE ALSO

SoXtDevice, SoLocation2Event, SoMouseButtonEvent

NAME

SoXtPlaneViewer — viewer component which moves the camera in a plane

INHERITS FROM

SoXtComponent > SoXtGLWidget > SoXtRenderArea > SoXtViewer >
SoXtFullViewer > SoXtPlaneViewer

DESCRIPTION

The Plane viewer component allows the user to translate the camera in the viewing
plane, as well as dolly (move foward/backward) and zoom in and out. The viewer
also allows the user to roll the camera (rotate around the forward direction) and seek
to objects which will specify a new viewing plane. This viewer could be used for
modeling, in drafting, and architectural work. The camera can be aligned to the X, Y
or Z axes.

METHODS

SoXtPlaneViewer(Widget parent = NULL, const char *name =
NULL, SbBool buildInsideParent = TRUE,
SoXtFullViewer::BuildFlag flag = BUILD_ALL,
SoXtViewer::Type type = BROWSER)
~SoXtPlaneViewer()
Constructor and destructor which specifies the viewer type. Please refer to
the **SoXtViewer** man pages for a description of the viewer types.

Methods from class SoXtFullViewer:

setDecoration, isDecoration, setPopupMenuEnabled, isPopupMenuEnabled,
getAppPushButtonParent, addAppPushButton, insertAppPushButton,
removeAppPushButton, findAppPushButton, lengthAppPushButton,
getRenderAreaWidget

Methods from class SoXtViewer:

setCamera, getCamera, setCameraType, getCameraType, viewAll,
saveHomePosition, resetToHomePosition, setHeadlight, isHeadlight,
getHeadlight, setDrawStyle, getDrawStyle, setBufferingType,
getBufferingType, setViewing, isViewing, setAutoClipping, isAutoClipping,
setStereoViewing, isStereoViewing, setStereoOffset, getStereoOffset,
setDetailSeek, isDetailSeek, setSeekTime, getSeekTime, addStartCallback,
addFinishCallback, re moveStartCallback, removeFinishCallback, copyView,
pasteView

Methods from class SoXtRenderArea:

setSceneGraph, getSceneGraph, setOverlaySceneGraph,
getOverlaySceneGraph, registerDevice, unregisterDevice,
setBackgroundColor, getBackgroundColor, setBackgroundIndex,
getBackgroundIndex, setOverlayBackgroundIndex,

getOverlayBackgroundIndex, setColorMap, setOverlayColorMap, setViewportRegion, getViewportRegion, setTransparencyType, getTransparencyType, setAntialiasing, getAntialiasing, setClearBeforeRender, isClearBeforeRender, setClearBe foreOverlayRender, isClearBeforeOverlayRender, setAutoRedraw, isAutoRedraw, setRedrawPriority, getRedrawPriority, getDefaultRedrawPriority, render, renderOverlay, scheduleRedraw, scheduleOverlayRedraw, redrawOnSelectionChange, redrawOverlayOnSelectionChange, setEventCallback, setGLRenderAction, getGLRenderAction, setOverlayGLRenderAction, getOverlayGLRenderAction, setSceneManager, getSceneManager, setOverlaySceneManager, getOverlaySceneManager

Methods from class SoXtGLWidget:

setBorder, isBorder, setDoubleBuffer, isDoubleBuffer, getNormalWindow, getOverlayWindow, getNormalContext, getOverlayContext, getNormalWidget, getOverlayWidget, setNormalVisual, getNormalVisual, setOverlayVisual, getOverlayVisual

Methods from class SoXtComponent:

show, hide, isVisible, getWidget, isTopLevelShell, getShellWidget, getParentWidget, setSize, getSize, getDisplay, setTitle, getTitle, setIconTitle, getIconTitle, setWindowCloseCallback, getComponent, getWidgetName, getClassName

INCLUDE FILE

```
#include <Inventor/Xt/viewers/SoXtPlaneViewer.h>
```

RESOURCES

*SoXtPlaneViewer.decoration: on (on | off)
*SoXtPlaneViewer.seekAnimationTime: 2.0 (float)
*SoXtPlaneViewer.seekTo: point (point | object)
*SoXtPlaneViewer.seekDistanceUsage: percentage (percentage | absolute)
*SoXtPlaneViewer.zoomMin: 1.0 (float)
*SoXtPlaneViewer.zoomMax: 179.0 (float)
*SoXtPlaneViewer.autoClipping: on (on | off)
*SoXtPlaneViewer.nearDistance: 2.4 (float, when autoClipping is off)
*SoXtPlaneViewer.farDistance: 2.8 (float, when autoClipping is off)
*SoXtPlaneViewer*BackgroundColor: black (color name or hex value)

SoXtPlaneViewer

USAGE

Left Mouse: Translate up, down, left and right.

Ctrl + Left Mouse: Used for roll action (rotates around the viewer forward direction).

<s> + Left Mouse: Alternative to the Seek button. Press (but do not hold down) the <s> key, then click on a target object.

Middle Mouse: Dolly in and out (gets closer to and further away from the object).

Right Mouse: Open the popup menu.

SEE ALSO

SoXtFullViewer, SoXtViewer, SoXtComponent, SoXtRenderArea, SoXtWalkViewer, SoXtExaminerViewer, SoXtFlyViewer

NAME

SoXtPrintDialog — dialog box for controlling printing

INHERITS FROM

SoXtComponent > SoXtPrintDialog

DESCRIPTION

This class provides an interactive widget for setting available options used in printing with the **SoPrintAction** and its subclasses. Options include whether to print with hidden lines or not, whether to print using the Landscape format, whether to print to a file or a printer.

METHODS

        SoXtPrintDialog(Widget parent = NULL, const char *name = NULL, SbBool buildInsideParent = TRUE)

        ~SoXtPrintDialog()

Constructors and destructor.

void	**setSceneGraph**(SoNode *root)
SoNode *	**getSceneGraph**()
void	**setSceneGraph**(SoPath *path)
SoPath *	**getSceneGraphPath**()

Sets/gets the root node or path to nodes to be used for printing.

void	**setPrintSize**(SbVec2f &inches)
void	**setPrintSize**(SbVec2s &)

Sets/gets the size of the printed image. This is typically the same size as the window displaying the scene to be printed.

void	**setBeforePrintCallback**(SoXtPrintDialogCB *f, void *userData = NULL)
void	**setAfterPrintCallback**(SoXtPrintDialogCB *f, void *userData = NULL)

Two callbacks are maintained, one which gets called just before a print is executed, and one which gets called after a print is executed. These two methods sets the appropriate callback function (set these to NULL to remove the callback).

Methods from class SoXtComponent:

show, hide, isVisible, getWidget, isTopLevelShell, getShellWidget, getParentWidget, setSize, getSize, getDisplay, setTitle, getTitle, setIconTitle, getIconTitle, setWindowCloseCallback, getComponent, getWidgetName, getClassName

SoXtPrintDialog

INCLUDE FILE

```
#include <Inventor/Xt/SoXtPrintDialog.h>
```

typedef void   **SoXtPrintDialogCB**(void *userData, SoXtPrintDialog *dialog)

SEE ALSO

SoPrintAction, SoCallbackList, SoXtComponent

NAME

SoXtRenderArea — Xt Component for rendering Inventor scene graphs

INHERITS FROM

SoXtComponent > SoXtGLWidget > SoXtRenderArea

DESCRIPTION

This class provides Inventor rendering and event handling inside a GLX Motif widget. There is a routine to specify the scene to render. The scene is automatically rendered whenever anything under it changes (a data sensor is attached to the root of the scene), unless explicitly told not to do so (manual redraws). Users can also set Inventor rendering attributes such as the transparency type, antialiasing on or off, etc. This class employs an **SoSceneManager** to manage rendering and event handling.

X events that occur in the render area can be handled by the application or by the nodes in the scene graph. When an event occurs, it is first passed to the application event callback function registered with the **setEventCallback()** method on **SoXtRenderArea**. If this function does not exist or returns FALSE, the X event is translated to an **SoEvent** for further processing. First, if an overlay scene graph exists, the **SoEvent** is sent to that scene graph by way of an **SoHandleEventAction**. If no node in the overlay scene graph handles the event (i.e., calls **setHandled()** on the **SoHandleEventAction**), **the SoEvent** is passed to the normal scene graph in the same manner.

METHODS

      SoXtRenderArea(Widget parent = NULL, const char *name = NULL, SbBool buildInsideParent = TRUE, SbBool getMouseInput = TRUE, SbBool getKeyboardInput = TRUE)
      ~SoXtRenderArea()

Constructor which is passed arguments which tell it whether to register the mouse and keyboard devices by default (**SoXtMouse** and **SoXtKeyboard**).

virtual void   **setSceneGraph**(SoNode *newScene)
virtual SoNode *   **getSceneGraph**()

Set/get the scene graph to be rendered in this component's window.

void   **setOverlaySceneGraph**(SoNode *newScene)
SoNode *   **getOverlaySceneGraph**()

Sets/gets the scene graph to render in the overlay bit planes.

Note: since the overlay bit planes are in color index mode, single buffer with a limited number of colors, the user should limit rendering in the overlay planes to simple objects.

Typically rendering in color index mode is done using the **SoColorIndex** node with a **SoLightModel** set to BASE_COLOR.

void	**registerDevice**(SoXtDevice *)
void	**unregisterDevice**(SoXtDevice *)

Register/unregister interest in devices. When a device is registered, events from that device will be processed by the render area, and passed into the scene graph. Events from unregistered devices will be ignored.

void	**setBackgroundColor**(const SbColor &c)
const SbColor &	**getBackgroundColor**() const

Set/get the background color for this window. Default is black (0,0,0).

void	**setBackgroundIndex**(int index)
int	**getBackgroundIndex**() const

Sets/gets the window background color when in color index mode. (default to black (index 0)).

void	**setOverlayBackgroundIndex**(int index)
int	**getOverlayBackgroundIndex**() const

Sets/gets the overlay window background color index. (default to 0 (clear color)).

void	**setColorMap**(int startIndex, int num, const SbColor *colors)

Sets the colors to use when displaying in color index mode. This will load the color map with the given colors at the starting index.

void	**setOverlayColorMap**(int startIndex, int num, const SbColor *colors)

Sets the colors to use for overlay bit planes.This will load the color map with the given colors at the starting index.

void	**setViewportRegion**(const SbViewportRegion &newRegion)
const SbViewportRegion &	**getViewportRegion**() const

Sets/gets current viewport region to use for rendering

void	**setTransparencyType**(SoGLRenderAction::TransparencyType type)
SoGLRenderAction::TransparencyType	**getTransparencyType**() const

Set/get the quality level for rendering transparent objects. See **SoGLRenderAction** for possible transparency types.

void	**setAntialiasing**(SbBool smoothing, int numPasses)
void	**getAntialiasing**(SbBool &smoothing, int &numPasses) const

Set/get the antialiasing for rendering. There are two kinds of antialiasing available: smoothing and multipass antialiasing. If *smoothing* is set to TRUE, smoothing is enabled. Smoothing uses OpenGL's line- and point-smoothing features to provide cheap antialiasing of lines and points. The value of *numPasses* controls multipass antialiasing. Each time a render action is applied, Inventor renders the scene *numPasses* times from slightly different camera positions, averaging the results. *numPasses* can be from one to 255, inclusive. Setting *numPasses* to one disables multipass antialiasing. You can use either, both, or neither of these antialiasing techniques. By default, both smoothing and multipass antialiasing are disabled.

void	**setClearBeforeRender**(SbBool trueOrFalse)
SbBool	**isClearBeforeRender**() const

Enable/prevent window clearing from happening before a rendering starts (default is clear TRUE). This can be useful to limit flickering when doing single buffering and geometry covers the entire window (used in the material editor).

void	**setClearBeforeOverlayRender**(SbBool trueOrFalse)
SbBool	**isClearBeforeOverlayRender**() const

Enable/prevent overlay window clearing from happening before a rendering starts (default is clear TRUE).

void	**setAutoRedraw**(SbBool trueOrFalse)
SbBool	**isAutoRedraw**() const

The render area will automatically redraw whenever something in the scene graph changes. Passing FALSE will disable this feature.

void	**setRedrawPriority**(unsigned long priority)
unsigned long	**getRedrawPriority**() const
static unsigned long	
	getDefaultRedrawPriority()

Sets/gets the priority of the redraw sensor and get the default priority number.

void	**render**()
void	**renderOverlay**()

Calling this forces the render area to be redrawn now. It is not necessary to call this method if auto redraw is enabled (which is the default).

749

void	**scheduleRedraw**()
void	**scheduleOverlayRedraw**()

Schedule a redraw to happen sometime soon (as opposed to immediately). This can be used to compress multiple redraws.

void	**redrawOnSelectionChange**(SoSelection *s)
void	**redrawOverlayOnSelectionChange**(SoSelection *s)

Call this convenience method to have this render area redraw whenever the selection list changes in the passed node. This is useful if using a highlight render action like the **SoBoxHighlightRenderAction** to correctly render whenever the selection changes. Pass NULL to turn this off.

void	**setEventCallback**(SoXtRenderAreaEventCB *fcn, void *userData = NULL)

X events which occur in the render area window are automatically translated to **SoEvents**, then passed into the scene graph (via the **SoHandleEventAction**) so that live scene graph objects can handle the event. This method allows the application to register a callback for handling events that occur in the window, instead of sending them down the graph. The callback is passed the X event, and should return TRUE if it handled the event. If the callback returns FALSE, then the event will be translated and sent to the scene graph.

void	**setGLRenderAction**(SoGLRenderAction *ra)
SoGLRenderAction *	
	getGLRenderAction() const

Sets/gets the GL render action to use. This is used to set selection highlighting with the **SoBoxHighlightRenderAction** and **SoLineHighlightRenderAction** classes.

void	**setOverlayGLRenderAction**(SoGLRenderAction *ra)
SoGLRenderAction *	
	getOverlayGLRenderAction() const

Sets/gets the GL render action for the overlay window.

void	**setSceneManager**(SoSceneManager *sm)
SoSceneManager *	
	getSceneManager() const
void	**setOverlaySceneManager**(SoSceneManager *sm)
SoSceneManager *	
	getOverlaySceneManager() const

Sets/gets the normal and overlay plane scene managers.

Note: for convenience most of the **SoSceneManager** methods have already been added to this class.

Methods from class SoXtGLWidget:

setBorder, isBorder, setDoubleBuffer, isDoubleBuffer, getNormalWindow, getOverlayWindow, getNormalContext, getOverlayContext, getNormalWidget, getOverlayWidget, setNormalVisual, getNormalVisual, setOverlayVisual, getOverlayVisual

Methods from class SoXtComponent:

show, hide, isVisible, getWidget, isTopLevelShell, getShellWidget, getParentWidget, setSize, getSize, getDisplay, setTitle, getTitle, setIconTitle, getIconTitle, setWindowCloseCallback, getComponent, getWidgetName, getClassName

INCLUDE FILE

```
#include <Inventor/Xt/SoXtRenderArea.h>
```

typedef SbBool   **SoXtRenderAreaEventCB**(void *userData, XAnyEvent *anyevent)

RESOURCES

*SoXtRenderArea*BackgroundColor: black (color name or hex value)

SEE ALSO

SoXtGLWidget, SoXtComponent, SoXtViewer, SoSceneManager, SoBoxHighlightRenderAction, SoLineHighlightRenderAction

SoXtResource

NAME

SoXtResource — used to retrieve X resources for SoXtComponents and widgets

INHERITS FROM

SoXtResource

DESCRIPTION

This class provides an easy to use interface for retrieving X resource values for widgets and components. Rather than use standard Xt calls to traverse up a widget hierarchy, this class performs its own traversal so that it may provide special care for widgets which are Inventor components. For instance, the Inventor Material Editor top level widget is a Motif form widget. Its class name is thus XmForm. **SoXtResource** knows that the editor is an Inventor component, though, so it uses the class name provided by the editor (in this case "SoXtMaterialEditor") when looking up resource values.

EXAMPLE:

```
SoXtResource xr( materialEditor->getWidget() );
xr.getResource("tile1Color", "Tile1Color", color);
xr.getResource("updateFrequency", "UpdateFrequency", freq);
```

METHODS

SoXtResource(Widget w)
~SoXtResource()

Constructor and destructor. The constructor takes the widget for which it will retrieve resource values.

SbBool	**getResource**(char *resName, char *resClass, SbColor &c)
SbBool	**getResource**(char *resName, char *resClass, short &i)
SbBool	**getResource**(char *resName, char *resClass, unsigned short &u)
SbBool	**getResource**(char *resName, char *resClass, char *&s)
SbBool	**getResource**(char *resName, char *resClass, SbBool &b)
SbBool	**getResource**(char *resName, char *resClass, float &f)

This returns the X resource value for the specified resource name and class. There is no need to specify the widget hierarchy; this is automatically computed in the constructor.

INCLUDE FILE

```
#include <Inventor/Xt/SoXtResource.h>
```

NOTES

Components will typically look up their own resources during **buildWidget()**. In order for a component to have its Inventor class name recognized by **SoXtResource**, it must call **SoXtComponent::registerWidget()** in its **buildWidget()** method. (This is done in every Inventor component.)

SEE ALSO

X Resources (Xrm), X Intrinsics (Xt), SoXt, SoXtComponent

NAME

SoXtSliderSet — base class for Motif-only slider components

INHERITS FROM

SoXtComponent > SoXtSliderSetBase > SoXtSliderSet

DESCRIPTION

This class is used as a base class for all editors which use sets of Motif sliders to edit fields in an Inventor scene graph node. The editor consists of a number of sliders each of which may change a different value in a field. This class is not meant to be instanced by programmers who want to use an editor in a program. It should only be used as a base class when designing new editors.

This class has no public methods. The internal methods deal with managing the layout of the subcomponents.

METHODS

Methods from class SoXtSliderSetBase:

setNode, getNode

Methods from class SoXtComponent:

show, hide, isVisible, getWidget, isTopLevelShell, getShellWidget, getParentWidget, setSize, getSize, getDisplay, setTitle, getTitle, setIconTitle, getIconTitle, setWindowCloseCallback, getComponent, getWidgetName, getClassName

INCLUDE FILE

```
#include <Inventor/Xt/SoXtSliderSet.h>
```

SEE ALSO

SoXtSliderSetBase, SoXtComponent, SoNode, SoXtLightSliderSet, SoXtMaterialSliderSet, SoXtTransformSliderSet

NAME
SoXtSliderSetBase — abstract base class for Motif-only slider components

INHERITS FROM
SoXtComponent > SoXtSliderSetBase

DESCRIPTION
This class is used as a base class for all editors which use Motif sliders to edit fields in an Inventor scene graph node. This class is not meant to be instanced by programmers who want to use an editor in a program. It should only be used as a base class when designing new editors.

SoXtSliderSetBase is derived from **SoXtComponent**, but adds three concepts. First, there is a node to edit. Second, there are subcomponents. When an **SoXtSliderSetBase** is shown or hidden, so are its subcomponents. (As an example, an **SoXtTransformSliderSet** is composed of many subcomponents). Third, an **SoXtSliderSetBase** has a layout size, which is used to lay out the subcomponents.

METHODS
virtual void   **setNode**(SoNode *newNode)
Sets a new node as the node to be modified by this editor component.

SoNode *   **getNode**() const
Returns a pointer to the node currently being modified by this editor component.

Methods from class SoXtComponent:
show, hide, isVisible, getWidget, isTopLevelShell, getShellWidget, getParentWidget, setSize, getSize, getDisplay, setTitle, getTitle, setIconTitle, getIconTitle, setWindowCloseCallback, getComponent, getWidgetName, getClassName

INCLUDE FILE
```
#include <Inventor/Xt/SoXtSliderSetBase.h>
```

SEE ALSO
SoXtComponent, SoXtSliderSet

SoXtSpaceball

NAME

SoXtSpaceball — translates and reports events for the spaceball

INHERITS FROM

SoXtDevice > SoXtSpaceball

DESCRIPTION

This class manages events generated by the spaceball, including spaceball motion (**SoMotion3Event**), and spaceball button press and release events (**SoSpaceballButtonEvent**).

METHODS

> **SoXtSpaceball**(SoXtSpaceball::Mask mask = SoXtSpaceball::ALL)
> **SoXtSpaceball**(Display *d, SoXtSpaceball::Mask mask = SoXtSpaceball::ALL)
> **~SoXtSpaceball**()

Constructor and destructor. Pass to the constructor an enumerated value specifying which spaceball events are of interest. Only those events will be reported to the callback routine registered on each widget. The first constructor uses the X display which was set in **SoXt::init**().

void	**setRotationScaleFactor**(float f)
float	**getRotationScaleFactor**() const

Set and get the rotation scale factor. The scale factor is applied to the rotation value generated by the spaceball device. The default rotation scale factor is .006.

void	**setTranslationScaleFactor**(float f)
float	**getTranslationScaleFactor**() const

Set and get the translation scale factor. The scale factor is applied to the translation value generated by the spaceball device. The default translation scale factor is .006.

static SbBool	**exists**()
static SbBool	**exists**(Display *d)

This returns TRUE if the spaceball exists, either on the X display which was set in **SoXt::init**(), or on the passed display.

Methods from class SoXtDevice:

enable, disable, translateEvent, setWindowSize, getWindowSize

INCLUDE FILE

```
#include <Inventor/Xt/devices/SoXtSpaceball.h>
```

enum **Mask** {

    SoXtSpaceball::MOTION

                Spaceball translation and rotation events

    SoXtSpaceball::PRESS

                Spaceball button press events

    SoXtSpaceball::RELEASE

                Spaceball button release events

    SoXtSpaceball::ALL

                All spaceball events

    }

SEE ALSO

    SoXt, SoXtDevice, SoMotion3Event, SoSpaceballButtonEvent

SoXtTransformSliderSet

NAME

SoXtTransformSliderSet — component with Motif sliders for editing SoTransform nodes

INHERITS FROM

SoXtComponent > SoXtSliderSetBase > SoXtSliderSet > SoXtTransformSliderSet

DESCRIPTION

This class defines an editor that uses Motif Sliders to edit fields in an **SoTransform** node. There are sliders for editing the translation, scale, rotation, and transform center.

METHODS

> **SoXtTransformSliderSet**(Widget parent = NULL, const char
> *name = NULL, SbBool buildInsideParent = TRUE, SoNode
> *newEditNode = NULL)
> **~SoXtTransformSliderSet**()

Constructor and destructor. At construction time the transform node to edit can be supplied.

Methods from class SoXtSliderSetBase:

setNode, getNode

Methods from class SoXtComponent:

show, hide, isVisible, getWidget, isTopLevelShell, getShellWidget, getParentWidget, setSize, getSize, getDisplay, setTitle, getTitle, setIconTitle, getIconTitle, setWindowCloseCallback, getComponent, getWidgetName, getClassName

INCLUDE FILE

```
#include <Inventor/Xt/SoXtTransformSliderSet.h>
```

SEE ALSO

SoXtSliderSet, SoXtSliderSetBase, SoXtComponent, SoTransform, SoNode

NAME

SoXtViewer — viewer component lowest base class

INHERITS FROM

SoXtComponent > SoXtGLWidget > SoXtRenderArea > SoXtViewer

DESCRIPTION

This is the lowest base class for viewer components. This class adds the notion of a camera to the **SoXtRenderArea** class. Whenever a new scene is specified with **setSceneGraph()**, the first camera encountered will be by default used as the edited camera. If no camera is found in the scene, the viewer will automatically create one. If the viewer type is **SoXtViewer::BROWSER** then the camera is told to view the supplied scene graph but is not added beneath that scene graph root. If the viewer type is **SoXtViewer::EDITOR** then the camera is added beneath the supplied scene graph root.

In addition to automatically creating a camera if needed, this base class also creates a headlight (directional light which is made to follow the camera), enables the user to change drawing styles (like wireframe or move wireframe), and buffering types. This base class also provides a convenient way to have the camera near and far clipping planes be automatically adjusted to minimize the clipping of objects in the scene.

Viewers allow the application to shadow event processing. When the application registers an event processing callback by calling **setEventCallback()** the viewer will invoke this callback for every X event it receives. However, unlike the render area, the viewer ignores the return value of this callback, and processes the event as usual. This allows the application to expand viewing capabilities without breaking the viewing paradigm. It is an easy way to hook up other devices, like the spaceball, to an existing viewer.

METHODS

virtual void	**setCamera**(SoCamera *cam)
SoCamera *	**getCamera**()

Set and get the edited camera. Setting the camera is only needed if the first camera found in the scene when setting the scene graph isn't the one the user really wants to edit.

virtual void	**setCameraType**(SoType type)
SoType	**getCameraType**()

Set and get the camera type that will be created by the viewer if no cameras are found in the scene graph (see **SoPerspectiveCamera** and **SoOrthographicCamera**). By default an **SoPerspectiveCamera** will be created if no camera are found.

Note: the set method will only take effect next time a scene graph is specified (and if no camera are found).

virtual void **viewAll**()
Changes the camera position to view the entire scene (the camera zoom or orientation isn't changed).

virtual void **saveHomePosition**()
virtual void **resetToHomePosition**()
Saves and restores the camera values.

void **setHeadlight**(SbBool onOrOff)
SbBool **isHeadlight**()
SoDirectionalLight *

getHeadlight()
Turns the headlight on/off (default on) and return the headlight node.

void **setDrawStyle**(SoXtViewer::DrawType type,
SoXtViewer::DrawStyle style)
SoXtViewer::DrawStyle

getDrawStyle(SoXtViewer::DrawType type)
Sets/gets the current drawing style in the main view — The user can specify the INTERACTIVE draw style (draw style used when the scene changes) independently from the STILL style (default VIEW_AS_IS for both STILL and INTERACTIVE). Possible draw styles are:

VIEW_AS_IS — Leaves the objects unchanged.

VIEW_HIDDEN_LINE — Renders the object as wireframe, but only show the object front faces. This is accomplished using a two pass rendering. In the first pass, the objects are rendered as FILLED using the background BASE_COLOR (this sets up the wanted z-buffer values). The second pass then renders the objects as LINES, while adjusting the z-buffer range to limit overlapping polygons problems.

VIEW_NO_TEXTURE — Renders the objects withought any textures. This is done by setting the override flag on an empty **SoTexture2** node.

VIEW_LOW_COMPLEXITY — Renders the objects withought any textures and with a low complexity. This is done by setting the override flag on an empty **SoTexture2** node, and by setting a low complexity value on an **SoComplexity** node with override set to TRUE.

VIEW_LINE — Renders the objects as LINES with lighting model set to BASE_COLOR.

VIEW_POINT — Renders the objects as POINTS with lighting model set to BASE_COLOR.

VIEW_BBOX — Renders the objects with complexity BOUNDING_BOX, lighting model set to BASE_COLOR and drawing style LINES.

void   **setBufferingType**(SoXtViewer::BufferType type)
SoXtViewer::BufferType
                       getBufferingType()
Sets/gets the current buffering type in the main view (default SoXtViewer::BUFFER_DOUBLE).

virtual void   **setViewing**(SbBool onOrOff)
SbBool   **isViewing**() const
Set/get whether the viewer is turned on or off. When turned on, events are consumed by the viewer. When viewing is off, events are processed by the viewers render area. This means events will be sent down to the scene graph for processing (i.e. picking can occur). Note that if the application has registered an event callback, it will be invoked on every event, whether viewing is turned on or not. However, the return value of this callback (which specifies whether the callback handled the event or not) is ignored when viewing is on. That is, the viewer will process the event even if the callback already did. This is to ensure that the viewing paradigm is not broken (default viewing is on).

void   **setAutoClipping**(SbBool onOrOff)
SbBool   **isAutoClipping**() const
Set and get the auto clipping plane. When auto clipping is ON, the camera near and far planes are dynamically adjusted to be as tight as possible around the objects being viewed. When OFF, the user is expected to manually set those planes within the preference sheet (default is on).

virtual void   **setStereoViewing**(SbBool onOrOff)
virtual SbBool   **isStereoViewing**()
void   **setStereoOffset**(float dist)
float   **getStereoOffset**()
Turns stereo viewing on/off on the viewer (default off). When in stereo mode, which may not work on all machines, the scene is rendered twice (in the left and right buffers) with an offset between the two views to simulate stereo viewing. Stereo glasses have to be used to see the effect and /usr/gfx/setmon needs to be called to set the monitor in stereo mode.

The user can also specify what the offset between the two views should be.

void	**setDetailSeek**(SbBool onOrOff)
SbBool	**isDetailSeek**()

When the viewer is in seek mode, left mouse clicks initiate a pick, and the viewer changes its orientation and position to look at the picked object. This routine tells the seeking viewer whether to orient the camera towards the picked point (detail on), or the center of the object's bounding box (detail off). Default is detail on.

void	**setSeekTime**(float seconds)
float	**getSeekTime**()

Set the time a seek takes to change to the new camera location. A value of zero seeks directly to the point without any animation. Default value is 2 seconds.

void	**addStartCallback**(SoXtViewerCB *f, void *userData = NULL)
void	**addFinishCallback**(SoXtViewerCB *f, void *userData = NULL)
void	**removeStartCallback**(SoXtViewerCB *f, void *userData = NULL)
void	**removeFinishCallback**(SoXtViewerCB *f, void *userData = NULL)

Add/remove start and finish callback routines on the viewer. Start callbacks are called whenever the user starts doing interactive viewing (for example, mouse down), and finish callbacks are called when user is done doing interactive work (for example, mouse up).

Note: The viewer "this" pointer is passed as callback data.

void	**copyView**(Time eventTime)
void	**pasteView**(Time eventTime)

Copy/paste the view. *eventTime* should be the time of the X event which initiated the copy or paste (e.g. if copy/paste is initiated from a keystroke, *eventTime* should be the time in the X KeyPress event.)

Methods from class SoXtRenderArea:

setSceneGraph, getSceneGraph, setOverlaySceneGraph, getOverlaySceneGraph, registerDevice, unregisterDevice, setBackgroundColor, getBackgroundColor, setBackgroundIndex, getBackgroundIndex, setOverlayBackgroundIndex, getOverlayBackgroundIndex, setColorMap, setOverlayColorMap, setViewportRegion, getViewportRegion, setTransparencyType, getTransparencyType, setAntialiasing, getAntialiasing, setClearBeforeRender, isClearBeforeRender, setClearBe foreOverlayRender, isClearBeforeOverlayRender, setAutoRedraw, isAutoRedraw, setRedrawPriority, getRedrawPriority, getDefaultRedrawPriority, render, renderOverlay, scheduleRedraw, scheduleOverlayRedraw, redrawOnSelectionChange, redrawOverlayOnSelectionChange, setEventCallback, setGLRenderAction, getGLRenderAction, setOverlayGLRenderAction, getOverlayGLRenderAction, setSceneManager, getSceneManager, setOverlaySceneManager, getOverlaySceneManager

Methods from class SoXtGLWidget:

setBorder, isBorder, setDoubleBuffer, isDoubleBuffer, getNormalWindow, getOverlayWindow, getNormalContext, getOverlayContext, getNormalWidget, getOverlayWidget, setNormalVisual, getNormalVisual, setOverlayVisual, getOverlayVisual

Methods from class SoXtComponent:

show, hide, isVisible, getWidget, isTopLevelShell, getShellWidget, getParentWidget, setSize, getSize, getDisplay, setTitle, getTitle, setIconTitle, getIconTitle, setWindowCloseCallback, getComponent, getWidgetName, getClassName

INCLUDE FILE

```
#include <Inventor/Xt/viewers/SoXtViewer.h>
```

typedef void   **SoXtViewerCB**(void *userData, SoXtViewer *viewer)

enum **Type** {
SoXtViewer::BROWSER	camera views scene, but is not added to scene
SoXtViewer::EDITOR	camera is added to user's scene
}

enum **DrawStyle** {
SoXtViewer::VIEW_AS_IS	unchanged
SoXtViewer::VIEW_HIDDEN_LINE	
	render only the front most lines
SoXtViewer::VIEW_NO_TEXTURE	
	render withought textures
SoXtViewer::VIEW_LOW_COMPLEXITY	
	render low complexity and no texture
SoXtViewer::VIEW_LINE	wireframe draw style
SoXtViewer::VIEW_POINT	point draw style
SoXtViewer::VIEW_BBOX	bounding box draw style
}

```
enum DrawType {
        SoXtViewer::STILL           applies to static rendering
        SoXtViewer::INTERACTIVE  applies to rendering while interactive viewing
}

enum BufferType {
        SoXtViewer::BUFFER_SINGLE
                                single buffer
        SoXtViewer::BUFFER_DOUBLE
                                double buffer
        SoXtViewer::BUFFER_INTERACTIVE
                                double buffer while interactive viewing
}
```

SEE ALSO

SoXtComponent, SoXtRenderArea, SoXtExaminerViewer, SoXtWalkViewer, SoXtFlyViewer, SoXtPlaneViewer

NAME

SoXtWalkViewer — viewer component which moves the camera in a plane

INHERITS FROM

SoXtComponent > SoXtGLWidget > SoXtRenderArea > SoXtViewer > SoXtFullViewer > SoXtConstrainedViewer > SoXtWalkViewer

DESCRIPTION

The paradigm for this viewer is a walkthrough of an architectural model. Its primary behavior is forward, backward, and left/right turning motion while maintaining a constant "eye level". It is also possible to stop and look around at the scene. The eye level plane can be disabled, allowing the viewer to proceed in the "look at" direction, as if on an escalator. The eye level plane can also be translated up and down — similar to an elevator.

METHODS

SoXtWalkViewer(Widget parent = NULL, const char *name = NULL, SbBool buildInsideParent = TRUE, SoXtFullViewer::BuildFlag flag = BUILD_ALL, SoXtViewer::Type type = BROWSER)

~SoXtWalkViewer()

Constructor and destructor which specifies the viewer type. Please refer to the **SoXtViewer** man pages for a description of the viewer types.

Methods from class SoXtConstrainedViewer:

setUpDirection, getUpDirection

Methods from class SoXtFullViewer:

setDecoration, isDecoration, setPopupMenuEnabled, isPopupMenuEnabled, getAppPushButtonParent, addAppPushButton, insertAppPushButton, removeAppPushButton, findAppPushButton, lengthAppPushButton, getRenderAreaWidget

Methods from class SoXtViewer:

setCamera, getCamera, setCameraType, getCameraType, viewAll, saveHomePosition, resetToHomePosition, setHeadlight, isHeadlight, getHeadlight, setDrawStyle, getDrawStyle, setBufferingType, getBufferingType, setViewing, isViewing, setAutoClipping, isAutoClipping, setStereoViewing, isStereoViewing, setStereoOffset, getStereoOffset, setDetailSeek, isDetailSeek, setSeekTime, getSeekTime, addStartCallback, addFinishCallback, re moveStartCallback, removeFinishCallback, copyView, pasteView

Methods from class SoXtRenderArea:

setSceneGraph, getSceneGraph, setOverlaySceneGraph,
getOverlaySceneGraph, registerDevice, unregisterDevice,
setBackgroundColor, getBackgroundColor, setBackgroundIndex,
getBackgroundIndex, setOverlayBackgroundIndex,
getOverlayBackgroundIndex, setColorMap, setOverlayColorMap,
setViewportRegion, getViewportRegion, setTransparencyType,
getTransparencyType, setAntialiasing, getAntialiasing, setClearBeforeRender,
isClearBeforeRender, setClearBe foreOverlayRender,
isClearBeforeOverlayRender, setAutoRedraw, isAutoRedraw,
setRedrawPriority, getRedrawPriority, getDefaultRedrawPriority, render,
renderOverlay, scheduleRedraw, scheduleOverlayRedraw,
redrawOnSelectionChange, redrawOverlayOnSelectionChange,
setEventCallback, setGLRenderAction, getGLRenderAction,
setOverlayGLRenderAction, getOverlayGLRenderAction, setSceneManager,
getSceneManager, setOverlaySceneManager, getOverlaySceneManager

Methods from class SoXtGLWidget:

setBorder, isBorder, setDoubleBuffer, isDoubleBuffer, getNormalWindow,
getOverlayWindow, getNormalContext, getOverlayContext,
getNormalWidget, getOverlayWidget, setNormalVisual, getNormalVisual,
setOverlayVisual, getOverlayVisual

Methods from class SoXtComponent:

show, hide, isVisible, getWidget, isTopLevelShell, getShellWidget,
getParentWidget, setSize, getSize, getDisplay, setTitle, getTitle, setIconTitle,
getIconTitle, setWindowCloseCallback, getComponent, getWidgetName,
getClassName

INCLUDE FILE

```
#include <Inventor/Xt/viewers/SoXtWalkViewer.h>
```

RESOURCES

*SoXtWalkViewer.decoration: on (on | off)
*SoXtWalkViewer.seekAnimationTime: 2.0 (float)
*SoXtWalkViewer.seekTo: point (point | object)
*SoXtWalkViewer.seekDistanceUsage: percentage (percentage | absolute)
*SoXtWalkViewer.zoomMin: 1.0 (float)
*SoXtWalkViewer.zoomMax: 179.0 (float)
*SoXtWalkViewer.autoClipping: on (on | off)
*SoXtWalkViewer.nearDistance: 2.4 (float, when autoClipping is off)
*SoXtWalkViewer.farDistance: 2.8 (float, when autoClipping is off)
*SoXtWalkViewer*BackgroundColor: black (color name or hex value)

USAGE

Left Mouse: Click down and move up and down for fowards and backwards motion. Move right and left for turning. Speed increases exponentially with the distance from the mouse-down origin.

Ctrl + Left Mouse: Allows motion in the "look at" direction, which is not necessarily in the "eye level" plane ("Escalator" mode).

<s> + Left Mouse: Alternative to the Seek button. Press (but do not hold down) the <s> key, then click on a target object.

<u> + Left Mouse: Press (but do not hold down) the <u> key, then click on a target object to set the "up" direction to the surface normal. By default +y is the "up" direction.

Middle Mouse: Rotate the viewpoint. This allows you to look around while stopped.

Right Mouse: Open the popup menu.

SEE ALSO

SoXtFullViewer, SoXtViewer, SoXtComponent, SoXtRenderArea, SoXtPlaneViewer, SoXtExaminerViewer, SoXtFlyViewer